MEILICHA DÔRA

Poems and Prose in Greek
from Renaissance and Early Modern Europe

Societas Scientiarum Fennica

The Finnish Society of Sciences and Letters

Address:
Pohjoinen Makasiinikatu 7 A 6, FI – 00130 Helsinki
In Swedish:
Finska Vetenskaps-Societeten, Norra Magasinsgatan 7 A 6, FI – 00130 Helsingfors
In Finnish:
Suomen Tiedeseura, Pohjoinen Makasiinikatu 7 A 6, FI – 00130 Helsinki

Commentationes Humanarum Litterarum

The series, founded in 1923, publishes monographs or other studies on antiquity
and its tradition.

Editor:
Prof. Mika Kajava
Address: Department of Languages, P. O. Box 24, FI – 00014 University of Helsinki.

Requests for Exchange:
Exchange Centre for Scientific Literature, Snellmaninkatu 13, FI – 00170 Helsinki,
or at the Secretary of the Society.

Distribution and Sale:
Tiedekirja, Snellmaninkatu 13, FI – 00170 Helsinki; tiedekirja@tsv.fi, www.tsv.fi.

Other series published by the Society:
Commentationes Physico-Mathematicae
Commentationes Scientiarum Socialium
Bidrag till kännedom av Finlands natur och folk
The History of Learning and Science in Finland 1828-1918
Årsbok – Vuosikirja (Yearbook), serie A sarja
Sphinx (Årsbok – Vuosikirja, serie B sarja)

Commentationes Humanarum Litterarum
138 2020

MEILICHA DÔRA

Poems and Prose in Greek
from Renaissance and Early Modern Europe

Edited by
MIKA KAJAVA, TUA KORHONEN AND JAMIE VESTERINEN

Societas Scientiarum Fennica

The Finnish Society of Sciences and Letters

Commentationes Humanarum Litterarum
is part of the publishing cooperation between
the Finnish Society of Sciences and Letters and
the Finnish Academy of Science and Letters

This book has received a subsidy granted by the Ministry of Education and Culture
distributed by the Federation of Finnish Learned Societies

ISSN 0069-6587
ISBN 978-951-653-441-4
ISBN 978-951-653-442-1 (PDF)

Layout by Vesa Vahtikari

Printed by Grano Oy, Vaasa 2020

Contents

IV. GREEK POEMS FROM THE "EDGES" OF EUROPE: PRAGUE AND UTRECHT

V. GREEK AND THE 18th AND 19th CENTURY NEUHUMANISMUS

Ἠνίδε γράμματα γραψάντων εὐγνώμονα δέξαι.
Ἐρῖκος ὁ ἐλάχιστος Σίρονεν

Introduction

Tua Korhonen

A startling detail in the history of Greek studies in Germany is Martin Crusius' thousands and thousands of sermons written in (ancient) Greek. Why did Crusius (1524–1607), a Greek professor in Tübingen, compose Greek sermons – and for what purpose? In fact, Crusius 'only' paraphrased or translated the sermons simultaneously as he was listening to them in church three times a week for over a 40-year period. Fortunately, he gave reasons for this practice: translating or paraphrasing German sermons into Greek helped him concentrate on the sermons. In addition, he wanted to practise his *ad hoc* writing in Greek. Exactly 6588 sermons have survived among Crusius' enormous manuscript collection, which has been published by Thomas Wilhelmi.[1] These sermons were not the only texts Crusius wrote in Greek. His *Germanograecia* came out in 1585 containing some of his own Greek texts as well as poems and prose by his students and acquaintances whom he had encouraged and stirred by his own example to express themselves in Greek. The explicit function of *Germanograecia* was, as Crusius states in his preface, to 'hellenize' the German peoples because Greece itself had been 'barbarized'.[2]

One of the causes that inspired the writing of poetry and prose in Greek, alongside pedagogical purposes, was to perpetuate Greek literature. Although Crusius was exceptionally prolific, many humanists not only in central Europe but also at its periphery – like in Sweden – showed quite amazing active skills in Greek. Nowadays, these Greek texts composed by humanists have been overshadowed by the vast amount of Neo-Latin texts. After all, Latin was the language of letters, the means of communication, the 'eternal' language by which to make oneself heard. Neo-Latin Studies have an established place among humanities nowadays, with journals, handbooks and international conferences. Greek, which was used by

---

[1] Wilhelmi, Thomas (ed.) 2002. *Die griechischen Handschriften der Universitätsbibliothek* Tübingen. *Sonderband Martin Crusius: Handschriftenverzeichnis und Bibiliographie*. Wiesbaden. See also, Grafton, Anthony. 2002. "Martin Crusius Read his Homer", *Princeton University Library Chronicle* 64:1, 64–65.

[2] Crusius, Martin. 1585. *Germanograecia libri sex*. Basel, 2v (dedicatory letter). See also Ludwig, Walter. 1998. *Hellas in Deutschland. Darstellung der Gräzistik im deutschsprachigen Raum aus dem 16. und 17. Jahrhundert* (Berichte aus den Sitzungen der Joachim Jungius-Gesellschaft der Wissenschaften E.V. Jahrgang 16, Heft 1). Hamburg, 29–31.

Renaissance and early modern humanists and which imitated ancient Greek, has aroused interest only recently, over the past twenty years of time.

The articles in this volume are based on the papers presented at the conference "Humanist Greek (HUG) – Perspectives for a New Field of Studies" that was arranged by the Finnish members (Tua Korhonen and Erkki Sironen) of the project *Helleno-Nordica* in Helsinki, August 2018.[3] In a way, the Helsinki conference was a continuation of the 'HUG' conference in Tartu that was organised within the framework of Janika Päll's research project in 2014. In her preface to the Tartu conference's acta (*Hellenostephanos*, published in 2018), Päll presents the much-discussed terminological problem for this field of studies: what should we call this form or register of Greek that is a kind of equivalent to Neo-Latin? For example, Émile Legrand used the term *la nouvelle Grèce* for the Greek literature that the Byzantine scholars created in the West. In English, *Neo-Greek* would easily be terminologically mixed with modern Greek.[4] In German, the term *Neualtgriechisch* captures the meaning very well, but the term would seem like an oxymoron in English ('New ancient Greek'). One option is Humanist Greek, which Dieter Harlfinger used in a catalogue for the exhibition 'Graecogermania' (an obvious pun on Crusius' *Germanograecia*) on Greek studies and the editorial work by German and Italian humanists. The exhibition was arranged at the Herzog August Library in Wolfenbüttel in 1987.[5] Many scholars have managed, however, to refer to this form of language just as 'Greek'.

---

[3] In organizing the conference, the Finnish members of the project were aided by students Jamie Vesterinen, Minna Vesa and Katja Sivonen. This preface and the editorial work for *Meilicha Dôra* was done under the auspices of the *Helleno-Nordica*, directed by Johanna Akujärvi; Swedish Research Council, grant 2016-01881.

[4] Päll, Janika. 2018. "Editor's Preface", in Päll, Janika & Ivo Volt (eds.) *Hellenostephanos: Humanist Greek in Early Modern Europe: Learned Communities between Antiquity and Contemporary Culture*, Tartu, 9–10. On the terminological problem, see also Korhonen, Tua. 2004. *Ateena Auran rannoilla*. Helsinki, 9–10 (http://ethesis.helsinki.fi/julkaisut/hum/klass/vk/korhonen2/). Recent studies on Humanist Greek, see for instance: Stefan Weise (ed.) 2020. *HELLENISTI! Altgriechisch als Literatursprache im neuzeitlichen Europa*. Stuttgart, and Weise's and Päll's articles in Constantinidou, Natascha & Lamers, Han (eds.) (2020). *Receptions of Hellenism in Early Modern Europe: 15th–17th Centuries*. Turnhout.

[5] Harlfinger, Dieter *et al.* (Hrsg.) 1989. *Graecogermania. Griechischstudien deutscher Humanisten. Die Editionstätigkeit der Griechen in der italienischen Renaissance (1469–1523). Ausstellung im Zeughaus der Herzog August Bibliothek Wolfenbüttel vom 22. April bis 9. Juli 1989.* Weinheim–New York, XVII. Following Harlfinger, I used the term *humanistikreikka* (Humanist Greek in Finnish) in my first articles on the subject in 1997.

Which term to use was also the question in the Renaissance Society of America congress in Berlin in 2015 at the panel discussion titled 'What is Renaissance Greek?' One may indeed make a distinction between Renaissance and Humanist Greek: the former would denote the Greek that was used by Byzantine scholars in the West and the first generations of Italian humanists. **Renaissance Greek** is then the title of the first section of this book. The first paper by **Grigory Vorobyev** discusses the Greek translation of an important letter written by Pope Nicholas V to Constantine XI Palaiologus in 1451. The Greek version was made by a Byzantine scholar famous for his Greek grammar, Theodore Gaza (c. 1398–1475). In his article 'Theodore Gaza's Translation between Diplomacy and Humanism: A List of European Countries in Nicholas V's Letter to the Last Byzantine Emperor', Vorobyev concentrates especially on the geographical names by comparing the Greek and Latin versions of the geographical expressions. He pays particular attention to Latinism, additions in the Greek translation and to some odd instances in Greek terms (like ἡ τῶν καλουμένων Δάμνων ἀξιόλογος χώρα for Denmark). **Angelo de Patto**, in his article 'Uberto Decembrio's Epitaph', presents instances of Greek by Italian humanists from a time before the production of books, namely Greek inscriptions. The use of Greek in funerary inscriptions was a practice of which there are some examples even in remote Sweden in the early modern period. Uberto Decembrio is remembered for his contribution to Manuel Chrysoloras' translation of Plato's *Republic* into Latin. Decembrio, who died in 1427, might be the first Italian humanist who used Greek in his Latin epitaph, which he composed himself.

According to the famous dictum by Constantin Lascaris, *Graecia transvolavit Alpes*, and Paris was then one of the first centres in which Greek attained a firm hold through the support of the King, Francis I (1494–1547). One topic that underlies the three articles in the section titled **Greek and the Kings** is the role of monarchs as supporters of Greek studies. **Luigi-Alberto Sanchi** discusses two Greek liminary prose epistles by the first Greek professor in Paris (and the namesake of a modern French series of Greek editions) in his 'Guillaume Budé's Greek *Manifesto*: the Introductory Epistles of the *Commentarii linguae Graecae* (1529)'. The first epistle is addressed to Francis I, and the other to "young Hellenists" willing to learn Greek. The letter to the king recalls the king's former promise to help found a collegium in Paris, which materialised in 1530. Both of the liminary epistles not only present the main lines of the content of *Commentarii* but also reveal something of Budé's working methods in creating this influential work.

Besides Budé and many other philologists, Francis I favoured poets and writers. For example, he secured the printing of François Rabelais' masterpiece *Pantagruel*. Rabelais, who was well-educated in *artes liberales*, used Greek words and phrases as icing for his satirical cakes. **Martin Steinrück** shows, in his 'Rabelais' *Quart livre* and Greek language', that the French genius could take advantage of the musical qualities of Greek words with his sharp ear. Rabelais' use of Greek is indicative of the status of Greek as the peak of humanistic education and a way to make a distinction – only the Hellenists could (and can) understand the deeper meaning of these seemingly randomly used Greek words, quotes and pseudo-quotes.

Johanna Akujärvi's paper 'Neo-Latin Texts and Humanist Greek Paratexts: On Two Wittenberg Prints dedicated to Crown Prince Erik of Sweden' also underlines the monarchical contribution to liberal arts, especially to poetry. The monarch in question was the son of Gustav I, the first Protestant king in Sweden. Four Greek poems were added, as paratexts, to two long Latin narrative poems that combined Swedish and Graeco-Roman history: Henricus Mollerus' *Stheno Sture* (1557) and Laurentius Petri Gothus' *Strategema* (1559). They were dedicated to the crown-prince, who later became King Erik XIV and who had received a thorough humanistic education. Akujärvi shows that these short Greek paratexts were not merely embellishments or displays of their writer's skill in composing in Greek to a Greek-knowing crown prince but that they also direct the readers to focus on the important nationalistic topics of the main Latin texts.

Both Mollerus' and Petri's publications were printed in Wittenberg, which was the centre of the Protestant movement and therefore also a promotor of Greek studies. The section **Greek in Protestant Germany** contains four papers. Due to the need to study the New Testament and the Greek Church Fathers, Greek studies attained a firm hold within German schools and universities, and the high status of Greek and the appreciation of active skills in Greek have lasted even today. **Stefan Rhein**, the keynote speaker at the Helsinki 2018 conference, presents a systematic description of how Greek became a valued subject in educational institutions in his paper 'Die Griechischstudien in Deutschland und ihre universitäre Institutionalisierung im 16. Jahrhundert. Ein Überblick'. Rhein chronologically lists 18 universities or other institutions of higher learning, beginning with Leipzig in which the first Greek chair was founded in 1515 – the professor, Richard Crocus, came from Scotland – and ending with Helmstedt, where Greek had a natural place – with an emphasis on active skills – among other subjects in the university founded in 1576. Rhein explains how the initiation and progress of Greek as a standard subject was combined with the Reformation and aided by the strong influence of Melanchthon, the second German-born Greek professor in a German university (Wittenberg 1518). Rhein also presents several passages of inaugural orations in which the newly-named professors defended the new subject. Sometimes, Greek chairs were combined with other chairs, like with mathematics and astronomy in Jena in 1551.

One of the most prolific early writers in Greek in Germany was Joachim Camerarius (1500–1574), a professor of Helmstedt, whom **Jochen Schultheiß** introduces both as a poet, translator and editor of Greek epigrams in his 'Profilbildung eines Dichterphilologen – Joachim Camerarius d.Ä. als Verfasser, Übersetzer und Herausgeber griechischer Epigramme'. Schultheiß shows how Camerarius, in his function as an editor of ancient and contemporary epigrams, endeavored to prove his independence from Aldus Manutius and Janus Lascaris by offering a collection radically different from the *Aldina* of the *Anthologia Planudea*. As a poet of Greek epigrams, however, Camerarius sticks to his poetological program of *imitatio*, so that his epigrams purposefully evoke the Greek tradition, including an epitaph to a "yellow-haired horse" (Camerarius also translated Xenophon's two works on horsemanship). However, due to the literary context of early modern poetry, epigrams were not purely literal but usually written for different types of occasions (e.g., weddings, funerals or academic festivities). Schultheiß shows how the typological variety of Greek epigrams offers Camerarius an outstanding challenge and opportunity to display himself according to the ideal of the humanist poet-philologist.

The corpus of Renaissance and Humanist Greek texts does not contain only epigrams or short occasional texts. Lorenz (Laurentius) Rhodoman (c. 1545–1606) wrote a Greek-Latin epic (c. 4500 lines) on biblical geography and history, *Palaestina*. The other keynote speaker at the Helsinki 2018 conference, **Stefan Weise**, presents Rhodoman's shorter Greek epics in his paper 'Griechische Mythologie im Dienste reformatorischer Pädagogik: Zur Epensammlung *Argonautica. Thebaica. Troica. Ilias parva* von Lorenz Rhodoman (1588)'. While much shorter than *Palaestina*, these epics are still impressive: *Argonautica* and *Thebaica* are c. 560 verses long, and *Troica* and *Ilias parva* more than twice as long (c. 1700). The collection also includes the 1248-verses long *Arion*, which is not mentioned on the title page. Weise, who published an edition of *Arion* in 2019, suggests that the erotic features of *Arion* are the reason for omitting it on the title-page. As Weise shows from the passages (mostly) of the prefaces of each epic, the four named epics had a pedagogical function. They were meant to be read by boys and young men who studied Greek and Greek literature. Another omission, as a peculiar inside joke, is the name of the author. The editor, Michael Neander, who was Rhodoman's teacher and a good Greek poet himself, presented the poems as if they had been the newly-found, genuine poems of an unknown Greek author (unfortunately, some did not understand the joke). Weise prefaces his presentation by giving a short history of Renaissance and Humanist Greek poetry beginning with Angelo Poliziano and emphasizing the quite strong tradition of composing long paraphrases in Greek on the Bible, especially on the Psalms. Despite the Christian themes, Humanist Greek poets always paraphrased and imitated "pagan" authors, taking whole verses from Homer and Hesiod (if writing in hexametre or elegiac couplet), among others.

As a background for Rhodoman's achievements as an epic poet in Greek, **Thomas Gärtner** presents, in his article 'Jonische Hexameter als Träger der norddeutschen Reformation', several sixteenth century writers of this genre, all of whom concentrated on Biblical themes. Gärtner begins and ends with passages by Rhodoman: from his Greek autobiography written during the 1560s and his Greek biography of Martin Luther (1579). The other passages are from Nikolaus von Reusner's "Herod's Infantcide" and "Christus' Triumph" (both published in 1593), Martin Crusius' "Susanna" (1567), Georg Koch's "Jonas" (1567), Johannes Melas' "Biography of Philipp Melanchthon" (1574), Matthaeus Gothus' "Daniel" (1573) – which, as originally in Latin, the author translated into Greek for the benefit of his students as he stated – Heinrich Eckstorm's "Biography of St. Laurentius" (1582), Matthaeus Domisius' "John the Baptist" (1594) and Jakob Steinbrück's "The Apostle Paul's Conversion" (1607). Many of these writers imitated the *Odyssey*, especially its first lines.

During the early modern period, Greek did not reach only France, Germany and England, but more remote parts of Europe as well. A Finn, Johan Paulinus (ennobled as Lillienstedt), used the expression that is reminiscent of Hesiod, ἄκροις ἐνὶ πείρασι γαίης, with positive connotations of his home country in his epic-like Greek poem on Finland.[6] Edges may be peaceful places to live – or to escape the COVID-19 in 2020 – or to occasionally write Greek poetry. The section titled **Greek Poems from Prague and Utrecht from the "Edges" of Europe** contains two papers that can loosely be seen from this perspective. **Marcela Slavíková** presents a general view on Greek studies in the Bohemian lands in her 'Γενεὴν Βοίημος: Humanist Greek Poetry in the Bohemian Lands'. The centre for humanism in this area was Prague, which was and is, of course, not at the edges of Europe as such. On the contrary, the medieval University of Prague was founded in 1348, and the department for Greek studies was established already in 1537, for which the contribution of monarchs was considerable. The peak of humanist Greek production in the Bohemian lands occurred between 1537–1622. In an Appendix to her more general presentation, Slavíková presents four Greek poems: a wedding poem (1551), a congratulation to students for receiving their degrees (1610), a congratulation for an oration, which concentrates more on the topic of oration than

---

[6] Paulinus, Johan. 1678. *Magnus Principatus Finlandia*, Uppsala, vv. 9, 60 (cfr. Hes. *Theog.* 731: ἔσχατα γαίης).

on eulogizing the student-orator (1610), and a congratulation for a dissertation (1611), in which the congratulation to the student-respondent is also in a minor role – the focus of the Greek poem being on the topic of the dissertation, that is, on death.

Access to knowledge in Greek was closed to most Renaissance and early modern women. Nevertheless, some women knew Greek and even composed in Greek, such as Angelo Poliziano's friend Alessandra Scala (1475–1506) and Olympia Fulvia Morata (1526–1555), an Italian who taught Greek in Heidelberg a short time before her early death. A Hollander also belongs to this small group, the Utrecht-born Anna Maria van Schurman, who corresponded in Greek with famous scholars and Greek Orthodox priests. **Pieta van Beek** presents in her article 'Οὐλτραϊεκτείνων μέγα κῦδος πότνια κούρη. Greek eulogies in honour of Anna Maria van Schurman (1607–1678)' five men who eulogised in Greek this *virgo docta*, focusing on her erudition and piety. Her teacher and later friend, Gisbertus Voetius, praises her as a shining (Protestant) light in Catholic Cologne where she stayed a couple of months. All in all, erudite women were exceptions and objects of wonder, and therefore they were placed at the edges of the general intellectual community.

Interest in the Greek language and culture have changed and will change as time goes by. German *Neuhumanismus* was a movement that had a strong influence on many countries. The last section of this book, titled **Greek and the 18th and 19th Century *Neuhumanismus***, concentrates on this phenomenon. **Janika Päll** introduces a remarkable regional corpus of Greek poems from the 17th and 18th centuries in her 'German New Humanism versus rising Professionalism: *Carmina Hellenica Teutonum* by Braunschweig Physician and *Philhellene* Karl Friedrich Arend Scheller'. K.A. Scheller (1773–1843) collected mostly occasional, paratextual, Greek poems from the Brunswick area in southern Germany and transcribed them or cut them from publications for his scrap-book-like collection that was never published. This regional corpus – the manuscript is preserved in the Herzog August Library – provides an interesting picture of what kinds of Greek poems were written in the Brunswick area in that time. Päll's aim is to 'rehabilitate' Scheller's notorious fame as a philologist (if he is known or remembered at all) by showing how the collector worked between the time of great respect for the autopoetic Humanist tradition (that is: writing in Greek) and of rising professionalism in classical philology.

Elena Ermolaeva's article deals with Russian *Neuhumanismus* that is closest of our time. Although there were many great classical scholars in the Russian empire (including the Soviet era), their active knowledge of Greek has hardly been studied at all. Ermolaeva's 'Three Greek Poems by the Neohumanist Vyacheslav Ivanov (1866–1949)' gives one example of a quite well-known person in the Russian context who wrote in Greek. Ivanov was a theorist of the theatre and a poet that belonged to the Russian symbolistic movement. In addition, he published his dissertation in ancient history, having first studied the subject in Moscow and then under the famous Theodor Mommsen in Berlin. Ivanov lived aboard for most of his adult life – for instance in Italy and in Athens during 1886–1905 and again in Rome from 1920 until his death. His Greek poems can be viewed as part of his poetic *oeuvre* containing classical and biblical allusions as well as gifts for his classically-orientated acquaintances.

The name of this volume, *Meilicha dôra*, 'Sweet gifts', is to be found in the *Homeric Hymn to Aphrodite* (v. 2). The phrase was imitated by Mimnermus (1.3 West) in his love elegy and can be found in several early modern gnomologies and (therefore) in many Humanist Greek poems.[7] One contribution of this volume is that it gives some examples – and their contexts – from this quite substantial but very unstudied corpus of Greek poems and prose written by Renaissance and early modern humanists in Europe.[8] How 'sweet' these gifts are depends on the reader's taste. Baroque poetry is often too verbose and ornate for the ear that is accustomed to modernist poetry. However, these poems and prose texts might have their peculiar charm in their attempts to give blood to the Greek spirits.

Sincere thanks are due to anonymous reviewers. Many thanks to the publisher, the Finnish Society of Sciences and Letters, for accepting this volume to be published in the series *Commentationes Humanarum Litterarum*, especially to Prof. Mika Kajava, the general editor of the series. Without the work of MA Jamie Vesterinen, this book would have many more mistakes and editorial inconsistencies than what it surely still has. Lots of thanks also to the members of the *Helleno-Nordica* project as well as to PhD Philip Lane, the final inspector of the English language of some articles, and to PhD Vesa Vahtikari, who did the book's layout and greatly supported us in the last phase of the editing.

Helsinki, August 2020
Tua Korhonen

---

[7] For instance, Laurentius Praetorius, a Swede, used the phrase in his *propemptikon*, written in Helmstedt in 1592, and Elaus Terserus, who had studied in Helmstedt, used it in his congratulation for a wedding, which was published in Turku (Finland) in 1644. See Korhonen (n. 4 above), 221 and 273.

[8] Mostly the writers have normalised their Greek texts according to modern standards; some with more specific editorial principles explain them in the footnotes.

I. RENAISSANCE GREEK

Theodore Gaza's Translation between Diplomacy and Humanism. A List of European Countries in Pope Nicholas V's Letter to the Last Byzantine Emperor

GRIGORY VOROBYEV

Introduction

As Donald M. Nicol put it, 'one thing that astonishes the reader of the Byzantine historians particularly of the later period is their evident ignorance of the history and geography of Western Europe.'[1] It is thus of special interest to investigate how the Byzantine view of Western geography evolved in the fifteenth century, when numerous Greek men of letters fled to the West, not only settling in Italy but also crossing the Alps and, sometimes, even the English Channel.[2]

One text that offers insight into this matter, at first glance, cannot be considered a Byzantine source on European geography – namely, a letter written by Pope Nicholas V (1447–1455) to the last Byzantine emperor. Its Greek translation, however, made in Rome by the Byzantine scholar Theodore Gaza (d. *ca.* 1475), is a particularly interesting case, since both the Greek version and its Latin original are extant, permitting a comparison of the two texts. In the letter,

---

[1] Nicol (1967, 315). A significant exception was Laonikos Chalkokondyles, who, in his *Histories*, demonstrated astonishing competence in European geography (Akışık 2013, 181–237; Kaldellis 2014, 85–100). Cf. in Ducellier (1995, 252): 'le désintérêt évident pour la topographie et les structures de l'Europe occidentale subsiste, au XVème siècle, chez la plupart des auteurs, à l'exception notable de Laonikos Chalkokondylis'; *ibid.*, 254: 'le solde des connaissances que les Grecs médiévaux laissent paraître de l'Occident serait donc extrêmement négatif si l'on n'abordait l'oeuvre d'un auteur, Laonikos Chalkokondylis.' On late Byzantine understanding of the ethnography and geography of the European West, see Kaldellis (2013, 166–186); Ducellier (1994); esp. Ducellier (1995); unfortunately, I could not access Ducellier (1996); it seems that none of Ducellier's articles was used in Kaldellis (2013). As for the Byzantine understanding about and nomenclature for foreign peoples and countries, see, e.g., the following studies on Byzantine views about and toponyms for the Turks, e.g., Moravcsik (1932); Moravcsik (1983); Bisaha (2004, 43–134); Meserve (2008, 123–142). I would like to express my profound gratitude to Han Lamers and the anonymous reviewer of this article as well as Jamie Vesterinen for their helpful suggestions.

[2] On France, cf. Sanchi (2019); on England, cf. Harris (2000).

the pope lists the European countries that serve as *testes* (witnesses) of the decree of the Church union stipulated at the Council of Ferrara-Florence (1438–1439). By comparing the Latin names of these countries with their Greek renderings and analyzing how they are introduced to the Greek readership, a perspective not yet undertaken on Gaza's version of the text, I thus aim to explore how Gaza's translation of the pope's letter reflects late Byzantine knowledge of Western geography.

Nicholas V's Letter to the Last Byzantine Emperor: The History of the Text

In April 1451, Andronikos Bryennios Leontaris, an envoy of the last Byzantine emperor Constantine XI Palaiologos (1449–1453), was sent to Italy to seek aid against the Turks.[3] One of the places he visited during his mission was Rome. It is not known when exactly he reached the city – though, most probably, he spent August and September there – but it is attested that he brought a letter from Constantine and held a speech before the pope. At the end of September or the beginning of October,[4] Nicholas sent an official reply to the emperor, where he specified that he was writing in response to both Constantine's letter and Bryennios' speech. He insisted that Constantine finally implement the decrees of the Council of Ferrara-Florence (1438–1439) – i.e., first of all, enforce the acknowledgement of the full supremacy of the papacy so as to accomplish the union of the Churches; otherwise, the West would not come to Constantinople's aid.[5] This letter is extant in two languages, though it remains unknown whether the one actually sent to Constantine was in Latin, in Greek, or in both.

Historians are well acquainted with the contents of the letter,[6] but the origin and transmission of the bilingual text deserve reassessment. To my knowledge, the most recent study on the letter is a 2007 article by Walter K. Hanak. While he prepared an English translation of the letter, printed as an appendix to his article,

---

[3] See Philippides & Hanak (2011, 362 n. 9); Leone (1994, 922) (both with references to further literature).

[4] Either 27 September or 11 October. See the discussion, below, on the date.

[5] For further details, see Leone (1994, 923–924); Hanak (2007, 339–345).

[6] See, e.g., Guilland (1953, 231–233); Gill (1959, 377–378); Dölger (1965, 135 No. 3533); Setton (1978, 105–106); Nicol (1992, 49–50); Philippides & Hanak (2011, 372–373). The letter is sometimes mentioned among the translations made by Theodore Gaza, Leone (1989, 71); Geanakoplos (1989, 77 n. 37); Bianca (1999, 740).

Hanak, however, did not study the history of the letter's transmission.[7] Moreover, he was not aware that Bryennios' speech, to which Pope Nicholas was replying, is extant and even published. Composed in elegant Latin, the text is contained in the miscellaneous manuscript Wrocław, Biblioteka Uniwersytecka, Rehdiger 36, ff. 51r–54v. In Conrad Ziegler's 1915 catalogue of the Rehdiger collection, the codex is dated to the fifteenth century,[8] and the Appendix contains an edition of Bryennios' oration.[9] The manuscript is also registered in Paul Oskar Kristeller's *Iter Italicum*, with a mention of the *Andronici Bryennii oratio ad Nicolaum V*. Kristeller drew the description of the codex from Ziegler 1915 and, as he adds, had it verified by Antoni Knot.[10] Still, as far as I know, only Pietro Luigi Maria Leone (1994), whose article will be introduced below, took note of the publication of Bryennios' speech. The scholars mentioned in the footnote 6 above seemed to make no note of either Ziegler 1915 or Leone 1994.[11] While Bryennios' oration is not of direct interest to the present study, it surely deserves more attention.

Now, the Greek version of Nicholas V's answer to the emperor exists in at least thirty codices, the earliest dated to 1479.[12] The Latin original survives in at least two manuscript copies, Vat. lat. 3878 (ff. 171r–174r), dating back to the third quarter of the fifteenth century, and the aforementioned manuscript

---

[7] Hanak (2007, translation on pp. 354–359).

[8] Ziegler (1915, 4).

[9] Ziegler (1915, 241–244).

[10] Kristeller (1989, 427).

[11] E.g., Hanak (2007, 337–338) writes: 'We do not possess the emperor's letter to the pope, which had been conveyed by his legate Andronikos Leontaris Bryennios, and we can only surmise its contents from the curt papal response'. Hanak does not mention that we do possess Bryennios' speech, which, as we know from the pope's answer, was held before him in oral form and considered by the pope an explanatory addition to the emperor's epistle: *Oratorem tuum nobilem virum Andronicum Brienium Leonardum* [!]*, quem ad nos serenitas tua misit, gratissime recepimus, et lectis litteris tuis ipsum gratius audivimus; nam gratissime et prudentissime omnia sibi a tua serenitate commissa seriosius explicavit. Intelleximus tum verbis suis, tum ex litteris* […] (Hofmann 1946, 131, ll. 3–6). When quoting from Hofmann's edition, I compared his text with its direct sources, Arcudius (1630) for Latin and Lampros (1930) for Greek (for these editions, see below), and corrected some minor typographical errors that appeared in Hofmann (1946); I followed Hofmann's orthography and punctuation.

[12] Lampros (1930, 49–51), used twelve manuscripts for his critical edition. In the database *Pinakes*, thirty-two can be found: https://pinakes.irht.cnrs.fr/notices/oeuvre/5239/; https://pinakes.irht.cnrs.fr/notices/oeuvre/5249/ (retrieved 3 January 2020). Codex Vat. gr. 1393, mentioned by Lampros, is not registered in *Pinakes* among those containing Nicholas' letter, since its contents are not described thoroughly enough in the database (as of 3 January 2020).

from Wrocław.[13] In the latter, Nicholas' letter is preserved as a separate quire (ff. 57r–60v) bound after that containing Bryennios' speech.[14] In addition, an official copy of the pope's letter was kept in the Vatican archives but can no longer be located.[15] Nicholas' letter was printed for the first time in 1630 by Peter Arcudius in Rome, both in Latin and Greek.[16] I did not consult the Wrocław manuscript for this article, so I only compared Arcudius' edition with Vat. lat. 3878. The Latin text of the latter betrays certain discrepancies from that of Arcudius' edition. Based on a sample collation of Vat. lat. 3878, f. 171r and selected fragments, I conclude that the readings of Vat. lat. 3878 are sometimes better;[17] nevertheless, in most cases, Arcudius' edition provides more plausible variants, which probably means that the *Vorlage* of his manuscript and the Vatican codex are not dependent on one another and thus represent different branches of the tradition. Arcudius' edition was reprinted with slight corrections in Jacques-Paul Migne's *Patrologia Graeca*.[18] As noticed above, the Wrocław codex seems to remain unknown to scholars of Nicholas' letter – apart from Leone 1994 (he was, however, much more interested in Gaza's letter to his brothers, which will be discussed below, than in Nicholas' epistle to Constantine).[19] Therefore, not only

---

[13] Lampros (1930, 50–51), in his edition of the Greek text, mentions the existence of more Latin codices but names only the Vat. lat. 3878: Τὸ δὲ λατινικὸν πρωτότυπον σώζεται ἐν ἄλλοις τε κώδιξι καὶ τῷ Vaticanus 3878.

[14] Ziegler (1915, 4); Kristeller (1989, 427).

[15] Archivio Segreto Vaticano, AA Arm. I–XVIII, 2047 [= AA Arm. IX, caps. 1, n. 9], so cited by Hofmann (1946, 130–131).

[16] Arcudius (1630, 685–701).

[17] For instance, while Vat. lat. 3878 reads *impedimenta illa tantae retardationis verissimulia* (for *verisimilia*) *esse viderentur* (f. 171r, ll. 12–13), the last word in Arcudius (1630, 686, l. 16) reads *videretur* – clearly, an error. Another case where the reading of Vat. lat. 3878 should be preferred to that of Arcudius' concerns the spelling of the Latin name of Sweden, which will be treated below. Further on readings of the Vatican codex that are better than those of Arcudius, see the apparatus of Hofmann (1946, 131–134). Cf., below, n. 22 of this article.

[18] Migne (1866, cols. 1201–1212). Sometimes, its text diverges from that of Arcudius (1630), so it should be investigated whether he used an alternative source or the discrepancies are just Migne's conjectures *ope ingenii*. Lampros (1930, 50) writes that Migne merely reprinted Arcudius (1630), but, in Arcudius, the address of the letter reads *Nicolaus episcopus etc.* [...] *imperatori illustri salutem etc.*, whereas Migne has *Nicolaus episcopus servus servorum Dei* [...] *imperatori illustri salutem et apostolicam benedictionem*.

[19] Leone (1994) does not mention the Wrocław manuscript, nor does he explore the transmission of the pope's epistle, but he does name Ziegler (1915) as the edition of Bryennios' speech (albeit with a mistake: Leone [1994, 922–923, n. 5] cites 341 as the page number instead of 241).

should the Wrocław codex be collated with the Vat. lat. 3878 and Arcudius' 1630 edition (and maybe with Migne 1866, cf. note 18), but a new *recensio codicum* should also be made, as the Latin text could have been preserved in still other manuscripts.

The only critical edition of the Greek text was prepared by Spyridon Lampros and appeared posthumously in 1930, in the fourth volume of his Παλαιολόγεια καὶ Πελοποννησιακά.[20] Later, Georg Hofmann, a historian of the Council of Ferrara-Florence, included the letter in his 1946 edition of the papal correspondence pertaining to the council. Hofmann cited the Greek text from Lampros and the Latin from Arcudius' edition, adding variant readings of Vat. lat. 3878 in the apparatus, at times preferring the readings of the latter.[21] Hofmann (1946, 131) admits that it was impossible to prepare a critical edition on the basis of only Arcudius 1630 and the Vatican manuscript. Indeed, his edition can be hardly referred to as critical.[22]

The Greek text had been usually referred to as a translation from Latin made by Theodore Gaza, a well-known Byzantine scholar active in Italy in the mid-Quattrocento.[23] Still, in the short introduction to his edition, Hofmann stresses the difference between the Greek and the Latin variant, confessing that he could not ascertain which of the two ought to be considered the original:

---

[20] Lampros (1930, 49–63).

[21] Hofmann (1946, 131–138).

[22] For instance, he includes insignificant orthographic variants, such as *charissime / carissime* (Hofmann 1946, 132), in his apparatus but omits some major discrepancies and tacitly implements his conjectural reconstructions. Thus, the Vatican codex (f. 171r, ll. 16–17) reads: *Accipe igi(tur) carissime fili que dicturi sumus ta(n)q(uam) ab amantissimo a(n)i(m)o, cui et libere colloquendi ap(?) db(?)*, the end of the sentence marked by a marginal *crux* of the scribe's hand. Arcudius (1630, 686, ll. 19–21) offers the plausible variant *Accipe igitur charissime fili, quae dicturi sumus, tanquam ab amantissimo animo, quem vere et libere te alloquentem deputa*, whereas Hofmann (1946, 132, ll. 1–2), in his supposed citation of Arcudius' version, tacitly substitutes 'amico' for *animo*, without any mention in the apparatus.

[23] Gaza's translations from Greek to Latin and vice versa have been studied in a number of works – e.g., Weber (1852, 52–55); Mohler (1942); Bevegni (1992a), (1992b), (1993), (1994), (2004); Santoro (1992); Kindstrand (1993); Perfetti (1995), (1996); Monfasani (1999), (2006a), (2006b); Repici (2003); Gionta (2004); Berger (2005 *passim*); Beullens & Gotthelf (2007); Beullens (2008 *passim*); Papanicolaou (2007); Ventura (2008); Salanitro (2014, 161–228) (a collection of his articles on Gaza, published since the late 1960s); Vorobyev (2018, 2019). On Gaza's life, see Bianca (1999); Leone (1989) (also Geanakoplos [1989], which contains not a few mistakes). New discoveries concerning Gaza are likely forthcoming due to the paleographical research introduced in Speranzi (2012).

Estne textus Latinus iam editus versioni Graecae Theodori Gazis praeferendus? Estne textus Graecus exemplar originale, secundum quod textus Latinus forsitan tamquam versio illius factus est?[24]

In his 2007 article, Hanak echoes Hofmann's uncertainty while noting that 'the language of the Greek rendition is more moderate in tone, unlike the Latin text, which is abrupt in a number of passages.' Hanak seems thus to consider the Latin text the original and the Greek text the translation. Therefore, Hanak makes his English translation from the Latin, not from the Greek variant.[25]

Indeed, in November 1451, about a month after the official letter had been dispatched, Gaza himself mentions his translation of it in a private letter he sent from Rome to his two brothers staying in Constantinople. This letter was studied in the aforementioned 1994 article by Pietro Luigi Maria Leone, who only touches upon Nicholas V's letter to the emperor as background information. In the epistle to his brothers, Gaza makes it clear that he had translated the pope's letter:

Θεόδωρος Ἀνδρονίκῳ καὶ Δημητρίῳ τοῖς ἀδελφοῖς εὖ πράττειν. Διανοουμένῳ μοι ἐπιστεῖλαι ὑμῖν, ὅπως τὰ περὶ τὴν βασιλικὴν πρεσβείαν διαπέπρακται, οὐδὲν οὕτως ἔδοξεν ἱκανόν, ὡς τὸ τὴν τοῦ μεγάλου ἀρχιερέως ἀπόκρισιν <u>μεταφράσαντι</u> πέμψαι· ἤδε γὰρ τά τε ἄλλα πάντα εὖ μάλα δηλοῖ καὶ τὴν τοῦ ἀποκρινομένου αὐτοῦ γνώμην, ἣν ἔχει περὶ τῶν ὅλων, φανερωτάτην καθίστησι. Ταῦτα μὲν οὖν εἴσεσθε, τὴν <u>ἑρμηνευθεῖσαν</u> τήνδε πρὸς τὸν βασιλέα ἐπιστολὴν ἀναγνόντες.[26]

---

[24] Hofmann (1946, 130): 'Should the published Latin text be preferred to Theodore Gaza's Greek version? Perhaps the Greek text is the original and the Latin one was created as its translation?' Joseph Gill (1959, 378) names Hofmann's edition as one 'where both the Latin and the Greek texts, which differ slightly, are given – neither is certainly authentic – and where the question of the date is discussed'. Why Gill considers both texts clearly inauthentic remains unclear. On Hofmann's treatment of the date, see below.

[25] Hanak (2007, 337)); he does not explain what intentions underlay that moderation.

[26] 'Theodore greets [his] brothers Andronikos and Demetrios. Since I was intending to inform you on how the matters of the imperial embassy had been accomplished, nothing seemed to me as adequate as to send the answer of the great pontiff, since I have translated it. Indeed, not only does it reveal all other things, but it also makes quite clear the opinion of the replier (i.e., the pope) concerning all the things. Thus, you will know these things if you read this translated letter to the emperor.' The English translation is mine; the Greek text is quoted from the edition prepared by the aforementioned Pietro Luigi Maria Leone (Gaza 1990, 48, ll. 1–10). As for the previous editor of Gaza's letters, Emilio Pinto, his dating (1441), as well as his interpretation of the addressees as

Therefore, the Greek text is definitely Gaza's version of the Latin original and not vice versa.[27]

The Purpose of Gaza's Translation

What remains unclear is whether Gaza translated the letter just for his brothers and friends or whether his version was officially commissioned by the pope to be sent to the Byzantine emperor.[28] The words μεταφράσαντι and ἑρμηνευθεῖσαν would corroborate either interpretation.[29] Scholars who have studied the letter have either passed over the question of the purpose of the translation or took for granted that it was commissioned by the pope.[30] If the latter is true, was Gaza's

---

members of the Byzantine imperial family (Gaza 1975; discussion, edition and translation printed, respectively, on pp. 29–32, 75–77, and 129–130), are certainly erroneous, as Leone (1994, 921, n. 2) first noticed. Cf. Leone's general negative assessment of Pinto's edition in Gaza (1990, 27). On Gaza's epistolary legacy, see also Leone (1993), where each letter is briefly paraphrased and commented upon (on his translation of Nicholas V's letter, see pp. 204–205).

[27] Interestingly, Ziegler (1915, 4) describes the Wrocław copy of the pope's Latin letter to the emperor as *Nicolai V. papae responsio ad Imperatorem Constantinum. Oratio e graeco in latinum a Theodoro Gaza versa, quae saepius typis expressa est*. Kristeller, apparently puzzled, adds *sic* (Kristeller [1989, 427]). Given the information provided by Gaza himself in his letter to his brothers, Ziegler must have made a mistake.

[28] The alternative that the translation might have been commissioned by Constantine XI can be hardly the case, given that Gaza lived in Italy in the early 1450s, and there is no evidence of him having travelled to Constantinople after 1440 (see, e.g., Leone 1989, 66). Besides, the above letter to his brothers indicates Rome as the place where the translation was made (Gaza 1990, 50, l. 50). Nevertheless, the possibility that the emperor's legate was the commissioner of the translation cannot be ruled out. Since we do not know any details of Leontaris' sojourn in Rome, nor of his possible interactions with the Greeks dwelling there, it is difficult to state anything for or against such a hypothesis.

[29] On the one hand, if he had been ordered to translate the letter by the pope, Gaza, addressing his brothers, would probably have expressed it explicitly – he would certainly have been proud of such an important task. On the other hand, this argument is not strong enough to rule out Gaza's translation as having originated from his own, unofficial initiative, as the possibility that he had informed his brothers of the pope's commission in a previous letter cannot be ruled out, such that it would not have been necessary to specify it in this letter. Since the letter cited above is the only extant evidence of Gaza's correspondence with his brothers, it is difficult to estimate the intensity of their epistolary intercourse.

[30] Domenico Giorgi, an eighteenth-century author of Nicholas V's biography, does not doubt that it was an official translation (Giorgi [1742, 99]), but, since Giorgi's knowledge of the letter is

version meant to be sent to Constantine XI as the official translation or made for circulation among Greeks in Italy? If, on the contrary, Gaza translated the letter *sua sponte*, how did he get access to the Latin text? Even though none of these possibilities can be proven with the current data, it is instructive to reflect on the purpose of Gaza's translation based on the information available.

Invited by Giovanni Tortelli, the pope's right hand in matters of humanist learning and books, Gaza arrived in Rome in February or March 1450,[31] and, by autumn 1451, when the letter to Constantine was composed, he had definitely started his activity as translator in the humanist circle patronized by Nicholas V.[32] By summer 1451, he had already finished his translation of Theophrastus' *Historia plantarum*.[33] Since the career of another Greek émigré as translator, George of Trebizond, Gaza's main rival in Rome, was declining by autumn 1451 and since George 'never approached the intimacy with Nicholas which a Giovanni Tortelli or a Giannozzo Manetti enjoyed',[34] Gaza, considered by then the main Hellenist of the papal court, was quite likely to have been commissioned to translate the letter, rather than George or anyone else in Rome (if, indeed, the pope had

---

apparently based only on Arcudius, his statement cannot be considered significant. Nevertheless, Giorgi was cited by Émile Legrand in his influential *Bibliographie hellénique* (Legrand [1885, XXXIV]), which is why, a century after Legrand, Giorgi's opinion was repeated by Deno J. Geanakoplos in his overview of Gaza's life (Geanakoplos [1989, 77, n. 37]). Leone, the above-mentioned editor of Gaza's correspondence, also follows Legrand in considering the translation an official one (Leone [1989, 71]; Leone [1994, 924]). In the most up-to-date biography of Gaza hitherto published, Concetta Bianca mentions Gaza's translation with a reference to Migne (1866), seeming likewise to take for granted that the translation was made at the pope's commission: 'In qualità di traduttore il Gaza fu inoltre coinvolto in progetti di politica ecclesiale: nell'ottobre 1451 tradusse la lettera di Niccolò V' (Bianca [1999, 740]).

[31] Leone (1989, 70).

[32] On Nicholas V's initiative to have ancient Greek authors translated to Latin, see Monfasani (1976, 69–83).

[33] Gionta (2004, 181); cf. Bianca (1999, 739–740). The reason for the broader dating proposed by Luciana Repici for the completion of Gaza's translation of Theophrastus is unclear, Repici (2003, 423): '[La versione della botanica teofrastea] fu forse completata verso il 1451 o in anni di poco successivi (1453–1454)'. Indeed, Daniela Gionta's argument for dating the text to around late spring 1451 seems quite plausible. Namely, she quotes Gaza's preface, dedicated to the pope, where he explicitly says that he had spent one year with him (*iam annum apud te manens*). Since we know precisely the time of his arrival in Rome (February or March 1450) and we also know that Gaza was invited by Tortelli – i.e., he was, most probably, presented to the pope directly upon arrival in the city – Gionta's dating should be considered secure.

[34] Monfasani (1976, 104).

ordered for it to be translated). All this seems to support the hypothesis that Gaza's translation could have been a task officially assigned by the pope. Indeed, Nicholas adored Greek antiquity and most probably would not have minded if Gaza had translated the letter in the humanist non-verbatim manner, so as to comply with the standards of Attic elegance, as he eventually managed to do (see below). Thus, the discrepancies between the Latin and the Greek text cannot alone be proof of the unofficial character of Gaza's version.

On the one hand, his diplomatic softening of the pope's tone,[35] which would explain part of the discrepancies, could be taken as corroborating the option that Gaza's translation was made officially and that its intended reader was Constantine XI. On the other hand, Gaza's friends and relatives, especially those dwelling in Constantinople and not in Italy, could have been offended by certain harsh words in the pope's letter, just as the emperor could have been; therefore, Gaza, who was (as we know, e.g., from his letter to his brothers discussed above) a supporter of the pope's politics, would have wanted the Greek version of the letter to sound softer also in case he intended it to be read only by his Byzantine friends.

Even though, to my knowledge, there are no extant Greek letters of Nicholas, it is attested that he did dispatch at least one letter in Greek – namely, to the despot of Morea Theodore II, in 1447 or 1448.[36]

Whether Gaza's Greek version was sent to the Byzantine emperor or not, its wide diffusion in Italy, demonstrated by the significant number of manuscripts present in Italian libraries, shows that it was eagerly read by the Greek émigrés in the Italian peninsula. Given the importance of the letter for the fate of Byzantium, it is no wonder that Gaza's Greek friends were interested in reading it in their mother tongue – as also with Gaza's brothers in Constantinople. Thus, either Nicholas himself, or rather a secretary or a group of secretaries, would have composed the Latin text of the letter, which would then have been translated into Greek by Gaza. Though the circumstances of his work remain unclear, Gaza in any case probably had a broader audience in mind than just the emperor and his court.

---

[35] Hanak (2007, 337) briefly notices the softer tone in Gaza's translation (cf. p. 6 above).

[36] Hofmann (1946, 119, No. 293). Nevertheless, the letters that the previous popes Martin V and Eugene IV sent to Byzantine emperors and patriarchs of Constantinople are extant only in Latin (Hofmann [1940, Nos. 2–4, 6, 9, 15, 17–18, 25, 27, 51, 75, 80, 82]; [1946, No. 249]).

The Date of the Letter

A striking example of textual discrepancies between the Latin original and the Greek version is the date provided at the end of the letter.[37] Arcudius puts it as *V Idus Octobris* in the Latin text and, accordingly, πρώτῃ ἐπὶ δέκα Ὀκτωβρίου in the Greek version, dating it clearly to 11 October.[38] On the other hand, ms. Vat. lat. 3878 reads *Qui(n)to K(a)l(endas) Octobris* – i.e., 27 September [see Ill. 1].[39]

Ill. 1. *Qui(n)to K(a)l(endas) Octobris* (Vat. lat. 3878, f. 174r, l. 4).

Although Domenico Giorgi (see n. 30) considered the *Kalendas* in the Vatican manuscript to be a scribal error, the tradition of the Greek version supports the reading *Kalendas*. According to the critical edition of the Greek text prepared by Lampros, all twelve collated manuscripts read πέμπτῃ πρὸ καλανδῶν ὀκτωβρίων – i.e., 27 September – except codex E, i.e. Modena, Biblioteca Estense, α.T.8.10 (Puntoni 148), ff. 29r–31r, which reads πρώτῃ ἐπὶ δέκα ὀκτωβρίων.[40] The latter reading was probably a conjecture made on the basis of the Latin text.

Given this ambiguity, it is apparently impossible to decide if the letter was originally dated 27 September or 11 October 1451. Nevertheless, since only Arcudius and codex E among the Greek texts and Arcudius among the Latin texts read 11 October, while eleven codices among the Greek texts and Vat. lat. 3878 among the Latin texts read 27 September, the latter appears to be more plausible.[41] The date '11 October' might have originated from a scribal error in the tradition of the Latin text (as Giorgi supposed, *mutatis mutandis*). Indeed,

---

[37] Hanak does not discuss this question, apart from a brief note on the discrepancy of the date in Hofmann's Latin and Greek texts (Hanak [2007, 359 n. 77]).

[38] Arcudius (1630, 698–699). Setton (1978, 107, n. 94) refers to Rinaldi (1694, 376) as a source for dating the letter to 11 October, but Rinaldi simply reprints the Latin text from Arcudius' edition.

[39] Vat. lat. 3878, f. 174r, l. 4.

[40] Lampros (1930, 63).

[41] Hofmann comes to the same conclusion, adding that the description of the copy once kept in the Vatican archives bears the date 27 September, too (Hofmann [1946, 131]). Still, even though he discusses the variant reading of Vat. lat. 3878 in his introductory note, he does not provide it in the apparatus. As noted above, a collation with the codex from Wrocław and other possibly extant manuscripts should be carried out.

given the wide use of the abbreviations *id* and *kl* for *Idus* and *Kalendas*,[42] *V kl octobris* could have been easily confused with *V id octobris* by a copyist (cf. Ill. 1, above). The latter reading could have been present in a manuscript that both underlay Arcudius' edition and served as *Kollationsvorlage* for the Greek codex now in Modena.

European Country Names in Gaza's Translation

In what follows, further discrepancies will be discussed – namely, those regarding the aforementioned list of European country names. These discrepancies are explicable partly paleographically, partly due to Gaza's diplomatic approach to translation.

The Latin text is far from elegant and can be hardly designated as humanistic. Gaza tries to embellish it, so his Atticist translation, made *ad sententiam*, not *ad verbum*,[43] often diverges from the Latin original for the sake of both clarity and elegance. I will confine myself to just one example:

> *Si qui vero sunt, qui in decreto unionis nonnulla posita minus intelligant, procures illos ad nos proficisci. Satisfaciemus Deo concedente eorum dubitationibus, honorabuntur a nobis et gaudebunt se apud nos non fuisse despectos.*

> Εἰ δέ τινες τῶν ἐν τῷ ὅρῳ λεγομένων ἄττα συνιέναι οὐχ οἷοί τε, ἔστω σοι διὰ φροντίδος πέμψαι αὐτοὺς πρὸς ἡμᾶς. Σὺν Θεῷ γὰρ ἱκανῶς τὰς αὐτῶν ἀπορίας ἀπομακρινάμενοι διαλύσομεν καὶ τιμήσαντες τοὺς ἄνδρας καὶ δωρησάμενοι ἀποπέμψομεν χαίροντας.[44]

Here, Gaza's attention to the rhythmic structure seems evident. Although most of his modifications are merely stylistic or clarifying, some seem to carry a diplomatic function, meant to soften certain harsh expressions, as Hanak noted (see n. 35 above). Thus, in the second sentence, Gaza omits the arrogant litotes *gaudebunt se apud nos non fuisse despectos*, which becomes ἀποπέμψομεν χαίροντας.

---

[42] Cf. Cappelli (1929, 172, 196).

[43] On the humanist *translatio ad sententiam* as opposed to the scholastic *translatio ad verbum*, see, e.g., Pade (2013), with further literature.

[44] Hofmann (1946, 134, ll. 33–35; 138, ll. 12–14).

Gaza's diplomatic attitude as a translator is even more evident when, other than softening the pope's harsh tone, he tries bridging a gap between the Latin and Byzantine cultures. Whether he made the translation officially for dispatching to the emperor or just for his friends and relatives, he modified some Latin words and expressions which would otherwise have sounded utterly incomprehensible to both a Greek general public and the Byzantine emperor – *inter alia*, the names of Western European countries.

As the pope asserts, the countries of the West have accepted the decree of the Florentine council and are awaiting union with the Eastern Church. He adds that the decree had been sent everywhere (*terrarum ubique transmissum* / διεπέμφθη ἀπανταχοῦ) and, apparently as a measure of persuasion and pressure, provides a list of countries as 'witnesses' (*testes* / μάρτυρες), meaning, apparently, that these are the places where copies of the decree had been dispatched. This catalogue thus constitutes an example of the denomination of different parts of Europe at an early stage of Humanist Greek, a balance between the humanist classicising approach and the diplomatic demands of adaptation to the Byzantine understanding of the world.[45] The list of countries begins with Spain:

> ut <…> decretum huiusmodi unionis concorditer publicaretur. Facta sunt ista teste toto orbe terrarum, et decretum unionis huiusmodi et Graecis et Latinis litteris editum cum subscriptione manuali eorum, qui interfuere, terrarum ubique transmissum. Testis est Hispania quatuor christianis regnis ornata, Castella, Aragonia, Portugallia, Navarra.

> ψήφισμα δὲ εἶτ' οὖν θέσιν καὶ ὅρον ἑνώσεως τοιοῦτον γνώμῃ ἐξενεγκόντες κοινῇ ἀνεκήρυξαν. Πέπρακται μὲν οὖν ταῦτα μάρτυρι πάσῃ τῇ οἰκουμένῃ καὶ ὁ τῆς ἑνώσεως ὅρος ἑλληνιστί τε καὶ ῥωμαϊστὶ γεγραμμένος διεπέμφθη ἀπανταχοῦ. Μάρτυς Ἰβηρία <u>πᾶσα πολυθρύλητος χώρα</u>, εἰς τέτταρας

---

[45] Not only was the use of the ancient names of countries and peoples an attribute of the humanist style, they had been employed throughout the Byzantine history, combined with more recent denominations, which created great confusion (see nn. 1 and 54). Gaza's use of names designating Byzantium and the Byzantines, as well as ancient Greeks and Romans, in comparison with the relevant instances in Gaza's other writings, is a peculiar topic that should be treated separately, discussed partly in Irmscher (1961); Lamers (2015, 59–61, 86, 170–171); I am currently working on one such article. On the transformation of the Byzantine Roman / Hellenic identity in general, see, apart from Lamers (2015), e.g., Mantouvalou (1985, 174, 182–183, 188, 191–192); Kaldellis (2007, esp. 317–388); Kaldellis (2017); Page (2008, 51–71); Kaplanis (2014); Lamers (forthcoming).

χριστιανῶν βασιλείας <u>εὐδαιμονεστάτας</u> διαιρουμένη, Καστελλίαν δηλονότι καὶ Ἀραγονίαν καὶ Πορτογαλλίαν καὶ Ναβαρίαν.[46]

Here, Gaza adds an epithet to Iberia, 'much spoken of, well-known country', maybe so as to distinguish it from the other Iberia – namely, Georgia – which was much better known in Constantinople. On the contrary, naming the four countries of the Iberian peninsula 'highly prosperous' is probably nothing more than rhetorical amplification, inserted to make the pope's argument stronger – i.e., great prosperous countries are wishing for the union to be completed. The text continues:

Testis est Britannia maior <u>Anglicorum regis</u>[47] <u>*subiecta ditioni.*</u>[48]

Μάρτυς Βρεττανία <u>νῆσος</u> μεγίστη <u>τῇ ἠπείρῳ παρακειμένη.</u>[49]

---

[46] Hofmann (1946, 133, ll. 35–40; 137, ll. 11–16). The same subdivision of the Iberian peninsula is found in Laonikos Chalkokondyles' *Histories*, the only difference being that Καστελλία is avoided in the latter, with Ἰβηρία clearly used for Castile: Λίβυες γὰρ διαβάντες τὸν πρὸς Ἡρακλείους στήλας πορθμὸν κατέσχον τε κατὰ βραχὺ προϊόντες τὴν Ἰβηρίαν, μετὰ δὲ ταῦτα Ναβάρην τε χειρωσάμενοι καὶ Πορτουγαλλίαν χώραν, ἔστε ἐπὶ Ταρακῶνα ἐλαύνοντες, τὰ ἐς τήνδε αὖ τὴν χώραν καταστρεψάμενοι ἐσέβαλλον ἐς τὴν Κελτικήν ('For the North Africans had crossed the straits at the Pillars of Herakles, had conquered and quickly passed through Iberia, and after that had seized the land of Navarre and Portugal, advancing as far as Aragon. When they had conquered that land, they invaded France', transl. by Kaldellis in Chalkokondyles [2014, vol. 1, 140–141]). On the double use of Ἰβηρία in Chalkokondyles – namely, to denote the whole peninsula *sensu lato* and Castile *sensu stricto* – see Chalkokondyles (2014, vol. 2, 525). Manuel Chrysoloras, whose knowledge of Western geography is far poorer than that of Chalkokondyles, distinguishes Spain from Iberia as two different Western countries (the latter here certainly not denoting Georgia): 'Θαῦμα ὄντως ἔστιν ἰδεῖν ἀπὸ Ἰσπανίας καὶ Ἰβηρίας, καὶ Γαλατίας, καὶ τῶν Βριτανικῶν νήσων' 'it is indeed marvelous to see [people] from Spain, Iberia, Gaul, and the British Isles' (Chrysoloras [1866, col. 32]; unfortunately, I could not consult the newer edition, Chrysoloras [2000]).

[47] Printed in Arcudius (1630) as *regi* (the same, clearly erroneous, reading is provided by codex Vat. lat. 3878, f. 173r, l. 10), corrected already by Migne (1866, col. 1208, l. 5), then by Hofmann, whose edition, for the Latin text, is based on Arcudius (1630).

[48] While Arcudius (repeated by Hofmann and Migne) reads *ditioni*, the Vat. lat. 3878 provides an orthographically better variant, *dicioni*, though the Vatican manuscript later reads *Scocia* instead of *Scotia* – see Ill. 4, below.

[49] Hofmann (1946, 133, l. 40; 137, l. 16). Hanak's (2007, 357) translation, 'the Anglican royal subjects of greater Britain witnessed this', is perplexing in terms of the syntax and his use of the word 'Anglican'.

Here, Nicholas mentions Great Britain as part of the English kingdom, apparently because he also kept in mind the continental territories that were under English rule. Gaza, on the other hand, thought that it would be too complicated to mention these circumstances to the Byzantines; instead, he informs his Greek readers that Britain is an island, situated not far from the continent.

Ireland and Scotland, on the other hand, are described in both versions as islands far from the mainland:

> *Testis Hibernia et Scotia insulae maximae extra continentem positae.*

> Μάρτυς Ἰβέρνη τε καὶ Σκοτία νῆσοι μεγάλαι πελάγιαι.[50]

Here, Gaza does not change anything, but it is certainly noteworthy that both the original and the translation name Scotland as an island. The text then moves on to Germany:

> *Testis Germania numerosissimis*[51] *populis culta et longissimo terrarum tractu distenta.*

> Μάρτυς Γερμανία, χώρα ἐπὶ πλεῖστον πλάτει τε καὶ μήκει ἐκτεταμένη καὶ πανταχῆ πολυανθρωποτάτη.[52]

Gaza's text is a bit more elegant than the original, but he does not change anything substantial; he probably just eliminates the ambiguity of *numerosissimis populis culta*, which could be interpreted as either 'inhabited by very populous nations' – i.e., 'densely populated' – as Gaza does, or 'inhabited by many different peoples', reflecting the number of independent states in the German-speaking region. The catalogue is especially fascinating when the pope progresses to the Nordic countries:

---

[50] Hofmann (1946, 133, ll. 40–41; 137, ll. 16–17).

[51] Codex Vat. lat. 3878 reads *innumerosissimis* (f. 173r, l. 12), not mentioned in Hofmann's apparatus.

[52] Hofmann (1946, 133, ll. 41–42; 137, ll. 17–18). Hanak (2007, 357), again, provides a syntactically strange translation: 'Outside the continental region, the great islands of Ireland and Scotland witnessed [this]; among the cultured populace of the numerous Germans and the extent to the most distant tracts of land witnessed this'. Dimensions and population are parameters specially noticed also by Chalkokondyles in the description of Germany: Ἔστι δὲ γένος τοῦτο μέγα καὶ ἐπὶ πολὺ διῆκον τῶν κατὰ τὴν οἰκουμένην (2014, 1:112; in Kaldellis' translation: 'This people is populous and occupies a large part of the world').

Testis Danorum regio, testis Norvegia. Testes sub Daciam extremi populi ad Aquilonem positi.

Μάρτυς ἡ <u>τῶν καλουμένων</u> Δάμνων <u>ἀξιόλογος</u> χώρα. Οἴδασι πάντες Νωρβέγιοι <u>καὶ Συέτιοι</u>, γένη ἔσχατα πρὸς ἄρκτον οἰκοῦντα.[53]

Gaza seems to be sure that his Greek readers are unfamiliar with Denmark, so he writes 'the remarkable country of the *so-called* Danes'. On the other hand, he might have added the words 'τῶν καλουμένων' to emphasize his deliberate labelling of Danes with such a peculiar Greek name. Indeed, I could not find further occurrences of this Greek designation of Danes. It is plausible that Gaza might have adopted the name of a people mentioned by Ptolemy, Δάμναι, even though they seem to be identified as a people living to the north of the Taklamakan desert, located in the northwest of modern-day China.[54] Since Vat. lat. 3878 reads *Dannorum* instead of *Danorum*, it cannot be excluded that Gaza's Latin *Vorlage* would have spelled the word with a double *n*, too, which, given Gaza's Italian entourage, could have led him to the idea that *Dannorum* was a corruption, well explicable both paleographically and linguistically, of *Damnorum*; such a reconstruction

---

[53] Hofmann (1946, 133, ll. 42–43; 137, ll. 18–19).

[54] Τὰ μὲν οὖν ἀρκτικώτατα τῆς Σηρικῆς κατανέμεται ἔθνη ἀνθρωποφάγων· ὑφ' οὓς Ἄννιβοι ἔθνος ὑπέρκειται τῶν ὁμωνύμων ὀρῶν, μεταξὺ δὲ τούτων καὶ τῶν Αὐζακίων Σίζυγες (v. Σίγυζες) ἔθνος, ὑφ' οὓς Δάμναι (Ptol. *Geog.* 6.16.4.1–3; cf. Stückelberger & Graßhoff [2006, 666]. The peoples Ptolemy names here are also dwelling in the extreme north, but it is explicitly specified as the extreme north of *Serica* (the latter standing for the northwestern part of China or China in general), so this passage could be hardly interpreted as referring to the ἀρκτικώτατα of Western Europe. Gaza might have found the name Δάμναι in a list of peoples where no precise geographical position of their region was given. Alternatively, though less probably, he might have thought that both *Serica*, according to Ptolemy, and *Dacia* (if understood roughly as present-day Romania and Hungary) had Scythians as their neighbours. The Byzantine tradition of applying ancient names to modern peoples, leading to frequent confusions, is well attested: '[The Byzantines'] ignorance of the West is to some extent excusable. Part of it stems from the Byzantine propensity for archaising. The nations beyond the boundaries of Byzantium had to be disguised or dignified with Herodotean names. The Serbs become Triballians, the Bulgars Mysians, the Hungarians Paeonians and the Mongols Scythians (though here confusion arises because some historians apply the name Scythians to the Bulgars as well)' (Nicol 1967, 315). Nevertheless, the possibility that Gaza called Danes Δάμναι since both Dacians (i.e., Danes) and Ptolemy's Δάμναι were neighboured by the Scythians becomes less probable if one considers that the Latin text of Nicholas' epistle that Gaza used read '*testis Suuvecia*' or similar, instead of '*testes sub Daciam*' (see below).

could have been the reason for Gaza's choice of the Greek name.[55] In any case, so as to give more weight to this unknown Danish land, he calls it ἀξιόλογος (important, remarkable).

Most stunning is that not only does Gaza explain where Norway is located, he also adds Sweden, which is absent from the Latin text. By the fifteenth century, *Dacia* had long since become the standard Latin name for Denmark[56] but could not just be transliterated as Δακία, because the Byzantines would have surely understood it in its original meaning, as the well-known region by the lower Danube.[57] One could hypothesize that this is why Gaza substituted *sub Daciam extremi populi ad Aquilonem positi* with the more precise Σουέτιοι. In fact, the explanation is much simpler and lies in the corruption of the Latin text. In this case, the Vatican manuscript offers a definitely better reading than Arcudius' edition. While Arcudius (1630, 694, ll. 26–27) reads:

> *Testis Norvegia. Testes sub Daciam extremi populi ad Aquilonem positi,*[58]

the codex Vat. lat. 3878 (f. 173r, ll. 26–27) offers the following variant:

---

[55] The Latin consonant cluster *mn* is usually simplified to a geminate *nn* in Italian (also in fifteenth-century Central Italy), cf. Rohlfs (1966, 381). Still, the reading *Dannorum* could be an idiosyncrasy of the Vatican manuscript, which misspells many of the foreign personal and place names (e.g., *Paleogulus*, f. 172v, l. 26, instead of *Paleologus* in Arcudius [1630, 694, l. 4]; *Britania* and *Panonia* in Vat. lat. 3878, f. 173, ll. 10 & 16, instead of *Britannia* and *Pannonia* in Arcudius [1630, 694, ll. 21 & 28]).

[56] It had been first established as the name of the church province and was then transferred to the kingdom. The origin of this toponym is due to Paulus Orosius' and Isidore of Seville's information about the vicinity of *Dacia* and *Gothia* (Jakobsen [2012], which is based mainly on Gallén [1957]).

[57] Laonikos Chalkokondyles speaks of Δανία (2014, vol. 1, 110, 138, 214), but Gaza for whatever reason does not use this name. Walter Hanak was apparently not aware that *Dacia* was the usual toponym for Denmark in the Middle Ages, since his English translation (2007, 357) transfers this passage to the Balkans: 'The Danish kingdom witnessed this; Norway witnessed this. The foreign populations under Dacia to the region of Aquileia witnessed this'. As it seems, Hanak simply misread *Aquileiam* (pro *Aquilonem*), since, if it had been his conjecture, he would have explained it in a footnote, as he does in other instances. He also translates ἔσχατα as 'foreign', not 'extremely far, utmost far', apparently because the people living between Dacia and Veneto could hardly be defined as living at the margins of the world.

[58] This is also the reading in Migne (1866, col. 1208, ll. 9–11), and Hofmann (1946, 133, ll. 42–43), which follow Arcudius, the only difference consisting of a comma instead of Hofmann's full stop after *Norvegia*.

Test(is) Norvvegia, test(is) Suvvecia extremi p(o)p(u)li ad Aquilonem po(s)iti.

The rare toponym 'Sweden' could easily have undergone distortions via scribal error. Illustration 2 shows how the word looks in Vat. lat. 3878.

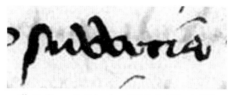

Ill. 2. *Suvvecia* (Vat. lat. 3878, f. 173r, l. 26)

The Vatican codex, as noted above, could hardly have served as Arcudius' *Vorlage*, since its textual disagreements with Arcudius' edition cannot be explained as the latter's conjectures *ope ingenii*. Still, Arcudius most probably used a manuscript in which *Suvvecia* had been written in a similar (maybe even more misleading) way.

That the word in the Illustration 2 should really be understood as *Suvvecia* is corroborated, for instance, by the presence of an identical group *vv* in the nearby *Norvvegia* (see Ill. 3).

Ill. 3. *Norvvegia* (Vat. lat. 3878, f. 173r, l. 26). Double *v*.

In *Suvvecia*, the long curvy stroke over the *i* is part of the same letter, but since it significantly inclines to the right, it could be misinterpreted as a *titulus* over the next letter, *a*, standing for nasalisation, whence would have derived the misinterpretation of the accusative form *-am* (cf. similar long supralinear strokes of the *i* in the Illustrations 4 and 5, where they also hang over the subsequent letter).

Ill. 4. *Scocia* (for *Scotia*, Vat. lat. 3878, f. 173r, l. 23). A long stroke over the *i*.

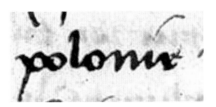

Ill. 5. *Polonie* (for *Poloniae*, Vat. lat. 3878, f. 173r, l. 7). A long stroke over the *i*.

From the Illustration 2 above, it is clear how easily the first *v* could have been misinterpreted as *b* (cf. *ubique* in the Illustration 6, spelled *vbiq(ue)*, where the *b* differs from the *v* only by the angle of inclination). This is likely why Arcudius' edition contains the preposition *sub* here.

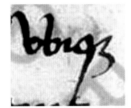

Ill. 6. *Ubique* (Vat. lat. 3878, f. 173r, l. 7). Similar *v* and *b*.

While the change from *suv* to *sub* is understandable, a less trivial question is how *ve* became *da*. I see at least two possible explanations. First, it might have been a conjecture of a later copyist who misread *sub baciam*, considered it a corrupted toponym, and deliberately changed the supposed accusative *baciam* to *daciam*, which would actually not have been an imperfect emendation, since, as discussed above, *Dacia* was a standard toponym for Denmark. Another possibility is yet another misreading. Namely, the second vertical stroke of the *u* in *Suvvecia*, together with the first stroke of the first *v*, could have been interpreted together as *d*, which would make the reader consider the curvy right part of the first *v*, together with the first stroke of the second *v*, as a second *d*; thus, the rest of the second *v*, together with the *e*, becomes similar to an *a*, rendering the whole word *siddaciam* (see Ill. 2; cf. Ills. 7 and 8 for this scribe's execution of the ligature *da*). Such a misreading, even though its first part, *sid*, is senseless, could have led to the notion of the presence of the word *Daciam* in the sentence.

As for the syntax, the word *testis* appears anaphorically ten times in the list of countries. After the first two full instances of the word (Ill. 7, instances a–b), the scribe of the Vatican codex opts for an abbreviated form, substituting the ending *-is* (or whatever case or number it should have been) with a loop-shaped element, resembling an enlarged *-e*, which allows for syntactic ambiguity (see Ill. 7, instance c].[59] Thus, *test(is) Norvegia, test(is) Suvvecia, extremi populi ad Aquilonem positi* could have been interpreted as *test(is) Norvegia, test(es) sub Daciam extremi populi ad Aquilonem positi* (see Ill. 8).

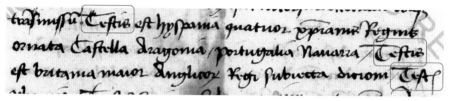

Ill. 7. [...] *tra(n)smissu(m). Testis est Hyspania quatuor chr(ist)ianis regnis ornata Castella Aragonia, Portugalia Navarra, testis est Britania maior Anglicorum regi subiecta dicioni, test(is)* [...] (Vat. lat. 3878, f. 173r, ll. 19–21): instances a and b: full forms *testis*; instance c: abbreviated form *test(is)*.

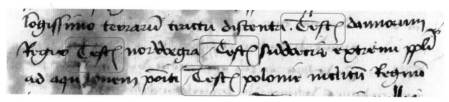

Ill. 8. [...] *lo(n)gissimo terraru(m) tractu distenta. Test(is) Dannorum regio test(is) Norvvegia, test(is) Suvvecia extremi p(o)p(u)li ad Aquilonem po(s)iti, test(is) Polonie inclitu(m) regnu(m)* (Vat. lat. 3878, f. 173r, ll. 25–27). The abbreviated form *test(is)* appears four times here.

Concluding this excursus on Nordic toponyms, it is worth repeating that Arcudius most probably used a manuscript other than Vat. lat. 3878; therefore, the above paleographical demonstration is valid just as an example of how Arcudius (or the scribe of his *Vorlage*, or of its parent manuscript) could have committed the error that led from *Suvvecia* to *sub Daciam*.

Leaving Scandinavia, Nicholas V passes on to Poland and Hungary. The latter is denoted with a *hendiadys, Ungariaque et Pannonia*. Strangely enough, Gaza completely omits this region (or is it, on the contrary, a later interpolation in the Latin text?), mentioning only Poland:

---

[59] Cappelli (1929, 374) registers this form as an abbreviation for *testonis*, meaning an Italian coin in use from the latter half of the fifteenth century onwards, yet it seems evident that, here, the abbreviation simply stands for *testis* (it cannot be an unabbreviated *teste*, since the scribe writes 'e' differently; moreover, the ablative *teste* would not agree with *insulae maximae, regio, regnum,* or *omnis Gallia*).

Testis Poloniae inclytum regnum, <u>testis Ungariaque et Pannonia</u>.

Οἶδεν ἡ Πολωνῶν ὀνομαστὴ βασιλεία.[60]

The list concludes with France. In describing its territory, Gaza adds the southeastern border – namely, the Ligurian sea (or gulf, as he puts it). Perhaps he thought that this addition would clarify the location of France to his Byzantine readers, who would have known Liguria better than the other borders of the French-speaking region mentioned in the original:

Testis omnis Gallia ab Occiduo mari ad Mediterraneum usque distentaque inter Germanos Hispanosque collocata, hac in re Germanis Hispanisque concordat.

Μάρτυς πᾶσα ἡ Κελτικὴ ἀπὸ τῆς ἔξω θαλάττης ἐπὶ τὴν ἐντὸς <u>μέχρι τοῦ Λιγυστοῦ καθήκουσα κόλπου</u>, μεταξὺ Γερμανῶν καὶ Ἰβήρων κειμένη καὶ τῶν περιοίκων αὐτῶν μηθὲν τὰ περὶ τὴν θρησκείαν διαφέρουσα.[61]

Conclusion

Thus, the presence of the Swedes in Gaza's translation, while absent from the original, is most probably just a later corruption of the Latin text due to scribal error; furthermore, the absence of *Ungariaque et Pannonia* in Gaza's version could mean that these two toponyms were later additions to the Latin text. At the same time, other discrepancies between the Greek translation and the Latin original attest to how the humanist predilection for clarity and elegance, combined with the archaizing use of toponyms and ethnonyms, characteristic both of the Byzantine tradition and of the humanist fashion, coincided with the diplomatic demands of rendering certain passages more readily comprehensible

---

[60] Hofmann (1946, 133, ll. 43–44; 137, ll. 19–20). This discrepancy between the Latin and Greek texts has not hitherto been discussed. Both Vat. lat. 3878 and Arcudius agree in including *testis Ungariaque et Pannonia*, the only difference being the spelling *Hungariaque* and *Panonia* in the manuscript; cf. n. 55, above. Hanak (2007, 357), though translating from Latin, not from Greek, omits Hungary exactly as Gaza does: 'the celebrated kingdom of Poland witnessed this.'

[61] Hofmann (1946, 133, ll. 43–134, 2; 137, ll. 20–22). Hanak's (2007, 357) version is again puzzling: 'All of Gaul to the Western Sea [Atlantic], to the Mediterranean, and stretching all the way between Germany and collocated with Hispania, here the Germanic Hispania agreed with the matter.'

to Greek readers. As a result, the translation is more reader-friendly than the original.[62]

It is difficult to compare the list of countries in Gaza's Greek text directly with the representation of Western geography in the writings of contemporary Byzantine historians, since Gaza is not authoring a text of his own but translating the words of the pope. Still, some conclusions can be drawn based on his changes, omissions, and additions. Gaza's intended audience would apparently not have been aware of Spain or Denmark; Gaza thus adds colourful epithets (resembling, to a certain extent, those in folkloric texts, when a fabulous country is being introduced) as in πολυθρύλητος χώρα, ἀξιόλογος χώρα, or εὐδαιμονεστάτη βασιλεία, or glosses – e.g., that Great Britain is an island located not far from the continent and that France lies upon the Ligurian sea. Perhaps the same reasons led Gaza to introduce the Danes, surely unknown to most Byzantines, as the 'so-called Danes' (τῶν καλουμένων Δάμνων).

These discrepancies between the original list of country names and Gaza's Greek version seem to confirm what is known from other sources – i.e., the paucity of Byzantines' knowledge of Western European geography.

---

[62] A comparison with the methods Gaza applied in his other translations, made both from Greek to Latin and vice versa (cf. the literature referenced in n. 23), while relevant here, would be beyond the scope of the present article. I can only suggest that the clarity and elegance achieved by Gaza's humanist, non-verbatim *modus vertendi* and his diplomatic bridging of the cultural gap, along with the historical significance of the text, were behind the popularity enjoyed by his Greek version of Pope Nicholas' letter.

Bibliography

Manuscripts

Vatican City, Archivio Segreto Vaticano, AA Arm. I–XVIII, 2047 [= AA Arm. IX, caps. 1, n. 9].
Vatican City, Biblioteca Apostolica Vaticana, Vat. gr. 1393.
Vatican City, Biblioteca Apostolica Vaticana, Vat. lat. 3878 (https://digi.vatlib.it/view/MSS_Vat.lat.3878).
Modena, Biblioteca Estense, α.T.8.10 (Puntoni 148).
Wrocław, Biblioteka Uniwersytecka, Rehdiger 36.

Books published before 1800

Arcudius, Petrus. 1630. *Opuscula aurea theologica quorundam clariss(imorum) virorum posteriorum Graecorum [...] circa processionem Spritus Sancti*. Rome.
Giorgi, Domenico. 1742. *Vita Nicolai Quinti Pont(ificis) Max(imi)*. Rome.
Rinaldi, Odorico. 1694. *Annales ecclesiastici ab anno quo desinit Card(inalis) Caes(ar) Baronius MCXCVIII usque ad annum MDXXXIV continuati*, T. 18: *Ab anno MCCCCXVII usque ad annum MCCCCLVIII*. Cologne.

Modern authors

Akışık, Aslıhan. 2013. *Self and Other in the Renaissance. Laonikos Chalkokondyles and Late Byzantine Intellectuals*. Diss. Harvard. Cambridge (Mass.).
Berger, Friederike. 2005. *Die Textgeschichte der* Historia Animalium *des Aristoteles*. Wiesbaden.
Beullens, Pieter. 2008. "Aristotle, His Translators, and the Formation of Ichthyologic Nomenclature", in M. Goyens *et al.* (eds.) *Science Translated. Latin and Vernacular Translations of Scientific Treatises in Medieval Europe*. Leuven, 105–122.
Beullens, Pieter & Allan Gotthelf. 2007. "Theodore Gaza's Translation of Aristotle's *De Animalibus*: Content, Influence, and Date", *Greek, Roman, and Byzantine Studies* 47, 469–513.
Bevegni, Claudio. 1992a. "Teodoro Gaza fra la cultura greca e la cultura latina", *Studi umanistici piceni* 12, 47–55.

Bevegni, Claudio. 1992b. "*Il De senectute nella traduzione greca di Teodoro Gaza: riflessioni e confronti*", in M. Cortesi & E.V. Maltese (eds.) *Dotti bizantini e libri greci nell'Italia del secolo XV*, Naples, 227–230.

Bevegni, Claudio. 1993. "Teodoro Gaza traduttore del *Maxime cum principibus philosopho esse disserendum* di Plutarco: primi appunti di un'edizione critica con particolare riguardo alla lettera dedicatoria ad Andrea Bussi", in S. Feraboli (ed.) *Mosaico. Studi in onore di Alberto Albini*, Genoa, 33–42.

Bevegni, Claudio. 1994. "Appunti sulle traduzioni latine dei *Moralia* di Plutarco nel Quattrocento", *Studi umanistici piceni* 14, 71–84.

Bevegni, Claudio. 2004. "Emendare e interpretare Plutarco tramite Teodoro Gaza", *Studi umanistici piceni* 24, 129–150.

Bianca, Concetta. 1999. "Gaza, Teodoro", in *Dizionario biografico degli italiani*, vol. 52, Rome, 737–746.

Bisaha, Nancy. 2004. *Creating East and West: Renaissance Humanists and the Ottoman Turks*. Philadelphia.

Cappelli, Adriano. 1929. *Dizionario di abbreviature latine ed italiane usate nelle carte e codici specialmente del medioevo*. 3rd ed. [1st ed. 1921]. Milan.

Chalkokondyles, Laonikos. 2014. *The Histories*. Vols. 1–2. Translated by Anthony Kaldellis. Cambridge (Mass.)–London.

Chrysoloras, Manuel. 1866. "Epistolae", in J.-P. Migne (ed.) *Patrologiae cursus completus. Series Graeca posterior*, vol. 156, Paris, 23–60.

Chrysoloras, Manuel. 2000. *Roma parte del cielo. Confronto tra l'antica e la nuova Roma di Manuele Crisolora*. Introduzione di Enrico V. Maltese. Traduzione e note di Guido Cortassa. Turin.

Dölger, Franz. 1965. *Regesten der Kaiserurkunden des Oströmischen Reiches von 565–1453*, 5. Teil: *Regesten von 1341–1453* (unter verantwortlicher Mitarbeit von Peter Wirth). Munich–Berlin.

Ducellier, Alain. 1994. "La notion d'Europe à Byzance dès origines au XIIIème siècle. Quelques reflections", *Byzantinoslavica* 55, 1–7.

Ducellier, Alain. 1995. "L'Europe occidentale dans les textes grecs médiévaux: Tradition impériale et redécouverte", *Byzantinoslavica* 56, 245–255.

Ducellier, Alain. 1996. "L'Europe occidentale vue par les historiens grecs des XIVème et XVème siècles", in P. Racine (ed.) *Byzance et l'Europe* (= *Byzantinische Forschungen* 22), Amsterdam, 119–159.

Gallén, Jarl. 1957. "Dacia", in *Kulturhistorisk leksikon for nordisk middelalder fra vikingetid til reformationen*, vol. 2, Copenhagen, coll. 608–610.

Gaza, Teodoro. 1975. *Epistole*. Edited and translated by Emilio Pinto. Naples.

Gaza, Theodorus. 1990. *Epistolae*. Edited by Pietro Luigi Maria Leone. Naples.

Geanakoplos, Deno John. 1989. "Theodore Gaza, a Byzantine Scholar of the Palaeologan 'Renaissance' in the Early Italian Renaissance", in *idem*, *Constantinople and the West. Essays on the Late Byzantine (Palaeologan) and Italian Renaissances and the Byzantine and Roman Churches*, Madison (Wisc.), 68–90.

Gill, Joseph. 1959. *The Council of Florence*. Cambridge.

Gionta, Daniela. 2004. "Il codice di dedica del Teofrasto latino di Teodoro Gaza", *Studi medievali e umanistici* 2, 167–214.

Guilland, Rodolphe. 1953. "Les appels de Constantin XI Paléologue à Rome et à Venise pour sauver Constantinople (1452–1453)", *Byzantinoslavica* 14, 226–244.

Hanak, Walter K. 2007. "Pope Nicholas V and the Aborted Crusade of 1452–1453 to Rescue Constantinople from the Turks", *Byzantinoslavica* 65, 337–359.

Harris, Jonathan. 2000. "Greek Scribes in England: The Evidence of Episcopal Registers", in R. Cormack & E. Jeffreys (eds.) *Through the Looking Glass: Byzantium through British Eyes*, Aldershot, 121–126.

Hofmann, Georg. 1940, 1944, 1946. *Epistolae pontificiae ad Concilium Florentinum spectantes*, pars 1 (1940), pars 2 (1944), pars 3 (1946). Rome.

Irmscher, Johannes. 1961. "Theodoros Gazes als griechischer Patriot", *La parola del passato* 78, 161–173.

Jakobsen, Johnny Grandjean Gøgsig. 2012. "Why Dacia? The Background for a Peculiar Province Name", in *Centre for Dominican Studies of Dacia*. http://www.jggj.dk/Dacia.htm (retrieved 1 March 2019); accessible also at https://www.academia.edu/16154257/Why_Dacia_-_The_background_for_a_peculiar_province_name. (retrieved 1 March 2019).

Kaldellis, Anthony. 2007. *Hellenism in Byzantium. The Transformations of Greek Identity*. Cambridge.

Kaldellis, Anthony. 2013. *Ethnography after Antiquity. Foreign Lands and Peoples in Byzantine Literature*. Philadelphia (PA).

Kaldellis, Anthony. 2014. *A New Herodotos: Laonikos Chalkokondyles on the Ottoman Empire, the fall of Byzantium, and the emergence of the West*. Washington (DC).

Kaldellis, Anthony. 2017. "The Social Scope of Roman Identity in Byzantium: an Evidence-Based Approach", Βυζαντινά σύμμεικτα 27, 173–210.

Kaplanis, Tassos A. 2014. "Antique Names and Self-Identification: *Hellenes, Graikoi*, and *Romaioi* from Late Byzantium to the Greek Nation-State", in D. Tziovas (ed.) *Re-Imagining the Past: Antiquity and Modern Greek Culture*, Oxford, 81–97.

Kindstrand, Jan Fredrik. 1993. "Notes on Theodorus Gaza's *Canis Laudatio*", *Eranos: Acta Philologica Suecana* 91, 93–105.

Kristeller, Paul Oskar. 1989. *Iter Italicum*, Vol. 4: *Alia itinera II, Great Britain to Spain*. London etc.

Lamers, Han. 2015. *Greece Reinvented. Transformations of Byzantine Hellenism in Renaissance Italy*. Leiden.

Lamers, Han. (forthcoming). "What's in a Name? Naming the 'Post-Byzantines' in Renaissance Italy (and Beyond)", in I. Deligiannis, V. Pappas & V. Vaiopoulos (eds.) *Post-Byzantine Latinitas: Latin in Post-Byzantine Scholarship (15ᵗʰ–19ᵗʰ cent.)*, London–New York.

Lampros, Spyridon P. 1930. Παλαιολόγεια καὶ Πελοποννησιακά, vol. 4. Athens.

Legrand, Émile. *Bibliographie hellénique ou description raisonnée des ouvrages publiés en grec par des grecs aux XVᵉ et XVIᵉ siècles*, Vol. 1. Paris.

Leone, Pietro Luigi Maria. 1989. "Appunti su Teodoro Gaza", *Quaderni catanesi di cultura classica e medievale* 1 (n. s.), 5–78.

Leone, Pietro Luigi Maria. 1993. "Le lettere di Teodoro Gaza", in M. Cortesi and E.V. Maltese (eds.) *Dotti bizantini e libri greci nell'Italia del secolo XV*, Naples, 201–218.

Leone, Pietro Luigi Maria. 1994. "In margine al Concilio: A proposito di una lettera di Teodoro Gaza", in P. Viti (ed.) *Firenze e il Concilio del 1439*, Florence, 921–929.

Mantouvalou, Maria. 1985. "Romaios-Romios-Romiossyni. La notion de *romain* avant et après la chute de Constantinople", Επιστημονική Επετηρίς της Φιλοσοφικής Σχολής του Πανεπιστημίου Αθηνών 28 (1979–1985), 169–198.

Meserve, Margaret. 2008. *Empires of Islam in Renaissance Historical Thought*. Cambridge (Mass.)–London.

Migne, Jacques-Paul. 1866. *Patrologiae cursus completus. Series Graeca posterior*, vol. 160. Paris.

Mohler, Ludwig. 1942. "Theodoros Gazes, seine bisher ungedruckten Schriften und Briefe", *Byzantinische Zeitschrift* 42, 50–75.

Monfasani, John. 1976. *George of Trebizond. A Biography and a Study of His Rhetoric and Logic*. Leiden.

Monfasani, John. 1999. "The Pseudo-Aristotelian *Problemata* and Aristotle's *De Animalibus* in the Renaissance", in A. Grafton & N. Siraisi (eds.) *Natural Particulars. Nature and the Disciplines in Renaissance Europe*, Cambridge (Mass.)–London, 79–121.

Monfasani, John. 2006a. "Aristotle as Scribe of Nature: The Title-Page of MS Vat. Lat. 2094", *Journal of the Warburg and Courtauld Institutes* 69, 193–205.

Monfasani, John. 2006b. "George of Trebizond's Critique of Theodore Gaza's Translation of the Aristotelian *Problemata*", in P. De Leemans & M. Goyens (eds.) *Aristotle's* Problemata *in different Times and Tongues*, Leuven, 275–294.

Moravcsik, Gyula. 1932. "Byzantinische Humanisten über den Volksnamen Türk", *Kőrösi Csoma-archívum* 2 (1926–1932), 381–384.

Moravscik, Gyula. 1983. *Byzantinoturcica*, vols. 1–2. 3rd ed. Leiden [vol 1:1st ed. 1942 Leiden, vol 2: 1st ed. 1943 Budapest].

Nicol, Donald M. 1967. "The Byzantine View of Western Europe", *Greek, Roman, and Byzantine Studies* 8:4, 315–345.

Nicol, Donald M. 1992. *The Immortal Emperor. The Life and Legend of Constantine Palaiologos, Last Emperor of the Romans*. Cambridge.

Pade, Marianne. 2013. "Renaissance translation", in *Encyclopedia of Ancient Greek Language and Linguistics*. http://dx.doi.org/10.1163/2214-448X_eagll_COM_00000398 (retrieved 28 March 2019).

Page, Gill. 2008. *Being Byzantine: Greek Identity before the Ottomans*, Cambridge (Mass.)

Papanicolaou, Maria. 2007. "Teodoro Gaza e Plutarco", *Rendiconti della Accademia Nazionale dei Lincei. Classe di scienze morali, storiche e filologiche*, Ser. 9, VIII, 363–428.

Perfetti, Stefano. 1995. "*Cultius atque integrius*. Teodoro Gaza, traduttore umanistico del *De partibus animalium*", *Rinascimento* 35, 253–286.

Perfetti, Stefano. 1996. "Metamorfosi di una traduzione: Agostino Nifo revisore dei *De animalibus* gaziani", *Medioevo. Rivista di storia della filosofia medievale* 22, 259–301.

Philippides, Marios & Walter K. Hanak. 2011. *The Siege and the Fall of Constantinople in 1453. Historiography, Topography, and Military Studies*. Farnham. Burlington (VT).

Repici, Luciana. 2003. "Teodoro Gaza traduttore e interprete di Teofrasto: La ricezione della botanica antica tra quattro e cinquecento", *Rinascimento* 43, 417–505.

Rohlfs, Gerhard. 1966. *Grammatica storica della lingua italiana e dei suoi dialetti*, vol. 1: *Fonetica*. Turin.

Salanitro, Giovanni. 2014. *Scritti di filologia greca e latina.* Catania.

Sanchi, Luigi-Alberto. 2019. "From a Thirsty Desert to the Rise of the Collège de France: Greek Studies in Paris, c.1490–1540", in N. Constantinidou & H. Lamers (eds.) *Receptions of Hellenism in Early Modern Europe (15th–17th Centuries).* Leiden–Boston, 53–71.

Santoro, Rosa. 1992. "La prima traduzione latina di Teodoro Gaza", *Studi umanistici* 3, 165–184.

Setton, Kenneth M. 1978. *The Papacy and the Levant (1204–1571),* vol. 2: *The Fifteenth Century.* Philadelphia.

Speranzi, David. 2012. "*De' libri che furono di Teodoro* [...]: una mano, due pratiche e una biblioteca scomparsa", *Medioevo e rinascimento* 23, 319–354.

Stückelberger, Alfred & Graßhoff, Gerd (eds.) 2006. *Ptolemaios. Handbuch der Geographie,* vols. 1–2. Basel.

Ventura, Iolanda. 2008. "Translating, Commenting, Re-Translating: Some Considerations on the Latin Translations of the Pseudo-Aristotelian *Problemata* and their Readers", in M. Goyens *et al.* (eds.) *Science Translated. Latin and Vernacular Translations of Scientific Treatises in Medieval Europe.* Leuven, 123–154.

Vorobyev, Grigory. 2018. "*Sylvia*: Zur Entstehung des wissenschaftlichen Namens der Grasmücke (Arist. *Hist. an.* 592b22)", *Philologia Classica* 13:2, 247–264.

Vorobyev, Grigory. 2019. "*Dubia* i *spuria* sredi sochinenij Feodora Gazy [*Dubia* and *spuria* among Theodore Gaza's Writings]", in A.K. Gladkov & I.H. Chernyak (eds.) *Kniga i knizhnaya kultura v Zapadnoy Evrope i Rossii do nachala Novogo vremeni. Sbornik v chest' A. H. Gorfunkelya* [Book and Book Culture in Western Europe and Russia before the Modern Times. Collected Essays in Honour of Alexander Gorfunkel]. Moscow–St. Petersburg, 111–130.

Weber, Karl Friedrich. 1852. *Dissertatio de Latine scriptis, quae Graeci veteres in linguam suam transtulerunt,* vol. 4. Kassel.

Ziegler, Conrad. 1915. *Catalogus codicum Latinorum classicorum qui in Bibliotheca urbica Wratislawiensi adservantur.* Wrocław.

Ill. 1. The sepulcher of Pier Candido Decembrio, St. Ambrose Church, Milan.

Uberto Decembrio's Epitaph.
A Fifteenth-century Greek-Latin Epigraph[1]

ANGELO DE PATTO

In the history of the return of Greek letters to the West and the resulting production in Greek (so-called Renaissance or Humanist Greek), an important chapter must be dedicated to epigraphy. The very first example of Renaissance Greek epigraphy is generally considered to be the rather long double epigraph engraved on the Malatesta Temple of Rimini.[2] The Greek inscriptions of the temple are dated to 1450 and they already display the characteristics that will be typical of the Greek epigraphy of Humanism and very different from contemporary Constantinopolitan epigraphy.[3]

In Italy there are two inscriptions that were written in Greek[4] before the production of the epigraphy of the Malatesta Temple: the epitaph of Joseph II, patriarch of Constantinople, who died in 1439,[5] and the epitaph of Uberto Decembrio (died in 1427), which is therefore probably the oldest known Greek inscription in the West. Uberto Decembrio's epitaph is inscribed on the wall of the external façade of the Basilica of St. Ambrose in Milan, next to the beautifully sculpted sepulchre of his son Pier Candido Decembrio,[6] 'the most eminent humanist of the Quattrocento born in the Ducate of Milano'[7] (see. Ill. 1–2).

---

[1] In view of the Helsinki conference about Humanist Greek in 2018, I thought it was worth proposing a topic somehow linked to the work and activity of the Finnish scholar Iiro Kajanto, who pursued his intellectual activity for many years in Helsinki. His works on medieval and renaissance epigraphy are still milestones: bibliography of Iiro Kajanto in Solin (1997). I would like to thank the following scholars for suggestions and important tips: Fabio Della Schiava, Tua Korhonen, Carla Maria Monti, Giuseppe Pascale, Marco Petoletti, Angelo Piacentini and Annamaria Terafina at the "Soprintendenza alle Belle Arti di Milano". All the photos in this article are taken by the author.

[2] Petrucci (1985, 90–93) and Muccioli (2003).

[3] Pontani (1992, 128–129).

[4] A special case is the well-known Pisanello's medal, dated 1438, with Greek capital inscriptions for the Byzantine emperor John VIII at the Council of Ferrara-Florence, see Pontani (1992, 130–133).

[5] In Santa Maria Novella at Florence, see Guillou (1996, 257) and Pontani (1992, 143–144).

[6] On Uberto Decembrio, see Viti (1987).

[7] Ferrari (1984, 247).

Born in Vigevano in *ca.* 1350, Uberto lived for many years in Milan as a friend and secretary of Pietro Filargis, "Pietro da Candia", the future pope Alexander V. He was also an important member of the Visconti chancery.[8] He was then appointed *podestà* of Treviglio, where he died in 1427. Most likely, it was Pietro da Candia who first

Ill. 2. The epitaph of Uberto Decembrio.

guided Decembrio in the study of the Greek language 'al cui apprendimento più aspiravano gli umanisti del tempo'.[9]

As a writer, Decembrio left letters,[10] speeches, moral treatises (*De candore* and *De modestia*, dedicated to his sons Pier Candido and Modesto respectively) and a political dialogue, published in 1422 under the title *De Republica* and inspired by Plato's *Republic*. In this dialogue, Decembrio emphasizes, among the various forms of government, the superiority of enlightened absolutism. In particular, he underlines the importance of a capable king in selecting the best staff members to create a trustworthy group of guardians of the State (*custodes rei publicae*) and guarantors of that *tranquillitas* which is the ultimate aim of politics: the connection with the Milan of the Visconti is clear.[11]

---

[8] Both Pietro da Candia and Uberto Decembrio obtained the title of Duke for Giangaleazzo Visconti from Emperor Wenceslaus, cfr. Zocco Ramazzo (2014, 142 n.1).

[9] See Petrucci (1960, 193); Mugnai Carrara (2005, 182–187). According to Rollo (2005, 260), Decembrio did not learn Greek from Pietro da Candia.

[10] Angelo Piacentini kindly enabled me to consult Uberto's letter collection: Piacentini is about to publish a complete and accurate critical edition of Uberto Decembrio's letters, see Piacentini (forthcoming).

[11] Viti (1987, 500–501); on Decembrio's *De Republica* see Ferraù (2005, 431–463), Pissavino (2005, 465–484) and especially Ponzù Donato (2019).

Father of two important fifteenth-century humanists, Pier Candido and Angelo, Uberto Decembrio is mainly known for his acquaintance with the distinguished Byzantine scholar Manuel Chrysoloras. Chrysoloras arrived in Pavia and Milan in *ca.* 1401 after about four years in Florence, where he had been holding the chair of Greek at the invitation of Coluccio Salutati. In Florence, Chrysoloras had as pupils, among others, Leonardo Bruni and Niccolò Niccoli.[12]

In Lombardy, Chrysoloras undertook, along with Uberto Decembrio, one of the most important cultural enterprises of that time, which had a great impact on the humanistic movement: the translation of Plato's *Republic*.[13] Chrysoloras translated the Greek text into Latin and Decembrio revised it, enabling him to improve his Greek while doing so.[14] The translation of the *Republic* was not a success: although the translated text did circulate among scholars,[15] it had little literary merit. In 1440 Uberto's son Pier Candido decided to produce a new version of the Platonic dialogue and his Latin style is undoubtedly superior.[16]

Indeed, both contemporary and modern scholars have considered Uberto Decembrio's knowledge of Greek inadequate.[17] Although Decembrio did not achieve a high level of Greek, he studied and copied Chrysoloras' *Erotemata*, the main elementary Greek grammar for a generation of fifteenth-century humanists, and he considered Chrysoloras his own *praeceptor*.[18] Uberto was surely proud of his knowledge of the Greek language and of his contribution to the translation of Plato's *Republic*. It is therefore not surprising that he mentions his skills in this language even in his epitaph.

According to a note written by Uberto's son, Pier Candido, the epitaph was composed by Uberto himself. As well as appearing in the St. Ambrose inscription, the epitaph occurs, with some transcription errors, in three manuscripts, which are presented in the Appendix of this article. One of them from Milan, namely A (Biblioteca Ambrosiana, B 123 sup., f. 79r), contains a few lines of commentary at the end of the epitaph transcription in the hand of Pier Candido:

---

[12] The arrival of Chrysoloras in Milan was most likely facilitated by the presence of Pietro da Candia, see Thorn-Wickert (2006, 56–57); see also Rollo (2005, 264–265).

[13] See Gentile (2002), Vegetti & Pissavino (2005) and Gusmini (2012).

[14] Uberto himself states this in the prologue to the translation of the *Republic*: Gentile (2002, 151–152); the prologue also in Hankins (1990, 525–528).

[15] Cfr. Viti (1987, 500, 502); Mugnai Carrara (2005, 185–186).

[16] Gusmini (2012); Sammut (1980); Zaggia (1993).

[17] See Bottoni (1984, 83–84); Gentile (2002, 153–155).

[18] Thorn-Wickert (2006, 57–59), Gentile (2002, 152).

MCCCCXXVII die veneris XXV Aprilis.[19] *Inter primam et secundam noctis horam, Ubertus predictus decessit in castro Trivilii, ibidem potestas et indilate corpus eiusdem translatum fuit et sepultum Mediolani iuxta portam principalem ecclesie Sancti Ambrosii, sinistrorsum introentibus ac ibidem in pariete excisum est lapide marmoreo suprascriptum epitaphium ab ipso editum latinis grecisque litteris.*

The words *latinis grecisque litteris* are a later addition by Pier Candido, intended to underline the uniqueness of this piece: indeed, excluding the epigraphs produced in the Byzantine territories, Decembrio's constitutes one of the first, if not the very first, epigraphs written in Greek in Western Europe.

Let us now focus on the Latin text (see Ill. 2 and p. 41, the Appedix), written in an epigraphic semi-gothic style,[20] still far from the beautiful *quadrata* recovered by Leon Battista Alberti:[21]

> By destiny, together with the body members, this place houses the bones of Uberto Decembrio. He took care of the secrets of the Duke of the Ligurians and he provided the multitudes with the translated volumes of the Platonic city, [5] supported by the knowledge of the Greek language and the Latin language. Born in Vigevano, he was buried in the famous city. Yet death did not extinguish everything with the cruel dart: The earthly part to the earth, the best part entered the heavens.[22]

The epitaph, composed in rhymed hexameters, recalls the most important merits of Decembrio. Since the epitaph was dictated by Uberto himself, we can be sure that he believed he had achieved two important goals in his life: serving as a secretary to the Visconti (the Duke of Ligurians, *Ligurum duces*, v. 3) and translating (in fact, helping to translate) Plato's *Republic* into Latin, enabled by his knowledge of both classical languages. Emphasis on this achievement suited the spirit of early humanism; when this translation of Plato was made, very few people in Western Europe were able to read Greek. Decembrio was one of them.

The epitaph, however, does not end with the Latin hexameters. On the gravestone, the Latin text is followed by five verses of the Psalms quoted from the

---

[19] The same expression for Uberto's date of death occurs at the end of the epitaph, see Ill. 2.

[20] Pontani (1992, 180) describes it as a 'bella testuale rotonda'.

[21] See Forcella (1890, 231–232).

[22] English translation is mine.

Greek version of the *Septuaginta* (see Ill. 2):

ἐλέησόν με, ὦ Θ(εό)ς μου, [cf. *Ps.* 55:2]
εἰς χεῖράς σου παραθήσομαι τὸ πνεῦμά μου [cf. *Ps.* 30:6]
ἐλυτρώσω με κ(ύρι)ε ὦ θεὸς τῆς ἀληθείας [ἀλείθηας *lapis*; cf. *Ps.* 30:6]
ἐλέησόν με, Κ(ύρι)ε, ὅτι θλίβομαι [cf. *Ps.* 30:10]
ἐγὼ δὲ ἐπὶ σοὶ Κ(ύρι)ε ἤλπισα[23] [cf. *Ps.* 30:15]

The reason for this Greek addendum to the Latin text is clear: Decembrio wanted to brandish his command of Greek as a sacred language in a place *par excellence* for sacredness, the tombstone. Interestingly, the transcription includes a few errors, most glaringly ἀλείθηας for ἀληθείας, which was also repeated by his son Pier Candido in manuscript A (see Appendix).

Uberto's emphasis on knowledge of Greek and Latin and his proud claim to have translated Plato (a 'pagan') are elements that fit perfectly within the framework of early modern epigraphy, as outlined by Iiro Kajanto, who defined the main feature of Renaissance Latin epigraphy with these words: 'The revival of interest in classical literature and in classical Latin, which we call Humanism, could not fail to make itself felt in the funeral inscriptions of the Renaissance. [...] It was especially the word *litterae* that was employed to denote humanistic studies. Renaissance Humanism meant first and foremost the study of literature, in particular the study of Latin and to lesser degree Greek classics.'[24] Kajanto's assessment applies to Uberto's epitaph. In contrast to the Middle Ages, the new humanistic élite of the early Renaissance – laypeople as well as clergy – began to emphasize their commitment to the classical languages and their pivotal role in the revival of the *humanae litterae*. The epitaph of Decembrio fits this pattern: in spite of the still very strong tie with the Christian and biblical tradition, the place he grants to the new humanistic approach is undisputable. And even if the Decembrio epitaph mirrors specific features of the gothic epigraphy (mainly in the graphic form), as Anna Pontani has demonstrated, several properties of the humanistic epigraphs have to be acknowledged: Decembrio underlines that he was an important man

---

[23] According to the paleographic analysis of Anna Pontani, the Greek inscription of this epigraph recalls the Greek handwriting of western scholars, for example that of Boccaccio: it is certainly a product of a western stonecutter who did not have Byzantine models to draw upon and which had not yet acquired the characteristics that would later be associated with humanist taste. In particular, the *sigma-omikron* ligatures in ἐλέησον are reminiscent of the Latin nexus *co* and that of ει reminiscent of the Latin *q* or the *alpha* without a horizontal bar. See Pontani (1992, 140–141).

[24] Kajanto (1980, 124).

in the Visconti court and that, through his knowledge of the Latin and Greek languages, he brought Plato's *Republic* to Italy.

If the stone was inscribed in Decembrio's year of death (1427), it is the first bilingual Latin-Greek epigraph in Milan.[25] In Italy, excluding the above mentioned epigraphs of Malatesta Temple (1450) and that for Joseph II (1439), all the inscriptions in Greek date back to the second half of the fifteenth century.[26] Moreover, we are aware of only one other carved inscription in Greek in Milan in the

Ill. 3. Palazzo Castani in Piazza San Sepolcro in Milan.

fifteenth century engraved on the front door of a building. It consists of only two words, ΑΓΑΘΗ ΤΥΧΗ ('With good fortune'), a common well-wishing formula in classical inscriptions. The words are cut on the architrave of the beautiful portal of Palazzo Castani in Piazza San Sepolcro, a palace now used as a police station

---

[25] See Forcella (1889–1893).

[26] See Kajanto (1980), Guillou (1996) and Pontani (1992, 144–149).

(see Ill. 3–4).[27]   It was in the Palazzo Castani that the so called *Fasci Italiani di combattimento* were constituted on 23 March in 1919, the organization that would later become the Fascist Party led by Benito Mussolini. Despite its message of hope, the inscription did not make the Palazzo the birthplace of good fortune for Italy.

Ill. 4. The architrave of the Palazzo Castani in Milan.

---

[27] Forcella (1892, 46). This epigraph is dated by Forcella to the fifteenth century, although a later dating to the beginning of the sixteenth century cannot be excluded, see Battaglia & Repishti (2003, 416–417). Another Greek epigraph, dated by Forcella (1892, 52) to the fifteenth century, originally located in Palazzo Rabia and now in the civic collections of the Castello Sforzesco in Milan is most likely from the sixteenth century, see Franco (2015, 364–365). From sixteenth-century Milan, in addition to the epigraph of Palazzo Rabia, there are only two Greek epigraphs: one from 1517 in S. Maria Incoronata, on the monument for Giovanni di Tolentino (see Forcella [1891, 86] and Gatti Perer [1980, 125–130]) and the other, perhaps from the end of the sixteenth century, in the church of San Marco, on the tomb of Alessandro Pusterla (see Forcella [1891, 321] and Pontani [1992, 149]). It is interesting that in Milan other sixteenth-century epigraphs concerning Greek scholars were written in Latin: the epitaphs of Demetrius Chalcondyles in S. Maria della Passione, written by Giorgio Trissino (see Forcella [1889, Vol. 1, 196]) and the epitaphs of Manuel Chrysoloras and his niece Theodora, wife of Francesco Filelfo, in Sant'Eustorgio, see Forcella (1889, Vol. 2, 99).

Bibliography

Battaglia, Antonio & Francesco Repishti. 2003. "Fra Giocondo, Giano Lascaris e lo studio di Vitruvio a Milano", in Gianluca Ciotta & Marco Folin, Marco Spesso (eds.) *Vitruvio nella cultura architettonica antica, medievale e moderna. Atti del Convegno Internazionale di Genova, 5-8 novembre 2001.* Genua, 414–421.

Bottoni, Diego. 1984. "I Decembrio e la traduzione della Repubblica di Platone: dalle correzioni dell'autografo di Uberto alle integrazioni greche di Pier Candido", in Rino Avesani *et al.* (eds.) *Vestigia. Studi in onore di Giuseppe Billanovich*, vol. I. Rome, 75–91.

Ferrari, Mirella. 1984. "Fra i «latini scriptores» di Pier Candido Decembrio e biblioteche umanistiche milanesi: codici di Vitruvio e Quintiliano", in Rino Avesani *et al.* (eds.) *Vestigia. Studi in onore di Giuseppe Billanovich*, vol. I. Rome, 247–296.

Ferraù, Giacomo. 2005. "Esemplarità platonica ed esperienza viscontea nel "De Republica" di Uberto Decembrio", in Paolo Pissavino & Mario Vegetti (eds.), *I Decembrio e la tradizione della Repubblica di Platone tra Medioevo e Umanesimo.* Naples, 431–463.

Forcella, Vincenzo. 1889–1893. *Iscrizioni delle chiese e degli altri edifici di Milano dal secolo VIII ai giorni nostri.* Vols. I–XII [1889 (vols. 1–2), 1890 (vol. 3), 1891 (vol. 4), 1892 (vol. 10), 1893 (vol. 11–12). Milan.

Franco, Laura. 2015. "Plinto da palazzo Rabia", in Maria Teresa Fiorio & Graziano Alfredo Vergani (*eds.*) *Museo d'arte antica del Castello Sforzesco. Scultura lapidea*, Milan, 364–365.

Gatti Perer, Maria Luisa. 1980. "Il tramonto di una certezza. Un monumento funebre del 1517", *Arte Lombarda* 53–54, 125–130.

Gentile, Sebastiano. 2002. "Note sulla traduzione crisolorina della Repubblica", in Enrico Maisano & Antonio Rollo (eds.), *Manuele Crisolora e il ritorno del greco in Occidente: atti del Convegno internazionale (Napoli, 26–29 giugno 1997).* Naples, 151–173.

Guillou, André. 1996. *Recueil des inscriptions grecques médiévales d'Italie.* Rome.

Gusmini, Franca. 2012. "Le traduzioni della *Repubblica* platonica di Uberto e Pier Candido Decembrio: primi accertamenti testuali", *Filologia Italiana* 9, 77–108.

Hankins, James. 1990. *Plato in the Italian Renaissance.* Vol. 2. Leiden–New York–Copenhagen–Köln.

Muccioli, Federicomaria. 2003. "Le epigrafi gemelle in lingua greca del Tempio Malatestiano", in Marco Musmeci (*ed.*) *Templum mirabile*. Rimini, 73–85.

Mugnai Carrara, Daniela. 2005. "La collaborazione fra Manuele Crisolora e Uberto Decembrio: ideologia signorile all'origine della prima versione latina della Repubblica di Platone e problemi di traduzione", in Mario Vegetti & Paolo Pissavino (eds.) *I Decembrio e la tradizione della Repubblica di Platone tra Medioevo e Umanesimo*. Naples, 177–235.

Petoletti, Marco. 2016. "Pier Candido Decembrio e i suoi libri: primi appunti", in Patrizia Carmassi (ed.) *Retter der Antike: Marquard Gude (1635–1689) auf der Suche nach den Klassikern*. Wiesbaden, 147–190.

Petrucci, Armando. 1960. "Alessandro V", in *Dizionario Biografico degli Italiani*, vol. 2, Rome, 193–196.

Petrucci, Armando. 1985. "Potere, spazi urbani, scritture esposte: proposte ed esempi", in Charles Pietri *et al.* (eds.) *Culture et idéologie dans la genèse de l'état moderne. Actes de la table ronde de Rome (15-17 octobre 1984)*. Rome, 85–97.

Piacentini, Angelo. (forthcoming). "L'*Epistolarum liber* di Uberto Decembrio".

Pissavino, Paolo. 2005. "Sistemi di potere e dinamiche istituzionali nel primo e maturo Quattrocento: il *De Republica* di Uberto Decembrio" in Mario Vegetti & Paolo Pissavino (eds.) *I Decembrio e la tradizione della Repubblica di Platone tra Medioevo e Umanesimo*. Naples, 465–484.

Pontani, Anna. 1992. "Le maiuscole greche antiquarie di Giano Lascaris: per la storia dell'alfabeto greco in Italia nel '400", *Scrittura e civiltà* 16, 77–227.

Ponzù Donato, Paolo. 2019. Uberto Decembrio's *Four Books on the Commonwealth (De re publica libri IV, ca. 1420)*. Leiden.

Rollo, Antonio. 2005. "Gli inizi dello studio del greco in Lombardia", in Mario Vegetti & Paolo Pissavino (eds.) *I Decembrio e la tradizione della Repubblica di Platone tra Medioevo e Umanesimo*. Naples, 237–265.

Sammut, Alfonso. 1980. *Unfredo duca di Gloucester e gli umanisti italiani*. Padova.

Solin, Heikki, 1997. "Kajanto, Iiro. Kansallisbiografia", *Studia Biographica* 4. Helsinki.

Thorn-Wickert, Lydia. 2006. *Manuel Chrysoloras (ca. 1350–1415): eine Biographie des byzantinischen Intellektuellen vor dem Hintergrund der hellenistischen Studien in der italienischen Renaissance*. Frankfurt am Main.

Vegetti, Mario & Pissavino, Paolo 2005 (eds.) *I Decembrio e la tradizione della Repubblica di Platone tra Medioevo e Umanesimo*. Naples.

Viti, Paolo. 1987. "Decembrio, Uberto", in *Dizionario Biografico degli Italiani*, vol. 33. Rome, 498–503.

Zaggia, Massimo. 1993. "La versione latina di Pier Candido Decembrio dalla *Repubblica* di Platone: per la storia della tradizione", *Interpres* 13, 7–55.

Zocco Ramazzo, Marco. 2014. "Sulla fortuna del *Romane historie compendium* di Uberto Decembrio", *Italia Medievale e Umanistica* 55, 141–166.

APPENDIX: Uberto Decembrio's Epitaph
according to the Manuscript Tradition

As mentioned earlier, Uberto Decembrio's stone epitaph, which I refer to here as
L (= *lapis*), is also to be found in three manuscripts (A, D and B).

Manuscript A (Milano, Biblioteca Ambrosiana, B 123 sup.) is considered
the Decembrio family codex prepared under the guidance of Pier Candido and
copied by him as well as by Uberto himself and his eldest son Modesto. It contains
a selection of Uberto's works (e.g., *De Republica, De candore,* the cotranslation
with Chrysoloras of Plato's *Republic*) and epistles; in addition, at f. 131r Pier
Candido marked the dates of death of the members of the Decembrio family.
The entire text of the epitaph (f. 79r), both in Greek and in Latin, is transcribed
in the hand of Pier Candido. A is the only ms that transmits the Greek text of
the epitaph. Moreover, Pier Candido's transcription closely recalls the graphic
solutions we are used to see in manuscript epigraphic collections. Pier Candido's
transcription of the Greek text (see Ill. 5)[28] reproduces exactly the content and
the graphic style of the text engraved on the tombstone (Ill. 6):

Ill. 5. Ambr. B 123 sup., f. 79r.

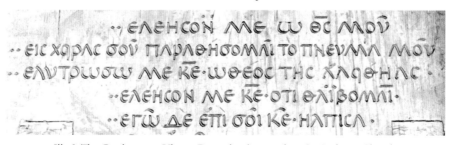

Ill. 6. The Greek text in Uberto Decembrio's epitaph in St. Ambrose Church.

---

[28] The text taken from the manuscript A. © Veneranda Biblioteca Ambrosiana / Mondadori
Portfolio.

The most peculiar features of this hand are the dots which separate the words, the ligature ει, the use of Γ, Δ, Η capital in the last psalm, the sign above αι of παραθήσομαι and θλίβομαι, and the error ἀλείθηας. I suggest that, as a token of respect to his father, Pier Candido wanted to transcribe the epitaph in the family's codex to resemble as closely as possible the inscription on the monument. Another element that reinforces this hypothesis is the word *telo* (v. 7) in the Latin part of the epitaph in this manuscript: *telo* seems to be rewritten over *tello*. *Tello*, which occurs on the tombstone (see Ill. 2 above), was most likely the stonecutter's mistake. Reporting the epitaph exactly as he read it, Pier Candido reproduced this misspelling, which was probably corrected by the deletion of an *l* by a later hand.

D (Milano, Biblioteca Ambrosiana, D 112 inf.) transmits only the Latin version of the epitaph (163v). This manuscript not only transmits several works of Pier Candido, but it was also written under his supervision and corrected by himself. This codex was part of the home library of the humanist and it is worth noting that the epitaph of Uberto appears in the section dedicated to the epigrams and epistles in verse by Pier Candido (*P. Candidi epigramatum et epistolarum liber*, f. 150r), as if it were his work. Instead, in B (f. 79r), Pier Candido stated that the epitaph was *ab ipso* [that is, by Uberto] *editum*.[29]

B (Bergamo, Biblioteca Civica Angelo Mai, MA 611) contains a few texts by Uberto Decembrio. The epitaph is transmitted (f. 48v) with two extra verses which are not displayed in the other two manuscripts: *Quem pariter coniux busto comitatur in isto / Ut fuerant animo, iaceant sic corpora mixto* (f. 48v). These verses refer to Uberto's wife, Caterina Marazzi, who died in 1430, and was buried along with her husband in the church of Sant'Ambrogio (Ambrose) in Milan. Angelo Piacentini, who discusses the epitaph in his forthcoming edition of Uberto's letters, argues that one of Uberto's sons wrote these two verses, as they were written long after the father's death.[30]

The differences between the three transcriptions can be summarized as follows: A transmits the whole text of the epitaph as it is displayed on the sepulcher, both in Latin and in Greek, and it is an autograph by Pier Candido Decembrio. D reports only the Latin text of the epitaph with a few minor transcription errors. B transmits only the Latin text with the addition of the two hexameters in memory of Uberto's wife. I have therefore decided to print the reading of A, as it is the

---

[29] For the bibliography on these two Ambrosiana manuscripts, see Petoletti (2016, 158).

[30] On this manuscript, in addition to the description in the aforementioned work by Piacentini (forthcoming), see Viti (1987, 502).

closest to the original epitaph on the tombstone (L), and I have placed in the *apparatus* the reading of D and B.

The edited epitaph according to these three manuscripts reads as follows:

Epitaphium Uberti Decembri viri optimi et eruditissimi ducis Mediolani secretarii

Sorte necis pariter stratis cum corpore membris,
Hic locus ossa tenet Uberti inclusa Decembris.
Iste ducis Ligurum secreta peregit, et urbis
Platonice dederat translata volumina turbis
Argive ac latie linguarum dogmate fultus.   5
Viglevani natus, famosa est urbe sepultus.
Non tamen extinxit sevo mors omnia telo:
Terrea pars terre, cessit pars optima celo.

ἐλέησόν με, ὦ Θεός μου,
εἰς χεῖράς σου παραθήσομαι τὸ πνεῦμά μου   10
ἐλυτρώσω με Κύριε ὦ θεὸς τῆς ἀληθείας
ἐλέησόν με, Κύριε, ὅτι θλίβομαι
ἐγὼ δὲ ἐπὶ σοὶ Κύριε ἤλπισα

MCCCCXXVII die veneris XXV Aprilis

Crit. Epitaphium […] secretarii] om. L;   Epitaphium Uberti Decembri B;
Epitaphium viri clarissimi Uberti Decembri Petri Candidi parentis D
4 Platonice] Platonis D
7 telo] tello L, telo A post corr., ut vid., forte manu seriore correctum e *tello*
8 terre, cessit pars] terre cessit, pars sic distinxerunt BD
8 celo] post celo "Quem pariter coniux busto comitatur in isto / Ut fuerant
animo, iaceant sic corpora mixto" addidit B
9–13 ἐλέησόν με, ὦ Θεός […] ἤλπισα] om. BD
11 ἀληθείας] ἀλείθηας LA
MCCCCXXVII […] Aprilis] om. BD

II. GREEK AND KINGS

Guillaume Budé's Greek *manifesto*.
The Introductory Epistles
of the *Commentarii linguae Graecae* (1529)[1]

In September 1529, Guillaume Budé (1468–1540)[2] published a manifesto of sorts, in two parts, on the importance of studying ancient Greek. The two works, written in Greek and in the form of introductory epistles, differ drastically from one another: one is a preface letter and the other an afterword to his *Commentarii linguae Graecae* ('Commentaries on the Greek language', 1529). Consisting of approximately a thousand folio pages, the *Commentaries* were printed by Josse Bade (Jodocus Badius Ascensius) and had a decisively favourable impact on Greek studies in France and beyond. The first Greek epistle, Φραγκίσκῳ τῷ τῆς Φραγκίας βασιλεῖ ('To Francis, king of France', comprising four-and-a-half pages in the original 1529 edition), addresses King Francis I, reminding him of his promise to fund a new royal college for ancient tongues and the liberal arts. In the latter work, Τῶν νέων τοῖς τῶν Ἑλληνικῶν λόγων ἐφιεμένοις ('To the students fond of Greek literature', three pages), Budé aims to explain to a new generation of specialists how he constructed the *Commentaries* and what to expect from reading them. Already well known among humanists for his scholarly contributions, which ranged from Roman law to ancient economic history, and for his Greek and Latin epistles, Budé was, together with Erasmus, one of Europe's most accomplished Hellenists of his day.

The *Commentaries on the Greek language* was undoubtedly Budé's masterpiece. Sixty-one years old at the time of its publication in 1529, Budé had studied Greek for thirty-five years, starting in 1494. The material for this work he had likely accumulated over the course of seven or eight years, recording the vocabulary of Greek authors in dozens of files. This was a typically humanist practice and would remain an important part of Budé's intellectual activity. After the publication of his *Commentaries* in 1529, Budé continued working on the project to expand it

---

[1] I warmly thank my colleagues Tomas Veteikis (Vilnius university, Lithuania) and Scott Blanchard (Misericordia university, Pennsylvania) for their careful revision of this paper.

[2] For a general introduction to Budé, see McNeil (1975), as well as Sandy (2002), in English, and, in French, Sanchi (2018a).

into a larger edition: in fact, he studied more Greek authors and re-read previous ones, making small additions to every single page of his book, as can be seen in his personal copy (Paris, BnF, *Réserve* X. 67).[3] The new edition would appear only eight years after Budé's death, edited and printed by Robertus Stephanus (Budé 1548).[4] This final edition, whose front page announces an ensemble 'one-third bigger' (*tertia parte aucti*), includes some 18,000 Greek quotations, taken from nearly a hundred Classical and Byzantine authors, as well as some 2,000 Latin quotations from seventy-five ancient and medieval authors. Each lexical item is studied inside its lexical family, its meanings linked to several quotations, demonstrating how the Greek authors use the particular word.[5] In offering a broad thesaurus of Greek literature, Budé's *Commentaries* thus marked a turning point in Greek studies. The elegant 1548 folio became the standard lexicographical work for Greek until 1572, when Henricus Stephanus, Robertus' son, published his *Thesaurus Graecae linguae* twenty-four years later. In his *Thesaurus*, Stephanus regularly quotes Budé's findings, thus acknowledging the scientific foundation Budé had laid for Greek studies. Indeed, the *Commentaries* would remain in many scholarly libraries long after the 16th century. Therefore, the dissemination across Europe of both introductory texts from the 1529 edition was aided by the broad impact Budé's *Commentaries* had on the French panorama of Greek studies.

The political context of early sixteenth-century Paris should also be noted: at the time, decades before becoming a modern "capital" of arts and letters, Paris was one of the "capitals" of theological studies, renowned for its many colleges—in particular, the Collège de la Sorbonne, where philosophy and theology were the principal subjects taught and discussed. Nevertheless, the Humanist movement soon gave way to the Reformation, which profoundly impacted the Latin Quarter: already by 1519, the Sorbonne was beginning to resonate with Luther's new theology, its impact beginning to be felt all throughout France. Suddenly, humanists interested in Greek literature were suspected of heresy.

---

[3] On the preparatory work that went into the original *Commentaries* and its second edition, see Sanchi (2006, 39–48).

[4] The two editions of Budé's *Commentaries* (1529 and 1548) are both available online, so the Greek liminary texts can be read in their original formats. For a standardized edition (with punctuation, word division, capital letters, and diacritics), see Sanchi (2006, 281–287 and 289–293); for a French translation of the afterword, see *ibid*. (296–298). The texts of the epistles are printed more compactly in the 1548 edition (a2r–3v and Aaa3v–Aaa4v, respectively).

[5] For an analysis of the book's contents, see Sanchi (2006, 49–119 and 173–236); for the Greek authors quoted by Budé in his *Commentaries*, see *ibid*. (121–153 and 237–259). See also Sanchi (2018b) for a recent study on Budé's intellectual and material library.

They were already under suspicion for having criticised the text of the Latin Vulgate, following the example of Lorenzo Valla. In Paris, some even claimed to be able to explain Holy Writ better than the doctors in theology at the Sorbonne could, arguing that those theologians could read the Bible neither in Greek nor in Hebrew.[6] Thus, at the time Budé published his *Commentaries*, Hellenists in Paris and elsewhere in France often found themselves besieged. While Budé, as a member of the king's Court and a Catholic, regularly interceded on behalf of his friends, they were of the opinion that only royal protection would put an end to the persecutions.[7] Budé and other influential men thus wanted to found a King's College in Paris devoted to both Classics and Oriental studies. The circumstances in Paris, however, meant that local and visiting intellectuals from other countries had to wait until 1530 to witness the inauguration of the college they had been dreaming of, with two Royal Lecturers in Greek and in Hebrew appointed, Pierre Danès (1497–1577) and Agathias Guidacerius (1477–1542), respectively, demonstrating the impact Budé's preface must have had on the king. Elsewhere in Europe – in Vienna, Rome, Alcalá and Leuven – trilingual colleges had already existed for some decades.

This paper briefly introduces the contents of Budé's two Greek texts in his *Commentaries* to encourage greater academic attention around them and to promote further discussion and especially synchronic and diachronic research on Budé's complicated Greek prose, rhetorical style, and his philosophical and cultural views. His rhetorical skill and originality in Greek become evident especially when his works are compared with the Greek prefaces that a contemporary French Hellenist, Jean Cheradame (*ca.* 1495–1543),[8] added to each of the nine comedies in his 1528 edition of Aristophanes, published just one year before Budé's *Commentaries*.[9]

---

[6] On the censorship of and negative reaction to humanism in Paris, see, e.g., Higman (1979), Farge (1992), Rummel (1995), Saladin (2000), Sanchi (2014).

[7] One famous case is Budé's intervention to prevent the condemnation of a nobleman, Louis de Berquin, see La Garanderie (1995, esp. 210–211 and 235–236).

[8] See Maillard and Flamand (2010, 571–680).

[9] Cheradame (1528, a3r; aa2r; aaa2r; A2r; AA1r; AAA2r; Aa2r; Aaa2r; AaA2r); see transcriptions in Maillard & Flamand (2010, 627–642).

The Letter to the King

Budé's preface to King Francis was so effective that its publication, advocating vibrantly for a *collegium trilingue*, is even regarded as the starting point of the Collège de France. In fact, the first two lecturers were appointed at the beginning of 1530, only a few weeks after the *Commentaries* had been published.[10] It should be noted, however, that Francis could not have read this preface directly, as he could not read Greek – nor Latin, for that matter. In its Greek form, Budé's preface was designed to be read by Hellenists throughout Europe. For the king, on the other hand, was issued a French version, one whose manuscript (Paris, BnF, *fr.* 25445, ff. 1r–15r) shows no substantial differences from the Greek original.[11] From this rather long text, I have chosen a few passages that exemplify Budé's role in swaying the king.

The address to King Francis reads: Φραγκίσκῳ τῷ τῆς Φραγκίας βασιλεῖ, τῶν χριστιανῶν μονάρχων τῷ πάνυ, Ἴλερμος Βουδαῖος ὁ τούτου θεράπων ἐφέστιος, εὖ τε πράττειν διαζῶντα, καὶ μακαρίως ποτ' ἀπαλλάττειν, 'To Francis, King of France, celebrated among Christian kings, Guillaume Budé, His domestic servant, wishes bliss throughout His earthly life and, one day, a blessed passing.'[12] The expression τῶν χριστιανῶν τῷ πάνυ, suggesting a comparison with other European monarchs, is noteworthy, as it shows that Budé was aware of writing for an international public and wanted to honour his country through his King. At the outset of his preface, Budé opens in complicated Greek prose, describing an 'illness' he had recently been afflicted with:

> Δεύτερον ἤδη μοι[13] τὸ ἔτος, ὦ μέγα δυνάμενε βασιλεῦ, διαγέγονε, καὶ μικρόν τι πρός, περὶ τοῦτο μὲν ἀσχολουμένῳ τὸ ὑπομνηματικὸν σύνταγμα, οὗ παρέργως δ' οὐδ' ὡς αὐτὸς τύχοιμι, μεταξὺ πραγματευομένῳ καὶ φροντίζοντι. ἐτύγχανε γὰρ ἐμὲ ὁ μὲν ἔνθεν ἐπισπεύδων ἀδιαλείπτως, ἔρως δεινὸς τῆς φιλομαθούντων κοινωφελίας.[14] ἡ δ' ἔνθεν ποιεῖν τὸ κελευόμενον προθυμουμένη φιλοπονία, ἐς τὸ ἐπιὸν ἀεὶ μᾶλλον αὐτῇ τῇ

---

[10] See Sanchi (2006, 21–22).

[11] For the edition of this early French version, see Sanchi (2006, 23–33).

[12] French version (f. 1r): 'A Françoys Roy de France, le tresrenommé des chrestiens monarques, Guillaume Budé, son domestique serviteur, félicité de longue vie et à la parfin yssue bienheureuse d'icelle.' The diacritics of the Greek texts have been standardised.

[13] After μοι, the adjective τόδε is added in the 1548 edition.

[14] The full stop after κοινωφελίας is changed to an interpunct (·) in the 1548 edition.

πραγματείᾳ προσλιπαροῦσα. πάμπολλά γε μὴν πρὸς τούτῳ διανοητικῶς τε καὶ ἐνθυμητικῶς ἐπικεκυφώς, ὅμως οὐκ ἐδυνήθην κατὰ τὴν προαίρεσιν τὴν ἐμὴν ἐπεξιέναι τῷ ἐπικεχειρημένῳ, ἠνώχληκε γὰρ ἡ νόσος μελετῶντι, ἣ δὴ ἐκ τῆς σφόδρα πρὸς τοῖς λόγοις ἐπιστάσεως πρὸ πολλοῦ μοι ἔφθη ἐντετηκυῖα, ὡς γοῦν διισχυρίζονται οἱ τῶν ἰατρῶν παῖδες. (lines 1–14)[15]

For more than two years, my powerful Lord, I have been working on this book of commentaries – neither a part-time occupation nor an episodic one, but a constant effort and care. For I was constantly prompted, on one side, by a strong desire to help the scholars, and, on the other side, by the love of a labour well done, encouraging me to do what was needed and always urging me to achieve it as soon as possible. Nevertheless, as I was totally absorbed in it, mind and soul, I could not complete the work in the form I had previously designed, since an illness prevented me from attending to it. According to the doctors, this illness has been consuming me for a long time and was provoked by an excess of study.[16]

By indicating that he had been working on his book for 'more than two years' (δεύτερον ἤδη [...] τὸ ἔτος [...] καὶ μικρόν τι πρός), Budé suggests that he had been compiling the materials he had previously produced. He employs the term ὑπομνηματικὸν σύνταγμα, the equivalent for Latin *commentarii*. Through two litotes, he insists on the intensity of his effort (οὐ παρέργως δ' οὐδ' ὡς αὐτὸς τύχοιμι), explaining that he was driven to work by an 'intense desire to help the scholars' (ἔρως δεινὸς τῆς φιλομαθούντων κοινωφελίας) and by φιλοπονία, 'love of labour', a concept rendered in French by an oxymoron, 'plaisir de la peine'. He expresses and summarises this effort in the second sentence: πάμπολλά γε μὴν πρὸς τούτῳ διανοητικῶς τε καὶ ἐνθυμητικῶς ἐπικεκυφώς ('totally absorbed in

---

[15] The line numbers provided in the present paper are based on the 1529 edition.

[16] French version (ff. 1r–v): 'Il y a jà deux ans et ung peu plus, trespuissant Roy, que je suis après ceste euvre de Commentaires, y besoignant tousjours et minutant non certes lentement ou par maniere d'acquict; car l'amour tresvehemente de la publique utilité des estudians m'esguillonnoit contiuellement d'ung costé, et de l'aultre m'eschauffoit ung certain plaisir de la peine se solicitant luy-mesmes; et m'[h]ate à vouloir achever l'euvre entreprise et qui tous les jours de plus en plus estoit assistant et fiché sur la besoigne. Toutesfoys, avecques ceste si grande instance de couraige, je n'ay peu faire ce que j'avoys entrepris et en venir à bout ainsy que je l'entendoye. Car le cours de ce progect a esté empesché par une maladie laquelle, ainsy que les medecins afferment, s'est en moy fourrée et enracinée jusques au plus profond, pour vouloir trop asprement et perserveramment estudier.'

this work, mind and soul').[17] Thus, our humanist was sick to the point of being unable to work. He finally notes that the most likely reason for his illness is what we might nowadays understand as burnout (ἐκ τῆς σφόδρα πρὸς τοῖς λόγοις ἐπιστάσεως).

In a subsequent passage, it is worth noting that the Greek text is shorter than the French, which adds one important clause—compare οὗ δὴ κακοῦ οἰκοφθόρου ἡ καθ' ἡμᾶς ἀπειροκαλία εἰκότως αἰτίαν ἔχει παρὰ πολλοῖς, ἡ τῷ καλῷ τὸ προσῆκον καὶ τὸ ἐπιβάλλον ἀπονέμειν οὐκ εἰδυῖα ('the probable cause for this trouble, which might end up ruining a household, is today's ignorance, making the people incapable of granting to an honest enterprise what it deserves and what is appropriate to it', lines 28–30) with the French version (3r): 'Duquel malheur – c'est assavoir que la plus belle chose de toutes ait commencé estre dommageuse à ses poursuyvans – le blasme en demeure emprès les hommes de nostre temps, qui ne scevent bailler et adjuger à chascune chose son pris.' In Greek, Budé alludes to a 'trouble' (κακός) that 'ruins [his] household' (οἰκοφθόρος), in the French text, he elaborates on this *malheur*: 'that the finest of all things has become harmful to those who pursue it'. He then offers a general reason: this trouble arises, because his 'contemporaries' (καθ' ἡμᾶς) do not care about literature and humanist ideals due to their ignorance of the good or the beautiful (ἀπειροκαλία) and thus do not support the liberal arts.

Eventually, Budé suggests solution to the problem. In his opinion, the King should be the main sponsor of humanism and science:

ἀλλὰ μὴν τῆς ἀρετῆς τε καὶ τῆς ἐπιεικείας τῆς σῆς τόν τε καρπὸν καὶ μισθὸν ζῶν τε καὶ θανὼν ἔκπλεων ἂν ἀπενέγκαιο, εἰ καὶ ταύτης τὸ μέρος οὐκ ἐλάχιστον παραπολαύσειαν οἱ μάλιστα φιλόχρηστοι τῶν ἀνθρώπων καὶ φιλόκαλοι. τοῦτο τοίνυν εὖ ἴσθι τότ' ἔσται ὁπόταν τήν τε φιλοδωρίαν ταυτηνὶ καὶ τὴν μεγαλουργίαν εἰς τὰ περὶ λόγους ἀποστρέψῃς καὶ εἰς παιδείας ἐλευθερίους. (lines 95–99)

But you would obtain, during your lifetime, abundant yield and, after passing, a reward for your excellence and mercy, if a fair share of these benefits those who love the good and the honest to the utmost. Be well aware that it will occur whenever you turn this generosity of yours in favour of learning and the liberal arts.[18]

---

[17] Here, the right word would be ἐνθυμηματικῶς, not ἐνθυμητικῶς.

[18] French version (9v): 'Mais tu auras en ce, finablement, perceu fruict tresabundant de ta bonté

Budé thus approach the matter indirectly: he first vaguely hints at 'the people who love the good and the honest to the utmost' (οἱ μάλιστα φιλόχρηστοι τῶν ἀνθρώπων καὶ φιλόκαλοι), after having said, in the previous lines, that these men should obtain a fair share of the 'excellence and mercy' (ἀρετὴ καὶ ἐπιείκεια) that so characterise the king. In turn, the king will receive a reward for this good deed not only during his life but also after his death. Budé only becomes more explicit in the following sentence, with phrases like 'this generosity of yours' (τήν τε φιλοδωρίαν ταυτηνὶ καὶ τὴν μεγαλουργίαν) and 'learning and the liberal arts' (εἰς τὰ περὶ λόγους […] καὶ εἰς παιδείας ἐλευθερίους).

Later, we learn that Budé's idea is, in fact, neither a new one nor entirely his own, as the King had already promised a few years earlier to create a sort of college for the humanities:[19]

> μέμνησαι δήπου, φημ' ἐγώ, κύριε ἐπιεικέστατε, πρῶτον μὲν αὐθαιρέτως τε καὶ διαρρήδην ἐπηγγελμένος, εἶτα δὲ πάλιν ἐρομένων μὲν ἡμῶν, καὶ ὡσπερεὶ ἐπίδοσίν τινα προικῴαν προμνωμένων Φιλολογίᾳ κοινῇ, ὡς ἀνεκδότῳ τινὶ κόρῃ, αὐτός γ' εὐπροσώπως τε καὶ ἡδέως αὐτολεξεὶ σχεδὸν καθωμολογηκώς, ἦ μὴν φροντιστήριον, καὶ νὴ Δία φυτευτήριον, ὡς ἄν τις φαίη, συντάξεσθαι τῶν τ' ἐλλογίμων ἀνδρῶν καὶ ἐνδόξων εἶναι μελλόντων. (lines 106–110)

> Most merciful Lord, you certainly remember, as I recall, that you had made a promise, at first spontaneously and explicitly, and then you promised again, as we had asked you to offer a dowry for Philology, as if for an unmarried young lady, and that you confirmed in a sweet and benevolent way, according to your own words, approximately, that you would order the creation of a school, or, by Zeus, a special class, as it were, to welcome a few men eager to become eloquent and glorious.[20]

---

et clemence, se d'icelle partie non petite est assignée à gens aymans bonté et l'honnesteté pour en joyr. Ce qui, certes, lors adviendra quant tu convertiras ceste tienne largesse à honorer les lectres et les sciences liberalles […].'

[19] On this promise, see Sanchi (2006, 21, n. 1).

[20] French version (10r–v): 'Doncques, je dy, sire tresclement, qu'il te souvient en premier lieu de ton bon gré et par parolles tresouvertes avoir promis et comme, après, je veinsse à demander et stipuler douaire à commune Philologie – ainsi que à une fille à marier despourveue de biens – avoir quasi par les mesmes parolles confermé de vouloir fonder un colliège et comme une pepiniere de gens de deviendroient à l'advenir par doctrine recommandables […].'

From the first word, 'you remember' (μέμνησαι), Budé reminds the King that he once 'made a promise' to found a royal college in Paris; the promise was made in 1521, eight years earlier. Budé recalls that the king uttered his promise twice: 'at first, spontaneously' (πρῶτον μὲν αὐθαιρέτως), 'and then again' (εἶτα δὲ πάλιν) when Budé asks him (ἐρομένων μὲν ἡμῶν) to do so, introducing his demand as if a dowry for a poor young lady, called Philology: ὡσπερεὶ ἐπίδοσίν τινα προικῷαν προμνωμένων Φιλολογίᾳ κοινῇ, ὡς ἀνεκδότῳ τινὶ κόρῃ. The French Hellenist insists that the King was 'willing', 'explicit' and 'benevolent' in uttering this promise, using no fewer than five adverbs: αὐθαιρέτως, διαρρήδην, εὐπροσώπως, ἡδέως and αὐτολεξεί.

Budé next describes in florid detail the college about which he dreams:

τοῦτο δὲ γενήσεσθαι ἐν τῷδε τῷ ἡμετέρῳ ἄστει τῷ ἐπιπρεπεῖ μὲν νῦν ὄντι, καὶ προσχήματι τῆς ὀνομαστοτάτης μοναρχίας σου ἐσομένῳ δὲ Μουσείῳ ἁπάσης τῆς Κελτικῆς. ἔφασκες δὲ δὴ ἵδρυμά τι λαμπρὸν τῇ πάνυ παιδείᾳ καὶ διγλώττῳ καταβαλεῖσθαί τε καὶ παμμεγέθη συνοικίαν ἐποικοδομήσεσθαι, ἐφ᾽ ἧς ἐξέσται τοῖς ἀμφὶ τὰ γράμματα σπουδάζουσι τὰ δόκιμα, τῆς ἐγκύκλου παιδείας τὸν δρόμον, καὶ τοῖς βουλομένοις δέ, τὸν δόλιχον ἐπιτελέσαι, ἅπαντά γε τὰ πρὸς ῥᾳστώνην ἐπιτήδεια συγκεκροτημένοις ἐκτενῶς. (lines 110–116)

This school would be located in this town of ours, as now becomes it, which would thus become the ornament of your renowned kingdom and the Muses' dwelling for all of France. You spoke of a magnificent building, to honour the celebrated ancient education in two languages, and a very large one, where those who study the finest literature would be allowed to complete the basic course and, if they so desire, the full course of a liberal education, well-trained with all the facilities that might ease their lives.[21]

After this short description, the rest of Budé's letter (lines 116–166) is a sort of respectful but firm remonstration, lamenting that Francis had not yet kept his

---

[21] French version (10v–11r): '[…] et que ce seroit en ceste nostre ville, laquelle, ainsi comme elle est à present capitale et maistresse de ton tresample Royaulme, seroit lors le sejour commun des Muses de toute la Gaule. À cela, tu adjusterois y devoir faire bastir et construire ung logeis d'ouvraige sumptueux et magnifique, dès les fondemens jusques à la couverture, qui seroit comme une lice de tournoyans en l'une et l'autre langue, où, en plantureuse abundance de toutes les choses requises pour l'entretenement du repoz, ils pourroient venir au bout non d'une science ou deux, mais aussi parfaire et achever, s'ilz vouloient, l'entier cours et cercle de toutes les ars […].'

promise. Budé speaks as if he were the complainant in a trial, stating that he had assumed the role of a warrant in this royal promise made to his fellow Parisian humanists. As noted above, Budé's words would prove to be effective.

The Letter to the Young Hellenists

The second Greek text is much less known yet remarkable for two reasons: it includes a short explanation of how Budé produced his *Commentaries*, and it shows how he conceived of educating a new generation of Hellenists. The address, Ἴλερμος Βουδαῖος τῶν νέων τοῖς τῶν Ἑλληνικῶν λόγων ἐφιεμένοις εὖ πράττειν, 'Guillaume Budé wishes wellbeing to the students fond of Greek literature', points out the 'passion', or *studium*, for Greek letters, through the participle ἐφιεμένοις. The first word of the *incipit*, the elegant conjunction ἐπειδήπερ, in correlation with διὰ τοῦτ(ο), is also the first word of Luke's Gospel, a Greek text that Budé had studied carefully, as shown in his *Annotationes in Pandectas* (1508):[22]

> Ἐπειδήπερ τοῖς ἀκριβῶς τῶν λόγων ἡμμένοις τῶν δοκίμων, οὐδὲν ἑώρων περισπουδαστότερον ἐν τῷ παρόντι, ἢ ὅπως τῆς παιδείας ἄντικρυς ἐφίξοιντο τῆς Ἑλληνικῆς, διὰ τοῦτ' ἐγὼ διὰ σπουδῆς ἔσχον, ὦ νέοι προσφιλέστατοι, καὶ ἐν τοῖς μάλιστα δὴ προὐθυμησάμην, τοῖς οὕτω τὴν προαίρεσιν διατεθεῖσι συμφιλοπονεῖν, ἐφ' ᾧ τούτοις συμποριοῦμαι ὧν μάλιστα δεῖσθαί μοι ἐοίκασιν, ἐφ' ὅσον δὴ ἔγωγε οἷός τ' ἦν διαπράττεσθαι. καὶ γὰρ δὴ ᾧτινί τε πρώτῳ καὶ χρόνον οὐ βραχὺν μόνῳ τῶν τῇδε φιλομαθησάντων, ἐποπτεύειν τε τὰ τῶν Ἑλλήνων καὶ πολυπραγμονεῖν ὑπῆρξεν, οὐδὲν ὅ τι δήπου μὴ ποιήσειν οὗτος ἤμελλεν, ὁρῶν τοῦθ' ὅ τι εἰσηγούμενος καὶ ὑποδεικνύων ἔτυχε, κατ' οὖρον νῦν φέρεσθαι. (lines 1–10)

Beloved young men, since I noticed that today those who are committed to thoroughly understand the finest literature were looking intensely for none other than to study the Hellenic culture directly, I tried hard and did my very best to help with my work those who had this goal, providing them, as much as I was able, with what seemed to me they lacked most. In fact, nothing is more worth doing for someone like me, the first scholar here [in Paris] (and

---

[22] On Budé's remarks on the Gospel, published eight years before Erasmus' *Novum instrumentum* (1516), see Sanchi (2020).

for a long time the only one) to begin to study and research Greek literature, especially as I see that what I had introduced and recommended by my own example is now doing well.

In the first sentence, the author notes the strength of the 'actual' (ἐν τῷ παρόντι) desire to 'study the Hellenic culture directly'—that is, in the Greek language— and how he has therefore decided to act to assist this desire, so much as he is able, underlining his efforts with several expressions: ἐγὼ διὰ σπουδῆς ἔσχον […] καὶ ἐν τοῖς μάλιστα δὴ προύθυμησάμην […] ἐφ' ὅσον δὴ ἔγωγε οἷός τ' ἦν διαπράττεσθαι. On a touching note, he expresses his joy in seeing that many more people are now passionate for the subject he had 'studied alone for a long time'. He uses the technical expression κατ' οὖρον νῦν φέρεσθαι ('pushed by favourable winds') to indicate that Greek studies were highly successful at the time.[23]

Subsequent passages elaborate on (A) how Budé tried to be useful to students of Greek and (B) how he had assumed that his potential public had high expectations for his work, too high perhaps for him to be able to fulfil all of.

(A) […] τοῦτο δὴ χρῆν ἐν τοῖς μάλιστα, ὅπως τοὺς λόγους τῶν ῥητόρων ἐπαΐοντές τε ἐπιλέξονται καὶ μεθ' ἡδονῆς διεξίασι. […] τούτοις τοίνυν τὰ τῶν λογογράφων τε καὶ τῶν ῥητόρων ἐπερχομένοις ἐνοχλήσειν ᾤμην οὐχ ἥκιστα τὰς δικανικὰς λέξεις, τάχα δὲ καὶ ἄγαν αὐτῶν προθυμίαν ἀποσπεύσειν. ἐφ' ᾧ δὴ προύργου τι ποιήσειν μοι ἐδόκουν, εἰ τῷδε τῷ μέρει ἐπιτυχῶς τῆς ἐξηγήσεως ἐπιθησοίμην, τοῦτό τε ποιῶν, κατὰ τὴν τῶν Ῥωμαίων γλῶτταν ἑκάστῃ φωνῇ τὴν προσήκουσαν ἑρμηνείαν ὅπῃ παρείκοι αὐτὸς ἀποδιδοίην. (lines 16–17 and 18–23)
[…]
καὶ δὴ καὶ ἐκ προσαγωγῆς πόρρω που ἔφθακα διεξελθών, ἐνδιδούσης δῆθεν τῆς συνεπείας, καὶ τοῦ ἐφεξῆς ἀεὶ ἐξεχομένου τὴν ὑφὴν παρεκτείνοντος. τοῦ γὰρ ἔμπροσθεν σκοποῦ ἀντεχόμενος, ἅττ' ἐν παρέργου μέρει οὕτως ἠδυνήθη τεθεῖσθαι, ὡς τὰ[24] ἄλλ' ἐπ' ἄλλοις ἐπερχόμενα, τῶν ἤδη παραπεπλεγμένων[25] ἁρμοττόντως ἔχεσθαι, τούτοις οὕτως ἐπεξῆλθον ὥστ' οὐδαμοῦ οὐδεπώποτε συνειδέναι μοι οὔτέ τι καθυφεμένῳ, οὔτε τὴν ὁδὸν ἐκτραπομένῳ ἣν εὐθυπορεῖν ἠρξάμην. καὶ μὲν δὴ καὶ ὅσα γε ἐνθυμεῖσθαι δυνατὸς ἦν ἐγὼ τῶν πραγματείας ἀκριβοῦς δεομένων, ἢ λόγου

---

[23] See Stephanus *et al.* (1846, *s.v.* οὖρος, col. 2415; cf. Aesch. *Pers.* 481, *Sept.* 690 and 854, etc.).

[24] After τά, the pronoun ἡμῖν is added in the 1548 edition.

[25] The 1529 and 1548 editions have παραπεπλεγμνέων.

οὐκ ἀναξίων, ἢ δυσεικάστων παρὰ τοῖς πάνυ συγγραφεῦσι, καὶ οἵας δὴ γλωσσηματικὰς λέξεις ἢ ἀπηρχαιωμένας οἱ πάλαι ἀποκαλοῦσι, ταῦτα δὴ πάντα διασαφηνίσαι τ᾽ ἐνεχείρησα, καὶ τὰ ἀνωμαλῆ τοῖς νέοις καθομαλίσαι σφόδρα διεφιλοτιμήθην. (lines 34–43)

Most of all, [the students] giving heed to the speeches of the orators needed both to carefully study them and to read them with pleasure. […] Therefore, I thought that those approaching the writings of lawyers and orators would be mostly annoyed by the legal expressions, which might quickly and effectively dissuade them from their zeal. That is why I thought I could provide some help by consistently applying myself to this part of the exegesis [of such authors] and, in doing so, giving the Latin equivalent of each word, whenever possible. […]
And so, I proceeded onward and was able to explain the items little by little, following the connections between the words, whose web was constantly enlarged. In fact, even though I continued to adhere to my first goal, I was able to add some extra words, one following another so consistently that I was never left with the impression that I had neglected anything or that I had lost my path. In particular, I undertook to make clear all the words that I could think needed careful explanation, or that were worth specific study, or that might sound obscure in the prose of the most celebrated authors, and such expressions that the ancients called idiomatic or archaic; also, I earnestly strove to smooth out any irregularity for the sake of younger students.

Budé's starting point in writing his *Commentaries* was to explain 'the legal expressions' (τὰς δικανικὰς λέξεις) used by lawyers and orators (τὰ τῶν λογογράφων τε καὶ τῶν ῥητόρων), as well as to 'read with pleasure' (καὶ μεθ᾽ ἡδονῆς διεξίασι) these texts. In fact, the first third of the *Commentaries* comprises explanations of several technical expressions typical of legal jargon. The *Commentaries* then shift to a systematic survey of each Greek lexical family, arranged by stem and derivation.

Budé tells how this happened, here starting from ἐκ προσαγωγῆς πόρρω, where the key expression being ἐνδιδούσης δῆθεν τῆς συνεπείας, 'the connection of words inviting me to go further'. He then lists the kinds of words he cared most about: those 'needing a careful study' (τῶν πραγματείας ἀκριβοῦς δεομένων), those 'deserving anyway some explanation' (λόγου οὐκ ἀναξίων), the 'difficult ones found in the major authors' (δυσεικάστων παρὰ τοῖς πάνυ συγγραφεῦσι), and the 'rare or the archaic' ones (γλωσσηματικὰς λέξεις ἢ ἀπηρχαιωμένας).

In two other passages, Budé stresses the role he played, almost despite himself, as the author of a long-anticipated reference work, finally declaring his expectation that the next generation provide new and better works on the same subject:

(B) προϊόντος μέντοι τοῦ ἔργου διευλαβεῖσθαί μοι παρέστη, μὴ φαῦλον εἶναι δοκοίη τὸ σύγγραμμα, ὡς πολὺ ἧττον δήπου τῆς προσδοκίας ἐσόμενον τῆς γ' ἐνίων ἀνθρώπων. ἐτύγχανε γὰρ ὂν ἐπίδοξόν τι παρ' ἡμῶν, ὡς τῶν συνήθων μοι καὶ γνωρίμων ἐπυθόμην, τῶν Ἑλληνικῶν περὶ ἐξηγημάτων, πολλῷ τε μεῖζον καὶ διεξοδικώτερον ἢ ὅπερ εἰς νοῦν ἐγὼ ἐμβεβλημένος ἦν τότε. ἐπὶ δὲ τούτῳ, τὸ τῆς ἐπιθυμίας τῶν νέων οὕτω θερμὸν εἶναι ᾐσθόμην, ὥστε τῶν ἐντυγχανόντων ἔνιοι (οὕτως ἐστὶν ἡ προσδοκία ἀκρατές τε καὶ ἐπισπευστικόν) ὡς ὑπερημέρους ἡμᾶς ἤδη τοῦδε τοῦ χρέους, εἰσεπράττοντο. ἦν δὲ τὸ χρέος οὐ τὸ ὑπ' ἐμοῦ ἐπηγγελμένον, ἀλλὰ τὸ δι' ἣν ἔτυχον αἰτίαν ὑπ' αὐτῶν προσδοκώμενον. (lines 25–32)

[…]

ἔστι γάρ τοι ἀμφιλαφὲς τὸ ἠργολαβημένον, καὶ οἷον προσίεσθαι τὸν διαδεξόμενον, ἕνα καὶ πλείους. ἐγὼ μὲν δὴ τὸ κατ' ἐμέ, μᾶλλον δὲ πολὺ μεῖζον ἢ κατ' ἐμὲ ἀπειργασμένος, τοῖς καθημένοις τοὐντεῦθεν ἐπὶ θέᾳ ἐντετάξομαι. γένοιτο δὲ πάνθ' ἕκαστον τῶν ἐπὶ τῷ αὐτῷ ἀγῶνι ἀνταρουμένων τε, καὶ ὡσαύτως παρενδειξομένων, τὸ ἐπιβάλλον εἰς ἑαυτὸν μέρος οὕτω συντελεῖν εἰς τὸ μέσον, ὡς τὸ ἡμέτερον τὸ τούτων παρευδοκιμεῖν. γένοιτο δέ τοι καὶ ἐμοὶ τοῦθ' ὁρᾶν ἐπιζήσαντι, ἵνα καὶ τόδε τῆς ἄγαν φιλοπονίας ἀπολαύσω τοῖς ἄλλοις συνηδόμενος τῆς τοῦ πράγματος ἐπιδόσεως. (lines 79–85)

As this work was in progress, I had the idea of ensuring that my book would not seem poor, even if it failed to meet the high expectations of some people. For I knew from my friends and associates that I was supposed to give a much larger and more complete exegetical work on the Greek language than the one I had initially conceived. Moreover, I felt that the desire of students was so passionate that some young friends of mine (so immoderate and urgent are their expectations!) were accusing me of having missed the day for the payment of this debt. Yet the 'debt' was not related to what I had announced but to the kind of expectation I happened to spark in them.

[…]

In fact, this enterprise is vast and asks for one or more successors. From now on, since I did the best at my task – far more than I could reasonably be certain about – I will take my place among the public and observe the game. May all those who will participate in this game, and in like manner make a showing in it, give to the public their own contribution in such a brilliant way that they overtake my own renown! And may I be able to see them succeed in my lifetime, that I might enjoy the fruits of my own excess of work and that I might congratulate others for the progress they will have accomplished in our discipline!

Budé ends his letter with a beautiful closing formula worth repeating here: Εὐδοκιμεῖτε νέοι, καὶ περὶ τὴν φιλολογίαν ἐρρωμένως εὐημερεῖτε (lines 107–108), 'Be honoured, young men, and be vigorously prosperous at philology!'

The two introductory texts give a sense of Budé's Greek prose style, the contemporary importance of which cannot be stressed enough, most of all because both works aimed to establish France's reputation in the humanist *respublica*. Considering the rapid development of Greek studies that would follow in France and, indeed, in the whole of Europe, Budé's two letters might be worth considering bona fide manifestos, not only because they were written in Greek, but also because they stand together as a statement of Budé's comprehensive method of scholarship and of his commitment to lofty cultural ideals and educational policies.

Bibliography

Manuscripts

Ms. Paris, Bibliothèque nationale de France, *français* 25445.

Books published before 1800

Aristophanes. 1528. *Aristophanis facetissimi comoediae novem*. Paris.
Budé, Guillaume. 1508. *Annotationes in XXIV Pandectarum libros*. Paris.
Budé, Guillaume. 1529. *Commentarii linguae Graecae*. Paris.
Budé, Guillaume. 1548. *Commentarii linguae Graecae accurate recogniti, atque amplius tertia parte aucti*. Paris.
Novum Instrumentum. 1516. *Novum Instrumentum omne a Erasmo diligenter recognitum et emendatum*. Paris.
Stephanus, Henricus. 1572. *Thesaurus Graecae linguae*. Geneva.

Modern authors

Farge, James K. 1992. *Le Parti conservateur en France au XVI siècle*. Paris.
Higman, Francis. 1979. *Censorship and the Sorbonne*. Geneva.
La Garanderie, Marie-Madeleine Payen de. 1995. *Christianisme et Lettres Profanes (1515–1535). Essai sur la mentalité des milieux intellectuels parisiens, et sur la pensée de Guillaume Budé*. Paris.
Maillard, Jean-François & Jean-Marie Flamand. 2010. *La France des Humanistes. Hellénistes II*. Turnhout.
McNeil, David O. 1975. *Guillaume Budé and Humanism in the Reign of Francis I*. Geneva.
Rummel, Erika. 1995. *The Humanist-Scholastic Debate in the Renaissance and Reformation*. Harvard.
Saladin, Jean-Christophe. 2000. *La Bataille du grec à la Renaissance*. Paris.
Sanchi, Luigi-Alberto. 2006. *Les Commentaires de la langue grecque de Guillaume Budé*. Geneva.
Sanchi, Luigi-Alberto. 2014. "Les imprimeurs humanistes et la censure", *Paris et Îles-de-France* 110, 233–249.

Sanchi, Luigi-Alberto. 2018a. "Producing Knowledge. Guillaume Budé's Encyclopaedic Horizon", in W. Scott Blanchard & Andrea Severi (eds.) *Renaissance Encyclopaedism: Studies in curiosity and Ambition*, Toronto, 433–451.

Sanchi, Luigi-Alberto. 2018b. "La bibliothèque de Guillaume Budé", *Arts & Savoirs* 10 [OpenEdition Journals], https://doi.org./10.4000/aes.1235.

Sanchi, Luigi-Alberto. 2020. "Guillaume Budé et la critique érasmienne du Nouveau Testament", in Thierry Amalou & Jean-Marie Le Gall (eds.), *Le Nouveau Testament d'Érasme (1516). Nouveaux regards sur l'Europe des Humanistes*, Turnhout, 31–38.

Sandy, Gerald. 2002. "Guillaume Budé: Philologist and Polymath. A preliminary study", in Gerald Sandy (ed.) *The Classical Heritage in France*. Leiden, 79–108.

Stephanus, Henricus, Carolus Benedictus Hase, Guilielmus Dindorfius & Ludovicus Dindorfius. 1846. *Thesaurus Graecae Linguae, ab Henrico Stephano Constructus. Volumen Quintum*. Paris.

Rabelais' *Quart livre* and Greek language

Martin Steinrück

But the calumny of certain cannibals, **misanthropes, agelastes**, has been so foul and excessive against me, that it had conquered my patience, and I had resolved not to write one **jot** more. For the least of their detractions were that my books are all stuffed with various **heresies**, of which, nevertheless, they could not show one single instance; much, indeed, of comical and facetious fooleries, neither offending God nor the king (and truly I own they are the only subject and only theme of these books), but of heresy not a word, unless they interpreted wrong, and against all use of reason and common language, what I had rather suffer a thousand deaths, if it were possible, than have thought; as who should make <u>bread to be stone, a fish to be a serpent, and an egg to be a scorpion</u>. This, my lord, emboldened me once to tell you, as I was complaining of it in your presence, that if I did not esteem myself a better Christian than they show themselves towards me, and if my life, writings, words, nay thoughts, betrayed to me one single spark of heresy, or I should in a detestable manner fall into the snares of the spirit of detraction, διάβολος, who, by their means, raises such crimes against me. (Rabelais: *Le Quart livre*, dedication, B2r-v[1])

This passage from the dedication of the *Quart livre* (1552),[2] the fourth book of Rabelais' pentalogy *The Life of Gargatua and of Pantagruel*, is addressed to the

---

[1] Peter A. Motteux (1708) is the translator of the *Fourth book* used throughout this article with some modifications to facilitate reading. The picture of Hergé's cartoon is from *Tintin au Tibet* p. 26, picture 8.

[2] The title page mentions Rabelais as 'docteur en Medicine'.

'tresillustre Prince, et reverendissime mon seigneur Odet cardinal de Chastillon.'[3] To enable the reader to appreciate it fully, the original in French is presented below, arranged in lines, for reading aloud with the prosody of Rabelais' times, pronouncing the plural -s fully and *oi* as a *uay*, in a prose-rhythm-style reminding us of the Atticist Dio Chrysostom rather than of the serial style of Lysias, and furthermore without Demosthenic or Ciceronian periodic *circuitus*:[4]

> Mais la **calumnie** de certains Canibales, **misantropes, agelastes**,
> avoit tant contre moy esté atroce & desraisonnee,
> qu'elle avoit vaincu ma patience:
> & plus n'estois deliberé en escrire un **Iota**.
>
> Car l'une des moindres contumelies dont ilz usoient,
> estoit, que telz livres tous estoient farciz d'**heresies** diverses:
> n'en povoient toutes fois une seulle exhiber en endroict aulcun:
>
> de folastries joyeuses hors l'offence de Dieu, et du Roy, prou
> (cest le subject & theme unicque d'iceulx livres)
> d'**heresies** poinct:
>
> sinon perversement & contre tout usaige raison & de languaige commun,
> interpretans ce que a poine de mille fois mourir, si autant possible estoit,
> ne vouldrois avoir pensé:
>
> comme qui <u>pain</u>, interpretroit <u>pierre</u>:
> poisson, serpent:
> <u>oeuf, scorpion.</u>
>
> Dont quelque fois me complaignant en vostre praesence vous dis librement,
> que si meilleur Christian je ne m'estimois,
> qu'ilz ne monstrent estre en leur part:
>
> & que si en ma vie, escriptz, parolles, voire certes pensees,
> je recongnoissois scintille aulcune d'**heresie**,

---

[3] Odet de Chastillon obtained from King Henry II (the son of Francis I of France) a *placet* for ten years for Rabelais' books, see Collectet (1970, 16).

[4] See my prosodic analysis of this passage in the Appendix.

ilz ne tomberoient tant detestablement es lacs de l'esprit **calumniateur,**
cest διάβολος qui par leur ministere me suscite tel crime. (*Le Quart livre,*
dedication, pp. A4r–A5r)

One can see from the curses of Rabelais' dedication what both the *Rabelaisians*
among scholars and the *Tintinologues* seem to take for granted, that Captain
Haddock's language (and his alcoholism, cf. Rabelais' anagrammatic pseudonym
Alcophrybas[5]) is an allusion to Rabelais by Hergé (cfr. the cartoon on Haddock
above). This observation is helpful for our inquiry into Rabelais' use of Greek
inasmuch as this sea dog does not seem to have the benefits of a classical
education, yet the curses of the cartoon picture above are of Greek origin, apart
from the American Indian word *canibale*,[6] and the German word for garlic,
Rockenbolle, although that may at least sound Greek. This tendency to use Greek
or Greek-sounding language could be Rabelaisian, even if the terms like *canibales,*
misantropes and *agelastes* in Rabelais' preface have a specific contemporary
referent: the *canibales* is likely representing the Greek suppressing Sorbonne; the
misantropes are those who reproached Rabelais as a human-hater like Timon of
Athens, *agelastos* is Calvin, and so on.[7]

    I do not think that the accumulation of consonants so characteristic of ancient
Greek, which sound so horrible in modern French (*ek-to-plas-me*), give Haddock's
and Rabelais' curses more maledictive power, even if Rabelais pronounced the
consonants that are silent in today's pronunciation.[8] A more promising approach
would be to hypothesize that Greek has, beyond the function as an ornamental
quotation, a specific semiotic function in Rabelais' style, somewhat like a secret
language. The present article is not the first to suggest this hypothesis.[9] The aim of
this paper is modest: to illustrate this interpretation by some well-known passages

---

[5] In the first book of the *Pantagruel* pentalogy, Rabelais signs with the anagram *Alcophrybas Nasier.*
Rabelais (1532).

[6] I am refering here to *Tintin au Tibèt*, but *cannibale* is to be found in Haddock's vocabulary in five
other books of Hergé as well.

[7] In 1533, the Sorbonne declared the *Pantagruel* obscene; Jean Calvin attacked Rabelais in his *Traité*
des scandales in 1550 (even if this was a misunderstanding to some, cf. Fatio [1984, introduction].
Gabriel du Puy-Herbault denounced Rabelais of misanthropy ('Quel Timon a médit davantage de
l'humanité?') in his *Theotimus* (1549).

[8] See Morin (2000).

[9] See Menini (2017). As Franciscan monk, Rabelais studied Greek in Fontenay-le-Comte around
1520, corresponding with Guillaume Budé; the result, Rabelais' high skills in Greek, can be seen in
his Greek letter to Erasmus (see below Ill. 1).

of the *Quart livre*, especially taken from its preface, the purpose of whose Greek references have not, to my knowledge, been fully understood.

Greek Words, Quotes and Translations

The first word printed in Greek letters in the excerpt of the dedication above is the word for the devil (διάβολος) which surely leads Greek-knowing readers to its derivation from the verb διαβάλλω, meaning 'to discredits someone' or 'calomnier' in French. It is a way to say that those who reproach Rabelais for heresy represent the devil themselves. Here the quarrel goes about in metonymies, but in general Rabelais seems to forbid metaphorical reading – without being too serious about this forbidding. The point here is that there is no need to use a Greek word and letters for the devil, but the simple change of type divides Rabelais' audience into those who know Greek and those who are ignorant of it. In addition, it is possible that the etymology and thus metonymy of the devil from discredit or slander is intended as a red herring, a diversion. For we could understand *diaballo* in the sense of 'splitting' as well. The strange spelling error of misanthrope without 'h' (*misantropes*), suggests the French *mise en trope*, putting into tropes, and thereby stresses the important function of the tropes, of the splitting into metonymy and metaphor. Rabelais' Greek quotation from the preface or prologue of the *Quart livre* at least hints at this:

> Santé est nostre vie, comme tresbien declare Ariphron Sicyonien. *Sans santé n'est la vie vie, n'est la vie vivable,* Α ΒΙΟΣ ΒΙΟΣ, ΒΙΟΣ ΑΒΙΩΤΟΣ *Sans santé n'est la vie que langueur:* la vie n'est que simulachre de mort. Ainsi donques vous estans de santé privez, cest a dire mors, saisissez vous du vif: saisissez vous de vie, c'est santé.
>
> J'ay cestuy espoir en Dieu qu'il oyra nos prieres, veue la ferme foy en laquelle nous les faisons: & accomplira cestuy nostre soubhayt, attendu qu'il est mediocre. <u>Mediocrité a esté par les saiges anciens dicte **auree**, cest a dire precieuse,</u> de tous louee, en tous endroictz agreable. (*Le Quart livre*, preface, pp. B2v–B3v)

Health is our life, as Ariphron the Sicyonian wisely has it; without health life is not life, it is not life worth to live: ἀβίος βίος, βίος ἀβίοτος. Without health life is only a languishment and an image of death. Therefore, you are deprived of your health, that is to say, are dead, seize the quick; secure life to yourselves, that is to say, health.

I have this hope in the Lord, that he will hear our supplications, considering with what faith and zeal we pray, and that he will grant this our wish because it is moderate and mean. <u>Mediocrity was held by the ancient sages to be **golden,** that is to say, precious</u>, praised by all men, and pleasing in all places. (Motteux B5r–v)

The end of Athenaeus' *Deipnosophists* contains a paean to Apollo Paean, attributed to Ariphron of Sicyon. [10] The paean states, as Rabelais points out, that without health life is unlivable.[11]

This quotation from Rabelais' preface appears in tune with his profession of a surgeon.[12] But there are some inconsistencies. It may or may not be significant that the quotation Α ΒΙΟΣ ΒΙΟΣ, ΒΙΟΣ ΑΒΙΩΤΟΣ is not metric (UU-U-UUUU-U),[13] neither cretic as in Delphic paeans nor aeolic as in Delic or other paeans, and it does not, in fact, even stem from Ariphron's paean. Furthermore, the Greek wording of the quotation does not seem to fit the translation (*Sans santé n'est la vie vie, n'est la vie vivable*): Ὑγίεια, health, is not mentioned in the quotation and βίος means neither health nor life in the biological sense. It usually means a way of living or wherewithal, or even money, from the *Odyssey* 4.90 on, which makes Rabelais' quotation a wordplay; life without money is not livable in the social sense. This makes sense to us, but is this second meaning of βίος possible beyond a "banker discourse"? At the very least, the larger context of this passage speaks in

---

[10] Athn. 15.63 Kaibel (Teubner 1887). Rabelais would have used the Basel edition of 1535 by Johann Walder.

[11] Ὑγέεια, πρεσβίστα μακάρων; / μετὰ σοῦ ναίοιμι τὸ λειπόμενον / βιοτᾶς σὺ δέ μοι / πρόφρων / σύνοικος εἴης / εἰ γάρ τις ἢ   πλούτου χάρις ἢ τεκέων / ἢ τᾶς ἰσοδαίμονος ἀνθρώποις / βασιληίδος ἀρχᾶς ἢ πόθων/οὓς κρυφίοις Ἀφροδίτας / ἄρκυσιν θηρεύομεν / ἢ εἴ τις ἄλλα θεόθεν ἀνθρώποισι τέρψις ἢ πόνων / ἀμπνοὰ πέφανται / μετὰ σεῖο, μάκαιρ᾽ Ὑγίεια / τέθαλε πάντα καὶ λάμπει Χαρίτων ὀάροις / σέθεν δε χωρὶς οὔτις εὐδαίμων ἔφυ· Translation: 'Health, Oldest of the Gods / may I dwell with you for the rest / of my life, may you be / my kind companion! / If one likes money or children / or, for men almost a god, / the power of a king, or the desire / we are hunting, ourselves / in the net of Aphrodite, / or what other toy or end of sorrow / the gods can give; / Only with you, divine Health / those things are success and softly whispering splendor / without you, no man is happy.' The translation is mine.

[12] Rabelais exaggerates of course, but the paean does say that money and power cannot render happy without Health.

[13] A denotes *alpha privativum*, so that the first words should, in fact, be written together as ΑΒΙΟΣ (ἄβιος βίος, βίος ἀβίοτος).

a very materialistic way of the *aurea mediocritas* that brings money. Furthermore, there is a certain Greek text that reader contemporary with Rabelais may have known from Pierre de Ronsard's translation, if not in its original language, namely, the *Plutus,* where Aristophanes links the quotation from Euripides' *Hippolytus* (ἀβίοτος βίου, 821) to both (personified) Wealth and health (*Plut.* 197 and 969):

Χρεμύλος.	Chremylus
σοῦ δ' ἐγένετ' οὐδεὶς μεστὸς οὐδεπώποτε.	Nobody ever has enough of you
ἀλλ' ἢν τάλαντά τις λάβῃ τριακαίδεκα,	If someone gets thirteen Talents
πολὺ μᾶλλον ἐπιθυμεῖ λαβεῖν ἑκκαίδεκα·	he would have preferred sixteen
κἂν ταῦτ' ἀνύσηται, τετταράκοντα βούλεται,	and once this is the case, he wants forty
ἤ φησιν εἶν ἀβίωτον αὑτῷ τὸν βίον.	**or else, he says, life is not livable.**
Γραῦς	Old woman
πέπονθα δεινὰ καὶ παράνομ' ὦ φίλτατε·	I go through terrible and not legit things, my dear,
ἀφ' οὗ γὰρ ὁ θεὸς οὗτος ἤρξατο βλέπειν,	since this god there started to see:
ἀβίωτον εἶναί μοι πεποίηκε τὸν βίον.	**he made my life unlivable.**

For Chremylus, the protagonist of this comedy, life is unbearable, unlivable without Πλοῦτος, or Wealth/Money, but in order to get the help of this god, he has to be healed. The Rabelais commentators have noted the link between Rabelais' Α ΒΙΟΣ ΒΙΟΣ, ΒΙΟΣ ΑΒΙΩΤΟΣ to the *Plutus*,[14] but not its consequences, that the Greek language offers the additional interpretation of "without money" to a Hellenist that is not available to the non-Hellenist.

If Rabelais really intends to make the link between health and money (the rich semantics of βίος), my third case, a quotation from the beginning of the preface of the *Quart livre,* seems to contradict this reading (i.e., a possible double meaning of βίος working at the same time):

Cl. Gal. non pour telle reverence en santé soy maintenoit, quoy que quelque sentiment il eust des sacres bibles: & eust congneu & frequenté les saincts Christians de son temps, comme appert lib. II. de usu partium, lib. 2. de differentiis pulsuum cap. 3. & ibidem lib. 3. Cap. 2. & lib de rerum affectibus (s'il est de Galen) mais par craincte de tomber en ceste vulgaire & Satyrique mocquerie.

---

[14] Cf. Defaux (1994). Edition of *Plutus* used here is Hall & Geldart (Oxford 1907).

ιητρος αλλων αυτος ελκεσι βρυων

Medicin est des aultres en effect:

Toutesfois est d'ulceres tout infect. (*Le Quart livre*, preface, p. B1v)

Galen had some knowledge of the Bible, and had conversed with the Christians of his time, as appears lib. 11. De Usu Partium; lib. 2. De Differentiis Pulsuum, cap. 3, and ibid. lib. 3. cap. 2. and lib. De Rerum Affectibus (if it be Galen's). Yet 'twas not for any such veneration of holy writ that he took care of his own health. No, it was for fear of being twitted with the saying so well known among physicians:

ιητρος αλλων αυτος ελκεσι βρυων

He boasts of healing poor and rich,

Yet is himself all over itch. (Motteux B4v)

Rabelais might have found, as so often, the quote about of the ailing doctor's inability to heal others in Erasmus' *Adagia*. True, Erasmus quotes the maxim: Ἄλλων ἰατρός, αὐτός ἕλκεσι βρύων, which occurs in several treatises by Plutarch (for example, in *De dignoscendo assentatore ab amico, Mor.* 71f). In fact, the verse is from Euripides' lost tragedy.[15] Furthermore, Rabelais has reformulated the verse by putting *Iatros* at its beginning, so modifying it according to Homeric prosody (cf. Ἰητρὸς γὰρ ἀνήρ πολλῶν ἀντάξιος ἄλλων, *Il.* 12.514). Therefore, he had mixed high-sounding epic verse and a low-key trimeter of the iambic tradition – or what Rabelais calls in his dedication a vulgar and satirist mockery ('much, indeed, of comical and facetious fooleries'). Rabelais even tries to reproduce the sound of the quote by rhymes, yet the allusion to Homer is neither visible nor audible to any readers except Hellenists.

The modified quote is without accents. This is strange if Rabelais revised and corrected the text for this second, much longer version of the *Quart livre* (1552).[16] Furthermore, the lack of accents is even more strange if we compare this Greek quote to the letter Rabelais wrote to Erasmus in accomplished Greek, which he probably composed without assistance:

---

[15] Fr. 1086 Kannicht, TrGF vol. V; Suda ε 3691.

[16] The first version of the *Quart livre* was published in 1548.

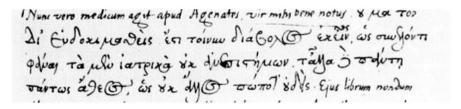

Ill. 1. Rabelais' letter to Erasmus, dated as 30 November 1532.[17]

Astonishingly, the same thematic connections as in the *Quart livre* are to be found in this autograph: οὐ μὰ τὸν Δί' εὐδοκιμασθεὶς ἔστι τοίνυν διάβολος ἔχειν, ὡς συνελόντι φάναι τὰ μὲν ἰατρικὰ οὐκ ἀνεπιστήμων· τἆλλα δὲ πάντη πάντως ἄθεος· ὡς οὐκ ἄλλος πώποτ' οὐδεὶς ('By Jove, the devil is justified to be, to say it that way, not ignorant of medicine, but for all the rest he is ungodly like none else'). In this kind of – always ironic – discourse, Rabelais is himself the devil, accepted only for his medical knowledge. However, once again the Greek text, addressed to a reader whose knowledge of Greek is unquestionable, functions as if it were a secret code, as if Rabelais feared that someone could intercept the letter and prevent its going to its addressee, Erasmus, if it were written in Latin.

One could add one passage from the *Quart livre*, not written in Greek letters. It is drawn not from the preface but from chapter IX, part of which is left out from Motteux's translation:

> Par sainct Treignan (dist Gymnaste) ce proces doibt estre souvent sus ce bureau. L'un appelloit une autre mon **verd**. Elle l'appelloit, son **coquin**. Il y a, bien la, dist Eusthenes, du Verdcoquin. Un aultre salua une sienne alliee disant. Bon di, ma coingnee. Elle respondit. & a vous mon manche. (*Le Quart livre* IX, p. 20r)

> Another greeted his buttock with a Farewell, my case. She replied, Adieu, trial. By St. Winifred's placket, cried Gymnast, this case has been often tried. [18]

This passage is from the catalogue of the family-titles on the isle of alliances. On this isle they do not say "mother" and "son" but use other names like *cognée* and

---

[17] The letter is reprinted in Allen, Allen & Garrod (1941, 130; No. 2743).

[18] Motteux (1708, 126). More complete and literal translation: 'By saint Treignan (said Gymnast) this case has to be frequent on this trial. One called a woman my "verd" and she called him her "coquin". "There is for sure some "Verdcoquin" underlying", said Eusthenes. Another greetes his date with the words "Goodday, my beaten". And she replies "to you too, my handle"'. The translation is mine.

manche, which seem to refer to the female and male sexual parts, but in fact allude to a binary analysis of language: In the Rabelais editions,[19] *verd* is translated into modern French by 'ver', worm, but the ending *d* suggests *viridis*, 'green'. But how then should one translate the name of the male part in this relation, the *coquin*? Boris Vian in his novel *Vercocquin et le plancton* (1946) thought about a coq, and its English associations are appropriate for the sexual part, but what has this to do with worm? Once again, the problem would not arise for some Catholic pupil of Byzantine Greek, where κόκκινος means red, so that an allusion in French to the *cochenille* becomes possible. *Verdcocquin* is today the name of a red wine in Lyon. *Verd* with a *d* would then have the sense of green, so that *verd* means 'green' and *coquin* 'red'. Thus the couples in Rabelais' isle of alliance use the category of color to refer to each other – which is evident only if you know Greek; otherwise you have to put up with different categories.

In the same line, there is a long passage – again from the prologue of the *Quart livre* – on *cogner*, 'striking' or 'banging', but mostly in the sexual meaning, which several scholars have worked on.[20]

> Ma coingnee Juppiter, ma coingnee, ma coingnee. Rien plus, ô Juppiter, que ma coingnee, ou deniers pour en achapter une autre. **Helas**, ma paouvre coingnee. Juppiter tenoit conseil sus certains urgens affaires [...] (*Le Quart livre*, preface, p. B4r)

> My hatchet, Lord Jupiter, my hatchet! my hatchet! only my hatchet, O Jupiter, or money to buy another, and nothing else! **alas**, my poor hatchet! Jupiter happened then to be holding a grand council about certain urgent affairs [...] (Motteux p. 26 [E2v])

We find here a joke that might have inspired Jean-Luc **God**ard, in 1993, in his transposition of the story of the Amphitryon (whom Captain Haddock mentions in his list of curses above), on the lake of Geneva. The title of Godard's film, starring Gerard Dèpar**dieu** as Amphitryon-Zeus, is *Hélas pour moi*, which means either 'What a poor fellow I am' or something like 'Greece (Hellas) to me' or 'Greece as I see it' and, as you can see, with an actor that matched etymologically the director's name.

---

[19] Defaux (1994).

[20] Rigolot (1996, 105).

A rather clear allusion to Greek literature is to be found at the end of chapter 18 of the *Quart livre*:

> Cest faict de moy. Je me conchie de male raige de paour. Bou bou, bou bou. **Otto to to to to ti. Otto to to to to ti.** Bou bou bou, ou ou ou bou bou bous bous. Je naye. Je naye. Je meurs. Bonnes gens je naye. (*Le Quart livre* XVIII, p. 43v)

> I am lost for ever. I conskite myself for mere madness and fear. Bou, bou, bou, bou, **Otto to to to to ti. Otto to to to to ti.** Bou, bou, bou, ou, ou, ou, bou, bou, bous. I sink, I'm drowned, I'm gone, good people, I'm drowned. (Motteux p. 58)

In this description of a tempest, Panurge, the crook directly imported from Aristophanic comedy, thinks his last hour is coming and expresses his anxiety by a phonic catalogue *Bou* [...] *bous*, nothing a 'barbaric' reader could not understand, but there is this strange sequence of *Otto to to to to ti* that might have inspired the Austrian poet Ernst Jandl to create his most famous sound-poem *ottos mops* ("Otto's Pug"). For this sequence, commentaries on Rabelais refer generally to ancient comedy and most usually to Aristophanes' *Birds* with its imitation of birds' songs.[21] However, it cannot be found from comedy because it is a θρῆνος, a tragic lamentation, that Aeschylus uses once in the *Supplices* (268: ὀτοτοτοῖ; cf. also 918), but repeating το three, not four times. Later manuscripts have often ὀττοτοῖ (cf. *LSJ*). In addition, in *Agamemnon* (1072) Cassandra, the barbarian who feigned not to understand Greek, suddenly cries out in sorrow with these sounds: ὀτοτοτοτοῖ. When one reads this with the catholic, i.e. Byzantine, pronunciation, the final τοῖ with its circumflex is to be read as *ti* – as if Panurge becomes Cassandra in a tragicomic scene.

Thus Rabelais both uses Greek letters with incorrect translations (Α ΒΙΟΣ ΒΙΟΣ, ΒΙΟΣ ΑΒΙΩΤΟΣ) and Greek in French letters (Otto to to to to ti. Otto to to to to ti) with a Greek subtext. Both divide the reading – and the readership – into those who know Greek and those who do not.

Classicists tend to find various meanings in Rabelais' text. The name of the ship *Thalamège* is easy to interpret as 'big sea', but may even refer to θάλαμος, the 'sleeping chamber'. There is the isle of the *macréons,* alluding to the μακραίωνες ('long-lived'), and in the ninth chapter we have the enigmatic name of the isle of

---

[21] Cf. Defaux (1994).

Ennasin, which a Greek philologist will easily link to the Greek number nine, but that Rabelais' text itself translates or comments as "isle of the nose-less", *énasés* – which is undoubtedly wrong, but taken at face-value by most of the Rabelais commentators.[22] The isle, which Thomas More called *Outopia*, 'Nowhere', is translated as *Meedamothi* by Rabelais,[23] that is, into Homeric Greek, just as the Euripidean verse mentioned earlier on the sick doctor (Ἄλλων ἰατρός, αὐτός ἕλκεσι βρύων) is transformed/translated into Homeric prosody.

Concluding Words

Greek was probably used by the humanists in Poliziano's circle as a secret code of the homosexual community, as I have argued before.[24] We cannot go this far in our interpretation of Rabelais' use of Greek, although it has many layers. Instead of a true secret code, we find, from the dedication of the *Quart livre* on, that it is as if the devil (*diabolos*) is dividing (*diaballein*) our understanding, our interpretation of the text, not as metaphor or metonymy or raw allegory, but moulding it into another way of translation.

---

[22] Cf. Defaux (1994).

[23] *Thalamège*, see the *Quart livr*e (1552, 2r, 2v, 71r); *macréons* (*ibid.*, 4r). On the influence of More's *Utopia* (1516) on Rabelais, cf. Marichal-Defaux (1947, 186 n. 1): 'On pense à l'*Utopie* de Thomas More. Encore un *non lieu*, un *nulle part*.'

[24] Steinrück (2018).

Bibliography

Literature before 1800

Motteux, Peter Anthony (tr.) (1708). *The whole works of F. Rabelais, M.D. In two volumes* [...] *Done out of French, by Sir Thomas Urchard, Knight, Mr. Motteux, and others* [...]. Vol. 2. London.

Rabelais, François. 1532. *Les Horribles et Épouvantables Faits et Prouesses du très renommé Pantagruel.* Paris.

Rabelais, François. 1552. *Le Quart Livre des faicts et dicts Heroiques du bon Pantagruel.* Paris.

Modern Literature

Allen, Percy Stafford, Helen Mary Allen & Heathcote William Garrod (eds.) 1941. *Opus epistolarum Des. Erasmi Roterodami* X. Oxford.

Collectet, G. 1970, *François Rabelais.* Reprint (1st ed. 1867). Geneva.

Defaux, Gerard. (ed.) 1994. *Rabelais: Le Quart livre.* Paris.

Fatio, Oliver. (ed.) 1984. *Jean Calvin: Des Scandales.* Geneva.

Marichal, Robert. (ed.) 1947. *Rabelais: Le Quart Livre.* Paris.

Menini, Romain. 2017. *Rabelais altérateur – "Græciser en François".* Paris.

Morin, Y. Ch. 2000. "La prononciation du français du XVIème siècle selon le témoignage de Jean-Antoine de Baïf", *Langue française* 126 (= Où en est la phonologie du français?), 9–28.

Rigolot, François. 1996. *Les langages de Rabelais.* Paris.

Steinrück, Martin. 2018. "Metric 'mistakes' in the Greek epigrams of Angelo Poliziano", in Janika Päll and Ivo Volt (eds.) *Hellenostephanos. Humanist Greek in Early Modern Europe.* Tartu, 318–335.

APPENDIX: A Prosodic Analysis of the Excerpt of the Dedication

Here is a detailed analysis of the passage quoted above in the beginning of this article, from Rabelais' dedication:

Mais la **calumnie** de certains Canibales, **misantropes, agelastes,**	3	20
avoit tant contre moy esté atroce & desraisonnee,	3	15
qu'elle avoit vaincu ma patience:	2/3	10
& plus n'estois deliberé en escrire un **Iota**.	2/3	15
Car l'une des moindres contumelies dont ilz usoient,	2	14
estoit, que telz livres tous estoient farciz d'**heresies** diverses:	2	18
n'en povoient toutes fois une seulle exhiber en endroict aulcun:	2	18
de folastries joyeuses hors l'offence de Dieu, et du Roy, prou	0	18
(cest le subject & theme unicque d'iceulx livres)	0	13
d'**heresies** poinct:	0	5
sinon perversement & contre tout usaige raison & de languaige commun,	2/1	22
interpretans ce que a poine de mille fois mourir, si autant possible estoit,	1	22
ne vouldrois avoir pensé:	1	7
comme qui <u>pain</u>, interpretroit <u>pierre</u>:	0	9/8
poisson, serpent:	1	4
<u>oeuf, scorpion</u>.	2	4
Dont quelque fois me complaignant en vostre praesence vous dis librement,	2	24
que si meilleur Christian je ne m'estimois,	2	11
qu'ilz ne monstrent estre en leur part:	2	8
& que si en ma vie, escriptz, parolles, voire certes pensees,	2	16
je recongnoissois scintille aulcune d'**heresie,**	2/3	18
ilz ne tomberoient tant detestablement es lacs de l'esprit ***calumniateur,***	2	21
cest διάβολος qui par leur ministere me suscite tel crime.	2	18

The repeated clusters of the same number of côla, being already en vogue in the democratic oratorical prose of Lysias, became, due to Caesar, a normative Roman state style the Greek had to adopt. The framing of the series of the clusters of three cola by two almost periodic clusters of four cola is rather imperial style, for instance Dio, but other interpretation are of course possible. The clausula rythm could be indicated according to the Latin *ars dictaminis* of Blois as *cursus tardus* (2) or *velox* (1) but since the final e-syllable can be muted even in Rabelais' times, I preferred the shorter notation of Byzantine accentual prose, indicating the number of unaccentuated syllables between the last two "appuis" or accents in the first column. The second column follows the Gorgian criterion of isocoly and shows that often the units are constituted by the same number of syllables, as in the second and fourth unit. The third unit combines 18 syllables in the first colon and 18 syllables in the second and third colon, a figure, which, e.g., Janika Päll has called *epiploke* in Gorgias.[1]

---

[1] Cf. Päll, Janika, *Form, style and syntax: Towards a method of description and analysis of Greek prose rhythm: The example of* Helen's encomium *by Gorgias*, Tartu 2007.

Neo-Latin Texts and Humanist Greek Paratexts. On Two Wittenberg Prints Dedicated to Crown Prince Erik of Sweden[1]

JOHANNA AKUJÄRVI

Τοῖς διδασκάλοις μου
Jerker καὶ Karin

This is a study of two Wittenberg prints that have many points of contact. Henricus Mollerus Hessus' (1528–1567) *Stheno Sture senior incluti Regni Sveciae gubernator* […] *carmine elegiaco celebratus* printed in 1557 (hereafter *Stheno Sture*),[2] and Laurentius Petri Gothus' (c. 1529–1579) *Strategema Gothici exercitus adversus Darium, periucundum, carmine redditum elegiaco* printed in 1559 (hereafter *Strategema*).[3] In addition to Latin introductory texts and the main texts, which in both prints narrate scenes from Swedish and ancient history in Latin elegiacs, they contain two paratexts each in Humanist Greek. Further correspondences between the two prints are that both exploit topics that floated in the propaganda of the day and that they are explicitly addressed to the well educated crown prince Erik, the future king Erik XIV of Sweden (1533–1577; reigned 1560–1568). Moreover, the authors were connected to the Vasa dynasty.

---

[1] Early versions of this paper were presented at the Renaissance Society of America meeting in New Orleans 2018 and at the International Association of Neo-Latin Studies congress in Albacete 2018; I thank the audience at those venues for comments and suggestions. Research for this paper has been made within the framework of the project *Helleno-Nordica. The Humanist Greek Heritage of the Swedish Empire*; I thank the Swedish Research council for making it possible (grant 2016-01881), my colleagues in the project for stimulating discussions on all aspects of our work, and Tua Korhonen in particular for carefully reading this paper.

[2] Mollerus (1557a); the copy in Lund University Library (*sign.* Paleot sv [1557]) has been used for this study. Note: the spelling of Latin is unified (except for chronostichs), ligatures are resolved and the nasal mark is replaced by the nasal in question.

[3] Petri (1559); the only known copy, in the Royal Danish Library (*sign.* NL 75:1, 181 00332) has been used for this study, together with the edition by Nordström (1922).

Mollerus and Petri often figure in the annals of Swedish (Neo-Latin) literature.[4] However, they are not only early authors of Neo-Latin poetry in Sweden, they are also the two first known authors of Humanist Greek poetry in a Swedish context; as such, they have been noted by scholars of Greek studies and poetic tradition in Sweden.[5]

The reception of the *Strategema* reflects the status of the author. In 1922 Johan Nordström published an edition of the *Strategema*, rediscovered in the collections of the Royal Danish Library in Copenhagen, but Swedish scholars had been searching for it since the 18th century at least. The print is cited by the title *Strategema Gothici exercitus adversus Danicum* (or *Danum* or *Danos*) by bibliographers like Anders Anton von Stiernman, Eric Benzelius Jr, and Elias Palmskiöld; little of the content of the Latin poem was known but a fairly accurate summary of the argument of the preface circulated.[6] The author, Laurentius Petri Gothus, the second Lutheran archbishop of Sweden, accounts for the interest in the print, apart from its age. For instance, in a letter inquiring about a number of old rare prints, Palmskiöld wished to learn more about the strategem used and to know whether the author was the later archbishop.[7]

One piece of new information about the print appears in Olof Plantin's review of Greek studies in Sweden: *huic Epigramma Graecum elegantissimum praemisit* ('he prefaces it with a very elegant Greek epigram').[8] Where Plantin learnt about the Greek epigram is unknown, but he must rely on second hand information. For, despite his knowledge of the first liminary Greek poem, he still cites the title incorrectly ([…] *adversus Danos*) and he does not appear to know about the concluding Greek poem. Eric Michael Fant, the next to publish on the Greek tradition in Sweden, repeats the information given by Plantin (the title is still incorrect, now […] *adversus Danum*), and adds a few notes on the men who have searched for the print (Benzelius and Palmskiöld) and explains that he has

---

[4] E.g. Schück & Warburg (1985, 87–8); Ijsewijn (1977, 184); in Ijsewijn (1990, 274) only Petri remains.

[5] On Mollerus: Floderus (1785–1789, 3–5); on Petri: Plantin (1736, 23); Fant (1775–1784, 17–20). These works are dissertations, but are cited by the name of the author only. On Petri, see also Collijn (1927–1931, 262–264).

[6] The following builds on Nordström (1922, 237–242).

[7] Printed in Anonymous (1760, 143; letter sent in 1702). See also the note in Warmholtz (1790, 32, no. 3026a).

[8] Plantin (1736, 23). Unless otherwise indicated, all translations of (Humanist) Greek and Latin are mine.

not been able to find a copy.[9] After him, Matthias Floderus simply declares that he has not been able to find a copy of the *Strategema*.[10]

Nordström's discovery, finally, revealed that the stratagem was one directed at Darius, the king of Persia (c. 522/1–486 BC) rather than the more expected Dane(s), and that the text is more than a panegyric of Gustav I of Sweden (Gustav Vasa, hereafter Gustav), as Henrik Schück had speculated before the rediscovery.[11] In addition to editing the print, both Latin and Greek texts, Nordström prefaces it with an introduction to the author, the context of its creation, its Gothicistic view of history, and a summary of the main Latin texts.

In studies on rhetoric, poetry and propaganda at the early Vasa court, viz. under the rule of Gustav of Sweden and his sons Erik XIV and Johan III, Kurt Johannesson has shown how the same topics recur in propaganda texts, in different forms, different degrees of elaboration, and always adapted for different recipients, both as regards language, form, and argument in order to argue the case of the Vasas in the propaganda war between Denmark and Sweden in the wake of the dissolution of the Kalmar Union.[12] Latin humanist poems, directed at a learned audience home and abroad, are one of the media; *Stheno Sture* and *Strategema* belong to the texts Johannesson considers. However, he shows no interest in the Greek paratexts of the prints.

The present study originated with an interest in the Humanist Greek paratexts of the prints, but it has by necessity developed into an investigation of how they relate to their context, that is, primarily, the main texts and their assumed message to the addressee(s). After short biographical sketches of Mollerus and Petri, as well as a sketch of the historical background, this paper offers a literary analysis of the two prints in question, beginning by studying the Latin texts and proceeding to editing and discussing their Greek poems, 36 elegiac verses in all (in *Stheno Sture* an epigram [4 eleg.] and a dedication [12 eleg.], in *Strategema* a liminary verse [8 eleg.] and a prayer [12 eleg.]). It is argued that while it is true that Mollerus and Petri argued issues that floated in the propaganda, other points were equally important. It is suggested that, in addition to arguing the case of the Vasas, both authors use pro-Vasa topoi to make what may have been their primary concern more appealing, and that they use the Greek paratexts to focus their message.

---

[9] Fant (1775–1784, 19f.).

[10] Floderus (1785–1789, 7f.).

[11] Schück (1890, 632f.).

[12] Johannesson (1969); (1974); (1982, 270–285); the latter translated into English in Johannesson (1991, 207–229).

The Authors

Henricus Mollerus Hessus, or Heinrich Möller of Hesse, was born 1528 in Witzenhausen in Hesse.[13] He studied at the universities of Rostock (matriculated in 1546 as *pauper*), Königsberg (1548 also as *pauper*) and came to Wittenberg (1554); before Wittenberg he taught in Kulm (at least in 1552) and visited the university of Frankfurt an der Oder (1553). In Kulm he published works for school use and occasional poetry addressed to local dignitaries; a practice he continued both in Wittenberg and elsewhere.

In Wittenberg Mollerus became praeceptor of the Swedish nobleman Åke Bengtsson Färla. He visited Sweden repeatedly on Åke's account and through Åke's relatives he came in contact with the Swedish royal family. On his first visit to Sweden he may have brought an *Epicedion* celebrating the life of the recently deceased Lars Siggesson Sparre (1554) dedicated to the nobleman Erik Trolle *fautori suo honorando*.[14] But soon he directed a series of Latin poems to Swedish royalty. Beginning with *Carolus Canuti cxxxix Svecorum rex* to king Gustav (1555), in 1557 he addressed *Stheno Sture* to the crown prince Erik and *Triumphus Christi* to his brother Johan, the future king Johan III, and an *Epithalamion* to the wedding of Gustav's daughter Katharina to Edzard II of East Frisia (1559). He was in the service of the Swedish royal court from August 1558 until 1560 when he returned to Wittenberg. From Wittenberg he proceeded to Danzig where he had been appointed rector of the gymnasium. Mollerus continued to celebrate Swedish royalty in occasional poems in Danzig: *Sertum Musarum* for the coronation of Erik XIV (1561), *Aulaeum gratiarum* to Johan upon his arrival to Danzig to court Catherine Jagiellon, daughter of Sigismund I of Poland (1562); *Elegia de adventu in Prussiam et civitatem Dantiscum* also celebrates Johan's arrival, and includes a series of epigrams in honour of other members of the royal family.[15] Mollerus died in 1567 only 39 years old. His poems for the Swedish royal family are only a small part of his poetic output.

---

[13] Biographical data after Johannesson (1974).

[14] The dedicatee is perhaps Erik Trolle (1533–1560), son of Ture Trolle, who studied in Rostock (enrolled 1549) and thereafter in Wittenberg and Paris.

[15] In addition to the above mentioned works, a series of portraits of the Swedish royal family is included among other portraits in Mollerus' *Imaginum liber* (1566).

Laurentius Petri Gothus was born 1529 or 1530, the son of a burgher of Söderköping.[16] There he received his primary education. Since the university of Uppsala, the only institution for higher education in Sweden, hardly functioned after the devastations of the reformation,[17] Petri, like all who needed university education, travelled to the continent. German protestant universities, particularly Rostock, Greifswald, and Wittenberg attracted Swedes.[18] Petri seems to have enrolled in Wittenberg in 1546, but due to the troubles that culminated in the Schmalkaldic war (1546–1547) after the death of Luther, he is likely to have returned to Sweden quickly. His studies were sponsored by crown prince Erik. Perhaps Petri went to the court upon his return; at least he was present there as preacher in 1554 (see below). In 1557 Petri returned to Wittenberg and became magister only one year later, which suggests that he had been able to continue his studies in the meantime. During this stay he also published the *Strategema* in 1559. He remained in Wittenberg until spring 1561, studying probably with the intent to become doctor of theology. After a short visit to Sweden, he travelled back to Germany in 1562. In 1565 he returned to Sweden for good. In 1566 he was appointed professor of Greek at the reopenned university of Uppsala; he advanced to rector (1572) as more professors were appointed to the university.[19] When the university fell out of royal favour, Petri had succeded his father-in-law, Laurentius Petri (Nericius), as archbishop of Sweden (1574). He died in 1579.

Petri's Latin poems are few. The *Strategema* is his first and largest poem. When he returned to Sweden, he published a small collection of elegies – one upon the death of Gustav, one upon the death of his sister, and one upon his return to Sweden – and a poem celebrating the coronation of Erik.[20] His other publications include a considerable number of works on matters of religion and church.

Mollerus and Petri were contemporaries, they knew each other,[21] they were in the service of the Vasas, and, to my knowledge, *Stheno Sture* and *Strategema*

---

[16] Biographical data after Nordström (1922, 221–235); Svalenius (1977–1979).

[17] Lindroth (1976, 15–35).

[18] On travel to German universities in the second half of the 16th century, see Wilner (1904); on confessional aspects of *peregrinatio* in the 16th century, see Göransson (1951, 1–16); for an overview of Swedish *peregrinatio academica* 1200–1800, see Eliasson (1992).

[19] On Petri's university career, see Annerstedt (1877, 60–64).

[20] *Aliquot elegiae* and *Urbs Stocholmia* both 1561. Both prints edited by Bergh (1973).

[21] When Petri left Wittenberg in 1561 he was sent off with a small collection of propemptic poems; one was written by Mollerus, who sends his best to colleagues in the chancellery and sings the praises of the Swedish royalty. *Non vidi*, but see Johannesson (1974, 79).

contain their only published Greek poems – with the caveat that in the case of Mollerus this statement may hold only as far as his prints directed at the Swedish royalty;[22] few of his publications are readily available.

Background of the Prints

In the tense relations between Sweden and Denmark after the dissolution of the Kalmar Union that had united the Nordic states under one monarch until 1523, and the ascendency of Gustav (1496–1560, reigned from 1523) as king of Sweden, propaganda was used by the Swedish court to consolidate the position of Gustav against both internal and external threats. Recurring topics concerned the interconnected issues of the legitimacy of Gustav's rule and relations between Sweden and Denmark.[23] The two Wittenberg prints describe the events that lead to the dissolution of the union as a righteous struggle for freedom by Swedes from Danish rule, they celebrate Gustav's role in that fight, and they remind of how Denmark played the dominant part in the Kalmar Union and of the iniquity of king Christian II of Denmark. A recurring motif, which figures especially prominently in the *Strategema*, was the so called Stockholm bloodbath, viz. the execution of a large number of leading opponents to Danish rule among the Swedish aristocracy at the coronation of Christian II to king of Sweden too (and not only to Denmark and Norway in 1520), an event that secured Christian the byword "Tyrant" in Swedish propaganda. Internally prominent issues were the legitimacy of Gustav's rule, and, in the 1550s, in Gustav's old age, the legitimate succession to the throne of his oldest son Erik. Sore points in this connection were the lineage of the House of Vasa – noble and only remotely connected to royalty; other families had nobler and more royal pedigrees – and the fact that Gustav had replaced the old institution of elective monarchy with a hereditary one.

In the 1550's two texts that circulated widely stirred new agitation in Sweden. One was the posthumously published *Gothorum sveonumque historia* (1554) by Johannes Magnus, the last Catholic archbishop of Sweden.[24] Gustav

---

[22] I thank Peter Sjökvist for helping me with prints in the Uppsala University Library.

[23] This section is indebted to Johannesson (1969).

[24] Johannes Magnus (1554); in the following, Johannes Magnus' text will be referred to not by page, but by book and paragraph. See also the recent Swedish translation and commentary by Johannesson & Helander (2018).

was displeased with many episodes in it that could be interpreted as critique of his policies regarding the reformation, reduction of church assets, and curtailment of the power of the prelacy, but the work was also valuable as a source of historical arguments for the Swedes in the propaganda war with Denmark: the account abounded in *exempla* of how trusting and brave Swedes are overcome by the deceptions of Danes, but, most importantly, the work was a well written history that presented Sweden with a long, Gothicistic past, streching as far back as to Magog, the grandson of Noah. Johannes Magnus' catalogue of rulers features an unbroken line of 'internal' rulers of Sweden until Gustav, the 143th king of the Goths and Swedes.[25] Erik was particularly taken with this grand and glorious version of Swedish history; he designated himself Erik XIV because of the thirteen earlier Gothic kings named Erik in Johannes Magnus' catalogue.

The other text was *De statu religionis et reipublicae* of Johannes Sleidanus, first published in 1555 and quickly reissued and translated into a number of vernaculars, including Swedish.[26] In this history of the reformation Sleidanus speaks of Sweden as a province of Denmark, calls the Swedish opposition against Danish domination in the union in the 1520s a *rebellio*, and describes its leader Gustav as an *ex nobilitate quidam, Gustavus Erixonius* etc.[27] This revived the old arguments against Sweden in relation to the dissolution of the Kalmar Union and the nobility and legitimacy of the House of Vasa.

Countermeasures were mobilized. Mollerus, who had not had immediate success with *Carolus Canuti* addressed to Gustav – indeed, his celebration of the wedding of Elizabeth of Denmark to Ulrich III of Mecklenburg-Güstrow in 1556 suggests that he tried his luck elsewhere – now received pay to write *contra Sleidanum* according to notes made by Karl Gera whom Mollerus had come in contact with through the above mentioned Åke Färla.[28] No such refutation by Mollerus is known, but Petri for his part refuted the most offensive passage in Sleidanus phrase by phrase in the *Strategema*. Moreover, prince Erik complains about Sleidanus' false depiction of the events in question in a letter to Philipp Melanchthon, and suggests that unlike Sleidanus, Melanchthon would give an accurate account of the (pre)history of the Swedes (here called Goths).[29]

---

[25] Printed before the main texts in Johannes Magnus (1554).

[26] Sleidanus (1555); Sylvius (1675).

[27] Sleidanus (1555, 48 [M iiijr]).

[28] Carlsson (1920, 51) and Johannesson (1969, 25).

[29] Letter to Melanchthon copied in Palmsk. 5 (pp. 80–81), ms. in Uppsala University Library; quoted in Wieselgren (1835, 122–124 n. *).

Mollerus' *Stheno Sture*

Stheno Sture is the third poem on Swedish matters by Mollerus, all of which
treat subjects important to Gustav. The first poem, *Epicedion Siggonis* (1554,
see above), dedicated to Erik Trolle, celebrated the life of the recently deceased
Lars Siggesson Sparre, councillor (*riksråd*) and constable (*riksmarsk*) to Gustav,
who together with Gustav had been one of the young noblemen taken hostages
to Denmark in 1518. In the two panegyric biographies *Carolus Canuti* (1555)
and *Stheno Sture* (1557) he celebrates the life and deeds of two men to whom
Gustav was related: Gustav's family ties to Karl Knutsson (Bonde) (1408–1470),
king of Sweden, were on his mother's side (his mother's (half) sister's father was
Karl Knutsson's grandson on his mother's side); to Sten Sture Sr (c. 1437–1503),
regent of Sweden after Karl Knutsson, the kinship was on his father's side (his
father's father was married to the sister of Sten Sture). Karl Knutsson (*rex*) was
succeeded by Sten Sture as regent (*dux*). Following Johannes Magnus' catalogue,
Mollerus designates Karl Knutsson the 139th and Sten Sture the 140th ruler of
Sweden.

   In his reading of the two latter poems, Johannesson has importantly positioned
them in the context of Johannes Magnus' history and the ongoing efforts of the
House of Vasa to legitimize their position and that of Sweden in relation to
Denmark.[30] In *Carolus Canuti* (38 pages with 24 verses each on average) other
leading men are pushed out or into the background of the narrative, and Karl
Knutsson is portrayed as a heroic protector, saviour, and liberator of Sweden from
Danish rule. By stressing the ties of kinship between Gustav and Karl Knutsson,
Mollerus creates a sense of continuity of Swedes rallying under the leadership of
one 'family' in their resistance and opposition to unjust Danish power, but also
suggests that Gustav has a hereditary claim to the throne. At the outset Mollerus
appeals to Gustav to look kindly upon the poem; the kinship between the subject
and the addressee of the text appears to be both part of the argument of the text
and a selling point for the poet in relation to the monarch. Introducing a short
panegyric of Gustav early in the text, Mollerus explains that Karl Knutsson is not
presented as an *exemplum* for Gustav to follow; instead, he should look upon the
actions of his ancestor as if he viewed his own, reflected in a mirror:

> *Cuius dum memori res gestas mente reuolues,*
> *Fortunæ uarias aspiciesque uices.*

---

[30] Johannesson (1969, 24f.); (1974); (1982, 276–278); (1991, 213–215).

> *Tunc uelut in speculo te contemplaberis ipsum,*
>   *Et cursum regni, factaque celsa, tui.* (*Carolus Canuti*, Bv)

As you reflect upon his (*sc.* Karl Knutsson's) deeds in your mind that remembers well, and behold the changing turns of fate; then you shall behold as in a mirror yourself, the course and lofty acts of your reign.

Mollerus uses the same strategy in *Stheno Sture*. In the dedication to *Stheno Sture*, addressed to prince Erik, Mollerus reminds of *Carolus Canuti* and explains that the praise of Karl Knutsson in that poem is to the credit of Gustav and Erik as much as to that of Karl himself, and he continues to elaborate on the theme of offspring inheriting both the reputation and the worldly goods of their (fore)fathers:

> *Nam cum non tantum regni sis ipse paterni,*
>   *Suecarumque hæres indubitatus opum.*
> *Sed quoque successor laudum, summique decoris,*
>   *Quae pater et proaui commeruere tui* [...]. (*Stheno Sture,* A iiir)

For as you are not only the certain inheritor of your father's kingship and the might of the Swedes, but also heir to the praises and the highest dignity that your father and forefathers earned [...].

In the beginning of the main poem (1404 elegiacs), Mollerus speaks of refuting the lies that are told about the obscure origins of Gustav and that he would be an illegitimate ruler.[31] Gustav is in fact, Mollerus stresses, descendant of one of the most renowned Swedes, Sten Sture, who in his turn took over the rule of Sweden after Karl Knutsson, another of Gustav's relatives (Bv–B iijr). That being established, the bulk of the poem consists of dramatic battle scene narratives in which Swedes fight off invaders, mainly Danish ones; Sten Sture plays a vital part by rousing battle speeches and crucial efforts in precarious situations (B iijv–Fr). The narratives in both *Carolus Canuti* and *Stheno Sture* are probably, as Johannesson suggests, moulded and elaborated on the account of Johannes Magnus; for *Stheno Sture* Mollerus may also have had additional Swedish informants.[32]

---

[31] *Ut confutemus vanae mendacia famae, / Quae passim falso vulgus in ore gerit. / Obscuro generis Gostaum* [!] *sanguine natum, non recto fasces iure tenere suos* (B ijr–v).

[32] Johannesson (1969, 24–5).

After the account of the death – from the plague – and funeral of Sten Sture, Mollerus summons the Muses to pay their respects to him. This the Muses do, and after that they enter Erik's castle and start to sing (Fv). Here begins the final part of the poem, a long speech by the Muses to Erik – all the more flattering as it is presented as delivered not by the poet but by the assembled song goddesses (Fv–G ijr). In light of the high expectations on Erik as heir to the throne, the Muses direct a series of precepts for a good ruler to him – to control his temper in all situations; to revere God, be pious, support true worship, protect the learned who preach the true word of God – *Haec est prosperitas florentis maxima regni, / Gloria nec maior regibus esse potest* ('This is the greatest success of a flourishing kingdom; there is no greater glory for kings', F ijv); to promote education of the young, and support the arts; to rule justly both of his own accord and by good counsel, and to purge the court of flatterers and parasites. As the Muses start to advise Erik on how he shall become an *exemplum* for Swedes to follow, they break off and change direction. They stop admonishing Erik and start praising him for his accomplishments: his learning and reading, his mastery of the martial arts, in short his possessing all the virtues and good qualities appropriate for a divinely sanctioned king.[33] They pronounce that with Erik *barbaries* will finally be exiled from Sweden and the Muses thrive,[34] as schools are opened, the youth is educated, poetry is practiced and the study of theology is encouraged (G iijr). In concluding this Mirror of Princes, the Muses invite Erik to consider his own reputation and to give continued support to Mollerus, for, they say, as he has celebrated Karl Knutsson and Sten Sture, he will surely celebrate Erik as well. The only way to secure posthumous fame is to favour the *Camenae* and to support poets, they say and depart.[35] In the final verses of the poem, the poetic I steps in and asks Erik to accept the words of the Muses that he himself brings as a gift.[36]

Mollerus' Greek poems

Not counting numerous passing remarks on praise becoming good/just/pious regents (e.g. *Reges laus decet ampla pios*, 'Ample praise befits pious kings,' E ivr), the conclusion is the fourth time that the theme of poetry and poets as providers

---

[33] *In te virtutum concursus et ordo bonarum est, / Quas in divinis Regibus esse decet* (Gv).

[34] *Te Duce barbaries sic Svecis exulat oris, / Et viget hic nutu gloria nostra tuo* (G iijv).

[35] *Sic, et non aliter, te laus aeterna sequetur, / Nos inopes, tanti iuris habemus opes* ([G ivv]).

[36] *Haec sunt, o Suecae Rex inclute gentis Erice, / Laudibus Aonides quae cecinere tuis. / Accipe […] Nuncius ipsarum quae tibi dona fero* (G ivr).

of eternal glory, and that of the necessity of the nobility to provide both subject matter and material support to poets are made topical by Mollerus in *Stheno Sture*. Mollerus has the Muses dwell on that Erik needs to cultivate a good relations to poets and to provide them with material for praise, if he wishes that his name be remembered.[37] He should be a Maecenas,[38] for the praise of poets is more incorruptible than monuments like pyramids and colossuses that fall to pieces by the ravages of weather and wind (F iijv). This is a topos in Greek and Roman poetry, but in view of Mollerus' choice of words, the intertext here is surely Horace's *Exegi monumentum aere perennius / regalique situ pyramidum altius* etc. (*Carm.* 3.30.1–2). But unlike Horace, Mollerus speaks about the permanence of the recipients' reputation rather than that of the poet himself; this is in line with the general orientation of the poem.

This is also one of the messages of the Latin dedication, and the sole message of Mollerus' two Greek poems. The wording of the epigram on the title page is stark:

ὡς χρὴ αἰνεῖσθαι μουσῶν ἥρωας ἀοιδαῖς,
    οὕτως ἐν τιμῇ τὰς πρέπον αὖθις ἄγειν.
ὑμεῖς οὖν βασιλεῖς δότε καὶ μούσαισιν ἀμοιβήν,
    ἀκαμάτῳ μὲν ὑμᾶς εὐλογέουσιν[39] ὀπί.[40]

As heroes ought to be praised in the songs of the Muses, so it is fitting that they
in their turn honour them. Thus, you kings must compensate the Muses; they
do honour you with untiring voice.

While the first couplet of this epigram is a gnomic description of the mutual obligations of poets, metonymically called the Muses, and nobles – as nobility is to be praised in poetry, so nobility ought to honour poets –, the second turns from the generic (heroes in general) to the specific (kings in particular), and, in the form of a conclusion drawn from the first couplet (note οὖν), exhorts

---

[37] *Vatibus esto bonis clemens, illisque canendi / De te, Rex, animum materiemque dato* (F iijv).

[38] *Maecenas igitur sis uatibus acer* (F iijv).

[39] Cf., e.g., Hil. *trin.* 3.7: *aeternis et indefessis in caelo vocibus laudant*; *indefessis vocibus* or *indefessa voce laudare, clamare, dicere* or other verbs of 'speaking' are a very common collocation in Christian Latin literature.

[40] Text as in Mollerus (1557a). Principles for quoting/editing Humanist Greek texts: spelling, accents and diacritical marks are normalised without comment, both when existing diacritics have been changed and when missing ones have been added, unless this changes the meaning of the word. In non-Greek words accents and diacritics are not added if there are none.

kings to compensate poets who fulfil their part of the mutual understanding. This epigram with its frank plea for patronage is placed on the title page but does not have the laudatory, commendatory or dedicatory function typical of liminary poetry,[41] but functions as a motto signalling a prominent theme of the print.

On the verso follows a twelve verses long dedicatory epigram that elaborates the message of the first poem:

'Επίγραμμα πρὸς Ἐρῖκον τὸν Σουιδῶν βασιλέα.
ὡς περιισταμένοιο εὔκρατος ἠέρος ἀτμὶς[42]
    ἠρέμα τῆς γαίης ἐξάγει εὐφορίαν.
τὴν δ' ἀντικρὺ κακῶς ἀποσβέννυσ' ἠδ' ἐπιθλίβει
    αἰθέρος ἡ στυγερὴ χειμερίη τε ζάλη.
οὕτως εὐλογίη τε φιλοφροσύνη τε ἀνάκτων   5
    μουσάων κραδίην καὶ ἀνεγείρει ὄπιν.
αἱ δὲ ἀτιμασθεῖσαι ὁμοῦ πάνυ ἀκρέες εἰσίν,
    τοῦθ' ἔρδει σκόλυθρος καὶ φρέν' ἄμουσος ἄναξ.
σὺ χθονὸς οὖν Γοθίας βασιλεῦ κύδιστε Ἐρῖκε
    ἐννέα ὦ κουρῶν ἐσθλὲ βοηθὲ διός.[43]   10
ἴσθι ἐλευθέριος δώροις, φρεσὶν ἤπιος ἴσθι,
    εἰ φιλέεις μουσῶν δῶρα ἰοστεφάνων[44].[45]

Epigram to Erik, king of Swedes: As a well-tempered steam of the surrounding air gently brings forth the fecundity of the earth, which, conversely, is badly extinguished and checked by the ether's odious and wintry squall, [5] so reasonableness and kindness of kings rouse the heart and care of the Muses. But, if dishonoured, they are quite mute – this is what a miserly king, with a rude mind, does. Thus, Erik, most illustrious king of Gothic land, [10] noble assistant of the nine daughters of Zeus, be generous with gifts, be kind in your mind, if you love the gifts of the violet-crowned Muses.

---

[41] Cf. van Dam (2015, 51 and *passim*).

[42] Cf. Arist. *Pr.* 915b4: δι' ἀνωμαλίαν τοῦ περιισταμένου ἀέρος, etc.

[43] Cf. Hes. *Theog.* 915–917; Clem. Al. *Strom.* 6.2.11.1: Μνημοσύνης καὶ Ζηνὸς Ὀλυμπίου ἐννέα κοῦραι, quoting Eumelus (fr. 16 Kinkel).

[44] Cf. Thgn. 1.250: ἀγλαὰ Μουσάων δῶρα ἰοστεφάνων.

[45] Text as in Mollerus (1557a) with the following emendations: **6** ἀνεγείρει conieci] ἀναγείρει ed. ‖ **10** κουρῶν correxi] κούρων ed.

This poem not only elaborates on the epigram on the title page but also applies the message to Erik specifically. Now the relation between poets and the powerful is not described as a matter of obligation, but one of inspiration, and the message is strengthened with an epic simile: as fair weather makes the crops grow and the cold winds of winter makes them wither and die, so a nurturing relationship makes the Muses sing and the opposite turns them mute, if the nobleman is an unrefined miser. The two final couplets exhort Erik to be generous to poets if their gifts please him. Finally, Mollerus' signature, used both here and in *Carolus Canuti*, created from his initials, repeats the message: *Honos Musis Habendus* ('the Muses are to be honoured').

As Mollerus' Latin is elegant,[46] so his Greek poems are well composed. Both poems have a moderate tinge of the Greek epic/poetic style; despite some irregularities, metre and prosody are adequately handled.[47] In addition to some poetic morphology, as well as vocabulary and/or word-forms,[48] Mollerus also uses the two rare adjectives ἀκρέες (acc. pl. of ἀκρής) and σκόλυθρος. The former appears to be attested only in Hesychius in the whole of the *TLG* corpus, while the latter is attested in a number of ancient lexicographical works beginning with the two 2nd century Atticistic lexica of Pollux and Pausanias.[49] Both adjectives were incorporated into early modern western Greek lexica from the Greek lexicographical tradition. The *Lexicon Graecolatinum* printed in Paris 1530, for instance, simply translates the entries on ἀκρής from Hesychius and σκόλυθρος from *Suda* or Photius.[50]

Prince Erik was most likely to have both understood and appreciated all parts of *Stheno Sture*, including the Greek paratexts. Gustav had no reputation for learning, but he had not neglected to give his sons a thorough humanistic

---

[46] On Mollerus as Latin poet, see Johannesson (1974).

[47] Note ὑμᾶς with short first syllable in poem 1 v. 4; hiatus is frequent and occurs without shortening in poem 1 v. 1 and poem 2 v. 6.

[48] Morphology: e.g. μούσαισιν, εὐλογέουσιν; περιισταμένοιο, γαίης, στυγερή, χειμερίη, εὐλογίη, μουσάων, κραδίην, φιλέεις. Vocabulary/wordforms: e.g. ὀπί; ἠέρος, ὄπιν, κύδιστε, ἰοστεφάνων.

[49] Hsch. α 2557; Poll. *Onom.* 10.164 (quoting the comic poet Telecleides [fr. 5 Meineke]); Paus. Gr. σ 18.

[50] See *Lexicon Graecolatinum* (1530) *s.v.* ἀκρής *mutus factus ob timorem, aut subitum terrorem* compared with Hsch. α 2557 ἀκρής· ὁ διά τινα ἔκπληξιν ἄφωνος γενόμενος; and *s.v.* σκόλυθρος *illiberalis, sordidus* compared with *Suda* σ 650, σκόλυθρον· σκνιπόν, καὶ ἀνελεύθερον, or the identical entry in Photius' *Lexicon s.v.* σκόλυθρον.

education.[51] Even Greek appears to have been included, as evidenced by book inventories and the occasional Greek word and phrase interspersed in Erik's Latin letters, as the one to Melanchthon, referred to above.[52] And the message was received, after this Mollerus was in the service of the House of Vasa.[53]

Petri's *Strategema*

The *Strategema* is a complex print in many parts: two Humanist Greek poems (one at the beginning, the other at the end), one Latin prose dedication (9 pages), the poem *Strategema Gothici exercitus* (520 verses, the last few in Greek). Petri touches on so many themes in the print that its several arguments defy concise summary. Johannesson, dismissing Nordström's reading of the text as an expression of the author's personal patriotic feelings of gratitude regarding the political and religious reforms in Sweden under Gustav, argues that the *Strategema* is to be understood in the context of contemporary propagandistic exertions and that the poem itself is to be read as a political allegory warning the Danes off an attack on Sweden in a time when the tension between the countries was intensifying.[54] The following analysis offers a complementary reading of the print, while indebted to Johannesson's study of its propagandistic context.

The prose dedication

In the prose dedication to prince Erik, Petri treats the Lutheran reformation, the independence of Sweden from Denmark, the rule of Gustav, and the legitimacy of Erik's succession as established states that are not argued; the severed ties to Rome and Denmark are described as fortunate developments and as liberation from foreign religious and political tyranny (A2r–A3r). He devotes more argumentative energy on two recent issues in the debate: the identity and great ancientness of Goths and a refutation of Sleidanus.

Petri introduces Sleidanus by stressing that his history contains audacious calumnies that must be refuted (A4v). After first quoting the whole objectionable

---

[51] On the princes' education, see Johannesson (1969).

[52] On the princes' Greek, see Collijn (1921, 117–118).

[53] Johannesson (1974, 73).

[54] Johannesson (1969, 25–28); Nordström (243–249).

passage,[55] Petri procedes to a refutation phrase by phrase in which he constantly stresses Sleidanus' impudence. For example, when he comes to Sleidanus' calling the struggle against Danish supremacy a *rebellio*, he just asks 'So you call defence of freedom, expulsion of tyranny, restitution of freedom a rebellion?'[56] Here more clearly than most, Petri shifts the focus from arguing the facts of the issue to attacking the reliability of the report, thereby implying that the author either is not fully informed or is informed but chose to slant the presentation, and, thus, suggesting that Sleidanus is not to be taken seriously. Indeed, to drive home that argument, Petri concludes the section on Sleidanus with a reflection on the deteriorated quality of historiographers, who, he says, used to be a truth-loving (φιλαλῆθες) species from whom one would expect 'the truth without affections' (*a quo veritas sine affectibus expectanda esset*). Quoting Josephus (*AJ* 1.3) he concludes that historians now write to please their masters (Bv).

Petri's choice of subject for the poem *Strategema* is inspired by the grand, Gothicistic view of Swedish history as promulgated in Johannes Magnus' *Historia* (not mentioned in the whole print[57]), according to which the invasion of Scythian territories by the Persians under king Darius I, son of Hystaspes, in 513 BC, is part of Swedish history. Since Sweden being the true home of the Goths (*verissima Gothorum Patria*, A3r) is a matter of controversy, Petri proceeds in the introduction to demonstrate that no people can compete with the Goths as to age, virtues, and achievements both military and cultural (A3r–[A4v]). For all that, all admire the power and glory of Rome, which was destroyed by the Goths (B2r).

This discrepancy, Petri explains, is due to a shortage of men to record the achievements of the Goths. For this is what the Goths need: a Homer to record their achievements; they have never suffered from a lack of Achilleses (*in hunc usque diem nunquam defuit Achilles, sed heu defuit Homerus*, B2r). In addition to the Greek liminary poems and a quote in Hebrew from the book of Isaiah (32.17) on the title page, Petri demonstrates his learning and fruits of his studies with numerous Greek quotes, allusions and scattered Greek and Hebrew words

---

[55] Sleidanus (1555, 48 (M iiijr)) = Petri (1559, Br): *Suecos ità debellatos, ex nobilitate quidam, Gustavus Erixonius, à Lubecensibus, ut creditur, instigatus et adiutus, iterum ad rebellionem incitat, et foeliciter quidem. Simulabat initiò, se negotium agere filiorum Stenonis: Confirmatior autem factus, regni possessionem arripit, et sui muniendi causa, Stenonis filiam in matrimonium ducit.*

[56] *Rebellionem vocas libertatis defensionem, tyrannidis expulsionem, pacisque restitutionem?* (Br).

[57] As Nordström (1922, 243) notes.

and phrases throughout the dedication.[58] His talk about Homer and Achilles here is one of many allusions to ancient Greek literature, but also a variation on the *topos* that without poets (and historians) the great deeds of great men fall into oblivion, perhaps by way of allusion to Cicero's *Pro Archia poeta* (24), where – as part of the argument on the value of poets – Cicero presents Alexander of Macedon contemplating Achilles' tomb at Sigeum and praising him fortunate to have had Homer as herald. For without the *Iliad* Achilles' memory would have been as covered in dust as his bones are. It is Petri's hope that someone in the future might rise to the challenge; his booklet is intended as a small contribution to the recording of the historical feats of his homeland, Petri explains; his aim is to restore events recorded by Greek historians to the truth of native history.[59]

Herodotus is the only historical source Petri refers to regarding the strategem of the Goths. It may be that Petri read the episode in Herodotus – perhaps even in recreational breaks from his study of theology, as he specifies (B2r) – but he paraphrases Johannes Magnus' version, as Nordström has shown.[60] Petri's dependence on Johannes Magnus is evident also in many parts of the dedication, inter alia in his discussion on the name and identity of the Goths – *Gether* in Swedish, *Gethae* in Greek and *Gothi* in Latin (A3r).[61] Petri explains that Herodotus, though he is the first historian to speak of their deeds and does distinguish the Goths from the Scythians, ascribes the deeds of the Goths to the Scythians, which is to be expected when a historian does not have access to the oldest and proper historical sources.[62] Petri even notes that Herodotus is cautious and indicates that he has reached the limit of his knowledge with κατ' ὅσον ἡμεῖς ἴδμεν ('as far as we know', Hdt 4.20) both here and elsewhere.[63] Thus, Petri

---

[58] Greek authors explicity quoted/cited: Pindar (*Ol.* 9.40; see below), Josephus (*AJ* 1.3), Herodotus (4.20, 4.118, see also below), Euripides (*Phoen.* 1623–1624, 1015–1018), Xenophon (*Cyr.,* see below); Greek proverb παρόντα ἀποδημεῖν (a witticism in Ar. *Eq.* 1120 that entered collections of proverbs); words e.g. ἀρχαιολογίαν, αὐτόχθονας; Hebrew particularly on p. A4v when arguing direct ties between the Hebrew and Gothic/Swedish languages. Many of the authors quoted were part of the curriculum in Wittenberg, see Nordström (1922, 228–230). For the authors alluded to in the Greek poems, see below.

[59] *ad patriae historiae veritatem* (B2r).

[60] Nordström (1922, 242–249); Johannes Magnus 3.6–9; Herodotus 4.83–143, particularly 118–143.

[61] Following Johannes Magnus *praef.* 7.

[62] *neglectis propriis et primis eius gentis historiis* (A3r).

[63] *ipse sibi cavens, saepe hanc addit correctionem* (A3v). Similar indications are indeed common in Herodotus' *Histories*.

argues, following Johannes Magnus, there is no reason to have greater confidence in Greek historians than in native ones who have direct access to the sources: a list of kings that streches further back in time than any, except perhaps the Hebrew one; knowledge about all Goths, not only the Asian ones; language; writing (i.e. runes, which are presumed to be much older than Greek and Latin letters); and inscribed ancient monuments (i.e. rune stones, also presumed older than the remains of antiquity, A3v–[A4r]).[64]

Petri concludes the dedication with a reflection on the use and necessity of reading and studying history of all times,[65] for history is a source of useful lessons both for character development, political deliberation, government, and theology.[66]

The Latin poem

While the dedication vehemently argues the case of Sweden and its regents against the conventional understanding of the history of Europe and the slander of its enemies, the *Strategema*, the poem itself, consists of three scenes in elegiac distichs. The poem as a whole reads like a series of lessons, one for each scene. The two first scenes come from the story of how the brave, warlike but peaceable, and freedom-loving Goths fought off the Persian invasion (from Johannes Magnus/ Herodotus);[67] the third merges two scenes of dying/old monarchs advising his heirs (from Xenophon and Petri's own observation). The scenes are clearly separated by extensive authorial comment on their significance.

First scene: When the king of the Goths was not intimidated into a humiliating alliance with Darius, the king of Persia, Gothic territory was invaded by Persians forces. As the lines of battle had been formed, the Goths forgot about the Persians and started to chase a hare that showed up between the armies – the military threat concerned them so little.[68] In Johannes Magnus this scene illustrates the Goths' bravery and contempt for the enemy (3.7). For Petri, too, it demonstrates

---

[64] On the parallels to Johannes Magnus, see notes in Nordström (1922, 255–257).

[65] *non minus necessarias quam utiles esse Historiarum omnium temporum lectiones et cognitiones* (Bv).

[66] Perhaps influenced by Melanchthon's view on the importance of historical studies for a better understanding of God's manifestations and workings, sacred history and biblical prophesies, and to properly judge theological controversies; see Ben-Tov (2009, 37–41).

[67] Johannes Magnus 3.6–8; Herodotus 4.118–143.

[68] B3v–Cr; vv. 29–134; Petri follows Johannes Magnus in placing the scene with the hare before the mystifying gifts.

the fearlessness of the Goths. Their playing proves them to be the very opposite of braggarts who flee the actual battle; in a just war no one can hope to defeat the Goths without much bloodshed.[69] But, he continues, the brave do not always have the advantage. In times of dirty warfare, tyrants easily defeat the virtuous and brave by deceit (*Fraude perit virtus* […] / *Quique nequit vinci robore, fraude potest*, v. 181f.), Petri says and reminds the youth of the blood that coloured the square (*memor esto* […] *qua clade, juventus / Tinxerunt proprio sanguine triste forum*). With this allusion to the Stockholm bloodbath – further described as stemming from deceit and dated with a chronostich ([…] *MagnaqVe*[70] *per fraVDes patrIa pressa fVIt*, '[…] by deceit our great homeland was overcome', v. 190)[71] which gives the year MDVVVII, viz. 1517[72]) – Petri links the Goths who faced the Persians, the Swedes who were slaughtered in Stockholm and the present day. This is a reminder that functions as a warning about the consequences of letting one's guard down as the Goths did when they started chasing the hare and as the Swedish nobility did when they trusted the Danes and were decimated. Thus, first lesson: do not be overconfident and do not underestimate your enemy.[73]

Second scene: The Persians, looking with wonder at the Goths' indifference towards themselves and their arms, next receive perplexing gifts: a mouse, a bird, a frog and an arrow.[74] Deliberating on the meaning of the gifts, not the ones that he had demanded as a token of submission, Darius heard the opinion of two men. One was a flatterer who could dupe wise Solomon – he interpreted the gifts

---

[69] Cr–C2r; vv. 135–196.

[70] I delete the comma after *magnaque*.

[71] A few verses later Petri weaves in his name: *LAUs RENovata TIbi PErfregit TRIstia GOTHE* (v. 193).

[72] 1517 is not the year of the bloodbath, but the year when the controversy between the regent Sten Sture Jr (with the anti-unionists) and archbishop Gustav Trolle (with the pro-unionists) had escalated so that Christian II of Denmark was drawn in and set in motion a series of events that led up to the the bloodbath in November 1520.

[73] Johannesson (1969, 27) reads this as a warning directed at the false Danes not to attack the braves Goths/Swedes, but it is difficult to support that reading in light of the repeated variations on the topic deceit easily conquers the brave, which must be taken as a warning to the brave (viz. Goths/ Swedes) not to trust those who are deceitful, either to be taken in a general sense or as referring to Danes.

[74] *Munera, Mus, Volucris, Rana, Sagitta simul* (v. 210); here Petri silently brings the account closer to Herodotus where the Scyths give ὄρνιθά τε καὶ μῦν καὶ βάτραχον καὶ ὀϊστοὺς πέντε ('bird, mouse, frog and five arrows,' 4.131); in Johannes Magnus the Goths give only *avem, murem, ranam* (bird, mouse, frog, 3.7).

to signify submission –, the other was a greyhaired old man who told the truth, however displeasing – he interpreted the gifts to signify resistance by all possible means against the aggressors.[75] Neither Herodotus nor Johannes Magnus has a scene of counselling at this point.[76] It is thus Petri who transforms the positive interpretation of the gifts – that they signify the submission of the Goths – from being Darius' wishful thinking to the fawning interpretation of a flatterer. Both this modification to the intertext(s) and the following commentary stress the difficulty but necessity of distinguishing good advice from bad.[77] Not only the harmful services of the bad advisor are to be avoided, but the good ones are to be recognised and cared for; they will secure the persistence of power.[78] Only the further development of events shows what is good advice, so Petri relates how the Persians barely escaped, and thereafter adds approving comments on the virtuous and moderate king who knows to listen to advise also when it goes against his desires.[79] Thus, second lesson: a good king must know how to recognize good advice.[80]

The last scene, or rather: double scene, does not continue the narrative on the Persian invasion, but begins with commentary that elaborates what is here taken as the final couplet of the second scene – *concordia* is the cause of victory[81] – and serves to establish the fundamental importance of *concordia* for well-functioning relations on all levels, both socially and societally.[82] Petri juxtaposes a short paraphrase of the deathbed speech of Cyrus, the founder of the Persian empire, from Xenophon's *Cyropaedia* (a highly popular text during the Renaissance),[83] with a scene of Gustav advising his sons,[84] an event that he says he witnessed.[85]

---

[75] C2r–C3v; vv. 197–286.

[76] Hdt. 4.132; Johannes Magnus 3.7.

[77] C3v–[C4r]; vv. 287–328.

[78] *Plurimus est usus, sapientum maxima cura, / Quorum consiliis robora fixa manent* (v. 307f.).

[79] *Crede mihi, decus est modesto principe maius / Nullum, cui facile est mentis habere satis* (v. 323f.).

[80] Taking into account only the flight of the Persians, Johannesson (1969, 27) reads this scene as advice to the Danish king not to provoke the Goths; this neglects too much of the text to be a convincing interpretation.

[81] *Haec etiam meminisse iuvat: Concordia fecit, / Victrici dextra, colla inimica premi* (v. 327f.).

[82] [C4r]; vv. 329–342.

[83] [C4r]–Dv; vv. 343–414; Xen. *Cyr.* 8.7.6–28; on Xenophon in the renaissance, and the *Cyropaedia* specifically, see Marsh (1992, 116–138).

[84] Dv–D2v; vv. 415–478.

[85] Johannesson (1969, 27f.) observes correctly that this juxtaposition serves to elevate Gustav to the

For also our own times give such examples,[86] Petri explains, and assures that he committed what he heard and saw to memory. A chronostich gives the year 1554, and specifies the event to one evening in spring time;[87] Petri also explains that he was then preacher at the royal court.[88] The speeches of the old, venerable monarchs who have built an empire, are held in the presence of their courts and directed to their sons. Both summarize their achievements and express a wish for the continued existence of their empire through their heirs; for this they advise unity, internal peace and harmony, that the sons respect the rules of succession; only one son, the oldest, shall be king (*sceptriger*, v. 465). Finally, Petri's commentary drives home the third lesson of the poem: *concordia* between rulers and ruled, between generations and between brothers preserves the people, as history shows – 'as long as you remember your forefathers' (*dum memor es patrum*, v. 481).[89]

Petri's Greek poems

Petri concludes the poem with a prayer for the well-being of the state – wishing for dutiful administration, lasting unity, and most of all that king and people know the religious dogmas.[90] Independence and lawful rule are good things, but to acknowledge Jesus is the only salvation for the wretched.[91] All three are united in Sweden/Gothia (*haec coëunt foelix* […] *ô Gothica tellus*, v. 507), a rare occurrence. Finally, argument shifts into prayer. First, a prayer for peace, in which Petri mixes in Greek words and verses (vv. 512–514; 519–520):

---

level of Xenophon's Cyrus, as builders of empire and wise rulers.

[86] *Talia, sed veteres, non soli, exempla, libelli / Praebent, dant etiam secula nostra pios* (v. 417f.).

[87] *TeMpVs erat, phoebI tV ponDVs onVste ferebas / HesperIosqVe tVI taVre reteXIs eqVos* ('It was the time when you, laden Taurus, bore the weight of Phoebus and you covered the evening horses', v. 423f.), that is, a spring evening the year MDXVVVVVVVVIIII, viz. MDLIV.

[88] *Astans tunc forte, et verbi de more paratus / Divini Praeco, nempe vocatus eram* (v. 435f.).

[89] The strong emphasis on *concordia* is significant in light of the discord between Gustav's sons. For example, Erik XIV was to imprison Johan; Erik was dethroned and imprisoned by Johan and Karl, and died before Johan III managed to execute him; during his reign Johan III had numerous conflicts with Karl; Sigismund, Johan's son and king of Poland as Sigismund III, was outmanoeuvred (on religious grounds) from the Swedish throne by duke Karl, later Karl IX, his uncle.

[90] *Sit pietas curae, maneat concordia* (v. 491); *Vera autem, verae pietatis maxima laus est, / Cum populo Regem dogmata nosse Dei* (v. 499f.).

[91] *Una salus miseris, Christum cognoscere Iesum, / Pernicies summa est, credere, nolle Deo* (v. 505f.)

ὄργανον *est pacis Rex pius ipse suae.*   512
Χρίστ᾽ εἰκὸν πατέρος, σῶτερ, λόγε, ὀλβιόδωρε,[92]
    Unica tu miseris spes animosa reis. [...]
Καρτίστη ἀρετῶν, οὔθ᾽ ἕσπερος οὔτε ἑῷος   519
    οὕτω θαυμαστός, ἐστι δικαιοσύνη.[93]
        Τέλος[94]

A pious king is himself the instrument of his own peace. Christ, the image
of your father, saviour, word, giver of bliss, you are the only resolute hope for
the wretched condemned. [...] The most excellent of virtues is righteousness;
neither the evening star nor the morning star is as admirable. The end.

The Latin fades into Greek, perhaps in order to accommodate the reference
to Aristotle, or because it is a more holy language than Latin. Next, after the
Strategema, follows a free standing, wholly Greek prayer:

Προσευχὴ περὶ τῆς ἐκκλησίας, ἀπὸ τοῦ Λαυρεντίου Γωθου
Πλάσμα σέθεν θνητοὺς γηραιὸν χριστ᾽ ἐλέησον,
    σοῦ γὰρ ἄνευ, δοῦναι μηδενός ἐστι βίον.
Νῶε κιβωτὸς ἔχει σε κυβερνήτην καὶ ἄνακτα
    μοῦνον, ἀλύξῃ ὅπως κύματα πίκρα μόρου.[95]
ἐν πατρίδος γαίῃ ὀρθῶς ἐκκλησία αὐξοῖ,   5
    δὸς ξένιον λάῳ ποιμένα παντὶ σέο.
ἑσπέρα ἦλθε, βροτῶν μετὰ ἡμῶν χριστὲ σὺ μεῖνον,
    μήποτε σεῖο φάος βούλου ἀπολλύμενον.
ἀνδροφόνου θυμὸς δεινόν γ᾽ ἐχθροῖο κακιστός,
    ἐν κόσμοιο τέλει, πλεῖά τε πάντα φόνου,   10
ἀλλὰ χρόνῳ, μῶλον πολύδακρυν παῦε μόναρχε,

---

[92] Verbal echoes from one of several poem εἰς τὸν Σωτῆρα, cf. *Anth. Pal.*: 1.22.1–4 Πατρὸς
ἐπουρανίου λόγε [...] ὁ βροτέην γενεὴν τιμήσας εἰκόνι σεῖο [...] ὄπαζε καὶ ὀλβιόδωρον ἀρωγήν.

[93] Cf. Arist. *Eth. Nic.* 5.1.1129b27–29 κρατίστη τῶν ἀρετῶν εἶναι δοκεῖ ἡ δικαιοσύνη, καὶ οὔθ᾽
ἕσπερος οὔθ᾽ ἑῷος οὕτω θαυμαστός. According to the ancient scholia this is a reminiscence of
Euripides' lost tragedy *Melanippe* (fr. 486 Nauck).

[94] D iijr. The text in Nordström (1922) follows the original print, except for diacritics; here it is
emended according to the following: **519** καρτίστη scripsi metri gratia] κρατίστη ed.; καρτίστη
Nordström. Note hiatus without shortening v. 519; in v. 520 θαυμαστός is apparently scanned
with a long final syllable.

[95] Cf. *Anth. Pal.* 9.276 (Crin.): πικροῦ κῦμ᾽ [...] θανάτου.

θρῆνον ἄπαντα μολὼν βέλτερε λῦσον ἄναξ.
AMEN[96]

A prayer for the church, by Laurentius Gothus. Christ, have mercy on mortals, your aged images, for, without you, no one is able to give life. Noah's ark has you as pilot and only lord, in order to escape the bitter waves of death. [5] May the church grow straight in our homeland; give the gift of a shepherd to all your people. Evening came; Christ, stay with us mortals, do not ever will your light to be fading. [9] The most evil spirit of the manslaughtering enemy is something to be feared in the end of the world, and all is full of slaughter, but with time, come, sovereign supreme ruler, end the tearful toil of war and dissolve all lament. AMEN

The final text of the print continues the concluding prayer, but concerns only the church and its congregation. Despite a number of minor linguistic lapses, mostly in the area of spelling with faulty accents and itacistic mistakes, declension, shaky syntax, and a general dearth of conjunctions connecting the clauses,[97] the poem, written in adequate elegiac distichs,[98] features some epic wordforms and vocabulary, even word play.[99] Both this and the first Greek poem are adequate and bear testimony to Petri's study of the Greek language. The first Greek poem, an address to the reader printed on the verso of the title page, supports a toning down of the propagandistic reading of the *Strategema* poem itself:

AMICO LECTORI
Φεῦ, πόλεμόν τε μάχαν τε θεοῖο ἄνευ, σὺ ἔασον,
    Πίνδαρος εἶπε σοφῶς·[100] πάντα γὰρ ἐστὶ θεοῦ.

---

[96] D iijv. The text in Nordström (1922) follows the original print, except for diacritics; here it is emended according to the following: **1** πλάσμα correxi] πλᾶσμα ed. ‖ **3** κιβωτός correxi] κυβωτός ed. ‖ **6** παντί conieci] πάντε ed. ‖ **10** τέλει correxi] τέλῳ ed. ‖ **11** πολύδακρυν correxi] πολυδάκρη ed. ‖ **12** θρῆνον correxi] θροῖνον ed. ‖ μολών correxi] μόλων ed.

[97] Accent: πλᾶσμα for πλάσμα, μόλων for μολών; itacistic mistakes: κυβωτός for κιβωτός, θροῖνον for θρῆνον; declension: τέλῳ for τέλει (an easy beginner's mistake in third declension neuters with sigma stem), πολυδάκρη for πολύδακρυν; shaky syntax: e.g., the participle ἀπολλύμενον for an expected infinitive.

[98] Note hiatus without shortening v. 5.

[99] Epic wordforms/vocabulary: e.g., σέθεν, σέο, ἐχθροῖο, βροτῶν, πολύδακρυν, μολών; word play μῶλον – μολών.

[100] Cf. Pind. *Ol.* 9.40f. ἔα πόλεμον μάχαν τε πᾶσαν / χωρὶς ἀθανάτων.

πράγματα τ᾽ ἀνθρώπων θεὸς αὐτὸς πάντα κυβερνᾷ,
  εὖχος δοὺς πολέμου τοῖσδε δικαιοτέροις.[101]
ὕβριν ἀμυνόμενοι ἐχθρῶν γλυκερῆς περὶ πάτρας,[102]   5
  ἀντιδίκων ἄλλων εἰσί δικαιότεροι.
τοῖον ἔχεις παράδειγμα ἐν ἱστορίᾳ, φίλε, ταύτῃ,
  ἥν σοι ἵησι φίλος. χαῖρε δὲ εὐτυχέων.[103]

To the kind reader. Alas! Let war and struggle without God be, said Pindar
wisely. For all is in God's hands. God alone governs all affairs of men, and grants
glory in battle to the more righteous. [5] Those who fight off the wantonness
of their enemies for their sweet homeland, are more just than other adversaries.
My friend, you have such an example in this piece of history, sent to you by a
friend. Farewell and prosper.

The same judgement applies to the quality of this poem as to that of the
former.[104] In this dedication, addressed to the reader, Petri warns against war
without God, with a reference to Pindar's wise words (*Ol.* 9.40f.). Petri evidently
interprets Pindar to say that man should not fight without God on his side; that
is perhaps also how Melanchthon's Latin interpretation is to be taken (*Omitte
bellum, omitte pugnam sine Deo*).[105] However, from the Pindaric context – this is
a narratorial comment marking a transition from the subject of mortals (Heracles
in particular) fighting against gods to the more immediate subject matter of the
poem – it appears that the words in essence say "no more talk about fights against

---

[101] Cf. *Il.* 5.285: εὖχος ἔδωκας etc.; εὖχος δίδωμι is a common collocation in the Homeric epics,
the *Iliad* in particular.

[102] Cf. *Il.* 12.243: ἀμύνεσθαι περὶ πάτρης etc.

[103] [A1v]. The text in Nordström (1922) follows the original print, except for diacritics and two
corrections, here with further emendations: **1** μάχαν τε sejunxi ‖ **5** πάτρας Nordström] πτράας
ed. ‖ **8** ἥν Nordström] υἵν ed. | δὲ εὐτυχέων scripsi metri gratia] δ᾽ εὐτυχέων Nordström; δὲ per
ligaturam ed.

[104] Itacistic mistake: υἵν for ἥν (may however simply be a typo); the demonstrative τοῖσδε appears
to be used as the definite article; no conjuctions connecting clauses (except τ᾽ v. 3, but probably
used to avoid hiatus); hiatus without shortening v. 5; one epic form (θεοῖο) and a few poetic
reminiscences; word play (ἀντιδίκων – δικαιότεροι).

[105] Melanchthon 1853, 204; the Pindar translation was edited by Caspar Peucer in 1558 (see
introduction to Melanchthon 1853, 187–188 with full title), who lectured on mathematics and
astronomy in Wittenberg when Petri studied there.

the gods."[106] Petri's interpretation of Pindar is evident from the following two couplets where he explains that God governs all, and gives the upper hand to the more righteous party, that is to the defenders rather than the aggressors.

Moreover, and most interestingly, the final couplet labels the piece of history a παράδειγμα, that is an example providing models to follow, sent by a friend to a friend. In addressing this to Erik, he could be certain that the recipient would be interested – Erik was an arduous reader of history, particularly of Johannes Magnus, whose history was to accompany him until the end of his life.[107] These two verses have the function of an interpretative key where Petri directs the readers towards identifying the lessons to be learnt from the historical *exempla* of his poem. In the prose dedication discussed above, Petri does not use the word *exemplum* or παράδειγμα, but speaks about the necessity and utility of history. Indeed, as the above analysis of the *Strategema* poem has shown, the three episodes serve as historical *exempla* to the three lessons to be drawn from the text; in each instance Petri makes the lesson clear with extensive commentary.

Concluding Words

The present study set out to show that Mollerus and Petri use pro-Vasa topoi to make what appears to be their primary messages more appealing to the addressee, and that this message is focussed by way of their Greek paratexts.

In *Stheno Sture* Mollerus argues exhaustively for Gustav's close relation to Sten Sture Sr, the regent of Sweden – thus, that Gustav's lineage is noble and that he has a hereditary claim to the throne – in addition to narrating the life and deeds of Sten Sture, with a focus on how Swedes under his leadership manage to fend off devious invaders, Danes in particular. These were all issues that floated in the propaganda. A recurring motif throughout the poem are poets as procurers of fame and the need, indeed necessity, of nobility to tend to a

---

[106] The whole section in Pindar: ἀπό μοι λόγον / τοῦτον, στόμα, ῥῖψον· | ἐπεὶ τό γε λοιδορῆσαι θεούς / ἐχθρὰ σοφία, καὶ τὸ καυχᾶσθαι παρὰ καιρόν // μανίαισιν ὑποκρέκει. / μὴ νῦν λαλάγει τὰ τοιαῦτ'· ἔα πόλεμον μάχαν τε πᾶσαν / χωρὶς ἀθανάτων· φέροις δὲ Πρωτογενείας / ἄστει γλῶσσαν ('But cast that story / away from me, my mouth! / for reviling the gods / is a hateful skill, and boasting inappropriately // sounds a note of madness. / Stop babbling of such things now! / Keep war and all fighting / clear of the immortals; apply your speech to Protogeneia's / city'). *Ol.* 9.35–42; transl. by Race (1997).

[107] On Erik's studies, see Johannesson (1969, 14–20); on his profound study of Johannes Magnus, see Johannesson (1982, 282–285) and (1991, 219–221).

good relationship to poets in particular and others who celebrate their deeds and thus provide lasting remembrance of past deeds. In the final part, celebrating the character and achievements of crown prince Erik, that motif becomes thematic, particularly in the concluding statement of the Muses – that the only means to secure posthumous fame is to support poets. And in the final verses Mollerus asks Erik to accept the words of the Muses – and the poem.

The print also begins on a similar note. The mutual obligations of princes and poets both on a general and specific level are the subject of the two Greek poems that precede the main texts of the print. The four Greek gnomic and hortatory verses on the title page function as a motto for the work. It is a starkly worded plea for the nobility to live up to their obligation to compensate poets for their work – remember that Gustav appears to have failed to remunerate Mollerus for the *Carolus Canuti*. The dedicatory verses on the verso elaborates on the first Greek poem in milder formulations and applies the message to Erik specifically; the final two couplets exhort Erik to be generous with his gifts if he is pleased by the poem. Thus the theme of the interdependence of poets and princes frame the whole print.

Memory of fame and glory by future generations is at the core of *Stheno Sture*, as Mollerus is selling his services to the crown prince. Fame and glory is an issue in the introduction to the *Strategema*, too, where Petri is concerned with the shortage of learned to relate the achievements of the Swedes/Goths and with setting the historical record straight, both that of contemporary history (the refutation of Sleidanus) and that of ancient history (the correct identification, ancientness, and achievements of the Swedes/Goths). Petri does not waste many words upon other issues that floated in propaganda, but simply takes the pro-Vasa side without much argument. The *Strategema* poem itself consists of three scenes from history that function as exempla for the three lessons for the preservation of power in relation to others and for internal harmony. The two first scenes form a continuous narrative from ancient Swedish/Gothic (not Scythian) history according to the Gothicistic reinterpretation of history that Petri presents in the introduction (without reference to Johannes Magnus' history), the last mixes two scenes, one from the Persian, the other from the Swedish court.

The introductory Greek verses function like an interpretative key; they label its history a παράδειγμα, that is, an example, and direct the readers towards identifying its lessons. In the prayer for peace that concludes the *Strategema*, where Petri switches gradually from Latin to Greek, and the wholly Greek prayer for the welfare of mankind, church and congregation that closes the print Petri changes both languages and the modes of delivery, from argument to prayer. This reminds the reader that Petri though a student in Wittenberg already had held the position of preacher at the Vasa court.

Thus, both Mollerus and Petri promoted a more positive image of Sweden and its rulers. Both dedicated the prints to crown prince Erik of Sweden. Both used liminary poems in Greek to draw the readers' attention to the primary message of their prints. The reasons for choosing Greek for these parts are likely a mixture of signalling exclusivity, showing off the authors' skills, and flattering the explicit addressee's accomplishments. The Renaissance was coming to Sweden, symbolized in Mollerus by the exiling of *barbaries* from Sweden, the arrival of the Muses, and the establishment of education – including Greek studies. In the case of Erik of Sweden, it is certain that he was able to not only appreciate the poets' effort to write in Greek, but also to understand the message.

Bibliography

Manuscript

Palmsk. 5 = *Den Palmsköldska samlingen* vol. 5 (*Acta ad historiam regum Sveciae*; *Acta ad Hist. R. Erici XIV* p. 1), Uppsala University Library.

Books published before 1800

Anonymous. 1760. "Herr Ärke-Biskop Doct. Eric Benzelii den Yngres Brefsamling", in Carl Christoffer Gjörwell (ed.) *Det Swenska Biblioteket*, 4, 38–174.

Fant, Eric Michael. 1775–1784. *Historiola Litteraturae Graecae in Svecia*. I–XII. Diss. Uppsala.

Floderus, Matthias. 1785–1789. *De poëtis in Svio-Gothia Graecis*. I–IV. Diss. Uppsala .

Johannes Magnus. 1554. *Gothorum sveonumque historia, ex probatis antiquorum monumentis collecta, et in xxiiii libros redacta […] cum indice rerum ac gestorum memorabiliorum locupletissimo*. Basel [copy used: urn:nbn:de:bvb:12-bsb10206684-3].

Lexicon Graecolatinum. 1530. *Lexicon Graecolatinum cui praeter omneis omnium additiones hactenus, sive in Italia, sive in Gallia, sive in Germania impressas, ingens vocabulorum numerus accessit: idque partim ex Graecorum Lexicis, partim ex recentium lucubrationibus: non quorumlibet, sed exquisitorum: nimirum: Guilielmi Budaei, Erasmi Roterodami, Laurentii Vallae, Harmolai Barbari, Angeli Politiani, Ludovici Coelii aliorumque eiusdem classis*. Paris.

Mollerus, Henricus. 1554. *Epicedion in morte […] D: Laurentii Siggonis, Equitis aurati in Sundby, regni Sveciae Marschalci, et capitanei arcis Orebröensis in Neritia*. Wittenberg.

Mollerus, Henricus. 1555. *Carolus Canuti cxxxix. Svecorum rex. Carmine elegiaco celebratus in honorem […] principis et domini D. Gostavi, Svecorum, Gothorum, Vandalorumque regis*. Rostock.

Mollerus, Henricus. 1556. *In honorem nuptiarum […] D. Ulrichi, ducis Megalburgii, principis Henetorum, comitis Sverini, domini Rostochiorum et Stargardiae, cum […] D. Elizabetha, prognata ex incluta Daniae regum, Holstatiaeque ducum familia*. Rostock.

Mollerus, Henricus. 1557a. *Stheno Sture senior incluti regni Sveciae gubernator. In honorem […] principis ac domini D. Erici, regis Suecorum, Gothorum et Vandalorum electi, carmine elegiaco celebratus […] Praecessit elegia ad eundem Upsaliae Svecorum scripta.* Wittenberg.

Mollerus, Henricus. 1557b. *Triumphus Christi ad Romanorum accommodatus et editus. In honorem […] principis ac domini D. Iohannis, nati ex Gostao potentissimo Svecorum, Gothorum et Vandalorum rege.* Wittenberg.

Mollerus, Henricus. 1559. *Epithalamion […] D. Esardo, Phrysiae orientalis comiti, et […] D. Catharinae, incluti Svedorum regis Gostavi filiae.* Stockholm.

Mollerus, Henricus. 1561. *Sertum Musarum in […] D. Erici Svedorum, Gothorum et Vandalorum regis coronatione.* Königsberg.

Mollerus, Henricus. 1562a. *Elegia de adventu in Prussiam et civitatem Dantiscum […] Domini Iohannis, ducis Finlandiae, Regnorumque Sveciae, Gothiae, Vandaliaeque haeredis. Adiecta sunt et alia quaedam in honorem Regiae apud Svedos familiae.* Königsberg.

Mollerus, Henricus. 1562b. *Aulaeum Gratiarum. Ursus Finlandicus – Aquila Polonica. In honorem […] principum ac dominorum D. Sigismundi Augusti […] D. Johannis […] D. Catharinae […].* Königsberg.

Mollerus, Henricus. 1566. *Imaginum liber.* Danzig.

Petri, Laurentius, Gothus. 1559. *Strategema Gothici exercitus adversus Darium, periucundum, carmine redditum elegiaco. Scriptum ad illustrissimum Principem ac Dominum, Dominum Ericum, Suecorum, Gothorum, Vandalorum, etc. electum Regem.* Wittenberg.

Petri, Laurentius, Gothus. 1561a. *Aliquot elegiae.* Stockholm.

Petri, Laurentius, Gothus. 1561b. *Urbs Stocholmia.* Stockholm.

Plantin, Olof. 1736. *Vindemiola literaria, in qua Hellas sub Arcto, sive merita Svecorum in linguam Graecam brevissime et modeste exponuntur.* Diss. Wittenberg.

Sleidanus, Johannes. 1555. *De statu religionis et reipublicae, Carolo Quinto, Caesare, Commentarii.* Strassburg.

Sylvius, Johannes (tr.) 1675. *Johannis Sleidani Historie-book. Hwilken beskrifwer tilståndet aff thet andelige och werldzlige wäsendet uthi keyser Carl then femptes tijdh.* Stockholm.

Warmholtz, Carl Gustaf. 1790. *Bibliotheca historica sveo-gothica; eller förteckning uppå så väl tryckte som handskrifne böcker, tractater och skrifter, hvilka handla om Svenska historien, eller därutinnan kunna gifva ljus; med critiska och historiska anmärkningar.* V. Stockholm.

Modern authors

Annerstedt, Claes. 1877. *Upsala universitets historia*. I. *1477–1634*. Uppsala.

Ben-Tov, Asaph. 2009. *Lutheran Humanists and Greek Antiquity. Melanchthonian Scholarship between Universal History and Pedagogy* (Brill's Studies in Intellectual History). Leiden

Bergh, Birger (ed.) 1973. *Laurentius Petri Gothus. En svensk latinpoet från 1500-talet. Textedition med inledning, översättning och kommentar*. Lund.

Carlsson, Gottfrid. 1920. "[Review of] G. Rudbeck: Skrifter till Sveriges historia, tryckta före år 1600, med en inledande redogörelse. Diss. Uppsala 1919", *Nordisk tidskrift för bok- och biblioteksväsen* 7, 41–54.

Collijn, Isak. 1921. "Catechesis Graeca christianorum Stockholm 1584. Den antagligen äldsta i Sverige på grekiska tryckta boken", *Nordisk tidskrift för bok- och biblioteksväsen* 8, 117–122.

Collijn, Isak. 1927–1931. *Sveriges bibliografi intill år 1600*. II. *1530–1582*. Uppsala.

Eliasson, Pär. 1992. "Resande studenter under 600 år", *Lychnos*, 71–102.

Göransson, Sven. 1951. *De svenska studieresorna och den religiösa kontrollen från reformationstiden till frihetstiden*. Uppsala.

Ijsewijn, Jozef. 1977. *Companion to Neo-Latin Studies*. Amsterdam–New York–Oxford.

Ijsewijn, Jozef. 1990. *Companion to Neo-Latin Studies*. I. *History and diffusion of Neo-Latin litterature*. 2nd ed.

Johannesson, Kurt. 1969. "Retorik och propaganda vid det äldre Vasahovet", *Lychnos*, 1–60.

Johannesson, Kurt. 1974. "Renässansens latinpoesi. Studier kring Henricus Mollerus", in Gunnar Eriksson, Tore Frängsmyr & Magnus von Platen (eds.) *Vetenskapens träd. Idéhistoriska studier tillägnade Sten Lindroth 28.XII. 1974*, Stockholm 1974, 55–94.

Johannesson, Kurt. 1982. *Gotisk renässans. Johannes och Olaus Magnus som politiker och historiker*. Stockholm 1982.

Johannesson, Kurt & James Larson (tr.) 1991. *The Renaissance of the Goths in sixteenth-century Sweden. Johannes and Olaus Magnus as politicians and historians*. Berkeley–Los Angeles–Oxford.

Johannesson, Kurt (tr., com.) & Hans Helander (com). 2018. *Johannes Magnus, Goternas och svearnas historia*. I–II. Stockholm.

Lindroth, Sten. 1976. *A history of Uppsala University 1477–1977*. Uppsala.

Marsh, David. 1992. "Xenophon", in V. Brown, P.O. Kristeller & F.E. Cranz (eds.) *Catalogus translationum et commentariorum: Mediaeval and Renaissance Latin translations and commentaries. Annotated lists and guides*, VII. Washington (D.C.), 75–196.

Melanchthon, Philipp. 1853. *Philippi Melanthonis opera quae supersunt omnia. Corpus Reformatorum.* XIX. C.G. Bretschneider & H.E. Bindseil (eds.) Brunschweig.

Nordström, J. 1922. "Laurentius Petri Gothus' *Strategema gothici exercitus.* Ett återfunnet humanistepos", *Samlaren* 3, 221–276.

Race, William H. (tr. & ed.) 1997. *Pindar. Olympian Odes. Pythian Odes.* Cambridge (Mass.).

Schück, Henrik. 1890. *Svensk Literaturhistoria*. I. Stockholm.

Schück, Henrik & Karl Warburg. 1985. *Illustrerad svensk litteraturhistoria.* Vol. 2. [1st ed. 1896–7, 3rd revised ed. 1927, reprint 1985]. Stockholm.

Svalenius, Ivan. 1977–1979. "Laurentius Petri Gothus", *Svenskt biografiskt lexikon* 22, 385–387.

van Dam, Harm-Jan. 2015. "Poems on the Threshold: Neo-Latin *carmina liminaria*", in Concetta Bianca *et al.* (eds.) *Acta Conventus Neo-Latini Monasteriensis. Proceedings of the Fifteenth International Congress of Neo-Latin Studies (Münster 2012)*, Leiden, 50–81.

Wieselgren, Peter. 1835. *Sveriges sköna litteratur.* III. *Statens sköna litteratur, fortsättning.* Lund.

Wilner, P.O. 1904. "Förteckning öfver svenskar inskrifna vid tyska universitet under 1500-talets senare hälft", *Samlaren* 25, 7–21.

III. GREEK IN PROTESTANT GERMANY

Die Griechischstudien in Deutschland und ihre universitäre Institutionalisierung im 16. Jahrhundert. Ein Überblick[1]

STEFAN RHEIN

Die Institutionalisierung der Griechischstudien an den deutschen Universitäten hat letztmalig Paul Pendzig 1921 in seinem Aufsatz „Die Anfänge der griechischen Studien und die deutschen Universitäten" vorgestellt. Auch wenn er die Kontinuität des Aristotelismus und des Neuplatonismus aus dem Mittelalter in die Renaissance betont, so markiert für ihn in Deutschland der Humanismus mit seiner pädagogischen Prägung den Beginn der Einführung des universitären Griechischstudiums. Zu Recht unterscheidet er eine Phase des eher privaten Unterrichts und informeller Interessensgruppen von der Institutionalisierung im Rahmen der Artistenfakultät durch Studienordnungen und Statuten, doch erscheint seine Feststellung, diese Entwicklung sei um 1520 abgeschlossen, allzu optimistisch.[2] Im Folgenden soll die Institutionalisierung der Gräzistik im 16. Jahrhundert an den deutschen Universitäten im Fokus stehen, ohne die die reiche

---

[1] Vor über 20 Jahren habe ich am Beispiel der Universität Rostock den langwierigen Prozess der Institutionalisierung der dortigen Griechischstudien dargestellt, vgl. Rhein (1996). Den damals begonnenen Faden führe ich mit diesem Beitrag in breiterer Perspektive fort. Für vielfältige Unterstützung bei der Beschaffung der Forschungsliteratur danke ich den Kolleginnen und Kollegen der Reformationsgeschichtlichen Forschungsbibliothek Wittenberg.

[2] Vgl. Pendzig (1921, 54): „Allgemein kann man sagen, daß um die Wende des 2. und 3. Jahrzehnts des XVI. Jahrh. dieser Prozeß als beendet angesehen werden muß." Er beruft sich dabei auf Friedrich Paulsens „Geschichte des Gelehrten Unterrichts": „Als Reuchlin 1522 starb, konnte man auf jeder deutschen Universität Griechisch lernen." Zusammenfassend Holzberg (1981, 83–86: „Zur Situation der Griechischen Studien in Deutschland um 1500"). Er nennt folgende Daten der Institutionalisierung: 1515 Leipzig, 1518 Wittenberg, 1519 Erfurt, 1520 Ingolstadt, 1521 Freiburg, Greifswald, Tübingen, 1522 Heidelberg, 1523 Wien und 1526 Rostock. Die Studie von G. Bauch (1896) ist aufschlussreich insbesondere für die Griechischstudien vor ihrer universitären Institutionalisierung, etwa zu Erfurt (49–76), Wittenberg (76–93), Frankfurt/Oder (93–98), Leipzig (163–189), Greifswald und Rostock (189–193). Zum Griechischunterricht an der Universität Wien vgl. Gastgeber (2012) mit ausführlicher Würdigung von Leben und Werk des 1523 berufenen ersten Wiener Griechischprofessors Georg Rithaymer. Zur Einrichtung gräzistischer Lehrstühle an deutschen Universitäten vgl. für die frühe Phase die – allerdings lückenhafte – Zusammenstellung von Saladin (2000, 333).

neualtgriechische Literatur des Humanismus kaum vorstellbar wäre. Dabei soll die Aufmerksamkeit neben der Institutionalisierung auch der damit einhergehenden, sich vor allem durch Festreden artikulierenden Repräsentation des Faches und seiner Fachvertreter gelten. Solche rhetorisch durchgefeilten Inauguralreden entstanden zunächst an italienischen Universitäten des 15. Jahrhunderts und widmeten sich als *laudes disciplinarum* den Vorzügen der Wissenschaften oder der jeweiligen Fachdisziplin. Für die Gräzistik setzte Demetrius Chalkondyles mit seiner Antrittsrede 1463 in Padua den Anfang, nachdem bereits über 100 Jahre zuvor, 1361, der erste gräzistische Lehrstuhl in Florenz eingerichtet und mit dem süditalienischen Griechen Leontius Pilatus besetzt wurde. Christian Gastgeber hat für Italien die Reden zur Verteidigung des Griechischen vorgestellt, die von Andronikos Kontoblakes (um 1450/69), Theodor Gaza (*ca.* 1460), Demetrius Chalkondyles (1463, 1464), Pietro Bembo (1494), Scipione Forteguerri (1504) und Marc Antonio Antimaco (bis 1552) stammen. Das Lob des Griechischen besaß durchweg apologetischen Charakter und bemühte sich, die zeitaufwändigen Schwierigkeiten des Lernens mit topischen Erläuterungen als erträglich und sinnvoll zu erweisen, etwa dass Latein ohne griechische Sprache nicht verständlich sei, dass jedes literarische Genus von den Griechen erfunden sei, ja dass in allen Wissensbereichen die Griechen die Grundlagen gelegt hätten.[3]

Der Redegestus von Lob und Verteidigung zeigt sich auch bei den deutschen Universitätsgräzisten. So soll im Folgenden neben den Darlegungen zu den institutionellen Anfängen der universitären Griechischstudien das Redegenus ‚gräzistische Antrittsvorlesung' mit ihren frühesten Beispielen erstmals für Deutschland vorgestellt werden, deren Argumentationen einen Zugang in die entstehende Wissenschaftskultur des Griechischen eröffnen. Dabei werden wie auch bei den italienischen Beispielen apologetische Argumentationsmuster sichtbar, die z. B. bereits bei Chalkondyles zur Anwendung kommen: Die Quellen aller Wissenschaften stammen von den Griechen. Wenn diese Fremdes übernahmen, haben sie es perfektioniert. Gerade die lateinischen Künste und Wissenschaften haben entscheidend von den griechischen profitiert. So ist die lateinische Grammatik ohne Kenntnis der griechischen nicht verständlich. Hinzu tritt bei den deutschen Rednern die Konstruktion einer Genealogie der Rezeption griechischer Sprache und Literatur aus dem italienischen Humanismus, um so die Dignität des eigenen Fachs zu unterstreichen. So sehr sich auch einzelne Argumente für den Nutzen des Griechischen etwa bei Chalkondyles und den

---

[3] Gastgeber (2014) verweist auch auf deutsche Beispiele: Melanchthon (1549), Heresbach (1551) und Esaias Priester (1571).

späteren deutschen Gräzisten ähneln, es liegt keine direkte Wirkung vor, da die lateinischsprachige *Oratio* des Paduaner Professors niemals veröffentlicht wurde, sondern nur abschriftlich in der Privatbibliothek des damaligen Zuhörers und späteren Nürnberger Arztes Hartmut Schedel überdauerte. [4]

Leipzig: Richard Crocus und Petrus Mosellanus mit Antrittsvorlesung des Mosellanus (1518)

Der erste gräzistische Lehrstuhl in Deutschland wurde in Leipzig eingerichtet – dank des sächsischen Herzogs Georg, der bereits seit 1502 die humanistischen Fächer etwa durch Berufungen an seiner Landesuniversität zu fördern suchte. So konnte 1515 der Schotte Richard Crocus gewonnen werden. Über dessen Vorlesungstätigkeit an der Leipziger Universität ist nur wenig bekannt. Herausgegeben hat er in dieser Zeit eine griechische Sprachlehre (*Tabulae*) und eine Ausonius-Ausgabe für Vorlesungszwecke; von seinem Schüler Joachim Camerarius wissen wir noch von einer Plutarch-Vorlesung. Der jüngst bearbeitete Nachlass eines weiteren Crocus-Schülers, Julius Pflug, erweitert unsere Kenntnisse nennenswert, da er Handschriften des Lehrers und Mitschriften des Schülers z. B. zu Pindars Olympischen Epinikien beinhaltet.[5] Doch Crocus verließ bereits 1517 Stadt und Universität mit Ziel Cambridge. Sein Nachfolger wurde Petrus Mosellanus und damit der erste deutsche Inhaber einer Griechisch-Professur. Seinen Amtsantritt nutzte er für eine programmatische Antrittsvorlesung und begründete damit die universitäre Auseinandersetzung um den Bildungswert des Griechischen.[6] In der Widmungsepistel, auf den 1. August 1518 datiert, gerichtet an seinen Landesherrn Herzog Georg von Sachsen, lässt Mosellanus bereits zentrale Themen anklingen: Der humanistische Optimismus von der „glückseligen Gegenwart" (A2v), in der der Buchdruck alle am Wissen teilhaben lässt, nährt sich aus der Entdeckung der drei Sprachen Hebräisch, Griechisch und Latein; nur sie gewähren einen direkten Zugang zur Theologie (A3r). In die Reihe

---

[4] Vgl. Geanakoplos (1974). Zur Frühgeschichte der Institutionalisierung der Griechischstudien in Italien vgl. auch Ricci (1952). Vgl. auch Saladin (2000, z. B. 81–86: „Florence, capitale de l'hellénisme"). Zur Gattung Antrittsvorlesung vgl. Schirrmeister (2018).

[5] Vgl. Cottin & Kunde (2017, 262 f.). Zu Crocus vgl. Bauch (1896, 177–183, auf S. 183 der Hinweis von Camerarius auf die Plutarch-Vorlesung des Crocus).

[6] Die Antrittsrede wird ausführlich paraphrasiert von François (2003). Vgl. auch Flood (2013, 243 f.). Die folgende Darstellung der Rede setzt andere Schwerpunkte und konzentriert sich auf die Auseinandersetzung mit der griechischen Sprache und Literatur.

der den Nebel durchdringenden Entdecker der Sprache setzt Mosellanus Papst
Nikolaus V., Bessarion, Nikolaus Cusanus, in Florenz die Medicifamilie und in
Venedig Hermolaus Barbarus sowie die Offizin des Aldus Manutius und Andreas
Asulanus (A3r). Besonders lobt der junge Dozent Kurfürst Friedrich den Weisen,
der in Wittenberg die humanistische Bildung in vorbildlicher Weise fördere
(A3v). Nicht weniger herausragend ist für ihn die Universität Leipzig mit ihren
wunderschönen Gebäuden und ihren Vertretern der Sprachenbildung, denen sich
allerdings immer wieder Vertreter der alten Sophisterei in den Weg stellen (A4r).[7]

Dieser Widmungsbrief an den Landesherrn erschließt sich mit seinen
Implikationen und Intentionen erst dann, wenn man die Situation des 25-jährigen
Dozenten in den Blick nimmt. Die Griechischprofessur war noch nicht in den
Fächerkanon der Artistenfakultät integriert, so dass auch ihr Inhaber keineswegs
Mitglied des Fakultätscollegiums war und deshalb nur mit einer geringen
Besoldung vorliebnehmen musste. Mosellanus kämpfte also in Brief und Rede für
die Akzeptanz des Griechischen, für die Aufnahme seines Faches in das universitäre
Curriculum und für eine Neubewertung seines Status als Griechischprofessor.
Dies gelang erst ein Jahr später, 1519, durch eine Studienreform, die sich an
Wittenberg orientierte, so dass sich Mosellanus Lob Friedrichs des Weisen als –
letztendlich erfolgreiche – Aufforderung an dessen Bruder Herzog Georg erweist.
Um in das Collegium aufgenommen zu werden, musste Mosellanus allerdings
erst die Magister-Prüfung ablegen, was ihm am 3. Januar 1520 gelang, so dass
er danach ordentlich besoldetes Mitglied der Artistenfakultät (mit Wohnrecht
in den Kolleggebäuden, denen ja auch sein besonderer Lobpreis gilt) werden
konnte – auf Veranlassung des Herzogs gegen den Willen der „Sophisten", wie
Mosellanus selbst berichtet.[8]

Die Antrittsrede des Mosellanus grundiert und verstärkt die
universitätspolitische Zielsetzung des Widmungsbriefs und konzentriert sich dabei
ganz auf das Griechische. Der durchweg in der Literatur zitierte eher allgemein
gehaltene Titel *De variarum linguarum cognitione paranda* wird nämlich präzisiert:
De variarum linguarum et praecipue Graecae cognitione paranda, ein Titel, der
bereits im Erstdruck von 1518 die Rede unmittelbar nach dem Widmungsbrief
einführt und klar zum Ausdruck bringt, dass für den Gräzisten Mosellanus das
Griechische naturgemäß den herausragenden Platz einnimmt, aber auch, dass hier
die institutionelle Akzeptanz des Griechischunterrichts im Mittelpunkt steht. Mit

---

[7] Mosellanus (1518). Die folgenden Zitate aus der Rede sind ebenfalls der Ausgabe 1518
entnommen.

[8] Vgl. Kusche (2009, 261 f., 786–788).

ihrem großen rhetorischen Aufwand erscheint die Rede selbst als *specimen* ihres Themas, als gelungenes Beispiel einer virtuosen Sprachbeherrschung, die sich in der Nachfolge der Sprachkraft eines Platon, Aristoteles, Demosthenes, Cicero, Quintilian und Plinius sieht (B1v–B2r). Mosellanus weiß von der Kritik am Studium des Hebräischen und Griechischen, das frommen Menschen angeblich unnütz sei; beide Sprachen aber sind, so seine Entgegnung, Geschenk des Heiligen Geistes, führen zu Gott und seinen Engeln und befördern die Kenntnis der Heiligen Schrift entscheidend. Die theologische Argumentationslinie wird weit gezogen und mit biblischen Autoritäten untermauert, so dass die Sprachmächtigkeit Gottes und der Engel, von heiligen Männern und insbesondere von Paulus den Menschen als vorbildlich vorgeführt wird (B4v–B5r). Mosellanus, der nach seinem theologischen Baccalaureat 1520 Vorlesungen über Augustinus und über Bibeltexte hielt, entwickelt ausführlich die Notwendigkeit von Sprachkenntnissen für jeden Theologen. Seine Argumentation betont den Nutzen der biblischen Schriftzeugnisse und der patristischen Literatur im Kampf gegen die Bildungsfeinde unter der Führung Christi, fernab von aristotelischer und platonischer Philosophendialektik (B6v). Ein zeitgenössischer Humanist wie Erasmus wird deshalb auch folgerichtig gepriesen als einer, der gleichsam von Gott geleitet und mit größter Kompetenz gegen viele Widerstände die biblischen und apostolischen Schriften gereinigt und sie wieder in die frühere Bedeutung zurückgeführt habe. Ja, Erasmus wird zum *dux* erklärt, der die griechischen Türen zur ursprünglichen Theologie wieder geöffnet hat (C3r–v). Auch die Kommentare der lateinischen Kirchenväter wie Hieronymus, Ambrosius und Augustinus seien ohne griechische Quellen nicht ausgekommen, so dass Mosellanus alle, die dies außer Acht lassen, als *impii* attackiert.

Nach dem ausführlichen Plädoyer für den Bildungswert des Griechischen in der Theologie nimmt sich Mosellanus die anderen Disziplinen vor, beginnend mit der Jurisprudenz, nach der Theologie die für ihn würdevollste (D1v). Auch hier insistiert er darauf, dass die römischen Rechtstexte ohne ihre griechischen Quellen, ohne Autoritäten wie Solon und ohne die Kenntnis griechischer Formulierungen nicht verständlich sind, was Zeugen wie Guillaume Budé, Poliziano, Alciato und Accursio belegen.[9] Auch für das Recht bedeutet die griechische Sprache die Quelle, ohne deren Kenntnis die späteren Flüsse

---

[9] Hier fügt der Redner einen zeichentheoretischen Exkurs ein, indem er die Bedeutung von Sprache durch den wechselseitigen Nexus von Zeichen und Bezeichneten unterstreicht, so dass das Vergessen der Zeichen die Unkenntnis der Sache mit sich bringt (D2v). Diesen epistemologischen Passus behandelt François (2003, 469–477) besonders ausführlich und verortet ihn philosophiegeschichtlich im Spannungsfeld von Nominalismus und Humanismus.

unverständlich bleiben. Ähnliches ist für die Medizin zu konstatieren, denn auch sie ist im damaligen (präexperimentellen) Zeitalter eine Textwissenschaft, die Heilmittel tradiert (D3r). Hier gilt das Lob außerdem der jüdischen Medizin, auf die sich sogar Päpste verlassen haben, und darüber hinaus der arabischen Medizin eines Avicenna, die Mosellanus zur Aufforderung ermutigt, sich mit der arabischen Sprache zu beschäftigen, ein Unterfangen, für das Giovanni Pico della Mirandola als Vorbild herangezogen wird (D3v). Für die herausragende Bedeutung der griechischen Medizin steht Galen, dessen Lehre nur im originalen Griechisch unverfälscht zugänglich sei. Wie in den anderen Wissenschaften kann Mosellanus für die Medizin zeitgenössische Vertreter der Verbindung von Sprach- und Fachkenntnis nur aus dem Ausland anführen: Niccolò Leoniceno, den Leibarzt des französischen Königs Wilhelm Kopp, Thomas Linacre und Jean Ruel (D4r). In der Philosophie ist die Reihe der griechischen Autoritäten besonders eindrucksvoll und reicht von Platon, Aristoteles über Plotin und Jamblich bis hin zu Theophrast. Doch auch die Mathematik und die Musik stehen auf griechischer Grundlage, was durch die Vielzahl der einschlägigen Fachtermini von *orthogonia* bis *symphonia* illustriert wird, demgegenüber sich die lateinische Sprache geradezu armselig ausnehme (D5v–6r).

Die Beschäftigung mit der griechischen Sprache übt den Geist also besser als die lateinische Sprache, so dass die Verbindung der beiden das Ideal darstellt. Kein Redner kann ohne das Griechische reüssieren, wenn Demosthenes als *norma dicendi* fungiert (D6v), wie auch kein Dichter ohne die griechischen Vorbilder eine der poetischen Gattungen betreiben kann (E1v). Eine Genealogie der griechischen und hebräischen Studien deutet Mosellanus nur an, da er von den Akteuren in Deutschland nicht sprechen will, im rhetorischen Modus des expliziten Verschweigens allerdings dann doch Johannes Reuchlin, Willibald Pirckheimer, Wolfgang Capito und – aus der Reihe der deutschen Humanisten fallend, aber als Pariser Lehrer seines Lehrers Crocus ihm wiederum bekannt – Hieronymus Aleander kurz nennt (E2v). Das Resümee der Rede kann nicht anders ausfallen, als dass Sprachkompetenz den Theologen nützlich, den Juristen vorteilhaft, den Medizinern angenehm und den Philosophen fruchtbringend, kurzum für alle Fächer höchst notwendig ist (*Theologis modis omnibus utilis, jureperitis commoda, Medicis etiam iucunda, Philosophis frugifera, breviter nulli disciplinae non vel maxime necessaria*, E3r). Zeitbedingt ist die Schlussargumentation, die den Zuhörern keine Fachautoritäten, sondern Machtautoritäten präsentiert, die Griechisch selbst beherrschen oder zumindest fördern: Papst Leo X. (also Giovanni de Medici), Kaiser Maximilian, König Franz von Frankreich, der spätere Kaiser Karl V., zu dessen Verdiensten die Förderung des Erasmus am Löwener

Hof zählt, und in Deutschland Herzog Ernst von Bayern, Kurfürst Friedrich der Weise und natürlich der Landesherr Herzog Georg von Sachsen als Förderer des Griechischen an seiner Landesuniversität Leipzig.

Diese erste Antrittsrede eines Gräzisten in Deutschland war übrigens zugleich Anlass einer Debatte um den Sinn humanistischer Sprachbildung. Denn Jakob Latomus, der Löwener Theologieprofessor, reagierte mit harscher Polemik, dass die Kenntnis von Griechisch und Hebräisch für einen Theologen eher schädlich sei.[10] Nach Mosellanus' frühem Tod 1524 verbot Herzog Georg den Griechisch- und Hebräischunterricht, da er die humanistischen Studien in engem Verbund mit der von ihm heftig bekämpften Reformation sah, so dass erst nach seinem Tod (1539) mit der von Melanchthon empfohlenen Berufung des Joachim Camerarius eine über 30 Jahre andauernde Blütezeit der griechischen Studien in Leipzig anbrach.[11]

Wittenberg: Philipp Melanchthon mit Antrittsvorlesung (28. August 1518)

Weitaus mehr Furore als Mosellanus erregte Melanchthon, der zweite deutsche Inhaber einer Griechischprofessur, mit seiner Antrittsvorlesung vom 28. August 1518 (*De corrigendis adolescentiae studiis*). Sie erlebte bis 1537 sechs eigenständige Drucke in Wittenberg, Basel und Paris, während Mosellanus' Leipziger Rede nur 1519 in Basel nachgedruckt und dann 1634 in Jena und 1665 in Hamburg jeweils zusammen mit einer Rede von Laurentius Rhodomannus zum gleichen Thema wiederaufgelegt wurde.[12] Melanchthons Antrittsrede ist ein kunstvolles Mixtum compositum, in dem das Lehrhafte einer Vorlesung, der rhetorische Prunk einer Festrede und das Dialogische eines Gesprächs durch die häufig direkte Anrede an die studentischen Zuhörer zusammenkommen. Diese Rede ist sich der Neuartigkeit ihres Themas sehr wohl bewusst und versteht die Emphase des Anfangs begeisternd zu formulieren. Dabei schildert Melanchthon seinen eigenen Bildungsweg, v. a. seine Abkehr von den scholastischen Kommentaren

---

[10] Vgl. ausführlich François (2003).

[11] Zur Entwicklung der griechischen Studien an der Universität Leipzig, vgl. Leipzig (2009, 1, 265–268 [Enno Bünz] und 4/1, 575–577 [Marcus Deufert & Kurt Sier]). Zu Leben und Werk des Camerarius vgl. Hamm (2011).

[12] Die verschiedenen Ausgaben von Melanchthons Antrittsvorlesung in Claus (2014), Nr. 1518.14 (Wittenberg), 1519.3 (Basel), 1527.28 (Paris), 1529.56a (Paris), 1534.40 (Paris), 1537.54 (Paris). Zu den Reden Melanchthons vgl. den Überblick von Gößner (2017). Die Ausgaben der Rede des Mosellanus in VD 16 (Nr. S 2133) und VD 17 (Nr. 39:145128Y und 32:674705M).

hin zur Beschäftigung mit dem Originaltext des Aristoteles, als Modell für den Bildungsgang seiner studentischen Zuhörer und entwickelt dadurch ein humanistisches Wir-Gefühl. Nach der Zeit des Verlusts der griechischen Bildung, die nicht nur einen allgemeinen Verfall der Wissenschaften, sondern auch einen Verfall des Religiösen mit sich gebracht habe, beschäftige man sich nun im Studium der Literatur mit der Sache selbst und nicht nur mit den Schatten der Dinge. Die griechische Gelehrsamkeit umfasse Naturkunde, Ethik dank der Schriften des Aristoteles und Platons und Theologie auf der Grundlage der biblischen Quellen, die uns befähigen, Christus zu begreifen. Theologisch, präziser formuliert: reformatorisch-theologisch geprägt ist Melanchthon in dieser Rede noch nicht, so dass er den bei den Anhängern der neuen, auf christliche Originalquellen fokussierten Theologie beliebten Anti-Aristotelismus seiner Zeit noch keineswegs teilt, der bei Mosellanus und später bei Johann Lang deutlich formuliert wird.

Eindrucksvoll gelingt es dem jungen Redner, eine Stimmung des Aufbruchs, die er in ganz Deutschland aufzublühen sieht, auch in Wittenberg zu etablieren. Gleichzeitig ist ihm bewusst, dass er das Griechischstudium zunächst nur als Parergon, gleichsam als Freizeitvergnügen, einführen kann, um Vorbehalte abzubauen:

> Mit Latein zusammen muss man gleichzeitig Griechisch lernen, was aber leicht zu bewerkstelligen ist. Widmet doch einige Stunden von der Freizeit, die euch das Studium lässt, dem Griechischen! Ich meinerseits werde all meinen Eifer und all meine Mühe daransetzen, dass ihr in der Erwartung, dass sich die zusätzliche Arbeit lohnt, nicht enttäuscht werdet. Denn gleich von der ersten Stunde an werde ich die Schwierigkeit der Grammatik durch die Lektüre der besten Schriftsteller mildern, damit das, was dort als Regel festgelegt ist, sich hier im Originaltext an Beispielen wiederfindet und bestätigt. Nebenbei wird euch bei der Autorenlektüre außerdem manches begegnen, was für die Charakterbildung oder auch für die Erkenntnis von geheimen Dingen wichtig ist. Wenn ihr alles zusammengetragen habt, werden sich eure Studien in schönster Weise zu einem vollendeten Kreis zusammenschließen.[13]

Im Gegensatz zu Mosellanus dekliniert Melanchthon nicht die Vorteile des Griechischen in den unterschiedlichen Disziplinen durch, noch führt er

---

[13] Melanchthons Antrittsvorlesung ist übersetzt von Gerhard Steiger in Beyer, Rhein & Wartenberg (2011, 46–67), Zitat: 64. Zur Rede Melanchthons vgl. Rhein (2018).

eine Galerie antiker und zeitgenössischer Zeugen an, sondern entfaltet ein Lebensgefühl, am Anfang einer Epoche zu stehen, und lädt ein, diesen Anfang zu erleben und mitzugestalten, und entwirft so die griechische Sprache und Literatur als Markierung der Neuzeit. Der Beginn von Melanchthons Griechischunterricht bedeutete zugleich eine wichtige Etappe für die humanistisch-gräzistische Lehr- und Lernkultur in ganz Deutschland, da hier die enge Verbindung von Reformation und griechischen Studien weit über die Leucorea hinaus initiiert wurde.[14]

Frankfurt/Oder: Gregor Schmidt (1518)

An der 1506 gegründeten Frankfurter Viadrina begann wie in Wittenberg der institutionalisierte Griechischunterricht im Jahr 1518 mit Gregor Schmidt, den Universitätsaufenthalte zuvor nach Köln, Ingolstadt, Leipzig, Erfurt und Wittenberg geführt hatten. 1518 wurde der aus dem schweizerischen Werdenberg stammende neue, fest besoldete Dozent in die Artistenfakultät aufgenommen. In der Matrikel steht *magister Gregorius Schmidt Werdenberg*, dazu ein Nachtrag: *professor grece lingue*. Er blieb bis zu seinem Tod Ende 1524 der Frankfurter Universität treu.[15] Von ihm ist nichts Schriftliches überliefert, also auch keine programmatischen Äußerungen zum Griechischstudium wie auch keine Ergebnisse seiner eigenen Beschäftigung, so dass er sich von Gustav Bauch die Qualifizierung „kleines Licht" gefallen lassen muss.[16] Nach diesem bescheidenen Anfang konnten mit Jodocus Willichius, Joachim Zierenberg und Matthäus Host kompetente Gräzisten gewonnen werden, so dass die griechische Sprache sogar zu einem Unterrichtsschwerpunkt in der Viadrina wurde.[17]

---

[14] Zur Entwicklung der Griechisch-Professur nach und neben Melanchthon vgl. Scheible (2015, 192–194): Auf Melanchthon folgten 1525/26 Joachim Camerarius und danach bis 1536 Franz Burchard; Melanchthon versah den dann vakanten Lehrstuhl, bis am 4.8.1541 Veit Örtel zum Griechisch-Professor ernannt wurde, ein Amt, das dieser bis zu seinem Tod (1570) bekleidete. Zum großen Einfluss Melanchthons auf die Rezeption des Griechischen in Deutschland vgl. Ben-Tov (2009, zu Melanchthons Rede *De studiis linguae graecae* von 1549: 140–148) und – mit Blick auf die neualtgriechische Dichtung des 16. Jahrhunderts – Rhein (2017).

[15] Vgl. Höhle (2002, 95 f.). Vgl. auch Höhle (2017).

[16] Bauch (1896, 98).

[17] So Asche (2001, 75). Zu Willichius, Höhle (2002, 100–105), zu Zierenberg, Höhle (2002, 106), zu Host, MBW 12, 327.

Erfurt: Johann Lang (Wintersemester 1519/20)

Melanchthons Berufung nach Wittenberg war das Ergebnis einer Studienreform, die Luther zusammen mit Johann Lang, Bartholomäus Bernhardi, Nikolaus von Amsdorf und anderen bereits seit längerem vorantrieb. Ziel war, im humanistischen Sinne die biblischen Sprachen Griechisch und Hebräisch im universitären Lehrangebot zu verankern. Dass dies parallel auch in Erfurt gelang, ist kein Zufall, denn zwischen den beiden mitteldeutschen Universitäten gab es enge persönliche Kontakte, die über Luther, Justus Jonas und Johann Lang liefen. Im Sommersemester 1519 kam es an der Erfurter Universität zu einer umfassenden humanistischen Strukturreform der Artistischen Fakultät, in deren Ergebnis sieben neue Professuren eingerichtet wurden, u. a. Griechisch. Im Unterschied etwa zu lateinischer Grammatik, Dialektik oder Physik wurde Griechisch allerdings als weniger relevant eingestuft, da der Besuch der Griechischvorlesungen nicht verpflichtend für das Magisterexamen war und zudem gesondert bezahlt werden musste, während die Pflichtvorlesungen gratis angeboten wurden.[18]

Der erste Inhaber der Griechischprofessur wurde Johann Lang, der von 1511 bis 1516 eng in die Wittenberger „Diskussionsgemeinschaft" rund um Luther eingebunden war und von dort das Interesse für eine quellenbasierte, antischolastische und patristisch orientierte Theologie in seine neue Stellung mitbrachte. Diese trat er im Wintersemester 1519/20 zunächst auf Honorarbasis und dann im Sommersemester 1520 offiziell an. Sein neues Amt konnte er allerdings nur wenige Semester wahrnehmen, denn sein Klosteraustritt im Januar 1522 machte den entlaufenen Mönch zu einem gesellschaftlichen Außenseiter, zumindest für die altgläubig gebliebene Universität Erfurt, so dass bereits im Sommersemester 1522 mit dem Katholiken Johannes Femel, der nach einem Wittenberger Aufenthalt sich gegen die Reformation entschieden hatte, ein Nachfolger amtierte. Langs wichtigste Publikation in der Zeit seiner gräzistischen Lehrtätigkeit ist die Übersetzung des Matthäus-Evangeliums aus der *Kriechsersprach [...] yns deutsch gebracht*, erschienen im Juni/Juli 1521, ein halbes Jahr bevor Luther seine Übersetzung auf der Wartburg begann, indessen mit völlig anderer Übersetzungshaltung, da Lang im Gegensatz zu Luther der griechischen Vorlage pedantisch folgte und eine wortgetreue Übersetzung vorlegte.[19] Eine

---

[18] Vgl. Asche (2003, 52–55).

[19] Zu Johann Lang als Teil der Wittenberger „Diskussionsgemeinschaft" vgl. Kruse (2002, 44–48 u. ö.). Zu seinen humanistischen Interessen vgl. ausführlich Lindner (2014).

grundsätzliche Rede zu den Zielen seiner Lehrtätigkeit hat sich aus der Feder
Langs nicht erhalten, nur ein offener Brief an den Erfurter Universitätsrektor
vom 24. Juni 1521, also bereits aus der Schlussphase seiner Lehrtätigkeit, in dem
er sich gegen den Vorwurf zur Wehr setzte, er habe die Autoritäten Platon und
Aristoteles angegriffen. Lang hingegen argumentiert in eigener Sache, dass er sich
gegen die Vermischung von säkularer und christlicher Weisheit gewendet und
dabei den Vorrang der biblischen Wahrheit verteidigt habe. Langs Einsatz gilt
also nicht allgemein dem Kampf für den Humanismus oder für den Nutzen der
antiken Sprachen, sondern gilt der neuen reformatorischen Lehre, die die alten
Sprachen als Mittel zum theologischen Zweck einsetzt und die zugleich gegen die
Aristoteles-Dominanz bei ethischen und metaphysischen Fragestellungen in der
scholastischen Theologie angeht – ganz wie Martin Luther in seiner Adelsschrift
vom Juni 1520:

> Hier wäre nun mein Rat, dass die Bücher des Aristoteles: Physica, Metaphysica,
> De anima, Ethica, welche bisher für die besten gehalten, ganz würden abgetan
> mit allen andern, die von natürlichen Dingen sich rühmen, so doch nichts
> darinnen kann gelehrt werden, weder von natürlichen noch geistlichen
> Dingen.[20]

Die religiöse, ja konfessionelle Fragestellung dominierte in Erfurt, da hier
reformatorische Gelehrsamkeit und katholische Institution konfliktreich
aufeinanderprallten.[21]

Ingolstadt: Johannes Reuchlin mit Einführungsrede des Johannes Gussubelius (5. März 1520)

Prägendes Vorbild für die Griechischstudien war für den jungen Melanchthon
Johannes Reuchlin, der in Pforzheim und Tübingen zum initiierenden Mittelpunkt
von Humanistenkreisen mit besonderen griechischen Interessen avancierte,
indessen erst im hohen Alter von 65 Jahren seine erste universitäre Stellung erhielt

---

[20] WA 6, 457. Vgl. Immenhauser (2003, 79).

[21] Lang (1521). Langs Brief ist von Eobanus Hessus zum Druck gebracht worden, wie dieser selbst
im Vorwort mitteilt. Zum Verständnis von Langs Brief vgl. Scribner (1976, 29 f.). Zur Geschichte
der Griechischstudien in Erfurt nach Lang vgl. Kleineidam (1983, 242–244).

und zwar an der 1472 gegründeten bayerischen Landesuniversität Ingolstadt.[22]
Zu Beginn seiner Lehrtätigkeit als Griechisch- und Hebräischprofessor hat nicht
Reuchlin selbst, sondern ein Kollege, Johannes Gussubelius, eine Einführungsrede
gehalten, in der die Person des neuen Professors ausführlich gewürdigt wird.
Reuchlin war am 29. Februar 1520 zum Professor ernannt worden, ein weithin
bekannter Intellektueller, Symbolfigur des humanistischen Kampfes gegen alle
Varianten bildungsferner Dunkelmänner, zweifelsohne eine besondere Zierde der
Universität Ingolstadt – so sieht es jedenfalls auch Gussubelius, der den Stolz seiner
Universität über den Neuzugang in seiner Festrede anlässlich der Einführung des
neuen Professors, gehalten am 5. März 1520 um 9 Uhr im größten Auditorium
des Alten Kollegs, nicht verbergen kann.[23]

    Gussubelius, bekannt auch unter dem Namen Longicampianus, hat sich
ansonsten nicht literarisch ausgezeichnet und ging später aus konfessionellen
Gründen nach Wittenberg, wo er 1525 zum Unterricht in den Grundlagen
der Mathematik und zugleich als Rhetor in den Kollegien, also als Aufsicht
über die Studenten, angestellt wurde. Er unterrichtete dort wie auch zuvor in
Zwolle Griechisch, doch gibt es davon keine schriftlichen Ergebnisse. Seine Rede
prunkt mit einem breiten griechischen Bezugsrahmen, in dem Autoritäten wie
Demosthenes, Aischines, Aristophanes, Sophokles, Euripides, Pausanias und
Aristoteles erscheinen, ohne dass eine nähere Kenntnis der Werke vermittelt wird.
Sprachkenntnis fördere die Kompetenz in Dichtung, Philosophie und Theologie,
was für Gussubelius mit Verweis auf die Beispiele der Alten als bewiesen gilt (A4v).
Ungewöhnlich im Genus einer Festrede sind seine ausführlichen Darlegungen zu
Übersetzungsfehlern, da sein Hauptargument für das Erlernen des Griechischen
und Hebräischen die Irrtümer der Übersetzer sind, die den Leser in Unwissenheit
belassen, so dass hier nur die eigene Kenntnis der Originalsprachen als Gegenmittel
helfen kann (B1v–B3r). Als Vorbild für den Kampf gegen falsche Übersetzungen
erwähnt Gussubelius Bessarion und dessen Schrift gegen die Verächter Platons
(B3r). Eine deutsche Genealogie der Griechischstudien kommt bei ihm nicht
vor, wohl v. a. aus dem Grund, da er Reuchlin als vorgängerlosen „Liebhaber der
Antike und Nachahmer der alten Autoren" (*antiquitatis* […] *amator et priscorum
imitator authorum*, A2v), als einzigen und ersten Praeceptor inszeniert, der – wie

---

[22] Zu Reuchlin (1455–1522) vgl. ausführlich Dörner (2013).

[23] Gussubelius (1520), auf A1v die exakten Daten zu Ort und Zeit der Rede. Zu Gussubelius vgl.
Biographisches Lexikon (1998, 162 [L. Böninger]). Ausführlich zu dieser Rede und zum Leben des
Gussubelius Volz (1964). Reuchlins Zeit in Ingolstadt wird vorgestellt in *Biographisches Lexikon*
(1998, 338–341 [St. Rhein]).

der antike Wundermann Apollonios zu den Indern – als gelehrter Heilsbringer nach Ingolstadt gekommen sei (A4v–B1r).

Reuchlin las in Ingolstadt über den *Plutos* des Aristophanes und bereitete Texte Xenophons als Vorlesungsgrundlage vor; die erhaltene studentische Mitschrift zur Aristophanes-Vorlesung ist bislang unbearbeitet.[24] Seine Lehrtätigkeit wurde im Frühjahr 1521 durch die Pest abrupt beendet. Doch die Saat für einen blühenden Griechischunterricht war gelegt, da in Ingolstadt ab 1522 Griechisch kontinuierlich gelehrt wurde: z. B. als Nachfolger Reuchlins Johannes Alexander Brassicanus von September 1522 bis Wintersemester 1523/24. Ein obligatorisches Prüfungsfach wurde Griechisch allerdings erst 1571 an der jesuitischen Universität Ingolstadt.[25]

Freiburg: Konrad Heresbach mit Antrittsvorlesung (Juli 1521)

Eine programmatische Antrittsrede ist erst wieder von Konrad Heresbach überliefert, der 1521 in Freiburg (im Breisgau) die erste Professur für Griechisch übernahm. Seine neue Position verdankte er seinem guten Verhältnis zu Erasmus, der den knapp 25-jährigen empfohlen hatte. In der Matrikel erscheint Heresbach als juristischer Bakkalar und als *litterarum Graecarum professor*. Die Rede ist erst 30 Jahre später gedruckt worden, als Heresbach schon in seinem Amt als Geheimer Rat zur politischen Führungsschicht der Herzogtümer Jülich-Kleve-Berg gehörte. [26] Nach einem ausführlichen Lob der Sprache als Proprium des Menschen unternimmt Heresbach einen Ausflug in die Ursprungsgeschichte der griechischen Sprache, preist Griechenland als reichste Nährerin der Begabungen (7v–8r) und das Griechische als die Sprache, die die Musen und Götter nutzen würden, wenn sie sich in menschlicher Sprache ausdrücken wollten (8v), und schildert die weite Verbreitung des Griechischen von Kleinasien, Ägypten, Syrien bis nach Mazedonien und Illyrien, ja bis zu den keltischen Druiden, deren Sakralsprache griechisch gewesen sei – nicht zu vergessen das Deutsche mit seinen zahlreichen Spuren der griechischen Sprache (8v–9r). Unter allen

---

[24] Die Handschrift befindet sich in der UB Salzburg vgl. Reuchlin (2013, 342 Anm. 17).

[25] Vgl. Liess (1964). Zu Brassicanus MBW 11, 201.

[26] Heresbach (1551). Zu Heresbach (1496–1576) vgl. ausführlich Szameitat (2010) und Sdzuj (2014); hier auch der Eintrag in die Matrikel vom 5.7.1521: *Conradus Hirzbachius Medumanus dioc. Coloniens. clericus artium mgr., baccalaureus legum ut asserit* [!]*, litterarum Graecarum professor* (Sp. 292); eine kurze Würdigung der Antrittsrede in Sp. 299.

Sprachen ist das Griechische herausgehoben, da es die Quelle aller Disziplinen ist, von Poesie, Rhetorik, Dialektik, Grammatik, Mathematik, Politik, Ethik, Medizin, Physik, Theologie und Philosophie, kurzum da es der Ursprung des ganzen enzyklopädischen Wissens ist (10r). Auch die Grammatik und Syntax des Lateinischen hängen eng vom Griechischen ab, so dass das Verständnis für die Wissenschaftssprache der damaligen Gegenwart ohne Griechischkenntnisse nach Heresbach nicht gelingen kann.

Der junge Griechischprofessor belegt nun seine Behauptung von der wissenschaftsbegründenden Bedeutung der griechischen Sprache in einem Parforceritt durch alle Disziplinen. Er beginnt mit der Poesie, bei der in allen Gattungen gerade die besten lateinischen Autoren ausnahmslos bei ihren griechischen Vorgängern in die Schule gegangen sind (10v–12r). In der Rhetorik hat sich der beste lateinische Redner Cicero an der Sprachkraft des Demosthenes, der Wortfülle Platons, der Liebenswürdigkeit des Isokrates, der Kraft des Perikles und der Ausgereiftheit des Thukydides gemessen und erst dadurch seine Qualität erworben (13r). Die Dialektik wäre ohne Aristoteles und Porphyrios ausgestorben, auch wenn sie nur in verderbten Übersetzungen überlebt haben (13v). Den griechischen Hintergrund der Mathematik expliziert Heresbach wie Mosellanus mit einer Aufzählung griechischer Fachbegriffe aus der Astronomie (13v). In der Philosophie gelten nur die griechischen Texte als rezeptionswürdig, da die Scholastik ausschließlich Albernheiten hervorgebracht habe. Hier erwähnt Heresbach eine eigene Lektürereminiszenz aus seiner Studienzeit in Paris 1517/18, als er mit dem Engländer Thomas Lupset abwechselnd Platon las (14v). Der Vorrang der griechischen Literatur für die Medizin und deren Rezeption wird mit den Zeitgenossen Theodor Gaza, Niccolò Leoniceno, Johannes Menardus, Wilhelm Kopp und Jean Ruel verknüpft; die weitgehende Übereinstimmung mit der entsprechenden Auflistung bei Mosellanus legt nahe, dass sich für die Renaissance der griechischen Medizin früh ein Kanon von aktuellen Zeugen und Autoritäten herausbildete oder – und dies erscheint naheliegender – dass Heresbach die Rede des Leipziger Kollegen als Steinbruch verwendete (15v).

Besondere Aufmerksamkeit widmet Heresbach der Rechtswissenschaft (15v–21v), hatte er doch selbst vor seiner Professur in Freiburg Jura in Orléans und Paris studiert, tat dies auch in Freiburg und sollte dieses Studium auch nach 1522 in Ferrara wiederaufnehmen. Gegen die Auffassung von der Nutzlosigkeit griechischer Bildung für die Jurisprudenz verweist er auf die griechische Kompetenz der römischen Juristen, auf griechische Formulierungen in römischen Rechtstexten und auf Rechtsregeln und Rechtsbeispielen, die sogar aus der griechischen Poesie, Epik, Rhetorik und Philosophie genommen sind. Auch hier kann Heresbach ein eigenes Erlebnis zur Beglaubigung beitragen, da zum Thema Schenkung eine Stelle aus der Odyssee erstmals von ihm richtig übersetzt und interpretiert worden sei, die dann der berühmte Jurist Cantiuncula seinem Buchexemplar entnommen habe, wodurch sie dann in die juristische Literatur gelangt sei (17v).[27] Andererseits sei es durch Fehlübersetzungen auch zu irrtümlichen Gesetzesinterpretationen gekommen, was nur die Griechischkundigen durchschauen könnten (19r). Dazu zählen Budé und Alciato, die solche Irrtümer etwa eines Accursio berichtigten (20v). Von seiner eigenen Beschäftigung mit originalen griechischen Rechtstexten berichtet Heresbach, dass er in Venedig die Bibliothek Bessarions besichtigte und dort Exzerpte anfertigte (21v).[28]

Die Theologie stellt in der Disziplinenpyramide den Höhepunkt dar und kommt deshalb in der Antrittsrede zum glanzvollen Abschluss (21v–25v). Das Neue Testament als das ehrwürdigste Buch der Welt und auch die wichtigsten Theologen wie Basilius, Chrysostomos, Gregor von Nazianz bis hin zu Athanasius und Epiphanius sind ohne griechische Sprachkenntnis nicht verständlich. Die *Vulgata* hingegen ist voller Irrtümer und deshalb keine verlässliche Glaubensbasis (21v–22v). Hier würdigt der junge Professor die editorische Arbeit des Erasmus als Werk von allergrößtem Nutzen für die Kirche; auf seine und die Kommentare von Lorenzo Valla wird der verwiesen, der noch weitere Irrtümer, als Heresbach zitiert, kennenlernen will (23r–24v). Der Redner ist von der Gewissheit erfüllt, dass die Wiederentdeckung der originalen Texte zum Ausbruch des Lichtes des Evangeliums führt, fernab von der Dunkelheit der Sophisten und Mönche (25r). Im Schlussteil wendet sich Heresbach gegen die alte scholastische Wissenschaft, die ohne Griechischkenntnisse ausgekommen sei und diese sogar scharf attackiert habe, und berichtet erschüttert von einem Prediger, der ein Buch in seiner Hand, das Neue Testament, als voller Gift und Stacheln vorgestellt habe (26r–v). Die Polemik gegen die griechische Sprache als vermeintliche Trägerin von Häresien bedeute ein Vergehen gegen den Heiligen Geist als Spender der Sprache. Dann müssten auch zahlreiche Päpste, Konzilien und Kirchenväter, ja sogar Paulus wegen ihrer Hochschätzung für die griechische Sprache der Häresie angeklagt werden (27r–v). Sollte es zu Irrtümern gekommen sein, dann liegt dies nicht an der Sprache, sondern an denen, die sie missbräuchlich verwenden (29r). Für Heresbach ist Guillaume Budé der gebildete und wortgewaltige Meister der beiden Sprachen Griechisch und Latein (30r), doch ist das Griechischlernen für jeden eine lohnende

---

[27] Zu Claudius Cantiuncula (1494/95–1549) vgl. Burmeister (2011).

[28] Zur Bibliothek von Kardinal Bessarion, berühmt v. a. wegen ihrer vielen griechischen Manuskripte vgl. z. B. Märtl *et al.* (2013).

Mühe, wie sie Augustinus noch im Alter auf sich nahm oder in der Gegenwart der Bischof von Rochester [sc. John Fisher]. Abschreckendes Beispiel sei hingegen ein bekannter Pariser Theologe, der gestand, noch niemals das Neue Testament gelesen zu haben, sondern nur die Teile, die in der Messliturgie vorkommen (30v–31r).

Heresbach beließ es nicht bei einer Laudatio auf die Griechischstudien, sondern beförderte diese z. B. durch eine Chrestomathie, die im gleichen Jahr 1521 unter dem Titel *Scriptores aliquot gnomici* in Basel erschien[29], und durch Ausgaben von Herodot, Thukydides und Strabo samt Übersetzung.[30]

Tübingen: Johannes Reuchlin (Wintersemester 1521/22)

Reuchlin, der am Beginn der Griechischstudien in Ingolstadt steht, wurde nach seiner nur ein Jahr dauernden Tätigkeit an der bayerischen Landesuniversität auch zum Begründer der Griechischstudien in Tübingen. Im April 1521 kehrte er vor der Pest flüchtend nach Württemberg zurück, las im Wintersemester an der Universität Tübingen über die *Erotemata* von Manuel Chrysoloras und bereitete für das kommende Sommersemester 1522 Aischines und Demosthenes vor. Von seinen Vorhaben berichtete er in Briefen, doch hielt er auch in Tübingen keine programmatische Antrittsvorlesung. Reuchlins Tübinger Lehrtätigkeit war nur von kurzer Dauer, da er bereits am 30. Juni 1522 starb. Ihn ersetzte wenige Wochen später der Engländer Robert Wakefield, der aber nur ein Jahr blieb. Den Griechischunterricht übernahm von 1523 bis 1526 (und 1533–1535) Caspar Churrer (oder Kurrer), der insbesondere als Erstherausgeber der Annalen Lamperts von Hersfeld bekannt ist (Edition von 1525), der aber auch als Schüler Melanchthons in Tübingen das Titelblatt von dessen erster Rede *De artibus liberalibus*, gedruckt in Hagenau im Juli 1518, mit einem griechischen Distichon schmückte.[31]

---

[29] Hieronymus (1992, Nr. 35).

[30] Zur weiteren Entwicklung der Griechischstudien im 16. Jahrhundert an der Universität Freiburg vgl. Schreiber (1859, 193–211 [v. a. zu Johannes Hartung]).

[31] Vgl. Claus (2014), Nr. 1518.6. Zu Churrer MBW 11, 285 f. Zu Reuchlins Verhältnis zur Universität Tübingen vgl. Lorenz (2009) und Lorenz (2013). Überliefert ist für Reuchlins Lehrtätigkeit 1521/22 nur eine Vorlesungsankündigung zu einer Hebräisch-Vorlesung, eigenhändig geschrieben am 20.2.1522, also kurz vor seinem Tod, mit der Reuchlin, der sich als *hebraicae linguae praeceptor* vorstellt, zu einer Ecclesiastes-Vorlesung einlädt, ediert in Reuchlin (2013, 424 f.). Zu Wakefield, der später in Cambridge Hebräisch lehrte, und Churrer vgl. Lorenz (2012, 27–29); ab 1535 war Joachim Camerarius Gräzist in Tübingen, vgl. Lorenz (2012, 47 f. u. ö.).

Heidelberg: Simon Grynaeus (1524)

Wie hartnäckig sich in Deutschland noch um 1500 Universitäten gegen die Institutionalisierung der Griechischstudien wehrten, belegt das Beispiel Heidelberg: Hier bemühte sich Kurfürst Philipp von der Pfalz, 1498 den Griechischunterricht an seiner Landesuniversität zu etablieren. Der jüngere Bruder von Johannes Reuchlin, Dionysius Reuchlin, sollte diese Aufgabe übernehmen. Doch Philipps Ersuchen an die Universität, einen Raum für den Griechischunterricht zur Verfügung zu stellen, wurde von der Artistenfakultät torpediert, da Dionysius Reuchlin sein Magisterexamen nicht nachgewiesen und nicht disputiert habe. Magister war Reuchlin allerdings vier Jahre zuvor in Tübingen geworden, so dass der Widerstand der Fakultät ganz offensichtlich dem Griechischunterricht galt, den sie auch zu verhindern wusste, da sie den strittigen Raum dann Jakob Wimpfeling als spezielles Privileg zusprach.[32] Ob Johannes Brenz als Griechischprofessor bezeichnet werden kann, nur weil er im Juni 1521 in den Universitätsakten als *interpres litteraturae Latinae, Graecae ac Hebraicae* vorkommt, erscheint fraglich, da keine Angaben zu einer Vorlesungstätigkeit überliefert sind.[33] So kommt der Titel des ersten ordentlichen Professors für griechische Sprache Simon Grynaeus zu, der ab Januar 1524 bis zu seinem Weggang Ende des Wintersemesters 1528/29 an der Universität Heidelberg Griechisch lehrte. Aus dieser Zeit sind allerdings keine Publikationen aus seiner Feder bekannt.[34] Zwei kurze Gastspiele auf der Heidelberger Griechischlektur schließen sich an, denn sowohl Johannes Sinapius, der in einer *Defensio eloquentiae* die Notwendigkeit des Sprachenstudiums für die Theologie wie auch für alle anderen Wissenschaften ausführlich begründete, als auch Johannes Werner Themar blieben nur jeweils zwei Jahre. Die 1520er Jahre waren an der Heidelberger Universität noch sehr von antihumanistischen Auseinandersetzungen geprägt.[35] 1533 wurde der Melanchthonschüler Jakob Micyllus berufen, dessen Bewerbung zunächst aus konfessionellen Gründen abgelehnt und erst nach seiner Distanzierung von der *lutterischen sect* akzeptiert wurde. Micyllus war aus Frankfurt am Main

---

[32] Drüll (2002, 125 f.).

[33] Drüll (2002, 51–53).

[34] Zu Grynaeus Drüll (2002, 190 f.) und MBW 12, 192 f.

[35] Zu Sinapius (1505–1560) vgl. Flood (2016). Ausführlich Flood & Shaw (1997, auf S. 264–273 Abdruck der Übersetzung des Sinapius von Lukians *Podagra*). Zu den Heidelberger Debatten um den Wert humanistischer Studien Flood (2003). Einen Überblick über die Griechischstudien in Heidelberg bietet Holzberg (1987).

gekommen, wo er die örtliche Gelehrtenschule leitete, und ging dorthin 1537 nach seiner Heidelberger Lehrtätigkeit auch wieder zurück. 1547 wurde er erneut auf die Griechischprofessur in Heidelberg berufen und vermochte als anerkannte Autorität 1551 die Statuten der Artistenfakultät im humanistischen Sinne zu reformieren.[36]

Marburg: Johannes Lonicerus (1527) mit Lobrede auf die griechische Literatur (nach 1527)

Als würde es eines lebensgeschichtlichen Belegs bedürfen, dass die Reformation besonders förderlich für die kontinuierliche Pflege der Griechischstudien war: An der 1527 gegründeten ersten protestantischen Universität bestand von Beginn an eine Griechischprofessur, die Johannes Lonicerus (1499–1569) inne hatte: 42 Jahre lang![37] Der Wittenberger Magister erhielt seine Marburger Stelle wohl durch Vermittlung Melanchthons, dem Lonicerus z. B. 1525 seine in Straßburg erschienene Homerausgabe gewidmet hatte und dessen naturtheologische Gedanken in den Werken des Schülers bis in die Formulierungen vorkommen. Er lehrte daneben aber auch Hebräisch (1536–1545) und Theologie (1554–1569) und konnte damit sein Einkommen entscheidend erhöhen. Lonicerus reiht sich mit einem *Encomium Graecae literaturae* in die Schar der Verteidiger und Lobredner des Griechischen ein. Die Rede ist in einem Basler Sammelband des Lonicerus abgedruckt, der 1536 erschien und als Haupttitel eine *Artis dicendi methodus* wiedergibt.[38] Das Encomium wendet sich an ein universitäres Publikum (*ornatissimi viri studiosissimi adolescentes*, L2v), ist aber wohl nicht die Antrittsvorlesung von 1527, sondern späteren Datums, da Lonicerus auf Argumente hinweist, die er bereits bei Reden in Freiburg, Straßburg und Marburg vorgetragen habe und denen er jetzt nur noch weniges hinzufügen könne (L3r). Der Einstieg ist ein allgemeines Lob der antiken Literatur, deren Beschäftigung schlaflose Nächte lohnt. Doch, so die rhetorische Frage des Lonicerus, „was magst Du größer, älter und ehrenhafter als die griechische

---

[36] Zu den Übersetzungen und Kommentaren des Micyllus, z. B. von Lukian, Homer und Hygin, und zu seiner Abhandlung über die griechische Tragödie vgl. ausführlich Seidel (2013). Zu Micyllus (1503–1558) vgl. Seidel (2015).

[37] Vgl. Gundlach (1927, 307). Vgl. Bauer (1999, v.a. 389–392). Zu Lonicerus' Marburger Zeit vgl. Reinermann (2018, 212–240 und v.a. 263–270).

[38] Lonicerus (1536, L2v–M3r: *Encomium Graecae literaturae Johannis Loniceri*).

Literatur einschätzen", denn die lateinische ist in allen Gattungen und Autoren eine Schülerin der griechischen (L5r). Sein Redeziel ist, die Größe, den Vorzug und die Notwendigkeit der griechischen Literatur zu entfalten. Dabei greift Lonicerus auch aktuelle Ereignisse auf, da nach ihm die Tragödie der Wiedertäufer nur wegen des Fehlens von Sprachkompetenz stattfinden konnte, was er sogleich selbst mit einer Texterläuterung der griechischen Einsetzungsworte untermauert. So muss das Griechische als die Sprache Christi besonders uns Christen lieb und wert sein (L6v–L7v). Weit mehr als die lateinischen und deutschen Bibeltexte sind die griechischen Quelle der Erkenntnis und notwendiges Mittel gegen Häresien. Dem Hofdienst mit all seinen Reichtümern ist der Dienst an Christus mit Hilfe des Griechischen weit vorzuziehen (L8v). Doch ist das Griechische mit dem Lateinischen eng verknüpft, so dass immer beide gelernt werden sollten (M1v–M2r). Lonicerus nimmt die Redesituation der zu Ende gehenden Wasseruhr als Einstieg in seinen Schlussabschnitt, der die herausragende Rolle der griechischen Literatur bei jeglicher Bildung als Weg zu den Sternen, zur Schrift und zum Wort Gottes betont, auch gegen Kritik am Griechischen durch die Altvordern. Er werde auch weiterhin die *Graeca* lehren, so das Versprechen Lonicers gegenüber seinen Zuhörern (M2v–M3r).

Der Marburger Gräzist zeichnete sich durch zahlreiche Übersetzungen aus, etwa von Pindar, Isokrates, Nikander, Sophokles, Theophylakt, Demosthenes, Aristoteles, Lykurg und als Autor einer griechischen Grammatik (erstmals 1536) sowie griechischer Verse.

Köln: Arnold Halderen (1528)

Die Universität Köln gilt insbesondere durch die Dunkelmännerbriefe als Hochburg einer reaktionären Scholastik, ein Bild, das durch intensive Forschungen tiefe Risse erhalten hat. Auch in Köln gab es um 1510 die ersten privaten Griechischlektionen, etwa von Johannes Caesarius oder von Richard Crocus, der nur kurz in Köln unterrichtete, bis er 1515 der erste ordentlich bestellte Griechischprofessor an der Universität Leipzig werden sollte. In den Matrikeln erscheint Crocus übrigens als *professor literarum grecarum*.[39] Doch die Professur konnte bei den Reformen von 1523 und 1525 nicht fest eingerichtet werden, obgleich die Forderung nach guten Griechischkenntnissen von den drei Gutachtern, Hermann von Neuenahr, Arnold Halderen und Quirin von Wylich,

---

[39] Meuthen (1988, 215).

erhoben wurde, da nach ihrer Ansicht der Niedergang der Studentenzahlen durch das Fehlen humanistischer Lehrangebote bedingt sei. Der Griechischunterricht konnte sich dann allerdings nur außerhalb der Fakultät in den Bursen etablieren. Hier setzte Arnoldus Halderen von Wesel den Anfang, der Mitglied des artistischen Consiliums und seit 1531 Kölner Domherr war und 1527 als hochgelehrter *vir trilinguis* gelobt wurde. Die Initiative ging ausschließlich von der Stadt als Dienstherrin aus, um den Forderungen der Studenten nach humanistischen Vorlesungen nachzukommen und so die wirtschaftlichen Folgen des Studentenrückgangs zu minimieren. Der Unterricht wurde 1528 vom Stadtrat beschlossen, so dass dieses Jahr als Gründungsdatum gelten kann.[40] Arnold Halderen hatte sich zuvor durch Editionen ausgezeichnet, die er 1527 zum *Somnium Scipionis* des Macrobius und zu den sieben Büchern *Saturnalium* publizierte.[41] Erst vier Jahre nach seinem Tod 1534, also 1538, wurde mit Christian Kellenaer wieder ein Gräzist ernannt, doch klagten die Studenten im gleichen Jahr, für die „griechische Lektur keinen Legenten oder Vorleser zu haben".[42] In rascher Folge lösten sich die Inhaber der Griechischlektur ab, Gisbert Longolius, dessen *Lexicon greco-latinum* (Köln 1533) und Erklärungen griechischer Mediziner seine Sprachkompetenz illustrieren, Bernardus Broickbern, der sich durch eine Schlägerei in der Badstube verewigte, Goedifridus Redanus, der als erzbischöflicher Kirchenmann reüssierte, und Gerardus Matthisius, der seit 1544 lehrte und sich wissenschaftlich durch Aristotelesstudien auszeichnete.[43] 1550 gab es durch Ratserlass den erneuten Versuch einer humanistischen Reform, die das Griechische neben Latein und Moralphilosophie zu profilieren suchte, doch konnte auch jetzt die Vorlesungstätigkeit dieser städtischen Professuren nicht in der Artistenschule stattfinden. Mathisius beendete 1557 seine „öffentliche" Griechisch-Professur und wurde Leiter einer Burse.[44]

Die mühselige Entwicklung der Griechischstudien illustriert, dass im Vorurteil gegen die scholastische Wagenburg Köln eine gehörige Portion

---

[40] Vgl. Nauert (2012, 73 f.). Freitäger (1997, 63) spricht hingegen schon für 1523 von einer *greickschen Lectura*, die durch Jakob Sobbe besetzt worden sei. Dieser starb 1528, so dass bei dieser Abfolge Arnold Halderen Nachfolger Sobbes war. Sobbe, ein *Doctor legum*, wurde nach Meuthen (1988, 245) 1523 städtischer Professor und Orator; sein Lehrgebiet beschreibt Nauert (1991, 60) als Rhetorikprofessur: „to teach rhetoric by lecturing on authors selected for excellence of Latin style".

[41] Vgl. Schmitz (1991, 96 f.).

[42] Zitiert nach Meuthen (1988, 249).

[43] Vgl. Meuthen (1988, 249–251). Zu Longolius Freitäger (1997).

[44] Vgl. Meuthen (1988, 286).

Wahrheit enthalten ist. Denn die Universität Köln war ganz offensichtlich nicht willens, ein humanistisches Curriculum zu konzipieren und umzusetzen, in dem das Griechischstudium seinen fest institutionalisierten Platz innerhalb der Artistischen Fakultät bekam.[45]

Greifswald: Petrus Vincentius (Wintersemester 1543/44)

In der Literatur wird für die Universität Greifswald das Jahr 1521 als Beginn der Griechischprofessur genannt. Die Quelle dafür ist das Dekanatsbuch der Philosophischen Fakultät, in dem zum Sommersemester 1521 der Dekan Faustinus Blenno aus Pyritz mit einem wahrhaft eindrucksvollen Vorlesungsprogramm eingeführt wird: Cicero *De officiis*, Albertus Magnus „Naturphilosophie", Sallust *Bellum Jugurtinum*, Lorenzo Valla „Dialektik", Vergil *Georgica*, Valerius Maximus *Exempla*, Cicero *Cato maior*, Erasmus *Ars epistolandi* und *Elementale introductorium in litteras graecas*. Darin spiegelt sich weniger die enzyklopädische Kompetenz des Dekans, aus dessen Feder sich im Übrigen kein wissenschaftliches Werk erhalten hat, wider als vielmehr die desolate Lage der Universität, der die Studenten und Professoren wegliefen, bis 1524 ihr kompletter Zusammenbruch eintrat. Um eine profunde originalsprachliche Beschäftigung mit griechischen Texten wird es sich also bei dieser Einführungsvorlesung nicht gehandelt haben, wenn sie denn überhaupt stattfand und es sich nicht vielmehr um eine Ankündigung geplanter Vorlesungsthemen handelt, die mangels Lehrpersonal nicht realisiert wurden. Aus dem zweiten Dekanat des Faustinus Blenno, Wintersemester 1522/23, ist wiederum eine stattliche Liste an Vorlesungen überliefert, doch fehlt hier jeglicher Verweis auf griechische Autoren oder Themen.[46]

Griechischunterricht ist demnach erst nach der protestantischen Neugründung der Universität 1539, nachdem ab 1525 nur am Paedagogium unterrichtet wurde, vorstellbar und beginnt mit dem Amtsantritt von Petrus Vincentius im Wintersemester 1543/44, der übrigens angesichts der noch geringen Zahl an artistischen Dozenten wenige Tage nach seiner Ankunft in Greifswald sogleich

---

[45] Zur katholischen Polemik gegen die *Graeca* vgl. Saladin (2000, 395 f.: *Qui graecizabant, lutheranizabant* […]).

[46] Thümmel (2008b, 148 [Sommersemester 1521] und 151 [Wintersemester 1522/23]). Vgl. Thümmel (2008a, 25) und Bauch (1896, 190), der die zahlreichen Vorlesungstitel nicht Blenno zuweist, aber in Blenno einen Humanisten und ohne nähere Anhaltspunkte vielleicht sogar einen Gräzisten vermutet.

das Dekanat übernehmen musste.[47] In der Liste der Professoren erscheint er 1543/44 als *arcium et philosophiae magister*, im Sommersemester 1544 als *artium, philosophiae magister publicusque professor*, im anschließenden Wintersemester als *artium et philosophiae magister*, im Wintersemester 1545/46 zu seinem Rektorat als *linguae Graecae professor ordinarius* und im Sommersemester 1546 ausführlich als *artium liberalium et philosophiae magister, bonarum literarum professor publicus et linguae graecae ordinarius*.[48] Der Beginn der Institutionalisierung der Gräzistik an der Universität Greifswald ist also auf das Wintersemester 1543/44 mit dem Lehrbeginn des Petrus Vincentius zu datieren. Die nachhaltige Festlegung wird dann mit den Statuten von 1545 vollzogen, in deren Gefolge Vincentius seinen Titel „ordentlicher Griechischprofessor" erhält und in denen über die engere Gräzistik hinaus die griechische Fachliteratur eine herausgehobene Bedeutung erhält und hier wie in zahlreichen anderen Fächern Melanchthon zur inspirierenden Autorität avanciert.[49]

Die Universität Greifswald zeigt sich in jenen Jahren als eindrucksvoller Beleg für die positiven wie negativen Einflüsse der Reformation auf die Universitäten. Diese konnten im Spätmittelalter in ganz Deutschland ständig wachsende Immatrikulationszahlen verzeichnen, bis ab 1521 ein starker Einbruch auf nur noch ein Viertel der bisherigen Neueinschreibungen eintrat. Die Ursache hierfür waren nicht (nur) wie bisher Kriege, Epidemien oder Missernten, sondern die Bildungskrise war (auch) Folge der Reformation, wie allein schon ihr Beginn nahe legt, denn die ersten starken Frequenzrückgänge entstanden in den mitteldeutschen Reformationslanden, nämlich in Wittenberg, Erfurt und Frankfurt/Oder. Binnen kurzem erreichte die Krise alle Universitäten: Leipzig, Rostock, Greifswald, Köln, Basel und Heidelberg, 1524 auch die weiteren Universitäten im Süden: Freiburg, Tübingen, Ingolstadt und Wien. Luthers Reformation griff das alte Universitätssystem mit zweifacher Stoßrichtung an: Die Universität wurde v. a. als Ausbildungsstätte des Klerus und damit als Teil der Papstkirche angesehen. Der Abbruch des Pfründenwesens beraubte das Universitätsstudium seiner beruflich-ökonomischen Attraktivität. Zugleich schien Luthers anti-aristotelische Polemik dem Unterricht die Grundlage zu nehmen, so dass die Artistischen Fakultäten erheblich an Attraktivität einbüßten. Für die Klagen über den Untergang der Wissenschaften soll pars pro toto das

---

[47] So schildert es Vincentius selbst im Dekanatsbuch (Thümmel 2008b, 157 f.). Zu Vincentius vgl. Freytag (2004) und Scheible (2010, 371 f.).

[48] Friedländer (1893, 207–214).

[49] Vgl. Thümmel (2008a, 41).

berühmte Dictum des Erasmus in einem Brief an Willibald Pirckheimer aus dem Jahr 1528 stehen: *Ubicunque regnat Luteranismus, ibi litterarum est interitus*. Diese Krise aber machte die Universitäten, insbesondere die protestantischen, auf Dauer stärker als zuvor. Denn hier setzte das breitgefächerte Wissenschafts- und Bildungsprogramm Philipp Melanchthons an, der unter den Vorzeichen eines versöhnten Miteinanders von *pietas* und *eruditio* neue Lehrbücher verfasste, neue Studienordnungen konzipierte und eine ganze Generation von wiederum einflussreichen Universitäts- und Schullehrern ausbildete. Die Universität Greifswald steht exemplarisch auch für diesen Neubeginn, da sie mit Petrus Vincentius einen Schüler Melanchthons als Griechischprofessor bekam und programmatisch die Bücher Melanchthons als Unterrichtsgrundlage festschrieb.[50]

Die Ausführungen der Greifswalder Statuten von 1545 zur Griechischprofessur bieten gleichzeitig einen Einblick in die Schwierigkeiten des Faches, denn sein Nutzen wird eher defensiv mit seinem Beitrag zum Verständnis der lateinischen Sprache formuliert, fast entschuldigend klingt der Hinweis auf die große Mühe, die mit dem Griechischstudium verbunden sei, die sich aber gleichwohl lohne:

> Die lateinische Sprache ist mit der griechischen nach dem Zeugnis Ciceros durch ein ewiges Band verbunden, so sehr, dass er glaubt, sie könnten beide besser zugleich als getrennt voneinander gelernt werden.

Zum Studium der Sprache werden dann die Grammatik Melanchthons, die ins Lateinische übersetzte von Theodor Gaza und die von Johannes Varennius empfohlen, da sie die Gemeinsamkeiten mit dem Latein hervorheben und dadurch das Verständnis erleichtern. Die Schwierigkeiten der Konjugationen und Deklinationen würden sich als weniger gravierend erweisen, wenn das Prinzip einmal erkannt sei und das Studium durch exemplarische Texte guter Autoren, die zudem Gottesfurcht und rechtschaffenen Lebenswandel befördern, unterstützt würden. Als Anfängerlektüre werden die Paulusbriefe, die *Tabula Cebetis*, Lukian, Plutarch und ganz besonders Hesiods *Werke und Tage* vorgeschlagen, danach Homer, Sophokles, Euripides, Aristophanes und Theokrit.[51]

Im Wintersemester 1547/48 tritt bereits ein neuer Griechischprofessor in Greifswald an, nämlich Georg Cracow, *ingenuarum artium et philosophiae magister*,

---

[50] Zur universitären Frequenzkrise in Deutschland im 16. Jahrhundert und ihren Gründen vgl. ausführlich Asche (2001) und Immenhauser (2003).

[51] Alvermann & Spieß (2011, 122 f.).

professor ordinarius mathematices et graecae linguae[52], während Vincentius nun als *professor Homeri et Virgilii* tituliert und im Sommersemester 1549 die Universität verlässt, wie übrigens auch Cracow.[53] Auch wenn Vincentius fast sechs Jahre an der Universität Greifswald wirkte, so erscheint das Fehlen jeglicher literarischer Ergebnisse – außer einigen Versen in den Matrikeln – umso überraschender, wenn man sein überliefertes reichhaltiges Werk an seinen späteren Wirkungsorten wie Lübeck, Wittenberg und Görlitz betrachtet. Das Fehlen von Antrittsvorlesungen oder anderen programmatischen Stellungnahmen zum Nutzen der griechischen Sprache kann auch einen medientechnologischen Grund haben: In Greifswald wurde erst 1581 eine Buchdruckerei gegründet, so dass auch fleißige Professoren vorher keine Möglichkeit des Publizierens besaßen.[54]

Königsberg: Abraham Culvensis (1544)

Nach dem Vorbild der Leucorea wurde 1544 als zweite protestantische Universität (nach Marburg) die Universität Königsberg gegründet.[55] Melanchthons Einfluss zeigte sich nicht zuletzt darin, dass sein Schüler und Schwiegersohn Georg Sabinus als erster Rektor eingesetzt wurde. Statuten sind aus den Jahren 1546 und 1554 überliefert, die für die Philosophische Fakultät einen *lector Graecus* vorsehen, dessen Vorlesungspensum mit Grammatik und den Autoren Homer, Hesiod, Euripides, Sophokles, Theokrit sowie einigen Reden des Demosthenes, „irgendetwas aus den griechischen Historikern" und der aristotelischen Ethik festgelegt war. So wurde der Griechischprofessur neben den einschlägigen Autoren auch die Unterweisung in Ethik zugewiesen.[56] Im Gründungsjahr war der erste Gräzist der Litauer Abraham Culvensis (oder Abraomas Kulvietis), der neben

---

[52] Friedländer (1893, 217, 220).

[53] Friedländer (1893, 222, 224).

[54] Vgl. Reske (2015, 312 ff.). In seiner Dissertation illustriert Wedow (2013) das Fehlen Greifswalder Druckerzeugnisse im 16. Jahrhundert anhand zahlreicher Statistiken (Messkataloge etc.). In Wittenberg hingegen war die Drucklegung von Universitätsreden Usus, so dass Vincentius zu Beginn seiner Rhetorik-Professur 1557 seine Antrittsvorlesung *De cura recte loquendi, recitata in initio praelectionis Wittebergae* veröffentlichen konnte.

[55] In der Forschungsübersicht von Manfred Komorowski wird der Griechischunterricht nur in seiner propädeutischen Funktion für die Theologische Fakultät kurz erwähnt, aber ohne jegliche Angaben zu Personen oder Publikationen, nur der Hinweis, dass die Reden und Dissertationen bislang nicht erforscht sind, vgl. Komorowski (2008, 20).

[56] Vgl. Arnoldt (1746,1, 175 f. und 126 f.). Vgl. Asche (2001, 75).

Krakau und Löwen auch in Wittenberg studiert, dort die lutherische Theologie und melanchthonische Philologie kennengelernt und bei Melanchthon z. B. den griechischen Astronomen Ptolemaios gehört hatte. Er amtierte zuvor als Rektor des Königsberger Gymnasiums und konnte sein universitäres Amt nur ein Jahr ausfüllen, da er bereits 1545 mit ungefähr 35 Jahren starb. Ob Melchior Isinder, den der Herzog auf Empfehlung Melanchthons berufen hatte, ebenfalls Griechisch unterrichtete, ist unklar. [57]

Jena: Michael Neander (1551)

Die 1548 gegründete Hohe Schule zu Jena, wie Marburg und Königsberg eine dezidiert protestantische Gründung, organisierte ihren Lehrbetrieb nach dem Vorbild der Wittenberger Universität und besaß bereits eine Professorenschaft in allen Fachgebieten, bevor sie 1557 das kaiserliche Universitätsprivileg erhielt. Als erster Professor der Beredsamkeit deckte Johannes Stigel anfänglich das artistische Themenfeld ab, doch las auch sein theologischer Kollege Victorin Strigel über griechische und römische Autoren.[58] 1551 erhielt Michael Neander, 1529 im böhmischen Joachimsthal geboren und nicht identisch mit dem gleichnamigen und vielfältig gräzistisch ausgewiesenen Rektor der Klosterschule Ilfeld, eine Professur für Griechisch und Mathematik/Astronomie. Seine Interessen konzentrierten sich auf Mathematik, Astronomie und Medizin, so dass er ab 1560 als Medizinprofessor in Jena wirkte, doch ist auch ein griechisches astrologisches Gedicht überliefert, das den ehemaligen Wittenberger Studenten Neander als Schüler Melanchthons ausweist.[59] In den ersten Statuten der Philosophischen Fakultät von 1558 wird nach dem Wittenberger Vorbild Melanchthons das Sprachstudium zur Grundlage aller Wissenschaften erklärt und für das Griechische ein Lektürekanon aus Hesiod, Homer, Sophokles, Euripides, Theokrit, Demosthenes, Lykurg, Aischines und Isokrates festgelegt. Nach Neander ist als nächster Griechischdozent Friedrich Pensold namhaft, der ab 1563 als Professor der griechischen Sprache und der Physik wirkte, nachdem

---

[57] Zu Culvensis MBW 11, 324 f. und Birziska (1947). Vgl. auch Pociute (2017, 554–557). Lawrynowicz (1999, 53 f.) nennt Culvensis als ersten Königsberger Griechischprofessor, von Selle (1956, 16) Isinder. Zu Isinder MBW 12, 355.

[58] Zu den Anfängen der Universität Jena Asche (2009).

[59] Vgl. Weißmann (2009, 181–187). Zu Strigels griechischen Vorlesungen, zu Neander und zu den im Folgenden zitierten Statuten von 1558 vgl. auch die Hinweise bei Gehrt (2015).

er zuvor (ab 1556) ebenfalls Griechischprofessor in Greifswald war. Als Anhänger Melanchthons musste er 1569 unter dem Druck der Gnesiolutheraner Jena verlassen, wohin er aber 1576 zurückkehren und bis 1580 wiederum als Gräzist tätig sein konnte.[60]

Würzburg: Conrad Dinner (1561)

Nachdem die Universität Würzburg 1402 gegründet wurde, indessen aber schon nach nur wenigen Jahren vor 1420 ihren Lehrbetrieb wegen finanzieller Schwierigkeiten einstellen musste, kam es auf Betreiben des Fürstbischofs Julius Echter von Mespelbrunn 1575 zu einer Wiederbegründung der dann 1582 feierlich eröffneten Universität unter jesuitischer Mitwirkung, also mit programmatisch gegenreformatorischer Ausrichtung. Als Vorläuferinstitution der Universität gilt das „Paedagogium" oder „Gymnasium illustre", das auch nach Gründung der Universität eng mit der Philosophischen Fakultät verbunden war und Ort des Sprachunterrichts blieb.[61] In einem Lektionskatalog von 1604 werden die Vorlesungsgegenstände aller Professoren der vier Fakultäten aufgelistet; in der Philosophischen Fakultät kommen dabei nur die Fächer Metaphysik, Physik, Logik sowie Ethik/Mathematik vor, so dass der Sprachunterricht ganz offensichtlich im Paedagogium organisiert war.[62] Es gab in Würzburg Überlegungen, den bekannten Gräzisten Johannes Hartung aus Freiburg / Brsg. nach Würzburg zu holen, doch dieser empfahl seine beiden Schüler Conrad Dinner und Kaspar Stüblin. Beide kamen im April 1561 an ihrem neuen Wirkungsort an, doch sollte ihre Tätigkeit bereits zwei Jahre später beendet sein, da in Folge der Pest Stüblin starb und Dinner nach Italien aufbrach. Dinner brachte sehr gute Griechisch-Kenntnisse mit, dichtete auch *graece*, so dass die Griechischstudien in Würzburg mit ihm einen respektablen Start hatten, wenn auch nur im präuniversitären Propädeutikum.[63]

---

[60] Zu Pensold vgl. Schmidt (1983, 50).

[61] Zur Geschichte und zum Profil des Würzburger Gymnasiums vgl. Süß (2007, 35–42). Die Schüler der beiden Abschlussklassen waren an der Philosophischen Fakultät immatrikuliert, was die enge institutionelle Verschränkung von Gymnasium und Universität illustriert.

[62] von Wegele (1882, 2, 225 f.).

[63] Vgl. Schubert (1973).

Rostock: Johannes Posselius (Wintersemester 1564/65) mit Rede über den Latein- und Griechischunterricht (vor 1589)

Die Universität Rostock erlebte zahlreiche Anläufe, bis mit der Errichtung eines Lehrstuhls das Griechischstudium einen festen institutionellen Platz erhielt. Nach einem frühen Beginn durch Nikolaus Marschalk, der von 1510 bis 1525 als Rechtsprofessor fungierte, gleichzeitig eine Druckerei mit griechischem Typensatz betrieb und auch Vorlesungen zur griechischen Antike, aber auf der Grundlage lateinischer Übersetzungen, anbot, kam 1526 Janus Cornarius an die mecklenburgische Landesuniversität und las an der Medizinischen Fakultät über die Aphorismen des Hippokrates mit einer griechischen Textgrundlage. Eine dauerhafte Einrichtung einer artistischen Griechischprofessur war damit nicht verbunden, ganz im Gegenteil, denn die Universität erlebte in den 1530er und 1540er Jahren einen massiven Niedergang, der auch durch Reformversuche von Christoph Hegendorff (1540) und Gisbert Longolius (1543) nicht dauerhaft aufgehalten werden konnte. Dem seit 1551 in Rostock wirkenden Melanchthonschüler David Chytraeus ist die Reorganisation der Universität zu verdanken, die auch eine feste Institutionalisierung des Griechischstudiums mit sich brachte. Johannes Posselius lehrte, so die Angabe in der Leichenrede auf ihn, seit dem Wintersemester 1553/54 öffentlich Griechisch, doch erhielt seine Tätigkeit erst mit der neuen Ordnung der Artistenfakultät vom 17. Oktober 1564 die offizielle Bezeichnung *Professor Graecae Linguae*.[64] Sein gräzistisches Werk ist vielfältig und umfasst u. a. lateinisch-griechische Schülergespräche (1588), eine *Syntaxis Graeca* (1560) und eine *Calligraphia Oratoria Linguae Graecae* (1584), die ihren Bildungszweck, nämlich mit Hilfe antiker Stilvorbilder die eigene schriftliche und mündliche (!) Sprachkompetenz im Griechischen zu perfektionieren, schon im Titel trägt: *ad proprietatem, elegantiam et copiam Graeci sermonis parandam utilissima*. Der Wert der Griechischstudien, so Posselius im Vorwort, ergibt sich aus ihrer Bedeutung für eine gereinigte Theologie und für das umfassende Verständnis von Recht, Medizin und aller artistischen Disziplinen, so dass den Verantwortlichen im Staat die wichtige Aufgabe zufällt, durch die Förderung der *Graeca* das Gemeinwesen vor der Barbarei zu bewahren.[65]

Seine pädagogischen Ziele und Methoden entwickelte Posselius in der Rede *De ratione discendae ac docendae linguae latinae et graecae*, die in einer Sammlung von acht Reden 1589 in Frankfurt am Main erschien, indessen nicht

---

[64] Vgl. ausführlich Rhein (1996). Zu Posselius (1528–1591) vgl. Elsmann (2016).

[65] Zur *Calligraphia,* Johnson (2006, 196–199).

näher datiert ist. Die Anrede an die *clarissimi viri et studiosi iuvenes* legt einen universitären Anlass nahe, wie auch der Titel der Redensammlung: *Orationes octo habitae in publicis congressibus Academiae Rostochiensis*. Langjährige eigene Erfahrung und Zeugnisse gebildeter Männer nennt er als Grundlage seiner Ausführungen. Der erste Teil behandelt den Unterricht in Latein, der im 6. oder 7. Lebensjahr beginnen soll, das intensive Einüben der Grammatikregeln erfordert, sprachlich umfassend gebildete und strenge Lehrer verlangt, Schreib- und Übersetzungsübungen umfasst, wobei nicht der Stil des Lehrers, sondern der Ciceros das Vorbild abgeben soll – die Warnung vor einem allzu freien, feste Regeln ablehnenden Gebrauch der klassischen Sprachen gehört zur Kritik des Posselius am zeitgenössischen Wissenschafts- und Bildungsbetrieb – und im eigenständigen *Latine loqui et scribere* münden soll. Der zweite Teil widmet sich dem Erlernen der griechischen Sprache; nach der Grammatik sollen die Schüler mit Texten von Sokrates, Plutarch, Lukian und Aesop üben und, da Abwechslung Freude bringe, noch Ps.-Pythagoras, Ps.-Phokylides, Hesiod und Homer hinzunehmen, außerdem Übersetzungen nach den Stilvorbildern Isokrates und Demosthenes anfertigen, z. B. die Briefe Ciceros ins Griechische übertragen, und durch eifriges Studieren auch das Griechisch-Sprechen erlernen. Denn keine Sprache sei angenehmer und bringe mehr Vergnügen mit sich. Beide Sprachen, Latein und Griechisch, sollten gemeinsam studiert werden, da sie voneinander abhängen wie auch Cicero viel von Platon übernommen habe. Eine solche Sprachbildung ertüchtige junge Menschen zum Nutzen von Kirche und Staat.[66]

Mainz: Petrus Tyraeus (1565)

An der Universität Mainz haben sich handschriftliche Statuten der Artistenfakultät von 1535 erhalten. Der Lektionsplan beginnt mit der Selbstverpflichtung, dass die Fakultät mit Eifer darauf aus sei, ihre Studenten durch die besten Autoren der beiden Sprachen zu bilden, an der Spitze Aristoteles. Doch der eigentliche griechische Sprachunterricht musste sich im Gegensatz zu anderen Fächern, bei denen z. B. die Lehrtexte mitgeteilt wurden, mit einer lapidaren Angabe begnügen: *Tertia hora Grecis literis vacabit.*[67] Mehr ist zur universitären Situation des Griechischunterrichts nicht überliefert, auch wenn es in Mainz wie allerorten Humanisten gab, an ihrer Spitze Dietrich Gresemund, der aber niemals eine

---

[66] Posselius (1589, 135–153).

[67] Vgl. Steiner (1989, 562).

Position an der Universität bekleidete. Vermutet wird als erster Griechischlehrer Nikolaus Fabri aus Karbach, dessen Griechischunterricht bereits 1518 gelobt wird, doch scheint sich dieser außerhalb institutionalisierter Lehrpläne und -strukturen abgespielt zu haben.[68]

Wie gering der Stellenwert des Griechischen war, lässt sich auch daran erkennen, dass „der Besuch der lectio greca weder für das Baccalaureat- noch für das Magister-Examen zu den Zulassungsvoraussetzungen [gehörte]".[69] Die Universität erlebte in den ersten beiden Jahrzehnten des 16. Jahrhunderts einen gewissen, bei rund 100 Studenten gleichwohl überschaubaren Aufschwung, der dann durch die Frequenzkrise der 1520er Jahre und v. a. durch die Ablehnung der Reformation und des dadurch provozierten Weggangs zahlreicher Professoren abrupt beendet wurde. Nicht ohne Grund setzen die Statuten von 1535 mit einer Klage über den drohenden Kollaps der Mainzer Gelehrsamkeit ein. Auch in den folgenden Jahren blieb die Lage desolat, verstärkt durch Kriege und Seuchen, die verbliebenen Professoren mussten mehrere Fächer abdecken, so dass der Lehrbetrieb allmählich zum Erliegen kam. Die Wende kam erst durch die Übernahme des Universitätsbetriebs durch die Jesuiten 1562, die mit straffer Organisation und theologischer Orientierung die Universität in erfolgreichere Bahnen führten. Erster Griechischprofessor wurde 1565 Petrus Tyraeus, der zugleich auch die Rhetorik-Professur inne hatte, bis dann ab 1566 Petrus Burgundus zumindest bis 1570 als *Professor Linguae Graecae*, ab 1569 zugleich als Theologieprofessor geführt wird.[70]

Dillingen: Theodorich Sprangius (um 1565)

In Dillingen an der Donau wurde 1551 auf Initiative des Augsburger Bischofs Otto Truchsess von Waldburg eine Universität gegründet, die 1554 ihren Lehrbetrieb aufnahm und 1563 zur ersten genuinen Jesuitenuniversität in Deutschland avancierte. Offenkundig gab es anfänglich an dieser Universität, die in den ersten Jahrzehnten nur aus einer Philosophischen und einer Theologischen Fakultät bestand, keinen gesonderten Griechischunterricht, da die Jesuiten 1565 die Forderung aufstellten, eine Griechischlektion erst dann einzurichten, wenn

---

[68] Zu Nicolaus Fabri von Carbachius oder Nikolaus Karbach („erster namhafter Kenner des Griechischen in Mainz") vgl. Bauch (1907, 81–84).

[69] Steiner (1989, 427).

[70] Vgl. die Liste bei Krafft (1977, 259–350).

sie die volle Finanzierung vom kirchlichen Landesherrn erhielten. Unter dieser
Voraussetzung verpflichtete sich der Jesuitenorden, neben zwei Theologie- und
drei Philosophieprofessoren auch einen Griechisch- und Hebräischprofessor zu
stellen.[71] Erstmals erscheint ein Theodorich Sprangius als *primarius professor
bonarum literarum et linguae graecae*, ohne dass nähere Angaben zu Leben und
Werk mitgeteilt werden.[72] In Dillingen prägte Aristoteles in Inhalt und Struktur
das Vorlesungsprogramm der Philosophischen Fakultät, so dass es nahe lag, in
einer Lizentiatsrede am 6. April 1575, gehalten von Johannes Pontanus, die
Kenntnis der griechischen Originalsprache als unersetzbar für das Verständnis,
ja als Grundlage jedes wissenschaftlichen Handelns zu preisen.[73] Die antiken
Sprachen und die Humaniora wurden in den jesuitisch geprägten Universitäten in
einer eigenen *facultas linguarum* unterrichtet, die dem artistischen Grundstudium
vorgeschaltet war, also eher einem voruniversitären Gymnasium entsprach. Auf
die *facultas philosophiae* folgte das Hauptstudium in der *facultas theologiae*, zu der
in Dillingen erst im 17. und 18. Jahrhundert Rechtswissenschaft und Medizin
hinzukamen.[74]

Helmstedt: Johannes Debelius (1576)

Der Einfluss Melanchthons bei der Entwicklung der griechischen Studien in
Deutschland ist durch seine Fachbücher, durch seine Schüler als Dozenten und
Professoren und durch die von ihm für Wittenberg aufgestellten Studienordnungen
vielfältig präsent. Dies gilt auch für die letzte Universitätsgründung im
Deutschland des 16. Jahrhunderts, für die 1576 gegründete Universität
Helmstedt. Zur Gründungskommission zählten mit Martin Chemnitz und David
Chytraeus zwei bedeutende Melanchthonschüler, für die *Artes superiores* galt als
Zugangsvoraussetzung die genaue Kenntnis von Melanchthons Dialektik und
Rhetorik, im Unterricht waren die Lehrbücher Melanchthons vorgeschrieben, z.
B. für die Lateingrammatik das entsprechende Werk des Wittenbergers, erstmals

---

[71] Rupp & Rüdiger (1999, 15).

[72] Specht (1902, 45).

[73] *In iis autem artibus, quae humanitatem complectuntur, nescire graece est nihil scire, nihil posse
discere: non grammaticus, non poeta, non orator evadet, qui hanc linguam non didicerit.* Vgl. Leinsle
(2014, 11).

[74] Vgl. auch Leinsle (2006, 65): Das Trivium verschwindet aus dem jesuitischen Universitäts-
programm und wird im Gymnasium unterrichtet.

erschienen 1525 und danach in vielen Auflagen und Bearbeitungen, für die Rhetorik seine *Elementa Rhetorices* oder für Geschichte Melanchthons *Chronicon Carionis*. Unter den Professoren des philosophischen Kollegiums war von Beginn an ein Gräzist, dessen Aufgaben die Statuten einen eigenen Abschnitt *De linguae graecae grammatica* widmen: Die griechische Sprache eröffne den Zugang zu allen Wissenschaften, erschließe die Quellen der wahren Gotteslehre und habe so die Reform der Kirche überhaupt erst möglich gemacht. Ihre wissenschaftliche Beschäftigung reiche von den griechischen Flüchtlingen Chysoloras, Gaza oder Chalkondyles über Reuchlin und Erasmus bis hin zu Crocus und Mosellanus, die die Griechischstudien in Sachsen einführten, und v. a. Melanchthon, der mit Fleiß und Erfolg die *studia sapientiae et eloquentiae graecae* in ganz Deutschland etablierte. Dem *graecae linguae doctor* wird ein auf die Ausbildung sprachlicher Kompetenz fokussierter Lektürekanon vorgeschrieben, für die Grammatik die *Institutiones linguae graecae* des Nikolaus Clenardus wegen ihrer didaktischen Kombination aus Regeln, Beispielen und christlichen Lebensweisheiten, danach u. a. Hesiod, einige Reden des Isokrates und Demosthenes und insbesondere Homer, der nach dem Grammatikunterricht in den verbleibenden vier Lektürestunden wegen seiner ethischen Qualitäten immer zwei davon beanspruchen sollte. Zur Lektüre sollte außerdem das Verfassen eigener griechischer Briefe und Gedichte nach den Stilvorbildern Demosthenes und Homer hinzukommen.[75]

Als erster Griechischprofessor amtierte Johannes Debelius, Jenenser Magister, der allerdings bereits nach drei Jahren in seine thüringische Heimat als Superintendent zurückging und später an der Universität Jena als Theologieprofessor wirkte.[76] Offensichtlich war die Griechischprofessur wenig attraktiv, denn auch für ihren nächsten Inhaber, Heinrich Boethius, stellte sie nur eine Zwischenetappe auf der Karriereleiter in die Theologische Fakultät und dann in das Amt des Generalsuperintendenten dar. Von dem zwischen Januar 1586 und November 1593 lehrenden Helmstedter Griechischprofessor Heinrich Papenberg ist immerhin ein griechisches Epitaphium auf einen Kollegen, den Mathematiker Erhard Hofmann, erhalten. Überliefert ist zudem das Teilprotokoll eines Examens von 1587 über Hesiods *Werke und Tage* mit Fragen Papenbergs zu *utilitas, occasio, doctrina* etc. des Gedichts, ein aussagekräftiges Dokument aus

---

[75] Die Statuten des Jahre 1576 sind ediert von Baumgart & Pitz (1963, 127–130: *De graecae linguae grammatica*).

[76] Vgl. Ahrens (2004, 61); Debelius (1540–1610) war Professor der griechischen und lateinischen Sprache.

dem gräzistischen Alltag des 16. Jahrhunderts.[77] Doch von einer Blüte waren die Griechischstudien an der Universität Helmstedt weit entfernt, so dass die Universität den Landesherrn um einen zusätzlichen *graecus professor* bat, der schließlich in Johannes Caselius gefunden wurde. Dieser Schüler Melanchthons und des Camerarius entwickelte seit seinem Antritt als Griechischprofessor am 24. Juni 1590 wie schon zuvor in Rostock eine stupende Produktivität an wissenschaftlichen und literarischen Aktivitäten durch Editionen, Lehrbücher und eigene Dichtungen und führte die *Academia Julia* zu ihrem Höhepunkt.[78]

Epilog

Die deutschen Universitäten waren durchweg in vier Fakultäten organisiert, von denen die Artistische die weitaus größte Anzahl an Studenten verzeichnete, nämlich durchschnittlich 80 Prozent. Mit dem Massenbetrieb verbunden war der geringe soziale Status der hier Lehrenden.[79] Wie auch bei den anderen humanistischen Fächern erfolgte der Griechischunterricht zunächst *extra ordinem*. Die Professionalisierung der Lehre konnte sich hier erst allmählich durchsetzen, indem inhaltlich definierte, besoldete Professuren eingerichtet wurden. Sie ersetzten das in der spätmittelalterlichen Artistenfakultät übliche Regenz-System, d. h. dass die Magister-Scholaren zugleich lernten und lehrten, alle Fächer des artistischen Curriculums unterrichteten und nur durch Hörergebühren honoriert wurden. Vorbildlich für das neue System wurde die Leucorea mit den Bildungsreformen Melanchthons, der 1526 für die Artistenfakultät elf fest besoldete Professuren einrichtete, von denen eine der Gräzistik gewidmet war, und der durch seine Lehrbücher und v. a. durch seine Schüler diese Studien- und Bildungsreform in den lutherischen Territorien etablierte.[80] So passte sich die Artistenfakultät den drei höheren Fakultäten an und wurde wie diese zu einer Ordinarienfakultät mit inhaltlich präzis definierten Professuren. Davon

---

[77] Vgl. Henze (1990, 93–99). Die Prüffragen folgten den Lehranweisungen der Universitätsstatuten und der Hesiodinterpretation Melanchthons. Zu Papenberg (oder Papenberger) vgl. Korhonen (2019, 47, 60).

[78] Zu Caselius (1533–1613) vgl. Sdzuj (2011) und Ahrens (2004, 46f.). Zu den ersten Griechischlehrern vgl. Ahrens (2004, 28f.: Boethius [1551–1622], 173: Papenberg [1558–1606]).

[79] Vgl. Schwinges (2008, 555–561).

[80] Zum Regenz-System vgl. Müller (1999, 152 f.). Zum Vorbild Melanchthon vgl. Hammerstein (2000, 388–401) und Asche (2001, 69 f.). Die Entwicklung zur Fachprofessur beschreibt für die Tübinger Artistenfakultät – mit Belegen auch zu anderen deutschen Universitäten – Lorenz (2012).

profitierte auch der Griechischunterricht, der dauerhaft institutionalisiert wurde. Gleichzeitig kam es zu Organisationsformen, bei denen die *Artes dicendi* in propädeutischen Institutionen, d. h. Gymnasien oder Pädagogien, unterrichtet wurden, vor allem in katholischen Universitäten, in denen sich das Griechischstudium auf das Erlernen der Sprache als Qualifikation für Philosophie und Theologie reduzierte. Hier – im katholischen Bildungskontext – wurde die höhere Stadtschule aufgewertet, die einst – in der Reformation – von Melanchthon 1526 in Nürnberg als neuer Schultyp begründet wurde und die sich auch in den protestantischen Bildungslandschaften als mehrklassiges Gymnasium, das die Artistenfakultät vom Sprachunterricht, allerdings vorrangig vom lateinischen, entlastete, ab Ende des 16. Jahrhunderts durchsetzte.[81]

Der Einfluss des Humanismus im gesamten 16. Jahrhundert war virulent – unabhängig vom konfessionellen Status der jeweiligen Universität. Während in der ersten Hälfte des 16. Jahrhunderts die Griechischstudien von Melanchthon und seinen Schülern geprägt waren, wurde nach 1550 auch in katholischen Universitätsgründungen der Griechischunterricht etabliert, insbesondere im Rahmen der jesuitischen Bildungskonzeption mit ihrer humanistisch orientierten Pädagogik. Griechisch wurde zum transkonfessionellen Bildungsgut und büßte erst im Lauf des 20. Jahrhunderts seine Bedeutung als Ausweis von Gelehrsamkeit ein.[82]

---

[81] Zu Melanchthons Schulgründung vgl. Scheible (2016, 54–60). Die Organisation des Sprachstudiums in einer der Universität vorgeschalteten und mit ihr institutionell eng verschränkten Schule lässt sich übrigens auch bei der 1584 eröffneten Hohen Schule Herborn beobachten. Sie wurde in diesem Beitrag nicht näher vorgestellt, da ihr wegen ihrer konfessionellen, d. h. calvinistischen, Ausrichtung der Status Universität verwehrt wurde. Sie war – auch wegen ihrer überschaubaren Größe – nicht in Fakultäten organisiert; die artistischen Fächer wurden überwiegend in einem „Paedagog" nicht von ordentlichen Professoren, sondern von Praeceptores unterrichtet, vgl. Menk (1981, 143–145, 170–174).

[82] Zum „überkonfessionellen humanistischen Bildungs- und Gelehrtenideal" vgl. Asche (2001).

Quellen und Forschungsliteratur

Literatur vor 1800

Arnoldt, Daniel Heinrich. 1746. *Ausführliche und mit Urkunden versehene Historie der Königsbergischen Universität.* Königsberg (ND Aalen 1994).

Gussubelius, Johannes. 1520. *Oratio […] pro D. Io. Capnione Phorcensi cum in lingua Hebraica et Graeca ludum literarium ex conducto aperiret.* Augsburg. (urn:nbn:de:bvb:12-bsb00015786-4).

Heresbach, Konrad. 1551. *De laudibus Graecarum literarum oratio olim Friburgi in celeberrimo conventu et Doctorum et Procerum habita.* Strassburg. (http://mdz-nbn-reso-eving.de/urn:nbn:de:bvb:12-brb11072860-1).

Mosellanus, Petrus. 1518. *De variorum linguarum cognitione paranda […] Lipsiae in magna eruditorum corona pronunciata.* Leipzig. (http://resolver. staatsbibliothek-berlin.de/SBB001A66200000000).

Lang, Johannes. 1521. *Epistola ad Excellentiss. D. Martinum Margaritanum Erphurdiensis Gymnasii Rectorem pro litteris sacris et seipso.* Erfurt. (http://mdz-nbn-resolving.de/um:nbn:de:bvb:12-bsb10201239-3).

Lonicerus, Johannes. 1536. *Artis dicendi methodus ex optimis utriusque linguae autoribus deprompta.* Basel. (urn:nbn:de:bvb:12-bsb00087229-2).

Posselius, Johannes. 1589. *Orationes octo habitae in publicis congressibus Academiae Rostochiensis.* Frankfurt am Main. (http://mdz-nbn-resolving.de/um:nbn:de: bvb:12-bsb10994702-2).

Moderne Literatur

Ahrens, Sabine. 2004. *Die Lehrkräfte der Universität Helmstedt (1576–1810).* Helmstedt.

Alvermann, Dirk & Karl-Heinz Spieß (Hrsg.) 2011. *Quellen zur Verfassungsgeschichte der Universität Greifswald 1456–1815*, Bd. 1. Stuttgart.

Asche, Matthias. 2001. „Humanistische Distanz gegenüber dem ‚Konfessionalisierungsparadigma‘. Kritische Bemerkungen aus der Sicht der deutschen Bildungs- und Universitätsgeschichte", *Jahrbuch für Historische Bildungsforschung* 7, 261–282.

Asche, Matthias. 2003. „Joachim Camerarius in Leipzig und Erfurt (1512/13– 1521). Studien- und Jugendjahre im Zeichen des Humanismus", in Rainer Kößling & Günther Wartenberg (Hrsg.) *Joachim Camerarius*, Tübingen, 43– 60.

Asche, Matthias. 2009. „Jena als Typus einer protestantischen Universitätsgründung im Zeichen des Humanismus", *Zeitschrift für Thüringische Geschichte* 63, 117–142.

Bauch, Gustav. 1896. „Die Anfänge des Studiums der griechischen Sprache und Literatur in Norddeutschland", *Mitteilungen der Gesellschaft für deutsche Erziehungs- und Schulgeschichte* 6, 47–98, 163–193.

Bauch, Gustav. 1907. „Aus der Geschichte des Mainzer Humanismus", in Julius Reinhard Dietrich & Karl Bader (Hrsg.) *Beiträge zur Geschichte der Universität Mainz und Gießen*, Darmstadt, 3–86.

Bauer, Barbara (Hrsg.) 1999. *Melanchthon und die Marburger Professoren (1527–1627)*. Marburg.

Baumgart, Peter & Ernst Pitz. 1963. *Die Statuten der Universität Helmstedt*, Göttingen.

Ben-Tov, Asaph. 2009. *Lutheran Humanists and Greek Antiquity. Melanchthonian Scholarship between Universal History and Pedagogy*. Leiden.

Beyer, Michael, Stefan Rhein & Günther Wartenberg (Hrsg.) 2011. *Melanchthon deutsch. Bd. 1: Schule und Universität*. 2. Aufl. (1. Aufl. 1997). Leipzig.

Biographisches Lexikon. 1998 = Laetitia Boehm *et al.* (Hrsg.) *Biographisches Lexikon der Ludwig-Maximilians-Universität München. Teil 1: Ingolstadt-Landshut 1472–1826*. Berlin.

Birziska, Vaclovas. 1947. *Abraham Kulvietis. The first Lithuanian humanist*. Pinneberg.

Bollbuck, Harald. 2015. „David Chytraeus in Rostock und Helmstedt", in Matthias Asche *et al.* (Hrsg.) *Die Leucorea zur Zeit des späten Melanchthon. Institutionen und Formen gelehrter Bildung um 1550*, Leipzig, 313–339.

Burmeister, Karl Heinz. 2011. Art. „Cantiuncula, Claudius", in *Frühe Neuzeit in Deutschland 1520-1620. Literaturwissenschaftliches Verfasserlexikon (VL 16)*, Bd. 1, Berlin–Boston, 458–465.

Claus, Helmut. 2014. *Melanchthon-Bibliographie 1510–1560*, Bd. 1–4. Gütersloh.

Cottin, Markus & Holger Kunde (Hrsg.) 2017. *Dialog der Konfessionen. Bischof Julius Pflug und die Reformation*. Petersberg.

Dörner, Gerald. 2013. „Reuchlin (Rochlin, Roechlin, Capnion), Johannes", in *Deutscher Humanismus 1480–1520. Verfasserlexikon*, Bd. 2, Berlin–Boston, 579–633.

Drüll, Dagmar. 2002. *Heidelberger Gelehrtenlexikon 1386–1651*. Berlin–Heidelberg.

Elsmann, Thomas. 2016. „Posselius, Johannes", in *Frühe Neuzeit in Deutschland 1520–1620. Literaturwissenschaftliches Verfasserlexikon (VL 16)*, Bd. 5, Berlin–Boston, 130–138.

Flood, John L. & David J. Shaw. 1997. *Johannes Sinapius (1505–1560). Hellenist and Physician in Germany and Italy*. Genf.

Flood, John L. 2003. „The crisis in Greek teaching at the University of Heidelberg around 1530", *Renaissance studies* 17, 84–95.

Flood, John L. 2013. „Mosellanus (Schade), Petrus", in *Deutscher Humanismus 1480–1520. Verfasserlexikon*, Bd. 2, Berlin–Boston, 239–255.

Flood, John L. 2017. „Sinapius, Johannes", in *Frühe Neuzeit in Deutschland 1520–1620. Literaturwissenschaftliches Verfasserlexikon (VL 16)*, Bd. 6, Berlin–Boston, 23–27.

François, Wim. 2003. „The Plea by the Humanist Petrus Mosellanus for a Knowledge of the Three Biblical Languages. A Louvain Perspective", *Revue d'Histoire Ecclésiastique* 98, 438–481.

Freitäger, Andreas. 1997. „Der Italienaufenthalt des Gisbert Longolius und seine Kölner Griechisch-Professur", *Düsseldorfer Jahrbuch. Beiträge zur Geschichte des Niederrheins* 68, 57–75.

Freytag, Hartmut. 2004. „Petrus Vincentius (1519–1581)", *Schlesische Lebensbilder* 8, 60–68.

Friedländer, Ernst (Hrsg.) 1893. *Aeltere Universität-Matrikeln. Universität Greifswald*. Bd.1. Leipzig.

Gastgeber, Christian. 2012. „Griechischhumanismus an der Wiener Universität. Der erste *Professor Linguae Graecae* Georg Rithaymer", *Graecolatina et orientalia*, 83–110.

Gastgeber, Christian. 2014. „Griechischstudium im italienischen Humanismus. Eröffnungsvorträge des Demetrios Chalkondyles zum Griechischlehrgang in Padua 1463 und 1464", *Jahrbuch der Österreichischen Byzantinistik* 64, 67–104.

Geanakoplos, Deno J. 1974. „The Discourse of Demetrius Chalcondyles on the Inauguration of Greek Studies at the University of Padua in 1463", *Studies in the Renaissance* 21, 118–144.

Gehrt, Daniel. 2015. „Die Harmonie der Theologie mit den studia humanitatis. Zur Rezeption der Wittenberger Bildungskonzeptionen in Jena am Beispiel der Pfarrerausbildung", in Matthias Asche *et al.* (Hrsg.) 2015. *Die Leucorea zur Zeit des späten Melanchthon. Institutionen und Formen gelehrter Bildung um 1550*, Leipzig, 263–312.

Gößner, Andreas. 2017. „Deklamationen, Reden und Postillen", in Günter Frank (Hrsg.) *Philipp Melanchthon. Der Reformator zwischen Glauben und Wissen. Ein Handbuch*, Berlin–Boston, 277–294.

Gundlach, Franz. 1927. *Catalogus Professorum Academiae Marburgensis 1527–1910*. Marburg.

Hamm, Joachim. 2011. „Camerarius (Kammermeister), Joachim d. Ä.", in *Frühe Neuzeit in Deutschland 1520–1620. Literaturwissenschaftliches Verfasserlexikon (VL 16)*, Bd. 1, Berlin–New York, 425–438.

Hammerstein, Notker. 2000. „Universitäten und Reformation", in Ulrich Muhlack & Walther Gerrit (Hrsg.) *Res publica litteraria. Ausgewählte Aufsätze zur frühneuzeitlichen Bildungs-, Wissenschafts- und Universitätsgeschichte*, Berlin, 388–401.

Henze, Ingrid. 1990. *Der Lehrstuhl für Poesie an der Universität Helmstedt bis zum Tode Heinrich Meiboms d. Ält. (+ 1625). Eine Untersuchung zur Rezeption antiker Dichtung im lutherischen Späthumanismus*. Hildesheim.

Hieronymus, Frank. 1992. *Griechischer Geist aus Basler Pressen*, Basel (2. Aufl. digital: http://www.ub.unibas.ch/cmsdata/spezialkataloge/gg/).

Höhle, Michael. 2002. *Universität und Reformation. Die Universität Frankfurt (Oder) von 1506 bis 1550*. Köln.

Höhle, Michael. 2017. „Kontinuität und Bekenntniswechsel an der Universität Frankfurt/Oder", in Enno Bünz *et al.* (Hrsg.) *Reformationen vor Ort. Christlicher Glaube und konfessionelle Kultur in Brandenburg und Sachsen im 16. Jahrhundert*, Berlin, 204–215.

Holzberg, Niklas. 1981. *Willibald Pirckheimer. Griechischer Humanismus in Deutschland*. München.

Holzberg, Niklas. 1987. „Olympia Morata und die Anfänge des Griechischen an der Universität Heidelberg", *Heidelberger Jahrbücher* 31, 77–93.

Immenhauser, Beat. 2003. „Universitätsbesuch zur Reformationszeit. Überlegungen zum Rückgang der Immatrikulationen nach 1521", *Jahrbuch für Universitätsgeschichte* 6, 69–88.

Johnson, Diane. 2006. „Musa Posseliana. Johannnes Posselius the Elder and the Lutheran Greek Program", *Reformation and Renaissance Review* 8, 186–209.

Kleineidam, Erich. 1983. *Universitas Studii Erffordensis III*, (2. Aufl.) Erfurt.

Komorowski, Manfred. 2008. „Die Universität Königsberg in der Frühen Neuzeit: Forschungsstand und -perspektiven im Überblick", in Hanspeter Martin & Manfred Komorowski (Hrsg.) *Die Universität Königsberg in der Frühen Neuzeit*, Köln, 1–26.

Korhonen, Tua. 2019. „Learned and Playful Farewells to Fellow Swedes. Two Greek Poems by Laurentius Praetorius from Gävle (Helmstedt, 1592)“, *Eranos* 110, 45–62.

Krafft, Fritz. 1977. „Jesuiten als Lehrer an Gymnasium und Universität Mainz“, in Helmut Mathy and Ludwig Petry (Hrsg.) *Tradition und Gegenwart. Aus der Zeit der kurfürstlichen Universität*, Wiesbaden, 259–350.

Kruse, Jens-Martin. 2002. *Universitätstheologie und Kirchenreform. Die Anfänge der Reformation in Wittenberg 1516–1522.* Mainz.

Kusche, Beate. 2009. *„Ego collegiatus“ – Die Magisterkollegien an der Universität Leipzig von 1409 bis zur Einführung der Reformation 1539. Eine struktur- und personengeschichtliche Untersuchung.* Leipzig.

Lawrynowicz, Kasimir. 1999. *Albertina. Zur Geschichte der Albertus-Universität zu Königsberg in Preußen.* Hrsg. [u. übersetzt] von Dietrich Rauschning. Berlin.

Leinsle, Ulrich G. 2006. *Dilinganae Disputationes. Die Lehrinhalte der gedruckten Disputationen an der Philosophischen Fakultät der Universität Dillingen 1555–1648.* Regensburg.

Leinsle, Ulrich G. (Hrsg.) 2014. *Akademische Reden aus der Universität Dillingen 1572–1582.* Münster.

Leipzig 2009 = *Geschichte der Universität Leipzig 1409–2009. Ausgabe in Fünf Bänden.* Hrsg. von Senatskommission zur Erforschung der Leipziger Universitäts- und Wissenschaftsgeschichte & Franz Häuser. Leipzig.

Liess, Albrecht. 1964. „Die Einführung des Griechischen als Lehrfach an der Universität Ingolstadt“, in Walter Fröhlich, Albrecht Liess & Helmut Wolff (Hrsg.) *Liber ad Magistrum. Festgabe Herrn Universitätsprofessor Dr. Johannes Spörl zu seinem 60. Geburtstag*, München, 113–119.

Lindner, Andreas. 2014. „Johannes Lang im Netzwerk des Humanismus“, in Michael Ludscheidt (Hrsg.) *Musik – Geschichte – Erfurt. Gedenkschrift für Helga Brück*, Erfurt, 117–142.

Lorenz, Sönke. 2009. „Johannes Reuchlin und die Universität Tübingen“, *Zeitschrift für Württembergische Landesgeschichte* 68, 139–155.

Lorenz, Sönke. 2012. „Scholastik und Humanismus. Zur Genese der Fachprofessur an der Tübinger Artistenfakultät“, in Sönke Lorenz et al. (Hrsg.) *Die Universität Tübingen zwischen Scholastik und Humanismus*, Ostfildern, 11–93.

Lorenz, Sönke. 2013. „Reuchlin und die Universität Tübingen“, in Sönke Lorenz & Dieter Mertens (Hrsg.) *Johannes Reuchlin und der „Judenbücherstreit“*, Tübingen, 15–53.

MBW = Scheible, Heinz (Hrsg.) 1977 ff. *Melanchthons Briefwechsel. Kritische und kommentierte Gesamtausgabe.* Stuttgart–Bad Cannstatt.

Menk, Gerhard. 1981. *Die Hohe Schule Herborn in ihrer Frühzeit (1584–1660). Ein Beitrag zum Hochschulwesen des deutschen Kalvinismus im Zeitalter der Gegenreformation.* Wiesbaden.

Meuthen, Erich. 1988. *Kölner Universitätsgeschichte.* Bd. 1. Köln.

Müller, Rainer A. 1999. „Struktur und Wandel der Artisten- bzw. Philosophischen Fakultät am Beginn des 16. Jahrhunderts", in Rainer Christoph Schwinges (Hrsg.) *Artisten und Philosophen. Wissenschafts- und Wirkungsgeschichte einer Fakultät vom 13. bis zum 19. Jahrhundert*, Basel, 143–159.

Märtl, Claudia *et al.* (Hrsg.) 2013. *„Inter graecos latinissimus, inter latinos graecissimus". Bessarion zwischen den Kulturen.* Berlin.

Nauert Jr., Charles G. 1991. „Humanists, Scholastics, and the Struggle to Reform the University of Cologne, 1523–1525", in James V. Mehl (Hrsg.) *Humanismus in Köln / Humanism in Cologne*, Köln–Weimar–Wien, 39–76.

Pendzig, Paul. 1921. „Die Anfänge der griechischen Studien und die deutschen Universitäten", *Neue Jahrbücher für das Klassische Altertum, Geschichte und Deutsche Literatur und für Pädagogik* 48, 49–62.

Pociute, Dainora. 2017. „The Reformation Experience in Sixteenth-Century Vilnius", in Heinrich Assel *et al.* (Hrsg.) *Reformatio Baltica. Kulturwirkungen der Reformation in den Metropolen des Ostseeraums*, Berlin–Boston, 553–572.

Reinermann, Heinrich. 2018. *Johannes Lonicerus 1499–1569. Ein Leben im Zeichen der Reformation.* Ubstadt–Weiher.

Reske, Christoph. 2015. *Buchdrucker des sechzehnten und siebzehnten Jahrhunderts im deutschen Sprachgebiet.* Wiesbaden.

Reuchlin, Johannes. 2013. *Briefwechsel.* Bd. 4, hrsg. von Matthias Dall'Asta & Gerald Dörner. Stuttgart–Bad Cannstatt.

Rhein, Stefan. 1996. „'De usu Graecae linguae'. Die Griechischstudien an der Universität Rostock", in Inger Ekrem *et al.* (Hrsg.) *Reformation and Latin Literature in Northern Europe*, Oslo, 42–55.

Rhein, Stefan. 1997. „Melanchthon and Greek Literature", in Timothy J. Wengert & M. Patrick Graham (Hrsg.) *Philipp Melanchthon (1497–1560) and the Commentary*, Sheffield, 149–170.

Rhein, Stefan. 2017. „Philipp Melanchthon und seine griechischen Dichterschüler", in Stefan Weise (Hrsg.) *Hellenisti! Altgriechisch als Literatursprache im neuzeitlichen Europa*, Stuttgart, 15–46.

Rhein, Stefan. 2018. „Vor 500 Jahren. Melanchthon kommt! Die Antrittsrede ‚Über die Neugestaltung des Universitätsstudiums' vom 28. August 1518“, *Luther* 88, 72–76.

Ricci, Paolo. 1952. „La prima cattedra di Greco in Firenze“, *Rinascimento* 3, 159–165.

Rupp, Paul B & Rüdiger May. 1999. *450 Jahre Universität Dillingen (1549–1999). Eine Ausstellung des Stadtarchivs Augsburg* […]. München.

Saladin, Jean-Christophe. 2000. *La Bataille du Grec à la Renaissance*, Paris.

Scheible, Heinz. 2010. „Melanchthons Beziehungen zu Stadt und Bistum Breslau (2000)“, in Ders. *Aufsätze zu Melanchthon*, Tübingen, 342–372.

Scheible, Heinz. 2015. „Lehrpersonal und Lehrprofil der Leucorea zwischen Neufundation (1536) und Tod Melanchthons (1560): die Philosophische Fakultät“, in Matthias Asche *et al.* (Hrsg.) *Die Leucorea zur Zeit des späten Melanchthon. Institutionen und Formen gelehrter Bildung um 1550*, Leipzig, 191–206.

Scheible, Heinz. 2016. *Melanchthon. Vermittler der Reformation*, München.

Schirrmeister, Albert. 2018. „Universitätsreden“, in Jan-Hendryk de Boer *et al.* (Hrsg.) *Universitäre Gelehrtenkultur vom 13.–16. Jahrhundert. Ein interdisziplinäres Quellen- und Methodenhandbuch*, Stuttgart, 559–577.

Schmidt, Siegfried (Hrsg.) 1983. *Alma Mater Jenensis. Geschichte der Universität Jena*. Weimar.

Schmitz, Wolfgang. 1991. „Das humanistische Verlagsprogramm Johannes Soters“, in James V. Mehl (Hrsg.) *Humanismus in Köln / Humanism in Cologne*, Köln–Weimar–Wien, 77–117.

Schreiber, Heinrich. 1859. *Geschichte der Stadt und Universität Freiburg im Breisgau*. T. 2. Freiburg.

Schubert, Ernst. 1973. „Conrad Dinner. Ein Beitrag zur geistigen und sozialen Umwelt des Späthumanismus in Würzburg“, *Jahrbuch für fränkische Landesforschung* 33, 213–238.

Schwinges, Rainer Christoph. 2008. „Zur Professionalisierung gelehrter Tätigkeit im deutschen Spätmittelalter“, in Ders. *Studenten und Gelehrte. Studien zur Sozial- und Kulturgeschichte deutscher Universitäten im Mittelalter*, Leiden–Boston, 553–578.

Scribner, Robert W. 1976. „The Erasmians and the Beginning of the Reformation in Erfurt“, *Journal of Religious History* 9, 3–31.

Sdzuj, Reimund B. 2011. „Caselius, Johannes“, in *Frühe Neuzeit in Deutschland 1520–1620. Literaturwissenschaftliches Verfasserlexikon (VL 16)*, Bd. 1, Berlin–Boston, 478–497.

Sdzuj, Reimund B. 2014. „Heresbach, Konrad", in *Frühe Neuzeit in Deutschland 1520–1620. Literaturwissenschaftliches Verfasserlexikon (VL 16)*, Bd. 3, Berlin–Boston, 292–303.

Seidel, Robert. 2013. „Jacob Micyllus in Heidelberg. Programm und Leistung eines humanistischen Philologen in kurpfälzischen Diensten", in Wilhelm Kreutz *et al.* (Hrsg.) *Die Wittelsbacher und die Kurpfalz in der Neuzeit. Zwischen Reformation und Revolution*, Regensburg, 333–359.

Seidel, Robert. 2015. „Micyllus, Jakob", in *Frühe Neuzeit in Deutschland 1520–1620. Literaturwissenschaftliches Verfasserlexikon (VL 16)*, Bd. 4, Berlin–Boston, 410–412.

Specht, Thomas. 1902. *Geschichte der ehemaligen Universität Dillingen (1549–1804)*. Freiburg im Breisgau.

Steiner, Jürgen. 1989. *Die Artistenfakultät der Universität Mainz 1477–1562.* Stuttgart.

Süß, Peter A. 2007. *Grundzüge der Würzburger Universitätsgeschichte 1402–2002.* Neustadt an der Aisch.

Szameitat, Martin. 2010. *Konrad Heresbach. Ein niederrheinischer Humanist zwischen Politik und Gelehrsamkeit.* Bonn.

Thümmel, Hans Georg. 2008a. „Die Universität Greifswald in den ersten hundert Jahren", in Dirk Alvermann & Karl-Heinz Spieß (Hrsg.) *Bausteine zur Greifswalder Universitätsgeschichte. Vorträge anlässlich des Jubiläums „550 Jahre Universität Greifswald"*, Stuttgart, 19–43.

Thümmel, Hans Georg (Übers.) 2008b. *Das Dekanatsbuch der Philosophischen Fakultät der Universität Greifswald 1456–1662.* Stuttgart.

Volz, Hans. 1964. „Johann Gusebel Longicampianus: ein unbekannter Humanist des 16. Jahrhunderts", in Elisabeth Geck & Guido Pressler (Hrsg.) *Festschrift für Josef Benzing*, Wiesbaden, 456–475.

von Selle, Götz. 1956. *Geschichte der Albertus-Universität zu Königsberg in Preußen.* [2. Aufl., 1. Aufl. 1944]. Würzburg.

von Wegele, Franz X. 1882. *Geschichte der Universität Wirzburg.* Wirzburg.

WA = D. Martin Luthers Werke. Kritische Gesamtausgabe (Weimarer Ausgabe), Bd. 1 ff., Weimar 1883 ff.

Wedow, Christian. 2013. *Die Rolle des deutschen Luthertums für Schweden zwischen 1600 und 1648*, Diss. Rostock.

Weißmann, Robert. 2009. „Kryptoradikale Ansätze und Emanzipation im Werk des Jenaer Polyhistors Michael Neander", in Günter Mühlpfordt & Ulman Weiß (eds.) *Kryptoradikalität in der Frühneuzeit*, Stuttgart, 181–204.

Profilbildung eines Dichterphilologen
– Joachim Camerarius d.Ä. als Verfasser, Übersetzer und Herausgeber griechischer Epigramme

Jochen Schultheiß

Joachim Camerarius der Ältere (1500–1574), Schullehrer in Nürnberg und Universitätsprofessor in Tübingen und Leipzig, trat nicht nur als bedeutsamer gräzistischer Philologe hervor, indem er Editionen etwa von Homer, Herodot, Thukydides oder an bedeutsamster Stelle Sophokles verfertigte und zahlreiche griechische Texte übersetzte und kommentierte. Er legte auch eine erstaunlich umfangreiche eigene literarische Produktion in griechischer Sprache vor.[1] Es liegt deshalb nahe, auch ihn zu den Dichterphilologen zu zählen, für die die philologische Beschäftigung mit der antiken Literatur – sei es in Edition, Übersetzung oder Kommentierung – und die eigene Produktion in den alten Sprachen untrennbar zusammengehörten.[2] Das Postulat einer Einheit von Produktion und Analyse dichterischer Texte war von Camerarius' Freund Philipp Melanchthon formuliert worden.[3] Die Kompetenz in dem einen Bereich betrachtete er als unabdingbare Voraussetzung für ein qualifiziertes Schaffen in dem anderen. Nur wer selbst in den alten Sprachen zu dichten vermochte, war auch imstande, über die antike Dichtung zu urteilen, nur wer über ein vertieftes Verständnis der literarischen Tradition verfügte, besaß auch die Voraussetzung, um seinerseits gute Poesie verfertigen zu können.

---

[1] Eine Gesamterfassung aller Drucke, Werke und Briefe des Camerarius findet sich in der Datenbank des Projektes *Opera Camerarii* (http://www.camerarius.de); hier auch genauere bibliographische Daten zu den in diesem Aufsatz besprochenen Epigrammen sowie Weiterleitungen zu aktuell verfügbaren Digitalisaten. Für weiterführende Hinweise zur Textkonstitution bedanke ich mich bei Thomas Gärtner (Köln), Martin Steinrück (Fribourg) und Stefan Weise (Wuppertal). Für Anmerkungen in Hinblick auf Camerarius bin ich Marion Gindhart, Manuel Huth und Moritz Stock (alle Würzburg) sehr verbunden. Wichtige Verbesserungsvorschläge kamen schließlich von Tua Korhonen (Helsinki) und den beiden anonymen Peer-Reviewern.

[2] Der Terminus „Dichter-Philologe" bei Rhein (1987, 29) zu Philipp Melanchthon, Weise (2016, 133) zu Lorenz Rhodoman.

[3] Zu Melanchthons Vorstellung einer unauflöslichen Interdependenz von Produktion und Hermeneutik vgl. Rhein (1987, 23–37).

So treffend das zusammengesetzte Nomen „Dichterphilologe" die in dem Konzept enthaltene Einheit zum Ausdruck bringt, so sehr stellt es für die literaturwissenschaftliche Forschung eine höchst bedeutsame Aufgabe dar, die Transmissionspunkte klarer herauszuarbeiten, an denen eine solche wechselseitige Vermittlung zwischen Exegese und Produktion möglich war. Als augenfälliges Beispiel für die angestrebte Konvergenz von Philologie und Dichtung kann bei Camerarius sicherlich seine Herausgabe der *Idyllen* des Theokrit bei gleichzeitiger kreativer Ausfüllung von (teils vermeintlichen) Überlieferungslücken durch zwei Supplemente angeführt werden.[4] Aber auch die Epigrammdichtung bietet sich Camerarius bestens dazu an, seinem Selbstbild als Philologe und Dichter deutlichere Konturen zu verleihen.[5] Gerade durch die Mannigfaltigkeit seiner Erscheinungsformen stellt das Epigramm den Herausgeber, den Übersetzer und den Dichter vor ganz besondere Aufgaben.

Betrachten wir den uns heute überlieferten Bestand, so hat Camerarius über 310 Werke auf Griechisch verfasst. Dabei deckt er eine sehr große Bandbreite an Gattungen ab, sei es in Dichtung, sei es in Prosa. Hierzu gehören unterschiedliche Formen der Fachschriftstellerei, so etwa seine *Versus senarii de analogiis* (Leipzig, 1554), ein Lehrgedicht über die drei unterschiedlichen Formen der Analogie. Auch der Geschichtsschreibung widmete er sich in griechischer Sprache. So verfasste er eine historische Monographie zum Schmalkaldischen Krieg, worin er eine aktive Thukydides-Nachfolge praktizierte. Einen weiteren Schwerpunkt bilden katechetische und homiletische Werke. Von seiner Korrespondenz in ausschließlich oder zumindest teilweise griechischer Sprache, etwa mit Adrien Turnèbe oder Bartholomaeus Latomus, sind 26 Briefe in den Drucken überliefert, die von Camerarius selbst oder seinen Söhnen herausgegeben wurden. Die Anzahl der tatsächlich in Griechisch verfassten Briefe dürfte jedoch deutlich höher gelegen haben, da Camerarius selbst in erster Linie lediglich diejenigen Briefe gesammelt und herausgegeben hat, die von anderen an ihn gerichtet waren.[6] Seine Söhne wiederum hatten bei den von ihnen erstellten Auswahleditionen ein Lesepublikum im Sinn, das des Griechischen nicht oder nur in Ansätzen mächtig war. Dies beweisen die in den Marginalien oder im unmittelbaren Anschluss

---

[4] Vgl. zu den Theokrit-Supplementen Weise (2018).

[5] Eine vergleichbare Studie zur „humanist self-definition in a learned and witty discourse" bietet in Hinblick auf die lateinische Epigrammdichtung der Frühen Neuzeit Enenkel 2009. Nicht nur über den Inhalt der Gedichte, sondern auch durch die poetische Technik positioniert sich der Dichter im gelehrten Diskurs.

[6] Vgl. Schlegelmilch (2017, 290).

beigegebenen lateinischen Übersetzungen zu griechischen Textpassagen, die in
den von ihnen verfertigten Ausgaben vorzufinden sind.

Camerarius hat in seinem Leben etwa 125 Epigramme in griechischer
Sprache verfasst und zur Veröffentlichung gebracht.[7] Als Epigramme sollen
diejenigen Gedichte aufgefasst werden, die entweder (a) von dem Humanisten
explizit als solche klassifiziert werden, (b) tatsächlich oder – was in der Regel der
Fall ist – in der Fiktion Auf- oder Inschriften darstellen, (c) inhaltlich und formal
in der Tradition eines bestimmten antiken Epigrammtypus stehen, (d) sich durch
ihre Kürze oder (e) durch eine Pointe auszeichnen und (f) in einem der für die
Gattung gängigen Versmaße abgefasst sind, wobei dem elegischen Distichon
eine dominante Stellung zukommt.[8] Somit wird hier eine sehr weite Definition
des Epigramms zugrunde gelegt, die auch zahlreiche Formen der epideiktischen
Kasualdichtung, wie etwa das Epitaphium oder das Begleitgedicht zu Drucken,
mit einschließen kann. Diese Auffassung spiegelt jedoch durchaus Camerarius'
eigene Vorstellung von dieser poetischen Gattung wider, wie die große Breite an
Formen von Gedichten zu erkennen gibt, die er selbst als Epigramme tituliert
und als Herausgeber unter dieser Bezeichnung sammelt. Die Konzeption dieses
Dichtungstypus ist bei Camerarius – wie auch bei Melanchthon – weiter gefasst,
als in den gängigen Definitionen der heutigen Literaturwissenschaften, die das
Epigramm als eine pointierte und konzise Form enger umgrenzen.[9] Schwer zu
beurteilende Grenzfälle zu anderen Dichtungsformen, insbesondere zur Elegie,

---

[7] Hiervon sind (mindestens) 119 im Kontext unterschiedlicher Drucke überliefert, (mindestens)
6 wurden als Briefgedichte versandt und von Camerarius oder seinen Söhnen im Rahmen von
Briefsammlungen veröffentlicht (vgl. http://wiki.camerarius.de). Vereinzelte Neufunde sind
nicht auszuschließen, dürften den quantitativen Befund jedoch nicht mehr merklich verändern.
Die handschriftliche Überlieferung bedarf noch einer gesonderten Erfassung. Beispiel für ein
nur in Form des Manuskripts bekanntes griechisches Epigramm ist das von Johannes Kepler ins
Lateinische übersetzte dialogische Epigramm des Camerarius auf Nikolaus Kopernikus (ediert
in Hübner, Jürgen *et al.* (Hrsg.) 1990. *Johannes Kepler, Gesammelte Werke, Band XII*, München,
417–419).

[8] Zur Definition und den unterschiedlichen Formen des Epigramms vgl. Keydell (1962) zur Antike;
Ciccolella (2014) zum Renaissance-Humanismus. Zur Relativität der *brevitas* bei neulateinischen
Epigrammen, die bis zu hundert Verse umfassen können, und zur metrischen Varianz, die auch
in der zeitgenössischen poetologischen Literatur behandelt wird, vgl. Enenkel (2009, 14, 19, 21).

[9] So werden beispielsweise in Camerarius' Epigrammsammlung von 1538 (132–137) die
Epitaphien mit der Kategorie Ἐπιτάφια ἐπιγράμματα – „Grabepigramme" – überschrieben. Eine
vergleichbare Variabilität des Epigrammbegriffs setzt auch Melanchthon voraus; vgl. Rhein (1987,
73); zum Epitaphium als weitverbreitete Form des neulateinischen Epigramms vgl. Enenkel (2009,
10–11).

sind hierbei nicht auszuschließen. Sehr viele Epigramme können somit der Gelegenheitsdichtung zugeordnet werden und sind als Begleitepigramme oder Epitaphien auf zahlreiche Drucke verstreut. Jedoch hat Camerarius auch eine große Epigrammsammlung erstellt, die im Jahr 1538 bei Johann Herwagen d.Ä. in Basel veröffentlicht wurde. Der erste Teil dieses Editionsunternehmens besteht aus einer von dem Bamberger Humanisten besorgten Ausgabe antiker und auch einiger frühneuzeitlicher Epigramme. Der zweite Teil bietet eine Edition von 11 Gedichten, die Jakob Micyllus verfertigt hat,[10] und 66 Werken, die der Feder des Camerarius entstammen.[11] Es folgen schließlich 52 lateinische Übersetzungen zu meist antiken Epigrammen, die ebenfalls von Camerarius erstellt wurden.

In Hinblick auf die Epigrammatik tritt Camerarius, wie bereits deutlich geworden ist, in ganz unterschiedlichen Formen der Autor- bzw. Herausgeberschaft in Erscheinung. Dabei zeichnen sich vier verschiedene Funktionen ab:

1. Camerarius als Herausgeber überlieferter Epigramme
2. Camerarius als Verfasser eigener Epigramme
3. Camerarius als Herausgeber selbst verfasster Epigramme
4. Camerarius als Übersetzer von Epigrammen

Alle diese Funktionen, sei es die des Verfassers, des Herausgebers oder des Übersetzers, werden von Camerarius nicht nur in der philologischen und dichterischen Tätigkeit praktisch ausgefüllt, sondern in Paratexten auch theoretisch reflektiert. Mit den Paratexten sind wichtige Quellen gegeben, die es erlauben, sowohl die Prämissen des philologischen Arbeitens als auch die Grundsätze des aktiven Gebrauchs der griechischen Sprache besser zu erfassen. Leicht drängt sich der Verdacht auf, dass es sich bei neualtgriechischen Werken um bloße Gelehrsamkeitsbeweise der jeweiligen Autoren handeln könnte. Eine solche Schlussfolgerung läge nicht fern, denn der Renaissance-Humanismus darf durchaus als eine Kultur der Selbstinszenierung (*self-fashioning*) gelten.[12] Allerdings wäre es unzutreffend, daraus die Vermutung abzuleiten, dass eine solche Bemühung um das Außenbild als bloßer Selbstzweck gedient habe. Vielmehr

---

[10] Camerarius (1538, 100–103): Ἰακόβου τοῦ Μικύλλου Ἀργεντορατέως ἐπιτάφια (Epitaphien des Jakob Micyllus aus Straßburg).

[11] Von Camerarius' Epitaphien waren sieben bereits in einer früheren, gemeinsam mit Helius Eobanus Hessus herausgegebenen Zusammenstellung von Sepulkraldichtungen publiziert worden (Nürnberg 1531).

[12] Das *Renaissance self-fashioning* rückte erstmals Greenblatt (1980) in den Fokus der Forschung.

muss man annehmen, dass sie bestimmte Funktionen erfüllte, nicht zuletzt im Kontext der Etablierung des Griechischen als Schul- und Universitätsfach.[13]

I. Camerarius als Herausgeber überlieferter Epigramme

In der Funktion als Herausgeber griechischer Epigramme tritt Camerarius insbesondere in der großen Edition von überlieferten und eigenen griechischen Epigrammen (Ἐπιγράμματα Ἑλληνικὰ τῶν παλαιῶν ποιητῶν) aus dem Jahr 1538 hervor.[14] Sein Vorgehen bei diesem Publikationsunternehmen thematisiert er in dem ebenfalls auf Griechisch abgefassten Widmungsbrief an die Nürnberger Patrizier Georg Römer und Hieronymus Baumgartner d.Ä. (S. 3–5):[15]

Ἰωαχεῖμος[16] Καμεράριος Ἱερωνύμῳ Βαμγαρτνέρῳ καὶ Γεωργίῳ Ῥωμαίῳ φρονήσει καὶ σοφίᾳ ἐπιφανεστάτοις χαίρειν.

Συγγραφέα τινὰ τῶν πάλαι διερχόμενόν φασι τὰς Ἑλληνίδας πόλεις καὶ συλλεξάμενον τὰ εὑρεθέντα ἐν αὐτοῖς ἐπιγράμματα ἐν ἑνὶ βιβλίῳ συλλήβδην ἀναγνωσθησόμενα προὐκτεθεικέναι τοῖς φιλίστορσι, τούτῳ δὴ καὶ ἡμεῖς ἐφεψάμενοι, οὐ μὴν κατά γε τὰς πόλεις ἀλλὰ βίβλους τὰς Ἑλληνικὰς διασπαρέντα ἐπιγράμματα ἔμμετρα συγκομίσαντες […].

τούτων μέν τοι τῶν ἐπιγραμμάτων ὧν ἡμεῖς, ὡς ὁρᾶτε, τὴν συγκομιδὴν ἐξιδιοποιοῦμεν, εἴ τινος[17] τυχὸν καὶ ἐν τοῖς πρότερον ὑπὸ τοῦ Ἀλδοῦ ἐκδοθεῖσιν εὑρεθήσεται οὐχ ἁπλῶς οὐδ᾽ ἠλιθίως οὐδ᾽[18] ἀλλότρια κἀνταῦθα κείμενα ὑπολάβησθε, ὄψεσθε γὰρ τὰ παρ᾽ ἡμῶν διερχόμενοι ἢ ἧττον ἀδιόρθωτα ἐκείνων, ἢ τῆς γραφῆς ἕτερόν τι ὑποβάλλοντα, ὥστε οὐκ εἶναι ταυτογραφίαν τήνδε, ἀλλὰ καθάπερ ἄν τις φαίη καινὴν ἀφ᾽ ἡμῶν.

---

[13] Zu Camerarius' Wirken als Universitätsreformer in Tübingen vgl. Schultheiß (2017, 200–203).

[14] Die Setzung von Akzenten und Spiritus wurde in den neualtgriechischen Texten, wenn nötig, stillschweigend normalisiert. Auch die Zeichensetzung wurde gegebenenfalls heutigen deutschen Gewohnheiten angepasst. Eingriffe in eine fehlerhafte Textgestalt werden in den Fußnoten zu den jeweiligen Stellen erläutert.

[15] Hieronymus Baumgartner d.Ä. (1498–1565) hatte bei Philipp Melanchthon studiert und stellte eine maßgebliche Figur bei der Umsetzung von Wittenberger Ideen in Nürnberg (z.B. Einrichtung der Hohen Schule) dar.

[16] Ἰωαχεῖμος] ΙΟΑΧΕΙΜΟΣ.

[17] Hier ist möglicherweise eine Emendation zu τι nötig.

[18] οὐδ᾽ ἠλιθίως οὐδ᾽] οὐ δ᾽ ἠλιθίως οὐ δ᾽.

Joachim Camerarius grüßt Hieronymus Baumgartner und Georg Römer, höchst herausragende Männer an Verstand und Weisheit.

Man sagt, einer von den alten Geschichtsschreibern[19] sei durch die griechischen Städte gegangen, habe die dort gefundenen Epigramme gesammelt, sie in einem einzigen Buch zusammengefasst und für die Wissbegierigen schon zu diesem früheren Zeitpunkt herausgegeben,[20] damit sie gelesen werden könnten. Diesem bin auch ich gefolgt und habe die zwar nicht über griechische Städte, sondern über griechische Bücher verstreuten metrischen Epigramme zusammengesammelt […].

Die Zusammenführung der Epigramme spreche ich, wie ihr seht, meinem eigenen Besitz zu.[21] Wenn von diesen eins zufällig unter den zuvor von Aldus herausgegebenen gefunden wird, solltet ihr dies nicht so auffassen, als ob auf naive und törichte Weise Fremdes auch hier liege. Ihr werdet nämlich sehen, wenn ihr das Meinige durchgeht, dass es entweder weniger unverbessert ist als jenes, oder dass es etwas Anderes als den (überlieferten) Text angibt.[22] Somit ist dies keine Abschrift, sondern, wie man sagen könnte, etwas Neues von mir.

Camerarius gibt hier wichtige Hinweise zur Genese seiner Epigrammsammlung. In der Antike sei ein Geschichtsschreiber durch die Städte Griechenlands gezogen, um Epigramme zu sammeln. Diese habe er dann in einem einzigen Buch zusammengefasst und für die Wissbegierigen herausgegeben, damit sie gelesen werden könnten. Diesem Vorbild sei auch Camerarius gefolgt, indem er die zwar nicht über griechische Städte, sondern über griechische

---

[19] Nach GG 300 sei dies der in der *Suda* belegte Historiker Agathias gewesen, der auch einen Epigrammzyklus herausgegeben hat. Dass er, wie bei Camerarius beschrieben, die Gedichte in ganz Griechenland gesammelt hat, lässt sich aus dem Lexikoneintrag jedoch nicht erhärten.

[20] Eine weitere Bedeutung von προεκτίθημι ist „vorab erklären" (etwa in Form eines Vorworts). Die in dem finalen Partizip ausgedrückte Intention des antiken Gelehrten, die Lektüre der Gedichte ermöglichen zu wollen, spricht jedoch eher dafür, dass es hier um die Publikation der Ausgabe und nicht um die Erläuterung geht. Entsprechende Kommentierungen sind auch nicht bezeugt. Die in dem Präfix προ- ausgedrückte Vorzeitigkeit muss sich dann auf Camerarius' Edition als Vergleichspunkt beziehen. Auch in der Paraphase bei GG 300 findet sich eine Wiedergabe mit „herausgegeben".

[21] Aufgrund der im Vergleich zur *Aldina* völlig andersartigen Zusammenstellung der Epigramme ist es hier unmöglich, ἐξιδιοποιοῦμεν in der Weise aufzufassen, dass Camerarius hier sagen wollte, er eigne sich einen fremden Besitz an, übernehme also eine andere Sammlung.

[22] Zur Übersetzung – τῆς γραφῆς: wohl die überlieferte Lesart der Handschrift. Vgl. *LSJ s.v.* II.2.d: „MS. reading"; ὑποβάλλοντα: Vgl. *LSJ s.v.* III: „suggest".

Bücher verstreuten Versepigramme (ἔμμετρα) zusammengesammelt habe. Die vorliegende Zusammentragung der Epigramme schreibe Camerarius seinem eigenen Besitz zu (τὴν συγκομιδὴν ἐξιδιοποιοῦμεν). Ein Blick auf die Herkunft der Gedichte in seiner Edition bestätigt in der Tat, dass Camerarius Epigramme von zahlreichen literarischen Überlieferungsträgern zusammengeführt hat.

Daraufhin nimmt er auf eine ältere Epigrammedition aus den Pressen des Aldus Manutius Bezug. Hiermit muss Camerarius die *Aldina* der *Anthologia Planudea* von 1503 meinen, die auf eine frühere Edition von Andreas Johannes (Janos) Laskaris zurückgeht und den Titel *Florilegium diversorum epigrammatum in septem libros* trägt, oder einen ihrer Nachdrucke. Eine erweiterte und korrigierte Neuauflage brachten Manutius' Erben 1521 auf den Markt.[23] Somit war also bereits eine maßgebliche Ausgabe zu den antiken Epigrammen vorhanden. In seinem Widmungsbrief macht Camerarius nun deutlich, dass er seine Edition als eine eigenständige Leistung gegenüber der vorausgehenden Ausgabe aufgefasst wissen will. Falls man zufällig ein Epigramm in beiden Ausgaben finde, werde man feststellen, dass es sich nicht um einen lediglich übernommenen Text handele, sondern infolge von Verbesserungen um ein neues Produkt.

Zieht man nun einen Vergleich zwischen den beiden Editionen, so gelangt man zu der Feststellung, dass Camerarius eine gänzlich eigenständige Zusammenstellung von Epigrammen vorgelegt hat, die sich als durchwegs unabhängig von den älteren, italienischen Ausgaben erweist. Er bezieht sein Textmaterial nicht aus der *Anthologia Planudea*, sondern nimmt eine eigenständige Zusammenstellung von Epigrammen vor, die er als Zitate in ganz unterschiedlichen Trägertexten vorfinden konnte. Die Gedichte stammen aus einer großen Bandbreite an Autoren wie Herodot (insbesondere die Orakelsprüche), Pausanias, Diogenes Laertios, Plutarch, Synesios oder Athenaios. Dass Camerarius die von ihm edierten Epigramme aus der *Anthologia Planudea* gewonnen haben könnte, lässt sich ausschließen, da diese Sammlung im Wesentlichen Epigramme umfasst, die ausschließlich durch sie und nicht anderweitig überliefert sind. Camerarius betont auch die Hinzufügung von „Leistungen jüngerer Autoren" (τῆς τῶν νεωτέρων σπουδῆς) in seiner Ausgabe. Letztlich geht es dem Tübinger Gräzist bei seiner Edition, wie er im Widmungsbrief angekündigt hat, in erster Linie um eine dezidierte Abgrenzung von der *Aldina*: Selbst im Falle unbeabsichtigter Überschneidungen – so gibt Camerarius vor – müsste sich seine Ausgabe als die bessere erweisen.

---

[23] Zur Druckgeschichte vgl. GG 300. Die Editio princeps der von Laskaris besorgten Ausgabe der *Anthologia Planudea* war 1494 in Florenz erschienen. Die Seitenangaben erfolgen in diesem Artikel nach der Edition von 1521, die der Epigrammausgabe des Camerarius zeitlich am nächsten steht.

Die Camerarius-Sammlung unterschiedet sich von der *Aldina* nicht nur im dargelegten Textmaterial, sondern wartet auch mit einer ganz anderen Gliederungssystematik auf. Die Ἐπιγράμματα Ἑλληνικὰ τῶν παλαιῶν ποιητῶν werden hier nach Typen von Epigrammen angeordnet:

S. 6–33: Χρησμοί (Orakelsprüche).
S. 33–35: Στίχοι Σιβύλλας (Sibyllinische Verse).
S. 35–38: Γρῖφοι Κλεοβούλου (Rätsel des Kleobulos).
S. 28–63: Ἐγκωμιαστικὰ καὶ σκωπτικὰ παροιμιακά τε καὶ γνωμικὰ καὶ ὅσσα παιγνιώδη ἢ τοιουτότροπα (Lobgedichte, Spottgedichte, Sprichwörter, Denksprüche, Scherzhaftes verschiedenster Art und Vergleichbares).
S. 63–79: Ἀναθηματικὰ καὶ εἰς εἰκόνας (Weihgedichte und Erläuterungen zu Bildwerken).
S. 79–97: Ἐπιτάφια Θέωνι αὐλητῇ Ἡδύλου (Epitaphien des Hedylos auf den Flötenspieler Theon).
S. 97–99: Νεωτερικὰ Πολιτιάνου (Modernes von Poliziano und anderen Autoren).

Camerarius' Aussage im Widmungsbrief, wonach es sich bei der Edition um eine tiefgreifende Neugestaltung handle, bestätigt sich nicht nur hinsichtlich der Auswahl der Gedichte, sondern auch in Hinblick auf das Prinzip ihrer Anordnung. Findet sich in der *Aldina* der *Anthologia Planudea* (und bereits davor bei Laskaris) eine Gliederung vorzugsweise nach thematischen Überpunkten (z.B. Εἰς θάλασσαν, Εἰς θάνατον, Εἰς θεούς, Εἰς ἰατρούς usw.), zeigt sich Camerarius deutlich stärker als systematisierender Philologe und ordnet die Gedichte nach einem formalen Kriterium gemäß den unterschiedlichen Typen des Epigramms an. Bemerkenswert ist auch die Hinzufügung von Werken jüngerer Autoren in einer gesonderten Sektion – Νεωτερικά. Neben seinen eigenen Gedichten und denen des Jakob Micyllus sind der Sammlung antiker Epigramme auch solche von Angelo Poliziano, Germain de Brie (Germanus Brixius) und Andreas Johannes Laskaris beigegeben.

Dass Camerarius bei den überlieferten Epigrammen textkritisch stark eingegriffen hat, wie er im Widmungsbrief angibt, lässt sich für die antiken Werke kaum noch verifizieren. Denn welche Handschriften und Drucke er hierfür heranzog, kann nicht mehr mit Sicherheit festgestellt werden. Zumindest hinsichtlich der Epigramme aus der Feder Polizianos sind die Analysen

Filippomaria Pontanis aber zu dem Ergebnis gelangt, dass Camerarius durchaus einschneidende Änderungen in der Textgestalt vornahm.[24]

II. Camerarius als Verfasser von Epigrammen

Explizite Äußerungen zur Poetik in Paratexten

Gemessen an der bloßen Anzahl der Werke, die Camerarius in griechischer Sprache verfasst hat, nehmen mit Sicherheit seine Epigramme mit etwa 125 Gedichten den größten Teil ein. Das Epigramm kann bei Camerarius sowohl eine Form der Gelegenheitsdichtung darstellen, wobei das Gedicht für einen bestimmten Anlass verfasst ist, als auch eine rein literarische Kunstform bilden, die entweder an einen fiktiven oder an überhaupt keinen konkreten Entstehungsgrund gebunden ist.

In seinem bereits behandelten Widmungsbrief, der der Epigrammsammlung von 1538 vorangestellt ist, geht Camerarius auch auf die griechische Epigrammdichtung zeitgenössischer Autoren ein. Hierbei formuliert er sein Programm, wie eine griechische Dichtung in der Gegenwart auszusehen habe. Hinsichtlich einer Bewertung der Qualität dieser Dichtung bestimmt Camerarius die *imitatio* antiker Vorbilder als unabdingbare Voraussetzung für ein erfolgreiches Dichten in der Gattung des Epigramms (S. 5):

τὰ δὲ μεταγενέστερα ταυτὶ ἐν ᾧπερ αὐτοὶ ἐθέλοιτε λόγῳ τε καὶ ἀριθμῷ θήσετε, οὐδὲν δ᾽ οὖν οἷον δεῖγμά τι παρασκευάσασθαι τῆς τῶν νεωτέρων σπουδῆς, καὶ ὥσπερ κατ᾽ ἴχνη τῶν προτέρων ὁδοιπορίας, ἐκείνοις γὰρ ἑπομένων προὔργου τάχα τί, ἀποχωρούντων δὲ οὐδὲν πώποτε οὔτε δέον οὔτε χρηστὸν ἂν γένοιτο.

Die Werke aus späteren Zeiten könnt ihr so bewerten, wie ihr wollt. Aber nichts ist so gut wie irgendein Beispiel darzubieten für die Bemühungen der Jüngeren und gewissermaßen für eine Wegbeschreitung in den Spuren der Früheren; denn wenn man jenen (sc. den Früheren) folgt, ist es vielleicht förderlich; wenn man aber von diesem Weg abkommt, dann dürfte wohl niemals irgendetwas herauskommen, was nötig oder brauchbar wäre.

---

[24] Vgl. Pontani (2002, LXXXIX–XC).

Nach Camerarius' Auffassung kann somit auch in der Gegenwart Dichtung nur dann gelingen, wenn sie nach dem Prinzip der *imitatio* antiker Vorbilder erfolgt. Der Humanist betont hier das Prinzip literarischer Imitation, eine Aussage, die im Kontext seines Werkes nicht isoliert dasteht, sondern sich in ein weitergefasstes Konzept einfügt, wonach die Nachahmung nicht nur das grundlegende Prinzip allen Lernens darstellt, sondern jeglicher kulturelle Fortschritt auf dieser beruht.[25]

Kategorisierung nach Unterklassen des Epigramms

Camerarius verfasst seine Epigramme gewöhnlich im elegischen Distichon, verwendet jedoch auch andere in der Epigrammdichtung geläufige Metren.[26] Viele der in seiner Edition antiker Gedichte ausgewiesenen Formen des Epigramms finden sich in seiner eigenen Produktion wieder, wenngleich es auch Unterschiede gibt. Eine Erfassung des Gesamtbefundes bei Camerarius erlaubt eine Einteilung in die folgenden Klassen des Epigramms:

- Widmungs- und Begleitepigramm
- Epitaphium
- Weihepigramm
- Ekphrastisches Epigramm auf ein Kunstwerk
- Weitere Formen des epideiktischen Epigramms (z.B. Lobgedicht auf Personen)
- Satirisches Epigramm / Spottepigramm
- Erotisches Epigramm
- Rätselepigramm
- Ὀνειροκριτικά (Traumdeutungen)
- Poetologisches Epigramm

---

[25] Vgl. Baier (2017a, 86f. mit Anm. 34) zu Camerarius' Schrift *De imitatione* (hier insbesondere S. 137), die als Teil seines Kommentars zu Ciceros *Tusculanen* wie die Epigrammsammlung im Jahr 1538 erschienen ist. In den ebenfalls in Camerarius' Tübinger Zeit entstandenen *Elementa rhetoricae* (Erstauflage: Basel 1541), S. 272–305, wird die Imitation von Vorbildern für den Sprachunterricht empfohlen.

[26] Weitere Versmaße (der Epigramme in der Sammlung von 1538): der iambische Trimeter, der Hexameter, der Hendekasyllabus/Phalaeceus sowie – als bemerkenswerte Ausnahmeerscheinung – das Distichon aus Hexameter und iambischem Dimeter; vgl. zu diesem ungewöhnlichen Metrum Weise (2016, 154f.). Ob Camerarius auch bewusste metrische Fehler in spielerischer Intention einflicht, wie dies wohl Poliziano getan hat – vgl. Steinrück (2018) –, müsste eigens untersucht werden. Entsprechende Fälle sind dem Autor dieses Aufsatzes bisher jedoch noch nicht aufgefallen.

- Briefgedicht in Epigrammform
- Epigramm als kurze, pointierte dichterische Form für beliebige Themen

Bei den ersten fünf Gruppen handelt es sich um Formen der Gelegenheitsdichtung. Gerade die ersten beiden erscheinen dementsprechend auf zahlreiche Drucke verteilt, in denen sie jeweils ihre Funktion erfüllen. Dies gilt insbesondere für die Begleit- oder Widmungsepigramme, die in verschiedenen Drucken als Paratexte erscheinen.[27] Epitaphien können in unterschiedlicher Form begegnen:[28] Sie können sowohl im Kontext eines aktuellen Todesfalles entstanden sein, aber sich auch als rein literarische Produkte auf Menschen, die schon seit längerem tot sind, auf Tiere oder fiktive Personen beziehen.[29] Weihepigramme oder Bildunterschriften, die tatsächlich irgendwo angebracht worden wären, sind für Camerarius nicht bekannt.[30]

Bei zahlreichen Formen des Epigramms handelt es sich um Gedichte, die nicht eigentlich Inschrift sein wollen, sondern die unter konziser Formulierung eines Gedankens oder eines Gefühls ein beliebiges Thema behandeln.[31] Auch hier bilden sich wiederum Gruppen aus, wie das ekphrastische,[32] das erotische oder das skoptische Epigramm, ferner das Rätselgedicht. Sie sind von gänzlich literarischer Natur.[33] Auch der poetologischen Selbstreflexion des Dichters können Epigramme dienen.[34]

Schließlich finden sich im Oeuvre des Camerarius auch Briefgedichte, die in Epigrammform verfasst sind. Dabei kann es sich sowohl um Gedichte

---

[27] Mindestens 31 Belege, als Paratexte auf zahlreiche Drucke verstreut.

[28] Mindestens 29 Belege, in der Regel in eigenen oder fremden Gedichtsammlungen.

[29] Eine Sammlung solcher literarischer Epitaphien hat Camerarius in seiner mit Hessus erstellten Ausgabe von Epicedien und Epitaphien publiziert (Nürnberg 1531).

[30] Beispiel eines fiktiven Weihepigramms: Τῇ ἐργατίδι παρὰ Θεσπιεῦσι, in Camerarius (1538, 106).

[31] Vgl. zu dieser Gruppe Keydell (1962, 540).

[32] Vgl. die Epigramme in Camerarius (1538, 308–309).

[33] Lateinische Rätselepigramme und deren Auflösungen haben sich Camerarius und Hessus vermutlich tatsächlich zugesandt.

[34] Hier ist in der Epigrammsammlung von 1538 an die poetologische Selbstbetrachtung im Epigramm Τοῦ αὐτοῦ (sc. Ἰωαχείμου). Οὐδ' ἐγὼ αὐτὸς ποιητὴν (Inc.), S. 119, zu denken oder an das Gedicht mit dem Titel Εἰς Οἴαγρον ἐξεῖναι τοῖς παλαιοῖς ῥήμασι χρησάμενον εὐσεβῆ μοῦσαν ἀσκεῖν, S. 121–122, worin der Sprecher gegenüber einem Schmäher den Rückgriff eines christlichen Dichters auf die pagane Mythologie verteidigt.

handeln, die selbst Briefe darstellen und als solche verschickt wurden, als auch um Dichtungen, die einem Brief beigegeben waren.[35] Diese verdeutlichen in ganz unmittelbarer Weise, dass die Verwendung der griechischen Sprache der Etablierung einer Gemeinschaft von Gelehrten und der Kommunikation innerhalb dieser dient.[36] Ein Brief in Gedichtform kann beispielsweise dafür bestimmt sein, eine Einladung zu übermitteln,[37] oder er kann als Begleitbrief der Übersendung eines Druckes beiliegen.[38]

Vergleicht man Camerarius' literarische Produktion mit den überlieferten Gedichten, die er herausgibt, so stellt man, was die Klassifikation der Epigramme anbelangt, vielfältige Überlappungen, jedoch auch Unterschiede fest. So finden sich etwa die Orakelsprüche, die in seiner Ausgabe antiker Epigramme einen weiten Raum einnehmen, nicht in seiner eigenen Dichtung. Bei den als Ὀνειροκριτικά kategorisierten Epigrammen wiederum, auf die Camerarius im Widmungsbrief eigens hinweist (S. 5), scheint es sich um ein Spezifikum unseres Tübinger Humanisten innerhalb der Epigrammdichtung zu handeln.[39] Deshalb ist diese Form wohl als eine Anverwandlung der für einen christlichen, humanistischen Dichter unbrauchbar gewordenen Gruppe der Orakelsprüche zu verstehen. Für das Epitaphium des Renaissance-Humanismus gilt es zu bedenken, dass es meist stark enkomiastische Elemente aufweist und somit auch in die Tradition des epideiktischen Epigramms tritt.

Hiermit sind größere Epigrammgruppen erfasst, die sich in der Geschichte dieser Dichtungsform, die sich von der ursprünglichen Inschrift zu einer immer freier handhabbaren Gattung entwickelt hat, ausgebildet haben. Dies schließt nicht aus, dass das Epigramm als eine sich durch Kürze und Pointe auszeichnende Form auch mit beliebigen anderen Inhalten gefüllt werden kann. So ist es durchaus möglich, auch ein Epithalamium als Epigramm zu gestalten. Dies gilt etwa für

---

[35] Da diese in der Regel im Kontext von Briefsammlungen ediert vorliegen, ist die Form der ursprünglichen Versendung heute meist nicht mehr genau bestimmbar.

[36] Vgl. zu dieser Funktion des Griechischen in der Neuzeit Weise (2016, 114f., 132).

[37] Z.B. Camerarius an Volland, in Camerarius, *Libellus alter, epistolas complectens Eobani et aliorum quorundam doctissimorum virorum necnon versus varii generis atque argumenti*, Leipzig 1557, F7v.

[38] Z.B. Camerarius an Beust (17.06.1571) als Begleitbrief in dichterischer Form in Joachim von Beust, *Christiados libellus*, Wittenberg 1572, 16–17. Das mit dem Titel Ἀνθῶν δῶρον versehene, rein literarische Epigramm aus der Sammlung von 1538 (Camerarius 1538, 111) ist wohl als Begleitgedicht zu einer Blumensendung zu verstehen.

[39] Unter der Kategorie der Ὀνειροκριτικά finden sich zwei recht umfangreiche Epigramme zur Traumdeutung (84 iambische Trimeter sowie 38 elegische Distichen) in der Epigrammsammlung von 1538 (Camerarius 1538, 138–142).

das Hochzeitsgedicht auf den Mediziner Johannes Kentmann (1518–1574), das
mit fünf elegischen Distichen sehr kurz gehalten ist.[40]

Camerarius' dichterische Praxis soll im Folgenden anhand ausgewählter
Epigrammtypen untersucht werden. Vorab ist an dieser Stelle jedoch noch
auf einen negativen Befund hinzuweisen: Wir bleiben bei Camerarius ohne
explizite Hinweise auf eine Entstehung oder Verwendung von griechischen
Epigrammen im schulischen Unterricht. Wenngleich bei anderen Humanisten
Epigramme nachzuweisen sind, die für den Schulbetrieb verfasst wurden,
und auch bei anderen griechischen Werken des Camerarius, insbesondere bei
seinen katechetischen Schriften und bei seinen Lehrdichtungen, die didaktische
Intention durchaus einen zentralen Raum einnimmt, so ist in seinem Œuvre
zumindest keine explizite Äußerung zu finden, bei der dieser Aspekt hinsichtlich
der Epigrammatik thematisiert würde.[41] Die Entstehungsgründe sind also
anderswo zu suchen.

Widmungs- oder Begleitepigramm

In frühneuzeitlichen Drucken fungieren Epigramme sehr häufig als Paratexte.
Sie sind folglich nicht als selbstständige Werke verfasst worden, sondern dienen
der Begleitung eines anderen Textes. Hier sind unterschiedliche Formen zu
unterscheiden. Die Termini „Widmungsepigramm" und „Begleitepigramm"
stehen sich sehr nahe. Denkt man bei dem Wort „Widmung" vor allem an
einen persönlich adressierten, individuellen Widmungsempfänger, dem das
Werk zugeeignet wird, so besitzt der Terminus „Begleitepigramm" einen
weiteren Gültigkeitsbereich. Ein solches kann ein Werk und einen Dichter
auch gegenüber einem nicht individuell angesprochenen Leser anpreisen. Als
Beispiel aus den mindestens 32 griechischen Begleitepigrammen aus der Feder
des Camerarius lässt sich das Eröffnungsgedicht zum Grammatiklehrwerk des
Johannes Metzler anführen, bei dem die Intention der Werbung für den Druck
und die Sichtbarmachung des Autors besonders deutlich wird.[42] Das griechische
Epigramm steht in diesem Fall in einem besonders direkten und evidenten

---

[40] Gedruckt in *Georgii Fabricii Chemnicensis epithalamiorum liber unus*, Leipzig 1551, D6v.

[41] Zu Epigrammen von Janos Laskaris, die im Griechischunterricht entstanden sind, vgl. Ciccolella
(2014, 312); generell zur didaktischen Zielsetzung neualtgriechischer Literatur vgl. Weise (2016,
114); zur doppelten Zielsetzung von katechetischer Unterweisung und Sprachunterricht bei
Camerarius vgl. Hamm (2011, 430f.) und Walter (2017, 40–42).

[42] Druck in Metzler, Johannes, *Primae grammatices Graecae partis rudimenta*, Hagenau 1529, A1v.

Zusammenhang mit dem Werk, zu dem es einen Paratext bildet, insofern die griechische Sprache gerade auch den thematischen Gegenstand des Lehrwerkes bildet.

Zum Entstehungskontext des Epigramms zur Metzler-Grammatik kann vorausgeschickt werden, dass Metzler Camerarius' Griechischlehrer in seiner Leipziger Studienzeit war, so dass bereits eine persönliche Verbindung zwischen den beiden bestand, aus der das Begleitgedicht hervorgehen konnte. Hier wird deutlich, dass sich die Verwendung des Neualtgriechischen sehr häufig in persönlichen Netzwerken vollzieht, insbesondere in Lehrer-Schüler-Verhältnissen:[43]

> Χρηστὴν ἐλπίδ' ἔχοιθ' ἁπαλῶν παιδεύματα Μουσῶν,
>   ὡς ἔτι σφῶν πλείστοις, καὶ μεγάλοισι μέλει.
> Μαικελερὸς κανόνων ἐπεὶ ἔκ ποτ' ἐς ἀκρὰ βεβηκὼς
>   γραμματικῶν, ταύτην δείκνυσι παίσιν ὁδόν.

> Möget ihr guter Hoffnung sein, ihr Lehren der zarten Musen, denn noch ist den Meisten und auch den Großen an euch gelegen. Weil Metzler sich einmal von den Vorschriften hin zu den Gipfeln der Grammatik begeben hat, zeigt er den Kindern diesen Weg.

In diesem Begleitgedicht preist der Sprecher das nicht explizit benannte Grammatikwerk als Hoffnungsschimmer für die geistige Bildung an (ἁπαλῶν παιδεύματα μουσῶν = Lehrwerk der zarten Musen). Metzler (Μαικελερός), der selbst von den elementaren Regeln zu den Höhen der Grammatik vorangeschritten sei, wird als kompetenter Autor präsentiert, der den Schülern einen gangbaren Weg für das Erlernen des Griechischen aufzeigen kann. Das Gedicht wird in den zahlreichen Neuauflagen der Grammatik stets wieder mitabgedruckt.

Etwas anders gestaltet sich der Bezug zwischen Paratext und Referenztext bei dem folgenden Gedicht. Hier soll der Rückgriff auf die griechische Sprache wohl gerade dazu dienen, die in dem Hauptwerk behandelte Thematik der Medizin auch als einen Gegenstandsbereich der Gräzistik herauszustellen. In dem Begleitepigramm zu der Disputation *De recta arte medendi* (1562), die unter dem Vorsitz des Leipziger Arztes und späteren Medizinprofessors Wolfgang Meurer stand, wird dessen Wirken vor dem Hintergrund der literarischen Tradition

---

[43] Vgl. Rhein (2017 *passim*).

beleuchtet:[44] Asklepios, der Sohn Apollos, habe die Menschen die Heilkunst gelehrt. Die Bemühung des Hippokrates habe diese dann schön ausgearbeitet. Galen sei allen anderen gefolgt, rage aber trotzdem über sie hinaus, denn er habe ihren Werken Ordnung verliehen. Nun aber solle ein Sprössling aus deutschen Landen, Meurer, es dem antiken Arzt gleichtun und diesem in methodischer Herangehensweise nicht nachstehen. Die griechische Sprache ist hier sicherlich absichtsvoll gewählt. Sie dient dazu, den Gegenstand der vorgestellten Schrift, die Medizin, als ein Wissensgebiet zu kennzeichnen, das der griechischen Tradition verpflichtet ist.[45]

Als Beispiele einer besonders kunstvollen Form der Widmungspraxis darf man die beiden Epigramme betrachten, die Camerarius für die *Ars bibendi* des Gräzisten Vincentius Opsopoeus (Erstdruck 1536) verfasst hat: In diesem Fall befinden wir uns in der glücklichen Lage, durch den Briefwechsel mit Opsopoeus noch nachvollziehen zu können, dass Camerarius diese Gedichte verfasst hat, nachdem der Briefpartner und Verfasser des Hauptwerkes dieses Drucks seinen entsprechenden Wunsch geäußert hatte.[46] Camerarius hat zwei Epigramme verfertigt, ein lateinisches und ein griechisches. Die beiden Epigramme finden sich im Druck direkt übereinander und bilden auch inhaltlich eine kontrastierende Einheit. Zunächst zum lateinischen Epigramm:

> *Ioachimus Camerarius lectori.*
>
> *Hoc viso Ebrietas oculo manante libello,*
>   *haec fertur tremulo verba loquuta sono:*
> *"Nunc minus inter ero externos despecta meosque,*
>   *cum mea iam certa pars ratione bibet.*
> *Ante erat ille furor, nunc est doctrina futura,*   5
>   *nunc etiam ars animi desipientis erit.*

---

[44] *Inc.*: Πρῶτει᾽ ἀνθρώποις πάρα τὴν ὑγίειαν ἅπασι, in Meurer, Wolfgang 1562, *De recta medendi ratione Vvolfgangi Meureri, artis medicae & philosophiae doctoris, disputatio. Proposita Lipsiae ad diem XXVII. Augusti. Respondente Georgio Masbachio, bonarum art(ium) magistro*, Leipzig.

[45] Vergleichbar in seiner Funktion ist das Begleitgedicht zu einer Disputation über die Hautkrankheit Erysipel. Das Epigramm mit dem Titel Εἰς τὰ περὶ ἐρυσιπελάτων προτεθέντα ὑπὸ Ἀνδρέα Ἐλλιγγηροῦ ἰατροδιδασκάλου erschien als Paratext zu *De erysipelate seu igne sacro disputatio ordinaria* (gedruckt Leipzig 1560).

[46] Den im Druck nicht datierten Brief hat Camerarius in seine Briefsammlung aufgenommen: Camerarius (1568, 317–318).

Quid dicam, an fieri credam potuisse? Quod iste
  insanire docet cum ratione liber.
Gloria magna mea est:" sed ut haec quoque magna futura
  est tua vinosae noctis amica cohors.   10
"Discite," ait, "bona res est discere." Plura volebat
  dicere, sed dubii vox erat illa soni.
Ergo caput figens cervice in pectore flexa
  incertum balbo murmur ab ore dedit.
Sed sicut quidam se percepisse putabant,   15
  autori grates visa referre fuit.

Joachim Camerarius an den Leser

Als die Trunkenheit dieses Büchlein mit feuchtem Auge gesehen hatte, soll sie
in zitterndem Ton Folgendes gesagt haben: „Nun werde ich weniger verachtet
sein unter den Fremden und unter den Meinen, wenn meine Partei bald nach
sicherer Art und Weise trinken wird. Zuvor war dies Raserei, nun wird es
Gelehrsamkeit sein, nun wird es auch eine Kunst des verstandlosen Geistes
geben. – Soll ich wirklich glauben, dass geschehen könnte, was ich sage?
Dass dieses Buch lehrt, mit Vernunft zu rasen? – Mein Ruhm ist (jedenfalls)
groß." Doch wie dieser wird auch deine Schar, die der weinreichen Nacht
zugetan ist, groß sein. „Lernt", sagte sie, „eine gute Sache ist es zu lernen."
Sie wollte noch mehr sagen, aber ihre Stimme hatte einen unsicheren Klang.
Also fügte sie ihr Haupt an den Hals, wölbte sich zur Brust hin und gab aus
dem stammelnden Mund ein unsicheres Murmeln von sich. Aber wie einige
meinten wahrgenommen zu haben, schien sie dem Autor Dank zu sagen.

Das griechische Epigramm:

Idem

Θαρσεῖθ' ὅσσ' ἀγαθῶν ἀνδρῶν νούσῳ[47] κατέχεσθε
  καὶ στρεβλόπουν[48] ἱλαραῖς φρεσὶ φιλεῖτε μέθην.

---

[47] Cf. Ar. *V.* 70: χρηστῶν ἀνδρῶν νόσος (Hinweis von Michael Fontaine, Cornell).

[48] **2** καὶ στρεβλόπουν] στρεβλύπουν ed. 1537; καὶ στρεβλόπαιν ed. 1536, 1578: οἰνώδη θ' ed.
1568.

εἰ μὲν θυμὸς ἐνὶ στήθει πρόφρων δύναμις δὲ[49]
  λείπετ' ἐν ἀβλήχρῳ σώματι δαμναμένη,
τοίης[50] Νικήτης δεινῆς πόρε φάρμακα τέχνης   5
  ὥστ' ὑμέας ἀδεῶς οἰνοποταζέμεναι.
μή τινα νῦν δείσητε μέγαν σμικροὶ θρασὺν ἄνδρα,[51]
  τέχνῃ παῖς ἵππον ποσσὸν ὁποῖος ἐλᾷ;[52]

Alle, die ihr von der Krankheit der guten Männer ergriffen werdet, seid
zuversichtlich und liebet frohen Mutes den krummfüßigen Rausch! Wenn
zwar das Verlangen in der Brust voranstrebt, die Kraft jedoch gebändigt im
schwachen Körper zurückbleibt, – [5] (für diesen Fall) schenkte Gewinn-
zenz die Heilmittel solch einer wirksamen Kunst, dass ihr bedenkenlos Wein
trinken könnt. Jetzt sollt ihr, die ihr klein seid, keinen großen, ungestümen
Mann mehr fürchten; denn kann nicht mit Kunst ein auch noch so schwaches
Kind ein auch noch so großes Pferd ziehen?

Zunächst zu Aufbau und Inhalt des lateinischen Epigramms: *Ebrietas* tritt als
allegorische Figur auf. Camerarius bedient sich des rhetorischen Mittels der
Prosopopoeie und lässt die Personifikation der Trunkenheit nach einer kurzen
Einleitung durch den Sprecher des Gedichts eine Rede halten. Sie spricht über
das erschienene Buch und freut sich darüber. Sie werde jetzt weniger verachtet,
da ihre Anhängerschaft nun auf eine festgelegte Art und Weise trinken werde. Wo
früher *furor* gewaltet habe, werde nun *doctrina* herrschen. Für die Personifikation
des alkoholischen Rausches besteht die Leistung des Werkes in der Auflösung eines
Paradoxons: Nun gebe es eine „Kunst des verstandlosen Geistes". Aufkommende
Zweifel daran, ob es dem Buch gelingen könne, „die Raserei mit Vernunft zu
lehren", räumt sie aus und mahnt zur Gelehrsamkeit. Der unstete Gedankengang
der *Ebrietas* in diesen Versen ist Ausdruck ihres eigenen Wesens. Dann endet
die Rede, und der Sprecher übernimmt wieder das Wort, denn die allegorische
Trunkenheit spricht nicht mehr verständlich und „beginnt zu stammeln".
Immerhin kann der Sprecher noch mit der Bemerkung schließen, dass einige
Zuhörer meinten verstanden zu haben, dass sie dem Autor Dank sagen wollte.

---

[49] **3** δὲ] Die Emendation zu τε (Ausgabe 1582) löst den Kontrast μὲν – δὲ auf.

[50] **5–6** τοίης Νικήτης δεινῆς πόρε φάρμακα τέχνης / ὥστ' ὑμέας] τοίης νικήτης τέχνης τάδε
φάρμακα πᾶσιν / θῆκεν ὑμῖν ed. 1568.

[51] **7** Punkt (.) am Ende des Verses ed. 1568.

[52] **8** ἐλᾷ] 3. Pers. Sg. Ind. Fut. ed. 1568 und 1582.

Das Gedicht thematisiert den Weingenuss in spezifisch lateinischen Denk-
und Ausdrucksformen. Die Vorstellung, dass es nun eine Lehre und Kunst
des rechten Umgangs mit Wein gebe, erinnert sehr an Ovids *Ars amatoria*, wo
Kunstfertigkeit und Lehre ebenfalls in einem paradoxen Verhältnis zu ihrem
Gegenstand, der Liebe, stehen. Nicht weniger ovidisch wirkt die humorvolle
Ausdeutung der Allegorie der Trunkenheit, deren Rede unverständlich wird,
da irgendwann nur noch ein unsicheres Lallen aus ihrem Mund zu vernehmen
sei.[53] In dieser spezifisch lateinischen Machart korrespondiert das Gedicht mit
dem nachfolgenden griechischen Gedicht, das seinerseits dezidiert griechisches
Kolorit trägt.

Besonders fällt im griechischen Epigramm die Darstellung der
menschlichen Affektstruktur auf, die in ihrer Wortwahl an die epische Dichtung
erinnert, jedoch ebenso an die philosophische Literatur denken lässt.[54] Die
Vorstellung vom Weingenuss als einer „Krankheit der guten Männer" –
ἀγαθῶν ἀνδρῶν νόσος geht auf Aristophanes' *Wespen* (v. 80) zurück. Mit den
beiden korrespondierenden Epigrammen präsentiert Camerarius somit zwei
unterschiedliche Gestaltungsformen, die sich an der literarischen Tradition des
jeweiligen Sprachraums ausrichten.

Das Epitaphium

Die gut 30 griechischen Epitaphien, die wir von Camerarius kennen, sind
ausschließlich in Drucken überliefert. Abgesehen von einigen Fällen von rein
literarischen Trauergedichten in den Gedichtsammlungen von 1531 und 1538
handelt es sich stets um Gelegenheitsdichtung im Kontext der Memorialkultur.
Hierbei ist der Anlass jedoch insofern literarisiert, als es nicht mehr um die Wahrung
der Erinnerung durch ein Grabmal, sondern durch eine gedruckte Publikation
geht, in der verschiedene Gedenkschriften, auch von unterschiedlicher Form,
zusammengetragen werden. Von einer wirklich an einem Grab angebrachten
Inschrift oder dem Vortrag eines Gedichts im Kontext einer Begräbnis- oder einer
Erinnerungsfeier ist nichts bekannt. Viele Epitaphien wurden für Gedenkdrucke
für bedeutende Dichter, Theologen und sonstige Gelehrten wie Helius Eobanus
Hessus (1553), Georg Helt (1548), Johann Stigel (1562) oder Martin Luther

---

[53] Man kann hier etwa an die Gestaltung der *Elegia* in *Amores* 1,1 oder 3,1 denken.

[54] So finden sich für φρεσί(ν) bei Homer nicht weniger als 207 Belege. Auch der Begriff θυμός
ist in der Bedeutung von „Verlangen" und „Mut" bei epischen und philosophischen Autoren sehr
präsent; für Belege vgl. *LSJ s.v.* II.1 und 3.

(1546) verfertigt, sowie für Fürsten, die sich wie Eberhard im Bart (1537) oder Moritz von Sachsen (1553) als Förderer des Bildungswesens hervorgetan haben. Zu der Gruppe der Professoren, für die Camerarius ein Epitaphium verfasst hat, gehört auch Petrus Mosellanus (1524), bei dem Camerarius in Leipzig studiert hatte.[55] Auch hier ist es wieder wie bereits bei Metzler ein Lehrer-Schüler-Verhältnis, das der Verwendung der griechischen Sprache zugrunde liegt.[56] Wenden wir uns zunächst dem Druckkontext zu:[57]

> Bl. A1v: *Ohne Autor – Epigramma, quo in epicedion praefatus est is, qui vice declamationis pronuntiavit.*
>
> Bl. A2r-A4v: Jakob Micyllus – *Epicedion Petri Mosellani auctore Ia(cobo) Micyl(lo).*
>
> Bl. A5r: *Philipp Melanchthon – Epitaphium Guielmi Neseni. Phil(ippi) Mel(anchthonis)* (Griechisch).
>
> Bl. A5v-B2r: Jakob Micyllus – *Epicedion in Nesenum, auctore Iacobo Micyllo.*
>
> Bl. B2r: Joachim Camerarius d.Ä. – *Epitaphium Petri Mosell(ani) Ioachimo Q(uaestore) auctore.* (Griechisch).
>
> Bl. B2r: Philipp Melanchthon – *Epitaphium Petri Mosellani, auctore Philip(po) Melanchth(one).* (Griechisch)

Betrachtet man die mit einzelnen Werken an diesem Druck beteiligten Personen (Micyllus, Melanchthon, Camerarius) sowie die betrauerten Verstorbenen (Mosellanus, Nesen), so wird deutlich, wie sehr die Verwendung des Griechischen im Dienste der Etablierung einer Gemeinschaft von Gelehrten innerhalb der *res publica litterarum* steht. Grundsätzlich darf man davon ausgehen, dass Philipp Melanchthon mit seinen Epigrammen der Impulsgeber zur griechischen Dichtung innerhalb dieser Gruppe war.[58]

---

[55] Neben den bereits erwähnten Personengruppen finden sich griechische Epitaphien auch auf Personen aus dem privaten Umfeld, seien dies eigene Verwandte oder Angehörige anderer Gelehrter.

[56] Auch das griechische Epitaphium, das Camerarius auf seinen Erfurter Griechischlehrer Georg Helt verfasst hat, ist in dieser Epigrammgruppe zu erwähnen (gedruckt in Luther, Martin, *Epistolae reverendi patris D. Martini Lutheri et Philippi Melanchthonis, ad [...] Georgium principem Anhaltinum etc. de morte [...] Georgii Helti, et epitaphium eiusdem*, Leipzig 1548, B7v–B8r). Es liegt jedoch kein Grabgedicht vor, das Camerarius für einen seiner Schüler angefertigt hätte.

[57] Druck in Micyllus (1524).

[58] Vgl. Ludwig (1998, 54f.); Rhein (2017 *passim*).

Die Sammlung unterscheidet zwischen „Epicedia" und „Epitaphia", wobei die Epitaphia als kürzere Grabaufschriften konzipiert sind. Das Epitaphium lässt die für das Epigramm typische Eigenschaft erkennen, dass der Text einen Sprechakt darstellt, der von einer Sprecherinstanz getätigt wird, etwa vom Grab, vom Toten oder von einem Passanten. Auch die Imagination eines Dialogs am Grab zwischen einem Ortsansässigen und einem Fremden sind in der Gattungstradition belegt.[59] Neben der Präsentation von mündlicher Kommunikation bildet ein weiteres Charakteristikum des Epitaphiums der deiktische Hinweis auf den Ort des Grabmals.[60] Das drei elegische Distichen umfassende Epitaph auf Petrus Mosellanus inszeniert den Redeakt eines Sprechers am Grab oder des Grabes selbst (ἐνθάδε), bei dem der Tote in der 2. Person adressiert wird (Πέτρε):

Ἐνθάδε γαῖα τεὸν νεκρὸν Πέτρε σῶμα καλύπτει,
    αὖθι γενησόμενον, ὡς πάρος ἦσθα, κόνιν.
Μηδέ σε Μουσάων θεράποντ' αἰδέσσατο μοῖρα,
    ὥστε κε γηραλέον εἰς Ἀίδαο βαλεῖν
ἀλλὰ σοῦ ἔν τε νέοις καὶ τοῖς ἁπαλοῖσι δαμέντος   5
    σοὶ μὲν ἔδωκ' ἀγαθόν, χ' ἄμμι δὲ πένθος[61] ἔχειν.

Hier birgt, Petrus, die Erde deinen Leichnam, der wieder zu dem werden wird, was du zuvor warst, nämlich Staub. Und das Schicksal hat sich nicht vor dir, dem Diener der Musen, gescheut, so dass es dich erst als Greis in den Hades geworfen hätte, [5] vielmehr hat es, indem es dich unter den noch Jungen und Zarten gebändigt hat, dir etwas Gutes gegeben, uns aber Schmerz.

Die dem Gedicht zugrundeliegende kommunikative Situation korrespondiert mit der des nachfolgenden, ebenfalls griechischen und dieselbe Verszahl umfassenden Epitaphs von Philipp Melanchthon, in dem der Verstorbene nicht angesprochen, sondern in der 3. Person beschrieben wird. Der Effekt ist eine kontrastive Variation. Camerarius' Gedicht verbindet christliche und pagane Bilder: Christlich ist der Gedanke, dass der aus Staub entstandene Verstorbene wieder zu Staub wird (*Ecl.* 12.7), wobei mit κόνις ein in der Bibel recht seltener,

---

[59] Vgl. Meyer (2005, 144–158).

[60] Vgl. Meyer (2005, 58–63).

[61] Cf. Hom. *Il.* 9.427.

wohl aber in der Tradition des griechischen Epitaphs sehr gut belegter Terminus verwendet wird.[62]

Das griechische Epitaphium auf Martin Luther von 1546[63] macht nicht nur deutlich, wie Camerarius antike Formen in den Dienst einer christlichen Erinnerungskultur stellt, sondern auch, wie er sie ganz spezifisch im Sinne der Reformation zum Einsatz bringt. Dieses Epigramm ist gemeinsam mit einem vorausgehenden lateinischen an Melanchthons Grabrede auf Martin Luther angefügt. Lässt sich bereits grundsätzlich feststellen, dass das Aufblühen des Griechischen Hand in Hand mit der Reformation ging, so ist dieses Epitaphium ein besonders anschauliches Beispiel für dieses Zusammenwirken:[64]

Μ. Λουτῆρος ἐπιτάφιον
　　Κοσμήτωρ τάφου καὶ ξένος
Ξε. Τοῦ τάφος ἐσθ᾽ ὅδε; Κ. Λουτῆρος. Ξ. Μῶν ἐνθάδε κεῖνος
　　σῶμ᾽ ἀπέθηκε θανὼν ἐν βιότοιο τέλει;
Κ. Οὐχ ὧδ᾽, ἀλλ᾽ ὁρίοις ἐνὶ πατρίδος. ὧδε δέμας δὲ
　　κεῖθ᾽ ὅθ᾽ ἀληθείας πρόσθεν ἔδειξεν ὁδὸν
εὐσεβέος θ᾽ ὑγιᾶ διδαχὴν ἐδίδαξε λόγοιο,　　　　　　　5
　　κηρύσσων θείου ῥήματος ἀγγελίην.
Ξ. Πολλοὶ δῆτα τὸν ἄνδρα καταφθίμενον ποθέουσιν.
　　Κ. Εἰσὶ δὲ καὶ τούτου ἡδόμενοι θανάτῳ.
Ξ. Αὐτοὶ δὴ τίνες εἰσί; Κ. Κακῶν μήστωρες. Ξ. ὅδ᾽ ἐσθλός.
　　Δῆλόν γ᾽ ὡς πᾶς τις δάκρυα τῷδε νέμει.　　　　　　　10
Κ. Σφάλλῃ μήν, ὦ ξεῖν᾽, ἐπεὶ οὐκ ἐπὶ δάκρυσι τούτου,
　　ἀλλ᾽ ἐπ᾽ εὐφροσύναις μᾶλλον ἔγεντο μόρος.
Εὐκτός γ᾽ τοῖς δὲ φίλοις. Ξ. Κλαίουσιν ἄρ᾽ ἐχθροί.
　　Κ. Καὶ ἀπ᾽ ἔβη ᾽ντεῦθεν κεῖσε μεθ᾽ ἡσυχίης,
ἀλλάξας σφαλεροῦ στυγερὰς βιότοιο μερίμνας　　　　　15
　　πρὸς μάκαρος ζωὴν τέρματος ἀιδίην.
Οἰχόμενός τε νόμον κοινὸν μεταθεὶς θανάτοιο.
　　Χαρμοσύνην ἀγαθοῖς πένθος ἔλειψε κακοῖς.

---

[62] In der *Anthologia Graeca* finden sich 68 Belege zu κόνις, im griechischen *Neuen Testament* und der *Septuaginta* nicht mehr als vier Belege in den *Büchern der Makkabäer*.

[63] Erstdruck: Melanchthon, Philipp (1546 A8r). Es folgen zwei Wiederabdrucke in Pollicarius, *Historia de vita et actis reverendissimi viri D. Martini Lutheri*, Wittenberg 1549, F8r–v und Melanchthon, Philipp. 1567. *Declamationes*, Straßburg, 35.

[64] Hierzu grundlegend Rhein (2017, 17f. u.ö.).

Ξ. Ἀλλὰ τίς ἐσσι φέριστε σύ; Κ. ὅστις; Τοῦδε τάφοιο
    κοσμήτωρ. Ξ. Τί δ' ἔχεις οὔνομ'; Κ. Ἐτυμολόγος.   20
Ξ. Θαυμάσιον τόδε γ' ἐστίν. ἐτυμολογεῖς δὲ τί; Κ. Λουτήρ
    ἐστιν ὁ βαπτιστής. Ξ. Πῶς; Κ. ὅτι λοῦτρα⁶⁵ φέρει.
Βαπτιστὴς δὲ θεοῖο βροτοῖς πρόσθ' ἀμνὸν ἔδειξεν.
    Ξ ὅς δὲ τί; Κ. Θηοῦ δή. Ξ. Εἰκόνα τήνδ'⁶⁶ ὁρόω
ἀμνὸν βαστάζοντος ἰδ' ἐνδεικνύντος ἅπασιν.   25
    Κ. Οὗτος ἄρ' ἦν λουτήρ. Ξ. ἦν ἄρα. Κ. νῦν τί λέγεις:
Ξ. ὅττι λόγος τέος ἐστὶν ἐτήτυμος. Κ. ἀλλ' ἀΐωμεν,
    ὡς πρὶν ἀπειθοῦσιν μήτι γένοιτο κακόν.
                      ἀπὸ Ἰωαχ(είμου)

Epitaphium auf M. Luther
Grabpfleger und Fremder
Fr.: Wessen Grab ist dies? Gr.: Das Luthers. Fr.: Hat etwa jener hier seinen Leib
zurückgelassen, als er am Ende seines Lebens (an diesem Ort auch) starb? Gr.:
Nicht hier, sondern im Gebiet seiner Heimat. Sein Körper aber liegt da, von wo
er vormals den Weg zur Wahrheit gezeigt, [5] die gesunde Lehre vom frommen
Wort gelehrt und die Botschaft der göttlichen Kunde ausgerufen hat. Fr.: Viele
vermissen also diesen Mann, nachdem er gestorben ist. Gr.: Es gibt aber auch
Leute, die sich über seinen Tod freuen. Fr.: Was sind das denn für Leute? Gr.
Solche, die Rat wissen im Unheil.⁶⁷ Fr.: Dieser ist gut. [10] Es ist doch klar,
dass jeder Tränen für ihn vergießt. Gr.: Du täuschst dich allerdings, Fremder,
denn nicht unter Tränen für ihn, vielmehr zur Freude ist der Tod eingetreten.
Den Freunden war er erwünscht. Fr.: Es weinen folglich die Widersacher. Gr.:
Und er ging von hier aus dorthin in Ruhe [15] und tauschte die verhassten
Sorgen eines unsicheren Lebens ein in das ewige Leben eines seligen Zieles.
Durch seinen Weggang veränderte er das allgemeine Gesetz des Todes. Freude
hinterließ er den Guten, Schmerz den Schlechten. Fr.: Aber wer bist du, Bester?

---

⁶⁵ Neben der gängigen Form τὸ λουτρόν ist auch τὸ λοῦτρον belegt. Man könnte bei λοῦτρα auch
an eine synkopierte Form des Akkusativs Singular von λουτήρ (λουτῆρα) denken. Dies stünde
dem Namen Luthers noch näher. Luther würde dann auf der fiktiven bildlichen Darstellung des
Grabmals ein „Weihwasserbecken" tragen (vgl. Montanari, Franco. 2004. *Vocabolario della lingua
Greca*, Torino, *s.v.* λουτήρ, 1273). Allerdings beginnt die ekphrastische Beschreibung in dem
Epigramm erst in v. 24 mit der Aufforderung des Grabhüters, näher auf das Grabmal hinzuschauen.
⁶⁶ τὴνδ'] τὴν δ' ed.
⁶⁷ Die lexikalisch mögliche Übersetzungsvariante „Solche, die auf Böses sinnen" fügt sich nur
schwer in den Gedankengang ein.

Gr.: Wer ich bin? Der Pfleger [20] dieses Grabes. Fr.: Welchen Namen trägst
du? Gr.: Etymologos. Fr.: Das ist aber wundersam. Welche Etymologien hast du
denn zu bieten? Gr. Luther ist der Täufer. Fr.: Wie (ist das denn zu verstehen)?
Gr.: Weil er λοῦτρα – Taufen – bringt. Der Täufer hat zuvor den Menschen das
Lamm Gottes gezeigt. Fr.: Dieser hat was (gemacht)? Gr.: Schau doch! Fr.: Ich
sehe dieses Bild [25] einer Person, die ein Schaf emporhebt und allen zeigt. Gr.:
Dieser also war Luther. Fr.: Dieser also war er. Gr.: Was sagst du nun? Fr.: Dass
deine Etymologie stimmt. Gr.: Aber lass uns hören, damit denen, die zuvor
ungläubig waren, kein Unheil geschehe.[68]

Das Epitaphium auf Martin Luther ist in Dialogform gestaltet. Das Gespräch
lässt sich in drei thematische Abschnitte gliedern. Zunächst erkundigt sich der
Fremde nach der Identität und dem Todesort des Verstorbenen (1–6). Auf seine
Nachfragen hin erhält er die Antwort, dass es sich um das Grab Luthers handele.
Dieser sei nicht an der Stelle des Grabmals – also in der Schlosskirche Wittenberg
– gestorben, sondern in seiner Heimat. Die Frage nach dem Todesort gibt dem
Grabhüter Gelegenheit zu einer Würdigung der Leistungen des Verstorbenen.
Hierauf steht die Reaktion der Hinterbliebenen im Blickpunkt (7–18). Der Fremde
meint, dass wohl viele den Tod einer solchen Persönlichkeit betrauern müssten.
Hierauf reagiert der Grabhüter mit der überraschenden Antwort, dass der Tod
für die Anhänger des Verstorbenen ein erfreuliches Ereignis bedeute. Das Paradox
hebt er schließlich durch den Hinweis auf die christliche Jenseitserwartung auf
(17). Der letzte Abschnitt ist geprägt von Wortspielen und Pointen (19–28). Auf
die Frage nach seinem Namen gibt der Grabhüter „Etymologe" / „Wahrheitssager"
(ἐτυμόλογος) an und präsentiert daraufhin seine Deutung des Namens „Luther".
Wortspiele mit dem Eigennamen des Verstorbenen waren bereits seit den antiken
Grabinschriften gängige Praxis.[69] Camerarius nutzt den ähnlichen Klang von
Luther und λοῦτρα, was „Taufen" bedeutet. Er habe den Sterblichen das Lamm
Gottes gezeigt. In dem Gespräch der beiden Dialogpartner wird hier das Grabmal
beschrieben, so dass das Epitaphium auch ein ekphrastisches Element enthält. Die
Verbindung, die der Sprecher zwischen Luther und dem Lamm Gottes herstellt,
verweist auf dessen Rolle bei der Öffnung des Abendmahls für alle Gläubige.

---

[68] Die Schlusspointe ist wohl als eine Aufforderung des Grabhüters an den Fremden zu deuten,
sich in der Kirche, dem (fiktiven) Anbringungsort des Epitaphs, auf die Verkündigung des Wortes
Gottes einzulassen.

[69] Vgl. zu sprechenden Namen im literarischen griechischen Grabepigramm Meyer (2005, 189f.).

Dieselbe Verbindung stellt Camerarius auch in seinen *Eklogen* her.[70] Auf den Hinweis des Grabhüters erkennt der Fremde eine Figur, die ein Schaf trägt. Der Grabhüter erklärt diese sodann als eine symbolische Darstellung Luthers.

Fiktive Epitaphien

Camerarius verfasst auch Tierepitaphien, wie etwa auf ein falbes, also graugelbes Pferd.[71] In dem Epigramm berichtet der Besitzer des Pferdes, wie er dem Tier mit seinem Schwert den Gnadenstoß versetzen musste:[72]

Ἵππῳ ξανθότριχι

Ὦ σὺν ἐμοὶ πολλὴν γαῖαν ξάνθ' ἵππε περήσας
    οὐδέ ποτ' ἠελίῳ τηκόμεν' οὐδὲ κρύει
κἄτθανες Ἁρματίας ἐκ γαίης ἐνθάδε σωθεὶς
    καὶ τεὸν ἑλκώδης ὕβρισε σῶμα νόσος.
Οὐδὲ ζῆν δύνασ' οὐδὲ θανεῖν ποσὶ δ' ἔκπεσον ὁπλαὶ   5
    ἀλλ' ὃ πάλ' ἦν ψυχῆς στέρρον, ἔμιμνε μένος.
ἥδε νόσος σε δάμασσεν, ἐγώ δ' οὐκ εἰσιδέν' ἔτλην
    σὸν πόνον οὐδεμίαν ἐλπίδ' ὑποσχόμενον.
Τὰς φρένας οὖν τύψας ξίφει ἔκτανον ἀμφὶ μελαίνας[73]
    καί σε βίου παύσας σύν χ' ἀμ'[74] ἔπαυσα πόνων.   10
νῦν δ' ὧδ' ἐκτερέιξα παρ' Ἀλβίδος ἱερὸν ὕδωρ.
    Δῶκέ τις ἀρχαίων ἀκρίδι τοῦτο γέρας.

Auf ein falbes Pferd

O du, falbes Pferd, das du mit mir viel Land durchschritten hast und weder einmal unter der Sonne über die Beschwernisse geklagt hast noch unter dem Frost. Du bist hier gestorben und aus dem Land der Wagen gerettet worden.

---

[70] Vgl. Mundt, Schäfer & Orth (2004, 229f.) zur Ekloge *Querela sive Agelaeus* εἰς ποτηριοκλέπτην (Erstveröffentlichung 1540).

[71] Camerarius hat insgesamt sechs Tiergedichte verfasst. Dem Epitaphium sind davon neben dem hier besprochenen Gedicht noch zwei weitere zuzuordnen: ein griechisches auf eine Nachtigall (Titel: Ἀηδόνι) und ein lateinisches auf eine Lerche (Titel: *Alaudae*). Sie folgen in Hessus & Camerarius (1531, F8r–v) unmittelbar auf das Grabgedicht auf das falbe Pferd.

[72] Druck: Hessus & Camerarius (1531, F7v), und Camerarius (1538, 136).

[73] Zu ἀμφὶ φρένας μελαίνας cf. Hom. *Il.* 17.83; 17.499; 17.573.

[74] Textgestalt nach Camerarius (1538); Im Druck Hessus & Camerarius (1531): σύν χ' ἄ μ' ἔπαυσα κακῶν.

Eine Krankheit mit vielen Geschwüren misshandelte deinen Körper. [5]
Weder konntest du leben noch sterben; von den Füßen fielen die Hufe. Aber
die Stärke der Seele, die von alters her hartnäckig war, bestand weiter. Diese
Krankheit bändigte dich, ich aber ertrug es nicht, dein Leid mit anzusehen,
das keine Hoffnung mehr gewährte. Ich stieß daher mit dem Schwert in das
ringsum dunkle Zwerchfell, tötete dich [10] und, indem ich dir das Leben
beschloss, beendete ich mit einem Streich zugleich auch mein Leid. Nun habe
ich dich hier beim heiligen Wasser der Elbe bestattet. Einer der Alten gab einer
Heuschrecke ein solches Ehrgeschenk.

Das Gedicht gibt eine sehr gefühlvolle Totenklage wieder.[75] Es oszilliert zwischen
realem Erleben und Literarizität. Zum einen wird der Realitätsbezug durch
die Ortsangabe an der Elbe gesucht, und der Leser, der etwas vertrauter mit
der Person und dem Werk des Camerarius ist, weiß, dass er immer wieder sein
Interesse an Pferden erkennen lässt.[76] Zum anderen wird das Gedicht in die
literarische Tradition eingebunden. Dies geschieht sowohl implizit durch Zitate
beispielsweise aus Homer – womit die literarische Technik antiker griechischer
Epigramme imitiert wird – als auch explizit durch die Herstellung eines Bezugs
zur Gattungstradition im Schlusssatz.[77] Hier spielt Camerarius auf einen ganzen
Zyklus von Epitaphien auf Heuschrecken im 3. Buch der *Anthologia Planudea* an
und markiert damit ausdrücklich seine Anknüpfung an das literarische Modell.[78]
In dieser Sammlung konnte Camerarius auch Gedichte auf Pferde vorfinden.[79]
Es zeichnet sich somit hier bereits ab, dass der Bezug des Dichters Camerarius
zur *Anthologia Planudea* anders zu bewerten ist als das distanzierte Verhältnis des
Herausgebers Camerarius zu der von Aldus Manutius verlegten Edition. Dies

---

[75] Herrlinger (1930, 14–51, 92–94) unterscheidet bei den antiken Trauergedichten auf Tiere
zwischen drei verschiedenen Macharten: den ernst-sentimentalen, den parodistischen und den
pointierten Epikedien. Das vorliegende Werk ist der ersten Gruppe zuzuordnen.

[76] Zentrale Werke auf diesem Gebiet sind Camerarius' Übersetzungen der xenophonteischen
Schriften „Περὶ ἱππικῆς" (1539) und „Ἱππαρχικός" (1543) sowie sein eigener Traktat zur Reitkunst
„Ἱπποκομικός" (1539); vgl. zu Camerarius und die Hippologie, Sannicandro (2017).

[77] Zum Anspruch, den das literarische Epigramm des Hellenismus an das literarische Vorwissen der
Leser stellt, vgl. Meyer (2005, 110–114).

[78] *Anth. Plan.* III, 153v (= *AG* 7.190; 7.192); *Anth. Plan.* III, 154r (= *AG* 7.189; 7.195); *Anth.
Plan.* III, 154v (= *AG* 7.197–198). Mit der Ausnahme von *AG* 7.195 handelt es sich bei allen
Epigrammen um Epitaphien.

[79] Vgl. *Anth. Plan.* II, 88r (= *AG* 11.259; 11.293). Hierbei handelt es sich allerdings nicht um
Epitaphien.

hat er auch schon im anfangs besprochenen Widmungsbrief zu seiner Ausgabe antiker Epigramme zu erkennen gegeben.

Satirisches Epigramm

Camerarius kennt aber auch die satirische Spielart des Epigramms. Diese begegnet beispielsweise in einem Dialog zwischen einem Fremden und der Frömmigkeit (Εὐσέβεια):[80]

Ξένος   Εὐσέβεια
Ξ. Οἴμοι τάλαινα, τίς σ᾽ ἄρ᾽ ὧδ᾽ ἀείκισε,
τὴν εὐσέβειαν τήν ποτε μακαρίαν ὁρῶ;
Φεῦ καὶ λέοντος δῆγμα, κ᾽ Ἀδριηνοῦ λύκου
κ᾽ Αὐσονίδος ἕλκημ᾽ αὖ τὸ δ᾽ ἄρκτου ὦ μελέα.
Οὐδεὶς δέ σ᾽ εὐσεβῶν βοήθησεν θεά;   5
Εὐσ. Ποῦ γῆς γάρ εἰσιν εὐσεβεῖς φίλε ξένων
Ξ. Οὐδέν᾽ ἀγαθὸν γοῦν ἡ δὲ[81] γαῖα νῦν τρέφει;
Εὐσ. Παύρους γ᾽ ἔτ᾽, ἀλλ᾽ ὅμως ἐμοὶ κεκακωμένους.
Ξ. Σπεύδ᾽ ἄγε πρὸς ἰητῆρας, πρὶν θανεῖν, κάλει.
ἤδη[82] γὰρ ἆσθμα νείατον ψυχῆς πνέεις.   10
Εὐσ. Οὔκ ἐστιν ἐμὲ θέμις θεάν γ᾽ οὖσαν θανεῖν.
Ξ. Ὅπως δέ τις παύσειε τῶν σε σῶν πόνων.
Εὐσ. Πολλῶν ἰατρῶν εἴσοδοι μ᾽ ἀπώλεσαν.

Fremder   Frömmigkeit
Fremder: O weh! Du Elende! Wer hat dich denn so verunstaltet? Sehe ich die Frömmigkeit, die einst glückselig war? Schrecklich! Ein Happen für den Löwen, eine Beute, die der adriatische und der ausonische Wolf fortschleppt oder ein andermal der Bär, o du Unglückliche. [5] Hat dir, Göttin, keiner von den Frommen geholfen?
Frömmigkeit: Wo auf Erden sind denn die Frommen, lieber Fremder?
Fremder: Nährt die Erde jetzt keinen einzigen guten Menschen?
Frömmigkeit: Nur wenige noch, aber ebenso wie ich wurden sie hart mitgenommen.

---

[80] Erstdruck: Camerarius (1538, 111). Später nochmals in Philipp Melanchthon (1563).

[81] ἡ δὲ] ἤδὲ ed.

[82] ἤδη] ed. 1563; ἤδου ed. 1538

Fremder: Beeil dich! Auf! Ruf Ärzte herbei, bevor du stirbst! [10] Denn schon
tut deine Seele ihren letzten Atemzug.
Frömmigkeit: Mir ist es nicht erlaubt zu sterben, da ich eine Göttin bin.
Fremder: Möge dich jemand von deinen Lasten befreien.
Frömmigkeit: Der Besuch vieler Ärzte hat mich zugrunde gerichtet.

Mit der Themenwahl schließt Camerarius an drei Epigramme der *Anthologia
Planudea* an (*APl* I, S. 22v–23r). Die allegorische Frömmigkeit jammert über ihren
schlechten Zustand. Die Behandlung durch die Ärzte habe sie endgültig zugrunde
gerichtet. Auch für dieses Gedicht liegt eine Anspielung auf die Zeitläufte nahe:
Hinter den Ärzten sind wohl die Theologen zu vermuten. Gerade dieses Epigramm
muss Melanchthons Aufmerksamkeit geweckt haben, denn er fertigte eine lateinische
Übersetzung dazu an.[83] Das Interesse des Reformators gerade für dieses Gedicht
spricht dafür, dass in dem Epigramm ein aktueller Zeitbezug gesehen wurde.

Einen weiteren bedeutsamen Gegenstand satirischer Behandlung stellen
bei Camerarius wie in der *Anthologia Planudea* bestimmte Berufsgruppen und
menschliche Charaktertypen dar. So nimmt etwa das mit Εἰς ἰατρούς betitelte
Epigramm (S. 116) eine Tradition auf, zu der sich in der *Anthologia Planudea*
eine ganze Gruppe von Gedichten unter der entsprechenden Überschrift
zusammengestellt findet (*APl* I, S. 34r-35r). In seinem Spottgedicht eignet
sich Camerarius aus einem antiken Einzeldistichon (*APl* I, S. 34r = *AG* 9,53)
den Gedanken an, dass die Kunst des Hippokrates in der Unterwelt für eine
allgemeine Flaute sorgte. Dieses Motiv baut der Humanist aus: Zu Hippokrates'
Zeiten war Charon aus Armut gezwungen, in Lumpen zu leben; nun aber,
wo es eine unermessliche Schar an Ärzten gebe, die durch ihre „Kunst" reich
geworden seien, könne sich auch der Fährmann in purpurne Gewänder kleiden
und entspannen.

Man darf somit zu der Feststellung gelangen, dass sich Camerarius
sowohl als Herausgeber als auch als Dichter intensiv mit der Tradition des
antiken Epigramms auseinandersetzt, dass sich aber je nach Funktion seine
Herangehensweise deutlich unterscheidet: Während Camerarius sich bei der
Erstellung seiner Sammlung antiker Epigramme möglichst unabhängig von
der *Anthologia Planudea* zeigt, orientiert er sich bei seiner eigenen literarischen
Produktion deutlich näher an dem antiken Modell. Dies wird durch konkret
greifbaren Prätextbezug ersichtlich.

---

[83] Gedruckt in Melanchthon, *Epigrammata*, 1563, O6r–O6v.

Noch eine weitere Beobachtung sei hier festgehalten: Allzu derber Spott, wie etwa bei Poliziano auf eine alte Frau, wo ein auf die Antike zurückreichender Motivstrang (Horaz, Martial, Iuvenal) noch verdichtet wird, findet sich bei den satirischen Epigrammen des Camerarius nicht.[84] Dies kann man sicherlich damit erklären, dass sich die griechische Tradition der Satire milder zeigt als die lateinische. Camerarius wird auf diese Weise aber auch Melanchthons Forderung nach einer Wendung der Dichtung ins Christliche gerecht.[85]

Weitere Epigrammtypen

Auch die Unterkategorie des erotischen Epigramms wird von Camerarius bedient. Der Humanist scheint hiermit demonstrieren zu wollen, dass er auch dieses Register beherrscht. Hierbei fällt in der Ἐπιγράμματα-Sammlung von 1538 (S. 116) ein Gedichtpaar mit den Titeln „Ἐρωτικόν" und „Ἐκ τοῦ ἐναντίου" ins Auge, welches das Motiv der Tränen und des inneren Brands in kontrastiver Gegenüberstellung behandelt. Bei dem von Eros entfachten „inneren Feuer" (ἐντὸς πῦρ με φλέγει, zweites Epigramm, v. 2) lässt sich die Spur zurück zur antiken Epigrammdichtung verfolgen.[86] Allerdings wird man auch hier feststellen, dass Camerarius insgesamt bei der erotischen Thematik Zurückhaltung walten lässt. Eine personalisierte Geliebte wie etwa eine Alessandra Scala, der Poliziano einen ganzen Gedichtband widmet, sucht man bei Camerarius vergeblich.[87] Auch hierin zeigt sich Camerarius wieder loyal gegenüber den Forderungen seines Freundes Philipp Melanchthon.

Eine ganz andere und zunächst nicht weniger überraschende Gattung in den Epigrammata von 1538 findet sich mit den fünf in Abfolge angeordneten Hymnen (S. 122–132).[88] An diesem Punkt entfernt sich Camerarius möglicherweise

---

[84] Zu Polizianos Epigramm *In anum* vgl. Gärtner (2015, 120–122).

[85] Ein wichtiges Dokument für Melanchthons christliche Konzeption der Literatur bildet seine 1545 erschienene *Cohortatio ad legendas tragoedias et comoedias*.

[86] Vgl. z.B. *APl*, VII.273r (= *AG* 5.124); *APl* III, 134v (= *AG* 7.217).

[87] Zur zyklenartigen Zusammenstellung der besagten Epigramme bei Poliziano vgl. Gärtner (2015, 123–125).

[88] Unter den Ἰοαχείμου ὕμνοι finden sich die folgenden Epigramme: 1) Εἰς τὸ ἅγιον πάσχα. (*Inc.*) Φωσφόρε νειοτόκοιο διὸς ἄμβροτον ἤματος αἴγλην (S. 122–123); 2) Χριστῷ Ἰησῷ νικητῇ τοῦ θανάτου. (*Inc.*) Τίπτε μόρ᾽ ἄμμορε τίπτ᾽ ἔτι σῇ βίηφι θρασύνῃ (S. 123–124); 3. Ἰησῷ Χριστῷ σωτῆρι ἀναβιωσκομένῳ. (*Inc.*) Χριστὲ πατρὸς θεὸς υἱὲ θεοῦ σύνθ᾽ εἷς τε δύω τε (S. 124–128); 4. Παράπτωμα τοῦ Ἀδάμου. (*Inc.*) Ὤμοι ἀναιδείην ἐπιειμένε κερδαλεόφρων (S. 128–129); 5. Τῷ ἁγίῳ πνεύματι. (*Inc.*) Πνεῦμα θεοῦ δύναμις μεγάλη μεγάλου θεὸς αὐτὸς (S. 129–132).

am weitesten von der antiken Tradition. Aber selbst für eine solche Form von geistlicher Dichtung konnte Camerarius an das antike Epigramm anknüpfen. So begegnen auch in Manutius' Ausgabe der *Anthologia Planudea* zwei Hymnen, einer auf Dionysos und einer auf Apollo.[89] Für die Einfügung von Hymnen in eine Epigrammsammlung konnte sich Camerarius also auf eine antike Traditionslinie berufen.

Man kann somit abschließend zu der Feststellung gelangen, dass bei den Dichtungen in Camerarius' Epigrammbuch in der Regel ein Gedicht der *Anthologia Planudea* als Modell zugrunde liegt.[90] Noch eine weitere wichtige Beobachtung zur Überlieferung der einzelnen Epigramme kann an dieser Stelle festgehalten werden: Mit der Ausnahme einiger weniger Epitaphien, die selbst zuvor schon Bestandteile einer Sammlung waren, sind sämtliche Epigramme im Druck von 1538 ausschließlich hier überliefert.[91] Dies ist als ein Indiz zur Genese des Werkes zu werten ist und legt die Vermutung nahe, dass Camerarius die Gedichte eigens für diese Sammlung konzipiert hat. Somit sind die Werke vor dem Hintergrund einer planvollen Gestaltung eines Ensembles zu betrachten.

III. Camerarius als Herausgeber eigener Epigramme

Für einen Dichter, der sich der *imitatio* verschreibt, sind nicht nur einzelne Epigramme sowie gängige Motive und formale Strukturelemente der Epigrammatik mögliche Gegenstände der Nachahmung, auch die Gedichtsammlung als ein Anordnungssystem kann ihm als Modell dienen.[92] In Hinblick auf Editionspraktiken hat die jüngere Forschung festgestellt, dass schon antike Epigrammsammlungen systematisch aufgebaut waren. Dies konnte Kathryn Gutzwiller für die *Anthologia Palatina*, oder genauer gesagt, für die Sammlungen,

---

[89] *APl* I.32r–33r = *AG* 9.524 und 525.

[90] Dies gilt ebenso für Poliziano, den Camerarius ja dafür lobt, dass er sich in den „Spuren der Alten" bewegt. Zu Polizianos griechischer Epigrammdichtung und seiner Beschäftigung mit der *Anthologia Planudea* vgl. Pontani (2002, XXXI–XLVIII).

[91] Eine seltene Ausnahme bildet das oben besprochene Eusebeia-Epigramm, das gemeinsam mit Melanchthons Übersetzung im Zusammenhang der Epigramme des Wittenberger Reformators wiederholt abgedruckt wurde.

[92] Mit diesem Unternehmen geht Camerarius einen Schritt weiter als etwa Janos Laskaris, der zwar ebenfalls eine große Anzahl an griechischen Gedichten verfasst hat, sie jedoch nicht selbst in Form einer Sylloge zur Publikation gebracht hat; vgl. Meschini (1976, 3f.).

auf denen diese beruht, feststellen.[93] Aber auch in der Frühen Neuzeit gab es Projekte von Epigrammsammlungen, die Camerarius bekannt waren und an denen er sich orientieren konnte. So etwa von Poliziano, der explizit von einem „griechischen Epigrammbüchlein" spricht, das er beinahe fertiggestellt habe: *composui propemodum libellum Graecorum epigrammatum.*[94] Aber insbesondere an der von Janos Laskaris herausgegebenen und von Aldus Manutius gedruckten Ausgabe der *Anthologia Planudea* konnte sich Camerarius, wie er es als Verfasser einzelner Epigramme getan hat, auch bei der Zusammenstellung seiner Gedichte orientieren. Und so zeichnet sich durchaus eine durchdachte Gliederung in seiner Epigrammsammlung von 1538 ab. In groben, aber erkennbaren Zügen folgt er einem Ordnungssystem wie es auch die Ausgabe der *Anthologia Planudea* ansetzt. Die Epigramme sind in beiden Sammlungen nach unterschiedlichen Themen geordnet (Über die Ärzte; Erotika usw.). Am Anfang stehen bei Camerarius` Epigrammen Gedichte zu verschiedenen abstrakten Themen. Dann folgen Spottepigramme, Weihepigramme, Rätselepigramme, poetologische Epigramme, Hymnen, Epitaphien und schließlich die Ὀνειροριτικά. Eine deutliche Gliederung innerhalb der Epitaphien ist insbesondere bei der früheren Sammlung von 1531 festzustellen, wo ein Übergang von den Sepulkraldichtungen auf reale Personen hin zu Grabepigrammen auf fiktive Personen und eben auch auf Tiere erkennbar wird. Sie sind also nach dem Prinzip der zunehmenden Literarizität angeordnet.

Es fällt somit auf, dass Camerarius bei der Zusammenstellung der selbst verfassten Epigramme eine andere Praxis verfolgt als bei der Herausgabe der überlieferten Gedichte im ersten Teil des Druckes: Bei der Edition antiker Epigramme versuchte sich der deutsche Humanist, wie wir gesehen haben, deutlich von der Leistung des Aldus Manutius abzusetzen, bei der Herausgabe von eigenen Epigrammen hingegen orientiert er sich wieder an den Formen der *Anthologia Planudea*. Strebte er einerseits in seiner Edition antiker Epigramme danach, etwas Eigenständiges gegenüber der früheren Edition zu bieten, folgt er hinsichtlich der Anordnungsprinzipien der selbstverfassten Gedichte wieder stärker dem tradierten Modell einer Epigrammsammlung.

---

[93] Gutzwiller (1998 *passim*).

[94] Der Text der *epist.* 5.7 findet sich in seiner gesamten Länge herausgegeben bei Pontani (2002, XXV–XXVI). Ediert werden sollten Polizianos Epigramme erst postum, aber festzuhalten bleibt, dass er den Plan eines Gedichtbuches verfolgte. Dies hat er wohl auch beinahe zu Ende gebracht, wie sein Editor Zanobi Acciaiuoli (Zenobius Acciaiolus) in der Vorrede zu der Ausgabe zu erkennen gibt: *Ang. Po. Graeca epigrammata sicut in archetypo volumine scripta erant publicanda curavi.*

IV. Camerarius als Übersetzer von Epigrammen

Camerarius verfasst ferner Übersetzungen von Epigrammen. Auch hier bietet die Ausgabe von 1538 eine besonders umfangreiche Sammlung. Im Blickpunkt stehen antike Epigramme. So überführt Camerarius etwa das literarische Epitaph des Kallimachos über den Suizid des Kleombrotos ins Lateinische. Jedoch erstellt er auch eine Version des griechischen Epigramms des Jakob Micyllus über die Weisheit (Εἰς τὴν σοφίαν).[95] An diesem Gedicht und seiner Wiedergabe im Lateinischen lässt sich beispielhaft Camerarius' Übersetzungstechnik aufzeigen. Micyllus beginnt sein Epigramm mit der gnomenhaft formulierten Feststellung, dass lange Zeitdauer alles zerstöre: „Πάντα χρόνος φθίνει μακρός". Darauf folgt eine Aufzählung der Bereiche, in denen sie vernichtend wirkt. Micyllus könnte hierfür Anleihen aus Sophokles' *Oedipus auf Kolonos* (vv. 609ff.) genommen haben, wo dieselbe Denkfigur begegnet. In der Übersetzung (*Micylli sapientia*) gibt Camerarius diesen Satz mit „*Quid non dies longa abstulit*" wieder. Für diese Formulierung greift Camerarius auf den römischen Epigrammatiker Martial zurück (*non me longa dies nec inutilis abstulit aetas*; Mart. 11,69,7). Die Martialreferenz in der Übersetzung ist kennzeichnend für Camerarius' Übersetzungstechnik und fügt sich ein in die von ihm in seinen *Elementa rhetoricae* (Erstdruck 1541) vorgebrachte Forderung, eine Übersetzung solle hinsichtlich der gebrauchten Wendungen an die Zielsprache angepasst sein.[96] Es wird bei der Übersetzung deutlich, was bereits bei den Begleitepigrammen zu Opsopoeus' *De arte bibendi* ersichtlich geworden ist: Camerarius versucht sich in die Traditionslinie der jeweils verwendeten Sprache einzureihen.[97]

Fazit: Camerarius als frühneuzeitlicher Dichter, Übersetzer und Herausgeber von Epigrammen

Die Ergebnisse dieses Überblicks über Camerarius und das griechische Epigramm lassen sich angesichts der unterschiedlichen Formen der Autor- bzw.

---

[95] Druck in Camerarius (1538, 102–103): griechisches Epigramm, 144: lateinische Übersetzung.

[96] Camerarius, Joachim, *Elementa rhetoricae, sive Capita excercitiorum studii puerilis & stili, ad comparandam utriusque linguae facultatem, collecta a Ioachimo Camerario, & proposita in Schola Tubingensi*, Basel 1541, S. 272–305.

[97] Von dieser Praxis lassen sich sicherlich auch Ausnahmen feststellen. Zu Reminiszenzen an Catull, *c.* 62 in der griechischen *Ekloge* XVI, einem Epithalamium, vgl. Mundt, Schäfer & Orth (2004, 275). In der Tendenz trifft diese Beobachtung jedoch zu.

Herausgeberschaft nicht auf einen einzigen Stichpunkt reduzieren. Stattdessen konnte eine Vielzahl von Erkenntnissen zutage gefördert werden:

(a) Bei Camerarius' Epigrammen wird das Bemühen deutlich, eine Form der Dichtung für seine Gegenwart zu schaffen. Dies wird insbesondere dann ersichtlich, wenn er wie bei dem Epitaphium auf Martin Luther am aktuellen reformatorischen Diskurs partizipiert.

(b) Die neualtgriechische Dichtung wird sehr häufig innerhalb von Lehrer-Schüler-Verhältnissen praktiziert, was etwa das Grabepigramm auf Petrus Mosellanus zeigt. Durch den Kontext des Druckes wird das Epitaphium zu einem Element der gemeinschaftlichen Erinnerungspflege einer ganzen Gruppe von Gelehrten.

(c) Die Begleitepigramme haben deutlich gemacht, dass die Verwendung der griechischen Sprache dazu dienen kann, bestimmte Wissensgebiete wie etwa die Medizin als Kompetenzbereiche antiker griechischer Autoren und somit auch der Gräzistik zu markieren. Epigramme fungieren somit auch als wichtige Instrumente bei dem Bemühen, Griechisch als Schul- und Universitätsfach zu fördern.

(d) In der Epigrammsammlung von 1538, in der Camerarius als Herausgeber, Verfasser und Übersetzer griechischer Epigramme hervortritt, wird das humanistische Konzept des Dichterphilologen in paradigmatischer Weise greifbar. Dabei werden die theoretischen Reflexionen des Widmungsbriefes in der Edition fremder und eigener Epigramme in die Praxis umgesetzt. Das Vorhaben des Camerarius, sich einerseits philologisch, andererseits auch dichterisch mit dem griechischen Epigramm auseinanderzusetzen und in beiden Bereichen sein Profil zu schärfen, umfasst sowohl Imitation als auch Innovation: Als Philologe versucht sich Camerarius möglichst stark von der Ausgabe der *Anthologia Planudea* durch Janos Laskaris, die von dem namentlich erwähnten Aldus Manutius gedruckt wurde, abzusetzen. Er wählt andere Epigramme aus der Überlieferungstradition aus und ordnet sie nach einem anderen, dem Anspruch des Philologen besser gerecht werdenden Gliederungsschema an. Für den Dichter hingegen gilt nach dem Widmungsbrief die *imitatio* als das einzig erfolgversprechende Prinzip. Dies führt Camerarius in seiner poetischen Praxis und als Herausgeber der eigenen Epigramme wieder näher an das Modell der *Anthologia Planudea* heran.

Schließlich wird jedoch eines deutlich: Gerade in der Zusammenführung von Herausgeber-, Dichter- und Übersetzerfunktion, die Camerarius in der Epigrammsammlung von 1538 leistet, zeigt sich exemplarisch das übergreifende humanistische Konzept des Dichterphilologen. Beim Epigramm ist es insbesondere die Mannigfaltigkeit seiner Erscheinungsformen, die für den humanistischen Gelehrten eine Herausforderung und auch eine Möglichkeit bieten konnte, seine Kompetenz sowohl in der Tätigkeit des Philologen als auch im Schaffen des Dichters gleichsam spiegelbildlich unter Beweis zu stellen.

Bibliographie

Frühneuzeitliche Drucke

Bocerus, Johann. 1556. *De origine et rebus gestis ducum Megapolensium libri tres Ioannis Boceri*. Leipzig. (VD16 B 5985).

Camerarius, Joachim. 1538. Ἐπιγράμματα Ἑλληνικὰ τῶν παλαιῶν ποιητῶν καὶ ἐπιτάφια μετὰ τῶν ἐπιγραμάτων Ἰωαχείμου Καμεραρίου καὶ Ἰακωβοῦ τοῦ Μικύλλου. *Epigrammata veterum poetarum, cum epitaphiis & epigrammatis Ioachimi Camerarii & Iacobi Micylli*. Basel. (VD16 C 406).

Camerarius, Joachim. 1568. *Libellus novus, epistolas et alia quaedam monumenta doctorum superioris et huius aetatis complectens* [...] *editus studio Ioachimi Camerarii Pabepergensis*. Leipzig.

Hessus, Helius Eobanus & Camerarius, Joachim. 1531. *Illustrium ac clarorum aliquot virorum memoriae scripta epicedia per Helium Eobanum Hessum. Epitaphia epigrammata composita ab Ioachimo Camerario Bombergensi*. Nürnberg. (VD16 E 1509, VD16 C 414).

Laskaris, Janos. 1521. *Florilegium diversorum epigrammatum in septem libros solerti nuper repurgatum cura M.D.XXI*. Ἀνθολογία διαφόρων ἐπιγραμμάτων [...]. Venedig.

Melanchthon, Philipp. 1546. *Oratio in funere reverendi viri D. Martini Lutheri, recitata Vitebergae a Philippo Melanchthone*. Wittenberg. (VD16 M 3849).

Melanchthon, Philipp. 1563. *Philippi Melanthonis epigrammatum libri sex recens editi studio et opera Petri Vincentii Vratislaviensis*. Wittenberg.

Metzler, Johannes. 1529. *Primae grammatices Graecae partis rudimenta, Iohanne Metzler authore*. Hagenau. (VD16 M 4974).

Micyllus, Jakob. 1524. *Epicedia in Petrum Mosellanum, et in Guielmum Nisenum. Wittenberg*. (VD16 M 6108; VD16 M 6104).

Opsopoeus, Vincentius. 1536. *De arte bibendi libri tres, autore Vincentio Obsopoeo*. Nürnberg. (VD16 O 808).

Forschungsliteratur und wissenschaftliche Editionen

Baier, Thomas. 2017. „Das Bildungsprogramm des Camerarius", in Thomas Baier (Hrsg.) *Camerarius Polyhistor. Wissensvermittlung im deutschen Humanismus*, Tübingen, 77–93.

Ciccolella, Federica. 2014. „Epigramm", *DNP Suppl*. 9, 308–315.

Enenkel, Karl A.E. 2009. „Introduction: The Neo-Latin Epigram: Humanist Self-Definition in a Learned and Witty Discourse", in Susanna de Beer, Karl A.E. Enenkel & David Rijser (Hrsg.) *The Neo-Latin Epigram. A Learned and Witty Genre*, Leuven, 1–23.

Gärtner, Thomas. 2015. „Lateinische und griechische Epigramme bei Polizian", in Thomas Baier, Tobias Dänzer & Ferdinand Stürner (eds.) *Angelo Poliziano. Dichter und Gelehrter*, Tübingen, 119–130.

GG = Hieronymus, Frank. 1992 / 2003 / 2011. Εν Βασιλείᾳ πόλει τῆς Γερμανίας. *Griechischer Geist aus Basler Pressen. Katalog der frühen griechischen Drucke aus Basel in Text und Bild*. Edited and prepared for the internet by Christoph Schneider and Benedikt Vögeli in co-operation with Andres von Arx, Andreas Bigger, Martin Cassani, Marie-Claire Crelier, Martin Leuenberger and Thierry Spampinato. Basel.

Greenblatt, Stephen. 1980. *Renaissance Self-fashioning: From More to Shakespeare*. Chicago.

Gutzwiller, Kathryn J. 1998. *Poetic Garlands. Hellenistic Epigrams in Context*. Berkeley–Los Angeles–London.

Hamm, Joachim. 2011. *„Joachim Camerarius d.Ä."*, VL 16, 425–438.

Herrlinger, Gerhard. 1930. *Totenklage um Tiere in der antiken Dichtung. Mit einem Anhang byzantinischer, mittellateinischer und neuhochdeutscher Tierepikedien*. Stuttgart.

Keydell, Rudolf. 1962. „Epigramm", *RAC* 5, 1962, 539–577.

LSJ = Liddell, Henry George, Robert Scott, & Henry Stuart Jones (Hrsg.) 1996. *A Greek-English Lexicon. With a Supplement*. 9. Aufl. Oxford.

Ludwig, Walther. 1998. *Hellas in Deutschland. Darstellungen der Gräzistik im deutschsprachigen Raum aus dem 16. und 17. Jahrhundert*. Hamburg.

Meschini, Anna (Hrsg.) 1976. *Giano Laskaris, Epigrammi greci*. Padova.

Meyer, Doris. 2005. *Inszeniertes Lesevergnügen. Das inschriftliche Epigramm und seine Rezeption bei Kallimachos*. Stuttgart.

Mundt, Lothar, Eckart Schäfer & Christian Orth (Hrsg.) 2004. *Joachim Camerarius, Eclogae / Die Eklogen*. Tübingen.

Pontani, Filippomaria (Hrsg.) 2002. *Angeli Politiani Liber Epigrammatum Graecorum*. Roma.

Rhein, Stefan. 1987. *Philologie und Dichtung. Melanchthons griechische Gedichte (Edition, Übersetzung und Kommentar)*. Inauguraldissertation. Heidelberg.

Rhein, Stefan. 2017. „Philipp Melanchthon und seine griechischen Dichterschüler", in Stefan Weise (Hrsg.) *Hellenisti! Altgriechisch als Literatursprache im neuzeitlichen Europa*, Stuttgart, 15–46.

Sannicandro, Lisa. 2017. „Joachim Camerarius e la traduzione latina del Περὶ ἱππικῆς (*De re equestri*) di Senofonte (1539)“, in Thomas Baier (Hrsg.) 2017. *Camerarius Polyhistor. Wissensvermittlung im deutschen Humanismus*, Tübingen, 187–196.

Schlegelmilch, Ulrich. 2017. „*Imagines amicorum*. Die Briefausgaben des Joachim Camerarius als literarisch gestaltete Werke“, in Thomas Baier (Hrsg.) *Camerarius Polyhistor. Wissensvermittlung im deutschen Humanismus*, Tübingen, 263–300.

Schultheiß, Jochen. 2017. „Joachim Camerarius in Tübingen. Reformation der Gelehrsamkeit – Gelehrsamkeit der Reformation“, in Jörg Robert, Evamarie Blattner & Wiebke Ratzeburg (Hrsg.) *Ein Vater neuer Zeit. Reuchlin, die Juden und die Reformation*, Tübingen, 198–211.

Steinrück, Martin. 2018. „Metric 'Mistakes' in the Greek Epigrams of Angelo Poliziano“, in Janika Päll & Ivo Volt (Hrsg.) *Hellenostephanos. Humanist Greek in Early Modern Europe. Learned Communities between Antiquity and Contemporary Culture*, Tartu, 318–335.

VD16 = *Verzeichnis der im deutschen Sprachbereich erschienenen Drucke des 16. Jahrhunderts*, https://www.bsb-muenchen.de/sammlungen/historische-drucke/recherche/vd-16/.

VD17 = *Das Verzeichnis der im deutschen Sprachraum erschienenen Drucke des 17. Jahrhunderts*, http://www.vd17.de/.

Walter, Jochen. 2017. „Die *Capita pietatis et religionis Christianae versibus Graecis comprehensa ad institutionem puerilem* des Joachim Camerarius (1545) und ihre kürzere Erstfassung in Melanchthons *Institutio puerilis literarum Graecarum* (1525)“, in Thomas Baier (Hrsg.) 2017. *Camerarius Polyhistor. Wissensvermittlung im deutschen Humanismus*, Tübingen, 23–57.

Weise, Stefan. 2016. „Ἑλληνίδ᾽ αἶαν εἰσιδεῖν ἱμείρομαι – Neualtgriechische Literatur in Deutschland (Versuch eines Überblicks)“, *Antike & Abendland* 62, 114–181.

Weise, Stefan. 2018. „*Alter Theocritus?* Joachim Camerarius' griechische Supplemente zu Theokrits *Herakliskos* und dem sogenannten *Herakles leontophonos*“, *Humanistica Lovaniensia* 67, 257–299.

Griechische Mythologie im Dienste reformatorischer Pädagogik: Zur Epensammlung *Argonautica. Thebaica. Troica. Ilias parva* von Lorenz Rhodoman (1588)

STEFAN WEISE

In diesem Beitrag soll eine Sammlung mythologischer Gedichte in griechischer Sprache von dem Renaissancedichter Lorenz Rhodoman (1545/46-1606) vorgestellt und auf ihre Funktion hin untersucht werden (Abschnitt II–V). Besondere Berücksichtigung finden dabei die Proömien, in denen sich der Dichter zum Teil programmatisch äußert (Abschnitt III). Zum Schluss wird den im Titel der Sammlung genannten Gedichten kurz der nicht genannte *Arion* Rhodomans gegenübergestellt, der scheinbar an Angelo Polizianos erotische griechische Dichtung anknüpft (Abschnitt VI). Zur weiteren kulturhistorischen Kontextualisierung wird zunächst jedoch allgemein auf die Rezeption griechischer Mythologie und die Wiederbelebung der griechischen Dichtung und Epik eingegangen (Abschnitt I).

I. Griechische Mythologie und die Wiederbelebung der griechischen Dichtung und Epik in der Renaissance

Auch wenn die griechische Mythologie in der einen oder anderen Form natürlich auch noch im Mittelalter begegnet, sticht ihre sichtbare und prägnante Wiederbelebung in Kunst und Literatur des italienischen Quattrocento dem fernen Betrachter besonders ins Auge. Als berühmte Beispiele könnte man etwa Angelo Polizianos *Stanze per la giostra* und Sandro Botticellis *Geburt der Venus* oder *Primavera* nennen.[1] In Verbindung mit antikisierender Liebesdichtung

---

[1] Zu den *Stanze* siehe Staiger (1974, mit deutscher Übersetzung). Zu Botticellis *Geburt der Venus* und *Primavera* siehe u.a. Dombrowski (2010, 53–61, 69–77) und Zöllner (2015, 62–80, 88–92). Zum Zusammenhang von Polizians *Stanze* und Botticellis mythologischen Gemälden siehe Warburg (1893) und Dombrowski (2010, 57f.; 72f.). Botticelli kann in dieser Hinsicht als „eigentlicher Erfinder" der neuen Gattung des mythologischen Gemäldes, vor allem des „monumentalen mythologischen Einzelbildes" mit komplexer Synthese von bild- und textlichen Vorlagen gelten. Siehe Zöllner (2015, 6, 92).

und sprachlicher Anlehnung an antike Vorbildautoren macht dieser Zug der Renaissance, die man freilich nicht darauf verengen und reduzieren kann, zweifelsohne einen der auffälligsten Züge der erneuerten Antikerezeption aus. Bald wimmelt es überall von Putten, Atlanten und allegorischen Götterfiguren. In Medaillen und Druckersignets erscheinen Grazien, Musen, Apoll und Minerva.[2] Zimmer und Schränke werden mit mythologischen Szenen dekoriert: Leda und der Schwan, das Parisurteil, Zeus und Ganymed.[3]

Wichtige Grundlage dafür ist die Wiedererschließung der lateinischen und griechischen Literatur, insbesondere der Dichtung, aber auch philosophischer Texte. Man denke an Edgar Winds berühmtes Buch über die *Heidnischen Mysterien in der Renaissance* (1958/dt. 1987). Zur besseren Orientierung stellte man bald auch neue mythologische Handbücher zusammen und griff freudig auf die mythographischen Texte der Antike zurück, die man im Druck neu edierte. Ein sehr frühes und bis weit ins 16. Jahrhundert einflussreiches Werk waren besonders Giovanni Boccaccios *Genealogie deorum gentilium* (1532). Aus diesen und den anderen Werken von Giovanni Battista Giraldi, Natale Conti und Vincenzo Cartari zogen Maler und Gelehrte ihre Inspiration, wie Seznec in seinem Buch über das *Fortleben der antiken Götter* (1940/dt. 1990) zeigte. Und natürlich wollte man dieses wiederentdeckte Wissen überall anbringen.

Insofern erstaunt es nicht, dass der Drang zur Erschließung und Nachahmung der Quellen sich nicht nur auf lateinische und italienische Literatur oder Malerei beschränkte, sondern bald auch eine eigenständige neu-altgriechische bzw. humanistengriechische Literatur hervorbrachte.[4] Wirksam hat dies in größerem Stil erstmals Angelo Poliziano (1454–1494) unternommen, der noch zu Lebzeiten einen *libellus epigrammatum Graecorum* zusammenstellte, der allerdings erst postum von Zanobi Acciaiuoli in der *Opera*-Ausgabe von 1498 bei Aldus Manutius erschienen ist.[5] Provozierend und neu ist an dieser Sammlung nicht nur das Medium der griechischen Sprache, die Vielfalt der Formen und Metren, sondern auch die Themen: insbesondere die explizite Erotik mancher

---

[2] Zu Druckersignets und Wappen siehe Ludwig (1999) und ausführlich Wolkenhauer (2002).

[3] Zur Verwendung und Verbreitung mythologischer Bilder im deutschen Kontext vgl. Matsche (1994 und 1996).

[4] Vgl. dazu bspw. Pontani (2017). Zur Diskussion der Begriffe „Neualtgriechisch" bzw. „Humanistengriechisch" siehe u.a. Päll & Volt (2018, 9); Weise (2016, 114); Weise (2019, 7 Anm. 5).

[5] Schon vor Polizian hat Francesco Filelfo (1398–1481) ein ähnliches Projekt verfolgt, hat seine griechische Gedichtsammlung *De psychagogia* allerdings nicht veröffentlicht. Siehe Cortassa & Maltese (1997, V. 1–4); Pontani (2017, 313–315).

Epigramme. Am deutlichsten tritt beides etwa in der kühnen Schöpfung eines Epigramms auf die *Aphrodite anadyomene* hervor, mit dem sich Polizian selbst ans Ende einer Reihe antiker Epigramme zum selben Thema setzt und damit direkt an die antike Tradition anknüpft.[6] Stolz hatte er in einem Brief (*epist.* 5.7) an Antonio Urceo genannt Codro (1446–1500) erklärt, dass er die griechischen Musen wieder aus ihrem Schlaf geweckt habe, da es seit 600 Jahren[7] kein von Griechen geschriebenes Gedicht mehr gebe, das man zu lesen ertragen könne: *non enim poema reperitur ullum citra sexcentos annos a Graecis conditum, quod patienter legas.*[8] Mit einem Federstrich schiebt er damit die byzantinische Literatur beiseite und propagiert so einen Neubeginn der antiken griechischen Dichtung. Doch was er uns bietet, ist in der Tat erstaunlich: das Bild einer Aphrodite, die auffällig an die Venus Botticellis erinnert, die Polizian selbst mit seinen *Stanze* inspiriert hatte (Nr. 54):[9]

Κύπριν Ἀπελλείας ἔργον χερός, ὡς ἴδον, ἔσταν
    δαρὸν θαμβαλέος, τὰν ἀναδυομέναν.
τᾶς ἅτε παρθενικᾶς, ἅτε καὶ φιλοπαίγμονος αἰδὼς
    τὰν ὄψιν μίγδαν ἔλλαχεν ἠδὲ γέλως.
καὶ τᾷ μὲν ῥαθάμιγγας ἁλιβρέκτοιο καράνου   5
    δεξιτερᾷ θλίβεν καὶ κελάρυζεν ἀφρός·
ἦν δ' ἄρα τᾶς νοτίδος τὶς ἐμοὶ φόβος. ἁ δέ γε λαιὰ
    ἔσκεπε τὰν ἄβαν τὰν ἔθ' ὑποβρύχιον
(καὶ γὰρ ἕως λαγόνων ὕφαλος πέλε), καί τις ἔτι φρὶξ
    ματρὸς ἀπ' ὠδίνων ὄμφακα μαστὸν ἕλεν.   10
εἰ τοίαν πόκ' Ἄρης ἔχε δέσμιος, οὐκ ἀποδῦναι
    οὐδ' Ἀφαιστείας ἤθελ' ἀλυκτοπέδας.[10]

Kypris, sobald ich sie sah, das Werk von der Hand des Apelles, blieb ich lange staunend stehen: Es war die *Anadyomene* (die [aus dem Meer] Auftauchende). Da sie Jungfrau ist und auch verspielt, hatten zugleich Scham und ein Lächeln ihr Gesicht erfasst. Und mit der Rechten drückte sie Tropfen von ihrem mit Meerwasser benetzten Kopf aus und es sprudelte der Schaum: [5] Ich hatte

---

[6] Siehe *Anth. Plan.* IVᵃ 8.22–26 (= *Anth. Graec.* 16.178–182).

[7] Vielleicht ist die Zahl auch unbestimmt im Sinne von „seit unzähligen Jahren" gemeint.

[8] Zitiert bei Pontani (2002, XXV).

[9] Griechischer Text nach Pontani (2002, 222). Siehe dazu auch Pontani (2017, 316f.).

[10] Alle Übersetzungen stammen von mir.

also eine gewisse Angst vor der Feuchtigkeit. Die Linke aber bedeckte ihre Scham, die noch unter Wasser war (denn bis zu den Hüften war sie unter Wasser) und noch ein Wassergekräusel erfasste [10] von den Geburtswehen der Mutter her ihre straffe Brust. Wenn Ares einstmals in Ketten eine solche Schönheit gehabt hätte, dann hätte er auch die unlösbaren Fesseln Hephaists nicht ablegen wollen.

In Verbund mit der Verwendung des Dorischen, der bis ins Detail ausgearbeiteten Stellung der Wörter und nicht zuletzt der expliziten Erotik ist das freilich in jeder Hinsicht kühn.[11] Nicht weniger herausfordernd sind seine griechischen Gedichte an Alessandra Scala (Nr. 28; 30–33; 48; 51), um die er mit Ianos Laskaris (1445–1534) in Versen wetteiferte. Von Polizian übernahmen dann auch die deutschen Humanisten das griechische Dichten. In einem Cento aus Polizian-Versen himmelt etwa Johannes Reuchlin (1455–1522) Konstanze Peutinger an und spielt dabei geschickt in Anlehnung an seinen Namen und sein Wappen (ein Altar mit glühenden Kohlen) mit der Feuermetaphorik.[12] Doch ist er im Gegensatz zu Polizian im Nachhinein eifrig bedacht, darauf hinzuweisen, dass seine Liebesbekundung rein platonisch zu verstehen sei. Das allzu offen „Pagane" und Erotische meiden die deutschen Humanisten.[13]

Einen prägenden Einfluss im protestantischen Bereich hatte dabei das Dichtungsverständnis Melanchthons, für den das Lob Gottes im Vordergrund der Dichtung zu stehen hatte, während er erotische Stoffe weitgehend verbannt wissen wollte: Auf keinen Fall sollte Dichtung zum Ehebruch einladen.[14] Dementsprechend wandten sich führende protestantische Neulateiner vor allem geistlicher Dichtung zu und suchten eine Erneuerung der christlichen Lyrik.[15] Prominente Figuren sind hier etwa Eobanus Hessus (1488–1540) mit seinen christlichen „Heroiden" (1514; 1532) und seiner Psalterparaphrase (1537) sowie später besonders Georg Fabricius (1516–1571) mit seinen christlichen Hymnen

---

[11] Entsprechend war die Reaktion des Freundes Urceo, der mit explizitem Verweis auf das *Anadyomene*-Epigramm antwortete: *Ede, ede quam celerrime.* Siehe Hutton (1935, 138f.).

[12] Das Reuchlin-Gedicht ist abgedruckt bei Rhein (1989, 74–79).

[13] Hier soll freilich nicht gesagt sein, dass Polizian ein getarnter „Heide" war. Man beachte auch, dass sich seine Aphrodite die Scham bedeckt und bis zu den Hüften unter Wasser steht (V. 8f.). Trotz aller Laszivität ist es also eine *Venus pudica*. Vgl. Dombrowski (2010, 73).

[14] Vgl. Ludwig (2001b, 35–43).

[15] Siehe Huber-Rebenich (2006, 69–74).

und Paeanen, die erstmals Walther Ludwig umfänglich untersucht hat.[16] Die Paraphrase rückte so zu einer der beliebtesten Formen auf, da sie sprachliche Eleganz mit christlichen Inhalten verband.[17]

Paraphrasen scheinen denn auch am Anfang der Wiederbelebung der griechischen Epik gestanden zu haben.[18] Bei Polizian finden wir, wie gesagt, nur kürzere griechische Epigramme. In Form von Begleitepigrammen (Paratexten) dringen sie mit dem Buchdruck auch um 1500 in den Norden vor. Größere Dichtungen fehlen zunächst. Ein erstes umfangreicheres Gedicht (200 Verse) findet sich dann in der Platon-Ode von Markos Musuros (um 1470–1517) aus dem Jahr 1513.[19] Diese ist allerdings noch im elegischen Distichon gehalten. Den Sprung zur epischen mehrere Bücher umfassenden Form wagt meines Wissens als Erster der im heutigen Frankreich geborene Sebastian Castellio (1515–1563) mit seiner epischen Paraphrase der Geschichte um Johannes den Täufer mit dem Titel *Prodromos seu Praecursor,* die 1545 bei Johannes Oporin in Basel zusammen mit einem lateinischen *Ionas propheta* erschienen ist. Die Verbindung mit Pindars erster Olympischer Ode im Proöm zeigt bereits den besonderen Anspruch des Werkes. In der Folgezeit entstanden eine Reihe weiterer griechischer Bibelparaphrasen unter den Melanchthonschülern[20] wie Paul Dolscius (1526–1589),[21] Johannes Posselius d.Ä. (1528–1591)[22] und dann besonders von den Schülern Michael Neanders (1525–1595),[23] der nach Melanchthon und Joachim Camerarius zweifelsohne einer der wichtigsten Initiatoren und Anreger griechischer Dichtung in Deutschland geworden ist, so dass es nicht zu viel gesagt ist, wenn man von ihm als Gründer einer ganzen Schule epischer Dichter im Griechischen spricht, der „Ilfelder Dichterschule".[24] Der profilierteste und bekannteste unter

---

[16] Siehe Ludwig (2001a); Ludwig (2001b, 44–49).

[17] Siehe Czapla (2013).

[18] Kürzere Paraphrasen liturgischer Texte gab es schon bei Griechischgelehrten in Italien. Siehe dazu ausführlich Pontani (2018).

[19] Siehe dazu Sifakis (1954); Dijkstra & Hermans (2015). Mit englischer Übersetzung auch bei Wilson (2016, 302–317).

[20] Zu Melanchthons griechischen Dichterschülern siehe Rhein (2017).

[21] Vgl. Weise (2016, 160).

[22] Zu Posselius siehe ausführlich Johnson (2006, speziell zu den Εὐαγγέλια καὶ Ἐπιστολαί, 200f.).

[23] Zu Neander siehe ausführlich Meister (1881–1882).

[24] Angedeutet in dem grundlegenden Beitrag von Ludwig (1998, 74). Zur „Ilfelder Dichterschule" siehe jetzt auch Weise (2019, 20–26).

Neanders Dichterschülern ist Lorenz Rhodoman (1545–1606).[25] Ihm zunächst ist weiterhin besonders Matthaeus Gothus (1548–1619) zu nennen.[26]

Im Zentrum der größeren Dichtungen dieser „Ilfelder Dichterschule" stehen dabei vor allem biblische oder theologische, speziell protestantische Stoffe. Mythologische Themen spielen hier also (außer in Okkasionaldichtung) zunächst keine Rolle mehr, mit einer signifikanten Ausnahme: Die 1588 in Leipzig erschienene Epensammlung *Argonautica. Thebaica. Troica. Ilias parva* von Lorenz Rhodoman, die uns im Folgenden näher beschäftigen soll.

II. Zur Epensammlung

Ungewöhnlich ist nicht nur eine Sammlung von epischen Gedichten über fast alle wichtigen Sagenkreise der griechischen Mythologie, – die Sage um die Fahrt der Argonauten unter Jason nach Kolchis zur Erlangung des Goldenen Vlieses, der thebanische Sagenkreis um Ödipus und schließlich die Geschehnisse um Troja –, ungewöhnlich ist besonders die Angabe zur Herkunft der Gedichte. Auf dem Titelblatt heißt es dazu:

> *Poematia Graeca Auctoris Anonymi, sed pereruditi, & incredibili planeque divinâ & Homericâ facilitate & suavitate composita; Ac nuper admodum sublata & prolata è bibliotheca summi & eruditi viri, ubi diu hactenus delituerant, & descripta non sine molestia & labore ex exemplari malè scripto & edita in usum studiosae iuventutis [...]*

> Kleine griechische Gedichte eines anonymen, aber sehr gelehrten Verfassers mit unglaublicher, ganz und gar göttlicher und homerischer Leichtigkeit und Anmut geschrieben; erst kürzlich wegnommen und ans Licht gebracht aus der Bibliothek eines hochstehenden und gebildeten Mannes, wo sie lange bisher verborgen waren; nicht ohne Anstrengung und Mühe abgeschrieben aus einer schlecht geschriebenen Vorlage und zum Nutzen der lernbegierigen Jugend herausgegeben [...]

---

[25] Zu Rhodoman als griechischem Dichter siehe v.a. Ludwig (2014; 2018), Gärtner (2016; 2017a; 2017b) und Weise (2016, 133–136; 2019).

[26] Gothus hat sich in besonderem Maße den Stil und die Verstechnik des Nonnos zu eigen gemacht. Siehe dazu demnächst Gärtner (2020).

Als Herausgeber wird dann Michael Neander genannt, Leiter der Klosterschule Ilfeld am südlichen Harzrand in der Mitte Deutschlands. Lange nach der großen Phase der Entdeckungen und *editiones principes* vom Ende des 15. und Anfang des 16. Jahrhunderts scheint es sich hier also um einen Neufund griechischer Gedichte zu handeln. Es werden die typischen humanistischen Topoi bedient, um dieser Entdeckung das entsprechende Narrativ zu geben und sie attraktiv zu machen: Die Gedichte waren lange in einer Bibliothek verborgen (*diu delituerant*), mussten daraus gleichsam heimlich entwendet werden (*sublata*) und mit viel Mühe (*non sine molestia & labore*) aus einem schlecht geschriebenen Exemplar (*ex exemplari malè scripto*) abgeschrieben werden. Neben diesen sensationellen Umständen der Entdeckung und Herausgabe wird zugleich jedoch die Qualität der Gedichte besonders gerühmt. Sie seien das Werk eines *auctor pereruditus* und gekennzeichnet durch *facilitas* und *suavitas* eines Homer. Das alles klingt in der Tat nach dem bedeutenden Neufund unbekannter antiker Texte. Hinzu kommt die „Geheimniskrämerei": *bibliotheca summi & eruditi viri* („die Bibliothek eines hochstehenden und gelehrten Mannes"). Sein Name wird freilich nicht genannt. Und auch der Dichter ist ein Anonymus. Bei den Titeln *Argonautica, Thebaica, Troica* und *Ilias parva* denkt man natürlich an die nur aus sekundärer Überlieferung bekannten kyklischen Epen. Dabei übersieht man bei dem ganzen auf der Titelseite betriebenen „Hokuspokus" schnell, dass gar nicht gesagt ist, dass es sich um antike Texte handelt (dies wird nur durch *diu delituerant* insinuiert).

Trotzdem sind einige auf diesen ohne Zweifel absichtlichen literarischen Coup hineingefallen und das nicht nur in der Zeit selbst, sondern auch noch später bis ins neunzehnte Jahrhundert hinein. Zu den prominenten „Opfern" zählt etwa der Jesuit Denis Pétau oder Dionysius Petavius (1583–1652), der in seiner Chronologie *Rationarium temporum* sowohl die *Thebaica* als auch die *Troica* als Autoritäten heranzog.[27] Ein anderes „Opfer" war der Philologe Karl Wilhelm Göttling, der zu Anfang des 19. Jahrhunderts in seinen *Animadversiones criticae in Callimachi epigrammata et Achillem Tatium* ebenfalls auf Belegstellen aus der Sammlung verwies.[28] In einem Brief des bekannten Lexikographen Franz Passow vom 23. März 1812 wird er freundlich auf seinen Irrtum hingewiesen (in Klammern sind die Abkürzungen von mir aufgelöst):

Endlich noch eine litterarische Berichtigung! Sie belegen den Gebrauch von ἐπινίσσομαι mit dem Accus(ativ) aus der *Ilias parva* und dem *Arion*; aber mit

---

[27] Siehe Petavius (1633, 156, 161–165).

[28] Göttling (1811, 22).

diesen Gedichten hat der alte Neander der gelehrten Welt einen muthwilligen Streich gespielt, indem der *auctor anonymus* niemand anders als Neanders Schüler Laurentius Rhodomannus ist. Was alsbald gegen die Aussage des Titels, der von einem *exemplari male scripto* redet […], Verdacht erregen kann, ist die wunderbar gute Erhaltung unserer *poematia graeca*. […] Den historischen Beweis gegen Alter und für den Verfasser, den ich Ihnen genannt, finden Sie in *Fabric(ii) bibl(iotheca) Graeca T(omus) I. p(agina) 377 Harl(es)*,[29] woraus Sie auch zu Ihrem Trost ersehn werden, daß Petavius, Morellus und Barnes eben so getäuscht worden sind, wie Sie.[30]

Damit ist also klar, dass Neanders Schüler Lorenz Rhodoman der Verfasser ist.[31] Wir brauchen dafür übrigens nicht auf Fabricius zurückgreifen, sondern Rhodoman und Neander enthüllen die Anonymität noch 1588[32] bzw. ein Jahr später selbst. So verrät Neander im Begleitbrief zu Rhodomans 1589 erschienenem *opus magnum*, dem neun Bücher umfassenden historischen Lehrgedicht *Palaistine*, dass die Gedichte von Rhodoman stammen.[33]

---

[29] Gemeint ist der erste Band der Neuauflage von Fabricius' *Bibliotheca Graeca* durch Gottlieb Christoph Harles (1790, 377), wo an der erwähnten Stelle ausgeführt ist: *Ceterum falsus est Petauius, qui in Rationario temporum part. I. lib. I. cap. 10. part. II. lib. II. cap. 9. 10. et alibi pro veteri illa parua Iliade habuit, tum* Federicus Morellus, *qui tamquam veteris poetae graeci cum versione et notis Parisiis in 8. edidit poema Iliacum graecum eruditi, sed recentis poetae,* Laurentii Rhodomanni, *quod sine auctoris nomine edidit* Michael Neander, *Lips. 1588. 8. vna cum eiusdem Rhodomanni Argonauticis, Thebaicis et Troicis, siue Epitome Homeri et Cointi totius historiae Troianae, stylo Homerico elegantissime expressa, Troicis item Manassae versibus politicis, et poemate Dorico Rhodomanni de Arione Methymnaeo. Troica eadem, praefixo, ne quis dubitet, Rhodomanni nomine, paululum mutata leguntur cum Metaphrasi Latina poetica ad Calcem Cointi Smyrnaei, Hanou. 1604 8.* Bei der Edition Morells handelt es sich im Übrigen nicht um ein Gedicht Rhodomans, sondern einen Ausschnitt von Tzetzes' *Antehomerica*.

[30] Der Brief ist abgedruckt bei Wachler (1839, 167f.). Gemeint sind hier der schon erwähnte Denis Pétau, Josua Barnes (1654–1695) und Fédéric Morell (1558–1630). Vgl. dazu auch Weise (2019, 28, Anm. 105).

[31] Auf wen genau die Idee der anonymen Veröffentlichung zurückgeht, ist nicht mit Sicherheit zu sagen. Da Rhodoman in zwei der Proömien (siehe unten) die „Neuheit" betont, könnte der Anstoß vielleicht von Neander ausgegangen sein, der ja auch als Herausgeber fungiert. Auf ihn werden wohl auch die lateinischen *argumenta* zurückgehen, die den Gedichten vorangestellt sind. Außerdem steht am Ende der Sammlung sein Motto *Vanitas vanitatum & omnia vanitas*.

[32] Rhodoman verrät seine Verfasserschaft schon 1588 in einem Brief an Nicodemus Frischlin. Siehe Frischlin (1588, 77).

[33] Siehe Rhodoman (1589, 6).

Interessant ist nun neben der Tatsache, dass die Gedichte anonym veröffentlicht worden sind, auch noch die weitere Ausstattung des Bandes, der folgende Textverteilung aufweist:

A 1r	Titelblatt
A 1v	Titelblatt zu den *Argonautika*
A 2r–A 3v	Argumentum Argonauticorum
A 4r–B 5v	ΑΡΓΟΝΑΥΤΙΚΑ
B 6r–v	De Apollodoro
[B 7r]–Γ 4v	Argonautica Apollodori
Γ 5r	Titelblatt zu den *Thebaika*
Γ 5v–Γ 6v	Argumentum Thebaicorum
Γ 6v–[Δ 8r]	ΘΗΒΑΙΚΑ
[Δ 8v]–E 5r	Thebaica Apollodori
E 5v	Titelblatt zu den *Troika*
[E 6r]–Z 1v	Argumentum Historiae belli Troiani
Z 1v–[I 7v]	ΤΡΩΙΚΑ
[I 8r]–[K 7r]	Troica Manassae versu politico scripta
[K 8r]	Titelblatt zur *Ilias parva*
[K 8v]–Λ 3r	De scriptoribus belli Troiani e Synopsi Chronicorum Neandri
Λ 3r–O 2v	ΙΛΙΑΣ Η ΚΑΛΟΥΜΕΝΗ ΜΙΚΡΑ
O 3r	Titelblatt zum *Arion*
O 3v–O 5r	Argumentum Arionis e libro primo Herodoti, et libro 16. cap. 19. Gellij noctium Atticarum, ubi his verbis scriptum reperitur
O 5r–Σ 2v	ΑΡΙΩΝ

Außer lateinischen *argumenta* und zusammenfassenden Marginalien zu den Gedichten (als Ersatz für durchgehende lateinische Übersetzungen) enthält der Oktavband also auch noch andere Texte, vor allem Exzerpte aus Pseudo-Apollodors *Bibliotheke*, so dass neben die Gedichte selbst noch sowohl Erklärungen als auch Paralleltexte treten, wodurch sie zusätzlich in den Rang zu erklärender antiker Texte aufsteigen. Gänzlich auf dem Titelblatt unterschlagen ist schließlich noch ein weiteres Gedicht Rhodomans, auf das weiter unten noch kurz einzugehen sein wird: der von Passow schon erwähnte *Arion*, der sich in seiner Gestaltung deutlich von den anderen Gedichten abhebt, formal betrachtet vor allem durch seinen, wie es bei Passow heißt, „wirklich schnurrige[n] und etwas schülerhafte[n] Dorismus, in welchem das sonst sehr anmuthige Gedicht geschrieben ist".[34]

---

[34] Wachler (1839, 167).

III. Analyse der Proömien von *Argonautica, Thebaica* und *Troica*

Nach diesem ersten Überblick über die Sammlung sollen die Texte selbst etwas näher betrachtet werden, um Genaueres über Machart und Intention dieser seltsam anmutenden Sammlung zu erfahren. Trotz der Bezeichnung als *poematia* sind die Gedichte von nicht unerheblicher Länge. *Argonautica* und *Thebaica* umfassen jeweils etwa um die 560 Verse, die *Troica* und die *Ilias parva* etwa 1700 Verse. Dazwischen steht der erwähnte *Arion* mit genau 1248 Versen, was also in etwa dem doppelten Umfang von *Argonautica* und *Thebaica* sowie etwa 2/3 des Umfangs von *Troica* und *Ilias parva* entspricht. Diese Zahlenverhältnisse lassen schon möglicherweise auf eine planvolle Gestaltung der Sammlung schließen. Um jedoch nicht nur bei den Zahlen zu verharren, empfiehlt sich zunächst ein Blick auf die Proömien der durchgehend hexametrischen Gedichte. Auch hier lässt sich rein quantitativ eine Entwicklung feststellen, indem sie von *Argonautica* über *Thebaica* zu den *Troica* immer ausführlicher und elaborierter werden. Die *Ilias parva* hat kein Proöm, was an ihrem besonderen Charakter liegt (siehe unten Abschnitt IV).

Fangen wir mit dem kürzesten Proöm, dem der *Argonautica*, an. Es umfasst lediglich zwei Verse (V. 1–2):

Ἥντιν' Ἰησονίης νηὸς[35] στόλος ἔλλαβεν ἀρχὴν
καὶ τέλος ἐξερέω. μοῦσαι δ' ὑποφήτορες εἶεν.[36]

Den Anfang, welchen die Fahrt von Jasons Schiff nahm, und das Ende will ich erzählen. Die Musen aber mögen Verkünder sein.

Ganz klassisch wird das Thema genannt und die Musen werden angerufen. Mit der Wendung μοῦσαι δ' ὑποφήτορες εἶεν greift Rhodoman einen Halbvers aus dem Argonautenepos des Apollonios Rhodios (1.22) auf. Besonders auffällig an der knappen Themenangabe ist der Anspruch auf Komplexität: ἀρχή und τέλος will der Dichter künden. In der Tat berichtet der Dichter in den folgenden

---

[35] Die Junktur Ἰησονίης νηός lehnt sich vielleicht an Theoc. 22.31 an.

[36] Folgende Adaptionen wurden bei den griechischen Texten von Rhodoman vorgenommen: a) Fehlende Akzente und Spiritus bei Majuskeln wurden stillschweigend ergänzt, b) die Interpunktion behutsam der deutschen Norm angepasst, c) die Großschreibung am Versanfang aufgegeben, d) vor Satzzeichen Gravis zu Akut geändert und e) Zusammenschreibungen mit einfachem kopulativem τε getrennt. Die Verszählung ist von mir ergänzt.

Versen die gesamte Argonautenfahrt. Dabei beginnt er deutlich früher als Apollonios mit der Genealogie Jasons, angefangen von Kretheus, dem Gründer von Iolkos und Großvater von Jason. Er bemüht sich also von Anfang an um eine umfassende Darlegung der genealogischen und mythologischen Voraussetzungen und schließt sich mit dem Beginn bei den Aioliden Kretheus und Salmoneus darüber hinaus an den Bericht von Pseudo-Apollodor an, der sich ja, wie schon dargelegt, in Neanders Edition auch unmittelbar an den Text anschloss (Apollod. *Bibl.* 1.107). Auch am Ende greift er über Apollonios hinaus, indem er mit den Geschehnissen in Korinth seinen Bericht beschließt. Im Mittelteil über die Abenteuer während der Fahrt aber folgt der Dichter sehr eng Apollonios und ergänzend den *Orphischen Argonautika* (zuerst 1500 in Florenz erschienen),[37] die er beide kürzend so textnah verbindet, dass man teilweise fast von einer centoartigen Epitome sprechen könnte.

Wesentlich ambitionierter präsentiert sich das Proöm zu dem zweiten Gedicht *Thebaica* (V. 1–7):

Θήβης ἑπταπύλοιο μόθον καὶ δύσμορον ἄτην
Καδμιαδέων, βαρύμηνις ὅσην πόρσυνεν ἐριννύς,[38]
ἐξ ἀρχῆς ἐνέπειν ἑλικώνιος οἶστρος ἐπείγει
Κασταλίῳ τε νέην κιρνᾶν ἐμὲ νέκταρι μολπήν,
ἣν καὶ πρόσθε κέρασσαν ἑοῖς θέλκτροισιν ἀοιδοί·   5
τὴν γὰρ ἀοιδὴν μᾶλλον ἐπικλείουσ᾽ ἄνθρωποι,
ἥτις ἀκουόντεσσι νεωτάτη ἀμφιπέληται.[39]

Den Kampf um das siebentorige Theben und die unglückliche Verblendung der Kadmos-Nachkommen, welche die heftig zürnende Erinnye bereitete, von Anfang an zu künden, drängt mich ein helikonischer Trieb und mit kastalischem Nektar neuen Gesang zu mischen, [5] den schon vorher die Dichter mit ihren Zaubermitteln mischten. Denn den Gesang preisen die Menschen mehr, welcher die Zuhörer jeweils als neuester umtönt.

Wiederum verwendet Rhodoman die kanonischen Elemente des epischen Proöms, variiert und erweitert sie aber signifikant zum ersten Proöm. Das Thema

---

[37] Zur frühen Rezeption der *Orphischen Argonautika* im Westen siehe Botley (2010, 110f.).

[38] ἑ- ed.

[39] Neander (1588, [Γ 6v]).

ist der Kampf um Theben (Θήβης ἑπταπύλοιο μόθον) und die Verblendung der Kadmos-Nachkommen (δύσμορον ἄτην / Καδμιαδέων). Neu ist, dass Rhodoman eine göttliche Instanz, die Erinnye, als Ursache für die Verblendung benennt. Der Musenanruf wird geschickt variiert, indem Rhodoman jetzt von einem ἑλικώνιος οἶστρος spricht, der ihn inspiriert habe, sein Thema ἐξ ἀρχῆς zu künden. Mit dem Stichwort ἐξ ἀρχῆς wird wiederum der komplexive Charakter angedeutet. Am Ende des Prööms folgt nun aber noch eine Aussage zu poetischen Vorgängern und zur Qualität des Gedichtes. Rhodoman macht deutlich, dass er einen schon vielbesungenen Stoff aufgreift: neben den nicht erhaltenen griechischen Thebais-Epen genügt es an die zahlreichen Tragödien zum Thebenstoff oder auch Statius' lateinisches Epos zu erinnern. Letzteres klingt hier sogar in dem Ausdruck ἑλικώνιος οἶστρος direkt an, den Statius mit den Junkturen *Pierius calor* (1.3) und *Pierius oestrus* (1.32) ebenfalls im Prööm seiner *Thebais* verwendet hat.[40] Die Tätigkeit der älteren Dichter wird mit dem Verb κεραννύναι (‚mischen') umschrieben. Dasselbe will auch Rhodoman tun. Er will ein neues Gedicht mit ‚kastalischem Nektar' mischen. Es geht also wesentlich um die sprachliche Ästhetik, wobei das Verb ‚mischen' eben offensichtlich auch den konstanten Rückgriff auf poetische Vorbilder einschließt. Die Pointe folgt am Schluss: Worin liegt der Reiz seiner Neubearbeitung? – Die Menschen preisen immer den neuesten Gesang! Hier greift Rhodoman auf ein Zitat aus dem ersten Gesang der *Odyssee* zurück (1.351–352). Anders als man nach den Insinuationen von der Titelseite der Sammlung vermuten könnte, wird hier also nicht ein vorgeblich alter Gesang präsentiert, sondern die Neuheit und Aktualität wird hervorgehoben.

In den folgenden Versen bietet Rhodoman tatsächlich wieder eine komplexe Darstellung des Mythos, angefangen von dem Gründer Thebens, Kadmos, bis zu den Epigonen, und greift dafür vor allem am Anfang auf Nonnos' *Dionysiaka*[41] und später auf die Dramen des Sophokles und Euripides zurück.[42]

---

[40] Für den Hinweis auf Statius danke ich Thomas Gärtner (Köln).

[41] Der Einbau der *Dionysiaka* wirft die Frage nach der Entstehungszeit auf. Entweder ist der Text erst nach der *editio princeps* 1569 entstanden oder Rhodoman hat eine Ilfelder „Urfassung" nach 1569 umgearbeitet oder in Ilfeld gab es schon vor 1569 eine Abschrift der *Dionysiaka*.

[42] Eine klare Reminiszenz aus Euripides' *Phoenissen* findet sich etwa in den Versen 406–408, in denen es um den Selbstmord des Menoikeus geht: μουνοβάτης πρὸς ἔπαλξιν ἀλεξιμόθων κίε πύργων, / εἴρυσε δὲ ξίφος ὀξὺ μελάνδετον οὗ παρὰ μηροῦ / καὶ λαιμοῖο διῆκε, πάτρην δ᾽ ἐρρύσατο μόχθων – Eur. *Phoen.* 1090–1092: ἐπεὶ Κρέοντος παῖς ὁ γῆς ὑπερθανὼν / πύργων ἐπ᾽ ἄκρων στὰς μελάνδετον ξίφος / λαιμῶν διῆκε, τῇδε γῇ σωτηρίαν, [...]. Auf Benutzung von Sophokles' *Antigone* deutet etwa das Adjektiv μελλόγαμος in V. 519 hin (dort von Haimon, bei Soph. *Ant.* 628 von Antigone).

Als Grundgerüst dient aber wiederum der ebenfalls abgedruckte Bericht Pseudo-Apollodors.

Das ausführlichste Proöm schließlich geht den *Troica* voran.[43] Hier sind es 22 Verse, in denen Rhodoman nicht nur Musenanruf und Themenangabe bietet, sondern auch eine ausführliche Poetik. Der erste Teil ist zunächst ganz traditionell (V. 1–10):[44]

Δεῦτε θεαὶ λιγυροῖσιν ἀγαλλόμεναι μελέεσσιν,
ἃς Διῒ Μνημοσύνη ποτ᾽ ἐγείνατο, δῶκε δὲ ναίειν
Παρνησοῦ κορυφὰς καὶ ἐΰφρονος ἄντρ᾽ Ἑλικῶνος
κρήνης θ᾽ ἱππογενοῦς[45] ζάθεον ῥόον ἀμφιπολεύειν,
δεῦτε θεαὶ πρὸς ἐμὸν νεοειδέος ἔργον ἀοιδῆς·   5
καὶ ταῖς νῦν θαλερῆσιν ὀρώρεται ἐν φρεσὶν ὁρμὴ
εἰπεῖν ἐξ ἀρχῆς Τρώων φάτιν ἄχρι τελευτῆς
Ἀργείων θ᾽ ἱδρῶτα κακόν τ᾽ εἰς πατρίδα νόστον
καὶ δέμας εἰς ἓν ἄγειν, σποράδην ὅσα χεῦαν ἀοιδοὶ
πλειοτέροις ἐπέεσσιν, ἐγὼ δ᾽ ὀλίγοισιν ἐνίψω.   10

Kommt hierher, ihr euch an helltönenden Liedern erfreuende Göttinnen, die Mnemosyne einst dem Zeus gebar und ihnen gewährte, die Gipfel des Parnass und die Höhlen des heiteren Helikon zu bewohnen und den heiligen Strom

---

[43] Vgl. dazu auch Gärtner (2017, 117).

[44] Siehe Neander (1588, Z 1v). In der zweiten Ausgabe der *Troica* von 1604 (als Anhang zu seiner Quintus-Ausgabe mit eigener Seitenzählung) hat Rhodoman die ersten fünf Verse ersetzt und an ihre Stelle den Gedanken einer *translatio* der Musen von Griechenland nach Deutschland ausgeführt: Μνημοσύνη λιγυράς [-ὰς ed.] ποτ᾽ ἐγείνατο πότνια μούσας, / δῶκε δὲ Παρνησοῦ ζάθεον κλέτας ἀμφιπολεύειν. / νῦν δὲ πατὴρ μετένασσεν ὀλύμπιος ἐς χθόνα σεμνῶν / Γερμανῶν καὶ ἄνωγε παλαιά τε καινά τ᾽ ἀείδειν, / ὅσσα θεῷ τ᾽ ἐπίηρα βροτῶν τ᾽ εἰς χρῆσιν ἱκάνει. / καὶ ταῖς νῦν κτλ. Siehe Rhodoman (1604, *Tr.* 2). In Responsion zum ursprünglichen Anfang erscheint damit die Aufforderung δεῦτε nun erfüllt und die Ankunft der Musen vollzogen.

[45] Das Kompositum ἱππογενής ist im *LSJ* nicht belegt. Es findet sich aber als Beiwort ebenfalls zu κρήνη in einem Epigramm von Joachim Camerarius: οὐδ᾽ ἐγὼ αὐτὸς ποιητὴν ἐμέ φημι γενέσθαι / οὐδέ τε Παρνασσοῦ βῆν᾽ ἐπ᾽ ὄρους κορυφήν, / οὐδ᾽ ἐμ᾽ [an ἔμ᾽ pro ἐμά?] ἐν ἱππογένους [sic!] ἐποτίσθη χείλεα κρήνης / οὐδέ με Πιερίδων ὅσσα προσῆλθε θεῶν […]. Siehe Camerarius & Micyllus (1538, 119). Dafür, dass Camerarius' griechische Dichtung rezipiert worden ist, spricht etwa auch die Übernahme der Junktur λυγκῶν αἰολοδέρμων aus Camerarius' Supplement zu Theoc. 24 (siehe Weise 2018, 290) in Johan Paulinus' späterer griechischer Dichtung *Finlandia* (V. 200: Λὺγξ αἰολόδερμος). Siehe Korhonen, Oksala & Sironen (2000, 56).

der pferdegeborenen Quelle zu umsorgen, [5] kommt hierher, Göttinnen, zu meinem Werk neuartigen Gesangs. Auch den jetzt blühenden (Musen) erhebt sich im Sinn der Drang, die Sage der Troer von Anfang bis Ende, die Mühe der Argeier und ihre üble Rückkehr in die Heimat zu künden und das in eine Gestalt zu bringen, was die Dichter verstreut [10] mit mehreren Worten gesagt haben; ich aber werde es mit wenigen (Worten) sagen.

Wiederum betont Rhodoman nach Anrufung der Musen die Neuheit (V. 5: νεοειδέος) und die Komplexität seiner Darstellung: ἐξ ἀρχῆς […] ἄχρι τελευτῆς (V. 7), ‚von Anfang bis Ende‘, will er die Sage über die Troer, die Mühe der Argeier und ihre Rückkehr schildern. Er verweist wiederum auf Vorgängerdichtungen und präzisiert seine Eigenleistung: Er will zusammenführen, was vorher verstreut (σποράδην) von Dichtern behandelt wurde, und er will dies mit wenigen Worten tun. Neben Komplexität und Neuheit tritt hier also noch die Kürze. In den restlichen Versen kommt nun noch weiterhin erstmals eine Aussage über das intendierte Publikum und den Zweck (V. 11–22):

οὐ μέλπω πινυτοῖσι καὶ ἀνδράσιν, οἷς ἅλις ἐστὶν
ἰδμοσύνης, ποθέω δὲ νέοις παίδεσσιν ὑφαίνειν
χρήσιμ’, ὅσοι φιλέουσιν Ἀχαιΐδος ἤθεα μούσης.
οὐ κρύπτειν γὰρ ἔοικε θεοῦ πολυκυδέα δῶρα,
ἀλλὰ βροτοῖς πολέεσσιν, ὅσον σθένος, ἔνθεν ἀρήγειν   15
χείρεσιν ἐσθλοπόνοισι καὶ εὐβούλοις πραπίδεσσι.
τοὔνεκεν εἰ ζητεῖ τις ἐς Ἑλλάδα ῥάδιον οἶμον,
ἡγεσίης ἀπόναιτο καὶ ἀγχινόοισι πεδίλοις
τῇδε μολὼν δρέψαιτο παλαιῶν καρπὸν ἀοιδῶν,
καρπὸν ἐπιστήμης τε καὶ ἤθεος ἠδὲ καὶ αὐδῆς.   20
νῦν δ’ ἄρ’ ἐγὼν ἄρχοιμι, φίλον δέ μοι ἔργον ἀρωγῆς
θεσπεσίης εὔκαιρος ἐλαφρίσσειεν ἀήτης.

Nicht singe ich für Kundige und Männer, die genug Wissen haben, sondern ich will für junge Knaben Nützliches weben, so viele den Charakter der griechischen Dichtung lieben. Denn es gehört sich nicht, die ruhmvollen Gaben Gottes zu verbergen, [15] sondern man muss vielen Menschen, soweit man vermag, von da her mit guter Tat und gutem Rat helfen. Wenn also jemand einen leichten Weg nach Griechenland sucht, möge er von meiner Führung Nutzen ziehen und, wenn er hierher mit scharfsinnigen Sohlen gekommen ist, die Frucht der alten Dichter, [20] die Frucht von Wissen, Moral und Sprache ernten. Jetzt aber möchte ich also anfangen, mein Werk jedoch möge mir zur rechten Zeit der Hauch göttlicher Hilfe erleichtern.[46]

Das Zielpublikum sind also παῖδες, Kinder, die sich für das Griechische interessieren. Ihnen will er einen Zugang zur griechischen Dichtung gewähren und zu Nutzen sein, damit sie so das Wichtigste aus der griechischen Dichtung ernten können: den καρπός von ἐπιστήμη (Wissen), ἦθος (Moral) und αὐδή (Sprache). Rhodoman will also nicht weniger als ein Konzentrat der griechischen Dichtung der Antike bieten. Und in der Tat umfassen seine *Troica* wiederum den trojanischen Krieg in komplexiver Weise, indem Rhodoman weit vor Homer quasi *ab ovo* anfängt und weit nach ihm aufhört. Die Erzählung beginnt mit den trojanischen Königen ab Dardanos. Endpunkt seines Gedichtes ist der Tod Helenas nach der Rückkehr der Griechen. Zwischendrin werden *Ilias*, Quintus' *Posthomerica* und die *Odyssee* jeweils kurz zusammengefasst. Neben weiteren Quellen greift Rhodoman für die Vorgeschichte wiederum auf Pseudo-Apollodor zurück (insbesondere für die Erzählung über die troischen Könige von Dardanos bis Priamos).[47] Als eigene philologische Leistung kann man dabei werten, dass Rhodoman für die Darstellung der Vorgeschichte natürlich auch auf die Rückblicke aus der homerischen *Ilias* mit längeren Zitaten zurückgreift und sie chronologisch anzuordnen versucht. Zwar zerstört er dadurch die schon von Aristoteles gerühmte thematische Konzentration bei Homer im Gegensatz zu den kontinuierlichen Erzählungen der kyklischen Epen (Arist. *Poetik* 1451e; 1459a–b), erlaubt aber Lesern, die das homerische Werk noch nicht in seiner Gänze kennen, einen Überblick und eine Einordnung der homerischen Verweise.

Damit ergibt sich also insgesamt als Kernanliegen der Sammlung die Zusammenfassung der wichtigsten Sagenkreise für Schüler in poetischer Form. Rhodoman verbindet dies mit den Zielen der sprachlichen, moralischen und wissenschaftlichen Schulung. Bevor jedoch näher betrachtet werden soll, wie Rhodoman diese Schulung in die Präsentation der Mythen integriert hat, soll noch ein kurzer Blick auf die *Ilias parva* und die Entstehung der Gedichte geworfen werden.

---

[46] Statt εὔκαιρος schreibt Rhodoman in der Edition von 1604 ᾧ πείθομ' (als christliche Note?). Ebenso könnte sich V. 14–16 vielleicht auf das Neue Testament beziehen (Mt 5,14–16). In der zweiten Edition von 1604 sind V. 14f. Anführungszeichen vorangesetzt. Siehe Rhodoman (1604, *Tr.* 2 u. 4).

[47] Vgl. Apollod. *Bibl.* 3.138–155, aber auch 2.103f. (Mauerbau durch Apollon und Poseidon); 134–136 (Herakles' Feldzug gegen Troia).

IV. Die *Ilias parva* und die Entstehung der Sammlung

Die *Ilias parva* fällt aus den kurz vorgestellten Gedichten *Argonautica, Thebaica* und *Troica* nicht nur durch den andersartigen Titel, sondern auch durch ihre Machart heraus. Als einziges der Gedichte der Sammlung hat sie kein Proöm. Dies hat seinen Grund darin, dass es sich bei der *Ilias parva* nicht wie bei den anderen Gedichten um eine zusammenfassende Darstellung des Mythos aus verschiedenen Quellen handelt, sondern um metrifizierte *argumenta* der einzelnen Gesänge von Homers *Ilias* und Quintus Smyrnaeus' *Posthomerica*. In gewissem Sinne ist also die *Ilias parva* das unselbstständigste der Gedichte, wenn Rhodoman wohl auch seinen Eifer darauf verlegt hat, nicht einfach wie in den *Argonautica* Zitate und Halbverse kompilierend zusammenzufügen, sondern durchaus eigenständig zu formulieren.[48] Man könnte daher von einer „poetischen Epitome" sprechen.[49] Dieser Punkt führt uns schließlich zur Entstehung der Gedichte.

Rhodoman selbst gibt uns besonders im Vorwort zu seiner epochemachenden Ausgabe von Quintus Smyrnaeus aus dem Jahr 1604, die im Übrigen auch eine Neuausgabe der *Ilias parva* und *Troica* mit lateinischer Versübersetzung enthält, einen Einblick in die Methode, mit der ihn Neander ans griechische Dichten herangeführt hat.[50] Danach habe Neander seinen Schüler zunächst zur intensiven Lektüre von Homer und Quintus angeleitet und ihn ermuntert, aus beiden Dichtern Phrasen und Einzelausdrücke zu sammeln. Neander führte Rhodoman also zu der auch von anderen bekannten *Phrase book*- bzw. *Commonplace book*-Technik[51] und stellte ihm dafür auch seine eigenen Ausgaben der Dichter mit entsprechenden Adnotaten zur Verfügung. Rhodoman sollte nun seine Sammlung in der Art von Georg Fabricius' lateinischen Sammlungen *Elegantiae poeticae* (1554 und öfter) und *De re poetica* (1556 u.ö.) anordnen und systematisieren. So wurde Rhodoman innerhalb von etwa anderthalb Jahren in die Lage versetzt, wie er sagt, jedes von Neander gestellte Thema in griechische Verse zu bringen.[52] Zu diesen Aufgaben gehörten wohl auch die Periochen von

---

[48] Dass auch hierin ein künstlerischer Anspruch liegt, zeigt sich etwa, wenn Rhodoman es schafft, den homerischen Schiffskatalog aus dem zweiten Buch der *Ilias* in seinem Gedicht auf 30 Verse zu kürzen. Zu antiken Homer-Epitomai, -Hypotheseis und -Periochen siehe bspw. Reitz (2007); Reitz (2010, 295–304).

[49] Diesen Begriff verwendet Reitz (2007) für die *Ilias Latina*.

[50] Siehe Rhodoman (1604, † 2v–3r).

[51] Vgl. dazu Adams (2015, 81–87).

[52] Siehe Rhodoman (1604, † 3r): *Annus interim effluxerat, iamque alter in cursu erat, cum tantum*

Ilias und *Posthomerica*, die dann in der *Ilias parva* zusammengeflossen sind. Dann scheinen die *Argonautica*, *Thebaica* und schließlich die *Troica* hinzugekommen zu sein. Ein weiteres Ergebnis dieser frühen Sammeltätigkeit waren die später von Johannes Volland herausgegebenen vier Bücher *De re poetica Graecorum*, eine gewaltige alphabetisch geordnete Sammlung von Epitheta, Phrasen, Beschreibungen und gelungenen Stellen aus beinahe der gesamten griechischen Dichtung, vor allem aber der Epik.[53] Man wird sicherlich bei diesem Werk von einer Art „Hausapotheke" der „Ilfelder Dichterschule" sprechen können. In dieser Sammelleidenschaft liegt sicher auch die besondere Sorgfalt der Ilfelder in der Auswahl von Epitheta und Formung von neuen Komposita begründet, die den vor allem von spätantiker Epik gekennzeichneten Stil bestimmen: Hier sind u.a. als Stilmuster neben Homer und Quintus vor allem Apollonios Rhodios und Nonnos, aber auch etwa Musaios, Kolluthos und Triphiodor zu nennen.

V. Umgang mit dem Mythos

Bleibt zum Schluss die Frage, wie Rhodoman nun die Mythologie für seine Zwecke zur schulischen Unterweisung nutzbar macht. Denn eine Wiederbelebung der griechischen Mythologie erstrebt Rhodoman nicht nur um ihrer selbst willen: Er schreibt für ein christliches Publikum, nennt explizit vor allem „Knaben". Und Neander hat sogar gefordert, dass man die Lektüre antiker paganer Dichtung zugunsten zeitgenössischer christlicher Dichtung einschränken soll. Besonders die lasziven Mythen um die Liebesabenteuer des Zeus waren ihm ein Dorn im Auge.[54] Dies wird als kritischer Punkt besonders deutlich, wenn Rhodoman in seiner überarbeiteten Version der *Troica* aus dem Jahr 1604 auf das Verhältnis von Zeus und Ganymed zu sprechen kommt. Dort heißt es in explizit antipaganer Weise:[55]

---

ex analectico illo studio utilitatis redundaret, ut quodvis argumentum vel à magistro propositum, vel arbitratu meo delectum, dictione Homerica non incommodè (ut ipsi tum videbatur) redderem. Vgl. Weise (2019, 115–117).

[53] Volland (1582). Eine zweite Auflage ist zehn Jahre später ebenfalls in Leipzig erschienen. Siehe dazu kurz Hummel (1994, 130).

[54] Siehe Neander (1565, 176 [*Prefatio*]). Mit dem Verweis auf Zeus' Liebschaften greift Neander einen Topos aus der christlichen Apologetik auf. Vgl. Schmitz (2013, 488f.). Zum Problemfeld siehe auch Kühlmann (1993).

[55] Siehe Rhodoman (1604, 8 [*Troica*]). Bei V. 103f. und 107f. handelt es sich um Zitate aus Gregor von Nazianz (PG 37,1558,4f. 7f.). In der Ausgabe von 1588 (ebd. Z 3r) folgt nach V. 101 ([…] εὔπτερον εἱμένος ὄρνιν) unmittelbar V. 111.

τοὔνεκα μὶν Κρονίδης ἀνερείψατο παῖδα μετεῖναι
ἀθανάτοις καὶ νέκταρ ἐΰχροον οἰνοχοεύειν
αἰετὸν ἐκπροϊεὶς τανυσίπτερον ἠὲ καὶ αὐτὸς   100
εἶδος ἀμειψάμενος καὶ ἐΰπτερον εἱμένος ὄρνιν.
παντοῖος γὰρ ἔγεντο λυγρῆς διὰ Κύπριδος ὁρμήν·
ταῦρος, κύκνος, ὄφις, χρυσός, πόσις, ἄρκτος, ἄπαντα,
ὅσσα μιν ὠκὺς ἄνωγεν ἔρως κοῦρός τ' ἀλαπαδνός.
ὦ μέλεοι τυφλοί τε καὶ ἄφρονες, οἵ ῥα σέβεσθε   105
νηοῖς εὐχωλαῖς τε πολυκνίσσοις τε θυηλαῖς
ψεύστας, ἀνδροφόνους, σκολιούς, ἐπίορκον ὀμοῦντας,
ἅρπαγας, ἀνδρογύνους, μοιχούς, ἐπιβήτορας ἀνδρῶν·
τοίους γὰρ τοίων τε χερείονας ἔθνεα γαίης
Ἑλλάδος ἀλλοδαπῆς τε θεοὺς σέβον ἄφρονι θυμῷ.   110

Deshalb (sc. wegen seiner Schönheit) entführte der Kronide den Knaben in die Höhe, dass er unter den Unsterblichen sei und schönfarbenen Nektar einschenke, [100] indem er einen breitflügeligen Adler schickte oder auch selbst seine Gestalt verwandelte und die des schönflügeligen Vogels annahm. Denn jegliche Gestalt nahm er wegen des Triebs der betrüblichen Kypris an: Stier, Schwan, Schlange, Gold, Ehegemahl, Bär, alles, was ihm der schnelle und schwache Erosknabe befahl. [105] Oh Ihr nichtigen, blinden und unverständigen Menschen, die Ihr mit Tempeln, Gebeten und fettdampfreichen Opfern Lügner, Mörder, Betrüger, Meineidige, Räuber, Schwächlinge, Ehebrecher und Männerbespringer verehrt! Denn derartige Götter und noch schlimmere als diese verehrten die Völker [110] Griechenlands und fremden Landes mit unverständigem Sinn.

Nachdem sich Rhodoman also als Verfasser zu erkennen gegeben hat, sieht er sich offensichtlich nochmals zu einer eindeutigen Distanzierung vom paganen Göttermythos gezwungen. Aber freilich fügt Rhodoman die Mythen schon in der ersten Sammlung von 1588 in sein pädagogischen Konzept ein, und zwar indem er sie als Exempel guten und schlechten Verhaltens moralisiert.[56] Die tragischen Ereignisse in Korinth, Theben und Troja erscheinen jeweils als Ergebnis ungezügelter *libido*. Der Fall Trojas wird als Folge des Ehebruchs von

---

[56] Entsprechend sagt Melanchthon im *Chronicon Carionis* bei der Besprechung der griechischen Mythen der Heldenzeit (*CR* 12, 772): *Etsi autem illae vetustae narrationes plenae sunt fabularum, tamen nihil dubium est, multas res veras illis involucris significatas esse.* Vgl. auch Matsche (1994 und 1996) zur moralisierenden Funktion von Cranachs mythologischen Bildern.

Paris und Helena, der Untergang der Labdakiden in Theben als Folge von Laios'
in Trunkenheit begangener Übertretung des Orakels, welches ihm die Zeugung
von Kindern verbot, und das Ende von Jason und seinen Kindern als göttliche
Strafe für die Ermordung von Medeas Bruder Apsyrtos gedeutet. Der griechische
Mythos dient hier also als Beispiel für das Prinzip der göttlichen Bestrafung
menschlicher Freveltaten, insbesondere der *libido*, und die Durchsetzung
göttlicher Gerechtigkeit. In allen drei Gedichten spielen daher die Erinyen
eine zentrale Rolle. So stellt Rhodoman etwa ans Ende der *Troica* einen durch
Pausanias (Paus. 3.19.9f.) inspirierten Bericht über die Tötung Helenas auf
Rhodos und bittet für sich als Dichter um einen νόος ἁγνός, einen keuschen
Sinn.[57] Mit der starken Betonung der *castitas* bewegt sich Rhodoman auf den
Spuren Melanchthons, der das Beispiel Troja schon in einem Epithalamium
(1562) für Rhodomans akademischen Lehrer David Chytraeus (1530–1600)
angeführt hatte.[58] Hier zeigt sich also klar die moralisierende Funktionalisierung,
die Rhodoman unter dem Stichwort ἦθος im Proöm der *Troica* genannt hatte
(V. 20: καρπὸν ἐπιστήμης τε καὶ ἤθεος ἠδὲ καὶ αὐδῆς). Was aber ist mit der
ἐπιστήμη?

    Diesen Punkt bedient Rhodoman, indem er in seine Mythenparaphrasen
Angaben zur Chronologie einbaut (weshalb später Pétau auch darauf
zurückgegriffen hat) und bisweilen rationalistische Mythenerklärungen bietet.
Zwei Beispiele mögen dies illustrieren. Besonders thematisiert Rhodoman etwa
in den *Thebaica* den mythischen Gründer Kadmos als Einführer des Alphabets
und Gründer von Schulen.[59] Warum? Es geht ihm darum, zu zeigen, dass das
Wissen der Griechen ursprünglich aus Palästina kam, die israelitische Kultur
also älter ist als die griechische![60] Außerdem erklärt er etwa in den *Argonautica*

---

[57] Vgl. Gärtner (2017, 118–120).

[58] Siehe Ludwig (2007, 221–223). Vgl. auch Fuchs (2008, 121–125).

[59] V. 27–35: Αὐτόθι γηγενέεσσι μετ' ἀνδράσιν ἡγεμονεύων / ἀγλαὰ πολλὰ τέλεσσε καὶ
ἐσθλομαθέεσσιν ἄνοιξε / γυμνάσιον μούσῃσι διδασκαλίης τ' ἐρατεινῆς / Ἑλλάδος ἐνναέτῃσι
φόως πάντεσσιν ἄειρε, / γράμματα δέ σφιν ἔδειξε σοφῶν θ' ἅμα κεύθεα μύθων. / ὧδε
Παλαιστίνης μὲν ἀπὸ χθονὸς ἦλθεν Ἀχαιοῖς / ἰδμοσύνη, Φοῖνιξ δέ μιν Ἑλλάδι Κάδμος ὄπασσε
/ θρεφθεὶς ἐν λογίοισι Παλαιστίνης περάτεσσιν. Kadmos gehört zu einer Reihe von Lehrerfiguren
in den Gedichten, die besonders hervorgehoben werden und damit nochmals die pädagogische
Absicht unterstreichen: in den *Argonautica* ist dies Chiron (Neander 1588, A 7r; V. 177–191) und
in den *Troica* Palamedes (Neander 1588, H 3r; V. 549–563). Vgl. zu Palamedes auch Melanchthon
in *CR* 12, 773.

[60] Vgl. dazu auch Melanchthon in *CR* 12, 772: *Inde intelligi potest, Graecam historiam multo
recentiorem esse Mosaica.*

das Goldene Vlies als reichen Goldschatz[61] und beruft sich dabei vielleicht auf Melanchthon, der in seinem *Chronicon Carionis* das Goldene Vlies u.a. als *venae metallicae*, also besonderes Erzvorkommen, erklärt hatte.[62]

Der letzte im Proöm der *Troica* genannte Punkt betrifft die Sprache (αὐδή). Die Nutzbarmachung der Dichtersprache zeigt sich in der steten Anwendung poetischer Phrasen aus der epischen Tradition der Griechen. Im Proöm der *Thebaica* hatte Rhodoman diesen Vorgang als „mischen" (κιρνᾶν bzw. κεραννύναι) umschrieben, was sehr gut auf seine Wiederverwendung poetischer Phrasen und Vorbilder passt. An neuralgischen Punkten, die für die moralische Unterweisung wichtig sind (in den Marginalnotizen stets als *loci* bezeichnet), gibt es ganze „Zitatennester", die gleichsam die wichtigsten Zitate aus der griechischen Literatur zum Thema zusammentragen. Ein signifikantes Beispiel dafür ist der Tod des Pelias in den *Argonautica*. Danach heißt es im griechischen Text (mit der Marginalnote *Locus de malo in autorem recidente*) (V. 536–543):

ὣς αὐτῷ κακὰ τεύχει ἀνὴρ ἄλλῳ κακὰ τεύχων.	= Hes. *Op.* 265
ταῖς δ' αὐταῖς τέχναις τὶς ἁλώσεται, αἶσπερ ὑπῆρξεν.	= Euseb. *praep.ev.* 5.27.1
ἡ δὲ κακὴ βουλὴ τῷ βουλεύσαντι κακίστη.	= Hes. *Op.* 266
οὐδ' ἀρετᾷ κακὰ ἔργα, κιχάνει καὶ βραδὺς ὠκύν.	= Hom. *Od.* 8.329
εἰ δὲ κακὸν τεύχῃ τις, ἔχει θεὸς ἔκδικον ὄμμα	~ *Batr.* 98
πάντα βλέπων καὶ πάντα νοῶν καὶ πάντ' ὑπακούων	~ *Orac. Sib.* 8.282
καὶ κωφοῦ ξυνιεὶς καὶ οὐ λαλέοντος ἀκούων.	~ *Orac. Sib.* 8.378
πολλά κεν εἰδείης, οἷς τὸν θεὸν ἐξαπατήσαις.[63]	= *Suda* π 1868 Adler; Apostol. 14.39 (*Paroemiogr.* II 615)

So tut sich selbst Übel der Mann, der anderen Übel tut. Und es wird einer mit denselben Listen gefangen, mit denen er angefangen hat. Der schlechte Ratschluss ist für den, der ihn ersann, am schlechtesten. Auch gedeihen

---

[61] V. 69–72: Καὶ τὸ μὲν ἦν χρυσοῦ μένος ἄπλετον, ὅν ῥα κόμισσε / κριοτύπῳ μετὰ νηῒ φυγὼν εἰς Κολχίδα Φρίξος / ἢ μεγάλου θησαυρὸς ἀπείριτος Αἰήταο, / ὅν ῥα πολυχρύσοισιν ἐν ἔθνεσι αὐτὸς ἄγειρεν.

[62] *CR* 12, 772. Neander (1588, A 2rv) weist allerdings schon im lateinischen *argumentum* auf Strabon hin: *Aureum vellus alij aliud quiddam fuisse existimant, de quo Strabo lib. 10. ubi de Colchis scribit. Suidas existimat fuisse Chymicum, in pellibus descriptum, qui tradiderit rationem conficiendi sive auri, sive lapidis Philosophici* […]. *Rectius faciunt, qui de thesauris & opibus immensis Colchici regis interpretantur, quas vel è fodinis metallicis, vel alijs regni reditibus quotannis colligebat.*

[63] Neander (1588, B5r). Im ersten Vers steht im Druck ὡς statt ὣς.

schlechte Werke nicht, der Langsame bekommt auch den Schnellen. [540] Und wenn jemand etwas Schlechtes tut, hat Gott ein strafendes Auge, er, der alles sieht und alles wahrnimmt und auf alles hinhört, er, der sowohl den Stummen versteht als auch den, der nicht spricht, hört. Viel dürftest du wissen, wenn du Gott damit täuschen kannst.

Sicherlich gehört dieses Cento von Sentenzen (die Quellenangaben sind von mir ergänzt) nicht zur gelungensten Partie des Gedichts, es zeigt aber, wie Rhodoman seinen Anspruch, einen καρπός der griechischen Bildung zu liefern, gerecht zu werden sucht.[64] Schließlich tritt als neues Element der Sprachbildung (und sicherlich auch der eigenen Profilierung) noch der dosierte Einsatz von Wortneubildungen hinzu.[65]

VI. Zusammenfassung und Ausblick auf Rhodomans *Arion*

Zusammengenommen zeigen Rhodomans mythologische Dichtungen typische Tendenzen späthumanistischer Gelehrtenkultur. Die Gedichte sind das Ergebnis einer ausgiebigen Sammeltätigkeit. In diesem Fall betrifft dies sowohl die Sprache wie auch die Mythologie. Rhodoman selbst hat dies in seinen Proömien betont, wenn er davon spricht, zusammenzuführen, was bei anderen verstreut (σποράδην) vorhanden sei (*Troica* V. 9).[66] Der enzyklopädische Charakter erinnert zudem

---

[64] Vgl. zum Aspekt der Sprachschulung durch eigene humanistengriechische Texte auch die Überlegungen von Walter (2017, 41f.) zu Camerarius' *Capita pietatis et religionis Christianae*.

[65] Es finden sich in *Argonautica*, *Thebaica* und *Troica* etwa folgende nicht im *LSJ* verzeichnete neue Adjektivkomposita (in der Reihenfolge ihres Vorkommens). *Argonautica*: κυκνοφανής, οἰστροτόκος, *Thebaica*: τεκνοφιλής, τερενόχνοος (aber belegt τερενόχρως), ἐσθλοδιώκτης, ἑλκεσίδιφρος, ἐθελόξενος, χαλινόδετος, λαμπροσίδηρος, λυρόκτιτος, λαοβόρος, μυσερόζυγος, δολερόπλοκος, πατεροσσόος, κυανόφρων, φριξεγχής, ἐγχεσίδουπος, μουνοβάτης, ἀλεξίμοθος, ἐρατόχνοος (aber belegt ἐρατόχροος), *Troica*: ἐσθλοπόνος, ἐσθλόφυτος, ἀεξίποθος, μονόλεκτρος, ἐσθλοτόκος, ὁμόπνευστος, φυξίγαμος, περισσόγονος (aber belegt περισσογονία), ἀγλαότεκνος, ἀμαυρόνοος, βαρύπνευστος (aber belegt βαρυπνείων), νοθόγραφος, ἀνεμοπλάνης, ἀγλαόδιφρος, ἀγρεκύδοιμος, ἐσθλοφυής, λιπόβλαστος, αἱματοραίστης, ἀκεσσίμοθος, στερεαύχην, ὀξύτυπος, παυσικύδοιμος, ῥαδινόχροος, νοοφλεγέθων, ἀλιτρόγαμος, ταραξίνοος, ἀφαντόλογος, ὀλβοτόκος, ῥηξίγαμος. Hierin kann man sicherlich auch einen Ausdruck des zeitgenössischen Manierismus sehen. Zu Neologismen Rhodomans vgl. auch Ludwig (2014, 165) und Weise (2019, 118f.). Siehe ferner die Beobachtungen von Sironen (2000, 144–147) zu Komposita in der viel später entstandenen *Finlandia* (1678) von Johan Paulinus.

[66] Auf dem Titelblatt der *Troica*-Fassung von 1604 heißt es unumwunden: *Totius historiae Troianae*

an die schon erwähnten mythographischen Handbücher der Zeit. Auch dort wurden Insignien der Götter gesammelt, wie dies Rhodoman, Neander und Volland in *De re poetica Graecorum* mit Epitheta getan haben. Außerdem hat sich Rhodoman sowohl in den *Argonautica* als auch in den *Thebaica* und *Troica* stark an der Darstellung von Pseudo-Apollodor orientiert. Conrad Bursian kommt deshalb in seiner *Geschichte der classischen Philologie in Deutschland* zu einem pragmatischen Urteil, wenn er schreibt:

> Rhodoman war einer der fruchtbarsten und gewandtesten griechischen Dichter der Neuzeit, wie seine sehr zahlreichen griechischen Gedichte beweisen, in denen er theils moderne, theils antike mythische Stoffe zwar ohne eigentlich poetischen Geist, aber mit großer Fertigkeit in der Handhabung der Form, besonders der Sprache der späteren griechischen Epiker, die er mit Vorliebe studierte, behandelt.[67]

Bursians einschränkendes Urteil „ohne eigentlich poetischen Geist" hängt wohl vor allem an dem besonderen Kontext von *Argonautica, Thebaica* und *Troica*. Die relative Kürze, aber auch der weitgehende Verzicht auf Reden und größere Gleichnisse, die eigentlich typisch für das mythologische Epos sind, liegt in dem Zweck begründet. Man muss diese Werke daher tatsächlich, wie schon Bursian hervorgehoben hat, vor allem von der sprachlichen Seite und der Nutzbarmachung der Mythen für pädagogische Zwecke her betrachten. Es geht Rhodoman um eine pädagogische Synthese. Dass er durchaus anders dichten konnte, zeigt das letzte im Titel der Sammlung nicht genannte Werk: der *Arion*.[68] In diesem Werk über den lesbischen Sänger, der auf der Rückfahrt von Unteritalien nach Korinth von Seeleuten bedroht und einem Delphin gerettet worden ist, entfaltet Rhodoman nochmals sein ganzes Können, was er in *Argonautica, Thebaica* und *Troica* weitgehend zurückgehalten hat. Dieses Gedicht ist nicht nur im dorischen Dialekt gehalten, es ist auch voll von langen Reden, eingelegten Gesängen und Beschreibungen. Damit nähert sich Rhodoman sogar dem hellenistischen bzw.

Epitome: Ex variis Auctoribus decerpta [...].

[67] Bursian (1883, 235).

[68] Erstmals ist der *Arion* wohl bereits um 1567 in einem heute verschollenen Basler Druck bei Johannes Oporin erschienen. Vgl. dazu Weise (2019, 30f.). Zum besonderen Charakter des *Arion* siehe Gärtner (2017b, 194f.) und Weise (2016, 134). Der griechische Text liegt jetzt in einer neuen Ausgabe mit Übersetzung vor. Siehe Weise (2019).

neoterischen Epyllion an.[69] Denn das Gedicht hat mehrere Einlagen, u.a. einen Hymnos auf die Zeugung der Dioskuren durch den in einen Schwan verwandelten Zeus mit Leda. Dieser Hymnos gehört vielleicht zu den kunstvollsten Passagen (alt)griechischer Literatur aus der Renaissance überhaupt und braucht den Vergleich mit Musuros oder Polizian nicht zu scheuen. Als Beispiel möge hier der Abschnitt genügen, in dem Zeus Leda umgarnt und sie ihn schließlich küsst (V. 1011–1022):

> ἤλπετο δ᾽ ὅττι τάχιστα φίλης παλάμαις κιχέεσθαι.[70]
> πρῶτα δέ μιν δολίοις τεχνήμασιν ἠπερόπευεν·
> ἁ γὰρ ὅταν μαλακαῖς ἐπορέξατο χερσὶ πιέσδειν,[71]
> ἄψορρον πάλιν ἔσσυτ᾽, ἀλυσκάζοντι δ᾽ ἐῴκει.
> εἰ δ᾽ ἀνασείρασε χεῖρας, ὑπέστρεφεν ἆσσον ἱκάνων.   1015
> ἁ δέ μιν οὐκ ἀέκοντα τέλος κίχεν,[72] ἀμφὶ δὲ πάχεις
> χεῦε καὶ οἷς στέρνοισιν ἐφάρμοσε, τῷ δὲ μάλ᾽ ἦτορ
> εὔφραινε πρόσπτυξις ἀριζήλοιο γυναικός.
> ἁ δέ μιν ἀφραδέοισα κύσε στόμα, καὶ λάθεν αὐτὰν
> σχετλίη ἀμφαφόωσα θεῶν σημάντορα πάντων.   1020
> Ζανὶ δὲ τοῦτο φίλαμα πολύλλιτον εἴσατο πάντως
> ἅδιον ἀμβροσίας καὶ νέκταρος ἠδὲ καὶ Ἥρας.

[Der Schwan] hoffte, so schnell wie möglich von den Armen der Geliebten erreicht zu werden. Zuerst täuschte er sie mit listigen Kunststücken. Denn als sie ihn mit ihren weichen Händen erreichen wollte, um ihn zu drücken, eilte er wieder rückwärts und schien zu fliehen. [1015] Wenn sie aber die Hände zurückzog, wandte er sich zurück und kam näher. Schließlich erreichte sie ihn, nicht gegen seinen Willen, legte ihre Arme um ihn und drückte ihn an ihre Brust. Die Umarmung der begehrten Frau aber erfreute ihm sehr das Herz. Ohne Überlegung küsste sie ihm den Schnabel und, ohne es zu merken, [1020] umfasste die Unglückliche den Lenker aller Götter. Dem Zeus aber

---

[69] Vgl. dazu Weise (2019, 103f.).

[70] Die Form κιχέεσθαι ist sonst nicht belegt. Hier ist sie wohl im Sinne eines Futur Passiv zu verstehen.

[71] Die Verwendung von ὅταν mit dem Indikativ ist eine Ausnahme innerhalb des Gedichtes, kann aber als typisch für humanistengriechische Literatur gelten. Vgl. bspw. Neuendorf (2017, 96).

[72] Die Darstellung erinnert an Boccaccios Bericht in den *Genealogie deorum gentilium* (11.7.1). Siehe Zaccaria (1998, 1088).

schien dieser erwünschte Kuss gänzlich süßer als Ambrosia, Nektar und selbst Hera.

Die explizite Erotik der Passage braucht hier nicht weiterverfolgt zu werden. Erstaunlich ist es aber schon. Hat Rhodoman also seine Meinung geändert? Verzichtet er hier auf den am Ende der *Troica* beschworenen νόος ἁγνός und folgt wieder den Spuren der erotischen Dichtung Polizians?[73] – Wahrscheinlich nicht: Die Szene ist wohl eher im Sinne einer „Götterburleske" zu verstehen. Darauf deutet innerhalb des Hymnos auch ein direkter Verweis auf die berühmte Ares-Aphrodite-Erzählung aus dem achten Buch der *Odyssee* (*Arion* V. 956–959). Zeus macht sich als Liebhaber lächerlich und verführt junge, unschuldige Mädchen.[74] Ähnlich ist es auch in Melchior Barlaeus' *De raptu Ganymedis* (1563).[75] Aber trotzdem lässt sich Rhodoman sichtlich von der Anmut der Szene hinreißen und zeigt die typisch zwiespältige Haltung, wie man sie auch von den Malern der Zeit kennt, die erotische Szenen zwar als Warnung deklarieren, aber zugleich auch so sehr in ihnen schwelgen.[76] Es sei nur daran erinnert, dass gerade die bekanntesten Leda-Bilder von Correggio und Michelangelo ganz oder zum Teil ihrer Erotik zum Opfer gefallen sind.[77] Das ursprünglich intendierte Publikum dieses Gedichts ist zweifelsohne ein anderes als das der vorgestellten Mythenparaphrasen: Es richtet sich eben an jene kundigen Männer, die Rhodoman in den *Troica* (V. 11f.) ausgeschlossen hatte.[78] Die Erotik wird vielleicht auch ein Grund gewesen sein, weshalb es im Titel der Sammlung nicht erwähnt worden ist. Das Gedicht feiert

---

[73] Eine interessante Parallele zu Polizians Gedicht auf die *Kypris anadyomene* besteht etwa noch in der Verwendung des dorischen Dialekts. Bei Polizian dürfte diese wohl durch die ebenfalls mit dorischer Färbung verfassten Vorlagen von Antipatros von Sidon, Aulus Licinius Archias und Leonidas von Tarent angeregt sein. Zur Verwendung des Dorischen in Rhodomans *Arion* vgl. Weise (2019, 106f.).

[74] Vgl. die ausführliche Diskussion in Weise (2019, 81–91).

[75] Vgl. Katona (2002); Korenjak (2012, 528f.).

[76] Vgl. Bonnet (1994) zu Lucas Cranachs Aktbildern und Zöllner (2015, 62–80) zu Botticellis *Primavera* und *Camilla und der Kentaur*. Eine kontrastive Lesart antiker Mythen, die zum Vergleich mit christlichen Pendants herausfordert, vermutet z.B. auch Accorinti (2015) für die *Dionysiaka* des spätantiken Dichters Nonnos.

[77] Vgl. Warner (2001, 278).

[78] Ein Katalog des Druckers Johannes Oporin verrät, dass der *Arion* schon einmal weit vor 1588 in einem Basler Druck um 1567 erschienen sein muss (vgl. oben Anm. 68). Im Erstdruck ist er laut Katalog mit einem nicht erhaltenen Gedicht *Vaticinium Nerei, cum Paris Helenam rapuisset* abgedruckt worden. Siehe Oporin (1567, 37).

die Autonomie der Dichtung und mit ihr auch den Drucker, dessen Signet durch
den delphinreitenden Arion damals die Verbreitung alter und neuer griechischer
Dichtung vorangetrieben hatte: Johannes Oporin (1507–1568).[79] Bei ihm war,
wie gesagt, 1545 Castellios epische Bearbeitung der Geschichte von Johannes
dem Täufer erschienen und damit haben wir wieder einen Bogen zum Anfang
der Wiederbelebung griechischer Epik gezogen und es zeigt sich die Vernetzung
humanistengriechischer Dichtung.[80] Ihre Bedeutung erschließt sich erst, wenn wir
sowohl Sprache als auch Traditionen und den zeitgenössischen Kontext beachten.
Altgriechische Literatur der Renaissance ist sicherlich sehr voraussetzungsreich,
aber ihre weitere Erschließung dürfte sich lohnen, wie in diesem Beitrag am
Zusammenspiel von Mythologie, Sprachschöpfung, gelehrtem Spiel, Kunst und
Pädagogik gezeigt werden sollte.

---

[79] Zu Oporins Signet siehe ausführlich Wolkenhauer (2002, 384–396).

[80] Direkte Belege für die Benutzung von Rhodomans mythologischen Gedichten durch andere
zeitgenössische Dichter konnte ich bisher noch nicht finden. Allerdings liegt in Kopenhagen eine
Handschrift mit einer Abschrift des *Arion* aus dem Druck von 1588 (Kopenhagen, Det Kongelige
Bibliotek, *sign.* GkS 1983,4°). Neben dem griechischen Text findet sich darin auch eine etwa bis
zur Hälfte ausgeführte lateinische Prosaübersetzung mit einigen Randkommentaren zu Realien und
Vorbildern. Die Handschrift und die Notizen stammen von Zacharias Lund (1608–1667) und sind
ein interessantes Zeugnis für eine frühe tiefer gehende philologische Beschäftigung mit dem Text.
Ob der Zweck der Annotierung eine Neuausgabe war, muss offenbleiben. Siehe dazu auch Weise
(2019, 32–36).

Literaturverzeichnis

Literatur vor 1800

Camerarius, Joachim and Jacob Micyllus. 1538. ΕΠΙΓΡΑΜΜΑΤΑ ΕΛΛΗΝΙΚΑ ΤΩΝ ΠΑΛΑΙΩΝ ΠΟΙΗΤΩΝ [...]. Basel (= VD16 C 406).

Castellio, Sebastian. 1545. *Ionas Propheta, heroico carmine Latino descriptus,* [...] ΠΡΟΔΡΟΜΟΣ, *sive Praecursor, id est. Vita Ioannis Baptistae, Graeco carmine heroico reddita, libris III.* [...]. Basel (= VD16 C 2133 u. 2134).

Frischlin, Nicodemus (ed.) 1588. ΤΡΥΦΙΟΔΩΡΟΥ ΑΙΓΥΠΤΙΟΥ, ΓΡΑΜΜΑΤΙΚΟΥ ΚΑΙ ΕΠΟΠΟΙΟΥ, ΙΛΙΟΥ ΑΛΩΣΙΣ. *Tryphiodori Aegypti, grammatici, et poetae, liber de Ilii excidio* [...]. Frankfurt am Main (= VD16 T 2140).

Neander, Michael. 1565. *Graecae linguae Erotemata* [...]. Basel [*Praefatio* [Prf.] mit eigener Seitenzählung] (= VD16 N 379).

Neander, Michael (ed.) 1588. *Argonautica. Thebaica. Troica. Ilias parva. Poematia auctoris anonymi, sed pereruditi* [...]. Leipzig (= VD16 R 2088).

Oporinus, Johannes. 1567. *Librorum per IOANNEM OPORINUM partim excusorum hactenus, partim in eiusdem Officina venalium, INDEX: singulis ad ordinem alphabeticum redactis, & adiecta impressionis forma.* Basel (= VD16 ZV 19007).

Petavius, Dionysius. 1633. *Rationarium temporum in partes duas, Libros decem tributum* [...]. Paris.

Rhodoman, Lorenz. 1589. ΠΟΙΗΣΙΣ ΧΡΙΣΤΙΑΝΗ. ΠΑΛΑΙΣΤΙΝΗΣ, ΗΤΟΙ ΑΓΙΑΣ ΙΣΤΟΡΙΑΣ, ΒΙΒΛΙΑ ΕΝΝΕΑ. *Poesis Christiana. Palaestinae, seu Historiae sacrae, libri novem.* [...]. Frankfurt (= VD16 R 2105).

Rhodoman, Lorenz. 1604. Ἰλιὰς Κοίντου Σμυρναίου; *seu Quinti Calabri Paraleipomena, Id est, Derelicta ab Homero, XIV. libris comprehensa*: [...] *Nunc accessit Epitome Gemina, tum Homeri & Cointi, tum universa Historiae Troianae.* [...]. Hanau (= VD17 3:004717X) [Der Druck enthält auch eine Neuausgabe der *Ilias parva* und *Troica* mit lateinischer Versübersetzung und eigener Seitenzählung].

Volland, Johannes (ed.) 1582. *De re poetica Graecorum, sive Epithetorum Graecorum Lib. I. Phraseoων* [!] *Poeticarum Lib. I. Descriptionum variarum & elegantiarum Poëticarum Lib. I. Elegantiarum secundum tria causarum genera distributarum Lib. I. Libri quatuor. E notationibus & multorum annorum observationibus viri clarißimi Michaelis Neandri* [...]. Leipzig (= VD16 N 415).

Moderne Literatur

Accorinti, Domenico. 2015. „Nonnos und der Mythos: Heidnische Antike aus christlicher Perspektive", in Hartmut Leppin (Hrsg.) *Antike Mythologie in christlichen Kontexten der Spätantike*, Berlin u.a., 45–69.

Adams, Matthew. 2015. *Teaching Classics in English Schools, 1500–1840.* Newcastle upon Tyne.

Bonnet, Anne-Marie. 1994. „Der Akt im Werk Lucas Cranachs. Bedeutung und Spezifität der ‚nacketen Bilder' innerhalb der deutschen Renaissance-Malerei", in Claus Grimm, Johannes Erichsen & Evamaria Brockhoff (Hrsg.) *Lucas Cranach. Ein Maler-Unternehmer aus Franken.* Regensburg, 139–149.

Botley, Paul. 2010. *Learning Greek in Western Europe, 1396–1529. Grammars, Lexica, and Classroom Texts.* Philadelphia.

Bursian, Conrad. 1883. *Geschichte der classischen Philologie in Deutschland von den Anfängen bis zur Gegenwart.* München–Leipzig.

Cortassa, Guida & Enrico V. Maltese (Hrsg.). 1997. *Francesco Filelfo. De psychagogia.* Alessandria.

CR = Bretschneider, Karl Gottlieb, Heinrich Ernst Bindseil (Hrsg.) 1834–1860. *Philippi Melanchthonis opera quae supersunt. Corpus reformatorum.* Bde. 1–28. Halle–Braunschweig.

Czapla, Rolf Georg. 2013. *Das Bibelepos in der frühen Neuzeit. Zur deutschen Geschichte einer europäischen Gattung.* Berlin–Boston.

Dijkstra, Roald & Erik Hermans. 2015. „Musurus' Homeric Ode to Plato and His Request to Pope Leo X", *Akroterion* 60, 33–63.

Dombrowski, Damian. 2010. *Botticelli. Ein Florentiner Maler über Gott, die Welt und sich selbst.* Berlin.

Dräger, Paul (Hrsg., Übers.). 2005. *Apollodor, Bibliotheke. Götter- und Heldensagen.* Düsseldorf–Zürich.

Fuchs, Thorsten. 2008. *Philipp Melanchthon als neulateinischer Dichter in der Zeit der Reformation.* Tübingen.

Gärtner, Thomas. 2016. „Rhodoman(nus), Lorenz (Laurentius)", in Wilhelm Kühlmann *et al.* (Hrsg.) *Frühe Neuzeit in Deutschland 1520–1620. Literaturwissenschaftliches Verfasserlexikon.* Band 5. Berlin u.a., 300–310.

Gärtner, Thomas. 2017a. „Der Troja-Mythos in den eigenen Dichtungen Lorenz Rhodomans", in Stefan Weise (Hrsg.) *HELLENISTI! Altgriechisch als Literatursprache im neuzeitlichen Europa*, Stuttgart, 109–123.

Gärtner, Thomas. 2017b. „Lorenz Rhodoman – ein homerisierender Dichter im Dienste der lutherischen Reformation", *Neulateinisches Jahrbuch* 19, 175–197.

Gärtner, Thomas. 2020 [Erscheinen geplant]. „Nonnos von Panopolis im protestantischen Philhellenismus des 16./17. Jahrhunderts. Zur Nonnos-Rezeption bei Lorenz Rhodoman und Matthaeus Gothus", in Berenice Verhelst (Hrsg.) *Nonnos of Panopolis in Context IV: Poetry at the Crossroads.*

Göttling, Karl Wilhelm. 1811. *Animadversiones criticae in Callimachi Epigrammata et Achillem Tatium.* Jenae.

Harles, Gottlieb Christoph (Hrsg.). 1790. *Ioannis Alberti Fabricii […] Bibliotheca Graeca […].* Volumen primum. Hamburg.

Huber-Rebenich, Gerlinde. 2006. „Neue Funktionen der Dichtung im Humanismus", in Thomas Maissen & Gerrit Walther (Hrsg.) *Funktionen des Humanismus. Studien zum Nutzen des Neuen in der humanistischen Kultur,* Göttingen, 49–75.

Hutton, James. 1935. *The Greek Anthology in Italy to the Year 1800.* Ithaca – New York.

Johnson, Diane L. 2006. „Musa Posseliana: Johannes Posselius the Elder (1528–91) and the Lutheran Greek Program", *Reformation & Renaissance Review* 8, 186–209.

Katona, Julianna. 2002. *Melchioris Barlaei de raptu Ganymedis liber. Edition und Kommentar.* Frankfurt am Main.

Korenjak, Martin. 2012. „Short Mythological Epic in Neo-Latin Literature", in Manuel Baumbach & Silvio Bär (Hrsg.), *Brill's Companion to Greek and Latin Epyllion and Its Reception,* Leiden–Boston, 519–536.

Korhonen, Tua, Teivas Oksala & Erkki Sironen. 2000. *Johan Paulinus (Lillienstedt): Magnus Principatus Finlandia […].* Helsinki.

Kühlmann, Wilhelm. 1993. „Poeten und Puritaner: Christliche und pagane Poesie im deutschen Humanismus – Mit einem Exkurs zur Prudentius-Rezeption in Deutschland", in Hanns Kerner (Hrsg.) *Humanismus und Theologie in der frühen Neuzeit. Akten des interdisziplinären Symposions vom 15. bis 17. Mai 1992 im Melanchthonhaus Bretten,* Nürnberg, 149–180.

LSJ = Liddell, Henry George, Robert Scott & Henry Stuart Jones (Hrsg.) 1996. *A Greek-English Lexicon. With a Supplement.* 9. Aufl. Oxford.

Ludwig, Walther. 1998. *Hellas in Deutschland. Darstellungen der Gräzistik im deutschsprachigen Raum aus dem 16. und 17. Jahrhundert.* Hamburg.

Ludwig, Walther. 1999. „Klassische Mythologie in Druckersigneten und Dichterwappen", in Bodo Guthmüller & Wilhelm Kühlmann (Hrsg.) *Renaissancekultur und antike Mythologie,* Tübingen, 113–148.

Ludwig, Walther. 2001a. *Christliche Dichtung des 16. Jahrhunderts – Die Poemata sacra des Georg Fabricius.* Göttingen.

Ludwig, Walther. 2001b. „Musenkult und Gottesdienst – Evangelischer Humanismus der Reformationszeit", in Walther Ludwig (Hrsg.) *Die Musen im Reformationszeitalter*, Leipzig, 9–51.

Ludwig. Walther. 2007. „Eine protestantische Ehelehre – die Sammlung der *Carmina et Epistolae de coniugio ad D. Davidem Chytraeum* (1562)", *Neulateinisches Jahrbuch* 9, 211–240.

Ludwig, Walther. 2014. „Der Humanist Laurentius Rhodomanus als griechischer Dichter Laurentios Rhodoman und seine Autobiographie von 1582", *Neulateinisches Jahrbuch* 16, 137–171.

Ludwig, Walther. 2017. „*Scitis, quanto semper amore Graecarum rerum flagrem.* Motive für den Höhepunkt des humanistischen griechischen Dichtens um 1600", in Stefan Weise (Hrsg.) *HELLENISTI! Altgriechisch als Literatursprache im neuzeitlichen Europa*, Stuttgart, 125–145.

Ludwig, Walther. 2018. „Der deutsche griechische Dichter Laurentios Rodoman", in Janika Päll & Ivo Volt (Hrsg.) *Hellenostephanos. Humanist Greek in Early Modern Europe. Learned Communities between Antiquity and Contemporary Culture*, Tartu, 249–259.

Matsche, Franz. 1994. „Lucas Cranachs mythologische Darstellungen", in Claus Grimm, Johannes Erichsen & Evamaria Brockhoff (Hrsg.) *Lucas Cranach. Ein Maler-Unternehmer aus Franken*, Regensburg, 78–88.

Matsche, Franz. 1996. „Humanistische Ethik am Beispiel der mythologischen Darstellungen von Lucas Cranach", in Winfried Eberhard & Alfred A. Strnad (Hrsg.) *Humanismus und Renaissance in Ostmitteleuropa vor der Reformation*, Köln–Weimar–Wien, 29–70.

Meister, F. 1881–1882. „Michael Neander", *Jahrbücher für Philologie und Paedagogik* 27, 180–186. 225–232. 309–315. 357–366. 390–400; 28, 188–196.

Neuendorf, Paul A. 2017. „Griechische Versepisteln im 16. Jahrhundert. Johannes Clajus d. Ä. (1535–1592) an die Gelehrten seiner Zeit", in Stefan Weise (Hrsg.) *HELLENISTI! Altgriechisch als Literatursprache im neuzeitlichen Europa*, Stuttgart, 63–108.

Päll, Janika & Ivo Volt (Hrsg.) 2018. *Hellenostephanos. Humanist Greek in Early Modern Europe. Learned Communities between Antiquity and Contemporary Culture.* Tartu.

Pontani, Filippomaria (Hrsg.) 2002. *Angeli Politiani Liber epigrammatum Graecorum*. Roma.

Pontani, Filippomaria. 2017. „*Graeca per Italiae fines*. Greek poetry in Italy from Poliziano to the present", in Stefan Weise (Hrsg.) *HELLENISTI! Altgriechisch als Literatursprache im neuzeitlichen Europa*, Stuttgart, 311–347.

Pontani, Filippomaria. 2018. „Hellenic Verse and Christian Humanism: From Nonnus to Musurus", *International Journal of Classical Tradition* 25, 216–240.

Reitz, Christiane. 2007. „Verkürzen und erweitern – Literarische Techniken für eilige Leser? Die ‚Ilias Latina' als poetische Epitome", *Hermes* 135, 334–351.

Reitz, Christiane. 2010. „Homer kürzen? Verkürzung und Paraphrase homerischer Epik in der antiken Kritik", in Marietta Horster & Christiane Reitz (Hrsg.) *Condensing texts – condensed texts*, Stuttgart, 289–305.

Rhein, Stefan. 1987. *Philologie und Dichtung. Melanchthons griechische Gedichte (Edition, Übersetzung und Kommentar)*. Diss. Heidelberg.

Rhein, Stefan. 1989. „Johannes Reuchlin als Dichter. Vorläufige Anmerkungen zu unbekannten Texten", in Hans-Peter Becht (Hrsg.) *Pforzheim in der frühen Neuzeit. Beiträge zur Stadtgeschichte des 16. bis 18. Jahrhunderts*, Sigmaringen, 51–80.

Rhein, Stefan. 2017. „Philipp Melanchthon und seine griechischen Dichterschüler", in Stefan Weise (Hrsg.) *HELLENISTI! Altgriechisch als Literatursprache im neuzeitlichen Europa*, Stuttgart, 15–46.

Schmitz, Christine. 2013. „Mythos. D. Christlich", *Reallexikon für Antike und Christentum* 25, 487–510.

Sifakis (ΣΗΦΑΚΗΣ), G. M. 1954. „Μάρκου Μουσούρου τοῦ Κρητὸς ποίημα εἰς τὸν Πλάτωνα", Κρητικὰ Χρονικά 8, 366–388.

Sironen, Erkki. 2000. „Notes on the Language of Johan Paulinus' *Finlandia*. A baroque eulogy in Greek verses", *Arctos* 34, 129–147.

Staiger, Emil. 1974. *Angelo Poliziano, Der Triumph Cupidos. «Stanze»*. Zürich–München.

Seznec, Jean. 1990. *Das Fortleben der antiken Götter. Die mythologische Tradition im Humanismus und in der Kunst der Renaissance*. Aus dem Französischen von Heinz Jatho. München (original unter dem Titel *La Survivance des Dieux Antiques*, London 1940, 2. Aufl. 1980 Paris).

VD16 = *Verzeichnis der im deutschen Sprachbereich erschienenen Drucke des 16. Jahrhunderts*, siehe https://www.bsb-muenchen.de/sammlungen/historische-drucke/recherche/vd-16/ [4.5.2020]

VD17 = *Das Verzeichnis der im deutschen Sprachraum erschienenen Drucke des 17. Jahrhunderts*, siehe http://www.vd17.de/ [4.5.2020]

Wachler, Albrecht (Hrsg.) 1839. *Franz Passow's Leben und Briefe*. Breslau.

Walter, Jochen. 2017. „*Die Capita pietatis et religionis Christianae versibus Graecis comprehensa* des Joachim Camerarius (1545) und ihre kürzere Erstfassung in Melanchthons *Institutio puerilis literarum Graecarum*", in Thomas Baier (Hrsg.) *Camerarius Polyhistor. Wissensvermittlung im deutschen Humanismus*, Tübingen, 23–57.

Warburg, Aby. 1893. *Sandro Botticellis „Geburt der Venus" und „Frühling." Eine Untersuchung über die Vorstellungen von der Antike in der italienischen Frührenaissance*. Hamburg–Leipzig.

Warner, Marina. 2001. „Leda and the Swan: The Unbearable Matter of Bliss", in John Marenbon (Hrsg.) *Poetry and Philosophy in the Middle Ages. A Festschrift for Peter Dronke*, Leiden, 263–265.

Weise, Stefan. 2016. „Ἑλληνίδ' αἶαν εἰσιδεῖν ἱμείρομαι – Neualtgriechische Literatur in Deutschland (Versuch eines Überblicks)", *Antike und Abendland* 62, 114–181.

Weise, Stefan. 2018. „*Alter Theocritus?* Joachim Camerarius' griechische Supplemente zu Theokrits *Herakliskos* und dem sogenannten *Herakles leontophonos*", *Humanistica Lovaniensia* 67:2, 257–299.

Weise, Stefan. 2019. *Der Arion des Lorenz Rhodoman. Ein altgriechisches Epyllion der Renaissance. Einleitung, Text, Übersetzung, Wortindex.* (Palingenesia 177). Stuttgart.

Wilson, Nigel Guy (Hrsg., Übers.). 2016. *Aldus Manutius. The Greek Classics.* Cambridge, Massachusetts–London.

Wind, Edgar. 1987. *Heidnische Mysterien in der Renaissance.* Mit einem Nachwort von Bernhard Buschendorf. Übersetzt von Christa Münstermann unter Mitarbeit von Bernhard Buschendorf und Gisela Heinrichs. Frankfurt am Main (original unter dem Titel *Pagan Mysteries in the Renaissance*, London 1958).

Wolkenhauer, Anja. 2002. *Zu schwer für Apoll. Die Antike in Humanistischen Druckerzeichen des 16. Jahrhunderts.* Wiesbaden.

Zaccaria, Vittorio (Hrsg.) 1998. *Tutte le opere di Giovanni Boccaccio. Volume VII–VIII: Genealogie deorum gentilium.* Tomo primo. Milano.

Zöllner, Frank. 2015. *Botticelli.* 2. Aufl. München.

Jonische Hexameter als Träger der norddeutschen Reformation

Thomas Gärtner

Lorenz Rhodoman, über dessen mythologische Epyllien mein Kollege Stefan Weise in seinem substanziellen Beitrag zu diesem Band[1] ausführlich gehandelt hat, beschreibt in einer griechischen Autobiographie mit lateinischer Übersetzung namens *Bioporikon*[2] (jeweils 268 Hexameter) seine Ausbildungszeit (*ca.* 1562 – 1567) an der Ilfelder Klosterschule unter seinem Lehrer Michael Neander. Dieser verordnete dem jungen Rhodoman einen Lektürekanon, dessen quantitativer Schwerpunkt bei der jonisierenden Epik liegt; Rhodoman übte sich gleich von Anfang an auch in der aktiven Komposition.

αὐτίκα δ᾽ Ἑρκυνίδων προσπτύξατο κύδιμος ἑσμὸς   *studia Ilefeldae*
κυδῆναι δώροισί με παντοίοισι μενοινῶν,
εἴτε μοι Ἑλλήνων πινυτὸς λόγος εἴτε Λατίνων   145   *poesis Graeca*
εἴτε καὶ Ἑβραίων θυμάρμενος. ἀλλὰ θεάων
κῆρ ἀμὸν μία θέλξε καὶ εἰς ἑὸν ἥρπασεν[3] ἄντρον
ὡς λάτριν οἰκίδιον καὶ Ἰωνίδος ἤθεα Μούσης
σκῆψεν[4] ὑπὸ πραπίδεσσιν. ὅσ[σ]ον[5] δ᾽ ἀπὸ θέλκτρον ἀοιδῆς
ἡμετέρης κνίζει πινυτόφρονος ἦτορ ἀκουστέω,   150
οὐ σαφές. ὅττι δ᾽ ἐπέων τερετίσμασι θυμὸν ἴηνα
νύμφαις ἡμεδαπῆσι, φατίζεται, εἰ τόδ᾽ ἀληθές.
            D. Neandri fida sedulitas in explicandis bonis auctorib(us)
σὴ χάρις, ἐσθλὲ Νέανδρε, τεὸν κλέος, εἴ τι λοχεύω
χρήσιμον ἠδὲ Θεῷ καταθύμιον Ἑλλάδι Μούσῃ.

---

[1] In diesem Band: „Griechische Mythologie im Dienste reformatorischer Pädagogik: Zur Epensammlung *Argonautica. Thebaica. Troica. Ilias parva* von Lorenz Rhodoman (1588)“, S. 185–215.

[2] Rhodoman (1582); deutsche Übersetzung mit kommentierenden Bemerkungen: Ludwig (2014). Eine Edition der Autobiographie Rhodomans erscheint demnächst bei Gärtner (2020a).

[3] ἥρπασεν *scripsi* : ἥσπασεν *ed.* : *an* ἔσπασεν *?*

[4] σκῆψεν *scripsi* : σκέμψεν *ed.* : πέμψεν *Ludwig*

[5] ὅσον *scripsi* : ὅσσον *ed.*

σῆς γὰρ ὑφ' ἡγεσίῃσι καὶ οὐ βρίζουσι κελεύθοις[6]　　　　155
γλώσσης ἐξεπέρησεν Ἀχαιΐδος ἄσπετον οἶδμα
λέμβος ἐμὸς τετόρων ἐτέων κατ' εὔδρομον ὁρμὴν
καὶ κέλσας λιμένεσσιν ἐμοὶ γνωτούς τε φίλους τε
θῆκεν, ὅσοι γραφίδεσσιν ἐν Ἑλλάδι πρῶτα φέρονται,
Ἰλιάδος γενέτην, Ἄσκρης ναστῆρα παλαιῆς,　　　　160
βουκολικῶν μήστωρα καὶ ἵστορα φορβάδος ἄγρης
καὶ λυρικὸν βασιλῆα καὶ ᾄσματα θέσκελα Νόννου
Γρηγορίου τ' ἐπὶ τῷδε θεόφρονος, ἐννέα βίβλους
Ἡροδότου πλείους τε, δίχ' ἑρμηνῆος ὁμιλεῖν
τῶν τε λόγους γραπτοῖσιν ὑφάσμασι μιμήσασθαι.　　*cognitio et usus*
πολλὰ γὰρ ἐνθάδ' ὕφηνα μίτ<ο>ις[7] εὐηχέσι Μουσέων,　　*Graecae linguae*
ὥς μοι μιμήτειρα[8] λόγους ἄσκησις ὀφέλλοι.[9]

Sogleich aber zog mich der ruhmvolle Schwarm der Harzmusen an sich heran und verlangte mich mit allerlei Geschenken zu ehren, [145] mochte mir die kundige Rede der Griechen oder die der Lateiner oder auch die der Hebräer am Herzen liegen. Aber eine einzige von den Göttinnen betörte mein Herz, zerrte mich wie ihren privaten Diener in ihre Grotte und heftete mir die Idiome der jonischen Muse tief in die Brust. Wieweit die von meinem Gesang ausgehende Betörung [150] das Herz eines gelehrten Hörers rührt, bleibt ungewiß. Aber es wird behauptet, daß ich den einheimischen Musen durch das Zwitschern meiner Lieder das Herz wärmte – wenn dies denn wahr ist.

---

[6] κελεύθοις *ed.* : *num* κελευσμοῖς ?

[7] μίτις *ed.*

[8] μιμήτειρα *Lenz* : μίου μήτειρα *ed.*

[9] Die Lateinische Übersetzung von Rhodomannus (143–167): *hic mox Hercynidum placide complectitur agmen, / divitiisque ornare suis me naviter ardent, / seu placeat Graii sapientia sive Latini / sive etiam Hebraei sermonis. at una dearum / occupat amplexus castumque abducit in antrum / devinctumque sibi reddens me nectare Musae / imbuit Ioniae. sed quas mea carmina doctis / auribus illecebras pariant, non dicere promptum est. / saepius at nymphis quod venerit inde voluptas / Hercyniis, memorant, si non palpantur, amici /. si pueris aliquid Graiis pario utile Musis / acceptumque Deo, tua laus est tota, Neander. / qui dum solicito clavum mihi corde gubernas, / exigua immensum cymba confecimus aequor / Graiugenum, quater in sese dum volvitur annus. / in portu excipiunt, socio et dignantur amore / auctores Graii scriptis ad sidera noti, / Iliados pater atque senex Ascraeus et inter / rex lyricos et, qui venatus versibus aptat, / et Siculus vates et grandis carmine Nonnus / et sacra Gregorius pangens Musaeque diserti / Herodoti pluresque alii, quos ore loquentes / agnovi patrio versusque effingere Achivos / assuevi calamo; cui multa negocia feci, / cognitio ut crebro linguae mihi cresceret usu.* Zu v. 147 *amplexus ed.* : *an amplexu[s]* ?

Dir ist es zu danken, edler Neander, Dein Ruhm ist es, wenn ich mit meiner griechischen Muse etwas Nützliches und Gott Gefälliges gebäre. [155] Denn unter Deiner Führung und schlaflosen Wegweisung (?) hat mein Kahn im geschwinden Lauf vierer Jahre die unsägliche Flut der griechischen Literatur durchlaufen, an verschiedenen Häfen angelegt und mir alle diejenigen zu Bekannten und guten Freunden gemacht, die durch ihre Schriften in Griechenland die ersten Preise gewinnen: [160] den Vater der Ilias [Homer], den Bewohner des alten Askra [Hesiod], den Erfinder der Bukolik [Theokrit] und den Kenner der nährenden Jagd [Oppian] und den König der Lyrik [Pindar] und den göttlichen Gesang des Nonnos und zudem denjenigen des gotterfüllten Gregor (von Nazianz), die neun Bücher Herodots und noch weitere – so daß ich mit ihnen ohne Dolmetscher verkehre [165] und deren Sprechweise mit dem Gespinst meiner Schriften nachahme. Denn vieles habe ich hier gesponnen mit den wohltönenden Fäden der Musen, damit mir nachahmende Übung die Rede verbessere.

Entsprechend machte ihn eine der in Ilfeld ansässigen Musen, nämlich diejenige, die für jonische Dichtung zuständig ist, zu ihrem privaten Diener (λάτριν οἰκίδιον, V. 148).[10] Die Dominanz dieser speziellen Muse bekam jedoch nicht nur Rhodoman zu spüren: Eine stattliche Reihe von Persönlichkeiten, die sich im Umfeld der Wittenberger Reformation, teilweise auch an der Ilfelder Schule entwickelten, befleißigten sich der jonischen Dichtung und bereicherten mit eigenen episierenden Dichtungen den protestantischen Lehr- und Literaturbetrieb. Ich möchte in meinem Beitrag eine Reihe solcher Persönlichkeiten – mit kleinen Textproben – vorstellen und hoffe, dass deren Zusammengehörigkeit im Laufe meiner Ausführungen deutlich wird.

Nikolaus von **Reusner** (1545–1602) begab sich gerade von seinem Breslauer Gymnasium zur Wittenberger Universität, um dort bei Melanchthon zu studieren, als dieser während Reusners Anreise starb (1560). Im zweiten Band von Reusners *Opera*, der 1593 erschien, finden wir unter den *Epica* zwei interessante griechische Stücke, zunächst ein *Infanticidium Herodis* (*ca.* 200 Hexameter).[11] Diese Darstellung des biblischen Kindermords nimmt thematisch zwei bekannte lateinische Barockwerke vorweg, nämlich die *Herodias* des Jesuiten Jakob

---

[10] οἰκίδιος i.q. οἰκεῖος begegnet gemäß *LSJ s.v.* nur bei Oppian *cyn.* I 473. Ludwig (2014) übersetzt irrig "wie in ein zum Dienst bereites kleines Haus".

[11] Reusner (1593, 102–109) unter *Epica*: *Infanticidium Herodis.*

Biderman,[12] dem es gelingt, dem Kindersterben durch ein Netz von typologischen Bezügen einen Sinn als einer Art von märtyrerhaftem Opfertod abzugewinnen, und die unglaublich düsteren *Herodis furiae* des Andreas Gryphius.[13] Reusner beginnt sein Werk dagegen schon im Prooemium mit einer deklamationsartigen empörten Apostrophe an den Erzverbrecher Herodes:

τίς[14] μὲν ἐρίννυος ἴς, ἀρχῆς τίς ἐπάρατος ὁρμή,
πάγκακε λωβητήρ, περὶ πάντων ἄγριε φωτῶν,
τίς σε κάτεσχε; φόνον τίς ἔπεισεν ἀπηνέα τεύχειν
νηπυτίοις ἐπιμαστιδίοις; τίνος οὕνεκεν αὐτοὺς
λυγρὸν ἔδει[15] θάνατον καὶ μοῖραν ἄωρον ἐπισπεῖν;   5
φεῦ ἀθέοιο θέας, πολυδακρύτοιο καὶ ἄτης.

Welche Kraft einer Furie, welcher verfluchte Trieb Deiner Herrschaft erfasste Dich, Du durch und durch böser Frevler, wild über alle Sterblichen hinaus? Wer brachte Dich dazu, grausamen Mord zu schaffen für kleine Kinder an der Brust ihrer Mutter? Weswegen mussten sie [5] einen leidvollen Tod und ein unzeitiges Geschick zeitigen? Weh ob des gottlosen Anblicks und des tränenreichen Unglücks!

Näher will ich auf ein fragmentarisches Stück Reusners eingehen, nämlich den Anfang eines *Triumphus Iesu Christi*:[16]

Χριστὸν ἄνακτα μέγιστον ἀείσομαι, ὃς <u>μάλα</u> <u>πολλὰ</u>
<u>πλάγχθη</u>, <u>ἐπεὶ</u> στυγερῆς θνητοὺς ἐρρύσατο μοίρας,
<u>αὐτῶν</u> οἳ <u>σφετέρῃσιν</u> <u>ἀτασθαλίῃσιν</u> <u>ὄλοντο</u>·
<u>πολλὰ</u> δὲ μοχθήσας καὶ ἐπισπὼν κῆρα μέλαιναν

---

[12] Biderman (1622).

[13] Gryphius (1634). Moderne Ausgabe : Czapla & Hintzen (2001).

[14] Τις *ed.*

[15] ἔπει *ed.*

[16] Reusner (1593, 110–112) unter *Epica*: *Triumphus Iesu Christi regis opt. max. (fragmentum)*. Vgl. Hom. *Od.* 1.1–10: ἄνδρα μοι ἔννεπε Μοῦσα πολύτροπον, <u>ὃς</u> <u>μάλα</u> <u>πολλὰ</u> / <u>πλάγχθη</u>, <u>ἐπεὶ</u> Τροίης ἱερὸν πτολίεθρον ἔπερσε· / πολλῶν δ᾽ ἀνθρώπων ἴδεν ἄστεα καὶ νόον ἔγνω, / <u>πολλὰ</u> δ᾽ ὅ γ᾽ ἐν πόντῳ πάθεν ἄλγεα ὃν κατὰ θυμόν, / <u>ἀρνύμενος</u> ἥν τε <u>ψυχὴν</u> καὶ <u>νόστον</u> ἑταίρων. / ἀλλ᾽ οὐδ᾽ ὣς ἑτάρους ἐρρύσατο, ἱέμενός περ· <u>αὐτῶν</u> γὰρ <u>σφετέρῃσιν</u> <u>ἀτασθαλίῃσιν</u> <u>ὄλοντο</u>, / νήπιοι, οἳ κατὰ βοῦς Ὑπερίονος Ἠελίοιο / ἤσθιον· αὐτὰρ ὁ τοῖσιν ἀφείλετο <u>νόστιμον</u> <u>ἦμαρ</u>. / <u>τῶν</u> <u>ἁμόθεν</u> <u>γε</u>, <u>θεά</u>, θύγατερ Διός, <u>εἰπὲ</u> <u>καὶ</u> <u>ἡμῖν</u>.

ἠοῖ σὺν τριτάτῃ †ἀπεδωκὼς†[17] <u>νόστιμον</u> <u>ἦμαρ</u>
ἐκ νεκύων ἀνόρουσε μετάρσιος· ὀψὲ δὲ μακρὸν   5
οὐρανὸν εἰσανέβη πατρὸς εἰς ἕδος ἀθανάτοιο,
<u>ἀρνύμενος</u> <u>ψυχὰς</u> ἀνθρώπων εἷό τε <u>νόστον</u>·
<u>τῶν</u> <u>ἁμόθεν</u> <u>γε</u>, Θεός, Θεοῦ υἱεῦ, <u>εἰπὲ</u> <u>καὶ</u> <u>ἡμῖν</u>.

Ich will von Christus, dem höchsten Herrn, singen, der reichlich viel
umherirren musste, als er die Sterblichen vor ihrem verhaßten Geschick rettete,
sie, die durch ihre eigenen Frevel zugrundegingen; nachdem er viele Mühen
geduldet und das schwarze Todesgeschick gezeitigt hatte, gab er ihnen mit der
dritten Morgenröte den Tag ihrer Heimkehr zurück [?] [5] und stürmte empor
von den Toten, sich wiederum erhebend; am Ende schließlich kehrte er in den
gewaltigen Himmel zurück in das Haus seines unsterblichen Vaters, die Seelen
der Menschen bewahrend und seine eigene Heimkehr. Aus dem Bereich dieser
Dinge verkünde auch uns, Gottes Sohn, selbst Gott.

Die Bezüge auf den Eingang der *Odyssee* sind evident. Im Gegensatz zu Odysseus
vermag Christus bei seinem Irrlauf über die Erde seinen Gefährten, die „durch
ihren eigenen Frevel zugrundegingen", den „Tag der Heimkehr" (nämlich ins
Himmelreich) zu sichern. Das Partizip ἀρνύμενος ist bei Reusner anders als
Homer nicht konativ zu verstehen, sondern bezeichnet den definitiven Erfolg der
Bemühung Christi.

Dieses Fragment, welches im zweiten Band von Reusners *Opera* enthalten
ist, lässt sich nicht sicher datieren; ich habe es an den Anfang gestellt, da hier
das *Odyssee*-Prooemium, das uns noch öfter begegnen wird, auf Christus selbst
umgebogen wird.

Als zweiten Autor bespreche ich Martin **Crusius** (1526–1607), der als
einziger nicht aus Norddeutschland stammt. Sein Wirkungskreis ist die Tübinger
Universität, und er gilt als einer der Begründer des deutschen Philhellenismus.
Seine Kontakte zu norddeutschen Protestanten zeigen sich jedoch u.a. darin,
dass Rhodoman seine wichtige Autobiographie in Crusius´ Sammelwerk
Germanograecia erscheinen ließ. In den *Poemata Graeca* des Crusius, die 1567
in Basel erschienen,[18] findet sich neben einer langen Evangelienversifikation
auch eine Bearbeitung des biblischen Susanna-Stoffes, die Stefan Weise jüngst

---

[17] *num* ἀποδωκὼς *perperam pro* ἀποδεδωκὼς *vel* ἀποδοὺς *? cf. Homericum illud* ἀφείλετο νόστιμον
ἦμαρ

[18] Crusius (1567). Die Susanna zuvor bereits in einer Separatausgabe, Crusius (1555).

auf einer Wuppertaler *Septuaginta*-Tagung gewinnreich besprochen hat.[19] Den Hexametern ist ein hendekasyllabisches Widmungsgedicht vorangestellt, in welchem Crusius seine *Susanna* dem Jakob Fabricius in Chemnitz, einem jüngeren Bruder des berühmten Dichters Georg Fabricius, widmete, der sich zu dieser Zeit bei Melanchthon in Wittenberg befand.

Μαρτῖνος Κρούσιος
Ἰακώβῳ Φαβρικίῳ τῷ Χεμ-
νικιεῖ χαίρειν ἐν Χριστῷ[20]

Martinus Crusius
Iacobo Fabricio Chemni-
censi salutem in Christo

τῷ θυγάτριον ἐδνόω φίλον μου
σπουδαίῳ γε νέῳ γάμον πρὸς ἁγνόν;
σοὶ καλῶς, Ἰάκωβε. συνεχὲς[21] γὰρ
πάντων μοι πλέον ἦς φίλος σὺ πιστός,
ὡς Στουρμίοιο[22] κλυτοῖο ῥητορείας   5
Ἀργεντινόθ᾽ ἄρ᾽ ἠκροώμεθ᾽ ἄμφω
νῦν δ᾽ αὖ Λευκορέης ἐνὶ πτόληϊ
Φιλίππου πολυωνύμου μαθητής
ὢν μέμνησ᾽ ἔτι μου[23] μακρὰν ἀπόντος.
καὶ δὴ κἀμὲ διδασκάλους τε κοινοὺς   10
τῇ μούσῃ σέο σώφρον᾽ ἄρτ᾽ ἐκόσμεις,
σώφρων αὐτὸς ἐὼν μάλ᾽ εὐσεβής τε.
δέξ᾽ οὖν θυγατέρ᾽, ὥς ποτ᾽ ἐστιν, ἀμήν,
τεχθεῖσάν ῥ᾽ ἀγάμῳ περ εἰσέτ᾽ ὄντι·
ἣν κἂν γράμμασι τὸ πρὶν ἐμνάου σοῖς.   15
ἄπροικον δέ θ᾽ ἑ δέξ᾽ ἴσως τ᾽ ἄωρον,
οὐ μὴν ἀλλὰ σαόφρον᾽ ἠγμένην τ᾽ εὖ

cuinam filiolam *locabo* charam
ad taedas iuveni bono pudicas?
te recte video, Iacobe. semper
prae cunctis aderas mihi fidelis,
una nos *ubi* Sturmium per altum
Argentina polivit arte fandi·
nunc et Leucorea studens in urbe
clari discipulus bonus Philippi
absentis procul es memor sodalis.
nostros inde didascalosque meque
ornabas modulis prius pudicis,
existens pius et pudicus ipse.
prolem *nunc capias, utut* sit, ergo,
quam coelebs genui carensque nupta:
quam scriptis etiam tuis petisti.
sed sumas sine dote forsque nigram,
at castam tamen optimeque cultam:·

---

[19] Weise (2020).

[20] *In ed. 1555 legitur* Μαρτῖ- / νος Κρούσιος ὁ νεώτερος / Ἰακώβῳ Φαβρικίῳ Χεμνικιεῖ τὴν / αὐτοῦ θυγατέρα Σώσανναν / μνηστευομένῳ χαίρειν ἐν /Χριστῷ. Die Streichung von ὁ νεώτερος im Exemplar der UB Tübingen reflektiert den Tod von Martin Crusius gleichnamigem Vater im Jahr 1554. Der griechische Text ist in der 1555-er Ausgabe ohne Variante gegen über den *Poemata Graeca* von 1567, eine lateinische Übersetzung fehlt dort noch.

[21] *an* συνν. ?

[22] *an* Στούρμοιο ?

[23] *an* ἔτ᾽ ἐμοῦ ?

οὗ δὴ καὶ χάριν ἂν φιλοῖς ἐ μᾶλλον.   *hinc (par est) etiam magis*[24] *placebit.*
κέκλησθ' οὖν ἀπὸ τοῦ σὺ μὲν φίλος μοι   *tu posthac gener ergo sis amatus,*
γαμβρός, τοὶ δ' ἀγαθοὶ κάσεις σέθεν τρεῖς 20 *at fratres mihi tres tui benigni*
κηδεσταί· φιλίη δ' ἐν ἄμμιν εἴη   *affines: et amor sit inter omnes*
ἄρρηκτος. σὺν ἀδελφεοῖσι χαῖρε.   *haud fractus. Valeas tuique fratres.*[25]

Martin Crusius sendet an Jacob Fabricius aus Chemnitz einen Gruß in Christus.

Welchem tüchtigen jungen Mann soll ich mein liebes Töchterlein zu reiner Ehe vermählen? Passenderweise Dir, Jacob [Fabricius]. Denn Du warst mir stets mehr als alle anderen ein zuverlässiger Freund, [5] seit wir beide die rhetorischen Unterweisungen des berühmten [Johannes] Sturm in Straßburg hörten. Jetzt aber, da Du wieder in der Stadt Wittenberg als Schüler des vielbekannten Philipp [Melanchthon] bist, denkst Du noch an mich trotz meiner weiten Entfernung. [10] Und Du hast ja fürwahr auch mich und unsere gemeinsamen Lehrer gerade noch mit Deiner besonnenen Muse ausgezeichnet, selbst gleichermaßen besonnen wie fromm. So nimm nun also meine Tochter, wie immer es mit ihr steht, die ich zeugte, als ich noch unvermählt war; [15] um diese hast Du ja auch schon zuvor in Deinen Schriften gefreit. Nimm Sie ohne Mitgift und vielleicht ohne jugendliche Schönheit, aber doch besonnen und unter guter Führung stehend: Deshalb wirst Du sie auch um so mehr lieben. So heiße denn von jetzt an mein lieber [20] Schwiegersohn, und Deine drei trefflichen Brüder seien meine angeheirateten Verwandten. Möge zwischen uns unzerbrechliche Freundschaft herrschen. Lebe wohl mit Deinen Brüdern!

Dieses Widmungsgedicht nimmt mit seiner chrakteristischen Frage „Wem soll ich meine Schrift zueignen?" unmissverständlich auf das Einleitungsgedicht Catulls bezug, variiert die catullische Poetologie jedoch durch eine Verheiratungsmetaphorik: Crusius tut so, als ob die *Susanna-Dichtung* seine Tochter sei, die er ehelos (ἄγαμος, V. 14) gezeugt habe – was immer das heißen mag – und für die er nun einen verständnisvollen Ehemann suche; für diese Stellung hat sich Fabricius in seinen Schriften geradezu als Freier beworben (ἐμνάου, V. 15). Diese sexuelle Metaphorik, welche die catullische Widmungsmotivik bei

---

[24] magnis *ed.*

[25] Vgl. Cat. 1: *Cui dono lepidum novum libellum / Arida modo pumice expolitum? / Corneli, tibi: namque tu solebas / Meas esse aliquid putare nugas, / [5] Iam tum cum ausus es unus Italorum / Omne aevum tribus explicare cartis / Doctis, Iuppiter, et laboriosis. / Quare habe tibi quicquid hoc libelli, / Qualecumque; quod, o patrona uirgo, / [10]Plus uno maneat perenne saeclo.*

Crusius einfärbt, mag man zumal im thematischen Zusammenhang mit der keuschen biblischen Susanna als unpassend empfinden.

Und in der Tat hat der nächste, der sich in griechischen Hexametern mit dem biblischen Susanna-Stoff befasste, auf solche Töne in seiner Einleitung ganz verzichtet und stattdessen die Keuschheit Gottes, seiner Diener und insbesondere die Bedeutung der *Susanna* als Exempel für die Keuschheit der Ehe hervorgehoben. Die strenge Unverbrüchlichkeit der Ehe wird ja auch in den mythologischen Epen Rhodomans, etwa in den *Troica*[26], anhand der beiden Frauen des Paris, Oenone und Helena, ins Licht gerückt.[27] Bei dem diesen Aspekt der *castitas* forcierenden Dichter handelt es sich um **Georg Koch** aus Heringen, seinerseits ebenfalls einen Ilfelder Schüler Neanders. Stefan Weise hat nachgewiesen, dass Koch die *Susanna* des Crusius rezipiert hat.

Koch versifizierte indes nicht nur die Susanna-Geschichte (1568),[28] sondern auch die Geburtsgeschichte des Täufers Johannes (1569);[29] ferner verfasste er ein *Eidyllion* über Christi Geburt[30] und stellte seine *Susanna* in den Kontext einer umfassenderen Versifikation des biblischen Buches Daniel[31] (beides 1569). Sein Erstlingswerk, zu welchem auch Rhodoman selbst beigetragen hat, ist indes der *Jonas* aus dem Jahr 1567,[32] dessen Prooemium ebenfalls deutlich auf die *Odyssee* bezugnimmt.

> δῖά μοι <u>ἔννεπε</u> <u>Μοῦσα</u> <u>θεηγόρον</u> <u>ἄνδρα</u> προφήτην,
> <u>ὅστις</u> πανδυνάμοιο Θεοῦ δακέθυμον ἐφετμὴν
> ἀνδράσ' ἀλυξάμενος ὑπερηνορέουσιν ἐνισπεῖν
> εἰναλίου μάλ' ἔλωρ γέγονεν καὶ κύρμα πελώρου·
> καὶ αὖ, ὡς[33] τριτάτη ἐφάνη ῥοδοδάκτυλος ἠώς,   5
> νηδύος εὐρυχόροιο ἐλύθη, πολιῆς τε ἀπήμων

---

[26] In Neander (1588) sowie (Zweitauflage) in Rhodoman (1604).

[27] Vgl. Gärtner (2017, 117–120).

[28] Cocus (1568).

[29] Cocus (1569a).

[30] Cocus (1569b).

[31] Cocus (1569c).

[32] Cocus (1567).

[33] ὥς *ed.*

ἐκ[34] ξηρῆσ’ ἀνεδύσσατ’ ἐπὶ ψαμάθοισι θαλάσσης
κ’ ἀγγελίην κρατερὴν Νίνου ἤγγειλε πολίταις.[35]

Göttliche Muse, künde mir den von Gott redenden Propheten, der, da er es vermied, den schmerzlichen Auftrag des allmächtigen Gottes an die frevelnden Menschen zu verkünden, Beute und Fund eines Meeresungeheuers wurde; [5] und dann, als die dritte rosenfingrige Morgenröte erschien, wurde er wieder aus dem geräumigen Leib (des Ungeheuers) erlöst und tauchte unbeschadet aus der gräulichen See auf am trockenen Meeresstrand und verkündete seine gewaltige Botschaft den Bürgern von Ninive.

Koch bekundet seine Frömmigkeit, indem er das charakteristisch am Werkanfang stehende ἄνδρα innerhalb des ersten Verses zurückzieht und an der Versspitze durch das neu hinzutretende Musenattribut δῖα ersetzt. Das aus acht Versen bestehende Prooemium Kochs gliedert sich in zwei Teilsätze zu je vier Versen; der erste beschreibt die Flucht des Jonas vor seinem göttlichen Auftrag, auf welche seine Verschlingung durch den Wal folgt, der zweite dagegen seine wundersame Rettung und die schließliche Befolgung des göttlichen Auftrags. Also führt Koch eine strukturelle Dichotomie ein, die Verirrung und Umkehr gegeneinanderstellt. Eine solche klassizistische Werkeinleitung ist keineswegs selbstverständlich: Noch wenige Jahre zuvor, 1565, hat Abraham Rockenbach eine vergleichsweise kurze griechische Jonas-Versifikation dem Dompropst zu Havelberg, Levin von der Schulenburg, gewidmet,[36] die auf jegliches Prooemium verzichtet und einfach mit dem Auftrag Gottes an den Propheten beginnt.

Unsere nächste Station ist **Johannes Melas** (ursprünglich wohl einfach Schwarz), Pastor in Unterglauchau, der sein Werk den Ratsherren von Bitterfeld widmet. Melas versifiziert im Jahr 1574 die *Vita Melanchthons* (dem er offenbar in der Gräzisierung seines Nachnamens folgt) auf der stofflichen Grundlage des Camerarius.[37] Das Werk fordert geradezu einen Vergleich mit Rhodomans etwas später (1579) erschienener *Luther-Vita*.[38] Anders als der sprachlich virtuose Rhodoman scheut sich Melas vor der Versifikation theologischer Sachverhalte

---

[34] ἐκ [...] ἀνεδύσσατο *per tmesin pro* ἐξανεδ. *ut vid.*

[35] Vgl. Hom. *Od.* 1.1–2: ἄνδρα μοι ἔννεπε Μοῦσα πολύτροπον, ὃς μάλα πολλὰ / πλάγχθη, ἐπεὶ Τροίης ἱερὸν πτολίεθρον ἔπερσε / [...]

[36] Rockenbach (1565).

[37] Melas (1574).

[38] Rhodoman (1579).

(Rhodomans Bravourstück ist eine metrische Umsetzung der *Confessio Augustana*). Daneben gibt es aber auch wichtige theologische Unterschiede: Während Rhodoman das Marburger Religionsgespräch, das eine jahrhundertelange Kluft zwischen Lutheranern und Calvinisten hinterließ, realistisch als ein „Unentschieden" wertet und nur einige unsachliche Boshaftigkeiten über das Todesgeschick Calvins und Zwinglis hinzuzusetzen weiß, wertet Melas dieses Gespräch etwas simplistisch als großen Erfolg Melanchthons. Sein Feindbild sind nicht etwa die Calvinisten oder der bei Rhodoman als böses Gegenbild zu Luther verteufelte Karlstadt, sondern vielmehr die sich mit den Philippisten zu dieser Zeit streitenden Gnesiolutheraner, insbesondere der „Illyrier" Matthias Flacius, dem Melas den Missbrauch von Melanchthons Gastfreundschaft vorwirft.

Auch die *Melanchthon-Vita* des Johannes Melas rekurriert in ihrem Prooemium auf die *Odyssee*:

ἄνδρα μοι ἔννεπε Μοῦσα φίλον Θεῷ ἠδὲ βροτοῖσιν
ἠγαθέοις ἀγαθοῖσί τε, ὃς μάλα πολλὰ δίδαξε
ῥῆμα Θεοῦ φῦλ' ἀνθρώπων ἐνὶ γαίη ἁπάση,
οὐκ ἀπολέσθ' αὐτούς, φυγέειν δὲ τὸν αἰπὺν ὄλεθρον·
αὐτοῦ γὰρ γραφαί εἰσι λιγυπνείοντες ἆῆται,   5
ἄνδρας ἀναψύχοντες ἀεί, ὅταν οἷσι[39] φίλον κῆρ
οὐκ ἐθέλει ζώειν καὶ ὁρᾶν φάος ἠελίοιο,[40]
εἴπερ χειρὶ Θεοῦ πᾶσαι γραφθεῖσαι ἔασι.
τῷ καί μιν Θεὸς ἠδ' αὐτοῦ κλέος εὐρὺ[41] ἔθηκεν,
ἐσθλόν τ' ἀθάνατόν τε καὶ ἄσβεστον περὶ πάντων.   10
τόν ῥ' ἅμα καὶ περὶ κῆρι φιλῶν ἐν γαστέρι μητρὸς
ὄργανον ἐκλεκτὸν προκρίνατο ὃν κατὰ δῆμον.[42]

---

[39] *an* ὅτε τοῖσι φ. κ. *?*

[40] Vgl. Hom. *Od.* 1.1–9: ἄνδρα μοι ἔννεπε Μοῦσα πολύτροπον, ὃς μάλα πολλὰ / πλάγχθη, ἐπεὶ Τροίης ἱερὸν πτολίεθρον ἔπερσε· / πολλῶν δ' ἀνθρώπων ἴδεν ἄστεα καὶ νόον ἔγνω, / πολλὰ δ' ὅ γ' ἐν πόντῳ πάθεν ἄλγεα ὃν κατὰ θυμόν, / ἀρνύμενος ἥν τε ψυχὴν καὶ νόστον ἑταίρων. / ἀλλ' οὐδ' ὣς ἑτάρους ἐρρύσατο, ἱέμενός περ· / αὐτῶν γὰρ σφετέρησιν ἀτασθαλίῃσιν ὄλοντο, / νήπιοι, οἳ κατὰ βοῦς Ὑπερίονος Ἠελίοιο / ἤσθιον· αὐτὰρ ὁ τοῖσιν ἀφείλετο νόστιμον ἦμαρ. Praeterea cf. Hom. *Od.* 4.539–540 / 10.497–498 (loco utroque de Ulixe ipso) οὐδέ νύ μοι κῆρ / ἤθελ' ἔτι ζώειν καὶ ὁρᾶν φάος ἠελίοιο.

[41] *an* εὐρὺ<ν> *?*

[42] *dic mihi, Musa, virum, Deo carum atque hominibus / piis honestisque, qui valde multum docuit / verbum Dei coetus hominum in universa terra, / ne pereant, sed effugiant tristem mortem. / eius enim scripta sunt stridentes spiritus, / homines refrigerantes semper, cum ipsis carum cor / non vult vivere et*

Muse, verkünde mir den Mann, geliebt von Gott und den gottesfürchtigen gütigen Menschen, der in vielerlei Dingen die Menschengeschlechter auf der ganzen Welt über das Wort Gottes belehrte, so dass sie selbst nicht untergehen, sondern dem jähen Verderben entkommen; [5] denn seine Schriften sind helltönende Winde, welche die Menschen immer wiederbeleben, wenn in ihnen ihr eigenes Herz nicht mehr leben und das Licht der Sonne sehen will, da sie [die Schriften] ja alle von der Hand Gottes geschrieben sind. Deswegen hat Gott auch ihm und seinem Ruhm weite Verbreitung gegeben, [10] auf dass dieser edel, unsterblich und über alle Menschen hinaus unvergänglich sei. So liebte er [Gott] ihn also in seinem Herzen und legte bereits, als er noch im Mutterleib war, fest, dass er sein auserwähltes Gefäß in seinem Volke sein sollte.

Melanchthon ist nicht „vielgewandt" bzw. „vielgetrieben" (πολύτροπον) wie Odysseus, sondern bei Gott und den guten Menschen geliebt (φίλον θεῷ ἠδὲ βροτοῖσιν/ ἠγαθέοις ἀγαθοῖσί τε); er wirkt nicht durch sein räumliches Umherirren, sondern durch seine in alle Länder ausstrahlende schriftliche Lehre (ὃς μάλα πολλὰ δίδαξε statt ὃς μάλα πολλὰ / πλάγχθη), und im Gegensatz zu Odysseus rettet er (wie Christus bei Reusner) ebenfalls seine Gefährten tatsächlich vor dem geistlichen Untergang, vor allem durch seine Schriften, welche die Menschen wie erfrischende Winde wiederbeleben. Nicht nur dieses Motiv der heilbringenden Winde kehrt das Vorbild der *Odyssee* um, sondern auch die Formulierung οἷσι φίλον κῆρ / οὐκ ἐθέλει ζώειν καὶ ὁρᾶν φάος ἠελίοιο, welche die okkasionelle Verzweiflung des homerischen Odysseus von Melanchthon selbst distanziert und auf die von diesem unterstützten hoffnungslosen Menschen überträgt.

Wenige Jahre später veröffentlichte **Matthaeus Gothus** aus Ellrich drei umfassende Werke in griechischen Hexametern: 1573 die *Historia vitae et doctrinae Iesu Christi*, „die Geschichte von Leben und Lehre des Jesus Christus, seiner Apostel und Schüler" in zwei Büchern großzügigen epischen Zuschnitts (das erste über Christus, das zweite über seine Schüler bis zur Zerstörung von Jersualem unter Titus);[43] dann 1574 einen *Katechismus*[44] und eine theologische

---

aspicere lumen solis, / siquidem omnia eius scripta manu Dei scripta sunt. / propterea etiam Deus ipsum atque eius famam dilatavit / honestam, immortalem atque inextinguibilem omnino. / quem simul etiam ex corde diligens in utero matris / organum electum elegit in suo populo.

[43] Gothus (1573a).

[44] Gothus (1574a).

Lehrdichtung mit dem Titel θεολογίας σύνοψις.[45] Bereits vor diesen Werken hat Gothus 1573 eine lateinische *Daniel-Versifikation* veröffentlicht[46] (in welcher er sich durchaus bewusst zeigt, dass er u.a. in Koch einen Vorgänger hat); beigegeben ist dem lateinischen *Daniel* ein griechisches Gedicht des Gothus an seine Ilfelder Schule, in welchem er sich geradezu entschuldigt, den *Daniel* noch auf Latein verfasst zu haben.

> *Eiusdem / ad scholam / Ilfeldensem*
> προτρεπτικόν
>
> ἱστορίην Δανιῆλος ἀγακλειτοῖο προφήτου
> ἡμῖν τετραθέλυμνα κυβερνητήρια κόσμου
> ἀμφαδὰ κλαγξαμένην Ἑβραΐδι μύστιδι φωνῇ,
> ἥν ποτε παντοδίδακτος ἐπεξύνωσε μαθηταῖς
> Ἰλβέλδης ἱεροῖσιν ὑπὸ σκοπέλοισι Νέανδρος   5
> στοίχοις παυροεπέσσι βίβλον βαθύπλουτον ἀείδων,
> ἥν τε Κόκος μετέπειτα κλυτῆς ὑποεργὸς ἀοιδῆς
> Ἑλλάδος αἰγλήεντι περιχλαίνωσε χιτῶνι
> θείης φραδμοσύνῃσι διδάκτορος ὑμετέροιο·
> ταύτην νῦν καὶ ἔγωγε Λατινίδος ἦχον ἰωῆς   10
> φθεγξαμένην προφόωσδε θορεῖν ἡρωΐδι ταρσῷ
> προὐτρεπόμην, ὅτι πάμπαν ὑπὸ στήθεσσι πέποιθα
> οὔτινα ῥηϊδίως γλυκερώτερον ἔμμεναι ἄλλην
> δέλτον, ἐπεσσομένων τὸ πάρος γραφθεῖσαν ἀοιδοῖς,
> πνεύματι παφλάζουσιν ἀειγενέταο τοκῆος·   15
> οὐδέ κεν ἔλπομαι ἄνδρα, κεκαδμένον ἀκροτάτῃ περ
> ἰδμοσύνῃ, τοσσοῦτον ἔπος μεγάλοιο προφήτου
> δυνάμεναι[47] κατὰ κόσμον ἅλις μελέεσσι λιγαίνειν,
> ἄρτον ἕως πέψειεν[48] ἐπὶ χθονὶ πουλυσοτείρῃ
> δυστήνου βιότοιο ταμὼν πλόον αἰνοθύελλον.   20
> ἔμπης καὶ πρέπον ἐστὶ τὰ θέσκελα μηχανάασθαι
> γράμματα σπουδαίῃ κραδίης φιλοπευθέος ὁρμῇ.
> ἀλλά νυ, γυμασίοιο Νεανδρείοιο παλαισταί,

---

[45] Gothus (1574b).

[46] Gothus (1573b). Einige Bemerkungen hierzu bei Ludwig (2016, 258–259).

[47] δυνάμεναι *scripsi* : δυνάμενον *ed.*

[48] πέψειεν *Stefan Weise* : πέψοιεν *ed.*

Κασταλίδων θέλγητρα θεοῖό τε σεμνὸς ὅμιλος
χρυσοκόμου, Δελφῶν ἱερὸν πέδον ἀμφιέποντος,   25
ἠπεδανὸν σπούδασμα φίλῃ ποτιδέρκετε γλήνῃ
καὶ νύμφαις δότε τοῦτο μελύδριον ὑμετέρῃσιν,
ὄφρα φιλοξείνοισι περισφίγξωσιν ἀγοστοῖς,
εἰ καὶ τυτθὸν ἔῃ· παῦρος χρόνος ἐστί, καὶ ἄλλο
φέρτερον ὕμμι φέρειν ἐθέλω, ῥυθμοῖσιν Ἀχαιοῖς   30
Χριστὸν ὅπερ παίδεσσι βιοσσόον ἐλπίδα κόσμου
καὶ λύκον Αὐσονίης γαίης ψυχάρπαγα δείξει.

Die Erzählung des berühmten Propheten Daniel, die uns die vier Säulen
der Führungsmächte über die Welt vernehmlich in der hebräischen Sprache
der Eingeweihten verkündigt hat, welche einstmals der allgelehrte Neander
seinen Schülern [5] unter den heiligen Felsen von Ilfeld vermittelte, indem
er in kurzen Merkversen dieses Buch mit seinem tiefen Reichtum dichterisch
wiedergab, und welche [Georg] Koch dann, [Neanders] Mitarbeiter im
berühmten Musengesang mit einem glanzvollen griechischen Gewandt
ummantelte auf das göttliche Geheiß Eures Lehrers hin [10] – diese Erzählung
ließ nun auch ich, die nunmehr im Klang der lateinischen Sprache spricht, ans
Licht vorspringen mit heroischem Fuße; denn ich bin tief in meinem Herzen
gänzlich davon überzeugt, daß kein anderes Buch, das zuvor geschrieben
wurde von den Propheten der Zukunft, [15] welche da schwärmen vom
Geiste des ewig zeugenden Gottvaters, leicht größeren Liebreiz entfalten
werde (als das Buch *Daniel*), und ich glaube, daß kein Mensch, mag er auch
mit dem schärfsten Verstandt ausgestattet sein, die so gewaltige Verkündigung
eines großen Propheten füglich in seinem Lied hinreichend besingen kann,
solange er jedenfalls Brot zu sich nimmt auf der viele [Menschen] erhaltenden
Erde [20] und die gräßlich bestürmte Irrfahrt des unseligen Menschenlebens
angetreten hat. Und dabei ist es trotzdem auch ziemlich, die göttlichen
Schriften (immer wieder) zu bearbeiten mit dem edlen Antrieb eines
forschungswilligen Herzens.

Doch jetzt, ihr Ringkämpfer von Neanders Gymnasium, Freude der
Musen und edle Gemeinde des goldhaarigen Gottes [Apollo], [25] welcher den
heiligen Boden von Delphi umwaltet, blickt auf meine schwächliche Bemühung
mit freundlichem Blick und gebt dieses Liedchen Euren Musen, damit sie es
in ihre gastfreundlichen Hände schließen, wenn es auch geringwertig ist. Es
währt nur noch kurze Zeit, [30] und ich will Euch etwas anderes Besseres
darbringen, das den (Schul-)Kindern in griechischen Rhythmen Christus, die

lebensrettende Hoffnung der Welt, und andererseits den seelenraubenden Wolf aus dem italischen Land (den Papst) darstellen wird.

Wichtig ist ferner ein Briefwechsel zwischen Gothus und Rhodoman, der in einer späteren, posthum erschienenen Gothus-Ausgabe[49] veröffentlicht ist. In diesem Briefwechsel wird deutlich, dass Rhodoman als ein neuer Homer, Gothus dagegen als eine Reinkarnation des Nonnos[50] angesehen wurde, was sich durch den Stil des Gothus verifizieren läßt, insbesondere seine Neologismen, aber auch durch nonnianische Junkturen. Gothus widmet Rhodoman die nicht erhaltene Zweitausgabe seiner Werke, in welcher diese (anders als in der Erstausgabe) jeweils mit lateinischer Übersetzung ausgestattet sind.

νῦν δὲ δὴ εἰς τεὸν[51] οἶκον ἐμὰς ποτιδέχνυσο Μούσας,
    εὐμενὲς ὄμμα φέρων ταῖς ἔπι προφρονέως.
παρθενικάς ποτ' ἐγὼ ταύτας ἐφίτυσα Νεάνδρου
    ξυνοῦ παιδευτοῦ βουλῇ ἀριστονόου·   60
ζῶσα δὲ καὶ κόσμησα νέον Ῥωμανίδι χλαίνῃ
    ξυμπάσας, κοινόν γ' εἰς φάος ὀρνυμένας.
δέχνυσο, καί μοι Ἀρίσταρχός τις ἐναίσιμος εἴης,
    μῶν κόσμος ταύταις ἄρκιός ἐσθ', ὁρόων.[52]

Jetzt aber nimm meine Musen in Dein Haus auf, freundlich Dein wohlwollendes Auge auf sie richtend. Einstmals habe ich diese jungen Damen auf den Rat unseres gemeinsamen Lehrers, [60] des herausragenden Geistes Neander, gezeugt; erst jüngst habe ich sie allesamt mit lateinischen Mänteln gegürtet und geschmückt, zumal sie sich ja jetzt gemeinsam ans Licht der Öffentlichkeit begaben. Nimm sie auf und sei mir ein trefflicher Aristarch;[53] sieh zu, ob sie über eine hinreichende Bekleidung verfügen.

---

[49] Gothus (1621).

[50] Vgl. hierzu: Gärtner (2020b). Hier findet sich eine Edition des vollständigen Briefwechsels zwischen Gothus und Rhodoman.

[51] εἰς ὂν τεοἶκον *ed.*

[52] *nunc vero nostras ne dedignare Camaenas / suscipere haud durus sub lare, quaeso* [quaesto *ed.*]*, tuo. / has ego progenui quondam monitore Neandro, / qui nos Pieriis imbuit auctor aquis: / et Latio cunctas decoravi nuper amictu, / publica cum vellent per fora carpere iter. / suscipe, Aristarchumque age non invitus, et omnes / perspice, num tali veste decenter eant.*

[53] Aristarch von Samothrake, 3./2. Jh. a, d.h. Prototyp eines Literaturkritikers

Diesen Umstand erklärt Gothus dem Rhodoman damit (V. 59–62), dass er die „Jungfrauen" (also die Musen), die er unter Beratung seines Lehrers Neanders gezeugt habe, nunmehr allesamt neu gegürtet und geschmückt habe mit einem lateinischen Mantel, zumal sie ja jetzt gemeinsam ans Licht drängen. Ähnlich sagte Rhodoman in seiner *Luther-Vita* über die zweite Auflage von dessen deutscher Bibelübersetzung, er habe der Bibel „einen glanzvolleren und besseren Mantel der deutschen Sprache als beim ersten Mal umgelegt".

> καὶ τότε καὶ βίβλῳ θεοτευχέϊ χεῖρα πελάσσας
> δεύτερον ἀγχίνοον Γερμανίδος ἔνδυε φωνῆς
> πέπλον στιλπνότερον καὶ φέρτερον, ἢ ὅτε πρῶτον
> βιβλία Γερμανῶν ὁμοχειλέα παισὶν ἔθηκε.[54]

> „Und damals auch, als er der von Gott geschaffenen Bibel zum zweiten Mal seine kundige Hand näherte, legte er ihr einen strahlenderen und besseren Mantel der deutschen Sprache um als zu dem Zeitpunkt, als er zum ersten Mal die Bibel mit den Kindern der Deutschen gleichsprachig machte."

Die Hinzufügung einer lateinischen Übersetzung oder Parallelversion wird also innerhalb der Metaphorik des Gothus so motiviert, dass man junge Mädchen ja nicht ohne angemessene Bekleidung an das Licht der Öffentlichkeit treten lässt, besonders dann nicht, wenn sie gemeinsam gehen. Diese Ausdrucksweise erinnert sehr an die sexualisierte Widmungsmetaphorik in der *Susanna* des Crusius: Wieder werden die Werke als vom Autor gezeugte junge Mädchen bezeichnet (wobei hier die Berechtigung dieser Metaphorik nicht wie bei Crusius in einer weiblichen Hauptfigur liegt, sondern ausschließlich in der Metonymie „Muse = dichterisches Werk"); allerdings hat Koch diese Werke nicht als ἄγαμος gezeugt wie Crusius, sondern mit Hilfe seines Lehrers Neander; die jungen Mädchen sollen von Rhodoman als Widmungsadressat gnädig aufgenommen werden wie die *Susanna* des Crusius von Jacob Fabricius.

---

[54] *atque tunc etiam cum libris divinis admovisset manum / solertem secundo, induit (eis) Germanicae loquelae / vestem nitidiorem et praestantiorem, quam ubi primum / biblia Germanorum labiis accomoda fecit.*

Auch theologisch bestehen Unterschiede zwischen Gothus und Rhodoman: Gothus betrachtet Luther vorzugsweise als einen Endzeitpropheten, dessen Botschaften dem Ende der Welt unmittelbar vorausgehen, während Rhodoman die Lutherische Reformation eher als eine Initialzündung für einen nachhaltigen wissenschaftlichen Aufstieg Deutschlands betrachtet (unter dieser Voraussetzung kann der Weltuntergang eigentlich noch nicht unmittelbar bevorstehen). Gothus assoziiert Luther intertextuell gelegentlich mit dem Täufer Johannes in der nonnianischen Versifikation des Johannes-Evangeliums, worin wohl impliziert sein soll, dass Luther dem letzten Gericht Christi ebenso unmittelbar vorausgeht wie der Täufer dem Messias. Außerdem bringt Gothus die lutherische Theologie mit spätmittelalterlicher Mystik, insbesondere mit Johannes Tauler und der vermeintlich von diesem stammenden *Theologia Teutsch*, in Verbindung, während Rhodoman in seiner *LutherVita* Luther eher in der Tradition von papstfeindlichen Reformationsvorläufern wie dem bömischen Jan Hus und dem italienischen Girolamo Savonarola sieht.

Auch der aus Elbingerode stammmende **Heinrich Eckstorm** (1557–1622) war Ilfeld-Schüler; eine gewisse Verbindung zu Rhodoman zeigt sich darin, dass er dessen Nachfolger als Rektor der Klosterschule in Walkenried wurde. Eckstorm versifizierte Teile des Matthaeus-Evangeliums[55] und schrieb zwei *Eidyllia*, eines über die heiligen Engel[56] und ein weiteres über den Geburtstag Christi[57] (alle 1578). Gegenüber diesen konventionellen Werken zeigt sich eine gewisse Neuerung in der *Historia Beati Laurentii* von 1582[58] – einer protestantischen Heiligenvita in episierenden griechischen Hexametern.

Gleich nach dem Prooemium geht Eckstorm auf die Problematik dieses Unterfangens ein:

οὐδ' ἄρ' ἐγὼ διὰ τοῦτο σεβάσμιον ἄνδρα ἀείσω,
ὥστε μιν εὐχωλαῖς ὁσίαις μετέπειτα καλέσσαι
δεῖ[59] θνητοὺς ἄνδρας χαλεπαῖς βεβαρηότας ἄταις·
Σφὶγξ ἄπερ Ἰταλίης Παππᾶς κακομήχανος ἔρδει·   30
τοῦ τρὶς μύριοί εἰσι θεοί, τοῖς ἱερὰ ῥέζει
καὶ τῶν εὐαγέως κέλεται ἰνδάλματα τίειν·

[55] Eckstorm (1578a).

[56] Eckstorm (1578b).

[57] Eckstorm (1578c).

[58] Eckstorm (1582).

[59] *an* δεῖ<ν> ?

σὸν δὲ κλέος μινύθει ἀδίκως ἀθεμίστιος ἀνήρ.
μᾶλλον δ’ ὑμνήσω πίστιν, τὴν εἰς σὲ κόμισε[60]
κεῖνος ἀνήρ· ἡμῖν δ’ ἔσται <u>παράδειγμα</u> <u>βίοιο</u>,   35
ὥστε μιν εὐσεβέως διάγειν καὶ ἐλπίδι πλείστῃ
ζωῆς ἐσσομένης πόλλ’ ἐνθάδε λυγρὰ μογῆσαι.
οὔπω δ’ ἀθανάτου σέο λήσομαι ἀφθίτου αἴνου·
σεῖο γὰρ ἀρχομένη καὶ εἰς σὲ λελήξεται ᾠδή.

Und so werde ich den ehrwürdigen Mann nicht deshalb besingen, daß ihn in der
Folge sterbliche Menschen, die von schwerem Unglück beladen sind, mit sakralen
Gebeten anrufen sollten; [30] wie es die Sphinx von Italien, der Übles sinnende
Papst, tut, der dreißigtausend Götter hat, denen er Opferhandlungen darbringt
und deren Standbilder er fromm zu verehren befiehlt; Deinen [Jesu] Ruhm aber
mindert dieser gesetzlose Mann ungerechterweise. Vielmehr will ich den Glauben
rühmen, welchen jener Mann [Laurentius] Dir gegenüber aufgebracht hat; [35] für
uns aber wird er ein Lebensvorbild sein, dass wir dieses in Frömmigkeit verbringen
und in reichlicher Hoffnung auf ein künftiges Leben hier viele traurige Mühen
auf uns nehmen. Und nicht werde ich Dein unsterbliches, unvergängliches Lob
vergessen; denn mein Gesang wird, wie er bei Dir beginnt, auch mit Dir aufhören.

Natürlich schreibe er eine solche Vita nicht, um diesen Heiligen dann anzurufen,
wie es der als Sphinx bezeichnete römische Papst mit seinen dreitausend Pseudo-
Gottheiten tue (V. 30–31) – vielmehr diene die hagiographische Lebensschilderung
nur als ein παράδειγμα βίοιο (V. 35).

Diese *Laurentius-Vita* könnte man gewinnreich vergleichen etwa mit der
zu Anfang des folgenden Jahrhunderts entstehenden griechisch episierenden
Genovefa-Vita des französischen Jesuiten Denis Pétau.[61] Hier dient das gesamte
zweite Buch dazu, die mit einem Tod im eigentlichen Sinne unvereinbare
postmortale Wirkung der Heiligen zu zeigen, und die Anbetung der Heiligen ist
nicht etwa Argumentationsziel des Jesuiten, sondern Voraussetzung für seinen
Wirksamkeitsbeweis; denn eine unwirksame Instanz würde niemand anbeten.

Auch Eckstorms Prooemium der *Laurentius-Vita* orientiert sich an der
Odyssee:

---

[60] *an* κόμισσε ?

[61] Petavius (1641, 86–145).

ἄνδρα μοι ἔννεπε Μοῦσα πολύστονον, ἔνθεον ἄνδρα,
ὅρρα πολυφλοίσβων ποτ᾽ ἀπ᾽ Ὠκεανοῖο ῥοάων,
ἧχι Ἴβηρ βαρύδουπος ἀπ᾽ εὐρυπόρου ποταμοῖο
χεύμασιν ἀενάοισι κυλίνδει ἄφθονον ὕδωρ,
Αὐσονίηνδ᾽[62] ἦλθεν μεγάλου κατὰ νεῦμα Θεοῖο   5
καὶ φρεσὶν ἀκλινέεσσιν ἀκαμπέα πίστιν ἀέξων
εἰς Χριστὸν κόσμου χραισμήτορα πολλὰ φρυγέτρῳ
ἄλγεα πέσσεν ἐνὶ κρυερῷ τετληότι θυμῷ
καὶ ἀδίκην ποινὴν Δεκίου θρασύχειρος ἔτισεν,
ἀστροδίαιτον ἑῷ πότμῳ βασιλῆα γεραίρων.[63]   10

Künde mir, Muse, den jammerreichen Mann, den gotterfüllten Mann, der einst
von den heftig rauschenden Strömen des Okeanos, dort wo der tiefdröhnende
Iber von seinem weiträumigen Flusslauf mit unablässigem Strömen reichliche
Wassermassen einherwälzt, [5] nach Italien kam auf die Weisung des mächtigen
Gottes hin und, in seinem unbeugsamen Herzen unverbrüchlichen Glauben
an Christus, den Helfer der Welt, nährend, auf der Folterbank viele Schmerzen
in seinem eiskalten, duldemutigen Geiste verdaute und die ungerechte Strafe
des unverschämt waltenden Decius abbüßte, [10] dabei den im Himmel
wohnenden König durch sein Todesschicksal verehrend.

Das Prooemium umfasst hier zehn Verse und zerfällt dichotomisch in zwei Teile
zu je fünf Hexametern, einen odysseischen (die Fahrt des Heiligen von Spanien
nach Rom) und einen iliadischen (seine Leiden in Rom, gipfelnd im Martyrium);
die vielen Schmerzen werden also vom odysseischen in den iliadischen Abschnitt
übertragen, und der πολύτροπος wird zum πολύστονος.

Doch jetzt verlassen wir den hagiographischen Bereich und kehren wieder in
den biblischen zurück: **Matthaeus Domisius**, Schulleiter in Taucha bei Leipzig,
dediziert sein Werk an Leipziger Honoratioren; es handelt sich um die *Historia de
s. Ioanne Baptista* von 1594.[64] Wenn man vergleichen möchte, bietet wiederum
Frankreich einen Vergleichstext: Sébastien Chateillon gibt seinem *Jonas Propheta*

---

[62] Αὐσονίην δ᾽ *ed.*

[63] Vgl. Hom. *Od.* 1.1–5: ἄνδρα μοι ἔννεπε Μοῦσα πολύτροπον, ὃς μάλα πολλὰ /πλάγχθη, ἐπεὶ
Τροίης ἱερὸν πτολίεθρον ἔπερσε· / πολλῶν δ᾽ ἀνθρώπων ἴδεν ἄστεα καὶ νόον ἔγνω, / πολλὰ δ᾽ ὅ
γ᾽ ἐν πόντῳ πάθεν ἄλγεα ὃν κατὰ θυμόν, / ἀρνύμενος ἥν τε ψυχὴν καὶ νόστον ἑταίρων.

[64] Domisius (1594).

heroico carmine Latino descriptus (Basel 1545)[65] eine griechische Versifikation der Geschichte des Täufers unter dem Titel πρόδρομος in drei Rhapsodien bei. Gleich im Prooemium heißt es bei Chateillon, es gebe keinen besseren als „den liebenswerten Zacharias-Sohn, den barfüßigen Propheten" (ἀνθρώπων δ' οὔ πώς τινα φέρτερον ἄσομεν ἄλλον / νηλίποδος προδρόμοι᾿ ἀγαπητοῦ Ζαχαρίαο). Solche Züge eremitenhafter Askese drängt Domisius bewusst zurück, der seinen Johannes lieber als einen aus bestem Elternhaus und vorzüglicher Heimatstadt stammenden jungen Mann darstellt, der in seiner Ausbildung dann „die Blüten der Musen abpflückt" und sich zu einem trefflichen protestantischen Musterschüler entwickelt, der als Schriftgelehrter seine soziale Umgebung unterweist. Hier wirkt also der protestantische Schulbetrieb möglicherweise etwas überformend auf die biblische Vorlage – ähnlich wie ja auch Rhodoman in seinem *Hymnus scholasticus*[66] (706 Hexameter) die gesamte Geschichte als eine Aneinanderreihung von Schulgründungen ausdeutet und aus dem von den Musen zum Dichter geweihten Hirten Quintus von Smyrna einen „Schulhirten" nach Art einer protestantischen Lehrerpersönlichkeit macht.[67]

Auch Domisius unterlässt es nicht, am Werkeingang nachdrücklich auf das *Odyssee*-Prooemium zu rekurrieren:

> Πνεῦμα Θεοῦ, τά τ᾽ ἐόντα, τά τ᾽ ἐσσόμενα πρό τ᾽ ἐόντα
> εὖ εἰδός (Θεὸς ἐσσὶ γάρ), <u>ἄνδρα</u> <u>μοι</u> <u>ἔννεπε</u> θεῖον
> τῷ ἱερῷ Σολύμων γεγαῶτα ἐνὶ <u>πτολιέθρῳ</u>,
> <u>ὅς</u> λέγετο Χριστοῦ κῆρυξ προκέλευθος ἄνακτος
> καὶ πάντεσσι μετέπρεπε γεννητοῖσι γυναικῶν·   5
> ἀλλ᾽ <u>ἐπὶ</u> <u>γῆς</u> μάλα <u>πόλλ᾽</u> <u>ἔπαθεν</u> καὶ πολλὰ μόγησε[68]
> ζωῆς ἀενάοιο θεόρρυτα χεύματα μύθων
> ἀμφιέπων· καὶ ἀλαζόνα τὸν βασιλῆα ἐλέγχων
> Ἡρώδην τοὺς ἀλλοτρίους θαλάμους μεθέποντα
> οἰκτίστῳ θανάτῳ ἀπὸ δουρὶ κτείνετο πληχθείς.[69]   10

---

[65] Castilio (1545).

[66] In Neander (1585).

[67] Hierzu demnächst: Gärtner (2020a) und Gärtner (2020c).

[68] Vgl. Hom. *Od.* 1.1–5: <u>ἄνδρα</u> <u>μοι</u> <u>ἔννεπε</u> Μοῦσα, πολύτροπον, <u>ὃς</u> μάλα πολλὰ / πλάγχθη, ἐπεὶ Τροίης ἱερὸν <u>πτολίεθρον</u> ἔπερσε· / πολλῶν δ᾽ ἀνθρώπων ἴδεν ἄστεα καὶ νόον ἔγνω, / <u>πολλὰ</u> δ᾽ ὅ γ᾽ <u>ἐν</u> <u>πόντῳ</u> <u>πάθεν</u> ἄλγεα ὃν κατὰ θυμόν, / ἀρνύμενος ἥν τε ψυχὴν καὶ νόστον ἑταίρων.

[69] *Spiritus alme Dei, qui noveris omnia praesens / quae fuerint (etenim Deus es), mihi sacra <u>virumque</u> / dicito divinum, <u>Solymae</u> <u>qui</u> natus in <u>oris</u> / praecursor Christi est dictus, quo foemina maius / nulla*

Hauch Gottes, der Du das Jetzige, das Künftige und das Vergangene gut kennst (denn Du bist selbst göttliche Instanz), verkünde mir den göttlichen Mann, geboren in der heiligen Stadt von Jerusalem, der als wegbereitender Prophet Christi des Herrn bezeichnet wurde [5] und unter allen von Frauen Geborenen herausragte; doch auf Erden litt und duldete er sehr Vieles, die von Gott fließenden Ströme seiner Worte über das ewige Leben umwaltend; und als er den prahlerischen König Herodes zurechtwies, wie dieser sich mit fremden Ehen abgab, [10] wurde er durch einen höchst grausamen Tod hingerichtet, vom Schwerte geschlagen.

Auch hier zerfällt die Prooemialpartie in zwei symmetrische Verspentaden; die erste hebt die hohe Bedeutung des Täufers hervor, die sich aus seiner göttlichen Auszeichnung ergibt, die zweite setzt sein irdisches Leiden dagegen, welches in der Hinrichtung durch Herodes gipfelt. Ich kann hier nur andeuten, dass Domisius auch einen lateinischen Paralleltext bietet, der in ähnlich sinnhaltiger Weise Bezüge zur vergilischen *Aeneis* herstellt, etwa durch Ersetzung des vergilischen *Arma virumque* durch *sacra virumque*.

Schließen möchte ich mit **Jakob Steinbrück** aus Salzungen, der im Jahr 1607 eine griechische Dichtung über den Apostel Paulus vorlegt: den *Paulus conversus Graeco carmine palliatus*, „den gewandelten Paulus, bekleidet mit einem griechischen Gedicht".[70] Hier ist also die Bekleidungsmetapher genau umgekehrt verwandt wie bei Gothus, bei welchem die lateinische Übersetzungen seine vorher nackten (d.h. nur griechisch verfassten) Musen bekleideten. Hier dagegen bekleidet das griechische Gedicht den theologischen Stoff neu.

Bei diesem Werk handelt es sich um eine Valediktionsarbeit am Gothaer Gymnasium, die eingeleitet wird durch ein Vorwort vom Rektor Andreas Wilk. Bei dem Verfasser, Jakob Steinbrück, handelt es sich um einen Sohn des bekannteren Melchior Steinbrück, der im Jahr 1563 in Gotha geboren wurde und ebendort spätere höhere kirchliche Ämter bekleidete. Dazu paßt, dass dieser Melchior Steinbrück im selben Jahr 1607 eine Predigtsammlung unter dem lateinischen

---

decus peperit, qui plurima passus acerba est, / dum vitam in terris miseramque brevemque trahebat, / instillans sacra et Christi monumenta propagans, / et qui, reginae incestum Herodisque nefandum / dum culpat, mortem indignam cervice resecta / oppetiit spurcae memorem meretricis ob iram. Vgl. Verg. *Aen.* 1.1–7: *arma virumque cano, Troiae qui primus ab <u>oris</u> / Italiam fato profugus Laviniaque venit / litora, multum ille et terris iactatus et alto / vi superum, saevae memorem Iunonis ob iram, / multa quoque et bello passus, dum conderet urbem / inferretque deos Latio, genus unde Latinum / Albanique patres atque altae moenia Romae.*

[70] Jacobus Steinbrück (1607).

Titel *Paulus conversus* veröffentlichte.[71] Was läge also näher als, dass dessen Sohn im gleichen Jahr am Gothaer Gymnasium als Abschlußarbeit den vom Vater traktierten Stoff mit dem „Mantel" eines griechischen Gedichts bekleidete?

Und auch der jüngere Steinbrück verzichtet nicht darauf, in seinem Prooemium auf die *Odyssee* zurückzugreifen:

> ἄνδρα μοι ἔννεπε Μοῦσα πολύτροπον, ὃς μάλα πολλὰ
> πλάγχθη, ἐπεὶ πόλει ἐν Σολύμων τῷ νηλέϊ χαλκῷ[72]
> μύστησιν Χριστοῖο ἀεικέα πότμον ἐφῆκε·
> λαμπρὸν[73] δ' οὐρανόθεν περὶ μιν φάος ἀστεροπῆς ὡς
> γνώσθη ἁμαρτοσύνην· ἠδ' ὃς πάρος ἔσκεν Ἰησοῦ   5
> ἐχθρός, καρπαλίμως γίνεται τότε[74] σκεῦος ἐκεῖνος
> ἐκλεκτόν· πάντη τόδε καὶ κατ' ἀπείρονα γαῖαν
> οὔνομα κηρύξειε Θεοῖο ἀγαυοῦ ἀγαυόν,
> θαρσαλέος τε Θεοῦ γίνεται θεράπων μεγάλοιο.

Künde mir, Muse, den vielgewandten Mann, der sich gar heftig verirrte, seit er in der Stadt Jerusalem mit seinem erbarmungslosen Schwert den Eingeweihten Christi ihr unziemliches Todesschicksal zusandte; vom Himmel aber strahlte (?) um ihn das Licht eines Blitzschlages, damit [?] [5] er seine Verfehlung erkenne [?][75]; und so wird schnell derjenige, der zuvor ein Feind Jesu war, dann dessen ausgesuchtes Gefäß; als solches sollte er auch überall auf der grenzenlosen Welt den erhabenen Namen des erhabenen Gottes verkündigen, und er wird zum mutigen Diener des gewaltigen Gottes.

Und zwar zitiert Steinbrück die *Odyssee* bis einschließlich πλάγχθη ἐπεί am Anfang des zweiten Hexameters wörtlich. In diesem über die anderen behandelten Autoren hinausgehenden wörtlichen Anschluß mag man auf den ersten Blick die

---

[71] Melchior Steinbrück (1607).

[72] Vgl. Hom. *Od.* 1.12: ἄνδρα μοι ἔννεπε Μοῦσα πολύτροπον, ὃς μάλα πολλὰ πλάγχθη, ἐπεὶ Τροίης ἱερὸν πτολίεθρον ἔπερσε/ …

[73] *voluitne* λάμψεν δ' […], ὡς/ γνοίη ἁμαρτοσύνην ?

[74] τόδε *ed.*

[75] Hier wurde die in der Fußnote 73 erwogene konjekturale Fassung übersetzt. Stefan Weise versucht die Überlieferung zu erklären: „,Ein helles Licht vom Himmel um ihn wie von einem Blitz [vgl. Hom. *Il.* 10.154] ließ ihn seine Sündhaftigkeit erkennen.' Dann wäre also λαμπρόν mit φάος die Klammer für den kühnen präpositionalen Ausdruck οὐρανόθεν περί μιν ohne ,Stützpartizip'. γνώσθη stünde dann anstelle eines Mediums."

schülerhafte Epigonalität des jungen Steinbrück sehen. Andererseits kann man ihm jedoch zugutehalten, dass πλάγχθη hier nicht nur das räumliche Umherirren bezeichnet, wie es Reusner von den irdischen Irrläufen Christi verwendete. Vielmehr impliziert μάλα πολλὰ / πλάγχθη bei Steinbrück vor allem die völlige innere Verirrung, welche Paulus (noch als Saulus) in Jerusalem seine gnadenlose Christenverfolgung betreiben ließ.

An dieser hier ist das Prooemium strukturell zweigeteilt: Die Verse 1–3 beschreiben die Verirrung des Paulus in seiner ersten Lebensphase, die Verse 4–10 dagegen seine innere und äußere Erleuchtung in der zweiten Lebensphase und seine anschließende Konversion vom Saulus zum Paulus. Diese Dichotomie entspricht exakt dem Prooemium zum *Jonas* des Georg Koch, wo zunächst die innere Abkehr des Propheten von Gott und sein äußeres Irren (der Schiffbruch), dann jedoch seine Rettung und seine innere wie äußere Rückkehr zum göttlichen Auftrag geschildert wurde.

An dieser Stelle schließe ich endet mein Überblick; den Anspruch, kein Werk übersehen zu haben, das noch gut in diese Reihe passen könnte, wage ich nicht zu erheben. Ich hoffe jedoch gezeigt zu haben, dass die von mir behandelten Autoren nicht nur bezüglich ihres protestantischen Sozialisationshintergrunds, der protestantisch-textnahen Stoßrichtung ihrer literarischen Tätigkeit, sondern auch in ihrer poetologischen Bildlichkeit und in ihrer Technik der Homerimitation eine homogene Gruppe von Literaten bilden, die man mit Recht im geistigen Umfeld der Ilfelder Schule und des Lorenz Rhodoman zusammenstellen darf. Odysseus im Gewande der homerischen Epik scheint für all diese Autoren ein literarisches Identifikationsmodell, das sich zur Beschreibung von Christus selbst, von alt- und neutestamentlichen Helden sowie Heiligen und führenden Repräsentanten der Reformation eignet. Teilweise handelt es sich bei den besprochenen Texten um bloße Reminiszenzen an das homerische Odyssee-Prooemium, teilweise wird aber auch durch detaillierte intertextuelle Strukturen eine genaue Beziehung zwischen den christlichen Helden und dem homerischen Dulder etabliert. Die für solches poetisches Vorgehen erforderliche Kunst des aktiven, aemulativen Griechischschreibens und die formale Imitationstechnik gehörten sicherlich zu den Fertigkeiten, die in der Ilfelder Schule unter Neander gelehrt wurden, wie schon die von Stefan Weise in diesem Band besprochene, von Neander selbst anonym edierte Epylliensammlung Rhodomans[76], die auf seine Ilfelder Schulzeit zurückgeht, beweist und sich aus dem oben ausgeschriebenen Selbstzeugnis Rhodomans über seine Ilfelder Zeit ergibt.

---

[76] Rhodoman (1588). Vgl. hierzu ausführlich Weise S. 185–215 im vorliegenden Band.

Rhodoman selbst, Neanders Meisterschüler, hat zwar in seiner *Luther-Vita* von 1579[77] seinen Helden nicht mit einem odyssee-artigen epischen Prooemium geehrt; vielmehr hat er einen solchen Kunstgriff bereits in seiner Totenklage um Luther (1573)[78] angewandt. Dort verbindet er den hellenistischen ἐπιτάφιος Βίωνος in dorischem Dialekt mit den beiden homerischen Proömien:

Πιερίδες νύμφαι τε θεαὶ καλυκώπιδες ἀγναί,
ταὶ ῥὰ νάπας ποταμώς τε καὶ ἄλσεα πυκνὰ φιλεῖτε,
μυρόμεναι στοναχεῖτε, γόῳ δ᾽ ἐξάρχετε πρᾶται·
ἀνέρα μοι κλαίοιτε θεόκριτον, ὃς κάμε πολλά,[79]
μυρία δ᾽ αὖ τέτλακε διὰ κλέος οὐρανόπαιδος,   5
Λουθᾶρον Χριστοῖο τὸν ἱμερόεντα προφήταν,
ὃς κνέφας ἀδυφαεῖ φθισίμβροτον ἤλασεν αὐγᾷ,
ἀντολίαν δ᾽ ἤνοιγε φαεσφόρος οἷά τις ἀστὴρ
ἀντέλλων φλογερῇσι μετὰ σκότος ἀκτίνεσσιν,
ἐκ δ᾽ ἐκάλεσσε φάος σωσίμβροτον ἠριγενείας·   10
ἔκτανε δ᾽ Αὐσόνιον λύκον, ὃς[80] φθόρος ἔπλετο μάλων,
πολλὰς δ᾽ ἰφθίμους ψυχὰς Ἄϊδι προΐαψε,[81]
ψεύδε᾽ ἐρῶν ἐτύμοισιν ὁμοῖα, λυγρὰ παρασχὼν
φάρμακ᾽, ἀλάθειαν τε λεωσόον ἀχλύϊ κρύψας.
ἄρχετε Τευτονικαὶ τῶ πένθεος ἄρχετε Μοῖσαι.[82]   15

Ihr Musen und Ihr Nymphen, keusche Göttinnen mit blütenfarbenen Augen, die ihr Waldschluchten, Flüsse und dichtbewachsene Haine liebt, klagt voller Jammer und beginnt die Totentrauer von Grund auf: Mögt ihr mir um den gotterwählten Mann trauern, [5] der viele Mühen ertrug und Zehntausendfaches erduldete um den Ruhm des Himmlischen Kindes willen, Luther, den lieblichen Propheten Christi, der die Menschen verderbende Finsternis mit seinen angenehm leuchtenden Strahlen vertrieb und den Sonnenaufgang

---

[77] Rhodoman (1579).

[78] In Martinus (1573). Edition der *Totenklage* geplant bei Gärtner (2020d, 115–154).

[79] Vgl. Hom. *Od.* 1.1–4: ἄνδρα μοι ἔννεπε Μοῦσα πολύτροπον, ὃς μάλα πολλά /πλάγχθη, ἐπεὶ Τροίης ἱερὸν πτολίεθρον ἔπερσε· / πολλῶν δ᾽ ἀνθρώπων ἴδεν ἄστεα καὶ νόον ἔγνω, / πολλὰ δ᾽ ὅ γ᾽ ἐν πόντῳ πάθεν ἄλγεα ὃν κατὰ θυμόν / […]

[80] ὡς *ed.*

[81] = Hom. *Il.* 1.3.

[82] Refrainvers des *Epitaphius Bionis* ἄρχετε Σικελικαὶ τῶ πένθεος ἄρχετε Μοῖσαι.

eröffnete wie ein lichtbringender Morgenstern, der mit flammenden Strahlen nach der Finsternis aufgeht, [10] und das menschenrettende Licht der Morgenröte hervorrief; und er tötete den italischen Wolf, welcher das Verderben der Schafe war und viele kraftvolle Seelen dem Hades vorwarf, indem er Trug verkündete, der der Wahrheit ähnlich sah, verderbliche Heilmittel anbot und die das Volk rettende Wahrheit im Schatten verbarg. [15] Beginnet mit der Totentrauer, beginnet, Ihr deutschen Musen.

Der charakteristische Refrainvers ἄρχετε Σικελικαὶ τῶ πένθεος ἄρχετε Μοῖσαι wird nur geringfügig durch Τευτονικαί statt Σικελικαί variiert. Nach der Anrede an die trauernden Musen und Nymphen wird die homerische Musenanrede ἄνδρα μοι ἔννεπε Μοῦσα πολύτροπον modifiziert zu pluralischem ἀνέρα μοι κλαίοιτε θεόκριτον. Möglicherweise kennzeichnet θεόκριτον nicht nur die göttliche Erwähltheit Luthers, sondern verweist zugleich auch subtil auf den führenden Vertreter der bukolischen Gattung, die hier mit dem archaischen Epos kontaminiert wird. Auch das *Ilias*-Prooemium fließt ein durch den wörtlichen zitierten Hexameter πολλὰς δ' ἰφθίμους ψυχὰς Ἄϊδι προΐαψε (V. 12), der sich allerdings auf das Wüten des feindlichen Papstes bezieht. Eine engere Symbiose zwischen Bukolischem, Odysseischem und Iliadischem ist kaum denkbar: Rhodoman trauert um Luther als den idealen Hirten, der durch seine mühevollen theologischen Irrfahrten das vernichtende spirituelle Morden des römischen Papstes unterband.

Literaturverzeichnis

Frühneuzeitliche Autoren

Biderman, Jacobus. 1622. *Herodiados libri tres*. Dillingen.

Castilio, Sebastianus. 1545. *Jonas Propheta heroico carmine Latino descriptus*. Basel.

Cocus, Georgius. 1567. *Ionas propheta Graeco heroico carmine redditus*. Leipzig.

Cocus, Georgius. 1568. *Historia Susannae, reddita Graeco heroico carmine*. Leipzig.

Cocus, Georgius. 1569a. *Carmen Graecum heroicum de nativitate Iohannis Baptistae* [...]. Leipzig.

Cocus, Georgius. 1569b. ΕΙΔΥΛΛΙΟΝ *in salutarem Domini ac Salvatoris nostri Iesu Christi* [...] *natalem*. Leipzig.

Cocus, Georgius. 1569c. ΤΑ ΤΟΥ ΔΑΝΙΗΛΟΥ ΤΟΥ ΠΡΟΦΗΤΟΥ ΜΕΤΑΦΡΑΣΘΕΝΤΑ ΕΛΛΗΝΙΚΟΙΣ ΣΤΙΧΟΙΣ ΗΡΩΙΚΟΙΣ [...]. Leipzig.

Crusius, Martinus. 1555. *Poemation de Susanna Helciade*. Straßburg.

Crusius, Martinus. 1567. *Poemata Graeca*. Basel.

Domisius, Matthaeus. 1594. *Historia de s. Ioanne Baptista*. Leipzig.

Eckstorm, Henricus. 1578a. *Historiae evangelicae Divi Matthaei xxvi. et xxvii. capita* [...]. Leipzig.

Eckstorm, Henricus. 1578b. ΕΙΔΥΛΛΙΟΝ de *sanctis angelis* [...]. Wittenberg.

Eckstorm, Henricus. 1578c. ΕΙΔΥΛΛΙΟΝ *de natali Domini* [...]. Wittenberg.

Eckstorm, Henricus. 1582. *Historia beati Laurentii martyris Graeco carmine conscripta*. Leipzig.

Gothus, Matthaeus. 1573a. Περὶ Χριστοῦ καὶ τῶν ἀποστόλων καὶ ἄλλων τινῶν ἁγίων μαθητῶν Χριστοῦ τε καὶ τῶν ἀποστόλων αὐτοῦ βιβλίῳ δύω. *id est: Historiae vitae et doctrinae Iesu Christi, apostolorum et discipulorum eorundem libri duo*. Basel.

Gothus, Matthaeus. 1573b. *Paraphrasis historiae Danielis prophetae* [...]. Leipzig.

Gothus, Matthaeus. 1574a. Κατηχητικὰ σὺν ἀντιθέσει τῶν ἐναντιουμένων, *Pietatis puerilis et doctrinae catecheticae expositio*. Frankfurt.

Gothus, Matthaeus. 1574b. Θεολογίας σύνοψις, *Theologiae Christianae synopsis*. Frankfurt.

Gothus, Matthaeus. 1621. Κατηχητικὰ σὺν ἀντιθέσει τῶν ἐναντιουμένων, *Pietatis puerilis et doctrinae catecheticae expositio; item* Θεολογίας σύνοψις, *Theologiae Christianae synopsis* [...] *Accessit nunc etiam Latina interpretatio*. Leipzig.

Gryphius, Andreas. 1634. *Herodis Furiae et Rachelis lachrymae*. Glogau.

Martinus, Joannes. 1573. ΚΑΤΗΧΗΣΙΣ ΛΟΥΘΗΡΟΥ Η ΜΙΚΡΑ. *Parvus Catechismus Lutheri carmine Graeco heroico redditus* [...] *a Ioanne Martino Soraviensi*. Frankfurt.

Melas, Johannes. 1574. *Vita reverendi D. praeceptoris Philippi Melanthonis* [...]. Wittenberg.

Neander, Michael. 1585. *Physice sive potius syllogae physicae rerum eruditarum* [...] *Michaelis Neandri* [...]. Leipzig.

Neander, Michael. 1588. *Argonautica, Thebaica, Troica, Ilias parva, poematia Graeca auctoris anonymi, sed pereruditi* [...]. Leipzig.

Petavius, Dionysius. 1641. ΔΙΟΝΥΣΙΟΥ ΤΟΥ ΠΕΤΑΒΙΟΥ ΑΥΡΗΛΙΑΝΕΩΣ τοῦ ἐκ τῆς ἑταρείας Ἰησοῦ Ἑλληνικὰ ἔπη παντοδαπά [...]. Paris.

Reusner, Nicolaus. 1593. *Operum pars secunda*. Jena.

Rhodoman, Laurentius. 1579. ΛΟΥΘΗΡΟΣ ἤτοι ΑΠΛΗ ΕΚΘΕΣΙΣ ΤΟΥ ΤΕ ΒΙΟΥ ΚΑΙ ΤΗΣ ΚΑΤΗΧΗΤΙΚΗΣ ΔΙΔΑΧΗΣ ΤΟΥ ΛΟΥΘΗΡΟΥ [...] ὑπὸ ΛΑΥΡΕΝΤΙΟΥ ΤΟΥ ΡΟΔΟΜΑΝΟΥ. *Lutherus sive expositio simplex vitae, doctrinae catecheticae et certaminum Lutheri*. Oberursel.

Rhodoman, Laurentius. 1582. „Bioporikon", in M. Crusius, *Germanograeciae libri sex*, Basel, 1585, 348–355.

Rhodoman, Laurentius, 1588. *Argonautica, Thebaica, Troica, Ilias Parva. Poematia Graeca auctoris anonymi, sed pereruditi* [ediert unter dem Namen Michael Neanders]. Leipzig.

Rhodoman, Laurentius. 1604. Ἰλιὰς Κοίντου Σμυρναίου *seu Quinti Calabri paraleipomena* [...]. Hanau.

Rockenbach, Abraham. 1565. *Propheta Ionas Graeco carmine redditus*. Wittenberg.

Steinbrück, Jacobus. 1607. *Paulus conversus Graeco carmine palliatus*. Erfurt.

Steinbrück, Melchior. 1607. *Paulus conversus*. Leipzig.

Moderne Autoren

Czapla, Ralf Georg & Hintzen, Beate. 2001. *Andreas Gryphius: Lateinische Kleinepik, Epigrammatik und Kasualdichtung*, Berlin.

Gärtner, Thomas. 2017. „Der Trojamythos in den eigenen Dichtungen Lorenz Rhodomans", in Stefan Weise (Hrsg.) *HELLENISTI! – Altgriechisch als Literatursprache im neuzeitlichen Europa*, Stuttgart, 109–123.

Gärtner, Thomas. 2020a. „Zwei Widmungstexte im Schrifttum des Philhellenen Lorenz Rhodoman", in Hartmut Wulfram (Hrsg.) *The Tradition of Dedication – La tradizione della dedica – Die Tradition der Widmung*. [in Kürze erscheinend]

Gärtner, Thomas. 2020b. "Nonnos von Panopolis im protestantischen Philhellenismus des 16. / 17 Jahrhunderts. Zur Nonnos-Rezeption bei Lorenz Rhodoman und Matthaeus Gothus", in Berenice Verhelst (Hrsg.) *Nonnus of Panopolis in Context IV. Poetry at the Crossroads*. Leuven. [in Kürze erscheinend]

Gärtner, Thomas. 2020c. "Zum Umgang Lorenz Rhodomans (1545 – 1606) mit den Posthomerica des Quintus Smyrnaeus", in Silvio Bär (Hrsg.) *Writing Homer Under Rome: Quintus of Smyrna In and Beyond the Second Sophistic*. Cambridge. [in Kürze erscheinend]

Gärtner, Thomas. 2020d. "Die diversen Reflexe des *Epithaphios Bionos* bei Lorenz Rhodoman", in Anne-Elisabeth Beron & Stefan Weise (Hrsg.) *Hyblaea avena – Theokritrezeption in griechischer und lateinischer Literatur der Kaiserzeit und Frühen Neuzeit*, Stuttgart, 115–154. [in Kürze erscheinend]

Ludwig, Walther. 2014. „Der Humanist Laurentius Rhodomanus als griechischer Dichter. Laurentios Rhodoman und seine Autobiographie von 1582", *Neulateinisches Jahrbuch* 16, 137–171 (= *Florilegium Neolatinum*, Hildesheim 2019, 185–219).

Ludwig, Walther. 2016. "Das protestantische Bild der Universalgeschichte im 16./17. Jahrhundert. Epigramme von Melanchthon und Stigel, die Daniel-Paraphrase des Matthaeus Gothus, Friedrich von Nostitz' Lehrdichtung über die vier Monarchien und das Theatrum historicum des Christian Matthiae", *Neulateinisches Jahrbuch* 18, 237–281 (= *Florilegium Neolatinum*, Hildesheim 2019, 243–285).

Weise, Stefan. 2020. "Χελκιάδος μέλλων θυμοῦ περὶ σώφρονος εἰπεῖν – Griechische Paraphrasen der Susanna-Geschichte aus der Renaissance (Martin Crusius und Georg Koch)", in Eberhard Bons, Michaela Geiger, Martin Meiser & Marcus Sigismund (Hrsg.), *Die Septuaginta. Themen - Manuskripte – Wirkungen*, Tübingen.

IV. GREEK POEMS FROM THE "EDGES" OF EUROPE: PRAGUE AND UTRECHT

Γενεὴν Βοίημος. Humanist Greek Poetry in the Bohemian Lands[1]

Marcela Slavíková

While extensive research into Neo-Latin poetry has a well-established tradition in the Czech lands,[2] Humanist Greek poetry, apart from sporadic individual efforts,[3] has mostly been left unexplored. The purpose of this paper is to discuss the general tendencies of Humanist Greek poetry in the Bohemian lands[4] from its origins

---

[1] This study is a result of research funded by the Czech Science Foundation as the project GA ČR 14-37038G "Between Renaissance and Baroque: Philosophy and Knowledge in the Czech Lands within the Wider European Context" and based at the Institute of Philosophy. The author of the present paper has recently contributed a chapter concerning Greek poetry in the Bohemian lands to the collective monograph titled *The Hellenizing Muse*; see Pontani & Weise (forthcoming). The concise introduction to the critical edition included in the chapter on the Bohemian lands comprises some similar information, although in less detail. The Greek quotation in the title (Γενεὴν Βοίημος) was taken from the beginning of Matthaeus Collinus' *epicedium* for Martin Hanno, see *Epicedia scripta honestis et eruditis viris M. Martino Hannoni* [...]. Wittenberg 1551, No. 3 and my chapter in Pontani & Weise (forthcoming)

[2] The first systematic research into Neo-Latin poetry in the Bohemian lands was conducted by A. Truhlář at the beginning of the 20th century; for his two-volume handbook of humanist literature in the Bohemian lands, see Truhlář (1908) and Truhlář & Hrdina (1918). The work was resumed in 1966 by J. Hejnic and J. Martínek, who then published a comprehensive handbook of humanist poetry entitled *Rukověť humanistického básnictví* (*RHB*) in six volumes; see Truhlář, Hrdina, Hejnic & Martínek (1966–2011). As a result of their work on the *RHB*, Hejnic and Martínek soon started to write essays in foreign languages, too, some of which might be mentioned in the present paper.

[3] In 1898, J. Král published an essay on Humanist Greek poetry in Bohemia. Apart from short biographies of the poets, the author presented his own transcriptions of the poems. Since then, however, not many essays on the subject have appeared (see Beránek, 1960, 331–333), although the *RHB* gives an extensive list of Greek poems by Bohemian authors. Besides the above-mentioned *Hellenizing Muse* (see note 1), major discussion and analyses of the Humanist Greek production in the Bohemian lands can be found in the two volumes of the series titled *Companion to Central and East European Humanism*, see Storchová (2020 and forthcoming).

[4] "The Bohemian lands" is a historical-geographical term indicating the area that included the historical regions of Bohemia, Moravia, and Silesia. The term "Bohemian" is sometimes used interchangeably with the term "Czech", although strictly speaking the latter concerns a much more recent concept of Czech nationality which dates back approximately to the early 19th century. Therefore, in this paper, the term "Bohemian" refers to the period of Renaissance Humanism, while the research conducted since the 19th century is classified as Czech.

to its decline. First of all, the political situation in the Bohemian lands from the founding of the University of Prague (1348) to the beginning of the early modern era will be depicted, for the politics of the times had a serious impact on the humanist production, Greek poetry included. Then the development of Greek studies in the early modern Bohemian lands will be described, the major scholars as well as authors will be mentioned and their connections, or the lack thereof, to the University of Prague will be determined. Finally, by specifying the genres and metres of Humanist Greek poetry in the Bohemian lands, its character will be defined and its purposes explained. A comparison will be made with the Latin production in the region and, at the same time, decisive conclusions will be drawn as to the frequency of Greek poems in comparison to the Latin ones. The Appendix presents some Greek poems from the Bohemian lands with translation, notes and references to ancient texts.

From the Founding of the University of Prague to the Battle of White Mountain

When the Emperor Charles IV founded the University of Prague in 1348, in many respects, the Bohemian lands were still behind the latest intellectual developments in Europe. However, the Emperor had a wide education[5] and maintained international contacts with some early Renaissance Humanists, Italian ones in particular.[6] Yet the period of growing prosperity that Charles' reign represented for the Bohemian lands was soon to come to an abrupt end. After Jan Hus, Rector of the University of Prague in 1409–1410 and a great reformer of the Catholic Church, was executed for heresy, the Hussite wars erupted which had a long-term impact on the Bohemian population.[7] The University of Prague, not unlike a great majority of the Bohemian people, was Hussite, for which it suffered serious consequences. In 1419, only the Faculty of Arts remained (it later came

---

[5] Besides a sound knowledge of civil and canon law and considerable diplomatic experience, Charles IV could speak five languages. See his autobiography *Vita Caroli*, chapter 8: *Ex divina autem gracia non solum Boemicum, sed Gallicum, Lombardicum, Teutunicum et Latinum ita loqui, scribere et legere scivimus, ut una lingua istarum sicut altera ad scribendum, legendum, loquendum et intelligendum nobis erat apta.* For Charles IV and his education, see also Thomson (1950, 1–20); for further information on the *Vita Caroli*, see Pichiorri (2003, 335–374).

[6] For the Emperor's correspondence with Francesco Petrarca, see Bayley (1942, 323–341).

[7] For the Hussite wars, see Soukup (2016, 19–44) and Kaminsky (2004).

to be referred to as the *Academia Pragensis*). The university was Utraquist[8] for the whole period of Renaissance Humanism, which had reached the Bohemian lands during the reigns of the Jagiellonian kings at the end of the 15th century. When the university openly supported the unsuccessful uprising of the Protestant Bohemian Estates in 1618–1620, the disastrous results of the rebellion[9] impinged seriously upon Bohemian intellectual circles. The University of Prague was officially united with the Jesuit college in 1622[10] and the Bohemian intellectual elite, for the most part Reformed,[11] was faced with either converting to the Catholic faith or emigrating. Since the majority chose the latter, the disaster entailed a dramatic decrease in literary production and essentially the end of Renaissance Humanism in the Bohemian lands.

The Beginnings of Humanist Greek Poetry in the Bohemian Lands: Bohuslav Hasištejnský of Lobkowicz

In the beginning of the Humanist Greek poetry production in the Bohemian lands, the ability to compose in Greek had to be acquired abroad, because the department of Greek studies was only established in 1537 at the University of Prague and it still took several years to find a professor who would be willing to teach it.[12] As far as is known, only a few Greek poems by a Bohemian author survive from before 1537, all composed by Bohuslav Hasištejnský of Lobkowicz (*ca.* 1461–1510), who is considered one of the first Bohemian humanist scholars. Being a nobleman of substantial wealth, Hasištejnský studied in Bologna and Ferrara in his youth, where he must have learned Greek during his theological studies. Apart from his correspondence and prose works, chiefly on moral

---

[8] The Utraquists, despite being originally a faction of the Hussite movement, were generally moderate in their views of the Catholic Church. For further information on the Utraquist church see Haberkern (2016; esp. 3-4, note 2).

[9] For the Battle of White Mountain (1620) and its repercussions, see Thomas (2010, 251–294).

[10] For further information on the history of the University of Prague, see Čornejová, Svatoš & Svobodný (2001).

[11] The Catholic Jesuit college, founded in 1556, does not seem to have been a major competitor to the University of Prague, certainly not until it was awarded university status in 1616. On the Greek production of the Jesuit college, see also the chapter "Other Centres of Humanist Greek in the Bohemian Lands" below.

[12] On Matthaeus Collinus, see the next chapter "The first Professor of Greek at the University of Prague: Matthaeus Collinus".

philosophy, several books of poems are extant, which were published after his death by Thomas Mitis[13] in a collection of poems entitled *Illustris ac generosi D. Bohuslai Hasisteynii a Lobkowitz, etc., Baronis Bohemici, Poetae Oratorisque clarissimi Farrago poematum in ordinem digestorum ac editorum* (1562; 1570).[14] Nevertheless, of more than five hundred poems preserved under Hasištejnský's name there are only two epigrams composed in Greek, both comprising a single elegiac couplet, and a third one combining Latin and Greek.[15] The poems, dating to between 1501/1502 and 1510, are, as stated above, the earliest extant Greek pieces by a Bohemian author. Hasištejnský was a skilled poet with a deep knowledge of ancient Greek authors,[16] but his efforts remained isolated, as no apparent continuity can be observed in Greek poems that later originated at the University of Prague.

The First Professor of Greek at the University of Prague: Matthaeus Collinus

The first professor of Greek studies at the University of Prague was Matthaeus Collinus (1516–1566). He learned Greek at Wittenberg University,[17] being supported by Jan the Elder Hodějovský, a prominent figure of Bohemian political as well as intellectual circles.[18] With Hodějovský's help, in 1541 Collinus finally

---

[13] Thomas Mitis (1523–1591), a graduate of the University of Prague, was a talented poet himself and an active editor of various humanist authors. He published an essential part of Hasištejnský's work in five books in the 1560s and 1570s. For Mitis, see Storchová (2014, 70–71).

[14] Only the edition of 1570 survives. A critical edition of Hasištejnský's extant poems has been published recently by Teubner, see Vaculínová (2012).

[15] For the poems, see Vaculínová (2012, 204–205).

[16] For further information on Hasištejnský, see Martínek (2010, 462–463); Müller (2008, 1032–1048).

[17] In Wittenberg, Collinus attended Philipp Melanchthon's classes, with whom he stayed in regular contact long after he had left Wittenberg, certainly until 1560, as his extant correspondence with Melanchthon suggests. However, Collinus seems to have studied other subjects under Melanchthon, while Vitus Winshemius and perhaps some others taught him Greek. See Říčan (1963, 237–260).

[18] Jan the Elder Hodějovský of Hodějov (1496–1566), a Bohemian nobleman of considerable political influence and fondness for learned poetry, was an important patron of humanist poetry in Bohemia in the mid-16th century. He had a circle of friends, clients and correspondents around him – there are almost 100 people associated with his name – whom he supported financially during their studies and even after their graduations. He also recommended them for offices or occasionally helped them achieve titles of nobility. In exchange for his generous support, he often dictated themes and consequently genres of the poems that originated in his circle. Because of this

obtained the Greek lectureship at the University of Prague where he gave Greek grammar classes and lectured on Homer's *Iliad*. Having founded his own private Latin school, Collinus could choose whom to recommend to Hodějovský and thus became the most influential member of his group.[19] Concerning Collinus' Greek, it appears that initially he was not very certain of his knowledge, judging by his confession that he had had "but a taste of the Greek language" and that "he was not able to interpret Homer satisfactorily."[20] While these words can be regarded as mere rhetoric, the truth is that there are perhaps only eight poems that he composed in Greek,[21] as opposed to dozens of Latin ones. Usually he also provided his Greek poems, of which the earliest two date to 1542, with literal Latin translations, presumably because he did not expect a very wide readership to understand Greek.[22] The most recent ones, however, dated to 1558 and 1561, are already longer, more refined and without Latin translations, which might suggest not only that his skills had improved,[23] but also that knowledge of Greek in Bohemia had generally increased. However, this increase was slow at first. Only a few students[24] attended Collinus' Greek classes, which he led in

---

practice, the range of genres in use in his circle was more varied than it would probably have been without his intervention. For the genres of Bohemian humanist poetry, see the chapter "Genres and metres" below. For further information on Hodějovský's life, see Storchová (2014, 109–110); for Hodějovský's circle, see *ibid.* (40–43).

[19] See Storchová (2014, 73–76).

[20] See Collinus (1557, 6r): *Argolicae vixdum gustavi grammata linguae*, and *ibid.* (6v): *Adde, quod autorem iubet enarrare Pelasgum, cui tradendo animus par meus esse nequit.* The quotations have been taken from Collinus' introduction to his first lecture on Homer's *Iliad*, which he gave in 1541.

[21] I have come across eight Greek poems by Collinus. For two of them, see Appendix (No. 1) to this paper and my chapter on the Bohemian lands in Pontani & Weise (forthcoming).

[22] Apart from Collinus' efforts, not many Greek poems by a Bohemian author have been preserved from before 1550, although he had colleagues who, being Wittenberg graduates like himself, must have known Greek. There is a piece consisting of five couplets by Collinus' friend and fellow student at Wittenberg university Sebastian Aerichalcus (*ca.* 1546, A1r) and also a short Greek *epithalamion* dated to 1546 which originated in the Hodějovský circle, but in general Greek poems were a rarity before 1550. For the Greek *epithalamion*, see Hodějovský of Hodějov (1561, 6v) (The author was Jan the Elder Hodějovský's nephew).

[23] In his late years, Collinus became associated with Jacobus Palaeologus (1520–1585), an antitrinitarian theologian of Greek origin who had sought refuge in Prague. This association gave Collinus a welcome opportunity to practice his Greek. For Palaeologus, see Balázs (2015, 185–194).

[24] Especially Petrus Codicillus (1533–1589) is worth mentioning, who continued Collinus' efforts as Professor of Greek at the University of Prague, where he gave lectures on Aristotle, Homer's *Iliad*, and Sophocles' *Antigone*. Another of Collinus' students was Thomas Mitis, see above, note 13.

Latin, with only occasional quotations of famous Greek passages from Homer, as his *Specimen studii ac laborum* (1557) attests.[25] Nevertheless, gradually the knowledge of Greek improved, and, after 1575, more Greek poems started to appear, although it is clear that the Greek production was always limited and was considered a proof of an exceptional skill and profound knowledge. While the ability to compose in Latin was indispensable for anyone who aspired to obtain an influential patron or a good position at the university, Greek composition was probably designed to impress.

Genres and Metres

The practical purposes of humanist poetry in the Bohemian lands, both Latin and Greek, strongly defined its genres[26] and its overall character, which was mostly occasional. It was customary to write a poem to congratulate or express condolences to teachers, colleagues and friends, and it is obvious that as an integral part of the school curriculum, the students were trained to write occasional poetry properly and elegantly, since it was a means of communication between learned people.[27] Important university events such as graduations were also regularly celebrated with collections of poems. Finally, the skill of writing good occasional poetry was instrumental for those who had ambitions but lacked noble birth or money, since it could help them gain the support of a powerful patron.[28] Apart from the congratulations to university graduates, the most common genres of Bohemian humanist poetry are *epithalamia*, *epicedia* and *genethliaca*, which could be addressed to various kinds of recipients such as friends and colleagues but also patrons. There were also dedications and other poems accompanying books of prose or learned dissertations that could sometimes qualify as epigrams. Thus the occasional poetry is at least partially linked to the non-occasional (purely artistic) one. The epigram is definitely the most frequently used genre of this 'artistic

---

[25] The *Specimen studii ac laborum* (1557), being a manuscript collection of lectures and notes Collinus had made on Homer's *Iliad* and Vergil's *Aeneid*, is an invaluable source of information on Collinus' university classes. See also Storchová (2012, 41–54) and Slavíková (2020 forthcoming).

[26] For the genres of Latin occasional poetry, see Martínek (2014, 200–212).

[27] See Storchová (2014, 36–40).

[28] See note 18 above on Jan the Elder Hodějovský of Hodějov. However, patronage could also be provided by a magistrate or a whole city council and some of the poems are even addressed to the emperor's family.

poetry'. In addition, some epics and elegies[29] that usually concerned religious matters were composed. In general, however, occasional genres were strongly predominant.

Considering that Greek was always exclusive to a limited number of scholars, it could be assumed that the spectrum of genres would have been far narrower than in Latin poetry. Yet all of the aforesaid genres are represented in the Greek production, even if only once.[30] However, there are some minor genres of the occasional poetry (such as *hodoeporica, strenae*, etc.) that are difficult to find in the Greek production. Also, the Greek poems are usually shorter than the Latin ones and sometimes they are provided with a Latin translation, probably for the benefit of the recipient. Congratulations to university graduates are the most common genre of Greek poetry in the Bohemian lands.

The observation that knowledge of Greek was hardly widespread and that Greek versification might have been considered difficult is corroborated by the distribution of metrical patterns. For as far as the metres of Humanist Greek poetry in the Bohemian lands are concerned, the poems are much less varied than the Latin ones. While the Latin poetry has a broad spectrum of metrical patterns including iambic metres, the Phalaecian, the Alcaic stanza and Anacreontics and Asclepiads, in Greek composition the elegiac couplet alone was used at first. From the 1570s, other metres are attested, such as the Sapphic stanza, but the elegiac couplet remained prevalent throughout the whole Greek production, although some skilled authors of the youngest generation[31] liked to experiment with iambic feet of various lengths. Hexameters were used quite frequently and a very few poems were composed in Anacreontics or in the Phalaecian, but apart from that, no other metrical patterns appear.

---

[29] In the Latin production, there are epic poems and laments (composed in the elegiac couplet). I also include in this group prayers, odes to God and poetic variations on psalms whose genres are sometimes difficult to discern. For an epic description of Christ's heroic descent to the underworld to save human souls, see Hynconius (1576). For an epic history of the Turks, see Campanus (1597). For an elegiac, yet dramatic depiction of plague, see Hynconius (1582). For a rare example of bucolic poetry, see Chorinnus (1589, 1598, 1604, 1605).

[30] Epic, elegy and other non-occasional genres mentioned in note 29 are very rare in Greek production. I have managed to find only a few such poems. For a variation on a psalm composed in the heroic verse, see Polanus (1599), see also my chapter in Pontani & Weise (forthcoming). For a prayer to God and a poetic allegory of the Church, see Saphirides (1594) and Sixtides (1580) respectively. These two poems were published in collections of occasional poetry.

[31] This applies especially to Johannes Campanus and Christophorus Crinesius, see below.

Some Composers in Greek at the University of Prague

The *RHB*,[32] the handbook on poetry composed by Bohemian authors, lists more than two thousand Neo-Latin poets,[33] of whom only some one hundred and twenty could compose in Greek. However, only twenty of these authors can be regarded as major, those who wrote more than one Greek poem or clearly displayed skills and experience in Greek composition, which reached its peak in the Bohemian lands in the first two decades of the 17th century. Although some authors still accompanied their Greek poems with a Latin translation even then, it was also the period when the most accomplished Greek pieces and some excellent Hellenists appeared. One of such scholars was Johannes Campanus (1572–1622), Professor of Classics at the University of Prague and a gifted poet whose Greek poetry surpasses that of his contemporaries both in frequency of composition and in poetic expression. Campanus worked at the University of Prague from 1603 until his death on the 13th of December 1622, giving lectures on Greek and Latin literature and on Bohemian history. He wrote dozens of Greek poems, which clearly show that he had a deep knowledge of classical authors and that he was especially well-read in the Homeric epic, Greek drama, and the Greek Anthology. He liked to experiment with metrical schemes and often inserted lyrical motifs into his occasional poems. Most importantly, there is a lightness to his Greek poems, which proves that he had a perfect command of the Greek language.[34]

Another important scholar was Johannes Prosdokonymus (died in 1625), who even seems to have preferred Greek to Latin. Born in the Central Bohemian town of Čáslav, he studied at the University of Prague and later worked as a notary at the Prague office (*cancellariae Pragensis notarius*). More than a half of his extant poems are in Greek, which is very unusual for Bohemian authors. This indicates a special liking for the language. Some of his Greek pieces are also exceptionally long, comprising around thirty verses or more.[35]

---

[32] *Sc. Rukověť humanistického básnictví* [A Handbook of Humanist Poetry]; see note 2.

[33] The cipher includes minor authors, too, some of whom wrote no more than one poem. The actual number of major authors would therefore be much smaller, probably in a ratio that would be similar to that between the major and minor Greek poets. However, to prove this point conclusively, further research is required, which exceeds the remit of this paper.

[34] For Campanus' graduation poem in Greek, see Appendix (No. 2). For another poem of his, see my chapter in Pontani & Weise (forthcoming).

[35] For one example of Prodokonymus' poems, see the Appendix (No. 3).

Finally, Christophorus Crinesius (1583–1629) should be mentioned, who, besides Latin and Greek, mastered oriental languages and often composed his poems in three or more language versions. Crinesius, having completed his studies at the local Latin school in his hometown of Schlaggenwald, left Bohemia and enrolled at Leipzig, Jena, and Wittenberg Universities in succession. From 1624 until his death, he was a Professor of Theology at the University of Altdorf. As far as is known, he never returned to Bohemia, so it is debatable whether he should be included among the Bohemian poets at all. It seems, however, that he stayed in contact with people in his hometown and that he considered himself Bohemian, if the epithet "Schlaccowaldo-Bohemus" he usually used after his name is any indication. He was a skilful poet and an exceptional linguist, and his Greek was perfectly natural, although he was mainly interested in oriental languages and theology.[36]

Other Centres of Humanist Greek in the Bohemian Lands

The Humanist Greek authors originated chiefly at the University of Prague. In addition, Greek poems were composed at the Jesuit college, which also gave Greek classes.[37] Finally, despite the success of the Greek Classes at the University of Prague, it was still customary to study abroad, the most frequent choices being the Wittenberg and Leipzig Universities. The graduates, unless they were offered a position at the university, usually proceeded to teach at local Latin schools. Some of the extant Greek pieces they composed while working at these schools[38] prove that they remained active, where Greek is concerned.

---

[36] For Crinesius' poems, see Appendix (No. 4) and my chapter in Pontani & Weise (forthcoming).

[37] It appears that the Jesuit college initially pursued similar aims to the University of Prague, judging by the three collections of poems published between 1584 and 1587. The poems were composed as congratulations to graduates, as they would have at the University of Prague. The few Greek poems, some of which are longer than average, display the same tendencies as those by graduates of the University of Prague. Nevertheless, the evidence is too scarce to draw any valid conclusions as to the development of Greek studies at the Prague Jesuit college while the University of Prague was still independent.

[38] There are two Greek poems by Jakub Strabo (*ca.* 1553–1582), both composed in 1575 when he was headmaster of the Latin school in Žatec, see Strabo (1575a, A2r–v; 1575b, A2v–A3r). For a critical edition of the first poem, see my chapter in Pontani & Weise (forthcoming).

It is therefore possible that they occasionally taught Greek there, too, although there is little direct evidence available to support this conclusion.[39]

As indicated above, the situation changed drastically after the University of Prague was closed in 1622. Some scholars who had been forced to emigrate still published abroad for some time and some collections of poetry continued to appear in the Bohemian lands, although their production decreased almost tenfold.[40] Once the Bohemian intellectual circles had been broken up, the demand for occasional poetry gradually vanished. The former Jesuit college, turned into a university, still had Greek classes, but the objectives for learning Greek were defined by the changes in society. Whatever Greek poems were published by the Prague Jesuit Order, they were so different from the humanist production that it is clear that there was no continuity at all.[41]

Conclusion

Due to the early reformation efforts of Jan Hus and the Hussite Wars that erupted after his execution, the Renaissance Humanism was late in coming to the Bohemian lands. In 1537, the department of Greek studies was established at the University of Prague; before that date it was only possible to learn abroad. The practice of studying abroad remained popular even after the department started to thrive. Humanist poetry was mainly occasional, designed to serve a particular purpose, such as communicating with colleagues and friends as well as

---

[39] In 1593, the Latin school in Hradec Králové published a collection of *epicedia* composed for a deceased student by his schoolmates. Two short pieces are in Greek, which might suggest that Greek was taught at the school. Unfortunately, it is not certain that the author of the poems was a student. See *Alumni scholae Hradecensium* (1593, A1v).

[40] For an illustrative diagram showing the exact numbers of books published before and after the Battle of White Mountain, see Martínek & Hejnic (2014, 31). The diagram indicates that while in 1619–1620 one hundred and twenty books were published, the subsequent years were definitely much less productive, with only twenty nine published books in 1621–1622, twenty two books in 1623–1624 and thirty eight books in the five year period from 1625 to 1630.

[41] There is an extensive book by a Jesuit priest Arnold Engel (1620–1690), entitled *Virtutis et honoris aedes in heroibus et poematis XXV Graeco-Latinis ordine litterarum deductis* and published in Prague in 1666. It is a collection of *epyllia*, which was a rare genre in humanist poetry. Its purpose was evidently educational. The same can be said about another Greek poem, which originated in the Jesuit Order: see *Oratoriae Facultatis Auditores Collegii Societatis Jesu* (1669, D2v–D3r). The poem, composed in the Alcaic stanza, is a part of a Jesuit school play. Both books include parallel Latin translations. For Engel, see also my chapter in Pontani & Weise (forthcoming).

procuring patrons. This applies to the Greek poetry too, which, compared to the Latin production, is distinctively less numerous in authors and poems. The most probable reason for this was that knowledge of Greek was not widespread in the Bohemian lands and that it was always regarded as an impressive rather than an indispensable skill. Greek poetry is also less varied in metrical patterns, although it encompasses most of the major occasional genres. The great majority of both Neo-Latin and Humanist Greek poetry in the Bohemian lands was associated with non-Catholic intellectuals and the University of Prague, so when the university was officially closed in 1622, humanist poetry suffered a massive decline.

Bibliography

Manuscripts

Collinus, Matthaeus. 1557. *Specimen studii ac laborum* [...]. Österreichische Nationalbibliothek Wien, Cod. 9910.

Books published before 1800

Aerichalcus, Sebastianus. *ca.* 1546. *Descriptiones affectuum, quae extant in libello de Anima* [...]. Prague.

Alumni scholae Hradecensium. 1593. *Naenia super honestum et eruditum Ioannem Albini Pragenum Hradecijcis Albim et Aquilam pie vita functum juxta et sepultum Annum et Die* [...]. Prague.

Anonymus. 1551 (ed.) *Epicedia scripta honestis et eruditis viris M. Martino Hannoni et Briccio Sithonio, natis in Bohemia, et ex Academia Germanica in celestem Academiam translatis.* Wittenberg.

Anonymus. 1669. *Oratoriae Facultatis Auditores Collegii Societatis Jesu. Melchisedech Panem et Vinum offerens* [...]. Prague.

Campanus, Johannes. 1597. *Turcicorum tyrannorum, qui inde usque ab Otomanno rebus Turcicis praefuerunt, descriptio* [...]. Prague.

Chorinnus, Joannes. 1589. *Idyllion de Maio mense* [...]. Prague.

Chorinnus, Joannes. 1598. *De quarta parte anni et eius occupationibus auctore Ioanne Chorinno.* Prague.

Chorinnus, Joannes. 1604. *De secunda parte anni, aestate. Auctore Joanne Chorinno.* Prague.

Chorinnus, Joannes. 1605. *De auctumno, parte anni quarta. Auctore Ioanne Chorinno.* Prague.

Engel, Arnold. 1666. *Virtutis et honoris aedes in heroibus et poematis XXV Graeco-Latinis ordine litterarum deductis* [...]. Prague.

Hodějovský of Hodějov, Bohuslav. 1561. "*Epithalamion Illustriss. Principis et D. D. Alberti Palatini Rheni*", in *Tertia farrago poematum scriptorum ad Nobilem et Clariss. virum D. Iohannem Seniorem Hoddeiovinum ab Hoddeioua, et in Rzepice, olim Viceiudicem Regni Bohemiae, Poetarum Mecoenatem, quinque libris comprehensa.* Prague, A7r.

Hynconius, Ioachimus. 1576. *Carmen de gloriosa et laetissima resurrectione a mortuis Filii Dei Salvatoris* [...]. Prague.

Hynconius, Ioachimus. 1582. *Glatovia urbs regni Bohemiae ardens ignibus* [...]. *Elegiaco carmine descripta à Ioachimo Hynconio*. Prague.

Polanus, Henricus. 1599. *Psalmus XCI. Graecolatino heroico carmine expressus.* [...]. Görlitz.

Saphirides, Paulus. 1594. "Εὐχή", in *Votum pro felici victoria in expeditionem contra Turcas* [...] *ad* [...] *Rudolphum II., Romanor. imperatorem* [...] *a M. Paulo Saphiride*. Prague.

Sixtides, Jacobus. 1580. "Navicula Christi quae allegoria suavissima [...]", in *Carmina aliquot in honorem virtute et doctrina praestantis viri D. Ioannis Adelphi Hermannomiesteceni* [...] *a Jacobo Sixtide Czaslaviensi et Iohanne Khern Pelzeno*. Prague.

Strabo, Jakub. 1575a. "Πρὸς Χριστὸν δέησις περὶ λύσεως τοῦ βίου", in *Symbolum viri pietate, doctrina, prudentia* [...] *praestantis D. Ioannis Balbini* [...] *ex coetu scholae Zatecensis*. Žatec. A2r–A2v.

Strabo, Jakub. 1575b. *Schola Zatecensis Iacobi Strabonis Glatovini* [...]. Prague.

Modern authors

Balázs, Mihály. 2015. "Antitrinitarianism", in Howard Louthan & Graeme Murdock (eds.) *A Companion to the Reformation in Central Europe*, Leiden–Boston, 171–194.

Bayley, Charles Calvert. 1942. "Petrarch, Charles IV, and the *Renovatio Imperii*", *Speculum* 17:3, 323–341.

Beránek, Karel. 1960. "Kdo to byl Vít Smečánský = Βῖτος Μουγκιφαγεύς?" [Who was Vít Smečánský = Βῖτος Μουγκιφαγεύς?], *Listy filologické/Folia philologica* 83:2, 331–333.

Čornejová, Ivana, Michal Svatoš & Petr Svobodný (eds.) 2001. *A History of Charles University. Volume I (1348–1802)*. Prague.

Haberkern, Phillip, N. 2016. *Patron Saint and Prophet in the Bohemian and German Reformations*. New York.

Kaminsky, Howard. 2004. *A History of the Hussite Revolution*. Eugene.

Král, Josef. 1898. "Řecké básnictví humanistické v Čechách až do konce samostatné university Karlovy" [Humanist Greek Poetry in Bohemia until the Charles University Lost its Autonomy], *Rozpravy filologické věnované Janu Gebauerovi*, 86–105.

Martínek, Jan. 2010. "Lobkowicz und Hassenstein, Bohuslaus von", in Wilhelm Kühlmann (ed.) *Killy Literaturlexikon. Autoren und Werke des deutschsprachigen Kulturräumes*. Vol. 7. Berlin, 462–463.

Martínek, Jan. 2014. "Lateinische Gelegenheitspoesie in den böhmischen Ländern und in Deutschland im 16. und 17. Jahrhundert", in Marta Vaculínová (ed.) *Martiniana, Studie o latinském humanismu v českých zemích*, Prague, 200–212.

Martínek, Jan & Hejnic, Josef. 2014. "Humanistické básnictví – periodizace, charakteristika, žánry" [Humanist Poetry – Periodization, Characteristics, and Genres], in Marta Vaculínová (ed.) *Martiniana, Studie o latinském humanismu v českých zemích*. Prague.

Müller, Jan-Dirk. 2008. "Bohuslav de Hassenstein", in Franz Josef Worstbrock (ed.) *Deutscher Humanismus 1480-1520 Verfasserlexikon*. Vol. 1. Berlin–New York, 1032–1048.

Murray, Augustus Taber (ed. & tr.) 1947. *Homer: The Iliad with and English Translation*. Vol. 2. Cambridge (Mass.).

Pavel, Jakub (ed. & tr.) 1979. *Karel IV., Vlastní životopis = Vita Caroli Quarti*. Prague.

Pichiorri, Flaminia. 2003. "L'autobiographie de Charles IV. Essai d'analyse lexicale", *Histoire & Mesure* 18:3/4, 335–374.

Pontani, Filippomaria & Stefan Weise (eds.) (forthcoming). *The Hellenizing Muse – An Anthology of Poetry in Ancient Greek from the Renaissance to the Present*. Leiden.

Říčan, Rudolf. 1963. "Melanchthon und die böhmischen Länder", in *Philipp Melanchthon: Humanist, Reformator, Praeceptor Germaniae*. Vol. 1. Berlin, 237–260.

Širka, Zdenko Š. 2017. "Czech Lands", in Mark A. Lamport (ed.) *Encyclopedia of Martin Luther and the Reformation*. 2. Lanham, 185–188.

Slavíková, Marcela. 2020 (forthcoming). "Lectures on Homer at non-Catholic Universities in Central Europe as Attested in Matthaeus Collinus's Specimen studii ac laborum (1557) and Joachim Camerarius's Commentarius explicationis primi libri Iliados (1538)", *Acta Universitatis Carolinae – Historia Universitatis Carolinae Pragensis* 60:1.

Slavíková, Marcela. (forthcoming). "The Bohemian Lands", in Filippomaria Pontani & Stefan Weise (eds.) *The Hellenizing Muse – An Anthology of Poetry in Ancient Greek from the Renaissance to the Present*. Leiden.

Soukup, Pavel. 2016. *"Religion and Violence in the Hussite Wars"*, in Wolfgang Palaver, Harriet Rudolph & Dietmar Regensburger (eds.) *The European Wars of Religion. An Interdisciplinary Reassessment of Sources, Interpretations, and Myths*, Farnham–Burlington, 19–44.

Storchová, Lucie. 2012. "Durchschnittliche Gelehrtenpraxis im Humanismus nördlich der Alpen? Der Umgang mit Homers und Vergils Epen in den Prager Universitätsvorlesungen des Matthaeus Collinus im Jahr 1557", *Acta Musei Nationalis Pragae* (Series C – Historia Litterarum 57:3), 41–54.

Storchová, Lucie (ed.) 2014. *Bohemian School Humanism and its Editorial Practices (ca. 1550–1610)*. Turnhout.

Storchová, Lucie (ed.) 2020. *Companion to Central and East European Humanism*. Vol. 2: Czech Lands (Part 1; A–L). Berlin.

Storchová, Lucie (ed.) (forthcoming). *Companion to Central and East European Humanism*. Vol. 2: Czech Lands (Part 2; M–Z). Berlin.

Thomas, Andrew L. 2010. *A House Divided, Wittelsbach Confessional Court Cultures in the Holy Roman Empire, c. 1550–1650*. Leiden–Boston.

Thomson, S. Harrison. 1950. "Learning at the Court of Charles IV", *Speculum* 25:1, 1–20.

Truhlář, Antonín. 1908. *Rukověť k písemnictví humanistickému, zvláště básnickému v Čechách a na Moravě ve století XVI*. Vol. 1 [A Handbook of Humanist Literature, Especially Poetry, in Bohemia and Moravia in the 16th Century]. Prague.

Truhlář, Antonín & Karel Hrdina. 1918. *Rukověť k písemnictví humanistickému, zvláště básnickému v Čechách a na Moravě ve století XVI*. Vol. 2, [A Handbook of Humanist Literature, Especially Poetry, in Bohemia and Moravia in the 16th Century]. Prague.

Truhlář, Antonín, Karel Hrdina, Josef Hejnic & Jan Martínek. 1966–2011. *Rukověť humanistického básnictví v Čechách a na Moravě od konce 15. do začátku 17. století / Enchiridion renatae poesis in Bohemia et Moravia cultae*. Vols. 1–6. [A Handbook of Humanist Poetry in Bohemia and Moravia from the End of the 15th Century until the Beginning of the 17th Century]. Prague.

Vaculínová, Marta (ed.) 2012. *Bohuslaw Lobkowitz von Hassenstein, Opera poetica*. Leipzig.

APPENDIX: Examples of Greek Poems
from the Bohemian Lands

1. Matthaeus Collinus (1516–1566): A Wedding Poem (1551)

Πνεῦμα ἐὼν θεὸς ἀΐδιος καθαρόν τε καὶ ἀγνόν
    τῶν ἀγνῶν δέχεται ἱερὰ μοῦνα φρενῶν,
κ' ἀνθρώπων γένεσιν σεμνοῖς διέταξε νόμοισι,
    τιμήσεις θεὸν οὖν ἐν γάμῳ εὐσεβέως.[42]

Sim.: 1 θεὸς ἀΐδιος] cf. Arist. *Metaph*.1072b29: θεὸν εἶναι ζῷον ἀΐδιον
ἄριστον; cf. etiam Plut. *Quest. conv.* 718A4: ἀγέννητον καὶ ἀΐδιον θεὸν ‖ **3**
διέταξε νόμοισι] cf. Hes. *Theog.* 74: διέταξε νόμους ‖

The God, being an eternal, pure and chaste spirit, only accepts offerings from
pure souls. And he imposed sacred laws of procreation upon people. Therefore,
fear God and be a pious husband.

Comprising only two elegiac couplets, Collinus' *epithalamion* for Sigismundus
Gelous (*De nuptiis clariss. Doctoris Sigismundi Geloi Pannonii.* Prague 1551,
A1v)[43] is one of the shortest poems Collinus ever wrote. Unlike Collinus' earlier
Greek poems, this *epithalamion* is not provided with a Latin translation. The
piece is simple in expression and the humorous vein at the conclusion, where
piety is based on sexual intercourse, is most welcome.

2. Johannes Campanus (1572–1622): A Congratulation to Graduates (1610)

῎Ιλιον αἰπὺ ἕλοντο Ἀθηναίης διὰ βουλὰς
    Ἀργεῖοι ὥσπερ διὸς Ὅμηρος ἔφη.

---

[42] The accents and other diacritical marks have been edited according to the modern editorial
practice.

[43] The complete title of the publication: *De nuptiis clariss. Doctoris Sigismundi Geloi Pannonii et
honestiss. puellae Euphemiae Magnifici ac doctiss. D. Georgii Vernheri etc. filiae, epigrammata aliquot,
a Boiemis poeticae studiosis scripta.* Prague: Ioannes Cantor Coluber, 1551.

Ταῦτα λέγων τί θέλει; εἰ μὴ λόγος ἐγγύθι ναίει,
    ἔνθ' ὄφελος ῥώμην σώματος οὐδὲν ἔχειν.
Ἔσπετε, ἡμετέροιο νέοι νέα ἄστρα λυκείου,   5
    σώματι τὴν νίκην εὕρετε ἠὲ νόῳ;
Χερσὶν Ἄρης βλάπτῃ· Ὑμῖν λόγος ἐστὶ τροπαίου
    αἴτιος, ἡ διδαχὴ τοῦτο ἔτευξε κλέος.
Χαίρετε, νικηταί, τῇ βαρβαρότητος ἁλώσει
    νοῦς δὲ πλέον κρατερῆς, ἔσπετέ, ἐστι χερός.   10

Sim.: 1 Ἴλιον αἰπὺ ἔλοντο Ἀθηναίης διὰ βουλὰς Ἀργεῖοι] cf. Hom. *Il.*
15.70–71: Ἀχαιοὶ Ἴλιον αἰπὺ ἔλοιεν Ἀθηναίης διὰ βουλάς ‖ **3** ἐγγύθι ναίει]
cf. Hom. *Od.* 7.29; cf. etiam Hes. *Op.* 343; 700 ‖ **7** Ἄρης βλάπτῃ] cf. Soph.
El. 697: ὅταν δέ τις θεῶν βλάπτῃ, δύναιτ' ἂν οὐδ' ἂν ἰσχύων φυγεῖν ‖ **8**
ἔτευξε κλέος] cf. Ap. Rhod. *Argon.* 3.992: τεύχων κλέος ‖ **10** νοῦς] cf. Stob.
Anth. 4.3.15.2: Γνώμη δὲ κρεῖσσόν ἐστιν ἢ ῥώμη χερῶν.

The Greeks took steep Ilios through the counsels of Athene,[44] as the divine
Homer said. What does he mean by saying so? He means that if there is no
reason inside, the strength of the body is of no use. [5] Tell us, youngsters, the
new stars of our academy, have you earned the victory with your bodies or your
minds? Let Ares do harm with his hands. You achieved your glory by reason,
your erudition brought you this fame. Rejoice in the conquest of barbarity,
champions, [10] and say that the mind has a much stronger hand.

The poem, included in the volume titled *Amicus amicorum virtute et doctrina
ornatiss. XII viris applausus* [...] (Prague 1610, A3r),[45] is one of numerous
congratulations Campanus wrote annually for new graduates of the University of
Prague. Despite it being a mere occasional poem, Campanus' knowledge of classical
texts and perfect command of Greek grammar and phraseology is evident from
the very first line. His enormous talent, great erudition, and creative inspiration
are even more apparent, if a direct comparison with his other gratulatory poems is
made. Although the occasion remains the same, Campanus always has new ideas.

---

[44] A.T. Murray's translation of the Iliadic passage has been used here. Murray (1947, 111).

[45] The complete title of the publication: *Amicus amicorum virtute et doctrina ornatiss. XII viris
applausus à Nobili et Clariss. viro Dn. Martino Bachacio Naumierzicio á Naumierzicz, in Universitate
Academiae Pragensis Rectore magnifico, Magisterii titulo 27. April. Anni M.DC.X insignitis scriptus.*
Prague: Georgius Hanussius, 1610.

3. Johannes Prosdokonymus (died in 1625): A Congratulation on a Thesis (1616)

Παντρόφον εἰν ἄστροις θνητοὶ θεὸν αἰτιόωνται
    καί τινες ἐξ ἄστρων φασὶ πονηρὸν ἔμεν.
Οὐ μὴν Πληϊάδων φοβερὴ δύσις, οὐδὲ θαλάσσης
    ὀρνύμενον στυφελῷ κῦμα περὶ σκοπέλῳ,
οὐδ' ὅταν ἀστράπτει μέγας οὐρανός, ὡς κακοεργούς   5
    ταρβῶ καὶ θνητῶν ἔργματα φαῦλα φύγω.
Κεῖνοι ἀτασθαλίαις ὄλλονται ἑῆς συνάπαντες,
    οἱ τεύχουσι καλοῖς ἄγκυλα πάντα βροτοῖς.
Οἵδ' ὀλοῇσι μέθης, κώμοις, τέρπουσι τὸ ἦτορ,
    οὗτοι φθείρονται νοῦν τε καὶ ἦτορ ὅλον.   10
Σχέτλια πράσσοντες, νεῖκος, δόλον ἀλλοπόταλλον,
    ἀμφαγαπῶσι στροφήν, ψεύδεα, κλέπτον, ἔριν.
Οἵτινες ἐν τούτοις ἀπολοῦσι κακὸν φρονέοντες,
    παντοίως κεῖνοι κεῖνται ὀλέθρῳ ἑῷ.
Καὶ μὴ ἔχουσι θεόν τινος εἵνεκα αἰτιόωνται,   15
    ἐξ ἄστρων λαμπρῶν μηδὲν ἔνεστι κακόν.
Τέκτονα γὰρ κόσμου θεὸν ἔμμεναι εὐρυμέδοντα,
    ἄστρων εὔτακτοι τοῦτο λέγουσιν ὁδοί.
Ἄστρα μὲν αὐτὰ πέλει θείας σημεῖα προνοίας,
    ἡ δ' ἄστρων μᾶλλον θεσπεσίη διδαχή.   20
Οἶδ' ὅτι Βζελεῖνος παιδευτὸς τοῦτο πιφαύσκει,
    ἰχνεύων κατὰ νοῦν λαμπετόωντα πόλον·
οὐκέτ' ἐπιψαύει γαίης ποσίν, ἀλλὰ παρ' αὐτῷ
    Ζηνὶ διοτρεφέος πίμπλαται ἀμβροσίης.

Crit.: 3 Οὐ μὴν] Ου μὴ ‖ **11** ἀλλοπόταλλον] ἀλλοπρόσαλλον *malim* ‖ **19** προνοίας] προνείας ‖ **22** πόλον] Γόλον ‖

Sim.: 1 Παντρόφον [...] θνητοὶ θεὸν αἰτιόωνται] cf. Hom. *Od.* 1.32: ὢ πόποι, οἷον δή νυ θεοὺς βροτοὶ αἰτιόωνται; cf. Clem. Al. *Paed.* 1.6.39.3.4: παντρόφου καὶ γενεσιουργοῦ θεοῦ ‖ **3–6** Οὐ μὴν Πληϊάδων φοβερὴ δύσις [...] ταρβῶ] cf. AG 11.31.1 ‖ **7** Κεῖνοι ἀτασθαλίαις ὄλλονται ἑῆς] cf. Hom. *Il.* 4. 409: κεῖνοι δὲ σφετέρησιν ἀτασθαλίησιν ὄλοντο; cf. etiam Hom. *Il.* 22.104; Hom. *Od.* 1.7, *et al.* ‖ **9** τέρπουσι τὸ ἦτορ] cf. Hymn. Hom. *In Apol.* 146: ἐπιτέρπεαι ἦτορ; cf. etiam Hom. *Il.* 1.474: ὃ δὲ φρένα τέρπετ'

ἀκούων ‖ **13** κακὸν φρονέοντες] cf. Hom. *Od.* 18.232: κακὰ φρονέοντες
‖ **16** μηδὲν ἔνεστι κακόν] cf. Thgn. 1.1154: μηδὲν ἔχοντι κακόν; cf. *ibid.*
1.1156 ‖ **17** εὐρυμέδοντα] cf. Pind. *Ol.* 8.31: εὐρυμέδων τε Ποσειδάν; cf.
etiam Pind. *Pyth.* 3.4: γόνον εὐρυμέδοντα Κρόνου ‖ **18** εὔτακτοι [...] ὁδοί]
cf. Ar. *Nub.* 964: βαδίζειν ἐν ταῖσιν ὁδοῖς εὐτάκτως ‖ **19** θείας [...] προνοίας
] cf. Eur. *Phoen.* 637: θείαι προνοίαι ‖ **21** τοῦτο πιφαύσκει] cf. AG Appendix
47.30: καὶ ταὐτὰ πιφαύσκει ‖ **22** λαμπετόωντα] cf. Hes. *Theog.* 110: ἄστρά
τε λαμπετόωντα καὶ οὐρανὸς εὐρὺς ὕπερθεν ‖ **23** ἐπιψαύει γαίης ποσὶν
] cf. Hes. *Sc.* 217: οὔτ᾽ ἄρ᾽ ἐπιψαύων σάκεος ποσίν; cf. etiam Diodor. Sic.
Bibliotheca historica 3.28.3.4: τοῖς ποσὶ τῆς γῆς ἐπιψαῦον ‖ **24** διοτρεφέος]
cf. Hom. *Il.* 2.847; 4.338; 5.464, *et al.* ‖

Mortals accuse the all-nurturing God, who lives among stars, and some say
that grief and pain are caused by stars. There is nothing to be afraid of when
the Pleiades set, nor when the sea waves rise and crash against the rocky cliffs.
[5] There is nothing to be afraid of when lightning flickers across the huge sky!
I rather fear evil people and abhor foul deeds of mortals. All those who lay
traps for good men die because of their wicked actions. Some find pleasure and
their end in drinking and banquets [10] where they destroy their mind and
soul. Others flinch from no cruelty, strife, deceit or treachery and love twists,
lies, thefts, and quarrels. But whoever get lost in causing harm, they are bound
to find their own doom. [15] They accuse God even though they have no
reason to do so, because there is no evil caused by shining stars. Orderly routes
of stars prove that it was the wide-ruling God who created the universe. The
stars themselves are signs of divine providence, [20] so the knowledge of stars
is just divine. I know that the learned Včelín proves this, he who has risen to
the shining celestial spheres through his mind. His feet do not touch the earth
anymore, but Zeus himself feeds him with his favourite ambrosia.

The piece is one of the seven accompanying poems included in a volume entitled
*Oratio de praesagiis astrologorum ex horoscopo pro consequendo primo in philosophiae
gradu* [...] (Prague 1616, C3r),[46] which is a bachelor's thesis by the University of

---

[46] The complete title of the publication: *Oratio de praesagiis astrologorum ex horoscopo pro consequendo
primo in philosophiae gradu per Nobilem ac Clarissimum virum D. M. Jacobum Zabonium a Wyssetina,
in celebri et vetusta Academia Pragensi p. t. Facultatis Philosophicae Decanum, Physicae Professorem
publicum, solenniter collato, habita et publice pronunciata in auditorio theologico, Collegii Caroli
IV. PP. alias Magni, 8. Augusti, anno a mystico θεογονίας conjugio: M DC XVI.* Prague: Jacobus
Wczelinus, 1616.

Prague student Jakub Včelín.[47] Prosdokonymus' vocabulary and phraseology show that he was well-read in the Homeric epic, Hesiod, and the Greek Anthology. The extent of the poem is exceptional, and its artistic quality is greater than was usual in Humanist Greek poetry of Bohemian origin. The volume includes another Greek poem, written by none other than Johannes Campanus, who held the position of vice-rector at the time. For this poem by Campanus, see my chapter on the Bohemian lands in Pontani & Weise (forthcoming).

4. Cristophorus Crinesius (1583–1629): An Epigram (1611)

Ἐπίγραμμα

in

Disputationem de morte, sepultura corporum et animarum statu

Οὐκέτι ἀνθρώποις πάντων φοβερώτατόν ἐστι
    πότμος, ἀτὰρ ζωῆς εἴσοδος ἐρχομένης.
Αὐτεξούσιος ἦν ῥα πάλαι βροτολοιγὸς ἄστοργος,
    νῦν δὲ καταθνητὸς καὐτὸς ὄλεθρος ἔφυ.
Πανθνητὸς θάνατος πέλει, ἡμεῖς σώμασι μούνως   5
    καὶ σμικρόν· τάχα γὰρ ζησόμεθ᾽ οὐράνιοι.

Sim. 1–2 φοβερώτατόν ἐστι πότμος] cf. Arist. *Eth. Nic.* 1115a26: φοβερώτατον δ᾽ ὁ θάνατος ‖ **3–4** ἄστοργος [...] ὄλεθρος] cf. AG 7.662.4: ἀστόργου [...] θανάτου

It is not death anymore that people should fear the most, but the moment when their lives begin. Death used to be absolute, destructive and cruel. Now, however, even death itself is perishable. [5] Death can die entirely, while we are only mortal in our bodies and just for an instant. For soon we will live in heaven.

---

[47] At the University of Prague, bachelor theses were produced, although they were not as frequent or important as the master theses. Včelín's thesis has a subheading *pro consequendo primo in philosophia gradu* and he had it six months after his matriculation at the University. His Master's degree followed a year later, in 1617.

The poem is an accompanying piece to a master's thesis on death, written by Jeremias Slovacius, native of Bohemia, at Wittenberg university in 1611.[48] The author titled it as an epigram, but it can easily serve as an epicedium. Like Crinesius' other poems, the epigram does not include many allusions to or quotations from classical authors, which seems to corroborate the idea that Crinesius' main interest did not lie in classical texts, but that he quickly mastered Greek grammar and vocabulary due to his considerable language abilities, while his principal focus was on the oriental languages.

---

[48] See *Partitionum Theologicarum Disputatio XXXIIX. De morte, corporum sepultura et statu animarum. In inclutâ et Florentissimâ Academiâ Wittenbergensi proposita praeside M. Iacobo Martini Professore publico, respondente Jeremia Slovatio Strenicensi Bohemo.* Wittenberg: Clemens Berger, 1611. Crinesius' poem follows immediately after the title page.

Οὐλτραϊεκτείνων μέγα κῦδος πότνια κούρη.
Greek Eulogies in Honour of Anna Maria van Schurman (1607–1678)[1]

PIETA VAN BEEK

A Prologue: van Schurman's Εὐχὴ Κυριακή

On a medieval illustrated parchment (dating from *ca.* 1450) Anna Maria van Schurman, the renowned 17th-century female scholar, wrote the following well-known prayer in gold lettering in Greek (see Ill. 1):

ΕΥΧΗ ΚΥΡΙΑΚΗ // Πάτερ ἡμῶν ὁ ἐν τοῖς οὐρανοῖς· / ἁγιασθήτω τὸ ὄνομά σου· / Ἐλθέτω ἡ βασιλεία σου· / Γενηθήτω τὸ θέλημά σου ὡς ἐν / οὐρανῷ καὶ ἐπὶ γῆς· / Τὸν ἄρτον ἡμῶν τὸν ἐπιούσιον δὸς / ἡμῖν σήμερον· Καὶ ἄφες ἡμῖν τὰ ὀφειλήματα / ἡμῶν, ὡς καὶ ἡμεῖς ἀφιέμην τοῖς / ὀφειλέταις ἡμῶν· / Καὶ μὴ εἰσενέγκης ἡμᾶς εἰς πειρασμόν, / Ἀλλὰ ῥῦσαι ἡμᾶς ἀπὸ τοῦ / πονηροῦ. Ἀμην. // Α.Μ. Σχύρμαν

Ill. 1. Anna Maria van Schurman, the Lord's Prayer. Museum Martena, Franeker.

---

[1] The Greek quote ('The great glory and mighty maiden of Utrecht') is from Gisbertus Voetius' eulogy for Anna Maria van Schurman, see below. With thanks to Antoine Haaker for his learned, and meticulous comments. Unless otherwise stated, all translations from Greek, Latin and Dutch are mine. The diacritics have been standardised and abbreviations have been written out in full.

She made this work of art in a similar way to the one by her hand which contains the beginning of the Koran in Arabic. It is actually a kind of 'destructive devotion', because both texts have been written on a palimpsest with the previous Catholic illustration or text removed.[2] The Lord's Prayer in Greek from the first century AD can be found both in the Gospel of Matthew (6:9–13) and in the Gospel of Luke (11:2–4) and was handed down via several manuscripts through the centuries. But which edition of the Greek New Testament did van Schurman use? Katlijne van der Stighelen dates the work of art to the period 1625–1650,[3] so the source could have been one of the printed versions of the New Testament by, for example, Desiderius Erasmus, Theodore Beza, or Daniel Heinsius.[4] The catalogues of the libraries of van Schurman's professor and neighbour Gisbertus Voetius and of the Labadists – a radical religious group she joined later in life, in 1669 – show that she had various New Testaments in Greek at her disposal, although the specific references, such as dates or names of the editors, are lacking.[5] Van Schurman chose the shorter version of the Lord's Prayer as it appears in Luke and left out the doxology 'For thine is the kingdom, and the power, and the glory, for ever and ever'. She added the title EYXH KYPIAKH, probably from the end of Clenardus' famous Greek grammar, which may also have served as a source for the reproduction of the prayer.[6] Van Schurman's work of calligraphic art in combination with the text of the Lord's Prayer is another surviving piece of evidence confirming her knowledge of and affective point of view regarding Greek.[7]

Van Schurman's Uses of the Greek Language

In the United Provinces of the Netherlands as well as in the rest of Europe, it was expected during the early modern period that members of the intellectual elite would have knowledge of the three languages of learning: Latin, Greek and

---

[2] Van Beek (2018a, 18–19).

[3] Van der Stighelen (1987, 321).

[4] De Jonge (1975, 64–90); Petzer (1990, 88–151); Van Miert (2018, 5–8, 105–106, 135–136).

[5] Voetius (1677a, i.a. I A1 No. 39, A3 No. 137); Van Beek (2016a, 61, 63, 67).

[6] Clenardus (*s.a.*, 251). With thanks to Henk Jan de Jonge for his help with the search after the title of the Lord's Prayer and to Luigi-Alberto Sanchi for discussing the exact transcription of van Schurman's manuscript's title of the Lord's Prayer.

[7] For an overview of van Schurman's Greek letters, see Van Beek (2018b, 414–437); Haaker (2018, 438–447); on her album *De Deo,* see Van Beek (2014).

Hebrew. The main language was Latin, but Greek was used quite extensively as well, as recent research shows.[8] The above mentioned professor, Gisbertus Voetius, a preacher and *rector magnificus* of Utrecht university, explicitly explains the reasons why one should know and use Greek in his *Sermoen* ("Sermon") given at the opening of the university in 1636. He grouped the reasons into three:

> [1] The knowledge of the Greek language is indispensable for Christianity, in particular since the New Testament, being written in Greek, contains many words, idioms and allusions, for a proper understanding of which one should be conversant with the Greek writers and the world of antiquity. Furthermore, it is highly recommended that the Greek translation of the Old Testament should be diligently compared with the corresponding ways of speaking in the New Testament, which are based on and refer to the aforementioned Greek translation and thus receive the light for their interpretation from this. [2] Added to this is the fact that through this language one can keep up correspondence with so many Greek churches in the East, which recently through God's blessing, now more than ever before, have started to blossom, and from which we expect greater outcomes in time to come. [3] Finally, one has to hold this language in high esteem if only for the excellent books and writings by the church fathers and councils as well as on church history; moreover, taking into account all learning concerning divine and human matters which has come to us from the Greeks. In order for us to remain modest, we as Western and African churches have to admit wholeheartedly, together with Saint Augustine, that we have evolved from the Greek churches and that from this has sprouted the Gospel and our faith.[9]

Although some women and girls were taught Latin, only a handful knew Greek.[10] Anna Maria van Schurman, polyglot and the first female university student in Europe (in 1636), was said to have mastered at least fourteen languages, including Greek. She was initially educated by her father, became an autodidact after his death (in 1623) and after 1634 was taught by professor Voetius, who became her *praeceptor* in Greek but especially in Hebrew.[11]

---

[8] In general, see Weise (2017); Päll & Volt (2018).

[9] Voetius (1636, 44–45); an unpublished translation of the original passage in Dutch by Dineke Ehlers.

[10] Stevenson (2014a, 87–111); Stevenson (2014b, 1199–1200).

[11] Van Beek (2010); Schotel (1853, 30–31, 98); De Niet & Goudriaan (2007, 182–185).

Ill. 2. Inscription (Rom. 12:2) by Anna Maria van Schurman in the *album amicorum*
of Johannes Voet. University of Amsterdam Library, Amsterdam.

Van Schurman put Voetius' *Sermoen* into practice, *inter alia* in her studies and
commentaries on the New Testament (as in her commentary on the Letter to the
Romans) as well as in her learned letters on some New Testament topics such
as the baptism for the dead (I Cor. 15:29), the shackling of Satan (Rev. 20:7–
15), the hyssop (John 19:29) and the transsubstantiation (Matt. 26:29). She
corresponded with Meletios Pantogalus, a representative of the Greek Orthodox
Church, and she read and translated Greek classical writers and the *Patres*, as
one can notice throughout her work.[12] Not only could van Schurman write in
Greek, she could perhaps speak it as well. Historian Jean le Laboureur remarked
that when the Queen of Poland, Maria Louise de Gonzaga, visited her in 1645,
van Schurman spoke fluently in Greek with Mr. Corrade, personal physician to
the queen.[13]

The Greek inscriptions in the *alba amicorum* and on her polyglot sheets often
contain her life motto, ὁ ἐμὸς ἔρως ἐσταύρωται ('my love has been crucified'),
taken from the martyr and second-century bishop of Antioch Ignatius' epistle
To the Romans (7.2). Three Bible verses also draw our attention: βλέπετε οὖν
πῶς ἀκριβῶς περιπατεῖτε (Ephes. 5:15) in a family album, οὕτω γὰρ ἠγάπησεν

---

[12] Van Beek (2010, 62–74, 192–194); Van Beek (2014); Van Beek (2018b).

[13] Le Laboureur (1647, 65–76).

ὁ Θεὸς τὸν κόσμον, ὥστε τὸν υἱὸν αὐτοῦ τὸν μονογενῆ ἔδωκεν, ἵνα πᾶς ὁ πιστεύων εἰς αὐτὸν μὴ ἀπόληται, ἀλλ᾽ ἔχῃ ζωὴν αἰώνιον (John 3:16) on a polyglot sheet, and μὴ συσχηματίζεσθε τῷ αἰῶνι τούτῳ (Rom. 12:2) in the *album amicorum* of Johannes Voet, grandson of Gisbertus Voetius (see Ill. 2).[14]

All in all, van Schurman's Greek letters and choosing of mottoes and quotations from the New Testament, inscribed in various *alba amicorum* as well as her commentaries on New Testament texts, indicate that she used Greek mainly within a religious context. However, her letters to Bathsua Makin, Johan van Beverwijck and Claudius Salmasius are mostly secular in nature.[15]

Van Schurman also received five more of less secular *eulogia*, four poems and one letter, written in Greek. They were composed by Wilhelmus Staackmans, Jacobus Crucius, van Beverwijck, Antonius Aemilius and Gisbertus Voetius. After a short introduction on *eulogia* in general and on those in honour of women specifically, I will translate and discuss these five *eulogia* written in Greek, which have gone largely unnotices so far.

Ill. 3. Crispijn van der Passe: Anna Maria van Schurman as a shepherdess. Rijksprentenkabinet, Amsterdam.

[14] Ephes. 5:15: 'See then that ye walk circumspectly'; John 3:16: 'For God so loved the world, that he gave his only begotten Son, that whosoever believeth in him should not perish, but have everlasting life'; Rom. 12:2: 'And be not conformed to this world'. English translation from the King James Version.

[15] Van Beek (2018b, 418–433).

Eulogia for Learned Women

Anna Maria van Schurman was part of the academic world, where praise writing was held in high esteem. From an early age, van Schurman had been used to glowing praise. Although van Schurman was not a royal herself, she – as a learned, polyglot and pious female author – received a lot of celebratory addresses or praise poems (*panegyrica*) separately printed, whereas normally these were only the prerogative of emperors, kings and other persons belonging to high society.[16] They were not only published in her own city of Utrecht, as was the *Epigrammes, consacrez à la vertu de Madamoiselle Anne Marie de Schurman* by Thomas Des Hayons (1649), but also in other cities and abroad. For example, *La Fama Trionfante* by Domenico Gilberto da Cesena was printed in Rome (1642), Jacobus Crucius' *Virgo Batava* in Amsterdam (1639), Augustinus Wisaeus' *De literaris virginibus tribus nostri saeculi* in Breslau (1643) and Rotger zum Bergen's *Epistola et non Epistola et Epigrammata ad nobilissimam clarisissimam doctissimam virginem Annam Mariam a Schürmann immortale sexus sui ornamentum ac vere stuporem* in Königsberg in 1649 and 1650, to mention just a few.[17] Her own life work, *Opuscula Hebraea Graeca Latina et Gallica, prosaica et metrica*, published several times (1648; 1650; 1652; 1749), ends with a section of *Elogia* dedicated to her, but these were all written in Latin, except for two in Dutch by Jacob Cats.

Written according to the rules of rhetoric as set out since antiquity, e.g., by Quintilian, the *eulogia* were adapted to suit specific circumstances. The central position in the *eulogia* is held by the *exemplificatio*, a form of rhetorical adornment where a person is praised and compared to famous mythological or historical figures. The comparisons are based on either resemblance or contrast. Van Schurman was likened to figures from antiquity – for example, as a poet she was compared to Sappho – but often the comparison ends with an *aemulatio*, in which a contrast is highlighted: thus, she was not only blessed with the light of nature, like the heathen Sappho, but also with the more valuable light of Christian truth shining through her.[18]

---

[16] Laureys (2014, 1148–1150).

[17] See also the other three *eulogia* printed in Königsberg: *Epistola altera* and *Epistola tertia cum nonnullis epigrammatibus ad nobilissimam clarisissimam doctissimam virginem Annam Mariam A Schürmann immortale Sexus sui Ornamentum ac Vere stuporem* (Johannis Reusner, both in 1650) and *Vita Bonum fragile est sive supremus honor nobilissimae clarissimae virgini Annae Mariae à Schurman sacro-sancto sexus sui stupor unico summae eruditionis exemplari* (Paschalis Mensenius, 1655). See Van Beek (2010, 134–135); Van Beek (2015, 20–26).

[18] Kajanto (1993, 42–55).

The *eulogia* for learned women show striking similarities. The women are nearly always compared to the same famous, mostly female, persons from mythology and history. They are, for instance, often described as the Tenth Muse, the fourth Grace or the new Sappho; as, for example, in the case of Anne Bradstreet, Sophia Elisabet Brenner, Sor Juana Inés de la Cruz, Birgitte Thott, Christina of Sweden and Elizabeth Weston.[19] No originality was needed in the *eulogia*: they consisted of variations on a well-known theme.[20] *Topoi* in the *eulogia* for learned women are virtues such as chastity, piety and erudition.

Van Schurman received praise for her aristocratic descent, her learning, her modesty, her country, her piety and her virginity, which was either praised or just hinted at. In the history of educated and learned women, it is striking how often the requirement of virginal purity features. Chastity was (and in many countries still is) regarded as the highest, the quintessential virtue of women. Van Schurman had promised her father on his deathbed in 1623 never to marry. He probably wanted her to blossom as a learned virgin.[21] From that time she had adopted her maxim for life, ὁ ἐμὸς ἔρως ἐσταύρωται, a motto that referred to both celibacy and the crucified Jesus. She kept her promise to his father and never married, in this regard too following, so to speak, in the footsteps of Christ. Remarks on her celibacy, whether negative or positive, accompanied her throughout her life. This was something erudite men never had to deal with.[22]

Greek *eulogia* in Honour of Anna Maria van Schurman

Wilhelmus Staackmans

While living in the Frisian town of Franeker during the studies of her brother Johan Godschalk (1623–1625), van Schurman befriended Wilhelmus Staackmans (1597–1640), mayor of Franeker, later delegate in the States General in The Hague

---

[19] Stevenson (2005, 421); Stolpe (1966, 250); Van Beek (2010, 136–141, 190–191). See also note 61 below.

[20] Van Beek (2010, 134–135); Van Beek (2015, 20–26).

[21] Van Beek (2010, 23–26, 124–129).

[22] See, for example, Van Beek (2010, 123–125, 137 (Meletios Pantogalus); 132–134, 137 (Crucius); 140 (Jacob Cats); 35–36, 54 (Caspar Barlaeus); 35, 54, 125, 224 (Constantijn Huygens); Van Beek (2015, 25–26, 38–40, 44–45 (Rotger zum Bergen)).

and patron of youthful practitioners of poetry.[23] He was a poet himself, writing in Dutch, Latin, French, Italian and Greek, but he did not publish his work in a volume of his own. His work has mainly survived in manuscript form, or was printed in books by others, like his long *encomium* in Latin for van Schurman. Some of the letters and poems exchanged between them were published in her *Opscula*.[24]

Staackmans' poem in Greek and Latin (see Ill. 4) forms part of a collection of twenty-six poems and letters addressed to different people, mainly by Staackmans to Anna Maria van Schurman, but also one by him to her brother and another to both her and her brother, and even a poem written by her father, Frederik van Schurman. The poems and letters were handed down as manuscripts through the centuries and ended up in the 19th-century estate of the Utrecht Professor of Medicine, Dr. Matthias van Geuns, later *rector magnificus* of Utrecht university. Mr. Nicolaas Frederik van Nooten from Utrecht took the manuscripts to Jonkheer Cornelis Anthony Rethaan Macaré, who had them published in a Utrecht historical journal *Kronijk van het Historisch Genootschap* in 1855. The manuscript itself has not been preserved, but a corrected proof of the article is stored in the Utrecht Municipal Archives.[25]

In his Latin eulogies to van Schurman, Staackmans enjoyed playing with all sorts of poetic devices, like *anagrammata* on her name: for example, *Humana rimans arcana* ('She who researches mysteries') or *Hanc ianam narra musa* ('Tell us, Muse, about this Iana') – Iana was an ancient Roman goddess, associated with Diana – or an acrostichon on her name, *AMAS* ('you love', or <u>A</u>nna <u>M</u>aria <u>à</u> <u>S</u>churman). For several of the poems and letters the reason for writing them is clear, for example the seven epigrams in Latin Staackmans wrote as an *antidoron*, as a New Year's present, in response to van Schurman's gift to him of a painted miniature depicting seven strawberries (now lost).[26] But the context for this poem in Greek, with a Latin translation added, has to be reconstructed.

---

[23] Schotel (1853, 119).

[24] Van Schurman (1652, 304, 326–333); Blom (2004, 122–132).

[25] Macaré (1855, 202–214); Blom (2004, 122–132).

[26] Staackmans (1855, 210–211).

Θέλω τὸν οὐρανόν τε
ὅλην τε τὴν ἄρουραν
ἀναπιμπλάναι ἀοιδῶν·
μενοῦντα[27] τῆς τὸν αἶνον
κατάρχομαι μελίζων,
τὸ σεβάσμιον μ’ ἀπείργει.

I want heaven as well as the whole
earth to be filled with songs. I
begin singing an everlasting praise
of her. But the reverence for her
withholds me.

Graecum.

Θέλω τὸν ἐρανόν τε
ὅλην τε τὴν ἄρεραν
ἀναπιμπλάναι ἄοιδῶν-
μενῦνγε τῆς τόν αἶνον
κατάρχομαι μελίζων,
τὸσεβάσμιον μ’ἀπείργει.

Ill. 4. Staackmans’ Greek praise poem for Anna
Maria van Schurman as published in *Kronijk van
het Historisch Genootschap* (1855).

In this Greek *encomium*, Staackmans wants to fill heaven and earth with his praise songs to honour her. Everyone is competing in praising her; it is almost like a contest. But his reverence for her is so great that he withholds his praise. That is why the poem is so short. The praise poem is followed by an even shorter Latin epigram of two disticha:

> *Sidera telluremque libet perfundere cantu,*
> *Insolitum genio suppeditante melos:*
> *Sed cuius meritis accingor strenuus, ausus*
> *Maiestate meos impedit ipsa suâ.*[28]

The content of the Greek and Latin poems is very similar and Staackmans stresses this fact by adding the words *Id est* before the Latin poem. This suggests that he wrote the Greek version first and translated it into Latin later, but we do not know this for certain (see discussion below). Also, in his Latin poem Staackmans states that he cannot do justice to van Schurman – because of her overwhelming "majesty". He does not compare her to a specific mythological god or goddess or to a divine person, but her majesty gives her such a divine allure that he cannot fill heaven and earth with his praise songs; thus he has to stop.

---

[27] μενοῦντα correxi [μενοῦνγε. ed.

[28] Translation: 'I would like to fill the sky and the earth with singing, / as my inclination provides me with an unusual tune. // But the person whose merits I am restlessly trying to praise, / hinders my attempts by her majesty herself.'

As mentioned earlier, we do not know the occasion for Staackmans' praise poems written in Greek and Latin. However, it is plausible that he wrote the poems after van Schurman's enrollment at Utrecht university in 1636. According to G.D.J. Schotel, 'the whole Parnassus came into motion. Anyone who could sing, grasped their lyre and the Dutch, French, Italian, Latin, Greek, Hebrew and Arabic poems that flooded Utrecht could have filled a volume'.[29] Since Staackmans died in November 1640, the poems were probably written between 1636 and 1640.

Jacobus Crucius

The Delft rector of the Latin School, Jacobus Crucius (1579–1655), who was also a preacher in the Walloon Church, contacted professor Voetius in 1637 by way of a letter in Latin. He asked him to give the enclosed letters in Latin to van Schurman, the young woman living next door, and to give 'a kiss from me to the dear maiden, but a kiss as the Vestal Virgins would have wanted or such as men like Cato would have given'.[30] Crucius managed to befriend van Schurman and, in 1639, he published the panegyric *Virgo Batava* in her honour. She seems to have had no problems with that love poem overflowing with innuendos, because she published parts of it in her own *Opuscula*. One cannot help but wonder if her favourable stance toward Crucius' poem came about because it was he who comforted her after the death of her dear mother in 1637. The correspondence in Latin, French, Greek and Hebrew between van Schurman and Crucius lasted from 1637 until his death in 1655.

Crucius' Latin letters and poems, as published in his books, were also used at his Latin School, which is probably why he did not add translations. To create *varietas*, he used a lot of lesser known words in Greek. His *eulogia* for van Schurman in Latin, French and Hebrew are included in his works published in the Low Countries and in Germany, in the above-mentioned *Virgo Batava* and *Mercurius Batavus*.[31] However, his two-page Greek letter to her, signed "from his study room in Delft", and which was published in *Mercurius Batavus*, is also a kind of prose eulogy to van Schurman (see Ill. 5). For reasons of space, I will summarise only the eulogising parts of this letter here.[32]

---

[29] Schotel (1853, 92); Van Beek (2010, 54); Van Beek (2015, *passim*).

[30] Crucius (1661, 512).

[31] *Mercurius Batavus* was printed several times (1642, 1643, 1647, 1650, 1660, 1661, 1662 and 1669).

[32] The chapter on Crucius' *eulogia* to van Schurman is based on my paper ('Crucius' Virgo Batava

Ill. 5. Beginning of a letter in Greek to Anna Maria van Schurman by Jacobus Crucius in his *Mercurius Batavus sive Epistolarum opus* (1662).

The common well-wishing formula (χαίρειν) has been put on the heading. Crucius begins his letter by explaining that he has not forgotten to mention van Schurman to all his correspondents who happened not to know her. Van Schurman sets her heart upon virtue and true faith, which are the noblest and most enduring possessions (cf. Isocr. *Ad Dem.* 5); the clear proof of this is her learnedness. He congratulates her for her mind, she is first among virgins, but neither does she neglect virtue: she does not live a frivolous life but exercises her body and soul willingly; she is well versed in the liberal arts because only wisdom is immortal (cf. Isocr. *Ad Dem.* 19). Crucius asks a rhetorical question: why does he need to enumerate all her praisworthy qualities? Because her offspring (βλάστημα, that is, her publications), for which she has gathered material as diligently as bees, speaks for itself. In all, he congratulates her for the utilisation of her education, because life is sweetest when one has sense (cfr. Soph. *Aj.* 554). Crucius ends the letter by requesting her to answer him as soon as possible, addressing her as 'goddess' (θεία κεφαλή), and asking her to carry on loving him: he is in awe of her education, her faith and her kindness.

As he did in his eulogising poems and letters in Latin, French, and Hebrew, here Crucius praises van Schurman's virginity and chastity, her faith and her scholarship and her accomplishments in publications. However, he mentions no

---

and ancient Women in the Renaissance') delivered on 24 January 2001 in the Congress of the Classical Assosiation of South Africa in Pretoria. I thank Tua Korhonen for the references to Isocrates and Sophocles in Crucius' letter. For further detail of this letter, see Van Beek (2010, 132–139). A discussion of the exchange of letters and poems in French, Latin, Greek and Hebrew between Crucius and van Schurman merits a separate article.

other famous names for comparison, although they appear to be compulsory in his other *eulogia* as part of an exemplification. Could this be because, in his view, she is 'number one' already, and that is why she does not need to be compared to other people, gods, or goddesses?

Johan van Beverwijck

Johan van Beverwijck (1594–1647), a scholarly physician from Dordrecht, corresponded with van Schurman in Latin, Greek, Dutch and Arabic and became a good friend of hers. He was involved in publishing some of her work, such as *De Vitae Termino, Vraaghbrief* ('The question letter', concerning the healing of the blind-born man) and her *Opuscula*. Van Beverwijck took his daughters to meet van Schurman during one of his visits to Utrecht. In 1639, he published his *Van de Wtnementheyt des Vrouwelijcken Geslachts* ("On the excellence of the female sex"). The entire second part, in which van Beverwijck discusses women's learning and wisdom, is dedicated to van Schurman. She was his greatest source of inspiration for this book. Not only did he include her Latin and French poems written in honour of Utrecht university, her *Apologia* (defence of her celibacy) and several echo verses[33] such as her poem on her life motto *Amor meus crucifixus est*, but also some *eulogia* written by others, e.g. the Latin, French and Italian poems by Staackmans and himself. Van Beverwijck incorporated a lot of Greek words and phrases (often not translated) in his Latin letters and in his books, but he also wrote letters in Greek. The letter van Schurman wrote to him in Greek was included in all four editions of her *Opuscula*.[34]

Ἑσπέριαι, Ῥωμαῖαι, Ἀχαΐδες, ὑκεῖε κίχλαι,
Οἴδαμεν ἢ φῦναι μείζονα τῆς Βαλαβῆς.

Hesperiæ, Graiæ, Romanæ, cedite, Gallæ,
Nescio quid majus nascitur hac Batava.

V Rancrijck, Spaengjen, Griecken, Roomen,
Hebben daer toe staeghgetracht,
Om vet wonders te vertoonen,
Van het vrouwelick geslacht:
Maer sy moeten Vtrecht wijcken.
Die de kroon heeft op haer hooft,
En de vlag voor Schurman strijcken,
Die haer van die eer berooft.
Wonder nergens oyt vernoomen,
Nergens soo gesegent brevn,
Niemants geeft soo hoogh gekomen
Van Frans, Spaengjaert, Grieck, Romtyn.

J. VAN BEVERWIICK.

Ill. 6. Van Beverwijck: *Van de Wtnementheyt des Vrouwelijcken Geslachts* (1649, 64). The author's eulogy for van Schurman in Greek, Latin and Dutch.

---

[33] Echo verse is a verse in which the final words or syllable of a line are repeated, sometimes as a response, for example in van Schurman's poem *In symbolum suum: clamat – amat, moriens – oriens*. Van Schurman 1685, [a1v].

[34] Van Beek (2018b, 426–430).

Although Latin was obviously the most natural language in which to write poetry for an educated Dutch person of the 17th century, van Beverwijck – like Staackmans above – puts the Greek version first in his poetic eulogy to van Schurman. It consists of three poems, i.e., a distichon in Greek, another in Latin and a longer, twelve-line poem in Dutch (see Ill. 6). The Greek distichon varies little from the Latin; differences are found mainly in word order and grammar (most notably the plural 'we' versus singular 'I'). He gives the ancient names for people living in Spain (the Hesperids) and in France (the Celts). The word Βαταβή (or -ά?) can either refer to her, as a Batavian maiden, or to the name of her country Batavia, as the Republic of the Seven United Provinces was often called Batavia by the scholars who constructed this historical myth.[35]

Ἑσπέριαι, Ῥωμαῖαι, Ἀχαΐδες, εἴκετε Κέλται,
    Οἴδαμεν οὐ φῦναι μείζονα τῆς Βαταβῆς.

Give way Hesperids, Romans, Greeks and Celts,
    We do not know anyone greater than the Batavian maiden.

Hesperiae, Graiae, Romanae, cedite, Gallae,
    Nescio quid majus nascitur hac Batava.[36]

In the Latin version, van Beverwijck is clearly following Propertius' famous distich (2.34.65–66) by which Propertius predicted that Virgil's *Aeneid* would be an exceptional poem: *Cedite romani scriptores, cedite Graii / Nescio quid maius nascitur Iliade.*[37] By this imitation, van Beverwijck states that van Schurman will be an exceptional person. Van Beverwijck expands these lines into a longer poem in Dutch of 12 lines, translated as follows in English:

France, Spain, the Greeks and Romans, all continuously tried to show something astounding regarding the female sex. But they have to yield to Utrecht [5] who is wearing the crown on its head, and they have to surrender to Schurman who strips them of that honour. A miracle never heard of elsewhere; nowhere

---

[35] De Glas (2017, *passim*).

[36] Translation: 'Give way, Hesperids (Spaniards), Greeks, Romans, Frenchwomen, I do not know anyone born greater than this Batavian woman.'

[37] Translation: 'Make way, you Roman writers, make way, Greeks! I don't know of anything greater than that the *Iliad* is born.'

such a blessed mind. [10] Nobody's spirit has risen so high, be it Frenchman, Spaniard, Greek or Roman.[38]

Only in the Dutch version does van Beverwijck mention van Schurman by name, in capital letters. Every country has to surrender to her, because nowhere on earth can a woman be found with such a blessed mind or intellect. No spirit or mind of a person has risen so highly in France, Spain, Greece or Italy. The Netherlands and Utrecht are number one, because van Schurman lives there and she gets the better of every country in Europe. Van Beverwijck mentions those countries twice to stress the importance of the Utrecht miracle van Schurman, rising above them. Probably because he published the poems in Greek and Latin in his book written in vernacular on the excellence of women (*Van de Wtnementheyt* ...) he added this extended poem in Dutch.

This entity of three poems have been reprinted several times, not only in van Beverwijck's own books (1639, 1643), but also in a number of other publications on van Schurman through the ages, although the Greek and Latin versions were often left out in later renditions. Van Schurman responded to van Beverwijck's book in general, not to the Greek, Latin and Dutch poems specifically. She told him that she loved his book but did not want a dedication to her put in the reprint as he had requested. She suggested a dedication to the young princess Augusta Maria of Orange instead – and so it happened.[39]

Antonius Aemilius (1589–1660)

Antonius Aemilius had befriended the van Schurman family after he came to live in Utrecht in 1619. He was Rector of the Utrecht Latin School (the Hieronymus Gymnasium), refused a professorship in Greek at Leiden university, but later became professor at Utrecht university teaching eloquence and history. Twice he

---

[38] Unpublished translation by Dineke Ehlers. The original: VRancrijck, Spaengjen, Griecken, Roomen, / Hebben daer toe staegh getracht, / Om yet wonders te vertoonen, / Van het vrouwelick geslacht: / Maer sy moeten Vtrecht wijcken, / Die de kroon heeft op haer hooft, / En de vlagh voor SCHURMAN strijcken, / Die haer van die eer berooft. / Wonder nergens oyt vernomen, / Nergens soo gesegent breyn, / Niemants geest soo hoogh gekomen / Van Frans, Spaengjaert, Grieck, Romeyn.

[39] Van Beverwijck (1639, 64); van Beverwijck (1643, D7v). Reprints of the Dutch poem in van Schurman (1728, 49), where it was wrongly assumed to be 'Noit voorheen in 't Nederduytsch gedrukt' ('never before printed in Dutch'); Schotel (1853, 104–105); Van der Aa (1864, 126–127); Van Elk (2017, 208); van Schurman (1652, 184–186).

was appointed *rector magnificus*, in 1644 and again in 1659. Aemilius was an elder in the Dutch Reformed Church as well[40] and wrote several Latin *eulogia* to van Schurman. One was written beneath a portrait the artist Steven van Lamsweerde made of her in 1657, the other was published in the third edition of her *Opuscula* (Utrecht 1652), reprinted in the 1749 edition and even appeared with translations in many 19th-century publications in Germany, Poland and Russia:

> *Non nisi dimidia spectatur imagine virgo*
> *Maxima, quod totam nulla tabella capit.*[41]

According to Pierre Bayle, the seventeenth-century writer of popular *Dictionnaire historique et critique*, Aemilius' poem is an imitation of an epigram on a portrait of Erasmus by Theodore Beza.[42] Aemilius thus praises van Schurman as the female counterpart of Erasmus.

Aemilius' Greek *eulogium* was printed in combination with the Latin version in his *Orationes* (see Ill. 7).[43] He introduces the Greek poem with some Latin lines:

> *AD Nobiliss. omnique literarum genere incomparabilem Virginem, ANNAM MARIAM à SCHURMAN, Musam Decimam: Quod gloriosum nomen longè minore jure, Antipater Sidonius olim tribuit Lesbiae poëtriae.*

> To the noblest virgin, incomparable in any genre of literature, Anna Maria van Schurman, the Tenth Muse: A glorious title, that, with much less justice, Antipater of Sidon once bestowed on the female poet of Lesbos.

---

[40] Van Lieburg (1989, 152).

[41] 'You view but half the Maid; to take in all, the Largest tablet would be far too small' (translator unknown); see Bayle (1735, 810).

[42] Bayle (1735, 810, *s.v.* 'Erasmus'); Libelt (1852, 18); Schotel (1853, aanteekeningen, 78, Nos. XXIII, XXIV); Libelt (1853, 145); Weber (1868, 252); Anonymus (1875, 127); Lange & Bäumer (1939, 50); Van Beek (1996, 90); Van Beek (2010, 213); Larsen (2016, 183).

[43] Aemilius (1651, 387–388). Aemilius published the Greek and Latin *encomia* without any portraits of van Schurman. See above about his Latin poem underneath van Schurman's portrait in her 1652 edition of the *Opuscula*.

Thus, the Latin lines function as a long heading for the Greek poem:

Εὐφυΐην ὅτε σὴν ἐπιθαμβῶ, πότνια Νύμφη,
    Παντοδαπήν τε σέβω πουλυμαθημοσύνην·
Ἐν δοιῇ πέλομαι, τί γένος σ᾽ ἐρέω ἔμεν, ἠὲ
    Ἔρνος ἀφ᾽ ἡμιθέων, ἠὲ θεῶν μακάρων.
Φασὶ μὲν ἐξ ἀΐδεω μελίφωνον Σαπφὼ ἀνελθεῖν,   5
    Ἀλλά μοι ἡ δεκάτη Πιερὶς αἰὲν ἔσῃ.

When I marvel at your talents, honourable
Nymph, and when I revere your erudition
of all sorts I am in doubt. Of what descent
shall I say you are: an offspring of the
semi-gods or of the blessed gods? [5] They
say that indeed the sweet-voiced Sappho
has returned from the Hades. But for me
you will always be the Tenth Muse.

Ill. 7. Aemilius' Greek eulogy in his
Orationes (1651, R1v).

The poem in Latin runs as follows:

CUm stupidus veneror genii solertis acumen,
    Omnigenasque artes, Nympha verenda, tuas:
Subdubito, quali dicam te sanguine cretam,
    Semideûm ne vocem, coelicolûmne genus.
Sunt mellita quibus Sappho rediviva videtur: 5
    Sed decima Aonidum Diva eris usque mihi.[44]

According to Aemilius, van Schurman is erudite, artistic and of (semi)divine descent. Some say she is Sappho, the great female poet of antiquity, who returned from Hades, or the underworld. He, on the other hand, thinks that she is even better than Sappho, who was named the Tenth Muse by Antipater of Sidon – but in Amelius' view with less justification than van Schurman. The question asked by the poet whether she is a goddess reminds us vaguely of how Odysseus asks Nausicaa the same question at their first encounter in the *Odyssey* (6.159) where

---

[44] Translation: 'When I with stupefaction venerate the acumen of your intelligent mind and your skills of all kinds, honourable Nymph, I hesitate: from what blood shall I say that you descend? Should I call you the offspring of semi-gods or of the gods? [5] To some the honey-sweet Sappho seems to have come back to life. But for me you will always be a goddess, the Tenth of the Muses.'

he asks her whether she is a goddess.[45] The Greek poem was never reprinted, but the Latin version of the poem was included in Caspar Burmannus' *Traiectum eruditum* (1737 and 1750).[46]

Gisbertus Voetius (1589–1676)

After his appointment as Professor of Theology and Semitic Languages at Utrecht university, Voetius became van Schurman's neighbour, *praeceptor*, teacher and minister. He was quite influential in her life and, although a strict Calvinist, he was the driving force behind her admittance to the university in 1636. She wrote a Dutch, a Latin and a French poem for the opening festivities of the university; the Dutch one responded specifically to Voetius' official *Sermoen* at the inauguration of the university. Van Schurman followed his classes, private as well as public ones (disputation classes and main classes) but also classes of others such as Johannes Hoornbeeck. Although they met each other quite often as she had befriended his wife as well as his children and he was acquainted with her family, we do not have much material evidence for their close relationship, except for his signature as witness on her wills and the references they made to each other in their letters, books and poems. The lack of evidence concerning their close relationship probably has to do with that they were neighbours: she lived on the street of Achter de Dom ('Behind the Cathedral', that is, the famous St. Martin's Cathedral, Utrecht Dom Church), just around the corner from Voetius' place. Van Schurman drew his portrait several times and wrote poems in honour of him. Her Hebrew letter to him, published in 1648 in her *Opuscula* and reprinted several times, is an extraordinary text, a *cento* consisting mainly of Bible verses. It proves that van Schurman was a student who loved and stood in awe of her teacher.[47]

We happen to know something about the context surrounding Voetius' Greek poem to van Schurman. In 1653, van Schurman had to leave Utrecht for her city of birth, Cologne. After the conclusion of the Thirty Years' War, her two aged aunts, Agnes and Sibyll von Harff, wanted to claim back their house and belongings in their hometown Cologne. Van Schurman and her brother Johan

---

[45] Another example is the exchange between Aphrodite and Anchises in the *Homeric Hymn to Aphrodite* (5.92–142), where Aphrodite assures the awed Anchises that she is no goddess at all, but a mortal maid.

[46] Burmannus (1738, 352), Burmannus (1750, 352).

[47] Duker (1989, 198); Van Beek (1992, 54–63); Van Beek (2003, 45–67); Van Beek (2010, *passim*); De Niet (2016, 467–479).

Godschalk assisted them with the court case, which took more than a year. To suppress her feelings of homesickness, van Schurman wrote a poem in Dutch entitled "Notes on the differences between Utrecht and Cologne" for the Utrecht Dom Church.[48] She missed Utrecht, the church, her friends, family and Voetius, as is expressed in the poem (ll. 1–4):[49]

> O Utrecht, beloved City, how could I ever forget you / although I must waste my days far away from you / ten times in a day I praise your city / which, in my judgement, surpasses everything else.[50]

Later in the poem, she complains about living in a Catholic city like Cologne, where it is dangerous to visit a Protestant church (ll. 33–34):

> Although there are many churches, they are all against us. / We have to cross the Rhine through wind, through snow, through rain.[51]

The poem contains much praise for the Utrecht Reformed theologians, including Voetius.

In 1655, Voetius published the second part of his "Selected Disputations" and dedicated it to van Schurman and her brother who had just returned to Utrecht from Cologne. In the dedication, dated 22 September 1654, he praises the study room in the van Schurmans' house on Achter de Dom:

> […] your family sanctuary of piety and school as well as treasury of all kinds of learning, really a private university within our famous university and an erected Republic of Letters within the Republic, but without fraud or treason […][52]

At the end of the foreword, Voetius included a Greek poem with an 'interpretation in Latin', sent earlier to Anna Maria van Schurman as a special token, as a consolation,

---

[48] *Aenmerkinghe over 't onderschijt tussen Uitrecht en Ceulen*; see Van Beek (1996, 69–85).

[49] Van Beek (1992, 66–78, 140–141); Van Beek (1996, 69–85).

[50] 'O Utreght, lieve Stadt hoe soud'ick U vergeeten / Almosten ver van U mijn dagen sijn versleten / Tien mael op eenen dagh verhef ik uwen stadt / Die soo mijn oordeel lyt et al te boven gaet.'

[51] 'Al sijn der kercken veel, sij sijn ons alle tegen / Wij moeten over rijn door wint doer sneu door regen.'

[52] Voetius (1655, ***2v).

even as a kind of Platonic love poem while she was in Cologne, missing the city of Utrecht and him so badly (see Ill. 8):[53]

Οὐλτραιεκτείνων μέγα κῦδος, πότνια κούρη,
    Μειλιχίων μουσῶν ἐννεάς, οὐ δεκάτη,
Οὐρανίου λευκῆς ἐξ αἴγλης ἤλασεν ἐχθρὸν
    Εἰς σκότος, οὗπερ ἐὸν ΔΥΝΣ ΣΚΟΤΟΣ ἔσχε τάφον.
Νῦν δ᾽ ἔνθ᾽ ἐν σκότεϊ[54] τηλαυγέα φάεα ῥείει,   5
    Φέρβουσ᾽ ἐν θείαις φῶς φρεσὶν ἐνδελεχές.
Εἶτα νέον παλίνορσος ἐοῖς, ὡς φοίνιος ἠώς,
    Οἴσει φῶς, ἅμα καὶ στήθεσιν ἡμετέροις.

Great glory of Utrecht, mighty young woman, the nonary of the gracious Muses, not the Tenth Muse. Out of the white brightness of the heaven she went down to the hated darkness, where DUNS SCOTUS had his grave. [5] Now there in the darkness she pours out far shining lights, feeding the light in her godlike heart continuously. Later, when back, as the red dawn, she will bring new light to her own and at the same time into our hearts.

Ill. 8. Page 3 from Voetius' book *Selectarum disputationum theologicarum, Pars Secunda* (1655) containing a Greek and Latin poem in honour of van Schurman.

---

[53] The manuscript of the poem is lost. The poems were published in 1655 in Voetius' *Selectarum disputationum theologicarum, Pars Secunda* and only the Latin poem was reprinted in Duker (1913, 198) and Duker (1989, 198); both poems were published in Van Beek (1987, 95–97) and in De Niet & Goudriaan (2007, 182–185).

[54] Line 5: σκότεϊ is metrically odd, unless the iota (with the strange trema) is lengthened, in which case the accent would be on the epsilon. I owe this notion to Jamie Vesterinen.

Interpretatio Latina.
MAgnum Ultrajecti decus, & veneranda virago,
  Blandarum Musωn enneas, haut decima,
Candido ad exosas coeli ex splendore tenebras
  Ivit, ubi jacuit DUNS SCOTUS in tumulo.
Nunc ibi per tenebras splendentia lumina spargit,   5
  Assiduum dio in pectore lumen alens.
Inde redux lucem, rosea ut matuta, recentem
  Adferet hic nostris, pectoribusque suis.[55]

Voetius refers to Duns Scotus (1266–1308), the famous Scottish philosopher, whose name in Greek means 'darkness' and which name is mentioned in the poem. Scotus was laid to rest in a sarcophagus in the Minoritenkirche in Cologne.[56] It is not known whether van Schurman visited his grave while in Cologne.

Voetius compares her to the light of dawn that will shine down on Utrecht, into his heart and her heart, but the light could also be a reference to the sun, as in the university's motto, *Sol Iustitiae, illustra nos* ('Sun of Justice, illuminate us'). According to Voetius, van Schurman is μουσῶν ἐννεάς, all the Nine attractive Muses together. That is an outstanding compliment for van Schurman. It was no secret that Voetius felt a deep connection to van Schurman and that they adored each other.[57] In her Hebrew letter to Voetius, she compares herself to Ruth, and, implicitly, Voetius to Boaz. Ruth and Boaz became a couple, but van Schurman and Voetius not, although some erotic sparks might have been in the air.[58] Voetius was not blind to her beauty and admired her talents and piety, but they remained faithful to their respective promises. Later in life, when she was

---

[55] 'A Latin interpretation. Great ornament of Utrecht and honourable, fearless, warriorlike woman, the Nine sweet Muses, not the Tenth Muse, who went from the white shine of the sky to the hated darkness, where DUNS SCOTUS lay down in his grave. [5] Now she is pouring out shining lights through the darkness, while she is cherishing a perpetual light in her godly heart. When returned like the rosy-fingered dawn, she will bring new light here, into our and her own heart.'

[56] In the margin, Voetius added the words *Ferunt Joh. Duns Scotum ad cujus nomen alluditur, Coloniae sepultum esse.* ('It is said that Joh. Duns Scotus, to which name is referred, has been buried in Cologne.')

[57] Although the differences are negligible, I prefer to give a separate translation for the Greek and Latin poems, unlike De Niet & Goudriaan (2007), who made one (but beautiful) poem to serve as the Dutch translation. Furthermore, they translate μουσῶν ἐννεάς as 'the Ninth Muse', but ἐννεάς refers to "nonary", the Nine Muses together. See De Niet & Goudriaan (2007, 182–185).

[58] Van Beek (2010, 75–76).

already sixty-one years of age, she chose Jean de Labadie as her spiritual leader instead of Voetius. He complained at home that de Labadie had lured her away, and at the university, he organised disputations against the Labadists without delay. De Labadie defended her choice and wrote to Voetius that Voetius 'had, so to speak, worshipped Miss van Schurman when she was young and idolised her, and now that she is of advanced years, he tramples on her and maligns her'.[59]

Voetius' poems are occasional poems (in *disticha*), using the contrast of light and darkness between the two cities Utrecht (the city of light) and Cologne (the city of darkness). They can be seen as replies to her above mentioned, earlier poem in Dutch on the differences between Utrecht and Cologne, based on Psalm 137, which refers to the Babylonian exile. Her poem has the rhetorical structure of a *comparatio* fleshed out with the general Christian theme of Augustine's two-city doctrine (*De Civitate Dei*). Utrecht is Jerusalem, the City of God; Cologne is Babylon, the city of the devil. As a young girl van Schurman had to flee Cologne, the city of her birth, due to religious persecution, and even in 1654 the Protestant churches had to remain underground.[60]

In the Latin version of his poem, Voetius uses the Greek words *Musωn enneas* again, to emphasise that she represents all nine charming Muses together, not only the Tenth Muse (as Aemilius had written). The Tenth Muse was an *epitheton ornans* that originally referred to Sappho and was often applied to early modern women writers like Anne Bradstreet, Juana Inés de la Cruz, Anna Roemers Visscher, van Schurman and Sophia Elisabet Brenner.[61] Van Schurman brings light from Utrecht to the other city (Cologne); she herself is like the goddess of dawn who, after her return from Cologne, will bring fresh light to Utrecht, to his heart and her heart. Voetius refers to her in Latin as a *virago*, an epithet that was also used for Pallas Athena, the goddess of wisdom.

---

[59] Van Beek (2010, 224); Koelman (1770, 34): '[…] hy juffrouw Schurmans, toen ze jong was, om zoo te spreeken, aangebeden en tot zyne Afgodinne had gemaakt en dat hy ze onder de voet trapt en leelyk uitmaakt, nu zy oud van jaaren […] is'.

[60] Van Beek (1996, 69–85).

[61] Van Beek (2010, 198, 248); on Bradstreet, see Bradstreet (1650); on Anna Roemers Visscher, Heinsius (1618, 33); on Juana Inés de la Cruz, Royer (2018); on Sophia Elisabet Brenner, Burman (1997) and Hiärne (1711, *passim*).

Concluding Words

Only a very small part (five that we know of) of the many hundreds of *eulogia* in honour of van Schurman was written in Greek. The eulogists used an exceptional language, Greek, to mark her exceptional qualities. Greek was not so widely known as Latin and had the added connotation of a holy language since the New Testament was written in Greek. Latin was the *lingua franca* in the *Res Publica Litteraria* and that is perhaps the reason that the poems, composed in Greek, appear in Latin versions as well (except for Crucius' praise letter in Greek). Writing good poems in Latin was already considered difficult and was only expected from students right at the end of their education in Latin, let alone writing poems in Greek. It is easier to compose a poem in Latin and subsequently translate it into Greek. But the order of the printed poems by Staackmans, van Beverwijck, Aemilius and Voetius suggests otherwise: first the Greek version followed by the Latin.

If one glances through other paratexts in front of books from the early modern period, it is often the case that praise poems (and letters) written in Greek were not translated. We do not know why it was done this way here. Maybe they were sometimes just versions of the same poem, even composed simultaneously, both influencing the other? Or indeed both translated from ideas preconceived in Dutch, in the minds of their authors? Or was it *variatio*? Piling up praise upon praise, first in Greek and then in Latin? Showing off the knowledge of Greek, especially in writing poems in Greek? We do not know. The differences between the Greek and the Latin texts are very small; for example, small changes in word order or variations in word choice and metrum. That is why C.A. De Niet and A. Goudriaan chose to make a single translation representing both of Voetius' poems. Often it is indicated in the text that the Latin version is an interpretation, and not a literal translation (except for van Beverwijck's poem).

The eulogists in other languages praise van Schurman's modesty, knowledge, celibacy, poetic and artistic excellence (by comparing her to Sappho and the Muses), her noble descent and her piety. She is often praised as Pallas Athena, the Greek goddess of wisdom, or as Minerva.[62] Topics in the Greek *eulogia* are her wisdom, learning and poetic excellence and her country. She is praised as being semi-divine, a halfgoddess, a goddess, Sappho, the Nymph, the Tenth Muse, or all Nine Muses together. According to van Beverwijck, she transcends women

---

[62] Van Schurman (1652, 322, 327); Van Beek (2010, 156, 218, 228–229).

in other countries, such as France, Spain, Italy and Greece; by virtue of her, her country Batavia is numbered first among the nations.

We are not aware of any reaction by van Schurman to any of the Greek praise poems dedicated to her, but she did protest in general against overblown *eulogia*. 'Praise is welcome if it coincides with the truth', she wrote in reply to the hyperbolic praise in a Greek letter written to her by the archbishop of the Greek Orthodox Church in Ephese, Meletios Pantogalus.[63] He should keep his overblown praise to himself. She had enough self-esteem to realise that she merited praise for the work she did. She even included the letters and poems by eulogists in the section of *Elogia* in her *Opuscula* and this may have been due to a combination of self-esteem, politeness, convention and a bit of vanity. She was bestowed with praise and she believed that in this way the eulogist would have read her books as well.[64]

Later in her life, as a radical Labadist, she deeply regretted the fact that she had given in to this kind of flattery. She should have protested much more vehemently against these 'trumpetters of her praise', who equalled her, an insignificant and mortal human being, a 'worm of earth', to the pagan gods; yes, even ascribing divine qualities such as omniscience to her. *Soli Deo Gloria*, glory to God alone, not to men. Just like Augustine, she recalled her writings, which smacked of vanity, and asked everyone to burn those praise writings that were branded by that particular sign of sinfulness. She herself burnt an unknown number of letters and poems that she had in her possession, including the Greek *eulogia* written by her *mendaces panegyrici*, 'lying eulogists'.[65]

---

[63] Van Schurman (1652, 159); Van Beek (2018b, 418–423).

[64] Schotel (1853, 92); Van Beek (2010, 54); Van Beek (2015, 20–26, 30–34); a book scroll on van Schurman's name and fame was published in 2016 (2016b) and digitised in 2017 (see http://objects.library.uu.nl/reader/index.php?obj=1874-357373&lan=nl#page//12/66/44/ 1266445257 909083930820714154284343134889.jpg/mode/1up; the accompanying book *Het wereldwonder van Utrechts Academie: Naam en faam van Anna Maria van Schurman (1636–2016)* is forthcoming.

[65] Van Schurman (1673, 10–11, 150–151); Irwin (1998, 77–79 (78)); Van Beek (2010, 230).

Bibliography

Books published before 1800

Aemilius, Antonius. 1651. *Orationes quarum pleraeque tractant argumentum politicum. Accedunt non nulla ejusdem utraque lingua poematia.* Utrecht.

Bayle, Pierre *et al.* 1735. *The Dictionary Historical and Critical of Mr Peter Bayle.* The second edition [...] Translated by Mr Des Maizeaux. Vol. 2: Bi–E. [*Dictionnaire Historique et Critique*, 1st ed. 1697]. London.

Bergen, Rotger zum. 1649. *Epistola et non-epistola et epigrammata ad nobilissimam clarisissimam doctissimam virginem Annam Mariam a Schürmann immortale sexus sui ornamentum ac vere stuporem.* Königsberg.

Bergen, Rotger zum. 1650a. *Epistola altera cum nonnullis epigrammatibus ad nobilissimam clarisissimam doctissimam virginem Annam Mariam A Schürmann* [...]. Königsberg.

Bergen, Rotger zum. 1650b. *Epistola tertia cum nonnullis epigrammatibus ad nobilissimam clarisissimam doctissimam virginem Annam Mariam A Schürmann* [...]. Königsberg.

Bergen, Rotger zum. 1655. *Vita Bonum fragile est sive supremus honor nobilissimae clarissimae virgini Annae Mariae à Schurmann sacro-sancto sexus sui stupori unico summae eruditionis exemplari.* Königsberg.

Bradstreet, Anne. 1650. *The Tenth Muse lately sprung up in America.* London.

Burmannus, Caspar. 1738. *Traiectum eruditum, virorum doctrina inlustrium, qui in urbe Trajecto, et regione Trajectensi nati sunt, sive ibi habitarunt, vitas, fata et scripta exhibens.* Utrecht.

Burmannus, Caspar. 1750. *Traiectum eruditum* [...]. Utrecht.

Gilberto, Domenico da Cesena. 1642. *La fama trionfante: panegirico alla bellissima, castissima, e dottissima signora Anna Maria Schurman.* Rome.

Clenardus, Nicolaus. *s.a.* [1600?]. *Rudimenta Linguae Graecae.* Brescia.

Crucius, Jacobus. 1639. *Virgo Batava.* Delft.

Crucius, Jacobus. 1661. *Mercurius Batavus, sive epistolarum opus, vi libros comprehendens, accuratius correctum et novis epistolis auctum.* Hanau.

Des Hayons, Thomas. 1649. *Epigrammes, consacrez à la vertu de Madamoiselle Anne Marie de Schurman.* Utrecht.

Heinsius, Daniel. 1618. *Nederduytsche Poemata.* Amsterdam.

[Hiärne, Urban.] (ed.) 1712. *De illustri Sveonum poëtria, Sophia Elisabetha Brenner, testimoniorum fasciculus.* Stockholm.

Koelman, Jakobus. 1770. *Historisch verhaal nopens der labadisten scheuring en veelerley dwalingen, met de wederlegginge derzelver.* Tweede druk. Leeuwarden.

Le Laboureur, Jean. 1647. *Relation du voyage de la royne de Pologne par la Hongrie* […]. Paris.

Van Beverwijck, Johan. 1639. *Van de Wtnementheyt des Vrovwelicken Geslachts.* Dordrecht.

Van Beverwijck, Johan. 1643. *Van de Wtnementheyt des Vrovwelicken Geslachts.* Dordrecht.

Van Schurman, Anna Maria. 1648. *Opuscula Hebraea Graeca Latina et Gallica, prosaica et metrica.* Leiden. [Reprinted in Leiden in 1650 and 1652 as well as in Leipzig 1749.]

Van Schurman, Anna Maria. 1673. ΕΥΚΛΗΡΙΑ *seu Melioris partis electio. Pars prima: Tractatus brevem vitae ejus delineationem exhibens.* (Altona) Hamburg.

Van Schurman, Anna Maria. 1685. ΕΥΚΛΗΡΙΑ *seu Melioris partis electio. Pars Secunda, Historiam vitae ejus usque ad mortem persequens.* Amsterdam.

Van Schurman, Anna Maria. 1728. *Geleerde brieven van de Edele, Deugt- en Konstrijcke Juffrouw Anna Maria van Schuurman gewisselt met de geleerde en beroemde Heeren Samuel Rachelius en Johan van Beverwijck.* Amsterdam.

Voetius, Gisbertus. 1677. *Pars Prior Bibliothecae Variorum et Insignium Librorum, Theologicorum et Miscelleaneorum, Reverendi et Celeberrimi Viri D. Gisberti Voetii.* Utrecht.

Voetius, Gisbertus. 1636. *Sermoen van de nutticheydt der Academien.* Utrecht.

Voetius, Gisbertus. 1655. *Selectarum disputationum theologicarum.* Pars Secunda. Utrecht.

Wiseaus, Augustinus. 1643. *De literatis virginibus tribus nostri saeculi. Schurmann, A. M., Memorata A., Corbiniana S.* Breslau.

Modern authors

Anonymus. 1875. *Allotria: Ungeflügelte Worte aus dem jocosen Citaten-Schatz des Gymnasial-Directors.* Berlin.

Anonymus. 1939. "Das Leben der gelehrten Anna Maria van Schurman", in Helene Lange & Gertrud Bäumer (eds.) *Die Frau, Monatsschrift fuer das gesamte Frauenleben unserer Zeit* Vol. 47, 48–52.

Blom, Frans R.E. 2004. "Constantijn Huygens en de Friese dichter Willem Staackmans", *De zeventiende eeuw* 20, 122–132.

Burman, Carina. 1997. *Den tionde Sånggudinnan.* Stockholm.

De Glas, Nico. 2017. *Holland is een eiland: De Batavia van Hadrianus Junius.* Hilversum.

De Jonge, Henk Jan. 1975. "The Study of the New Testament", in Th.H. Lunsingh Scheurleer & G.H.M. Posthumus Meyjes (eds.) *Leiden University in the Seventeenth Century. An Exchange of Learning*, Leiden, 64–90.

De Niet, C.A. 2016. "Voetius", in *Encyclopedie Nadere Reformatie*, Deel 2. Utrecht.

De Niet, C.A. & Niet A. Goudriaan. 2007. "Piëtistisch erfgoed. Voetius over de negende muze Anna Maria van Schurman", *Documentatieblad Nadere Reformatie* 31, 182–185.

Duker, A.C. 1913. *Gisbertus Voetius.* Vol. 3. Leiden.

Duker, A.C. 1989. *Gisbertus Voetius.* Vol. 3. Reprint. Leiden.

Haaker, Antoine. 2018. "An unpublished Greek letter of Ismaël Bullialdus to Anna Maria van Schurman", in Janika Päll & Ivo Volt (eds.) *Hellenostephanos. Humanist Greek in Early Modern Europe. Learned Communities between Antiquity and Contemporary Culture.* Tartu, 438–447.

Irwin, Joyce L. 1998. *Anna Maria van Schurman, Whether a Christian Woman Should Be Educated and other Writings from her Intellectual Circle.* Chicago.

Kajanto, Iiro. 1993. *Christina Heroina: Mythological and historical exemplification in the Latin panegyrics on Christina, Queen of Sweden.* Helsinki.

Larsen, Anne. 2016. *Anna Maria van Schurman, the Star of Utrecht. The Educational Vision and Reception of a Savante.* New York.

Laureys, Marc. 2014. "Praise and Blame", in Philip Ford, Jan Bloemendal & Charles Fantazzi (eds.) *Brill's Encyclopaedia of the Neo-Latin World. Macropaedia*, Leiden–Boston, 1148–1150.

Libelt, Carl. 1853. "Frauen und Gelehrtheit aus dem 'Humor und Wahrheit'", *Belletristische Blätter aus Russland. Aus dem Feuilleton der St. Petersburger Zeitung.* Vol.1. St. Petersburg, 138–147.

Libelt, Karol. 1852. *Humor i Prawda w Kilku obrazkach.* St. Petersburg.

Macaré, Jonkheer Cornelis Anthony Rethaan. 1855. "Onuitgegeven brieven en gedichten van Anna Maria van Schurman, Willem Staackmans, Constantijn Huygens enz.", *Kronijk van het Historisch Genootschap gevestigd te Utrecht* 11, 202–214.

Päll, Janika & Ivo Volt. 2018. *Hellenostephanos. Humanist Greek in Early Modern Europe Learned Communities between Antiquity and Contemporary Culture (Acta Societatis Morgensternianae VI–VII).* Tartu.

Petzer, Kobus. 1990. *Die teks van die Nuwe Testament. 'n Inleiding in die basiese aspekte van die teorie en praktyk van die tekskritiek van die Nuwe Testament.* Pretoria.

Royer, Fanchon. 2018. *The Tenth Muse: Sor Juana Inés De La Cruz.* Chicago.

Schotel, G.D.J. 1853. *Anna Maria van Schurman.* 's-Hertogenbosch.

Staackmans, Wilhelmus 1855. "*De VII. Fragis a nobilissima domina A.M. à Schurman vividissime pictis et in strenam datis epigrammatibus totidem*", *Kronijk van het Historisch Genootschap gevestigd te Utrecht* 11, 210–211.

Stevenson, Jane. 2005. *Women Latin Poets. From Antiquity to the Eighteenth Century.* Oxford.

Stevenson, Jane. 2014a. "Women's Education", in Philip Ford, Jan Bloemendal & Charles Fantazzi (eds.) *Brill's Encyclopaedia of the Neo-Latin World. Macropaedia*, Leiden–Boston, 87–111.

Stevenson, Jane. 2014b. "Women Prodigies. Anna Maria van Schurman, Elena Piscopia and Others", in Philip Ford, Jan Bloemendal & Charles Fantazzi (eds.) *Brill's Encyclopaedia of the Neo-Latin World. Macropaedia*, Leiden–Boston, 1199–1200.

Stolpe, Sven. 1966. *Christina of Sweden.* London.

Van Beek, Pieta. 1987. '*Aan Babylons stromen': Anna Maria van Schurman in Keulen.* Master thesis. Utrecht.

Van Beek, Pieta. 1992.*Verbastert Christendom. Nederlandse gedichten van Anna Maria van Schurman.* Houten.

Van Beek, Pieta. 1996. "'O Utreght, lieve Stadt'. Poems in Dutch by Anna Maria van Schurman", in Mirjam de Baar *et al.* (eds.) *Choosing the better part Anna Maria van Schurman (1607–1678).* Dordrecht, 69–86.

Van Beek, Pieta. 2003. "'Pallas Ultrajectina, bis quinta dearum': Anna Maria van Schurman en haar Neolatijnse dichtkunst", in Jan Bloemendal (ed.) *De Utrechtse Parnas: Utrechtse Neolatijnse dichters uit de zestiende en de zeventiende eeuw.* Amersfoort.

Van Beek, Pieta. 2010. *The first female university student. Anna Maria van Schurman (1636).* Utrecht.

Van Beek, Pieta. 2014. '*On God': An Unknown Florilegium by Anna Maria van Schurman (ca. 1625).* Translated by Dineke Ehlers. Ridderkerk.

Van Beek, Pieta. 2015. *Herrezen uit de as. Verbrande lofgeschriften van Rotger zum Bergen voor Anna Maria van Schurman (1649–1655).* Ridderkerk.

Van Beek, Pieta. 2016a. *Ex libris. De bibliotheek van Anna Maria van Schurman en de catalogi van de Labadistenbibliotheek.* Met medewerking van Joris Bürmann. Ridderkerk.

Van Beek, Pieta. 2016b. *Het wereldwonder van Utrechts Academie: Naam en faam van Anna Maria van Schurman (1636–2016)*. Book scroll. Ridderkerk. http://objects.library.uu.nl/reader/index.php?obj=1874-357373&lan=nl#page//12/66/44/12664452579090839308207141542843431 3489.jpg/mode/1up.

Van Beek, Pieta, 2018a. "Het gebed des Heeren en de Sura Al Fatiha: Destructieve devotie van Anna Maria van Schurman", *Handreiking* 48:5, 18–19.

Van Beek, Pieta, 2018b. "ῬΩΣ ῬΟΔΟΝ ἘΝ ἈΚΆΝΘΑΙΣ – As a Rose among the thorns: Anna Maria van Schurman and her correspondences in Greek", in Janika Päll & Ivo Volt (eds.) *Hellenostephanos. Humanist Greek in Early Modern Europe. Learned Communities between Antiquity and Contemporary Culture*, Tartu, 414–437.

Van Beek, Pieta. (forthcoming). *Het wereldwonder van Utrechts Academie: Naam en faam van Anna Maria van Schurman (1636–2016)*. Ridderkerk.

Van der Aa, A.J. 1864. *Nieuw Biografiesch, anthologiesch en krities woordenboek van Nederlandsche dichters*. Amsterdam.

Van der Stighelen, Katlijne. 1987. *Anna Maria van Schurman of 'Hoe hooge dat een maeght kan in de konsten stijgen'*. Leuven.

Van Elk, Martine. 2017. *Modern Women's Writing: Domesticity, privacy, and the public sphere in England and the Dutch Republic*. London.

Van Lieburg, F.A. 1989. *De Nadere Reformatie in Utrecht ten tijde van Voetius. Sporen in de gereformeerde kerkeraadsacta*. Rotterdam.

Van Miert, Dirk. 2018. *The emancipation of Biblical philology in the Dutch Republic, 1590–1670*. Oxford.

Weber, Karl Julius. 1868. *Demokritos oder hinterlassene Papiere eines lachenden Philosophen*. Achte Ausgabe, Volume 2. Stuttgart.

Weise, Stephan. 2017. *Hellenisti: Altgriechisch als Literatursprache in neuzeitlichen Europa*. Stuttgart.

V. GREEK AND THE 18th AND 19th CENTURY *NEUHUMANISMUS*

German Neo-Humanism *versus* Rising Professionalism. *Carmina Hellenica Teutonum* by the Braunschweig Physician and *Philhellene* Karl Friedrich Arend Scheller (1773–1842)

JANIKA PÄLL

Introduction[1]

Gradual changes in teaching and study of ancient languages and literature in the last decades of the 18th and the beginning of the 19th century brought a certain growth in teaching of Greek and Latin in the gymnasia and universities as the foundation of general education; this cultural movement is known as Neo-Humanism (German new humanism, *Neuhumanismus*).[2] Although "Neo-Humanism" has not been in favour in recent research, I believe that it is a suitable term to describe the main trends in the humanities during this period and preferable to the terms *Enlightenment*, (Neo-)Classicism, Romanticism or Philhellenism.[3]

During the first half of the 19th century, new professional teaching and research methods were developed in comparative and historical linguistics (Franz Bopp, Jacob Grimm) and textual criticism (Friedrich August Wolf, Karl Lachmann), resulting in text editions and *corpora* that were compiled and edited according to the new criteria. These methods became an absolute must for the professionals and

---

[1] My greatest thanks go to the Herzog-August Biblitothek in Wolfenbüttel for the scholarship for autumn 2017, Frau Dr Gillian Bepler and Herr Dr Volker Bauer and Dr Bertram Lesser, as well as other helpful staff members of HAB, and Kai Anne Kröger and Christina Eggers from Braunschweig libraries. This article has been written in the framework of the Swedish Research Council's project Helleno-Nordica (grant 2016-01881), led by Johanna Akujärvi (Lund University).

[2] See Bommel (2015, esp. pages 3–18), cf. also Landfester (1988), (2003), Paulsen (1897) in general. Weise (2016, 121–123) puts the renewed love for writing in Greek in the framework of *Neuhumanismus/Philhellenismus*.

[3] For the notion of classicism in art and 'classical' as something cold (Hegel's remark), see Oechslin (2011, 195). In recent scholarship on the reception of antiquity in the 19th century, the notion of Neo-Humanism is rare, e.g., only in Axer & Tomaszuk (2007, 148–150) (in Poland), Riedel (2007, 178–184) (in Germany), Skafte Jensen (2007, 260–263) (in Scandinavia) in Kallendorf (2007), it is completely absent in Grafton, Most & Settis (2013) etc.

made a clear distinction between the specialists who used them and the amateurs who did not.[4] The university reform which followed changes in sciences helped to create a significant gap between the old and the new approaches.[5]

Thus, at the same time as the democratisation of studies which brought education in classical languages to a broader range of people and gave them access to the culture of antiquity, the emerging professionalism in the field of *Altertumswissenschaften* divided the amateurs (in the case of Greek, the *Philhellenes*) and the professionals (classical scholars), thus "flattening"[6] some achievements of Neo-Humanism. This gap was cemented by the newly developing discipline of classical philology (study of ancient languages and cultures), named *altclassische Philologie* by the Tartu-Halle scholar Johann Karl Simon Morgenstern (1770–1852), who could be classified in both groups ("amateurs" and professionals) without too much damage to his scholarly reputation.[7]

This period of emerging professionalism and Neo-Humanism coincides with the life of a passionate and sedulous German *Saxonophile* and *Philhellene*, Braunschweig (Brunswick) physician Karl Friedrich Arend Scheller (1773–1842). He compiled the first comprehensive regional corpus of Hellenising Greek poetry,[8] *Carmina Hellenica Teutonum,* which is presently held in Wolfenbüttel,

---

[4] See Bommel (2015) for the role of Neo-Humanism in general, Riedel (2007, 183–184) for the clash between humanist ideals and the real situation in schools, cf. Grafton & Most (1997, 46). For the development of philology and specialisation, see, e.g., Sandys (1908, 51–60, 127–132, 205–206), Pfeiffer (1976, 176–190), Hunger (1997), Dover (1997), Delz (1997), Grafton & Most (1997). Today's distinctions do not always work for earlier periods: Polizian was an "amateur" of classical languages, but his contribution to the development of textual criticism is significant Pfeiffer (1976, 44–46).

[5] For role of the university reform of Wilhelm von Humboldt, see, e.g., Spranger (1960), Irmscher (1989), Humboldt (1903).

[6] This notion has been used by Riedel (2007, 184) for the description of classical tradition in the 19th century. The antiquarianism was still vigorous then, although it had been criticised from the 17th century onwards, see Herklotz (2011, 159, 167).

[7] See Classen (2002). For Morgenstern, see Süss (1928–1929).

[8] Georg Lizel's overview of Humanist Greek in Germany (*Historia poetarum Graecorum Germaniae,* 1730) must have been based on some sort of collection that has not been preserved. Lizel's account is bio-bibliographical, focusing on both the study and practice of ancient Greek and including few example, see Weise (2020). Scheller seems to have been unaware of Lizel's work; Johann Albert Fabricius' bio-bibliographic *Bibliotheca Graeca* (Hamburg 1705–1728) and Hieronymus Freyer's anthology *Fasciculus poematum Graecorum* (Halle 1715), which also include some examples of Humanist Greek poems, were apparently also unknown to him. See Weise (2011).

Herzog August Bibliothek (hereafter: HAB), *Cod. Guelf. 870–873 Novi.*[9]

This article presents the first introduction of this corpus. After discussing Karl Scheller and his role as amateur philologist, I will then describe generally the organisation and indices of his corpus, in the process discussing its "scrapbook" quality and Scheller's editorial technique as well as the omitted authors. Volumes I–III of the corpus, *Carmina Hellenica Teutonum*, are analysed from different aspects, including the distribution of authors by their origin and the number of represented poems, the meaning of 'Teutonic' and represented printing towns, which reveals the mostly regional nature of his corpus, and the genres used. The last chapter will conclude with general evaluation of the corpus and Scheller as a Hellenist.

The Life and Activity of Karl Friedrich Arend Scheller (1773–1842)

Although the name of Karl Scheller is unknown to Hellenists and Latinists,[10] he has a certain fame, or perhaps infamy, among scholars who study Low German. He can be described as an unlucky man, as suggested by his pseudonym, Karl Notwehr ("Miserable Karl").[11] Scheller's life-work combined antiquarianism and a love for languages, starting with the study of languages at home and in Wolfenbütteler Gelehrtenschule and continuing with the study of medicine at Jena University (where he was possibly also influenced by early Jena Romanticism and philhellenism). He continued his professional career by qualifying in medicine in Helmstedt and practiced for a long time in Braunschweig as a physician.[12] Most of

---

[9] Scheller's collection came to my notice accidentally during a search in the manuscript database of HAB for the word 'graeca'. For Scheller's life and activities concerning Low German, I follow Blume (1992) (cf. Blume [2009]), who is most thorough, even including a reference to *Carmina Hellenica Teutonum* (Blume [1992, 63 n. 79]).

[10] With the exception of a reference to his translations of Horace (Wolkenhauer [2015, 91]).

[11] For Scheller's biography: loss of his mother at birth, brutal father, incurable illness (hip dysplasia) in childhood and later, studies and promotion, emergence and loss of hopes for positions in the Ducal Library of Wolfenbüttel or Helmstedt university, the French occupation and the ruin of his family fortune, work as a military doctor, poverty, marriage and death (accidental or by suicide, following high fever and falling out of the window), see Blume (1992) and Schröder (1890) (the entry of Schmidt [1845] ends appropriately with a word 'Fleiß'). His portrait can be found in Hoffmeister (2003, 93).

[12] See Blume (1992); for the clash 'Gelehrtenschule vs modern education', Bommel (2014, 100–148) and Paulsen (1896–1897), for philhellenic tendencies and early romanticism in Jena, Irmscher (1966, 78–79).

his adult life was spent in the Duchy of Braunschweig-Lüneburg in Lower Saxony.

Scheller's life in Braunschweig has been described as a conflict between his real interest, his love for the study of languages (first and foremost Low German), and his duties as a physician (Blume 1992, 56). The linguistic interest won, although he received little praise for his scholarly input to the study of Low German (or 'altsässisch' as he preferred to call it) from professional linguists. It was criticised especially by Jacob Grimm.[13] Modern scholars have given him more credit for his studies on Low German: an extended bibliography *Bücherkunde der Sassisch-Niederdeutschen Sprache* (Scheller 1826a), a lexicon and several transcripts of poetry. However, he was also the author of literary works, including an anti-Napoleon (unfortunately also Francophobic and anti-Semitic) epic *Jeromiade*. Most of his other poems and prose are unknown and survive only in manuscripts.[14] He conducted his research for his bibliography, lexicon and transcripts mostly in the Ducal Library of Wolfenbüttel, where he fulfilled small incidental commissions, without ever becoming, to his disappointment, a staff member.[15]

In addition to his beloved 'altsässisch', Scheller had a passion for ancient languages. He published German translations of Horace, which he had started already as a young man, and even attempted to translate Horace into Low German.[16] But he had also started to collect Greek poetry by German authors, in tune with the philhellenic trends of his time. However, his first reference to this kind of poetry in the preface to *Bücherkunde* is not entirely favourable. After introductory words about the early history of the German language, which resemble Johannes Goropius' views on the history of Dutch,[17] and which irritated (not without reason) Jacob Grimm, Scheller complains that his beloved idiom ('sässisch') is gradually disappearing and that scholars prefer to write poetry in

---

[13] Grimm (1869, 290–296); a review of Scheller's edition of *Layen-Doctrinal,* starting with a grudging acknowledgement for making the work known to the public, but proceeding to an indignant condemnation, see Grimm (1869, 385–397, 412–415).

[14] See Blume (1992, 57–63, *passim*), Blume (2009), already Eckart (1911).

[15] Scheller's biographers mention some income from translation and small jobs commissioned by the Ducal library and museum (*Nekrolog* 1843: 709–710, Schröder 1890; Blume 1992: 54), resulting probably in two of his manuscripts, now in HAB: *Catalogus librorum Sassonicorum*, about 1800 (Sign. BA I, 496) and *Dublettenkatalog* ca. 1833, bound together with a printed catalogue which appeared in 1833 (Sign. BA I, 442). It seems that he was not always welcome in the libraries; see his wish to be able to see Helmstedt manuscripts (Scheller 1826a, 345).

[16] See Scheller (1830) (especially pp. III–IV on his other attempts), a reprint of an edition from 1826, and Scheller (1821), for his translations into Low German, see Blume (1992, 57).

[17] See Considine (2008, 143–144).

Greek and Latin and abandon their own language. He compares this activity to a burial:

> The scholars believed it worthy to wrap their work in the burial cloth of antiquity and put it into the grave. The best ever Saxon and German heads wrote at the very least Latin and Greek poems, when they did not write in Hebrew, Syrian and Chaldean – for the moles! – and taught people in a language which they did not understand (and do not understand completely even today), because they were unable to understand and even to learn to understand how the people spoke.[18]

Scheller continues by criticising the superfluous attention to High German and so-called Biblical and Oriental languages, but soon reveals that he is not entirely indifferent to the latter, especially Greek:

> The farmer did not learn to read or write at all, the townsfolk and more educated people learned only High German (*Oberländisch*) and the real scholars and writers preferred to write more in Latin and Greek than in High German (I do not even mention the Saxon) during more than two hundred years, so that I alone have discovered almost 500 producers of Greek verses from Germany, of which at least 2/3 were Saxons. Poetry, the real constructor of one's own language, did not find its own Hans Sachs or Martin Opitz in Saxony.[19]

This reference indicates that by 1826, Scheller's collection was already at an advanced stage. This is also attested to by another passing reference to a transcript

---

[18] Scheller (1826a, XI): 'Die Gelehrten setzten einen Werth darin, ihre Arbeiten in das Leichengewand des Alterthums zu hüllen und – ins Grab zu legen. Die besten Sassischen und Deutschen Köpfe überhaupt schrieben mindestens Lateinische und Griechische Gedichte, wo nicht Ebräische, Syrische und Chaldäische, für – die Motten, und unterrichteten das Volk in einer Sprache, dies es nicht Verstand, und noch heute nicht völlig versteht, weil sie selbst die Sprache nicht verstanden, und nicht verstehen lernen konnten, wie das Volk sprach.'

[19] Scheller (1826a, XIII): 'Der Bauer lernte überhaupt weder lesen noch schreiben, der Bürger und Gebildetere nur Oberländisch, und der eigentliche Gelehrte und Schriftsteller schrieb länger als zwei Jahrhunderte hindurch lieber Lateinisch und Griechisch; als auch nur Hochdeutsch, geschweige Sassisch, so dass ich allein nahe an 500 Griechische Versmacher in Deutschland aufgefunden haben von denen wenigstens zwei Drittel Sassen gewesen sind. Die Dichtkunst, die eigentliche Bildnerinn jeder Sprache, fand im Sassischen weder ein Hans Sachs noch Martin Opitz.'

of a Greek poem (by Gottfried Schrader) in his collection[20] and a date 1822 in one part of his *Carmina Hellenica Teutonum* (see below).

Following his antiquarian instincts to assemble different kinds of information, Scheller also presented some references to the translations of Horace, Propertius and Aratus in his *Bücherkunde*.[21] But in spite of these remarks, Scheller's collection of Greek poetry by German scholars clearly stands apart from his works about (and in) Low German.

General Description and Characteristic Features of Scheller's Greek Corpus

Scheller's collection of Humanist Greek poetry from Germany (*Cod. Guelf. 870–873 Novi* in the HAB) consists of four folio-size volumes. The written text is in Scheller's own hand, except for the library's notes (numeration in pencil, signature and a note about the acquisition).[22] The metadata to these volumes in the catalogue of the manuscript collection of the HAB includes links to the digitalisations of Otto von Heinemann's descriptions of these volumes (1870–1871) together with a list of authors,[23] but because some items are missing, the addenda to the list is included in the Appendix to this article.

The first three volumes, beginning with an index by Scheller, bear the title *Carmina Hellenica Teutonum* and include a collage (scrap-book) of transcripts and cut-outs from various prints, as well as references to publications which include Greek poems by German authors from (mostly) the 16th and 17th century. The

---

[20] *S.a.*, XXIII (No. 1341), occasional poems for Johann Ernest Schrader in different languages with a reference to the book in HAB and transcript in Scheller's collection *Wolfenb. Bibl. R. A. und Abschrift in meiner Sammlung* (Scheller 1826a, 481). Today the transcription of this poem is in his collection (Cod. Guelf. 870 Novi, p. 215v) and the corresponding printed version in HAB (Db 4618 (41)).

[21] See Blume (1992, 61–62). There are some misunderstandings concerning a manuscript of a translation of Aratus, No. 274 in *Bücherkunde* (*ARATI SOLENSIS, des Grekeschen Poeten* [...] *Ut dem Grekeschen in de nedersasseshe sprake forandered dorg Johannem Macrowarinum anno 1563*), now Cod. Guelf. Helmst. 1016 in HAB, see Ebert (1827, 22) and the Catalogue of Heinemann (1884, No. 1118), as well as Scheller's transcription of it (HAB, Ms Cod. Guelf. 701 Novi). Scheller seems to have thought that it could be the Flemish poet Claeskyn's (van Klaeskijn) *Astronomia en Fleubotomia* (No. 1847 in the Catalogue, see Scheller [1826a, 53, 472]). For Claeskyn, see Jansen-Sieben (1968, 264–265).

[22] These were acquired by HAB in 1859 with two other of Scheller's manuscripts.

[23] See, http://diglib.hab.de/?db=mss&list=ms&id=870-novi&catalog=Heinemann&hi=870.

fourth volume of the corpus includes added material. Each of the four volumes bears its own title:

1) *Carmina Hellenica Teutonum. I. Catalogus c. Brunsvicens. Mscr.*
(Cod Guelf. 870 Novi).
According to the title, the first volume includes a catalogue (index) and manuscripts by Braunschweig authors. To be more precise, it starts with two catalogues of the authors of Greek poems and includes the transcriptions and clippings of printed Greek poems by authors from the Duchy of Braunschweig-Lüneburg.[24] Most transcribed poems have been written directly on the pages of the present-day volume, but some have been cut out from their initial place and glued into it. This indicates that there was a previous version of Scheller's collection. The volume also includes cutouts from occasional poetry collections with Greek poems, similarly glued onto the pages of the present-day volume, as well as handwritten references to prints with Greek poems (including print information or cross-references to other volumes). The authors (and their poems) are arranged alphabetically by surnames.

2) *Carmina Hellenica Teutonum II. Originalia Brunsvic. impressa.*
(Cod Guelf. 871 Novi).
The title of the second volume suggests that it includes original prints with poems by Braunschweig authors, and there are indeed 55 numbered occasional poetry quires (sometimes only partial) which include poetry in Greek by (mostly) Braunschweig authors, arranged alphabetically according to the surnames of the authors of Greek poems.[25] *Pace* the title, several pages with transcripts of poems are also bound in the volume, as well as references to other prints.

3) *Carmina Hellenica Teutonum. III. Variorum, impr. & manuscr.*
(Cod. Guelf 872 Novi).
The third volume is dedicated to different "German" poets, as the title says, and includes both types of transcripts, cutouts and (parts of) occasional poetry collections. The authors have not only been alphabetically arranged, but also

---

[24] This part starts on page 18r of Cod. Guelf. 870 Novi with a short indication: *Brunsvicens.* and ends with page 235 (also bearing an old item number (?) '425').

[25] When there are several Greek poems by different authors in the same quire, the arrangement usually follows the names of the author of the first Greek poem in the quire.

numbered.[26] When an author is represented by several poems, the poems are usually numbered with Roman numerals. As will be explained below, 'Germany' is to be understood in a loose sense.

4) ΜΙΧΑΗΛ ΝΕΑΝΔΡΟΥ του Σωρανεως Ποιηματα Ἑλληνικα [*sic*].
(Cod. Guelf. 873 Novi).
Although I refer to this volume as Volume 4 of the collection, it was not presented as part of *Carmina Hellenica Teutonum* by its compiler.[27] According to the title, it includes transcripts of the poetry of Michael Neander, but it is incomplete, as there is a *lacuna* after poem VII by Neander. The present volume also includes poems by other authors: after the *lacuna*, it continues with some as yet unidentified *Carmina sacra* and ends with some occasional poems by Lorenz Rhodoman (some of which are earlier transcripts, glued into the volume).[28]

In general, the arrangement of Scheller's *Collectanea* reveals the following features:

a) The corpus in its present state is a rearrangement of an earlier one, including two types of transcripts, some on the greenish paper of the (present-day) volumes, some on a slightly better white paper. The poems on the white paper (from the earlier corpus) have been cut out and glued onto the pages of present-day volumes. Scheller has also occasionally added cross-references to the initial positions and numbers of poems.[29]

b) In addition to transcripts, *Carmina Hellenica Teutonum* includes a great number of cut-outs from occasional prints (sometimes entire prints or their parts) which have been added to the scrap-book (glued on or bound between the pages of the volumes), following each volume's individual alphabetic arrangement. Sometimes the cut-out poems continue (or are followed by another poem) on the verso[30] side of an added page; such cuttings have been glued into the scrap-book so that both sides of the paper slip are readable.

---

[26] For example, the last numbered item is a print with two Greek-Latin poems by M. Zuber, under No. III. 279.

[27] There are *lacunae*, pages (except the first) have not been numbered by Scheller, and the modern numeration in pencil occurs only after each 10 pages.

[28] Both Neander and Rhodoman are included in Scheller's index with a reference: *vi*[*de*] *separ.*

[29] Such as references to the numbers in the original collection: *orig.* I.15. *orig.* I.34 etc.

[30] Not always corresponding to recto-verso sides of the original print.

c) All three volumes of *Carmina Hellenica Teutonum* are arranged alphabetically, with each volume starting anew from the letter A. When one author is represented by more than one poem, the poems are numbered. The information for each poem includes the names of the authors and the addressee(s), the occasion (often corresponding to the short title of the print), the year and the town of printing.

d) Occasionally (mostly in Vol. 2), when whole quires of occasional poetry or their parts with poems by different authors are included, the alphabetic arrangement by surnames is disturbed. In such cases Scheller added cross-references in the expected positions of the authors, indicating the location of the poem with a volume and item number or/and the surname of the author, whose poems occur in correct positions according to the alphabet (usually these are the authors of the first Greek poem in a quire).[31] In addition to texts (transcripts or cut-outs), Scheller also added references to books including Greek poems, both in his indices and in the corpus proper.

Thus we see certain clear principles of organisation, such as the division of the poets according to their origin between volumes 1–2 and 3, alphabetic arrangement by surnames of the authors, referencing, cross-referencing and indexing, which all to differing degrees characterise both the antiquarian collections and the specialist *corpora*. However, the heterogeneous nature of these manuscripts and the lack of explanation of Scheller's arrangement principles and his editorial technique (explained below) mean that we have to classify it as an album or scrap-book of an amateur antiquarian.

Indices to Carmina Hellenica Teutonum

Scheller, who was used to bibliographical work, furnished his collection with two indices:

---

[31] For example, a collection of wedding poetry for Auctor Hustetus (VD16 ZV 13816, Helmstedt [1590]) included several Greek poems: two by Martin Baremius (rector of *Schola Martiniana*), one by Auctor Rennebocius (rector of *Schola Aegidiana*), a poem and its Latin translation by Christoph Hagius (subconrector of *Schola Aegidiana*) and single poems by Adolph Hageman and by Ludolph Reuter. The whole print is bound into the second volume (Cod. Guelf. 871 Novi, II–21), but the poems of Baremius are also separately transcribed in Volume 1 and furnished with cross-references to their location (in what was originally Vol.1, but now Vol. 2).

1) *Catalogus. Poetar. Graecobarb.*

This index ('The catalogue of Barbaro-Greek poets', i.e., Germans or other non-Greeks who wrote Greek poems) introduces Volume 1.[32] It is alphabetically ordered by the surnames (underlined) of the authors, inserting the letters of the Latin alphabet as headings; a few names in the Greek alphabet are inserted among the Latin ones.[33] After each name, the position of each author is indicated with an abbreviation *Br.* (for Braunschweig poets in Vol. 1 and 2)[34] or with a reference to Vol. 3 ('Teutonic' poets), with the number of the volume in Roman numerals and the poet in Arabic numerals.[35] The index also includes the names of several poets whose works are not presented in the collection, furnished with references *vide separ.* or short information about the print.[36]

2) *Cat. Collect. lib.*

The second index is a list of books including Greek poems, which are not represented in *Carmina Hellenica*, under title *Cat. Collect. Lib.* ('The catalogue of collected books').[37] This list is also arranged alphabetically by surnames (underlined) of the authors of poems or these books. Most entries are furnished with references to the locations, with the library shelf-mark *Bibl. Ridd.* or with an abbreviation *m.ppr,* as in the one case where both occur together:

> Joann. <u>Caselii</u> Carminum [...] *Goett. 1668. (Bibl. Ridd. N.253. 8º.)*
> *(Graec.m.ppr.).*

The first reference indicates that the Göttingen 1668 edition of Johannes Caselius'

---

[32] *Carmina Hellenica Teutonum. I. Catalogus c. Brunsvicens. Mscr.* (Cod Guelf. 870 Novi, 2r–13v).

[33] In case of 'Illyricus', a cross-reference to 'Matthias' is added in the index, in case of K. Ουδενωβιος under 'O', a cross-reference is given to 'Utenhovius' and Jacob Κηπωρυς [!] for J. Ceporinus.

[34] The works of the same author can be presented in two volumes, for example works by Werner Cuno, Justus v. Dransfeld, Johannes Groteianus, Adolph Hagemann, Christoph Hagius etc. In such cases Scheller furnished such entries in Vol. 1 with cross-references to Vol. 2.

[35] Cod. Guelf. 870–872 Novi. Double numbering was used by Scheller, who occasionally retained his original numeration in cross-references (e.g., orig. I–15), even before more numbers were added; however, later new numbering was added in pencil by a librarian (continuous numeration including the folio leaves of the bound volumes and the inserted and gluedin pages; as a result, one page often has more than one number in pencil on it).

[36] For example: *Dan. Heinsius vid. Separ.* or *Syphardus Saccus, vid. Neandri Erotem. Gr.*

[37] Cod Guelf. 870 Novi, 14r–17v. The abbreviation *Collect.* could stand for either *collectionum* or *collectorum.*

collected poems belonged to the collection of books from Riddagshausen monastery (Die Riddagshäuser Bibliothek) under the 'signature' N. 253 of octavo volumes.[38] Today this collection is held in the Theologisches Zentrum in Braunschweig and still includes (under new shelfmarks) most of the 20 books, which in Scheller's list are furnished with *Bibl. Ridd.* In Scheller's time, the collection was at HAB and he had been commissioned to catalogue these books: indeed, several of these books in the Braunschweig library include the librarian's notes in his handwriting.

The second type of reference is an abbreviation *m.ppr*, referring either to transcripts in Scheller's own hand (*manu propria*) or to the books (or transcripts) owned by him (*in manibus propriis*). Although the first explanation seems more plausible, there is a difficulty: only a few of such entries can be matched to transcripts of poetry in the present-day collection at HAB. However, the above-mentioned reference to Caselius' poetry could mean that Greek (but not Latin) poems from this edition of his poetry were transcribed by Scheller. Similarly, the following entry could refer to his transcripts of Caselius' paraphrases of the Lord's Prayer:

Joann. Caselii Orat. Dominic. [...] Helmst.1610 (M.ppr.)

In both cases we can find the transcripts of Caselius' poems in Scheller's collection.[39] Another entry, referring to the Psalm paraphrases by Maximos Margounios – edited by Konrad Rittershausen – mentions a transcript (ἀπογραφή) in Scheller's collection (Scheller's orthography here):

Μαξίμου του Μαργουνίου Ὕμνοι ἀνακρεόντειοι [...] *ed. C. Rittershusius 1601* (ἀπογρ. *ppr.*).[40]

Margounios (1552–1602), a descendant of Byzantine Greeks, does not belong to the category of "Barbaro-Greek" (that is: non-Greek) poets.[41] This edition

---

[38] Today in the library of Evangelisch-Lutherische Landeskirche Braunschweig in the Theologisches Zentrum Braunschweig, under a new signature R II 48 (3). For the history of this collection, see Eisenberg & Müller-Jelina (1997).

[39] See Cod. Guelf. 870 Novi 58e–100r and 91r–100v. However, in the case of *Opera omnia* Scheller certainly worked with original prints too, because he also presents the original print information, which is not found in the reprint.

[40] See Cod. Guelf. 870 Novi, 2v and 26r. The book could have been in the Riddagshausen library; at least a copy of this edition is now available in the Library of Evangelisch-Lutherische Landeskirche Braunschweig in the Theologisches Zentrum Braunschweig (*sign.* R II 24).

[41] Margounios had been born on Crete, worked as a Greek unionist bishop on Cythera and as a

is included in Scheller's index because of one of its paratexts: a versification of the Lord's Prayer in Anacreontics by Matthias Berg (1536–1592) from Braunschweig on pp. H2v–H3v. Berg was the editor Rittershausen's maternal uncle (*avunculus*).[42] Scheller names Berg among the Braunschweig poets in his first Index and provides in Volume 1 a reference (without a text) to the above-mentioned edition of Margounios', with an addition: *collect. apogr.* 426.

However, I have only rarely been able to find matching transcripts for books furnished with a reference *m.ppr.*[43] If other transcripts were made, they could still be hidden among Scheller's other manuscripts in the archives.[44] Thus, in general, both indices add more unsolved questions rather than help to explain the arrangement and nature of his corpus.

Scheller as an editor and a scrap-book compiler

As noted above, Scheller as an editor of Low German texts was criticised harshly by Jacob Grimm, although, according to Herbert Blume, Grimm probably misinterpreted Scheller's intention, which was not to present philological editions but to promote Low Saxon together with his own new orthography.[45] Similarly, in the case of his corpus of Greek poetry, we have to accept that Scheller acted as an antiquarian and amateur, not as a professional editor and textual critic. Following features characterise his approach to texts and their sources:

1) Orthography:
Modern classicists will be puzzled by Scheller's orthography. Nowadays, even the orthography of Greek in an early modern printed book might seem strange with its ligatures and peculiar usage of diacritic signs and other features, then used mostly for typographic reasons.[46] Scheller neither follows the orthography

---

teacher in Venice, see Geanakoplos (1966, 165).

[42] For Berg, see Deufert (2011).

[43] There are some exceptions: J. Caselius, M. Neander and L. Rhodoman, as well as transcriptions from Gosky's *Arbustum* (1650), which are present in the volumes now at HAB.

[44] It is just possible that when HAB bought six of Scheller's manuscripts in 1859 the library chose only the manuscripts that included local or rarer material and did not consider it important to buy manuscript copies of printed books which they either already had in their collections or which were easy to find.

[45] See references to Grimm and Blume above, notes 13 and 14.

[46] For the ligatures in Greek prints, see Ingram (1988) and Barker (1992), Päll (2005) for the analysis of principles.

of his early modern sources nor adheres to contemporary principles. However, his orthography is not unsystematic: he always opens the ligatures that occur in his sources (in a similar way as any professional Hellenist of his time would have done), and he usually follows the usage of majuscule and minuscule of his sources. As in many early modern prints, he does not use diacritics (especially accents) on or before the majuscule letters, although he occasionally uses the spiritus on majuscule, and always on minuscule letters. However, Scheller's differs from early modern prints in that he generally omits the acute and the gravis accents but retains the circumflex accents and the iota subscripts. The reasons for this practice are unclear, but do not seem to result from a lack of knowledge of Greek, because he seldom makes orthographic or grammatical mistakes in his transcripts.

2) Scheller as a compiler of printed sources from the 16th and 17th centuries:
Unlike in his study of Low German, Scheller focuses almost exclusively on printed sources from (mostly) the 16th and 17th centuries, with the two exceptions of his contemporary *philhellenes* and an inscription in Greek.[47] Not all the sources of poems in his corpus have yet been identified, but his manner of giving references to a short title, town and exact year makes it unlikely that his corpus will reveal transcripts from unique manuscript sources in the future. However, the corpus still includes texts and even entire prints which do not (to present knowledge) exist elsewhere, thus providing valuable source material for further studies.

3) Using books as reusable material and the status of occasional poetry:
In the history of the book, there have been practices that can be seen as destructive, such as reusing the parchment for writing or binding material, cutting out the woodcuts or other illustrations from old prints or manuscripts, and using books to make new paper, cartons, boxes, lamp covers and so on. The practice of making cuttings to place in a scrap album or recycling is acceptable to us when the materials destroyed are newspapers or battered old schoolbooks, but unacceptable when valuable old books are damaged. Scheller's attitude was not very different from ours as he seems to have similarly distinguished between books that could be destroyed for making his scrap-book and those that should remain intact. This is evident from an examination of the sources of his transcripts and the cuttings.

---

[47] There is at least one transcript of an inscription in Greek in Cod Guelf 872 Novi, f. 564. The two contemporary authors are Karl August Böttiger and Friedrich Thiersch (correspondingly in Dresdener *Abendzeitung*, No. 24, 27 January 1827 and No. 52, 1 March 1827), which also gives us the *terminus post quem* for the later (present-day) version of the corpus. For Böttiger, see Witzmann (2017); for Thiersch, Weise (2016, 147f).

The paratexts to humanist editions of ancient authors or manuals and the poems from humanist or religious poetry collections have either been transcribed by Scheller or referred to with source information. He (to my knowledge) never destroyed such prints. In the case of occasional prints, the situation is different. Entire quires of occasional poetry (a recommended treatment of an archival nowadays) have been included, but many are only partially included, and in numerous cases only a Greek poem (or poems) have been cut out from the original quire. The reason behind this practice lies in the status of occasional poetry collections in small quires which in the 19th century (and most of the 20th century) was much lower than the status of a printed book and more close to a status of modern newspapers.[48]

Thus we see that Scheller's approach to his 'material' was close to traditional antiquarian habits in many cases. Another question, to be discussed later, is whether he compiled his "Teutonic" corpus according to the standards of his contemporary scholars.

Authors and works not included in Scheller's corpus

Before turning to the authors who are represented with texts in Volumes 1–4 of Scheller's corpus, it is of some interest to look at the omitted authors. Curiously, these are often the best known German Humanist Greek poets. The book list (i.e. index 2 in the beginning of Volume 1) proves that Scheller was aware of these poets and valued their works. Did he intend to present these works separately in the future? We do not know, but it is possible that because of the fame and availabity of these editions, as well as the great number and length of these poems, he decided not to transcribe them (at least initially) and instead to present only references to the prints.

The above-named book list refers to a 'special collection' of about 40 printed books, which include Greek poems by "German" authors as main texts (in poetry collections) or as paratexts.[49] Currently it looks like a "virtual" collection (to use an anachronistic term), including:

---

[48] Except some funeral collections, which had source values for biographic literature, see Garber (2001, 7–10). For the status of Humanist Greek poetry, see Weise (2020, 381–383).

[49] On the definition of occasional and liminary texts, see Dam (2015). It is, however, clear that Scheller (like Lizel before him) does not distinguish between poetry proper and occasional or liminary poetry, although Scheller's editorial choices sometimes seem to follow these categories.

a) humanist editions of ancient Greek authors, such as *Ajax* of Sophocles (ed. by Josephus Justus Scaliger), Aristophanes' comedies (ed. by Nicodemus Frischlin), *Opus Aureum* (ed. by Michael Neander), Nonnus' *Paraphrasis* (ed. by Franciscus Nansius), Joachim Camerarius' commentary to the tragedies of Sophocles and a yet unidentified edition of Theocritus;

b) humanist manuals or different editions of school texts, such as *Erotemata Graeca* by M. Neander, Neander's translation of Luther's catechesis and J.J. Scaliger's translations of Cato and the Latin Mimes;

c) editions of poetry collections by humanist poets, such as Lampertus Alardus, Joachim Camerarius, Johannes Caselius, Martin Crusius, Heinrich Decimator, Daniel Heinsius, Nicolaus Leutinger, Hiob Magdeburgus, Johannes Mylius, Wilhelm Pistorius (included because it contained Greek poems by other authors), Joseph Justus Scaliger, Johannes Vagetius, Johannes Vorstius and Joseph Wurtzler. All of these collections are known to scholars and well documented.[50] We also find some more enigmatic references to the collected poems of Balthasar Crusius, Zach. Faber, Arnold Staubsand and Thomas Hopmann.[51] The first index contains vague references to a separate collection (*v. Separ.*) that includes Lorenz Rhodoman whose poems – but only some – appear at the end of the defective Volume 4;

d) so-called *Carmina sacra*, such as collections of Psalm paraphrases by Aemilius Portus, Paulus Dolscius and Maximos Margounios; other editions that include biblical paraphrases, such as Johann Caspar Schweizer's Ἐμπύρημα εὐσεβείης (with Joh. Ailmer's Greek paraphrases); and a reference to Christian verse oration by Justus Tetzelerus, Ἱστορία τῶν τοῦ κυρίου Ἰησοῦ θαυμάτων, διὰ στίχων ἡρωικῶν (Hamburg 1592);

---

[50] They were not all known to Lizel, who omits Lampertus Alardus, Heinrich Decimator, Daniel Heinsius, Wilhelm Pistorius, Joseph Justus Scaliger, Johannes Vagetius, Johannes Vorstius and Joseph Wurtzler, see Weise (2020, 407–408). Some (Scaliger, Heinsius) were possibly excluded because of their non-German origin, but not all.

[51] Some books have been difficult to find: M. Balth. Crusii [...] *Hymni Lips* 1591 (*M.ppr.*); M. Zachaeus Faber *Prima & II. pars Medullae*, Halle in Sachsen 1619 (*M.ppr.*); M. Arnoldi Staubsandi *Chatti, Cithara Casselii*s 1641.12vo. (*Gr. M.ppr.*). The work by Thom. Hopmann, *de IV. seculis ad imit. l.i. Hesiodi* ἔργων καὶ ἡμερων *in ejusd Hexaemero.* Rinteln 1665. 4to. (*M.ppr.*) is probably available in Oldenburg Landesbibliothek.

e) editions of poetry by Greek authors from late antiquity to the Renaissance, such as Gregory of Nazianzus, Christophoros Pelargos and Maximos Margounios, or a collection including different texts from the antiquity to Gemisthios Plethon, under a title *Doctrina recte vivendi et moriendi* (Basel 1577);

g) some occasional poetry collections, for example a collection by Martin Gosky (*Arbustum vel Arboretum,* Wolfenbüttel 1650) for Duke August of Lüneburg, or a collection of occasional poetry by Naumburg poets which is also referred to in several cases in the first index as *separ.*[52]

All these references in the indices and the collection proper point to two conclusions: firstly, as far as collecting and transcribing poems is considered, Scheller's *Carmina* was still a work in progress, and secondly, perhaps only a part of his Greek poetry collection (which did not include all the best known authors) was acquired by HAB.

Scheller as a Compiler of a 'Teutonic' Corpus

Scheller's casual remark in his *Bücherkunde,* referring to almost 500 authors of whom 2/3 are Saxons, is a valid description of *Carmina Hellenica* in its present state: according to my initial counts, 497 authors (including 5 anonymous) are mentioned in his corpus, of whom 445 are represented with a total of 726 poems, while 52 more authors are mentioned (see above).

The distribution of poems by authors

The ratio of the number of poems to the number of authors in the corpus is 726 to 497 (or 445 when only authors whose poems are included are counted) which means that, on average, a poet is represented with 1.5 poems in a corpus. However, the number of poems representing each author varies considerably, as seen from Chart 1.

---

[52] *Arbustum vel Arboretum* includes reprints of dedicatory poetry for celebrating different occasions in the history of the dynasty, among others 12 Greek poems, but only one anonymous author is referred to as transcribed in the book-list (others, all transcribed, are referred to in the first index).

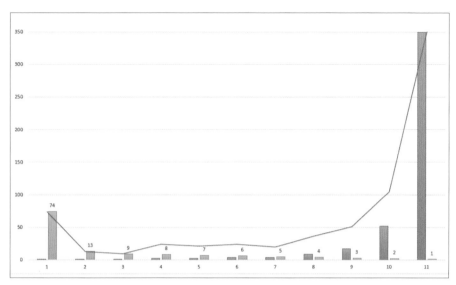

Chart 1. Distribution of poems by authors. Left column: number of authors, right column: number of poems by one author.

The chart reveals that in addition to the 350 authors who are represented in the corpus with only one poem and 52 authors who are represented with two poems, there are only 43 authors who are represented with three or more poems and only one author, Johannes Caselius, who is represented in Scheller's corpus with as much as 78 poems. Within the last group of 43, the greater the number of representative poems the lower the number of authors: only 17 authors are represented with more than five and only two with more than 10 poems (counting the transcripts of poems, not references).

The high percentage of authors from Braunschweig-Lüneburg who are represented with one or two poems (103 out of 126, with 206 Braunschweig poets listed in the index), suggests that Scheller's intention was to include all authors of Greek poems from his home region, Braunschweig-Lüneburg, where he collected his poems. For other regions there appears to be no rigorous selection principle, if we do not count a connection to the region via printing place (there are about 20 other prints from Braunschweig, Goslar, Helmstedt, Wolfenbüttel and Lüneburg with Greek poems by other authors) or the addressees.

The most represented authors in the collection

The most represented author in the collection is Johannes Caselius with 74 poems, which corresponds to his status as the most prolific Humanist Greek poet in the

Duchy of Braunschweig-Lüneburg.[53] His poems in *Carmina Hellenica Teutonum* are introduced by a separate title, its reference to the year 1822 indicating an earlier stage of Scheller's collection (orthography unchanged):[54]

ΙΩΑΝΝΟΥ τοῦ ΚΑΣΗΛΙΟΥ| ΕΛΛΗΝΙΚΑ ΑΠΑΝΤΑ | ἀπο | Καρολου Φρεδ. Ἀρενδ. Σχελλερ.| 1822. | Βρουνωνος ἐν ἄστεϊ. |

This sub-part starts with Konrad Horn's *epicedium* commemorating Caselius' death and includes transcripts of Caselius' poems, most of which can be found in two editions: *Johannis Caselii Carminum Graecorum et Latinorum Centuria Prima* (Göttingen 1668) and *Oratio Dominica aliis atque aliis* (Helmstedt 1610), the latter presenting Greek verse paraphrases of the Lord's Prayer and entirely transcribed by Caselius. Although there are manuscripts and prints with Caselius' other Greek poems at HAB, Scheller has not included them.

Apart from Caselius, eight of the other best represented 15 authors of the collection come from Braunschweig-Lüneburg. The rector of Braunschweig St. Aegidius School, Werner Cuno (1600–1657), is represented with eight occasional poems in different verse forms; he can be regarded as a poet of local importance, because he is not included in Lizel's account of German Greek poets.[55] The same is true for the rector of Braunschweig St. Martin School (afterwards Superintendent in Goslar), Martin Baremius (–1625), whose five occasional poems (*epithalamia* and book epigrams) are presented in Scheller's corpus.[56] The status of local poet can also be ascribed to Carl Bumann (ca. 1551–1610), who is best known for his long period of activity in Braunschweig (as the rector of St. Catherine and of St. Martin School), and to the Conrector and Rector of St. Martin School

---

[53] He worked in Dresden and Rostock for long periods and has also been regarded as a representative of Rostock, but his letters from this time reveal that he desperately wanted to obtain a post in Braunschweig-Lüneburg, in which he succeeded, finally becoming a Professor of Law in Helmstedt University.

[54] Cod. Guelf. 870 Novi, 58r–101r.

[55] See http://d-nb.info/gnd/1055508821. He is also mentioned in Bollmeyer 2014, 111. For the list of poets mentioned by Lizel (here and further), see Weise (2020, 405–409).

[56] See http://d-nb.info/gnd/115782702. There are seven texts of poems by Baremius in Scheller's collection, but two of these (for the wedding of Auctor Hustetus) appear twice, as transcriptions in Vol.1 and included in an occasional poetry collection in Vol. 2. Scheller also gives a reference to another poem by Baremius.

in Braunschweig Christoph Hagius (died 1640).[57] Bumann and Hagius are both represented with seven occasional poems and also omitted by Lizel.

In Scheller's corpus there are some other Braunschweig poets who gained national fame, at least in the eyes of Lizel. The professor of Greek at Helmstedt University, Johann Brennecius (1599–1655),[58] and the professor of Theology in Helmstedt University, Konrad Horn (Conrad Horneius, 1590–1649),[59] are both represented with six occasional poems. A relatively unknown *Poeta Laureatus* and the Rector of Lüneburg St. Johannes School, Johann Georg Kettembeil (1624–1675), is represented with five occasional poems.[60] Of these authors Horn is the best known to modern scholars, albeit more for his role as an Evangelical theologian than for his poetry.

Other authors represented with more than five poems are not from Braunschweig. The most famous among them is Martin Crusius (1526–1607) from Tübingen, who is represented with 13 occasional poems, including a presently unidentified transcript of a funeral poem for Caspar Hedio and several dedicatory epigrams in humanist editions, for example for Neander and Melissus.[61] Illfeld School rector Michael Neander (1525–1595) is represented with transcriptions of seven poems in Volume 4 and references to many others.[62] The Rostock scholar Johannes Posselius the Elder (1528–1591)[63] is represented with six poems, and a little less famous but no less prolific Johannes Lundorp (active 1575–1600) with five occasional poems.[64] These authors belong to the heyday of Humanist Greek poets in the second half of the 16th century and are

---

[57] Bumann had also worked in different schools in Berlin, Jena and Königsberg, see http://d-nb.info/gnd/12343839X and http://thesaurus.cerl.org/record/cnp01303464, as well as Bollmeyer (2014, 357). For Hagius, see http://d-nb.info/gnd/119696940 and Bollmeyer (2014, 267).

[58] http://d-nb.info/gnd/104308761, Bollmeyer (2014, 76).

[59] http://d-nb.info/gnd/116993901, Bollmeyer (2014, 74, 76, 94, 109, 138, 149, 327, 488).

[60] http://d-nb.info/gnd/104368624. In Gosky's *Arbustum* (1650), under No. XXIV of the dedicatory epigrams to Gosky, he is named *Poeta Laureatus Caesareus*, but Flood (2006) does not include him in his account.

[61] Cod. Guelf 872 Novi, pp. 88–99 (Scheller's initial order Vol. III–41). For Crusius, see Widmann, Hans, "Crusius, Martin", in NDB 3 (1957), 433–434, URL: https://www.deutsche-biographie.de/pnd118677446.html#ndbcontent and for him as a Hellenist, see Ludwig (2014), Ludwig (2017, 125–131) (and also his earlier works).

[62] http://d-nb.info/gnd/116901675 and G. Baur, "Neander, Michael", in ADB 23 (1886), 341–345, URL: https://www.deutsche-biographie.de/pnd116901675.html#adbcontent.

[63] For Posselius, see Johnson (2006).

[64] http://d-nb.info/gnd/119748630 and http://thesaurus.cerl.org/record/cnp01105176.

today mostly known for their epic, didactic or religious works, but (with the exception of Neander) Scheller includes mainly their occasional poetry.

Alongside these nationally and internationally known poets, Scheller includes works by some other authors who are omitted from Lizel's account of German *Hellenisers*. Two of them were medical doctors like Scheller himself. The Altdorf professor of Medicine, Caspar Hofmann (1572–1648), is represented by nine transcripts from one collection: *Poematum sacrorum centuria* [...] *Novenarius poematum graecorum*.[65] The Leipzig professor of Medicine, Johannes Siglicius (Siegelitz) from Halle (1576–1620), is represented by five transcripts of occasional poems and three references to others. Siegelitz is important as the author of the first known Greek disputation (with Latin translation) from Basel, and of other almost macaronic medical disputations.[66] Scheller also includes transcriptions of six occasional poems by Wittenberg Theologian and *Poeta Laureatus* Johann Förster (1576–1613)[67] and five occasional poems by Sebastian Winterstein (died 1626), colleague in Eisleben Gymnasium and cantor in St. Nicholas church.[68] These include dedicatory epigrams for books, but mostly *epicedia* and *epithalamia*. Scheller also included five transcripts of poems by the famous humanist scholar and Hellenist Karel (Carl) Utenhove (1536–1600), who was possibly omitted by Lizel because of his Flemish origin, although he was active mainly in Germany.[69]

Thus we see a mixture of very well known and relatively unknown Greek poets and a focus on Braunschweig-Lüneburg and Saxony. An analysis of printing towns will further explain Scheller's choice of authors.

The meaning of 'Teutonic' for Scheller

Scheller's understanding of 'German' or 'Teutonic' was criticised from the linguistic point of view by Grimm but explained by Blume (see above). In fact, Scheller's usage does not differ much from that of his early modern sources, taking

---

[65] Altdorf (1651), VD17 23:283719P, Cod. Guelf. Novi 872, p. 228–238. For biography, see Hirsch, August, "Hofmann, Kaspar", in ADB 12 (1880), 635, URL: https://www.deutsche-biographie.de/pnd116951753.html#adbcontent.

[66] For Siglicius, see http://thesaurus.cerl.org/record/cnp01022907 and Päll (2020, 730–731).

[67] See http://d-nb.info/gnd/117520918. Possibly omitted by Lizel because he wrote only occasional poetry in Greek and was better known as an Evangelical Theologian? See also http://thesaurus.cerl.org/record/cnp02076134, and Flood (2006, 136).

[68] See Ellendt (1846, 61).

[69] See NDB, https://d-nb.info/gnd/121650723, see also "Utenhove, Karel" in DB, https://www.deutsche-biographie.de/pnd121650723.html.

'German' (or Teutonic) to refer to different regions speaking German dialects or Germanic languages, as was done by Frank Hieronymus' in his catalogue of Basel Greek prints: Ἐν Βασιλέᾳ πόλει τῆς Γερμανίας ('In Basel, city of Germany').[70]

Accordingly, we find several Swiss (Jacob Ceporinus, Conrad Gessner and Johann Caspar Schweizer) and Flemish (Isaac Casaubon, Geraart Falkenburg, Jacob Gruter, Daniel Heinsius, Karl von Utenhove, Bonaventura Vulcanius) authors in Scheller's corpus. Some 'foreign' authors could have been included because of their activity in Germany or the Low Countries, such as Joseph Justus Scaliger, Matthias Flaccus Illyricus and Karl von Utenhove.[71] Aemilius Portus (1550–1614/1615) also spent most of his life in Switzerland (Geneva) and Germany (Heidelberg); Scheller refers to his 1581 Basel edition of the Psalms.[72]

Even the inclusion of seemingly very distant persons can be explained by their connections to Germany. For example, the above-mentioned Maximos Margounios is named in both of Scheller's indices. However, we do not find Margounios' Psalm paraphrases, which were published in Strassburg 1601 (*Maximi Margunii Hymni Anacreontici*) in Scheller's corpus. There is just a reference to one of its paratexts, an Anacreontic version of the Lord's Prayer by the editor Rittershausen's uncle Matthias Berg. Rittershausen came from an old Lüneburg family and studied Law in Helmstedt, and although he worked for most of his life as a professor of Law in Altdorf, he and Berg both fall under the category of Braunschweig poets.[73]

However, most of the last-named authors are represented with only one or two poems (the only exception is Karl von Utenhove with five poems). Thus it is clear that Scheller's understanding of 'Teutonic' included the Low Countries and Switzerland, but his focus is on Germany proper. Whether it is enough for a classification of Scheller's corpus as national, the following analysis of printing towns will reveal.

---

[70] See Hieronymus (1992), online as GG since 2004: https://ub.unibas.ch/cmsdata/spezialkataloge/gg/.

[71] There are some exceptions to the rule: some French authors (Guillaume Budé and Pierre Belon du Mans) and two more authors of Greek descent, such as Janus Lascaris and Maximos Margounios.

[72] Hoche, Richard, "Portus, Aemilius", in ADB 26 (1888), 447–449, URL: https://www.deutsche-biographie.de/pnd124362427.html#adbcontent.

[73] Duve, Thomas, "Rittershausen, Konrad", in NDB 21 (2003), 670–671, URL: https://www.deutsche-biographie.de/pnd104288639.html#ndbcontent.

Scheller's Carmina as a regional corpus: an analysis of printing towns

As the sources of almost all poems in the collection are printed works, an overview of printing towns is useful. The poems in Volumes 1–3 have been printed in 62 towns (see Chart 1), mainly in Germany, but also in Switzerland (Basel, Geneva), France (Strasbourg, Paris), Netherlands (Leiden), Prussia (Königsberg), Poland/ Silesia (Olsna), Sweden (Stockholm) and Austria (Vienna). However, most of the towns outside Germany (except for Basel and Strasbourg) are of low significance statistically and occur in the list largely because they include poems by 'German' authors.[74]

Therefore, although Scheller included some works printed in Switzerland, Alsace and the Low Countries, we see that he had as a rule excluded books from other German-speaking regions such as Prussia, Silesia and Austria.[75] The rarity of works printed outside Germany indicates that Scheller did not focus on detecting every work by German authors.

Another question, to what extent Scheller's corpus can be regarded as representative of Humanist Greek poetry from 16th–17th century Germany, can be further answered by analysing the numbers of poems from different towns.

As Chart 2 shows, the poems in the corpus were printed in 62 towns. However, this number includes 20 towns that are represented by one poem only (including such important centres of Greek studies as Augsburg, Erfurt and Dresden) and 14 towns that are represented by 2–4 poems (including important printing towns like Lübeck, Greifswald and Geneva). That leaves only 25 towns where more than 5 poems were printed, 15 towns where more than 10 poems were printed and only 8 towns (Helmstedt, Leipzig, Braunschweig, Wittenberg, Göttingen, Frankfurt am Main, Jena, Hildesheim) where 20 or more poems were printed.

Helmstedt, with 103 printed poems, owes its highest place to 26 transcripts of different versions of the Lord's Prayer by Johannes Caselius, from the 1610 Helmstedt collection.[76] Similarly, Wolfenbüttel has 16 poems owing to transcripts

---

[74] For example, a poem published in Stockholm by Petrus Pachius, of Pomeranian origin, or a poem by Ceporinus pubished in Vienna.

[75] There are only a few exceptions: Königsberg is represented by a poem by Henning Henningi from Holstein; Memel and Danzig are absent, whereas Stettin in Pomerania is not regarded as 'Prussian' and is represented by 14 poems; Olsna in Silesia is included because of a poem by a Saxon author, Johann Siglicius, but Breslau is completely ignored.

[76] Although Scheller usually refers to original publishing dates, it is also possible that he transcribed most of Caselius' other poems from their reprints in his *Opera Omnia*, Göttingen edition, as he did in the case of Gosky's *Arbustum*.

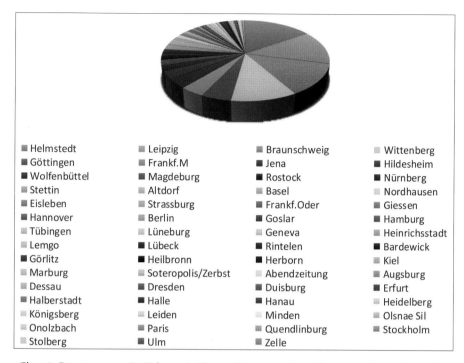

■ Helmstedt	■ Leipzig	■ Braunschweig	■ Wittenberg
■ Göttingen	■ Frankf.M	■ Jena	■ Hildesheim
■ Wolfenbüttel	■ Magdeburg	■ Rostock	■ Nürnberg
■ Stettin	■ Altdorf	■ Basel	■ Nordhausen
■ Eisleben	■ Strassburg	■ Frankf.Oder	■ Giessen
■ Hannover	■ Berlin	■ Goslar	■ Hamburg
■ Tübingen	■ Lüneburg	■ Geneva	■ Heinrichsstadt
■ Lemgo	■ Lübeck	■ Rintelen	■ Bardewick
■ Görlitz	■ Heilbronn	■ Herborn	■ Kiel
■ Marburg	■ Soteropolis/Zerbst	■ Abendzeitung	■ Augsburg
■ Dessau	■ Dresden	■ Duisburg	■ Erfurt
■ Halberstadt	■ Halle	■ Hanau	■ Heidelberg
■ Königsberg	■ Leiden	■ Minden	■ Olsnae Sil
■ Onolzbach	■ Paris	■ Quendlinburg	■ Stockholm
■ Stolberg	■ Ulm	■ Zelle	

Chart 2. Printing towns (in Volumes 1–3) according to numbers of poems in diminishing order, from left above to right.

from one source, Gosky's *Arbustum* (1650), which includes prints or reprints of 12 Greek poems by eight different authors dedicated to the Braunschweig-Lüneburg ducal dynasty.

If we omit these exceptions, we can see that there are four preeminent printing towns, each represented by more than 70 poems in Greek and clustered around Braunschweig-Lüneburg. Helmstedt and Braunschweig prints represent the region and include the greatest number of occasional poems such as *epicedia* and *epithalamia*; in Scheller's day Wittenberg was nationally and internationally the most important Lutheran university town and pioneer of Greek studies: its prints include a lot of *epicedia* but also poetry connected to university studies such as gratulations for graduations or university dissertations. Leipzig was an important centre of humanist printing and therefore furnished a large amount of the liminary poetry found in the corpus.

This analysis has revealed that some of the regions comprising modern Germany are underrepresented, such as Bavaria, Swabia (Baden-Württemberg), Schleswig-Holstein (with Lübeck), Mecklenburg-Western Pomerania and Saxony. Although Scheller includes poems printed in different parts of Germany, his collection can be regarded as representative for the Braunschweig-Lüneburg region only, with some admissions for Saxony-Anhalt and Lower Saxony. Thus, despite its title, we can speak only of a regional corpus within Germany and not a national one.

Scheller's Corpus of Humanist Greek Poetry: the Distribution of Genres

The next question is whether Scheller's corpus can be regarded as representative in respect of all genres of humanist Greek poetry. Because this study is in its preliminary phase, only some general features can be brought out.

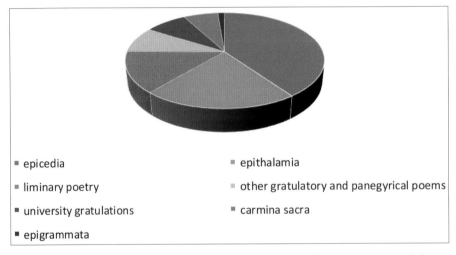

Chart 3. Genres of poems in *Carmina Hellenica*. The percentages of *epicedia* (40%), *epithalamia* (21%), liminary poetry (14%), other gratulatory poetry (9%), university poetry (8%), *Carmina sacra* (7%), epigrams and lyric poetry (1%)

If we look in the corpus for the genres with the highest status, we will see at once that Scheller has excluded epic poetry, probably because of the length of the epic poems. For instance, Lorenz Rhodoman's epic poetry is not even mentioned, although some of his occasional poems are included in the corpus.[77] But we will see examples of a related genre of a very high status, religious poetry, which was immensely popular in the second half of the 16th century. This genre is represented with 47 poems, including Greek prayers in verse (mostly Lord's

---

[77] For Rhodoman, see Ludwig (2014), Weise (2019, esp. 12–26).

Prayers by Caselius) and Greek versifications of the Psalms and other Biblical paraphrases, as well as four verse orations for Christian Holidays. The boundaries between these genres are not very clear and in case of poetry in hexametre they have often been classed together as biblical epic, which was very popular from the 1540s to the mid-1700s.[78] However, in the above statistics *Carmina sacra* are underrepresented, because Scheller often gives references only to the collections of religious poems, but not the texts themselves.

The third most elevated genre in the second half of the 16th century, Pindaric ode, is missing from the chart, because the statistics are based on generic division by occasions in order to compare the results with the analyses of Neo-Latin poetry. However, Scheller's corpus includes five Pindaric odes by different authors which are classified as belonging to different occasional genres (*epicedia*, an *epithalamion* and a gratulatory poem). Some of these are by well-known authors of Pindaric odes, such as Nicolaus Reusner and Erasmus Schmidt, some by less known authors, such as the Braunschweig authors Jacob Käseberg, Michael Würtzler and Jeremias Spiegel.[79] Another extremely popular genre, epigram, is represented by fewer examples than expected because many epigrams have been classified as liminary poetry (such as dedicatory book epigrams), but also because epigrams (as well as lyric poems proper) that were published in the editions of collected poetry of different humanists (such as Alardus or others) are not represented in *Carmina Hellenica* as texts but only as references to publications.

If we look at Chart 3, we can see that the prevailing genre in the corpus is *epicedium* with almost 290 (287) poems. The poetic features of such *epicedia* can differ considerably: in Scheller's corpus we find Psalm paraphrases and Pindaric odes, but also many typical funeral poems in elegies and hexametres. This corresponds to our picture of occasional poetry in Neo-Latin. Also, the second most represented genre *epithalamia* or wedding poetry with about 150 (151) poems, is similar to the genres of Neo-Latin poetry. As in the case of the *epicedia*, the choice of poetic features and meters varies greatly.[80]

The third group by importance in the corpus is liminary poetry with 100 examples, including congratulatory epigrams (the most eminent subgroup), but

---

[78] The number of Psalm paraphrases could even be bigger, because sometimes poems for weddings or funerals were in the form of versified psalms. See Weise (2020) (39 examples) and Czapla (2013) (11+4 examples), my figures include 32 examples of paraphrases, 36 other biblical orations and a further (3) orations on more loosely Christian subjects.

[79] For this genre, see Päll (2017).

[80] See for Greek poetry, Päll (2014), Veteikis (2004), Korhonen (2004), Akujärvi (forthcoming), for Latin, Dam (2014).

also addresses to the public and dedications by the authors of humanist editions. In fourth place we see a varied group of 62 poems for different occasions: poems for inaugurations, panegyrics (for the members of Braunschweig-Lüneburg dynasty or other important persons), *genethliaca*, *propemptica* and some other congratulatory verses for rarer occasions.

In fifth place we find poems for students: mostly poems for graduation (obtaining a master's or doctor's degree), but also some gratulatory poems for presenting orations and dissertations. However, when we compare the distribution of genres in Scheller's corpus and Nordic Greek corpuses, the much greater prominence of the genres connected to academic studies in the Nordic corpora appears surprising, as congratulatory poems for disputations and orations or for promotions and other events of academic life are much more frequent and hold the first place.[81] Whether this is the result of a much greater importance of universities in the practice of Humanist Greek in the case of Nordic countries (as I tend to believe),[82] or the lack of relevant studies for German university dissertations is something that needs to be ascertained by future research.

Evaluation and Conclusions

Scheller's activities in Germanic studies were vehemently criticised by Jacob Grimm: although Scheller brought many works in Low German which professional scholars had missed to the attention of readers, Grimm thought he did it in a totally unprofessional and unacceptable manner, among other things by using strange orthography, not distinguishing between different manuscripts, failing to specify his sources exactly and not taking into account the discussions of specialists. Herbert Blume has pointed out that Grimm missed the point: Scheller was not a linguist and editor, but a language moderniser like Johannes Aavik in Estonia and several scholars in the Nordic countries, who have all been praised by later generations.[83] However, all these men achieved most of their goals and promoted the development of their mother language (Aavik's ideas

---

[81] For a general picture of the Nordic corpora and Estonia, see Päll (2020), Päll (2013), for Sweden, Akujärvi (forthcoming), for Finland, Korhonen (2004), for Germany (focusing on Lizel), Weise (2020).

[82] Päll (2020).

[83] Blume (1992); philhellenism harmonizing with Romanticism in Poland, see Axer & Tomaszuk (2007, 148–150).

on orthography did not prevail, but hundreds of his newly coined words have become a accepted as part of the everyday Estonian language), whereas Scheller's 'sässisch' died out.

We can make a similar qualified judgement on Scheller's Greek corpus. His lack of editorial principles (strange orthography of diacritics, no clear references to sources, no clearly stated principles behind his compilation of the corpus) are as unacceptable for modern scholars as they would have been for contemporary Hellenists (had they been aware of his work), although even stranger orthographies can be seen in the output of less well-equipped printing-houses of that time. In addition, every book historian must wince when they look at his scrapbook, for which numerous valuable early modern occasional poetry collections were sacrificed. However, his activity as a collector of information and texts (which were usually transcribed without mistakes) demands respect: he compiled something valuable, a regional corpus of Braunschweig Greek poets, and also provided a lot of information on other German Hellenising poets.

The main goal of this article (and the paper at the Helsinki conference) was to bring Scheller's corpus to the attention of scholars who study the Greek tradition in Germany. I believe that this has been achieved. Another aim was to look into the relationships between philhellenism as part of Neo-Humanism and the contemporary emergence of professionalism and specialisation. In the context of today's crowdsourcing we need to think more about the role of amateurs in research.

There, is, however, more research to be done. Taking Scheller's *Bücherkunde* (and Blume's references to his manuscripts) as a basis, some (Low) German translations of ancient authors (Horace, Propertius, Aratus) could find their place in the study of classical reception in Germany, as could Scheller's own translations of Horace. On the basis of Scheller's corpus and the HAB corpus of digitised Helmstedt University dissertations, it would be relatively easy to create a complete Braunschweig-Lüneburg corpus of Humanist Greek, which could be compared to other regional and national humanist Greek corpora and reveal the nature of Greek poetry in Welfenland, including identification of the favoured forms and the features which reflect the social context (poems for courts, clerics, universities or learned gymnasia).

As a scholar who studies texts, I would have liked to present some exciting details from Scheller's corpus. However, this must wait for the future, and perhaps then "Miserable Karl" will become known as "Persistent Karl" and receive a little appreciation for the fruits of his passion.

Bibliography

Manuscripts

Carmina Hellenica Teutonum impressa necnon manuscripta. Collecta a Carolo F. A. Scheller medico Brunswicensi. Tom. I & II continent poemata graeca Brunswicensium. Herzog August Bibliothek, Cod. Guelf. 870–873 Novi.

Books printed before 1800

Gosky, Martin. 1650. *Arbustum vel Arboretum Augustaeum, aeternitati ac domui Augustae Selenianae sacrum, satum autem & educatum.* Wolfenbüttel.
Lizel, Georg 1730. *Historia Poetarum Graecorum Germaniae.* Frankfurt–Leipzig–Ulm.

Modern works

ADB = *Allgemeine Deutsche Biographie*, https://www.deutsche-biographie.de/pnd116951753.html#adbcontent.
Akujärvi, Johanna (forthcoming). "*Versificandi mania*. University Teaching of Greek and Greek Verses in Dissertations in Sweden", in Federica Ciccolella & Luigi Silvano (eds.) *Graecia transvolavit Alpes: The Study of Greek in Early Modern Europe* (Brill's Studies in Intellectual History). Leiden.
Axer, Jerzy & Tomaszuk, Katarzyna. 2007. "Central-Eastern Europe", in Craig W. Kallendorf (ed.) *A Companion to the Classical Tradition*, Malden (Mass.)–Oxford, 132–155.
Barker, Nicholas. 1992. *Aldus Manutius and the Development of Greek Script & Type in the Fifteenth Century.* New York.
Blume, Herbert. 1992. "Karl Friedrich Arend Scheller und das "Sassische"", in *Braunschweigisches und Ostfälisches. Gedenkschrift für Werner Fleissig*, Braunschweig, 51–68.
Blume, Herbert. 2009. "Zweimal "Henneke Knecht". Hoffmann von Fallersleben und Karl Friedrich Arend Scheller als editoren mittelniederdeutscher Texte", in Norbert Otto Eke & Kurt G.P. Schuster & Günter Tiggesbäumker (eds.) *Hoffmann von Fallersleben. Internationales Symposion Corvey/Höxter 2008*, Bielefeld, 195–226.

Bollmeyer, Matthias. 2014. *Lateinisches Welfenland: eine literaturgeschichtliche Kartographie zur lateinischen Gelegenheitsdichtung im Herzogtum Braunschweig-Lüneburg im 16. und 17. Jahrhundert.* Hildesheim.

Bommel, Bas van. 2015. *Classical Humanism and the Challenge of Modernity. Debates on Classical Education in 19th-century Germany.* Berlin.

Classen, Carl Joachim. 2002. "'Über das Alter der "klassischen Philologie"', *Hermes* 130:4, 490–497.

Considine, John. 2008. *Dictionaries in Early Modern Europe.* Cambridge.

Dam, Harm-Jan van. 2009. "Some facts and figures on Neo-Latin occasional poetry", in W. Verbaal, Y. Maes & J. Papy (eds.), *Latinitas perennis*, Vol. II: *Appropriation and Latin Literature*, Leiden, 125–126.

Dam, Harm-Jan van. 2015. "Poems on the Threshold: Neo-Latin *carmina liminaria*", in A. Steiner-Weber *et al.* (eds.) *Acta Conventus Neo-Latini Monasteriensis*, Leiden–Boston, 50–81.

Delz, Josef. 1997. "Textkritik und Editionstechnik", in Fritz Graf (ed.) *Einleitung in die lateinische Philologie*, Wiesbaden, 51–111.

Deufert, Diane. 2011. *Matthias Bergius (1536–1592). Antike Dichtungstradition im konfessionellen Zeitalter* (Hypomnemata 186). Göttingen.

Dover, Kenneth. 1997. "Textkritik", in Hans-Günther Nesselrath (ed.) *Einleitung in die griechische Philologie*, Stuttgart–Leipzig, 45–58.

Ebert, Friedrich Adolf. 1827. *Zur Handschriftenkunde. Bibliothecae Guelferbytanae Codices Graeci et Latini Classici.* Leipzig.

Eckart, Rudolf. 1911. *Handbuch zur Geschichte der plattdeutschen Literatur*, Bremen, 334–339.

Eisenberg, Christian & Müller-Jerina, Alwin. 1997. "Bibliothek des Predigerseminars der Evangelisch-Lutherischen Landeskirche in Braunschweig", in Bernhard Fabian *et al.* (eds.) *Handbuch der historischen Buchbestände in Deutschland. Digitalisiert von Günter Kükenshöner*, Hildesheim, 71–74. http://fabian.sub.uni-goettingen.de/fabian?Bibliothek_Des_Predigerseminars_Der_Evangelisch-Lutherischen_Landeskirche_In_Braunschweig (retrieved 30 July 2020).

Ellendt, Friedrich. 1846. *Geschichte des Königlichen Gymnasiums zu Eisleben. Eine Jubelschrift.* Eisleben.

Flood, John L. 2006. *Poets Laureate in the Roman Empire.* Berlin.

Garber, Klaus. 2001. "Vorwort zum Gesamtwerk", in Klaus Garber *et al.* (eds.) *Handbuch des personalen Gelegenheitsschrifttums in europäischen Bibliotheken und Archiven*, Bd. I, Abt. I. Teil 1, Hildesheim, 7–12.

Geanakoplos, Deno John. 1962. *Greek Scholars in Venice: studies in the dissemination of Greek learning from Byzantium to Western Europe.* Cambridge (Mass.).

Geanakoplos, Deno John. 1966. *Byzantine East and Latin West: Two Worlds of Christendom in Middle Ages and Renaissance* (*Studies in Ecclesiastical and Cultural History*). New York.

Grafton, Anthony & Glenn W. Most. 1997. "Philologie und Bildung seit der Renaissance", in Fritz Graf (ed.) *Einleitung in die lateinische Philologie*, Wiesbaden, 35–48.

Grafton, Anthony, Glenn W. Most & Salvatore Settis (eds.) 2013. *The Classical Tradition.* Cambridge (Mass.)–London.

Grimm, Jacob. 1869. *Kleinere Schriften IV.* Berlin.

Heinemann, Otto von. 1884. *Die Handschriften der Herzoglichen Bibliothek zu Wolfenbüttel. Abth. 1: Die Helmstedter Handschriften.* Bd. 3. Wolfenbüttel.

Herklotz, Ingo. 2011. "Der Antiquar als komische Figur. Ein literarisches Motiv zwischen Querelle und altertumswissenschaftlicher Methodenreflexion", in Ulrich Heinen & Elisabeth Klecker (eds.) *Welche Antike? Konkurrierende Rezeptionen des Altertums im Barock.* Band 1. Wiesbaden, 141–182.

Hieronymus, Frank (ed.) 1992. Ἐν Βασιλέᾳ Βασιλείᾳ πόλει τῆς Γερμανίας. *Griechischer Geist aus Basler Pressen* [= GG]. *Universitätsbibliothek Basel 4. Juli bis 22. August 1992. Staatsbibliothek zu Berlin – Preussischer Kulturbesitz – 28. Januar bis 6. März 1993. Gutenberg-Museum, Mainz 8. Juni bis 29. August 1993.* Basel.

Hoffmeister, Kurt 2003. *Braunschweigs Literaten: Über 150 Autorenportraits.* Braunschweig.

Humboldt, Wilhelm von. 1903. "Über das Studium des Altertums und des Griechischen insbesondere" – Werke, Bd. I Abteilung I. Berlin, 255–281.

Hunger, Herbert. 1997. "Die Handschriftliche Überlieferung in Mittelalter und früher Neuzeit; Paläographie", in Hans-Günther Nesselrath (ed.) *Einleitung in die griechische Philologie*, Stuttgart–Leipzig, 17–44.

Ingram, William H. 1966. "The ligatures of Early Printed Greek", *Greek, Roman and Byzantine Studies* 7, 371–389.

Irmscher, Johannes. 1966. "Der deutsche Philhellenismus als politisches Anliegen", *Byzantion* 36, 74–96. https://www.jstor.org/stable/i40174178 (retrieved 22 February 2020).

Jansen-Sieben, Ria. 1968. *De natuurkunde van het geheelal: Een 13de-eews Middelnederlands Leerdicht.* Volumes 1–2. Bruxelles.

Kallendorf, Craig W. (ed.) 2007. *A Companion to the Classical tradition.* Malden (Mass.)–Oxford–Carlton.

Korhonen, Tua. 2004. *Ateena Auran rannoilla. Humanistikreikkaa Kuninkaallisesta Turun akatemiasta.* Diss. Helsinki (with an English Summary), http: // ethesis.helsinki.fi/julkaisut /hum/klass/vk/korhonen2/ateenaau.pdf.

Landfester, Manfred. 2003. "Neuhumanismus", in Gert Ueding *et al.* (eds.) *Historisches Wörterbuch der Rhetorik. Bd. 6 Must-Pop*, Tübingen, 223–231.

Landfester, Martin. 1988. *Humanismus und Gesellschaft im 19. Jahrhundert. Untersuchuchen zur politischen und gesellschaftlichen Bedeutung der humanistischen Bildung in Deutschland.* Darmstadt.

Lizel, Georg. 1730. *Historia Poetarum Graecorum Germaniae.* Frankfurt–Leipzig–Ulm.

Ludwig, Walther. 2014. "Der Humanist Laurentius Rhodomanus als griechischer Dichter Laurentios Rhodoman und seine Autobiographie von 1582", *Neulateinisches Jahrbuch* 16, 137–171.

Ludwig, Walther. 2017. "*Scitis quanto semper amore Graecarum rerum flagrem.* Motive für den Höhepunkt des humanistischen griechischen Dichtens um 1600", in Stefan Weise (ed.) *Hellenisti! Altgriechisch als Literatursprache im neuzeitlichen Europa* (Palingenesia 107), Stuttgart, 125–145.

NDB = *Neue Deutsche Biographie* (Bayerische Akademie der Wissenschaften & Historische Kommission [eds.] [1953]. *Neue deutsche Biographie.* Berlin), http://www.ndb.badw-muenchen.de/.

Oechslin, Werner. 2011. "'Das Wort 'klassisch' hat für uns etwas Erkältendes' (Heinrich Wölfflin)", in Ulrich Heinen & Elisabeth Klecker (eds.) *Welche Antike? – Konkurrierende Rezeptionen des Altertums.* (*Wolfenbütteler Arbeiten zur Barockforschung* 47), Wiesbaden, 183–206.

Paulsen, Friedrich. 1896–1897. *Geschichte des gelehrten Unterrichts auf den deutschen Schulen und Universitäten.* Bd. 1–2 [2nd ed.]. Leipzig.

Pfeiffer, Rudolf. 1976. *History of Classical Scholarship from 1300–1850.* Oxford.

Päll, Janika. 2005. "Far Away from Byzantium: Pronunciation and Orthography of Greek in the 17th Century Estonia", in Ivo Volt & Janika Päll (eds.) *Byzantino-Nordica 2004. Papers presented at the international symposium of Byzantine studies held on 7–11 May 2004 in Tartu, Estonia* (Acta Societatis Morgensternianae II), Tartu, 86–119.

Päll, Janika. 2018. "Humanist Greek in Early Modern Estonia and Livonia: the contexts and Principal Genres", in Janika Päll & Ivo Volt (eds.) *Hellenostephanos. Humanist Greek in Early Modern Europe: Learned Communities between Antiquity and Contemporary Culture* (Acta Societatis Morgensternianae VI–VII), Tartu, 57–112.

Päll, Janika. 2020. "Hyperborean Flowers: Humanist Greek around the Baltic Sea (16th–17th Century)", in Natasha Constantinidou & Han Lamers (eds.) *Receptions of Hellenism in Early Modern Europe. 15th to 17th Centuries*, Leiden & Boston, 410–438.

Päll, Janika. 2020 (forthcoming). "Greek disputations in German and Swedish Universities and Academic Gymnasia in the 17th and Early 18th Century", in Hanspeter Marti, Robert Seidel, & Meelis Friedenthal (eds.) *Early Modern Disputations and Dissertations in an Interdisciplinary and European Context*, Leiden–Boston, 728–778.

Riedel, Volker. 2007. "Germany and German-Speaking Europe", in Craig W. Kallendorf (ed.) *A Companion to the Classical Tradition*, Malden (Mass.)–Oxford–Carlton, 169–191.

Sandys, John Edwin. 1906–1908. *History of Classical Scholarship*, 1–3. Cambridge.

Scheller, Karl Friedrich Arend. 1821. *Horaz: Oden und Epoden.* Helmstädt.

Scheller, Karl Friedrich Arend. 1826a. *Bücherkunde der Sassisch-Niederdeutschen Sprache, hauptsächlich nach den Schriftdenkmälern der herzogl. Bibliothek zu Wolfenbüttel.* Braunschweig.

Scheller, Karl Friedrich Arend. 1826b. *Q. Horatius Flaccus: sämmtliche Werke.* Braunschweig.

Scheller, Karl Friedrich Arend. 1830. *Q. Horatius Flaccus: sämmtliche Werke.* [2nd ed.]. Halberstadt.

Schmidt, Friedrich August (ed.) 1845. *Nekrolog 1843. Neuer Nekrolog der Deutschen. Einundzwanzigster Jahrgang. Zweiter Theil.* Weimar.

Schröder, Edward. 1890. "Scheller, Karl", in *Allgemeine Deutsche Biographie* 31, 1–3. https://www.deutsche-biographie.de/gnd10112970X.html#adbcontent (retrieved 20 February 2020).

Skafte Jensen, Minna. 2007. "Scandinavia", in Craig W. Kallendorf (ed.) *A Companion to the Classical Tradition*, Malden (Mass.)–Oxford–Carlton, 252–264.

Spranger, Eduard. 1960. *Wilhelm von Humboldt und die Reform des Bildungswesens.* Tübingen.

Süss, Wilhelm. 1928–1929. *Karl Morgenstern (1770–1852). Ein kulturhistorischer Versuch* (Acta et Commentationes Universitatis Tartuensis [Dorpatensis]) B 16:2). Dorpat.

VD16 = *Verzeichnis der im deutschen Sprachbereich erschienenen Drucke des 16. Jahrhunderts*, https://www.bsb-muenchen.de/sammlungen/historische-drucke/recherche/vd-16/.

VD17 = *Das Verzeichnis der im deutschen Sprachraum erschienenen Drucke des 17. Jahrhunderts*, http://www.vd17.de/

Veteikis, Tomas. 2004. *Greek Studies and Greek Literature in 16–17ᵗʰ Century Lithuania*. A Summary of Doctoral Dissertation. Humanities, Philology (04H). Vilnius.

Vierhaus, Rudolf (ed.) 1985. *Wissenschaften im Zeitalter der Aufklärung aus Anlass des 250jährigen Bestehens des Verlages Vandenhoeck & Ruprecht [1735–1985]*. Göttingen.

Weise, Stefan. 2011. "Μοῦσα Ἑλληνική. Griechische Gedichte hallescher Gelehrter," *Archiv für Papyrusforschung und verwandte Gebiete* 57:2, 399–429.

Weise, Stefan. 2016. "Ἑλληνίδ' αἶαν εἰσιδεῖν ἱμείρομαι – Neualtgriechische Literatur in Deutschland (Versuch eines Überblicks)", *Antike und Abendland* 62, 114–181.

Weise, Stefan. 2019. *Der* Arion *des Lorenz Rhodoman. Ein altgriechisches Epyllion der Renaissance. Einleitung, Text, Übersetzung, Wortindex* (Palingenesia 117). Stuttgart.

Weise, Stefan. 2020. "*Graecia transvolavit Alpes*: Humanist Greek Writing in Germany (15ᵗʰ to 17ᵗʰ Centuries) through the Eyes of Georg Lizel (1694–1761)", in Natasha Constantinidou & Han Lamers (eds.) *Receptions of Hellenism in Early Modern Europe. 15ᵗʰ to 17ᵗʰ Centuries*, Leiden–Boston, 379–409.

Witzmann, Peter. 2017. "Der Hofrat und der Prinz. Karl August Böttigers *carmina Graeca* für den Prinzen Johann von Sachsen", in Stefan Weise (ed.) *Hellenisti! Altgriechisch als Literatursprache im neuzeitlichen Europa* (Palingenesia *107*), Stuttgart, 253–283.

Wolkenhauer, Anja. 2015. "Gefälschte und supplementierte Lyrik. Überlegungen zur Publikations- und Wirkungsgeschichte von Horaz' *Carmina* 1.39 und 1.40", in Martin Korenjak & Simon Zuenelli (eds.) *Supplemente Antiker Literatur* (Pontes 8), Freiburg im Breisgau, 79–96.

Appendix: Addenda to the Catalogue Information of HAB

The list of authors in HAB catalogues seems to follow Scheller's own index which does not (always) distinguish between authors whose poems are included in the collection and the authors whose poetry is only referred to. Addenda to the list of Otto von Heinemann (1884):

Authors represented with poems: Pierre Belon du Mans, Theodor Beza, Karl Böttiger, Joachim Camerarius, Martin Crusius, Albertus Damius, Konrad Gessner, Daniel Hoffmann, Johann Höpner, Heinrich Andreae Käseberg (Keseberg), Thomas Koch, Erhard Lauterbach, Georg Leuschner, Friedrich Mollerus/Möller, Johannes Rhellicanus, Caspar Ringelmann, Chr. Fr. Schmidt, Heinrich Schrader, Sigismund Strophius, Nicolaus Volckmar, Justus Vultejus, Joachim Zimmermann, and J.F. Br., J. F. H. Hamb., F.F.F., H.P.H., S.N., I.U.P.M.D, C.T. with four other anonymuses (the authors represented in corpus with transcripts or cut-outs of their poems).

Referred authors: Guillaume Budé, Heinrich Decimator, Joachim Dreier, Nicodemus Frischlin, Johannes Gardesius, Jacobus Gruterus, Daniel Heinsius, Johannes Heinsius, Janus Laskaris, Laurentius Mitternacht (pro: Conrad), Chr. Mörichen, Heinrich Volckmar.

The electronic catalogue also includes some mistakes (Aladus pro Alardus, Joh. Seeliger pro Jos. Scaliger) and omits some authors listed in Heinemann's manuscript: Caspar Kirchmayer, Seibeneicheros [Jer. Seibeneicheros Mageiros/Koch], Friedrich Thiersch (all three present with poems in the *collectanea*), as well as Maximos Margounios.

Three Greek Poems by the Neohumanist Vyacheslav Ivanov (1866–1949)[1]

Elena Ermolaeva

The Russian symbolist poet Vyacheslav Ivanov, a classical scholar and significant thinker in Russian cultural history, was a prominent figure of new Russian humanism. He wrote poems in modern languages but also composed some dedications in Latin and ancient Greek. In a way Russian scholars and men of letters experimented in composing Greek verses like their colleagues in Germany and other parts of Europe, but so far only a few studies of Greek versifying in Russian universities and literary circles have been published.[2] In Ivanov's case, the reasons why he wrote in Greek were to occasionally appreciate the men of his circle, classical scholars, the proponents of new humanism in Russia akin to the German *Neuhumanismus* movement focusing on Greek language and culture.[3]

Vyacheslav Ivanov was not only a poet, literary critic, and historian of religion but also a translator from ancient Greek, Latin, Italian, German, and French.[4] When he was a pupil in the First Moscow Gymnasium he achieved excellent results in ancient Greek and Latin. His first poems in Russian and his poetic translations from classical languages, e.g., a passage from the *Oedipus Rex* in Russian trimeters, were completed during his school years.[5] Unfortunately, we know too little about his gymnasium years to determine when he started his exercises in Greek and Latin versification. After school, he first studied history, philology and philosophy at the University of Moscow, and later, in 1886–1891, he was a student at the Berlin University where he attended lectures by many famous classical scholars such as Theodor Mommsen, Eduard Zeller, Ernst Curtius, Otto Hirschfeld,

---

[1] My thanks go to the anonymous reviewers of my article for their helpful comments.

[2] Ermolaeva (2018, 165–180; 2019a, 120–129; 2019b, 375–386); Zeltchenko (2018, 115–137).

[3] Ivanov's attitude to *Humanismus* and its spiritual descendant *Neuhumanismus* was complicated and controversial, especially at the time of his passion for Nietzsche. For Ivanov's views on *Neuhumanismus*, see Iwanow (1934). The first part of the article concerns his reflections on nature and the essence of humanism.

[4] Davidson (1996). For materials on Ivanov's biography, archives and literature on him, see the Research Center of Vyach. Ivanov in Rome, see http://www.v-ivanov.it/ (retrieved 26 April 2020).

[5] Zobnin (2011).

Johannes Vahlen and Emil Hübner, preparing his dissertation under Hirschfeld.[6] Ivanov completed his studies by travelling quite extensively. In Rome, he studied archaeology at the German Archaeological Institute, and in Athens he attended the lectures of Adolf Wilhelm and Wilhelm Dörpfeld. He was influenced by the German Romantics, like Novalis and Friedrich Hölderlin, and the philosophy of Friedrich Nietzsche. In his treatises on Dionysus "The Hellenic Religion of the Suffering God" (1904) and "Religion of Dionysus" (1905), Ivanov followed the ideas of Nietzsche's *The Birth of Tragedy*.[7] After staying in Paris, London, Athens, Rome, Egypt and Geneva, among other places, Ivanov came back to Russia in 1905 and dwelt mainly in St Petersburg and Moscow. In literary circles, Ivanov was generally called 'Vyacheslav the Magnificent';[8] he attracted large audiences and his words enthralled many who were susceptible to his charm.

In 1924, Ivanov emigrated from the Soviet Union to Rome, where he found employment *inter alia* as a professor of Old Church Slavonic at the *Collegium Russicum*. His most important articles on ancient topics at that time were "Vergils Historiosophie" (1931) and "Humanismus und Religion: Zum religionsgeschichtlichen Nachlass von Wilamowitz" (1934). His translations of almost all tragedies of Aeschylus[9] as well as the poems of Pindar (1899), Sappho and Alcaeus (1914), and some other Greek poets[10] into Russian are still considered classics – Sappho and Alcaeus were even recently republished.[11]

Ivanov's three Greek poems were published in his poetry collection *Nezhnaja tajna*. ΛΕΠΤΑ ("Soft Secret. Light verses") in St Petersburg in 1912. The Greek poems (and one poem in Latin) were included in the part titled *Humaniorum studiorum cultoribus*.[12] In his introduction to ΛΕΠΤΑ, Ivanov hinted at the Alexandrian character of his poems – not only the Greek poems but his Russian

---

[6] On Ivanov as a student of Th. Mommsen and Otto Hirschfeld, see Wachtel (1994, 35, 1–2, 352–376).

[7] Ivanov's treatises were republished in 2012, see Ivanov 2012.

[8] 'Vyacheslav the Magnificent' is a title of the chapter dedicated to Vyach. Ivanov in Lev Shestov's book "Potestas clavium" (2007).

[9] On the history and edition problems of Vyach. Ivanov's translations from Aeschylus see Kotrelev (1989, 497–522); Yermakova (2015, 215–229). Ivanov translated all the tragedies of Aeschylus except the *Prometheus Bound*, while his translation of *The Suppliants* (vv. 1–323) and *Seven against Thebes* (1–777) are incomplete.

[10] See Lappo-Danilevsky (2014).

[11] See Ivanov (2019).

[12] Ivanov (1912, 112–113); Ivanov (1979, 59).

ones. Some of the poems are indeed quite obscure, full of allusions that would have been fully understandable only to the poet himself and his recipients, poets and friends.

Ivanov's three Greek poems were dedicated to his friends who were active in Russian *Neuhumanismus*, the classical scholars Mikhail I. Rostovtsev (Rostovtzeff) and Tadeusz F. Zieliński, and the philosopher of religion Grigory A. Rachinsky. This article provides a translation, context and a commentary on these poems, arguing that they all can be dated to between 1910–1912, that is, around the time when they were published. Ivanov was then already forty-six years old.

The Poem to M.I. Rostovtsev

The shortest of Ivanov's three Greek poems published in the ΛΕΠΤΑ consists of three verses in iambic trimeters and is addressed to Mikhail Ivanovich Rostovtsev (1870–1952), a historian of the ancient world and professor at St Petersburg University (1901–1918), later at Yale University (1925–1944). His most important books include *Iranians and Greeks in South Russia* (1922) and the very influential *Social and Economic History of the Roman Empire* (1926; 1957[4]).

The friendship between Ivanov and Rostovtsev began in 1893 when they were conducting their research at the German Archaeological Institute in Rome. They studied the ancient Roman wall paintings at Pompeii, listening *in situ* to the famous August Mau (1840–1909), who initially delineated them. Ivanov was writing his dissertation about tax farming in the Roman Empire. Rostovtsev, who was going to complete his dissertation about the wall paintings at Pompeii, changed his mind under the influence of Ivanov, among others, and began to work on his own dissertation on the same subject.[13]

After returning to Russia, Rostovtsev and Ivanov went their separate ways. Rostovtsev completed his master's and doctoral dissertations (1899, 1903); he was appointed a Professor at St Petersburg University (1901), and later a member of the Russian Academy of Science (1908). Ivanov saw himself more as a poet, a leader of the symbolic poetry movement and a philosopher of mysticism. Nevertheless, they maintained their friendship and close family relations, meeting either in "The Tower", Ivanov's famous literary salon, or in Rostovtsev's *jour-fixes* at his flat in the centre of St Petersburg.[14]

---

[13] Bongard-Levin (1997, 248–258).

[14] Bongard-Levin (1997, 249).

Rostovtsev persuaded Ivanov to complete his dissertation (in Latin), which to his mind was really valuable.[15] As the result, Ivanov published his dissertation *De societatibus vectigalium publicorum populi Romani* (St. Petersburg, 1910); he dedicated it to his former supervisor in Berlin (*Ottoni Hirschfeldio magistro*). It seems that Ivanov's Greek poem to Rostovtsev appeared shortly after that:

Φθορᾶς μὲν ἐκσώσαντι τὸν πάλαι σπόρον,
πόνου δ' ἄελπτον καρπὸν ἀντείλαντί σοι
σπείρας ἀπαρχῶν αὐξίμῳ φέρω χάριν.[16]

To you, who saved the seed of old from death, who made rise up the unhoped-for fruit of work, who promoted the growth of the first offerings, I, the sower, bring [my] thanks.

In lines 1–2, Ivanov expresses his gratitude for Rostovtsev's efforts in encouraging him to complete and publish, i.e. to save his *opus magnum* which he calls 'the seed of old' (τὸν πάλαι σπόρον) from perishing (φθορᾶς μὲν ἐκσώσαντι […] σοι), in promoting its growth (ἀντείλαντί σοι […] αὐξίμῳ), and in causing the 'unhoped-for fruit' (ἄελπτον καρπόν) to rise. It seems that in these lines Ivanov, a religious philosopher, gives a *sui generis* poetical paraphrase of two famous parables in the New Testament. The first one is the "Parable of the Sower" (Mark 4:3–8): Ἰδοὺ ἐξῆλθεν <u>ὁ σπείρων</u> τοῦ <u>σπείρειν</u>. καὶ ἐν τῷ <u>σπείρειν</u> αὐτὸν ἃ μὲν ἔπεσεν παρὰ τὴν ὁδόν, καὶ ἐλθόντα τὰ πετεινὰ κατέφαγεν αὐτά. ἄλλα δὲ ἔπεσεν ἐπὶ τὰ πετρώδη ὅπου οὐκ εἶχεν γῆν πολλήν, καὶ εὐθέως <u>ἐξανέτειλεν</u> διὰ τὸ μὴ ἔχειν βάθος γῆς. ἡλίου δὲ <u>ἀνατείλαντος</u> ἐκαυματίσθη καὶ διὰ τὸ μὴ ἔχειν ῥίζαν ἐξηράνθη. ἄλλα δὲ ἔπεσεν ἐπὶ τὰς ἀκάνθας, καὶ ἀνέβησαν αἱ ἄκανθαι καὶ ἔπνιξαν αὐτά. ἄλλα δὲ ἔπεσεν ἐπὶ τὴν γῆν τὴν καλὴν καὶ ἐδίδου <u>καρπόν</u>, ὃ μὲν ἑκατόν, ὃ δὲ ἑξήκοντα, ὃ δὲ τριάκοντα.[17] The second one is

---

[15] Rostovtsev was even ready to proofread Ivanov's dissertation, when Ivanov, who seemingly got lost in his text, delayed making corrections to it. Furthermore, Rostovtsev pressed Ivanov into agreeing with the academician Sergey Zhebelev (1867–1941) to publish his dissertation in the journal of the Imperial Russian Archaeological Society. At that time, Zhebelev was the Society's secretary. Bongard-Levin (1997, 249–251).

[16] The Greek text follows the one published in the ΛΕΠΤΑ.

[17] 'A sower went out to sow. And as he sowed, some seeds fell on the path and the birds came and ate them up. Other seeds fell among thorns where they did not have much soil, and they sprang up quickly, since they had no depth of soil. And when the sun rose, they were scorched; and since they had no root, they withered away. Other seeds fell among thorns, and the thorns grew

the "Parable of the growing seed" (Mark 4:26–29): Καὶ ἔλεγεν, Οὕτως ἐστὶν ἡ βασιλεία τοῦ θεοῦ ὡς ἄνθρωπος βάλῃ <u>τὸν σπόρον</u> ἐπὶ τῆς γῆς καὶ καθεύδῃ καὶ ἐγείρηται νύκτα καὶ ἡμέραν, καὶ <u>ὁ σπόρος</u> βλαστᾷ καὶ μηκύνηται ὡς οὐκ οἶδεν αὐτός. αὐτομάτη ἡ γῆ <u>καρποφορεῖ</u>, πρῶτον χόρτον, εἶτεν στάχυν, εἶτεν πλήρη σῖτον ἐν τῷ στάχυϊ. ὅταν δὲ παραδοῖ <u>ὁ καρπός</u>, εὐθὺς ἀποστέλλει τὸ δρέπανον, ὅτι παρέστηκεν ὁ θερισμός.[18]

In line 3, Ivanov portrays himself as the farmer-sower (σπείρας) in the famous parables. It appeared that his seed fell on good soil, and a harvest was obtained due to the efforts of his friend. Worth noting are the lexical borrowings from the parables in Ivanov's lines: σπόρον (1), καρπόν (2), ἀντείλαντι (2), σπείρας (4); to which Ivanov added a rare adjective αὐξίμῳ (3) 'promoting growth'.[19] Stylistically, Ivanov uses such literary devices as the emphatic position of the cognate words σπόρον (1), σπείρας (3), at the end of the first line and the beginning of the last one; and *hyperbaton*: ἐκσώσαντι (1) […] ἀντείλαντί σοι (2) […] αὐξίμῳ (3).

Ivanov can be seen to follow the poets Friedrich Schiller, Alexander Pushkin and Dmitry Merezhkovsky (one of the founders of the Symbolist movement), who all wrote a poem called the "Sower".[20] Additionally, the epigraph to Fyodor Dostoevsky's *The Brothers Karamazov* (1880), a novel of great significance for Ivanov, comes from the parable of the growing seed, although not from Mark but John (John 12:24). Ivanov's Russian poem *Samoiskanije* ("Self Seeking"), which came out in his poetry collection *Kormchije Zvezdy* ("Sailing Masters Stars", 1903), contains the image of perishing and growing seed as a metaphor of human life.

---

up and choked them, and they yielded no grain. Other seeds fell on good soil and brought forth grain, some a hundredfold, some sixty, some thirty.' Translations are from *The Holy Bible*. English Standard Version. Crossway Bibles, 2001.

[18] 'He also said, "The kingdom of God is as if someone would scatter seed on the ground, and would sleep and rise night and day, and the seed would sprout and grow, he does not know how. The earth produces of itself, first the stalk, then the head, then the full grain in the head. But when the grain is ripe, at once he goes in with his sickle, because the harvest has come."'

[19] *LSJ, s.v.* αὐξιμος.

[20] Schiller in 1795, Pushkin in 1823 and Merezhkovsky in 1892. On Schiller's "Sower", see Ivanov's article "Athena's Shield" (1909) in his book *Po zvezdam* ("By Stars"), reedited in 2018 (I, 45–46; II, 141).

The Poem to F.F. Zieliński

Tadeusz Stefan (in Russian Faddey Frantsevich) Zieliński (1859–1944) was a classical philologist and professor at St Petersburg University (1887–1921) and later at the University of Warsaw (1922–1939). 'Zieliński was Polish by origin, German by scholarship, and Russian by way of living, but Classical Hellas was his real motherland', as his student Salomo Luria wrote.[21] Zieliński's translations of ancient poetry, and especially the complete tragedies of Sophocles from 1914–1915, are still considered classics. He was an irresistible orator and a charming lecturer with a romantic appearance. In his Russian poem, "Drugu gumanistu" ("To the fellow-humanist", 1933), Ivanov compared Zieliński's appearance to the famous statue of Sophocles in Rome, the Lateran Sophocles.[22] After Zieliński's house in Warsaw was bombed and ruined in 1939, he took shelter with his son's family in Schondorf in Germany, where he passed away in 1944.[23]

The friendship between Ivanov and Zieliński seems to have formed in 1905 in St Petersburg, and their correspondence confirms that it was maintained until Zieliński's last period in Germany.[24] Soon a greater understanding and close collegial relationship developed between the two. Ivanov may have met Professor Zieliński at Rostovtsev's place because Rostovtsev was one of his favourite students, and, after Rostovtsev's appointment, university colleagues. In 1910, Zieliński helped Ivanov obtain the position of lecturer in ancient literature at the private women's institute founded by Nikolay P. Raev called "Higher Historical, Literary, and Law Courses for Women" by writing a recommendation for Ivanov to the Minister of Education.[25] The following year he invited Ivanov to take part in the editorial house so he could participate in the project of the Sabashnikov brothers, Mikhail and Sergei,[26] to publish the complete translations of Aeschylus, Sophocles and Euripides' tragedies. The translation work was divided so that

---

[21] Luria (1959, 14, 407). Zieliński's autobiography *Mein Lebenslauf* was translated from German into Polish in 2005, and, in 2012 published in its original language (Zieliński 2012a) and in a Russian translation (Zieliński 2012b). Zieliński's ideas of his national identity and cosmopolitanism could now be better understood.

[22] Ivanov (1979, 350–351).

[23] Gavrilov (2012, 32–45).

[24] Takho-Godi (2002, 181–276)

[25] Lappo-Danilevsky (2011, 4, 66–79).

[26] The publishing house operated from 1891 until 1934.

Zieliński himself translated Sophocles; the poet Innokenty Annensky[27] Euripides and Ivanov Aeschylus. The date of Ivanov's Greek epigram to Zieliński is uncertain. However, Ivanov could have composed it in the period from 1910 until 1912, when they both begun their translations of tragedies.

In his Greek elegiac couplets, Ivanov compares Zieliński to an ancient prophet, an interpreter of Apollo and Dionysus. Ivanov may imply that Zieliński, who was both an extremely popular and charismatic lecturer on ancient religion and literature and a brilliant translator and scholar, could be seen as a kind of mediator between antiquity and his contemporaries:[28]

Δελφίδος ἑρμηνεῦ καὶ βακχευτῶν ὑποφῆτα,[29]
    ἐξ Ἀίδαο δόμων ἀγκαλέσας Ἑλένην,
ἧς φάτιν ἡδυμελῶς ἑλληνίδα φωνησάσης
    ἔκλυες ἀνταυδᾶν καλὰ διδασκόμενος,
ὄλβιε, χαῖρε φίλει τε συνένθεον, Ἑλλάδος εἴπερ   5
    μουσοπόλω συνερᾶν εὐχόμεθ᾽ ἀμφοτέρω.

You, interpreter of Pythia and expounder of the Bacchants, who has invoked the ghost of Helen from Hades, to whom you listened face to face, learning beauties, when she was speaking sweetly in Greek. [5] [You] blessed, rejoice and love [me] full of the god together [with you], if we, the servants of the Muses, boast to love Hellas together.

The word ὑποφήτης in line 1 means basically 'suggester, interpreter, expounder of divine will or judgment, e.g., of a priest who declares an oracle' (cf. *LSJ*, *s.v.*). In a letter sent on 8 July 1933 from Warsaw to Ivanov, who was then staying in Pavia, Zieliński calls himself Ivanov's "juror *hypophetes*",[30] because he was then writing an article on Ivanov for an issue of the Milanese journal *Il convegno* (the issue was specially dedicated to Ivanov).[31] In his letter, Zieliński reminds Ivanov

---

[27] Innokenty Annensky (1855–1909) was a symbolist poet, philologist, translator and a teacher of ancient languages.

[28] Zieliński (1926).

[29] In the edition of the ΛΕΠΤΑ 1912, there is a misprint ὑποφτῆα.

[30] See Takho-Godi (2002, 240). Takho-Godi edited the letters by Zieliński to Ivanov and the articles by Zieliński about Ivanov.

[31] Zieliński (1933–1934, 8–12); Zieliński (1934, 12, 9).

of his previous publications about him: 'I have already *hypopheted* on you […].'[32] Here Zieliński is definitely alluding to Ivanov's poem published in the ΛΕΠΤΑ in 1912, that is, 21 years earlier, when Ivanov called him ὑποφήτης.

In line 2, Zieliński is said to invoke the ghost of Helen from Hades. Ivanov uses here the verb ἀνακαλέω, 'to call up the dead' from below. The verb was especially used of magical invocations (cf. Aesch. *Pers.* 621; Eur. *Hel.* 966). Ivanov uses here its poetical form (ἀγκαλέω), which is attested in Apollonius of Rhodes' *Argonautica*, where first Medea (3.861), and later Jason (3.1212) call up Hecate from the underworld. Presumably, Ivanov implicitly compares Zieliński even to Goethe's Faust, who summoned Helen of Troy from Hades so he could peruse eternal beauties. Zieliński was known as a woman charmer and admirer.

The verb ἀνταυδάω ('to address face to face', l. 4) is attested only in Sophocles' *Electra* (1478). Zieliński published his translation of *Electra* into Russian during February and March of 1912.[33] It is noteworthy that Ivanov published his three Greek poems, among them the one to Zieliński, relatively soon afterward, at least before Christmas of the same year. Obviously, it is impossible to prove that Ivanov took this verb from Sophocles with the objective of alluding to Zieliński's translation.

The adjective συνένθεον in line 5, which means 'together [with you] full of the god', seems to be *hapax legomenon,* coined by Ivanov from the adjective ἔνθεος under the influence of συνερᾶν and *dualis* in the next line, μουσοπόλω συνερᾶν εὐχόμεθ' ἀμφοτέρω. By μουσοπόλω, 'two servants of the Muses', in line 6, Ivanov means Zieliński and himself as poets and translators (cf. μουσοπόλοι, Eur. *Alc.* 445; Μουσάων ὑποφῆται, Theoc. 16.29, 17.115). Thus, the two last lines seem to hint at Zieliński and Ivanov's conceptions of the new renaissance of classical antiquity then occurring in the Slavic world.[34] The use of the dual emphasises the shared nature of their ideas.

---

[32] Zieliński thus jokingly inserted a Greek word in Russian letters by shaping it like a Russian verb. In other words, the sentence means, 'I have already been your *hypophetes*'.

[33] Zelinsky (1912, 47 (3), 34).

[34] On the fate and failure of the Slavic Renaissance ideas of Zieliński and Ivanov, see Nikolaev (1997, 343–350).

The Poem to G.A. Rachinsky[35]

The most enigmatic of Ivanov's Greek poems is that addressed to Grigory Alekseyevich Rachinsky (1859–1939).[36] Rachinsky was a Moscow philosopher of religion who chaired the open-minded forum called the Moscow Religious-Philosophic Society in Memory of Vladimir Solovyov. Rachinsky translated literature and philosophy from German and French into Russian (Nietzsche, Goethe, Maupassant and Balzac, among others). He was an expert in theology, and in 1906 he published his translation of "The Canon on the Great Saturday" from ancient Greek into modern Russian.[37] We know about Rachinsky mostly from the memoirs of two men: Andrey Bely,[38] a symbolist poet and novelist, and Nikolay Berdyaev,[39] a religious philosopher. However, he is mentioned very often in the correspondence and diaries of his contemporaries involved in religious philosophy.[40] We know very little about his fate in Soviet times.[41]

Ivanov's archives in Rome and Moscow contain some unpublished letters written to him by Rachinsky between the years 1910–1914.[42] The correspondence indicates that cordiality and even friendship between the two developed during 1910–1911. Ivanov dedicated two poems to Rachinsky in his ΛΕΠΤΑ (1912), one in Russian and one in Greek, in iambic dimeters and trimeters respectively. The Russian poem was called "On receiving a Greek Prayer". Indeed, Rachinksy sent a Greek prayer from Moscow to Ivanov in St Petersburg on a Christmas card dated 25 December 1910.[43] The greeting in Rachinksy's Christmas card consists

---

[35] My thanks go to Ksenia Kumpan, Gennady Obatnin, Alexander Sobolev for the expert consultations, and Andrey Shishkin for the possibility to read Grigory Rachinsky's unpublished letters to Ivanov.

[36] For a detailed commentary on the two poems, in Greek and Russian, by Ivanov dedicated to G. A. Rachinsky, specifying the date of both, and a comprehensive bibliography, see the article of Ermolaeva (2019, XIV, 120–129).

[37] However, during services the Old Church Slavonic translation is normally used, not modern Russian.

[38] Bely (1990, 339–349); Lavrov (2014, 499–518); Malmstad (2005, 127–147).

[39] Berdyaev (1983, 181–183, 224).

[40] Keydan (1997, 312–385).

[41] Guchkov & Kotrelev (2007, 266–269).

[42] On Rachinsky's unpublished letters to Ivanov, see above note 35.

[43] Russian State Library. F. 109, 33, 44.

of three Greek lines, which form the beginning (*Irmos*) of the fifth ode of the choir in the morning service for Christmas:

Θεὸς ὢν εἰρήνης, Πατὴρ οἰκτιρμῶν,
τῆς μεγάλης Βουλῆς σου τὸν Ἄγγελον,
εἰρήνην παρεχόμενον, ἀπέστειλας ἡμῖν.

As Thou art God of peace and Father of mercies, Thou hast sent unto us Thine Angel of great counsel, Granting us peace.

The wording of Ivanov's Greek poem to Rachinsky is reminiscent of Rachinsky's Christmas greeting:

Πρόμαντις οἰκτιρμῶν τε τοῦ Πατρός φίλοις
πέφυκας εἰρήνης τε συντεθλιμμένοις,
αὐτὸς συνοικτείρας μέν, ἐν καιρῷ δέ πως
θεοπροπήσας εὐστόμως νέαν χάριν
σὺν τοιγαροῦν χαῖρ' ὠγάθ' ἐν Χριστῷ φίλε.   5

You are a preacher of the Father of mercies and peace, for friends distressed, you yourself having pity upon them, but over time becoming somehow a prophet of a new delight with propitious words: [5] hence, good friend in Christ, rejoice together.

As well as recalling the wording of the *Irmos* (Θεὸς ὢν εἰρήνης, / Πατὴρ οἰκτιρμῶν), the expression οἰκτιρμῶν τε τοῦ Πατρός […] / πέφυκας εἰρήνης τε (in the first line) evokes formulas from the New Testament: ὁ Πατὴρ τῶν οἰκτιρμῶν καὶ Θεὸς πάσης παρακλήσεως (2. Cor. 1:3) and Παρακαλῶ οὖν ὑμᾶς, ἀδελφοί, διὰ τῶν οἰκτιρμῶν τοῦ Θεοῦ (Rom. 12:1). Taking into account the context of the verse and Ivanov's recognition of Rachinsky's identity as a poet, prophet, and preacher,[44] the first, emphatic word of the poem, πρόμαντις, can be understood here as a 'preacher' in more than a religious sense. As an efficient rhetorical device, the poem employs the deliberate repetition of *clausulae* in the beginning and in the end: τοῦ Πατρὸς φίλοις (line 1) – ἐν Χριστῷ φίλε (line 5).

In line 2, the participle συντεθλιμμένοις is a *hapax*, coming from θλίβω, 'to squeeze', metaphorically 'to oppress'; thus in the passive voice it means 'a heavy-

---

[44] See Kotrelev (*s.a.*).

laden person, distressed person'.[45] In line 3, there is another *hapax* with the same prefix. The verb συνοικτείρας comes from οἰκτείρω, 'to have pity upon' (the variant οἰκτίρω is used in the Gospels) but the verb never occurs with the prefix συν in the ancient or Byzantine corpus. The *hapax* could have been coined by Ivanov himself to stress the meaning of compassion (cf. συν-τεθλιμμένοις, συν-οικτείρας and σύγ-χαιρε *in tmesi*). The expression ἐν καιρῷ δέ πως (l. 3) seems implicitly to refer to the Christmas time.

In line 4, we find the Homeric verb θεοπροπέω, 'to be a prophet (θεοπρόπος)'. In Homer, this verb refers to the seer Calchas (*Il.* 1.109, 2.322; *Od.* 2.184), whereas Pindar uses it of the seer Mopsus in his fourth Pythian ode: μάντις [...] θεοπροπέων (*Pyth.* 4.190). Subsequently the verb was rarely used and it is not attested in the New Testament.[46] It is possible that Ivanov adopted the verb from Pindar. As mentioned earlier, his translation of Pindar's poems was published in 1899. Furthermore, Ivanov might have modified Pindar's expression μάντις [...] θεοπροπέων into προμάντις [...] θεοπροπήσας in his poem. The reference to 'new delight' (νέαν χάριν) in the same line may simply refer to the approach of Christmas or even to Rachinsky' openminded philosophical ideas on religion.

Concluding Words

The three Greek poems by Vyacheslav Ivanov belong to a genre of cordial dedicatory poetry, the key words of which seem to be related to the semantic field of friendship and thankfulness: φέρω χάριν (poem to Rostovtsev), χαῖρε φίλει τε συνένθεον (poem to Zieliński), νέαν χάριν / σὺν τοιγαροῦν χαῖρ' ὠγαθ' ἐν Χριστῷ φίλε (poem to Rachinsky).

Ivanov, a translator of ancient Greek poetry, uses such literary devices as 1) expressive repetitions, e.g., in his poem to Rachinsky: οἰκτιρμῶν – συνοικτείρας (lines 1 and 3); σύν- in συντεθλιμμένοις (l. 2), συνοικτείρας (l. 3) and σὺν [...] χαῖρ' (l. 5); and in that to Zieliński: συνένθεον, Ἑλλάδος εἴπερ / μουσοπόλω συνερᾶν εὐχόμεθ' ἀμφοτέρω (l. 5–6); 2) emphatic positioning of cognate words and, 3) *hyperbaton* in his poem to Rostovtsev, as well as 4) alliterations in all his three Greek poems. His lavish use of metaphors is remarkable. Furthermore, Ivanov incorporates elements from the New Testament into his dedication to

---

[45] Lampe (1961, 1331).

[46] It is noteworthy that in *The Paraphrase of John* attributed to Nonnus, Caiaphas (11.51) and Jesus (4.29) were said to be θεοπρόποι. See Lampe (1961, 632), Bauer (1988, *s.v.* θεοπρόπος).

Rostovtsev. He uses the image of the ancient Greek prophet and poet as well as that of the medieval philosopher (Faust) in his poem to Zieliński. In his iambic trimeters to Rachinsky, there is evidently a deliberate mixture of pagan (πρόμαντις, θεοπροπήσας) and Christian vocabulary (οἰκτιρμῶν τε τοῦ Πατρός φίλοις πέφυκας εἰρήνης τε; ὠγάθ᾽ ἐν Χριστῷ φίλε).

Ivanov was clearly following the humanist tradition of versification in ancient Greek with Christian elements, which has been quite a popular practice, especially in Germany in previous centuries but also of his time. The influence of the German tradition on him needs further study. A single Russian predecessor whose verses Ivanov might have known was Fyodor Korsch (Theodorus Korsch Mosquanus), an honored professor of Classics and Oriental languages at Moscow University and a member of the Imperial Academy of Sciences. His scope was broad enough to include Slavistics, Indo-European linguistics, theory of versification, metrics, and translations. Korsch published his collection of Latin and ancient Greek verses in Copenhagen in 1886. The small book was titled ΣΤΕΦΑΝΟΣ. *Carmina partim sua Graeca et Latina, partim aliena in alterutram linguam ab se conversa.* It consists of 17 Greek[47] and 88 Latin poems, both original and translated into ancient Greek and Latin from Russian, German (e.g., Goethe and Schiller), Arabic, Persian, Sanskrit, Armenian, and Slovenian. The poet and scholar Vyacheslav Ivanov seems to have had more humble goals: he wished to express his thanks to his friends in ancient Greek. However, these short Greek poems offer insights into Ivanov's complicated poetic style and personality as well as into Russian *Neuhumanismus*.

---

[47] Korsch 1886, Nos. IV, XIV, XVIII, XXV, XXVIII, XXXV, XLIII, XLIX, LXIII, LXV, LXXIV, LXXX, LXXXIV, LXXXVII, XCIV, XCVII, C.

Bibliography

Bauer, Walter. 1988. *Griechisch-deutsches Wörterbuch zu den Schriften des Neuen Testaments und der frühchristlichen Literatur.* Berlin.

Bely, Andrey. 1990. "Iz vospominanij o russkih filosofah [From Memoirs on Russian Philosophers]", *Minuvshee* [Past]. *Istoricheskii almanakh* 9, 339–349.

Berdyaev, Nikolay. 1983. *Samopoznanie: opyt filosofskoi avtobiografii* [Self-Knowledge: an Essay in Philosophical Autobiography]. [1ˢᵗ ed. 1949]. Paris.

Bongard-Levin, Grigory M. 1997. "M.I. Rostovtsev i Vyach. I. Ivanov [M.I. Rostovtsev and Vyach. I. Ivanov]", in Grigory M. Bongard-Levin (ed.) *Skifskii Roman* [Scythian Novel], Moscow, 248–258.

Davidson, Pamela. 1996. *Viacheslav Ivanov: A Reference Guide (Reference Guide to Literature).* New York.

Ermolaeva, Elena L. 2018. "Friedrich Schiller and Gavriil Derzhavin in Greek: Translations by Christian Friedrich Graefe (1780–1851)", *Philologia Classica*, 13 (1), 165–180.

Ermolaeva, Elena L. 2019a. "Grecheskoje poslanije Vyach. Ivanova G.A. Rachinskomy [The Greek poem by Vyach. Ivanov to G.A. Rachinsky]", *Philologia Classica* 14 (1), 120–129.

Ermolaeva, Elena L. 2019b. "Neo-Hellenic poetry in Russia: Antonios Palladoklis (1747–1801) and Georgios Baldani (about 1760–1789)", *Hyperboreus* 25 (2), 375–386.

Gavrilov, Alexander K. 2012. "Faddej Frantsevich Zelinskij v kontekste russkoj kultury" [Faddei Frantsevich Zieliński in the context of Russian culture], *Antiquitas Perennis* 4, 32–45.

Guchkov, Sergey M. & Nikolay V. Kotrelev. 2007. "Rachinsky Grigory Alekseevich", in Petr A. Nikolaev (ed.) *Russkiye pisateli 1800–1917. Biografichesky slovar* [Russian writers 1800–1917. The Biographical Dictionary] Vol. 5. (Bolshaya rossijskaja enziklopedia), Moscow, 266–269.

Ivanov, Vyacheslav (tr.). 1899. "Pindar. Pervaja Pifijskaja oda [The First Pythian Ode]", *ZMNP* [Journal of the Ministry of Public Instruction] III, 49–56.

Ivanov, Venceslaus. 1910. *De societatibus vectigalium publicorum populi Romani scripsit Venceslaus Ivanov.* Diss. St. Petersburg.

Ivanov, Vyacheslav. 1912. *Nezhnaja tajna.* ΛΕΠΤΑ ["Soft Secret. Light verses"], St Petersburg.

Ivanov, Vyacheslav. 1931. "Vergils Historiosophie", *Corona* 6, 761–774.

Iwanow, Wiatscheslaw. 1934. "Humanismus und Religion: Zum religionsgeschichtlichen Nachlass von Wilamowitz", *Hochland* 10 (Juli), 307–330.

Ivanov, Vyacheslav. 1979. *The Complete Works in four Volumes*. Vol. 3. Brussels.

Ivanov, Vyacheslav. 2012. *Dionysos und die vordionysischen Kulte*. Hrsg. von Michael Wachtel & Christian Wildberg. Tübingen.

Ivanov, Vyacheslav. 2018. *Po zvezdam* [By Stars]. Vol. I–II. Ksenia A. Kumpan (ed.). St Petersburg.

Ivanov, Vyacheslav. 2019. *Alkej i Sapfo: Sobranije pesen i liricheskih otryvkov v perevode razmerami podlinnikov Vyacheslava Ivanova* [Alcaeus and Sappho. A Collection of Songs and Fragments translated by Vyach. Ivanov in original metres]. Konstantin J. Lappo-Danilevsky (ed.) Sergey A. Zavyalovm (com.). St Petersburg.

Keydan, Vladimir I. (ed.) 1997. *Vzyskuyuschije grada. Hronika chastnoy zhizni russkih filosofov v pis'mah I dnevnikah S. A. Askoldova, N. A. Berdyaeva, S. N. Bulgakova, E. N. Trubetskova, V. F. Erna* [Those who seek a city to come. Chronicle of the private life of Russian religious philosophers in letters and diaries of S. A. Askoldov, N. A. Berdyaev, S. N. Bulgakov, E. N. Trubetskoy, V. F. Ern]. Moscow.

Korsch, Theodorus Mosquanus. 1886. ΣΤΕΦΑΝΟΣ. *Carmina partim sua Graeca et Latina, partim aliena in alterutram linguam ab se conversa* […]. Copenhagen [Reprinted in *Aristeas* 2012, 6, 13–67].

Kotrelev, Nikolay V. 1989. Vyacheslav Ivanov v rabote nad perevodom Eskhila [Vyacheslav Ivanov translating Aeschylus], in Ivanov, Vyacheslav. (tr.) *Eskhil. Tragedii* [Aeschylus. Tragedies]. Ed. Nikolay I. Balashov, Dmitry Vyach. Ivanov, Mikhail L. Gasparov, Gasan Ch. Guseinov, Nikolay V. Kotrelev & Victor N. Jarcho, Moscow, 497–522.

Kotrelev, Nikolay V. (*s.a.*). "Vyacheslav Ivanov. Curriculum vitae. Neizdannaia avtobiograficheskaia spravka Vyacheslava Ivanova [Vyacheslav Ivanov. Curriculum vitae. Unpublished autobiographical note by Vyacheslav Ivanov]", in http://www.v-ivanov.it/files/208/works/kotrelev_ivanov_curriculum_vitae.pdf. An article published during 2007–2013 on the Russian web-page of the Research Center of Vyach. Ivanov in Rome. http://www.v-ivanov.it/ (retrieved 3 May 2020).

Lampe, Geoffrey Willliam Hugo (ed.) 1961. *A Patristic Greek Lexicon*. Oxford.

Lappo-Danilevsky, Konstantin J. 2011. "O prepodavanii Vyacheslava Ivanova na kursah N. P. Raeva [Vyacheslav Ivanov as a lecturer at the N.P. Raev Courses]", *Russkaya Literatura* 4, 66–79.

Lappo-Danilevsky, Konstantin J. 2014. "Perevody Vyach. Ivanova, prednaznachavshijesya dlya antologii 'Grecheskije liriki v russkih perevodah' F.E. Korsha i V.O. Nilendera [Vyach. Ivanov's Translations for the Anthology 'Greek Lyric Poetry in Russian Translations' edited by F.E. Korsh and V.O. Nilender]", *Russkaya Literatura* 1, 178–205.

Lavrov, Alexander V. (ed.) 2014. *Belyj A. Nachalo veka: Berlinskaya redactsija (1923)* [Bely A. The Beginning of the Century: The Berlin Version (1923)]. St. Petersburg.

Luria, Salomo J. 1959. "Wspomnienia o prof. Tadeuszu Zielińskim i jego metodzie motywów rudymentarnych", *Meander* 14, 407.

Malmstad, John. 2005. "Andrej Belyj i G.A. Rachinskij [Andrey Bely and G.A. Rachinsky]", *Russkaja Literatura* 58, 1–2, 1 July – 15 August, 127–147.

Nikolaev, Nikolay I. 1997. "Sud'ba idei Tret'ego Vozrozhdeniya [The fate of the third Renaissance idea]", ΜΟΥΣΕΙΟΝ. [Collection of articles in honor of the seventieth birthday of Prof. Alexander I. Zaicev], St. Petersburg, 343–350.

Shestov, Lev. 2007. *Potestas clavium* [1st ed. 1923]. Moscow.

Takho-Godi, Elena A. (ed.) 2002. "Dve sudby nedarom svyazuet vidimaya nit' [A visible thread connects two destinies not by chance]", in Daniela Rizzi & Andrey Shishkin (eds.) *Europa Orientalis* 2: Archivio russo-italiano II, 181–276.

Wachtel, Michael. 1994. "Vyacheslav Ivanov – student Berlinskogo universiteta [Vyacheslav Ivanov a Student of the Berlin University]", *Cahiers du Monde Russe Anné*e *1994. Fait partie d'un numéro thématique: Un maître de sagesse au XXe siècle Vjačeslav Ivanov et son temps* 35, 1–2, 352–376.

Yermakova, Liya L. 2015. "Tragedii Eskhila v perevode Vyach. Ivanova: editsionnyje problemy" [Vyach. Ivanov's Translations of Aeschylus' Tragedies: Editing Problems], *Russkaya Literatura* 2, 215–229.

Zeltchenko, Vsevolod. 2018. "Innokentij Annenskij kak drevnegrecheskij poet" [Innokenty Annensky as an ancient Greek poet], *Traduire la Poésie, Lyon*, 115–137.

Zelinsky, Faddey F. (tr.). 1912. Sophocles. *Electra*, in *Vestnik Evropy* [Herald of Europe], 47 (2) 25–59; (3) 3–36.

Zieliński, Thaddeus. 1926. *The Religion of Ancient Greece*. Tr. George R. Noyes. London.

Zieliński, Thaddeo. 1933–1934. "Introduzione all'opera di Venceslavo Ivanov", *Il Convegno*, 8–12.

Zieliński, Thadeusz. 1934. "Poeta Odrodzenia Siowiacskiego: Wikcysiaw Iwanow", *Pion* 12, 9.

Zieliński, Thadeusz. 2005. *Autobiografia. Dziennik 1939–1944*. Ed. Hanna Geremek & Piotr Mitzner, Warszawa.

Zieliński, Tadeus. 2012a. *Mein Lebenslauf. Erstausgabe des deutschen Originals und Tagebuch 1939-1944*. Herausgegeben und eingeleitet von Jerzy Axer, Alexander Gavrilov & Michael von Albrecht. Frankfurt am Main.

Zieliński, Thaddeus. 2012b. *De vita sua*. Anatoly I. Ruban (Rutenice reddidit atque notis illustravit), *Antiquitas Perennis* 4, 46–197.

Zobnin, Jurii V. 2011. *Materialy k Letopisi zhizni i tvorchestva Vyach. I. Ivanova*. Chast' 1 (1866–1907) [The Materials to Chronicle of Vyach. I. Ivanov's Life and Works. Part 1 (1866–1907)]. E-Book 2011. http://www.v-ivanov.it/files/208/works/zobnin_materialy_k_letopisi_ivanova_2011.pdf (retrieved 26 April 2020).

Index nominum

Names are mostly in Anglicized forms except German names with titles.

Commentationes Humanarum Litterarum

Vol. 90 (1990)

Solin, Heikki: Namenpaare. Eine Studie zur römischen Namengebung. 1990. 92 p.

Vol. 91 (1990)

Roman Eastern Policy and Other Studies in Roman History, edited by Heikki Solin and Mika Kajava. 1990. 174 p.

Vol. 93 (1991)

Bruun, Christer: The Water Supply of Ancient Rome. A Study of Roman Imperial Administration. 1991. 468 p.

Vol. 94 (1991)

Koskenniemi, Erkki: Der philostrateische Apollonios. 1991. 101 p.

Vol. 95 (1992)

Löfstedt, Leena (ed.): Gratiani Decretum. La traduction en ancient français du Décret de Gratien. Edition critique. Vol. I: Distinctiones. 1992. 213 p.

Vol. 96 (1991)

Forsén, Björn: Lex Licinia Sextia de modo agrorum – fiction or reality? 1991. 88 p.

Vol. 97 (1992)

Salomies, Olli: Adoptive and Polyonymous Nomenclature in the Roman Empire. 1992. 179 p.

Vol. 99 (1993)

Löfstedt, Leena (ed.): Gratiani Decretum. La traduction en ancient français du Décret de Gratien. Edition critique. Vol. II: Causae 1–14. 1993. 276 p.

Vol. 102 (1994)

Leiwo, Martti: Neapolitana. A Study of Population and Language in Graeco-Roman Naples. 1994. 232 p.

Vol. 103 (1995)

Chydenius, Johan: The Spirituality of Fénelon in his Latin Writings 1700-1712. 1995. 60 p.

Vol. 104 (1995)

Acta colloquii epigraphici Latini Helsingiae 3.– 6. sept. 1991 habiti, ediderunt Heikki Solin, Olli Salomies, Uta-Maria Liertz. 1995. 425 p.

Vol. 105 (1996)

Löfstedt, Leena (ed.): Gratiani Decretum. La traduction en ancient français du Décret de Gratien. Edition critique. Vol. III: Causae 15–29. 1996. 275 p.

Vol. 108 (1996)

Mehtonen, Päivi: Old Concepts and New Poetics. Historia, Argumentum, and Fabula in the Twelfth- and Early Thirteenth-Century Latin Poetics of Fiction. 1996. 173 p.

Vol. 109 (1996)

Kuisma, Oiva: Proclus' Defence of Homer. 1996. 157 p.

Vol. 110 (1997)

Löfstedt, Leena (ed.): Gratiani Decretum. La traduction en ancient français du Décret de Gratien. Edition critique. Vol. IV: Causae 30– 36 et De Consecratione. 1997. 224 p.

Vol. 111 (1998)

Lampela, Anssi: Rome and the Ptolemies of Egypt. The Development of their Political Relations 273–80 B.C. 1998. 301 p.

Vol. 112 (1998)

Nummenmaa, Tapio: Divine Motions and Human Emotions in the Philebus and in the Laws. Plato's Theory of Physic Powers. 1998. 151 p.

Vol. 113 (1999)

Thesleff, Holger: Studies in Plato's Two-Level Model. 1999. 143 p.

Vol. 114 (1999)

Dimitropoulos, Panagiotis: Untersuchungen zum finalen Genetiv des substantivierten Infinitivs bei Thukydides. 1999. 117 p.

Vol. 115 (2000)

Heinonen, Sirkka: Prometheus Revisited. Human Interaction with Nature through Technology in Seneca, 2000. 232 p.

Vol. 116 (2000)

Lehtonen, Tuomas M. S. & Mehtonen, Päivi (eds.): Historia. The Concept and Genres in the Middle Ages. 2000. 142 p.

Vol. 117 (2001)

Löfstedt, Leena (ed.): Gratiani Decretum. La traduction en ancient français du Décret de Gratien. Edition critique. Vol. dV: Observations et explications. 2001. 482 p.

Vol. 118 (2002)

Kivistö, Sari: Creating Anti-eloquence. Epistolae obscurorum virorum and the Humanist Polemics on Style. 2002. 256 p.

Vol. 119 (2002)

Salmenkivi, Erja: Cartonnage Papyri in Context. New Ptolemaic Documents from Abū Sir al Malaq. 2002. 182 p., 20 plates.

Vol. 120 (2003)

Kuisma, Oiva: Art or Experience. A Study on Plotinus' Aesthetics. 2003. 207 p.

Vol. 121 (2004)

Korhonen, Kalle: Le iscrizioni del Museo civico di Catania. 2004. 418 p.

Vol. 122 1–2 (2007)

Proceedings of the 24th International Congress of Papyrology. Helsinki, 1–7 August, 2004, edited by Jaakko Frösén, Tiina Purola and Erja Salmenkivi. 2007. 1075 p., plates.

Vol. 123 (2007)

Steinby, Christa: The Roman Republican Navy. 2007. 236 p.

Vol. 124 (2009)

Halla-aho, Hilla: The non-literary Latin letters. A study of their syntax and pragmatics. 2009. 190 p.

Vol. 125 (2008)

The Konikovo Gospel (Bibl. Patr. Alex. 268), edited by Jouko Lindstedt, Ljudmil Spasov and Juhani Nuorluoto. 2008. 439 p., 82 plates.

Vol. 126 (2009)

Sipilä, Joonas: The Reorganisation of Provincial Territories in Light of the Imperial Decision-making Process. Later Roman Arabia and Tres Palaestinae as Case Studies. 2009. 328 p.

Vol. 127 (2010)

Saastamoinen, Ari: The Phraseology of Latin Building Inscriptions in Roman North-Africa. 2010. 646 p.

Vol. 128 (2011)

Building Roma Aeterna. Current Research on Roman Mortar and Concrete. Proceedings of the conference, March 27–29, 2008. Editors Åsa Ringbom and Robert L. Hohlfelder, assistant editors Pia Sjöberg and Pia Sonck-Koota. 2011. 260 p.

Vol. 129 (2011)

Eikonopoiia. Digital Imaging of Ancient Textual Heritage. Proceedings of the international conference Helsinki, 28–29, November, 2010, edited by Vesa Vahtikari, Mika Hakkarainen, Antti Nurminen. 2011. 267 p.

Vol. 130 (2013)

Maurizi, Luca: Il cursus honorum senatorio da Augusto a Traiano. Sviluppi formali e stilistici nell'epigrafia latina e greca. 2013. 324 p.

Vol. 131 (2014)

Papyri Turkuenses (P. Turku). Die Papyri im Besitz der Universitätsbibliothek Turku herausgegeben von Heikki Koskenniemi unter Mitwirkung von Erkki Koskenniemi und Johannes Koskenniemi. 2014. 135 p., Tafeln.

Vol. 132 (2015)

Second Sailing: Alternative Perspectives on Plato. Edited by Debra Nails and Harold Tarrant in Collaboration with Mika Kajava and Eero Salmenkivi. 2015. 366 p.

Vol. 133 (2016)

Korkiakangas, Timo: Subject Case in the Latin of Tuscan Charters of the 8th and 9th Centuries. 2016. 276 p.

Vol. 134 (2018)

Kivistö, Sari: *Lucubrationes Neolatinae*. Readings of Neo-Latin Dissertations and Satires. 2018. 244 p.

Vol. 135 (2018)

Buchholz, Matias: Römisches Recht auf Griechisch. Prolegomena zu einer linguistischen Untersuchung der Zusammensetzung und Semantik des byzantinischen prozessrechtlichen Wortschatzes. 2018. 236 p.

Vol. 136 (2019)

Domus Pompeiana M. Lucretii IX 3, 5.24. The Inscriptions, Works of Art and Finds from the Old and New Excavations. Edited by Ria Berg and Ilkka Kuivalainen. 2019. 323 p.

Vol. 137 (2019)

Studi storico-epigrafici sul Lazio antico II. A cura di Heikki Solin. 2019. 168 p.